Also by Wayne Winterrowd

ANNUALS FOR CONNOISSEURS

A YEAR AT NORTH HILL (WITH JOE ECK)

LIVING SEASONALLY (WITH JOE ECK)

ROSES: A CELEBRATION (ED.)

ANNUALS & TENDER PLANTS

for North American Gardens

ANNUALS & TENDER PLANTS

for North American Gardens

Wayne Winterrowd

Principal Photography by Cynthia Woodyard

RANDOM HOUSE / NEW YORK

All rights reserved under International and Pan-American Copyright Conventions.
Published in the United States by Random House, an imprint of The Random House
Publishing Group, a division of Random House, Inc., New York,
and in Canada by Random House of Canada Limited, Toronto.

RANDOM HOUSE and colophon are registered trademarks of Random House, Inc.

All photographs by Cynthia Woodyard and Joe Eck.

LIBRARY OF CONGRESS CATALOGING-IN-PUBLICATION DATA
Winterrowd, Wayne.
Annuals and tender plants for North American gardens / Wayne Winterrowd.
p.   cm.
Includes index.
ISBN 0-679-45736-4
1. Annuals (Plants) I. Title.
SB422.W54 2004
635.9'312'097—dc21   2003047069

Random House website address: www.atrandom.com

Printed in China on acid-free paper

246897531

FIRST EDITION

Book design by Casey Hampton

For Joe Eck and Fotios Bouzikos

ACKNOWLEDGMENTS

*A*nyone who publishes a book, and particularly one of this size and scope, must feel the need to express gratitude to many people. So many have contributed to this volume, in fact, that I see them almost as members of a small nineteenth-century factory, lined up in stiff suits and uniforms, according to rank, for the annual company photograph. No such hierarchy would be possible here, however, for the people I must thank are scattered all over my human acquaintance, and some who have done the most to help me along are not part of the editorial staff at Random House.

So I must begin with two splendid growers of annual and tender plants, Jack and Karen Manix of Walker Farm, in Dummerston, Vermont, who, over our fifteen years of friendship, have been willing to conduct crazy experiments with plants of this group and share their knowledge and experience freely. They have been wonderful partners in the making of this book, and their nursery is one of the first places I would go to acquire something new, something unknown to me. Luckily, they are nearby.

To them I must add Brian and Alice McGowan of Blue Meadow Farm, in Montague, Massachusetts, who have been in the forefront of the explosion of interest in annual and tender plants and who have always been ready to propagate unusual new species and also to share their encyclopedic knowledge of annuals and tender plants. Their excellent catalogues alone have been a major research tool for this work.

Though a book about plants must depend first on direct hands-on experience, and then on the borrowed experience of one's best gardening friends, it gets between two covers through the efforts of other people who may love gardens but whose primary expertise lies in knowing how books get published. Within that group, I must first thank Helen Pratt, my agent, who has always tirelessly put up with my fits and starts and patiently nudged me along to conclusion. It was she who first conceived of this book with Jason Epstein, senior editor of Random House, now retired, who nevertheless provided early encouragement and support. Susanna Porter inherited both me and this unwieldy book from him, and has borne the heavy burden it imposed on her and her staff with patience, intelligence, and enthusiasm. Her former assistant, Matt Thornton, provided efficient communication as the book progressed, and her current assistant, Evelyn O'Hara, continued that function while also proving to be an amusing and engaging correspondent.

The actual production of a book involves more people than the reader can perhaps imagine. Within that group I must thank Kathy Rosenbloom, who oversaw the book's entire production, Casey Hampton, whose hard job it was to design an interior that would squeeze so vast a text into printable form, and Janet Wygal, who has monitored the book's progress through all its final stages to publication. Special thanks go to Robbin Schiff, who designed the cover in such a way that it would convey both the beauty and the ethereal nature of its subject.

Several people who participated in the production of this book lie outside the structure of Random House. One is Elizabeth McHale, rather surprisingly my near neighbor here in Vermont, who was given the job of line editing the manuscript and then of creating a functional index for it. As a gardener herself, she did an amazingly sensitive job, both with my text and in the creation of a ready reference to the many facts the book contains.

Once again, I have also had the luck of collaborating with Cynthia Woodyard, the principal photographer of the book, whose sensitive eye conjoins with a deep knowledge and love of plants, and who, as a close friend, has always been ready with sympathy and humor whenever the task on which I had embarked began to seem hopeless.

Most especially, however, I must thank Elizabeth Harbin Hunter, who, on a sabbatical from her many years as an editor at *House Beautiful* magazine, edited the entire text, bending all her experience and her insistence on "story" to prose that might occasionally have been most charitably described as leisurely (and, less charitably, as rambling). A sensitive textual editor is the greatest luxury a writer can have, and over the difficult winter of 2002, Betsy offered that.

Writers of books do not usually work in offices. They work at home, and it is always to be hoped, in the case of garden books, that they work in houses surrounded by gardens within which the very plants they have chosen to write about are flourishing on any fine summer morning. But I must be frank. I have gardened with annual and tender plants for more than fifty years. Still, some of the firsthand experience in this book has not been mine. For really, you cannot garden and write about gardens at the same time. You can observe, and certainly you should do that. But the actual work of gardening—of weeding and fertilizing and staking and collecting seed and all that, must be left, for a time at least, to someone else—left, that is, if any of your accumulated knowledge, however it came to you, is to strike paper. So I have depended on (treasured would be a better word) the help of our gardeners here at North Hill, Wendy Girardi, Timothy Butterer, and Renee Lowe. Without them, I would certainly have been working in the garden myself. That could have been a great satisfaction to me. But I would hardly have written a book.

Finally, I must thank the two people most involved in this book, not so much—though often enough—while a page was written but more often when supper was delayed, or worse, served with a distracted air and, I fear, sometimes, with a most foul temper. It is to those two that the book is dedicated.

Wayne Winterrowd
North Hill
Readsboro, Vermont

CONTENTS

ACKNOWLEDGMENTS

ix

INTRODUCTION

xv

ZONE MAP

xxvii

ALPHABETICAL ENTRIES

3

APPENDIX I: TECHNIQUES FOR GROWING ANNUALS

499

APPENDIX II: MAIL ORDER SOURCES

511

INDEX OF COMMON NAMES

513

INDEX

521

INTRODUCTION

*I*n the minds of many American gardeners, the idea of a rare annual is still an oxymoron, and the concept of an annual that is sensitively used seems as absurd as expecting tasteful decor in the restroom of the Greyhound bus station. For too many gardeners, annuals are common things, quick fixes grabbed up in the local garden center to fill gaps, to provide color, or to do the planters. At the beginning of the garden year, planting annuals is about equal to raking leaves at the end of it. Necessary, but boring. And what is worse, most plantings of annuals seem to show the results of this attitude. Half whiskey barrels without number are refurbished each year with a perfectly centered spike plant clustered round with red geraniums and variegated myrtle straggling off the sides. Patriotic plantings of screaming red *Salvia splendens,* blue ageratum, and white petunias grace the fronts of post offices and other public buildings, and wherever orange marigolds are planted, the cooling influence of silver foliage—provided by one of several plants popularly called "dusty miller"—is felt to be obligatory. Busy Lizzies top the charts each year as America's best-loved annual (or, at least, most-used), for their tireless, garish endurance. Few American gardeners could imagine any of these plants in a natural environment any more than they could describe the process that produces Saran Wrap or the ingredients from which it is made. And until fairly recently, few really cared.

About ten years ago, however, this attitude began to shift. Through the '70s and '80s, hardy perennials were the principal focus of most American gardeners, who were encouraged by several splendid books whose influence culminated in Ruth Rogers Clausen and Nicolas H. Ekstrom's *Perennials for American Gardens* (Random House) and Allan M. Armitage's *Herbaceous Perennial Plants* (Varsity Press). Both appeared in the same year—1989—and in America, they marked the high-water point of interest in hardy herbaceous perennials. What might be called the Hardy Perennial Movement has scarcely abated since, though a positive thicket of other books and articles have served to educate the American gardening public pretty thoroughly in its knowledge of perennials. The Perennial Movement has taught American gardeners about a huge range of hardy plants they can grow, and the consequence is that our gardens are richer in perennial plants than they have ever been before. That is all gain.

But gardening, which seems to the world outside it to be so orderly and so full of sweet, seasonal predictability—rather like Sunday dinner at Grandma's—is really a very restless activity. It never stops searching for the new, the wonderful, the unknown, undreamed of, undiscovered . . . rediscovered. At the top of its bent, it is as greedy for new sensation as any fashion reporter, notebook in hand, hunched beside the runways of fashion shows in Milan. One would certainly not say that the interest in hardy perennials is over, for there are always wonderful new ones to grow, and certain ones—so proven, so true—must always be depended on as a backdrop against which the gardener might experiment with novelties. Still, the Perennial Movement left American gardeners, in a sense, wondering—after so heady a ride—what was next?

Annuals Redefined

In direct response to the hunger for garden plants beyond hardy perennials, several books appeared in a cluster about ten years ago, among them my own *Annuals for Connoisseurs*. Like most others on the subject, it contained portraits of favorite annuals, with cultural advice and suggestions for landscape use, but it was by no means intended as a thorough treatment of its subject. That daunting task had partially been undertaken by *Taylor's Guide to Annuals* (Macmillan, 1986), and four years later by Jennifer Bennett and Turid Forsyth in their excellent *The Harrowsmith Annual Garden* (Camden House, 1990). However, both books limited themselves to a consideration of true annuals, plants that could be grown from seed to maturity in a single growing season, with lives that usually extended only from spring to fall, after which they died.

But the subject of annuals began to seem much broader to many gardeners than they had previously thought. Plants began to appear in garden centers and in good seed catalogues that actually were biennials, tender perennials, or shrubs, but that were sufficiently fast of growth and decorative in character that they could be included in borders and in containers for a single season of pleasure, after which they were usually discarded. The wave of gardening enthusiasm that began to sweep America in the late '70s and early '80s created an appetite for new and unusual garden plants, and owners of garden centers quickly perceived that many species, often costly and slower to produce than seed-grown plants, might nevertheless result in a fuller cash register at season's end. Nurseries that produced their own plants for sale began to comb houseplant catalogues (such as the venerable Logee's Greenhouses in Danielson, Connecticut) for unusual or forgotten tender perennials, and to bring back tropical plants for propagation from vacations to Florida. They also eagerly accepted cuttings from customers who had preserved heirloom plants on their windowsills for years, or had been given a slip of a mystery plant by a cousin or friend. Large wholesale companies with vast ranges of greenhouses began to supply cutting-grown plants to garden centers, usually as rooted plugs, though often as fully grown specimens, and to sow biennials and half-hardy or tender perennials early in the year under controlled glasshouse conditions, in order to produce plants that would flower their first year outdoors in the garden. Gardeners began to cast a speculative eye on familiar "houseplants" and wonder how they might look bedded out among the hostas and astilbes. The consequence of all this activity was that the concept of an "annual"—never very clear from the start—came to mean anything one wanted to plant in spring (or later) and discarded in the fall (or earlier), when its decorative seasonal use was over.

Actually, though I have gardened for many years in Vermont (Zone 4/5), I had the good luck to be well prepared for this explosion of interest. I grew up in Louisiana, with gardening grandparents, aunts, uncles, cousins, and family friends among whom the passion for plants—all plants, whatever their technical categories of annual, perennial, or shrub—was extraordinarily well developed. Shreveport is perhaps not the most favored climate in North America for growing the largest number of garden-worthy species (San Diego is probably that), but it still exists within the fairly privileged Zone 7, where bananas are root-hardy, cannas live happily over winter in the ground, gardenia bushes are permanent features of the landscape, and figs ripen reliably. The end of February signals the arrival of spring, but camellias have been picked from backyard bushes a month or more before that. All my earliest experiments as a gardener were in that climate, and I can still remember the excitement of discovering that sansevieria, for example (popularly called "mother-in-law's tongue"), looked far more interesting planted among the hardy ferns in the backyard than it did standing in a pot in the upper stairway window.

New Orleans lies a full two gardening zones away from Shreveport, but I was often there also in the summer, where an aunt of mine, a passionate gardener, had a summer house across Lake Pontchartrain in the sleepy little village of Madisonville. Her garden was magical to me as a child, for it contained plants that I only later could call zantedeschias, setcresias, achimenes, and hedychiums. They grew in her beds and borders like any ordinary perennials, and could be divided to share with a child already passionate about gardening at the age of five. Before I was fifteen, my father, who was born in Fort Lauderdale, often took us on summer vacations to Florida, and to Cuba, of which he was particularly fond. There, another whole range of plants grew, enlarging even more my sense of all the magical things that could be planted once one broke away from the limitations of mere hardiness.

So when I came to write *Annuals for Connoisseurs* (1992), I knew already that my subject was far larger than so slight a book (or such a title) could cover. I am sure I am not alone—even among garden writers—in making a first, tentative attempt at a subject that I knew I would have to return to eventually and in a much more serious way. For even in its most traditional use, the term *annual* covers a huge territory beyond zinnias and marigolds and other summer bedding plants familiar to most American gardeners. And even if they are concerned merely with furnishing two window boxes outside a city apartment, there really is a brave new world of annual and tender plants available, quite suddenly, richer even than that known by the Edwardians, whose passion for gardening matched ours of the present day.

What Is an Annual?

Most gardeners will be keen to know the botanical classification of their plants, first, simply to know, but second, because the way a plant is classified often provides an important key to its cultivation or to the possibility of carrying it over the winter on a sunny windowsill, in a heated sun porch, home greenhouse, or even under fluorescent light in a heated basement. To that end, I have listed the technical classification of a plant in the heading that discusses each genus, and again in the text where individual species are discussed. But a little additional explanation may be useful here.

TRUE ANNUALS

If a plant is described as a **true annual,** it may be expected to develop reasonably rapidly from seed, which should in most cases be sown about six to eight weeks before the last anticipated frost date in one's area, or even later. Familiar, no-fuss plants within this class include marigolds, zinnias, and sunflowers. But within the class are also many that transplant with difficulty or not at all, such as larkspurs, sweet alyssum, and several flowering vines, including annual morning glories and sweet peas. When plants that resent transplanting also develop relatively slowly, they will have to be sown indoors in peat pots or flexible plastic cell packs that will allow their root mass to be slipped gently out, rather like an ice cube from a plastic tray. The persistent myth that all annual plants should be messed up about the roots at transplant time is just that, myth, for that practice would be either damaging or fatal to at least 70 percent of the plants discussed in this book. Plants that resent root disturbance, and so must be transplanted with extra care, are always noted.

TENDER AND HALF-HARDY PERENNIALS

In contrast to true annuals, **tender** and **half-hardy perennials** will usually require being sown under glass early in the year, as much as three to four months before the last anticipated frost date. The difference between these two classes is that **half-**

hardy perennials will accept cool spring weather and often even frost, whereas **tender perennials** are damaged even by light frosts and sulk at raw spring weather. Within these groups are some of the most popular "annuals" grown in America, such as pansies and violas, petunias, verbenas, and snapdragons. Plants within both these classes may also often be reproduced from cuttings, sometimes quite easily, as is the case with verbena or portulaca, for example. Often, choice forms of perennial plants grown as annuals can only be reproduced in this way, either because they are sterile and therefore set no seed, or their seed-born progeny will revert to another and less desirable form. Examples would include many of the finest new petunias, dubbed "Supertunias" and "Superfinias," and most verbenas, such as 'Sissinghurst Pink' or 'Homestead Purple'.

As plants in both groups will often regrow when cut back to tough, woody stems at their base, it is always worth shearing them by about a third when they become shabby and cease to produce flowers. Given a dose of fast-acting, water-soluble fertilizer, they will often produce a second flush of growth and flower before summer's end, or may be brought into a greenhouse or placed on a bright windowsill for a few flowers throughout the dark months of the year. From stock plants of tender or half-hardy perennials carried over winter, cuttings can also be made in early spring for additional plants, and some that form crowns of growth from the base may even be divided then for additional increase.

BIENNIALS

Included among plants that may be tricked against their nature to flower in their first season of growth are also several **biennials,** such as foxgloves, hollyhocks, forget-me-nots, and sweet William. Usually, such plants are old-fashioned cottage garden favorites that may be difficult to manage in small gardens, since they normally occupy their space for a full growing year before they produce bloom. They will not, therefore, normally bloom until their second year in gardens, after they have spent one full growing season producing leafy growth. But when tricked into precocious flowering by an extended period of growth in a cool greenhouse, they are useful for bedding schemes. The best example within this class is perhaps forget-me-nots, ubiquitously but often beautifully used as an underplanting for tulips. Most biennials can never be reproduced from cuttings. But once introduced into a garden as "annuals," they will often self-seed copiously, their progeny occupying out-of-the-way places and germinating in midsummer of one year and flowering in spring of the next.

TENDER SHRUBS

Shrubby plants grown as annuals used to be a fairly small group, though they included some great favorites, such as lantanas, pelargoniums, fuchsias, heliotropes, and hibiscus. In the last ten years, however, the number of popular plants that fit into this class has grown enormously, with the addition, for example, of abutilons in many forms, brugmansias, bouvardias, tibouchinas, anisodonteas, and many shrubs with variegated leaves, such as acalyphas, strobilanthes, and alternantheras. As these plants generally root with relative ease, they have traditionally been grown from cuttings, thus producing sizable plants more quickly than when grown from seed, and also preserving their desirable characteristics of flower, leaf shape, and color. If facilities for overwintering them exist—such as a home greenhouse, a heated sun porch, or the proverbial sunny windowsill—shrubby plants may be cut back and brought indoors to overwinter. Often, they may be sent into a state of semi or complete dormancy by holding them in a poorly lit cellar or garage heated to just above freezing. During this time they will take up little valuable growing space and require little care, asking only to be kept barely moist to prevent shriveling of the wood. In spring, however, they must be brought into warmer conditions and given more care as they resume active growth.

Within the class of tender shrubs are also plants often grown as **standards,** the old-fashioned gardener's term for woody plants trained into little trees—small, single-trunked, mop-headed specimens that look something like a child's first drawing of a tree. Such plants add great sophistication when used as single specimens in pots or in the ground. With patience, any woody-based tender shrub commonly grown as an annual may be trained into this form. Given the appropriate facilities, standards are always worth carrying over from year to year, as they gain in beauty and authority with each passing season.

Annuals: A Working Definition

All these classes of plants—true annuals, tender and half-hardy perennials, biennials, and tender shrubs—may now embellish our gardens, creating a richer possibility of choices than has ever been known before. Originating from every continent on the globe except Antarctica, they differ widely in their cultural requirements. To the gardener, that is a great advantage: At least a few may be found for the most difficult garden conditions, such as deep shade or permanently saturated earth, though most will require moderate to bright light, adequate drainage, and a reasonably fertile, free-draining humus-rich soil. Though diverse in their technical classifications, most may be comfortably thought of as annuals, in the way that impatiens, for example, have always been, even though most gardeners know that cuttings may be taken for pleasantly, if shyly, flowering windowsill plants through the winter, and that therefore the plant is actually a tender shrub that produces permanent growth above ground.

The word *annual,* then, is conveniently employed by most gardeners just as the word *vegetable* is, the first indicating a more-or-less cold-sensitive plant primarily valued for ornament in the summer garden and generally not surviving over winter, and the second designating a plant valued for culinary use. Most vegetable gardeners will not be concerned with the fact that tomatoes, peppers, and eggplants are technically shrubs, that

Swiss chard will be perennial in mild regions, or that beets are actually biennials. But the curious gardener might like to know such details, and the gardener who plants annuals always should, since the information often affects the way plants should be treated.

HARDY, HALF-HARDY, AND TENDER

In addition to the classifications of plants as annual, biennial, perennial, or shrub, plants grown for ornament in the summer garden are also often classified as hardy, half-hardy, or tender, depending on their tolerance for cold weather.

Hardy annuals will accept a few degrees of frost, and the early, spring-blooming ones such as pansies and English lawn daisies (*Bellis perennis*) will revive even after being covered with ice and snow. But they will only perform this feat of endurance if they are well **hardened off,** a traditional gardener's phrase that indicates a gradual process of exposure to real outdoor conditions before they are plunged directly from the grower's greenhouse into the open garden. Indeed, any plant taken from a protected environment in a nursery or garden center should experience a few days of hardening off, by being moved gradually from a sheltered environment—say, against a house foundation, just inside an open garage door, or beneath a shrub casting light shade—into the conditions in which it must finally grow, for frost and cold are not the only elemental difficulties greenhouse plants may experience. Broiling sun, dry air, and wind may be just as harmful, even fatal, to overcoddled plants.

Within the class of hardy plants are many that will self-seed from year to year once they have been grown, even in the colder gardens of Zone 4 (see Zone Map, page xxvii), where winters reach −20°F and the ground may freeze to a depth of three feet. Occasionally they may be a nuisance, or even an ecological threat, as the magnificent and prolific Himalayan jewelweed (*Impatiens glandulifera*) appears to be. Mostly, however, self-seeded hardy annuals are easy to scuffle away with a trowel or hoe, and many, such as English daisies, larkspurs, poppies, and Johnny-jump-ups would be sorely missed if they did not return from year to year as volunteer seedlings. Often, also, annuals that self-seed provide plants that behave far more splendidly than those that are transplanted into spaces assigned by the gardener, assuming they appear spontaneously in the right place. If not, of course they must be weeded out, or transplanted where they are wanted.

But plants that self-seed, or **volunteer,** as old gardeners say, sometimes show an uncanny aesthetic sense, appearing in unexpected spots where gardeners would never have thought to plant them, and where we cannot do better than to hold back the disturbing trowel. Quick-growing hardy annuals that are difficult to transplant, such as larkspurs, poppies, and nigellas, may often also be sown in place directly in the garden, and later thinned to stand an appropriate distance from one another. Such plants will behave essentially as self-seeded ones, producing results far more effective than even the most carefully transplanted seedlings.

Half-hardy annuals comprise the largest group grown in gardens, and are represented by familiar plants such as impatiens, fibrous-rooted begonias, zinnias, and marigolds. Though still sensitive to temperatures below 32°F, they will tolerate, and indeed sometimes relish, cool growing conditions. The mainstay of nurseries and garden centers—what the trade calls "bread-and-butter plants"—they generally behave well in pots and plastic six-packs, usually transplant readily, and often show a perky, precocious bloom or two in the first warm days after spring has settled in for good. That is about the time when the petals of apple blossoms fall from the trees, when all danger of frost is assumed to be past and lawns are green. In a good year, one never looks back. But the last frosts and the first ones are capricious things, and so one must be ready with old sheets, blankets, bedspreads, curtains, paper boxes, whatever is on hand, to protect young plants from a sudden and unexpected dip of temperatures toward freezing. Most times, these cautions represent wasted effort because the frost that was predicted on the evening news does not come. But gardeners are often superstitious in their way, and many would be convinced that if they hadn't protected newly transplanted half-hardy annuals, frost would have been a certainty.

Tender annuals all originate in climates that never know a touch of frost, chiefly parts of Central and South America, India, tropical Asia, and South Africa. Temperatures below freezing will surely blacken them in death, at both the beginning and the end of the season. However, even temperatures well above freezing but that still cause the gardener to don a sweater will make them sit still through the drizzles of June until really warm weather arrives. For this reason, it is never wise to hurry their transplanting, for most will fare better if kept in a warm but bright protected environment, fertilized and pinched to encourage bushy growth, hardened off carefully, and transplanted into their permanent homes only when really good beach weather arrives.

In this class belong many of the tender perennials and shrubs that are most exciting to gardeners at present, such as salvias, lantanas, abutilons, anisodonteas, and brugmansias. The group is of particular value to gardeners who endure the stress of summer heat in steamy eastern cities, in much of the middle and upper South, in parts of the Midwest, California, and the Southwest—for such plants will stand, and even relish, the hot, muggy days of August when many hardy or half-hardy annuals will pack up and be off.

Using Annuals in the Garden

However annuals are classified, certain generalizations may be made about their uses in the garden. To begin with, it is fair to say that annuals cannot of themselves make a garden. For a garden is best understood as structured space, much as a house or other building is instinctively understood by those who look at it. The solidity of a garden depends on its permanent elements, its paths, walls, hedges, trees, and the furniture provided by its shrubs and hardy perennials. Annuals are by definition transitory. And though a summer's lease at the shore might cause one—and with some success—to create the illusion of a well-structured garden using annuals alone, the first frosts of autumn would fell one's tall hedges of castor bean and malva, one's specimen shrubs of lavatera and abelmoschus, one's perennial-looking drifts of everything, even one's little ground covers of laurentia and diascia, leaving the ground—sooner or later—just about as bare as it was when one came. That would not of course stop any gardener required by necessity to occupy temporary digs, but neither would it conceal the real truth.

Which is this: All annuals are *carpe diem* plants, conditioned by botanical identity or by geographic circumstance to make the most of their short day. Many of them grow fast and bloom abundantly, often producing waves of color or incredible luxuriance of leaf with surprising speed. Among plants used as annuals, such plants are the most treasured and the most frequently purchased in garden centers, which, after all, are owned by people who must make a living, and so must understand what is called "shelf appeal."

Still, the most precious of all annual plants may be the most ephemeral, those that offer only a few magical flowers, sparingly born in a single summer month. And those will never appear in garden centers, but must be sown by the careful gardener in place, on a patch of prepared earth raked smooth, usually "as soon in spring as the ground may be worked," and pressed in lightly with the flat side of a board. But as a class, whether common or rare, all annuals seem to know that either sheer exhaustion or unendurable cold wait for them at the end of whatever show they may produce, which is always more-or-less brief.

Valuing Annuals

For this reason, plants classed as annuals are never to be thought of as permanent elements of a garden's design, but rather as garnish or enlivenment, sources of amusement and joy. The committed perennial cranks will have little use for them, for miserlike, they generally believe that if a plant is not reliably hardy, capable of returning year after year to furnish its space and provide divisions, they have poured money into the ground, and worse, wasted valuable space in the garden.

But a garden—a *real* garden—is not a static thing, reduced forever to unchanging elements, constant through the seasons and the years. Nothing constructed for the amusement of humans is that. And at their best, true annuals—and thousands of other plants grown as such—provide something that even relative permanence cannot offer. That is a sense of accidental beauty, a lightening of the heart that comes just because beauty is brief, rather like the pretty secretary that leaves after six months, or even a haunting face seen in a departing subway window. Annuals lend themselves to fantasy and to dreaming, for hedges cannot be moved about at will, and after a time trees must remain stubbornly where they are planted. Only the very wanton gardener rips up and discards his perennials on a yearly basis, restlessly pursuing subtleties of leaf and color harmony that he will perhaps never achieve. But any winter's dreaming over catalogues of annuals might suggest new possibilities, new color schemes, new scents, shapes, forms of temporary plants that might be brought into the garden. That is endless fun.

On Plant Choices

Readers who still think of annual and tender plants in terms of the traditional offerings of the average roadside plant stand may be surprised at the size and scope of this book, which treats more than 250 genera and an uncounted number of species. Still, in order to keep it within even its present bounds, many plants have been excluded, usually because they were not sufficiently garden worthy or were either hopelessly rare or impossibly difficult to grow. The most sophisticated gardeners will find the greatest number of omissions, of course, but then it is to be hoped that they are already sufficiently familiar with the plant they are checking on. It may still be true, however, that I must occasionally echo Dr. Johnson's reply, when asked by a woman why a certain word had not been included in his great *Dictionary:* "Simple ignorance, Madam."

But beyond all these reasons for omitting plants, two others must be pointed out. Again because of considerations of size, two important classes that might have been covered have been excluded—ornamental grasses and summer-blooming plants that grow from bulbs, corms, tubers, or rhizomes. There is much renewed interest in both, and tempting offerings—of species either newly discovered or simply forgotten—appear in catalogues each year. There would be enough to say about each class to fill two other books (though smaller, blessedly, than this). Sadly, that must wait a while.

Botanical Names

Plants within the book are listed under their botanical names. "More Greek and Latin!" the gardener will cry, though in fact, botanical names (which may also come from ancient Arabic or many native vernacular tongues) often tell their own fascinating tales, most of which, as they apply to one plant or another, have been explained within the entries of this book. Phonetic transcriptions have also been offered next to the first mention of each botanical name, in an attempt to help the reader with sometimes difficult pronunciations.

Every effort has been made to make sure that botanical names are current, though botany, like most science, is not static, but rather a rapidly evolving body of knowledge, and changes in botanical designations occur yearly. For the moment, what is offered here is as correct as it can be gotten, though occasionally, when both gardeners and seed catalogues still recognize a familiar plant under a previous name, it has been so listed, and its newer, more current name provided within the text.

Finally, all known common names have been listed as well. It is true that common names can create great confusion, as in the case of the notorious "creeping Jenny," which may designate half a dozen different plants. But common names are also charming, and often they attest to the history of a plant in gardens, its medicinal uses, or the ancient lore that surrounds it. Both botanical and common names offer gardeners information about their plants. And about gardening—as about any of the other important pursuits with which humans are concerned—the more we know, the more satisfaction we may obtain. It is to that single end that this book is devoted.

USDA Plant Hardiness Zone Map

AVERAGE ANNUAL MINIMUM TEMPERATURE

Temperature (°C)	Zone	Temperature (°F)
-45.6 and Below	1	Below -50
-42.8 to -45.5	2a	-45 to -50
-40.0 to -42.7	2b	-40 to -45
-37.3 to -40.0	3a	-35 to -40
-34.5 to -37.2	3b	-30 to -35
-31.7 to -34.4	4a	-25 to -30
-28.9 to -31.6	4b	-20 to -25
-26.2 to -28.8	5a	-15 to -20
-23.4 to -26.1	5b	-10 to -15
-20.6 to -23.3	6a	-5 to -10
-17.8 to -20.5	6b	0 to -5
-15.0 to -17.7	7a	5 to 0
-12.3 to -15.0	7b	10 to 5
-9.5 to -12.2	8a	15 to 10
-6.7 to -9.4	8b	20 to 15
-3.9 to -6.6	9a	25 to 20
-1.2 to -3.8	9b	30 to 25
1.6 to -1.1	10a	35 to 30
4.4 to 1.7	10b	40 to 35
4.5 and Above	11	40 and Above

0 100 200 300 400 500 600
Scale in Kilometers

0 100 200 300 400 500 600
Scale in Miles

Scale 1:6,000,000 (Approximately)

COURTESY AGRICULTURAL RESEARCH SERVICE, USDA

ANNUALS & TENDER PLANTS

for North American Gardens

ABELMOSCHUS SPECIES

FAMILY: *Malvaceae* or hibiscus family.

CLASSIFICATION: Tender annuals or tender perennials grown as tender annuals.

COMMON NAME: Abelmoschus.

HARDINESS: Resents temperatures much below 40°F. Extremely frost sensitive.

GROWING CONDITIONS: Very rich, humusy, well-drained soil. Full sun.

PROPAGATION: By seed, sown indoors in peat pots 8 to 12 weeks before last frost. Plants resent root disturbance.

HEIGHT: From 18" to 7', depending on species.

ORNAMENTAL VALUE: Grown for flower.

LEVEL OF CULTURAL DIFFICULTY: Easy.

SPECIAL PROPERTIES: *A. esculentus* valued for edible pods.

PRONUNCIATION: a-bel-MOS-kus

For gardeners who assume that all botanical language is drawn from Latin or Greek, the name of the genus *Abelmoschus* provides an interesting lesson, for it is derived from the Arabic *abu-l-mosk,* which translates as "parent of musk," attesting to the ancient use of the seeds of some species in perfume. Several species of *Abelmoschus* are grown in gardens, but none for fragrance in any of their parts. When crushed, they simply smell green, and when dried and crumbled, they merely smell dusty. Still, they are valuable ornamental plants, particularly for gardens that experience long, hot, humid summers, conditions that remind them of their African origins and cause them to flourish and bloom wonderfully well.

To most gardeners, the most familiar species in the genus is probably *A. esculentus* (es-cue-LEN-tus). Called "okra" after its ancient African name

and brought by slaves into colonial America, it quickly became almost a staple food in the American South, where its edible pods are stewed with tomatoes, dipped in cornmeal and fried, or best of all, added to thick, savory gumbos. For all its tastiness (the species name *esculentus* is Latin for savory), it is in itself a quite pretty plant. Though dwarves have been bred, the species naturally produces tall shrublike plants to as much as seven feet, their branches studded here and there with three-inch, lemon-yellow, five-petaled flowers stained with deep purple at their centers.

Among species of *Abelmoschus,* only okra is grown for food, though another closely related species, *A. manihot* (MAN-uh-hot), is a splendid garden subject. It improves on the ornamental qualities of its kitchen cousin by offering a plant that is elegant in all its parts. In the hot weather of high summer, *A. manihot* quickly forms a six- to eight-foot-tall, loosely branched plant, shrublike though open in growth, with beautifully crafted upturned, dark green leaves of three, five, or even seven lobes. The stature of the plant and the beauty of its foliage would almost be reason alone to grow it. But from midsummer to frost, each branch is ornamented by five- to six-inch-wide, hibiscus-like flowers, of a beautiful primrose yel-

ABELMOSCHUS MANIHOT

ABELMOSCHUS MOSCHATUS

against which the flowers seem to glow. They are predominately a rich, coral pink, though darker or lighter colors may result from the same seed sowing. Of whatever related tint, however, the flowers are given special beauty by the shading of each petal toward the center of the blossom, where white is brushed over deeper pink. Individual flowers last for only a day, but in warm weather, they are so abundantly produced that the plant always seems rich in bloom.

All members of the genus *Abelmoschus* love hot, steamy weather, and so little is gained by starting them very early indoors, for they will sulk in the cool, damp conditions of early spring, even when frosts are past. However, for earliest flower, seed of *A. manihot* might be sown about four to six weeks before the last anticipated frost date. Young plants are severely set back by root disturbance, and so should be sown three seeds to a peat pot, clipping out all but the strongest at transplant time. Germination is rapid at temperatures around 70°F, and young seedlings should be grown on in bright, sunny conditions until the weather is quite warm and settled, at about the time it is safe to transplant tomatoes, peppers, and eggplants.

Seed of *A. moschatus* is rarely available, but as it is a more compact plant requiring a longer period of development, it might well be sown in warm conditions as early as twelve weeks before the last anticipated frost date and grown on in sunny conditions at temperatures around 65° to 70°F. It will more often enter gardens, however, as a lusty, well-branched young plant in plastic six-packs, perhaps already showing the first precocious furled buds. Both *A. manihot* and *A. moschatus* require as much sun as possible, and rich, well-drained, humusy soil. Like their edible cousin, *A. esculentus,* both are also greedy feeders, benefit-

low with a deep burgundy stain at their throats. Like all members of Malvaceae, the hibiscus family, the fertile parts of the flower are worth looking at, made up here of bright yellow stamens crowned by a five-branched pistil of rich, plush red. Because of its height, one might suppose that *A. manihot* would look fine at the back of a border, and so it does. But its beauty of branch, leaf, and flower suggests that it might look even finer when pulled forward to the edge of a path or terrace, or planted anywhere as a single, solitary specimen.

Though a separate genus entirely from true hibiscus, all members of *Abelmoschus* are "hibiscus-like," some more so than others. Anyone who first saw *A. moschatus* (mos-KA-tus) growing in a garden would assume it to be a dwarf hibiscus, a genus in which it was once included. Its flowers are five petaled, as are hibiscus, though they never overlap, but rather flare out from the center and fold down at their edges, nicely displaying prominent anthers and pistil, another signature characteristic of the family. The plant is small, hardly ever more than a foot in height, though often twice as wide, shrubby in growth and clad with dark green, lobed leaves

ing from weekly applications of a general, water-soluble fertilizer at half the strength recommended on the package, or, when grown in the open ground, from a sprinkling of balanced, granular garden fertilizer—10-10-10 or the like—applied just after transplants have caught and again a month later.

ABRONIA SPECIES

FAMILY: *Nyctaginaceae* or four o'clock family.

CLASSIFICATION: Tender perennial grown as tender annual.

COMMON NAMES: Sand verbena, wild lantana, abronia.

HARDINESS: Hardy in Zones 9 and 10. Sensitive to light frosts elsewhere.

GROWING CONDITIONS: Thin, sandy soil. Full sun.

PROPAGATION: From seed, sown indoors 12 weeks before last anticipated frost. Tip cuttings root easily.

HEIGHT: To 12".

ORNAMENTAL VALUE: Grown for flower.

LEVEL OF CULTURAL DIFFICULTY: Moderately difficult.

SPECIAL PROPERTIES: Used to stabilize sandy soil where hardy. Drought tolerant.

PRONUNCIATION: a-BRO-nee-a

For eastern gardeners there are so many low-growing, floriferous plants for the front of a border or the edge of a pot that sand verbenas may well be of interest only to native plant specialists, rock gardeners, or other connoisseurs of unusual plants. In coastal California, however, or the Southwest, they are of greater value for they thrive in poor, sandy soil, and are able to stabilize it wherever their lax or procumbent stems touch ground and root.

The genus name, from ancient Greek *abros,* means delicate, attesting to the fragile bracts surrounding each flower, borne in thick, verbena-like clusters atop each stem. But the plants themselves are not at all verbena-like, bearing thick, fleshy leaves—roundish or kidney-shaped—capable of storing water during periods of drought. The species most widely cultivated are native to very temperate climates in the southwestern United States, particularly the coastal regions of California, and though true perennials all may be expected to flower in their first season from an early spring sowing. The three species most commonly grown are *Abronia fragrans* (fra-GRANS), upright to ten inches, with umbels of white, night-scented flowers; procumbent *A. latifolia* (la-ti-FO-lee-a), growing into foot-wide mats, furnished in high summer with lemon-yellow flowers; prostrate *A. umbellata* (um-be-LA-ta), especially in the desirable cultivar 'Grandiflora', which produces abundant, rose-pink to purple flowers, ideal for hanging baskets.

Seed of any species of *Abronia,* difficult to find and difficult to germinate, is best sown at temperatures of around 60°F, about twelve weeks from the last anticipated frost date. The outer husks should be removed by gently rubbing the seed between the palms of one's hands, before soaking it for a day in tepid water. It should then be drained and patted dry on paper towels so that it may be easily dispersed across the potting compost and lightly pressed in. Germination may still be erratic, and young seedlings, prone to mildew and to damping off, must be grown in bright, airy conditions, and possibly treated with a fungicide. Once any abronia has been grown in the garden, it may be carried on from year to year by cuttings taken from tip growths. Inserted in damp, sharp sand in moist, shaded conditions, they should root within three weeks or so. Rooted cuttings may then be potted in free-draining compost, and taken into bright, frost-free conditions for the winter, where they should be watered sparingly to prevent rot. As the days lengthen, water may be increased, and a light application of water-soluble fertilizer be given before transplanting after all danger of frost is past.

ABUTILON X HYBRIDUM

FAMILY: *Malvaceae* or hibiscus family.

CLASSIFICATION: Tender shrubs grown as tender annuals.

COMMON NAMES: Flowering maple, parlor maple, Chinese lantern bush, abutilon.

HARDINESS: Hardy to Zone 10. Damaged elsewhere by temperatures much below 40°F. Extremely frost tender.

ABUTILON MEGAPOTAMICUM

GROWING CONDITIONS: Humus-rich, well-drained soil. Abundant moisture. Full sun or very bright shade.

PROPAGATION: From tip cuttings, which root readily in spring and early summer.

HEIGHT: Varies, from 1 to 6'.

ORNAMENTAL VALUE: Grown for flower and in some cultivars for ornamental leaves.

LEVEL OF CULTURAL DIFFICULTY: Easy.

SPECIAL PROPERTIES: Excellent when trained as standards.

PRONUNCIATION: ab-YOU-ti-lon hi-BRI-dum

*B*ecause abutilons are winter-hardy in only the warmest parts of North America, they are most familiar as potted shrubs, either for winter bloom or for standing about in the summer garden. And while they may also be bedded out as striking woody accents in mixed borders, all abutilons are flowers to study up close, and so are best featured in pots or planted at the edge of a bed, along a path, or near a terrace, where their beauty may be closely observed.

The species name comes from an ancient Arabic word for many mallowlike plants, and gardeners will quickly recognize in these flowers their kinship to other plants in the family Malvaceae—hibiscus, abelmoschus, lavatera, and anisodontea. The distinction of abutilons, however, is that whereas most other members of their family produce their abundant, five-petaled flowers facing outward, abutilons bear theirs discreetly, as little cups dangling from two-inch stems. But as the color of their flowers is unusually vivid, their modesty exists only in the way they carry themselves. In the very limited areas where abutilons are hardy—chiefly southern Florida and the milder areas of the West Coast—gardeners will want to search out both pure species and the finest hybrids to use as free-growing shrubs, espaliers, or even scandent, vinelike plants. In such privileged places, an extensive collection of abutilons would be a wonderful idea, for there are approximately 150 species in the genus, and many showy hybrids.

Gardeners in other parts of North America will find all the abutilons they need grouped under the name *Abutilon* x *hybridum,* indicating (as the word *hybridum* always does) a complex intermingling of species and back crosses of hybrids to produce interesting, garden-worthy plants. Within this group will be plants compact or rangy of growth, with leaves lobed like those of sugar maples or arrow-shaped, dark green, white-margined, or speckled over with gold or white. Flowers may be as small as a thimble or as large, almost, as a shot glass, but they are always bell-shaped and down-hanging, and their petals are gossamer-thin, though prominently veined. Flower color will range through pure white and cream to pale and deep yellow, coral, orange, crimson, and deep red. One of the special charms of all abutilons is that their petals emerge from a prominent calyx, which is itself beautifully colored often in some shade of brick red.

The hybrid origin of most abutilons in gardens means that they are generally acquired as rooted cuttings, rather than from seed, which is rarely available. Softwood cuttings taken in spring and early summer, when plants are growing lustily, root easily in a mixture of half sharp sand or perlite and half peat, under warm, closed conditions, after which they may be potted and grown on in rich, free-draining compost. Like most members of the mallow family, abutilons demand a rich, humusy soil, abundant light—in the form of full sun or very bright shade—and plenty of moisture, though with perfect drainage at their roots. They are quick and rank of growth, and so frequently pinching out the tip of each shoot promotes bushy, attractive plants.

ABUTILON *X 'SAVITZII'*

Like two close members of their family (hibiscus and anisodontea), abutilons are prime candidates for training into standards—small, mop-headed miniature trees. The work takes time and patience—at least two full growing seasons and also a place where the plants may be protected throughout the winter from frost—a greenhouse or heated sun porch. First a strong, central trunk is developed from a rooted cutting, and then, when it has reached the desired height (usually around four feet) its growing tip is pinched, and subsequent growth pinched again, to develop a full, rounded head. Grown this way, abutilons display their dangling flowers to great advantage, and the plant, because of its interesting shape, becomes an important ornament in the summer garden.

ACALYPHA SPECIES

FAMILY: *Euphorbiaceae* or spurge family.

CLASSIFICATION: Tender shrubs grown as tender annuals.

COMMON NAME: Acalypha (other common names vary with species).

HARDINESS: Hardy in Zone 10. Damaged by temperatures much below 40°F. Extremely frost sensitive. Relish heat.

GROWING CONDITIONS: Humus-rich, moisture-retentive, well-drained soils. Full sun in cooler gardens, afternoon shade in warmer ones.

PROPAGATION: From tip cuttings, rooted in spring.

HEIGHT: To 2′ when grown as an annual. To 5′ if carried over as a cool greenhouse plant.

ORNAMENTAL VALUE: *A. hispida* grown for ropelike inflorescences; *A. wilkesiana* for colored leaves.

LEVEL OF CULTURAL DIFFICULTY: Easy.

SPECIAL PROPERTIES: Interesting winter cool greenhouse or houseplants.

PRONUNCIATION: a-KAL-i-fa

ACALYPHA HISPIDA

*A*calyphas, probably original to the Malay Archipelago and now naturalized in all tropical parts of the world, were much treasured by Victorian gardeners. They kept them through the winter in conservatories heated to 55° or 60°F, building them up into stout shrubs five or six feet tall, after which they became outrageous additions to bedding schemes, along with palms, croton, bananas, and other tropical plants. *Acalypha hispida* (HI-spi-da), the "chenille plant," the only member of its genus cultivated for its flowers, was especially beloved of Victorian gardeners for its extraordinary blooms: foot-long, dangling ropes in rose-pink shading to red.

Lately, as with so many other plants that passed out of fashion with the Victorian practice of tropical bedding, acalyphas have begun to reappear in nurseries and garden centers. They can be quite beautiful, but except for large specimens grown over the winter in a greenhouse heated to 70°F, it is hard to imagine any bedding scheme in which *A. hispida* would look its best. Its ropes of bloom, precociously produced, would dangle off plants that may be only two or three feet tall and draggle in the mud. It does, however, make a very interesting potted patio plant, and has lately appeared as a hanging basket plant, which shows off its blooms to perfect advantage, borne from the axils of its rich green, glossy, heart-shaped leaves. Grown this way, however, it must be watered frequently, as dryness at its roots will be fatal.

By contrast, *Acalypha wilkesiana* (wilks-ee-A-na), popularly called "copper leaf" or "beefsteak plant," and sometimes "match-me-if-you-can," is grown not for its flowers, which are insignificant, but for its colored leaves, the vividness of which can surpass almost any bright-leaved foliage plant, as its most amusing popular name attests. Though where it is hardy (Zone 10), it can

ACALYPHA WILKESIANA

summer conditions. It is striking when bedded out as an accent among plantings of annuals, perennials, and tender shrubs, or as a component to mixed plantings in containers. But two or three young plants are also effective in a bay within a border of hardy, spring-blooming shrubs, where their leaves make a vivid contrast to the more-or-less undistinguished foliage of forsythias, azaleas, spireas, and the like.

Most gardeners will acquire acalyphas as well-grown young plants from nurseries that specialize in unusual annuals and tender plants, but pliable tip cuttings root easily in spring, when inserted in half sharp sand or perlite and half peat, preferably with some bottom heat, and half-ripe cuttings will root with similar treatment later in the summer. Older plants can also be cut back and divided in spring, potted on in well-draining, rich compost, and kept just moist until new growth appears.

ACNISTUS AUSTRALIS (IOCHROMA AUSTRALE)

FAMILY: *Solanaceae* or deadly nightshade family.

CLASSIFICATION: Tender shrub grown as tender annual.

COMMON NAME: Acnistus.

HARDINESS: Sensitive to light frosts.

GROWING CONDITIONS: Humus-rich, fertile, well-drained soil. Full sun. Relishes heat.

PROPAGATION: From seed and cuttings.

HEIGHT: 2 to 3' in a season.

ORNAMENTAL VALUE: Grown for flower.

LEVEL OF CULTURAL DIFFICULTY: Difficult.

SPECIAL PROPERTIES: None.

PRONUNCIATION: ak-NIS-tus aus-TRA-lis (eye-o-KRO-ma aus-TRA-lee)

reach shrubby proportions to eight feet tall, small plants reach a height of a foot or two in summer gardens elsewhere. The triangular leaves, which are about six inches across and as long, are vividly marked with maroon, crimson, or orange-rose, often with creamy white edges. From a small plant, it can develop splendidly in gardens that experience hot, steamy late-

ACNISTUS AUSTRALIS

*H*orticultural data on *Acnistus australis* is so rare that its exact hardiness is unknown. Certainly it survives well over the winter in Zones 9 and 10, though it may be at least root-hardy in warm Zone 8, and in a favored location with the protection of a warm wall, it may even retain some wood throughout the winter. To most American gardeners, however, acnistus will be of greatest interest as a tender shrub for the summer garden.

A close relative of daturas and brugmansias, it is, like them, very fast growing, building up into two- to three-foot-tall bushes by summer's end, clad in arrow-shaped, four-inch-long medium green leaves. Its flowers are pendant bells, borne several to a cluster, each two to three inches long, typically of a beautiful slate blue, though California gardeners have made other color selections, ranging from every shade of blue and lilac to a powder blue almost white. Even a few blooms make the plant worth growing.

"Few" is all most American gardeners will ever get from acnistus, at least in summer, and even then only at the very end of summer, though plants taken into a warm winter greenhouse or conservatory can bloom profusely all winter long. Acnistus may, therefore, be one of those Southern Hemisphere plants (like many Central American *Salvias*) that require short days and long nights to flower. Gardeners who live where those conditions obtain (where, for example, okra grows well) might try the plant for summer bloom. The intense summer heat and humidity that usually exist in such gardens will certainly be very much to its liking, though plants must never be allowed to dry out, particularly when grown in pots, for that will usually be fatal.

Seed of acnistus is occasionally offered, and where it can be obtained, it should be sown at temperatures around 65°F, and pricked out as soon as the seedlings may be handled. They should then be grown on in bright, sunny conditions at temperatures around 70°F, until the weather is warm and settled, when they may be transplanted into permanent positions outdoors. Like most solanums—tomatoes, peppers, eggplants, and the like—they are very sensitive not only to frost, but also to the cool, damp conditions that occur in most American gardens in May and early June. Therefore, a late sowing is always best, so that plants may be shifted outdoors only when the weather is warm and settled. They are also very heavy feeders, and thrive best on fertilizers fabricated for tomatoes, their near relatives, according to the manufacturer's directions.

A random sowing of acnistus seed will produce flowers in a very wide range, from a pale, bluish white through paler, medium, and deeper blue, down to a blue that is almost royal purple, if one is lucky. None of their colors is positively ugly, though if one produces a seedling with particularly beautiful flowers—or buys such a plant as a rooted cutting—then it will be worth carrying over the winter for bloom the following year. Just before frost, such a plant should be cut back

hard, dug and potted in rich, free-draining compost, and brought into cool, sunny conditions,
at temperatures of around 55° to 60°F. Water
should be given sparingly until new growth appears in the spring, when it may be increased and
supplemented by frequent applications of dilute
liquid fertilizer. When the plant is growing vigorously and has filled its pot with roots, it should be
moved on to a larger pot, eventually to produce a
full-flowered specimen perhaps as much as six
feet tall and as broad.

The name of the genus *Acnistus* is of uncertain
meaning. The synonymous genus name *iochroma*
derives from ancient Greek *ion,* meaning violet,
and *chroma,* color or tint, and describes the typical
flower color of the species most frequently
grown. *Australis* or *australe* simply means southern, and indicates a plant originating in the
Southern Hemisphere, in this case Central and
South America.

ADONIS AESTIVALIS

FAMILY: *Ranunculaceae* or buttercup family.

CLASSIFICATION: Hardy annual.

COMMON NAMES: Blood poppy, annual adonis.

HARDINESS: Withstands frosts.

GROWING CONDITIONS: Humus-rich, moist, well-
drained soil. Full sun. Cool temperatures.

PROPAGATION: From seed, sown in place in September or October.

HEIGHT: To 1'.

ORNAMENTAL VALUE: Grown for flower.

LEVEL OF CULTURAL DIFFICULTY: Moderately difficult.

SPECIAL PROPERTIES: Will self-seed in most gardens.

PRONUNCIATION: a-DON-is es-ti-VAL-is

Of the forty or so Eurasian herbs in the genus
Adonis, only the one commonly grown as an annual—*Adonis aestivalis*—fits the legend of Adonis,
the mythical youth whose life was extraordinarily
tangled and tragic. Born from the heart of a tree
into which his mother was transformed when she
discovered that her own father was also the father
of her child, Adonis was rescued by Aphrodite and
delivered to Persephone to rear. When Aphrodite,
smitten by the extraordinary beauty of the child
when he grew to manhood, attempted to reclaim
him, Persephone refused to give him up. Eventually he was gored by a wild boar and as he died, his
blood flowed into the ground, which sprang up
with flowers of great beauty, blood-red in hue.

Most adonis are charming, early spring-
blooming perennials with sheeny, yellow butter-
cup-like flowers and dark centers, which give the
entire genus its common name, pheasant's eye.
But the flowers of *Adonis aestivalis* are a rare, clear
blood-red, about an inch wide, and borne profusely on single stems as five-petaled cups atop
finely divided, fernlike foliage.

There is great confusion about the botany of
the annual adonis, since *Adonis aestivalis, A. annua*
(AN-u-a), and *A. autumnalis* (au-tum-NA-lis)
may be three separate species, or merely variants
of one. In gardens, however, their effect is very
similar. Because they are hardy, annual forms of
adonis may be sown in all but the coldest gardens
in September or October, or as soon as the
ground is workable in early spring. Like most
hardy annuals, they resent root disturbance, and
so develop best when sown where they are to
grow, and later thinned to stand six to eight
inches from plant to plant. They prefer a rich,
humusy but free-draining soil, in full sun or in
early morning or evening shade, and are at their
best in early summer, after which, when warm
weather occurs, they tend to wither away.

AGASTACHE SPECIES

FAMILY: *Lamiaceae* (*Labiatae*) or mint family.

CLASSIFICATION: Hardy or half-hardy perennials grown as half-hardy annuals.

COMMON NAME: Agastache.

HARDINESS: Root hardy to Zone 7 on light, well-drained soils. Withstands light frosts.

GROWING CONDITIONS: Well-drained, moderately rich garden loam. Full sun.

PROPAGATION: From seed, sown 12 weeks before last anticipated frost.

HEIGHT: 1 to 6′ depending on species.

ORNAMENTAL VALUE: Grown for flower.

LEVEL OF CULTURAL DIFFICULTY: Easy.

SPECIAL PROPERTIES: Excellent container plants. Many species bear scented leaves.

PRONUNCIATION: a-ga-STA-kee

*U*ntil fairly recently, the only agastache familiar to American gardeners was *A. foeniculum* (fu–NI-cu-lum), the anise hyssop cultivated by herbalists and occasionally grown in perennial borders. It might charitably be described as a serviceable plant, for it is nothing special to look at, though it blooms the first year from seed, has upright tidy growth (to five feet), and four-inch cobs of flower, either blue or white, from late June until autumn. Were that all there is to say about the genus *Agastache,* it would merit only a short note in many manuals, and none in most. But in the last ten years or so, whole new races of agastache have burst into prominence, mostly species, hybrids, or selections from plants native to Central America and the southwestern portions of the United States. The genus name, composed of two Greek words, *aga,* meaning numerous, and *stachys,* an ear of grain, seems apt for many of these most recent introductions. The compact, bushy plants, hardly a foot in height, produce fragile-seeming flowers atop thin stems about eighteen inches tall and look—when planted in generous drifts—something like a patch of wheat.

Their flowers, however, are hardly wheatlike in hue, for they are more often colored a warm pink, apricot, orange, or heather purple, according to species, selection, or cross. The individual flowers, hardly half an inch long, are borne over a long period of time from whorled bracts and are often described as "salvia-like," because they possess the same narrow hood and extended, broad lower lip of most salvia flowers. The flowers, though tiny, are so profuse that plantings of many agastaches seem to be a haze of color.

All species of agastache appear to flower in their first year from an early sowing, and so,

AGASTACHE RUPESTRIS

though they are true perennials, they may be treated as half-hardy annuals. Their gene pool is easily as rich as that of zinnias, marigolds, and petunias, and if the breeders of those plants had been looking for a fine, hazy mass of color rather than full, rounded, individual blossoms, there might be many interesting agastaches available from seed. At present, they are being recognized as very valuable garden plants, and more selections and crosses will be offered in the future.

Meanwhile, gardeners should look for *Agastache anisata* (a-NIH-sa-ta) with silver-green foliage and blue flower spikes in summer, and *A. aurantiaca* (au-ran-TI-a-ca) 'Apricot Sunrise', widely available in nurseries that specialize in unusual annual and tender plants. Perhaps the best cultivar now available, it has apricot-yellow flowers that bloom profusely on eighteen-inch stems above gray-green, fruity-scented foliage. *A. cana* (CA-na) 'Heather Queen' is excellent, with much-branched stems topped by four-inch flower spikes from mid to late summer in a rich, heather-pink. *A. mexicana* (mex-i-CA-na) grows into a tall—up to six feet—slender plant, with pale green, lemony-scented foliage and clear pink flower spikes. A hybrid plant, *A. coccinea* (co-CHIN-ee-a) x *mexicana,* currently marketed as 'Pink Panther', produces brilliant, dusky pink flowers on stems as much as thirty inches tall, above purple-tinged leaves. Another hybrid of uncertain parentage, offered simply as *A.* x 'Fragrant Delight', might bear any flower color from blue, yellow, pink, red, or white, and leaves of any scent: anise, licorice, peppermint, or bergamot.

Most agastaches will be acquired as young plants, but they are also easy to grow from seed, which is becoming more available. It should be sown at temperatures around 60°F about twelve weeks from the last anticipated frost date. Young plants, which transplant readily, should be pricked out and grown on in bright, sunny con-

AGASTACHE *'APRICOT SUNRISE'*

ditions at about the same temperature or slightly warmer, until they may be transferred to their permanent positions in the garden. Easy plants to grow, they ask little beyond well-drained garden soil, not over-rich in nutrients, which sends them up into leaf rather than abundant flower. They make superb container plants, providing upright growth, abundant bloom, and a certain softness to combinations of tender plants in containers. Many may be much hardier than is generally supposed, and so, when grown in the open garden, it is worth cutting them back and mulching them lightly, rather than yanking them up by the roots. In a mild year, even gardens in Zone 5 may see them return for another season of bloom.

AGERATUM HOUSTONIANUM

FAMILY: *Asteraceae* or aster or daisy family.

CLASSIFICATION: Half-hardy annual.

COMMON NAMES: Floss flower, blue fleece flower, ageratum.

HARDINESS: Withstands light frosts.

GROWING CONDITIONS: Rich, water-retentive soil.
Perfect drainage. Abundant moisture. Full sun.
PROPAGATION: From seed, sown indoors 6 to 8
weeks before last anticipated frost.
HEIGHT: From 6" to 3', depending on cultivar.
ORNAMENTAL VALUE: Grown for flower.
LEVEL OF CULTURAL DIFFICULTY: Easy.
SPECIAL PROPERTIES: Excellent cut flowers. Accepts
transplanting even when fully grown.
PRONUNCIATION: a-jer-A-tum hew-sto-nee-AH-num

The genus name for *Ageratum* seems particularly apt. It comes from ancient Greek and means something like "never aging," attesting to the fact that all the tiny, fluffy blossoms in a flower head seem fresh until the whole corymb fades. Thus the plants look tidy with a minimum of deadheading.

Ageratums are even more valuable, however, for their clear blue forms. Blue is a color fairly rare in annuals (or in any other flowers, for that matter), and it is always treasured for the way it draws the sky to earth and for its capacity to make almost any other color more beautiful. Nicely, therefore, the breeding of ageratums has tended to concentrate on bluer and bluer forms, eliminating the mauvy quality older cultivars often had. Good, clearer, and deeper pinks and purer whites have also been bred for specialized color schemes.

Though the genus *Ageratum* includes about thirty species, all those generally available are offered under the name *houstonianum,* memorializing Dr. William Houstoun (1695–1733), a Scottish physician who collected seed of the plant in Central America. (It is probable, however, that there is a mixture of several species in some cultivars offered, particularly in the taller varieties such as 'Cut Wonder'.) Ageratums may come in any height from six inches to three feet, and generally the taller the variety, the more open and graceful its growing habit. The smallest varieties are tight little cushions six to eight inches tall, so smothered in flowers that almost no leaves are apparent. They have always been popular for edging, the practice that park superintendents so love, of planting regimented rows of small plants in a uniform hedge along the front of a bed. But as American flower gardens have become looser and more natural looking, the taller varieties have gained popularity, particularly when used in mixed borders, where they are valuable for filling gaps and where their flower color is always effective over a very long period of time, usually well into October.

Ageratums are very easy to grow from seed, which should be sown at temperatures around 65°F about six to eight weeks before the last anticipated frost date. Young seedlings should be transplanted as soon as they may be handled into plastic cell packs or individual pots, and grown on in bright, sunny, cool conditions around 70°F in the daytime and ten or so degrees cooler at night. Taller varieties benefit from being pinched once or twice to encourage branching. Young plants may be hardened off and established in their permanent positions as soon as all danger of frost is past. They require a rich, moist, water-retentive soil with perfect drainage, and while they are becoming established, they are very sensitive to drought, which will discourage full development or even result in the death of young plants. At all times in their life cycle, they will require deep irrigation in dry spells because powdery mildew, their one great scourge, sets in quickly when periods of drought are followed by rainy or humid weather. Ageratums are also grateful for a sprinkling of granular food—10-10-10—shortly after they have been transplanted and have "caught." Feeding at this time will discourage their precocious bloom, but it will increase the richness of their handsome, heart-shaped crinkled leaves. And as their flower should be most abundant in late summer and into autumn, the loss of a little early bloom will not be noticed.

It is also a nice feature of ageratums, as of some other members of the family Asteraceae, such as chrysanthemums, marigolds, and calendulas, that they will accept transplanting even when in full flower, if the work is done on a cloudy day. This makes them well suited for dropping in, the practice of holding plants in the vegetable garden or in special beds until they are needed in mid to late summer to fill gaps that develop in the border. For this purpose, ageratums should be grown on strong, with plenty of air around each plant. When needed, they should be carefully lifted with a generous mass of earth about their roots, watered well after transplanting, and shaded for a day or two from hot sun.

AGROSTEMMA GITHAGO

FAMILY: *Caryophyllaceae* or carnation family.

CLASSIFICATION: Hardy annual.

COMMON NAMES: Corn cockle, agrostemma.

HARDINESS: Withstands light frost.

GROWING CONDITIONS: Poor sandy to moderately fertile soil. Perfect drainage. Cool growing conditions. Full sun.

PROPAGATION: From seed, sown in place in autumn in warmer gardens, and elsewhere in very early spring.

HEIGHT: To 2'.

AGERATUM HOUSTONIANUM

ORNAMENTAL VALUE: Grown for flower.

LEVEL OF CULTURAL DIFFICULTY: Moderately difficult.

SPECIAL PROPERTIES: All parts of plant are poisonous.

PRONUNCIATION: a-gro-STEM-a gi-THAG-o

*A*grostemmas are seldom grown in European gardens since they have widely naturalized on agricultural land, and are, like the beautiful Veterans Day poppy, *Papaver rhoeas,* noxious weeds in cultivated fields. They were very popular in nineteenth- and early twentieth-century American gardens, where a patch or two was always sown, if only for cut flowers. They have fallen out of favor principally because they resent root disturbance (along with many other hardy annuals, such as poppies and larkspurs) and will not survive when torn from a flat and planted. They may return to popularity, however, with the widespread use of thin-walled plastic six-packs. For with their use, even the most delicately rooted annual can be slipped out in its cube of soil and into the garden.

A very pretty plant, agrostemma takes its name from the Greek word *agros,* meaning field, and *stemma,* meaning crown or garland. It grows up to two feet tall and is furnished with narrow, blade or grasslike leaves two or three inches long, downed with silky hairs that give them a silvery appearance. Flowers are five-petaled, satiny in texture, borne singly on long stems. Each petal curves down gracefully at its edge and is given special beauty by a streak of a darker color, beginning in the center of the flower as a row of tiny dots that become progressively closer, eventually forming a solid line. The flower color of the wild plant might be called purple, but is in fact a strong magenta, pretty when it occurs among green or golden wheat, but not so pretty when combined with other flowers. The cultivar 'Milas' (MEE-las), superior to the wild plant in every way, is taller by a foot, more freely branched and more floriferous, with flowers up to three inches wide, of a clear, rose-purple shading to white at the center. A very elegant pure white form has also begun to be offered, its petals beautifully marked with dark brown dotted lines.

Unless agrostemma can be found in nurseries that specialize in rarer annuals, it must be seeded in the garden in early spring where it is to grow, or, in gardens warmer than Zone 5, in late autumn. Agrostemmas grow best on rather poor soil, open in texture and perfectly well drained, for they are sensitive to excess water at their roots, which quickly causes them to rot, especially when they have grown fat on nitrogen-rich soil. For best development, plants should be thinned to stand eight inches apart, though they are often grown in thicker masses, as they would grow in wheat fields. When grown separately, however, individual plants may topple over just as they reach full development and so will require staking.

It is important to note that all parts of *A. githago* are poisonous when eaten, the seed especially so.

AGROSTEMMA GITHAGO

ALCEA ROSEA

FAMILY: *Malvaceae* or mallow family.

CLASSIFICATION: Hardy biennial grown as hardy annual.

COMMON NAME: Hollyhock.

HARDINESS: Hardy to Zone 4. Leaves are frost tolerant.

GROWING CONDITIONS: Rich, well-drained loam. Full sun.

PROPAGATION: From seed, sown indoors in peat pots in late February.

HEIGHT: From 4 to 7', depending on culture.

ORNAMENTAL VALUE: Grown for flower, and for vertical shape.

LEVEL OF CULTURAL DIFFICULTY: Easy.

SPECIAL PROPERTIES: None.

PRONUNCIATION: al-SEE-a RO-see-a

Only a person willfully ignorant of the world of plants would be unable to call up a mental image of a hollyhock, or to recognize it in flower. Though a native of China, and cultivated there for perhaps a thousand years, the plant was introduced into England in the sixteenth century and brought by the earliest colonists to North America, where it throve. And thrives still, though not as well as it used to, because a fungal disease called "rust" disfigures its great hairy leaves, eventually causing them to drop away, leaving the towering flower stalks looking naked and ill.

Alcea rosea is technically classed as a biennial, which is to say that seed is sown in late spring or early summer, and the plant is grown on through its first year to flower in its second. Being a biennial, it has all the problems of that class of plants, namely that they take up space for a year before flowering, and thus one must plan well ahead to have them in the garden, always keeping a young crop going to replace the plants that will be discarded after they flower. When they are rare or specially colored forms, a few plants at least must be left to set seed, and both because of rust and the general, chaffy gauntness they take on after flowering, they are not generally attractive assets in the garden.

Beyond all these problems, hollyhocks have one more or, if not a problem quite, a difficulty at least. Being mallows, they tend to form long taproots, and like most members of that family, resent transplanting. So it is not easy to keep a row of young plants in an out-of-the-way place, to slip into gaps left by the previous generation (as one can, for example, with other popular biennials, such as foxgloves). Young plants also become exposed to rust during their first year of growth, which overwinters on their leaves and under-

ALCEA ROSEA

ground parts, ready to infect them the following year just as they begin to flower. Still, hollyhocks always carry an air of romance and old-fashioned charm, and their stature and vertical form make them difficult to replace with any other plant. So there are those who will do anything to have hollyhock, and growing them as annuals has therefore become more popular. For though they never develop to their fullest magnificence, they are nevertheless not hideously disfigured by rust when they bloom.

Seed companies now offer strains of hollyhock that will flower reliably in the first year. For this purpose, seed should be sown in February and germinated at temperatures around 55°F. Though they resent root disturbance as they mature and develop a taproot, very young plants with two or three true leaves transplant readily. They should be pricked out individually into five- or six-inch pots that will allow for healthy root development, and grown on in bright, quite cool conditions at temperatures around 50°F without experiencing a check. Though hollyhocks are classed as hardy biennials, young plants grown under glass will be tender, and so they should be hardened off carefully and transplanted to their permanent positions in the garden after all danger of frost is past. Many may then settle down to become biennial, and a few may even return for a third year. That is not actually so desirable, for the main point of the "annual" hollyhocks is that, started anew each year and grown as fresh plants, they are not as susceptible to rust as are those grown as biennials or short-lived perennials.

It should be said, however, that the annual strains of hollyhock are not nearly so beautiful as some of the heirloom plants that used to grow in every garden. They are generally shorter, hardly reaching four and a half feet in height, and most are double or "powder puff" in flower, lacking the elegant, five-petaled grace of single forms. Seed is so far also fairly unstable, and so one may get from a single packet some unexpected surprises in flower form or color—perhaps pleasant, perhaps not. Better forms of annual hollyhocks are sure to be developed, however, as breeders concentrate on their capacities to be annuals at all.

Meanwhile, the appearance of hollyhocks grown as annuals may be improved by a simple planting trick. Plants grown as biennials generally produce three, five, or even more rods of flower from a well-established single plant. Annual strains will generally produce only one flower rod, and so three young plants may be planted fairly close together, almost in one hole. When this trick is employed, however, it is to be hoped that all three plants produce flowers of the same form and color, or at least of complementary shades.

ALONSOA SPECIES

FAMILY: *Scrophulariaceae* or snapdragon family.

CLASSIFICATION: Tender perennials grown as tender annuals.

COMMON NAMES: Mask flower, alonsoa.

HARDINESS: Sensitive to temperatures below 40°F. Damaged by light frosts.

GROWING CONDITIONS: Humus-rich, moisture-retentive soil. Abundant moisture. Cool growing conditions. Full sun.

PROPAGATION: From seed, sown indoors 12 weeks before last anticipated frost. Cuttings taken in spring from nonflowering shoots root easily.

HEIGHT: To about 18" with support.

ORNAMENTAL VALUE: Grown for flower.

LEVEL OF CULTURAL DIFFICULTY: Moderately difficult in cool gardens. Difficult elsewhere.

SPECIAL PROPERTIES: None.

PRONUNCIATION: a-lon-SO-a

Several species and interspecific hybrids of alonsoa are offered by nurseries that specialize in rare annuals and tender plants. In bloom and in growth habit they are all similar, with flowers that are quite small, never achieving, even in the largest-flowering forms, more than half an inch in width. But the blooms, freely produced from new growth in unusually clear colors—red, scarlet, blood orange, rich and shell pink—are vivid enough to make them always noticeable. And like their close cousins of the family Scrophulariaceae—snapdragons, wishbone flowers, monkey flowers, and toadflax—they seem curiously animated, as if possessing a sense of humor. Each alonsoa blossom, though lobed, is not tubular as are snapdragons, but rather flattened out into a little face, often with a darker center. Hence the common name, first applied to *Alonsoa warsewiczii* (war-sha-VICH-ee-ee), "mask flower," and now appropriated by all species. All alonsoas form loose bushes with many wiry stems furnished with small, bright green, linear leaves, attaining about eighteen inches in height, but becoming lax and tumbling over as they develop flower and seed pods. They may be staked, but they are just as attractive tangled together or weaving among other plants.

Whether the several species and hybrids (or possible hybrids) of the genus *Alonsoa* offered by nurseries specializing in rare annuals and tender plants are designated as tender shrubs, tender sub-shrubs, or tender perennials will depend on the reference the gardener consults. Native to sunny open slopes in the western sections of tropical and subtropical South America, they may behave as all three, but because they are precocious in their flowering from seed or cutting-grown plants they may be treated as annuals in most North American gardens. Flower time may be brief, hardly a month or more from plants established in the garden in late May. But when

ALONSOA LINEARIS

bloom begins to falter, new sprays of flower will arrive quickly if plants are cut back to vigorous basal growth and fed with an application of water-soluble fertilizer such as Rapid Gro, Miracle-Gro, or Peters 20-20-20.

A. warsewiczii is a somewhat rangier, looser-growing species than other members of the genus, typically with half-inch flowers of red or orange, usually with a darker eye, though forms have been selected in many other colors of pale and dark peach to pink. *A. acutifolia* (a-cu-ti-FO-lee-a) is bushier, to eighteen inches, with even smaller flowers borne in terminal racemes, but very showy because of their profusion and the vivid, deep red of their blossoms. *A. meridionalis* (me-ri-dee-o-NA-lis) (or *A.* x *meridionalis*) is the alonsoa most commonly offered at present, for though its flowers range from orange to dark red in the wild, beautiful shell pink and salmon forms have been selected or bred, and those are colors treasured by most gardeners. Very charming also is *A. linearis* (lin-ee-AR-is), which produces many upright stems sprinkled with tiny, quarter-inch-wide flowers of an unusually vivid, clear orange.

Alonsoas are not easy plants to grow well, for they are very tender, sensitive to temperatures

ALONSOA WARSEWICZII

below 45°F or so, and they are equally intolerant of hot, dry summers. Where fuschias thrive, they may be expected to thrive as well, and under similar growing conditions—cool summer nights and warm (but not hot) bright sunny days, a deep, humus-rich, fertile soil that drains well, and abundant moisture at their roots and in the atmosphere. Where those conditions cannot be met, alonsoas may be most useful as conservatory or greenhouse plants, where they will flower abundantly all winter long and into early spring.

All species of *Alonsoa* come easily from seed, which should be sown about twelve weeks from the last anticipated frost date, at temperatures around 60°F. Seedlings should be pricked out and grown on in bright conditions, fertilized regularly, and kept evenly moist. When they have reached a height of about five inches, they should be pinched once to encourage bushy growth. If necessary, they may be pinched again to retard flowering, as they should not be transplanted into the garden until the weather is quite warm and settled.

The usual method of propagation for alonsoas, however, is not from seed, but from cuttings, which root readily. They should be taken from vigorous, nonflowering shoots, best obtained from stock plants carried over the winter in a cool greenhouse or heated sun porch, and cut back hard in March to produce vigorous new growth. Cuttings are inserted in half peat, half sharp sand or perlite, and kept moist and shaded until rooting occurs, usually within two weeks. Young plants can then be potted up and grown on for use in the summer garden. A few may then be cut back hard in early July, to provide cuttings for stock plants to carry through the winter.

The genus name *Alonsoa* is a bit of an oddity in botanical language, as it commemorates the first rather than the last name of a person connected with it. Alonzo Zanoni was an obscure

eighteenth-century Spanish diplomat who was Secretary of State for Colombia when it was still a Spanish colony. Joseph Warsczewicz (1812–1866) botanized widely in South America and eventually became director of the botanic gardens at Krakow.

ALTERNANTHERA SPECIES

FAMILY: *Amaranthaceae* or amaranth family.

CLASSIFICATION: Tender perennials or shrubs grown as tender annuals.

COMMON NAMES: Joseph's coat, parrot leaf, alternanthera.

HARDINESS: Hardy in Zone 10. Sensitive to light frosts.

GROWING CONDITIONS: Humus-rich, well-drained soil. Abundant moisture. Full sun to part shade.

PROPAGATION: From tip cuttings, taken in late spring. Seed may be sown indoors in late winter.

HEIGHT: To less than 1'.

ORNAMENTAL VALUE: Grown for vividly colored leaves.

LEVEL OF CULTURAL DIFFICULTY: Easy.

SPECIAL PROPERTIES: Excellent container plant. Useful as winter houseplant or greenhouse plant.

PRONUNCIATION: al-ter-NAN-thu-ra

When carpet bedding was routinely practiced in public parks and on wealthy estates, alternantheras had certain remarkable advantages. Victorian gardeners could make them do almost anything in a design. Small plants, seldom more than ten inches tall when left to grow freely, they accept severe shearing, down to four inches or even less. They could thus be made into tidy little hedges to border complicated beds of other annual or tender plants, to spell out names of towns or institutions, or to supply one of the elements for a floral clock. Best of all, their leaves, which are never more than two inches long and often much smaller, are fantastically colored in shades of crimson, blood red, burgundy, pink, cream, or orange.

The recent return to favor of alternantheras is not, however, because the practice of carpet bedding is enjoying a revival. But the love of leaves—for shape, for freshness of green, for somber bronze, or for fantastic variegation—is an enthusiasm that has recently returned to gardeners, and so alternantheras, like coleus, are finding themselves once more in demand. And, like coleus, alternantheras are newly popular for their ease of culture and for the valuable contributions they can make to looser bedding schemes and especially to containers of mixed plantings of annuals and tender perennials and shrubs.

We can hope that the return to popularity of alternantheras will help to untangle the botany of the genus, which is unusually confused. (It takes its name, rather flat-footedly, from the fact that each alternating anther carries no pollen, and so is barren.) In old catalogues, several species were offered according to the color of their leaves. Many of them now appear to be variants of *A. ficoidea* (fi-KOY-dee-a), such as *A. bettzickiana* (bet-sik-ee-AN-a) with spoon-shaped leaves, variegated creamy yellow and red. Many color variants were selected under this name in the Victorian period, all quite interesting and some very beautiful, but difficult at present to find. *A. amoena* (a-MEE-na), among the tiniest of these plants, grows only four inches tall, with shiny green leaves blotched with red and orange, and it now, too, is listed as a variety of *A. ficoidea*. So is *A. versicolor* (ver-SI-co-lor), with leaves that are crimson and coppery, and may approach blood red. Lately a new species has begun to appear in catalogues, *A. purpurea* (pur-PUR-ee-a) 'Tricolor', with leaves colored deep burgundy, magenta, and lime, which probably is simply a variety of *A. ficoidea*.

With alternantheras, as with coleus of named varieties, the best approach is to choose among those that become available, trying those one likes and ruthlessly discarding others. Also like coleus, all the best forms must be propagated from cuttings, and so only those nurseries that specialize in tender plants will be sources.

But one distinct species that is clearly outside the *ficoidea* group will be of special interest to gardeners who enjoy complicated arrangements

ALTERNANTHERA DENTATA 'RUBIGINOSA'

of plants grown in containers—*Alternanthera dentata* (den-TA-ta) in its variety 'Rubiginosa'. A plant of sprawling vigor, quick of growth, it is well furnished with burgundy-colored, glossy leaves. Deep purple foliage makes almost any other flower color more beautiful (as gardeners have learned with another annual, *Perilla frutescens*) but the behavior of *A. dentata* 'Rubiginosa' makes it specially valuable in containers. Rather than seeming to plunge off the edge of the pot in a desperate search for more space, it tends to weave among other plants, knitting them all together.

Alternantheras are normally grown from softwood cuttings taken in late spring or summer, inserted in half peat, half sharp sand or perlite, and kept moist and shaded until rooting occurs, which should be within two weeks or so. Where seed is available, it should be sown in late winter at temperatures around 55°F, though unless it is very fresh or has been carefully stored, germination will be erratic. Young seedlings will usually show wide variations in the color and shape of their leaves, though they must be grown on to some size before their desirability in the garden may be evaluated. In the garden or in containers, alternantheras require a rich, humusy, well-drained soil, and they benefit by weekly applications of water-soluble fertilizer at half the strength recommended on the package. Leaf color develops best in full sun, though in warmer gardens, alternantheras are useful in part shade, either for bedding or for containers and hanging baskets. All forms make excellent winter houseplants for the sunny windowsill, though they should be clipped frequently to maintain compact form, and they may be unusually troubled by all the familiar insects that attack windowsill plants, such as aphids, red spider, mealy bug, and white fly.

AMARANTHUS SPECIES

FAMILY: *Amaranthaceae* or amaranth family.

CLASSIFICATION: Hardy to half-hardy annuals.

COMMON NAME: Amaranth (other common names vary with species).

HARDINESS: Seed-hardy to Zone 5. Sensitive to light frost.

GROWING CONDITIONS: Average, well-drained garden soil. Full sun. All species relish humid, hot weather.

PROPAGATION: By seed, sown 4 to 6 weeks before last anticipated frost. Young plants resent root disturbance.

HEIGHT: From 2 to 5' depending on species and cultivar.

ORNAMENTAL VALUE: Grown for ornamental seed heads. Several species valued for highly colored leaves.

LEVEL OF CULTURAL DIFFICULTY: Easy.

SPECIAL PROPERTIES: Several species valued for protein-rich seed, and as a cooked or salad green.

PRONUNCIATION: a-ma-RAN-thus

*T*he genus *Amaranthus* is composed of about fifty species originating in both hemispheres in tropical or very temperate areas—that is, so far as we can know for sure, for all amaranths are annuals of quick growth, most with considerable seed hardiness, and many species appear to have naturalized throughout the world, either as escapees from deliberately cultivated crops, or simply as weeds. Although some of these weeds are remarkably troublesome—*A. albus* (AL-bus), the tumbleweed of western ranches and Hollywood movies, and *A. hybridus* (HI-bri-dus), the pigweed hated by vegetable gardeners everywhere—the genus *Amaranthus* has been of great importance to humanity. It may be of even greater importance in the future as the search for nutritious and highly productive staple foods accelerates. Those amaranths that may be grown for food (and there are many) accept and even thrive on poor, dryish soils, and can produce more nutritious, protein-rich seed than any other common grain crop—as much as one metric ton per acre.

Interestingly, several of the species of *Amaranthus* that have had the greatest economic importance are also valued in ornamental gardens for their complexly shaped and colored seed heads, their brilliantly colored and variegated foliage, or often for both. The genus takes its name from the Greek word *amaranthos,* meaning never fading, and attests to the fact that several species produce chaffy, brightly colored seed heads that retain their color when picked and dried. In this they are like many other "everlasting flowers"

such as celosia and gomphrena that are valued in the garden and in dried arrangements not for their flowers—generally insignificant—but for the structures that bear or surround them.

There appears to be much confusion in the botany of those amaranths grown for garden ornament, since many plants originally listed as separate species are now considered to be either varieties or cultivars of other species. For simplicity, the plants discussed below are treated as separate species, just as they generally are in most botanical manuals, seed catalogues, and nurseries.

Perhaps the oddest of the amaranthus cultivated in gardens is *A. caudatus* (cau-DA-tus). Few plants bear a stranger collection of popular names, ranging from the comforting "chenille plant" and romantic "kiss-me-over-the-garden-gate," to "love lies bleeding," and "nun's scourge." Very much a hot weather annual (like all garden

AMARANTHUS TRICOLOR

amaranths), *A. caudatus* does little until warm settled days arrive. Then it shoots up to four or even five feet in height, making a much-branched shrubby bush clothed in coarse leaves that might be as long as ten inches and could frankly be called ugly. Were that all the plant could do, it would be summarily yanked out of any garden. But in mid- to late summer, it begins producing the extraordinary structures in which its minute flowers are borne, consisting of long, down-hanging ropes the color and texture of Victorian plush upholstery. In those varieties cultivated for their flower structures, the tassels can be as long as two feet, and are often borne in thick clusters at the tips of the branches. Though typically a purplish-red, the variety 'Viridis' (VIR-i-dis) bears ropes colored chartreuse and sometimes greenish-white. Like most garden amaranths, *A. caudatus* looks best in casual borders as a free-standing, single specimen, where its dramatic architecture can be appreciated. A shorter-tasseled form of *A. caudatus* is sometimes offered as an ornamental and is also the grain amaranth most valued in India as a food crop.

Two amaranths are commonly cultivated under the name "prince's feather," *Amaranthus hypochondriacus* (hi-po-kon-DRI-a-cus) and *A. cruentus* (cru-IN-tus). Both would probably be correctly listed as varieties of *Amaranthus hybridus* (HI-bri-dus), in which case the first would be *A. hybridus* var. *erythrostachys* (er-i-thro-STA-kis), though it is hard to shake off a name like "hypochondriacus." The word means somber or gloomy in appearance, but the garden plant is merely an interestingly colored pigweed with a large, much-branched chaffy cluster in which its insignificant flowers are borne. Like most amaranths, it is a tall plant, growing from two to four feet, and coarse in appearance, with leaves that may be as long as six inches. Foliage is reddish to blood-red, burgundy, or even an intense purple

AMARANTHUS HYBRIDUS

in selected forms, and the plant is surmounted in high summer by graceful flower-bearing structures treasured by dried flower arrangers.

The second prince's feather is often listed as *Amaranthus cruentus* or *A. paniculata* (pa-ni-cu-LA-ta), but is also probably a variety of *A. hybridus*. It is a taller plant, to six feet, much-branched and copious in its production of seed-bearing structures. Generally, the colors of the flowering cones will be reflected in the leaves, so that golden forms will have coppery foliage, bronze-leaved forms shading into rose will have deep rose heads, and the deeper, burgundy-leaved forms will bear seed heads of a dusky, plush purple.

But among amaranths, the most vividly colored foliage belongs to *Amaranthus tricolor* (TRI-co-lor). It can equal almost any bright-leaved foliage plant, even including *Acalypha wilkesiana,* which vaunts the popular name "match-me-if-you-can." *Amaranthus tricolor* can do that, and even win the higher prize, since in selected forms it is among the most vivid of all garden plants. It shares another common name with acalypha, "Joseph's coat," for in the most familiar forms its narrow, five-inch leaves may be scarlet, orange, cream, yellow, and bronze, all in combination. Many other forms have been selected that bear deep or light red foliage, or all yellow and cream. They are somewhat quieter in effect than Joseph's coat, but only by comparison with it, and not with other plants. The most intense colors are always at the top of the plant, which typically reaches five feet. Lower leaves change their

AMARANTHUS CAUDATUS *'VIRIDIS'*

color to dark green, a nice and somewhat comforting contrast to what is going on above. Many forms of *A. tricolor* have been bred, some quite dwarf, and those are especially effective in pots and containers, and most especially when grown in greenhouses for indoor winter decoration, as a refreshing alternative to poinsettias. In its green form, *A. tricolor* is cultivated under the name "tampala," and is "cooked like spinach," as so many exotic greens are said to be prepared. It is worth noting, however, that the colored-leaved forms are also edible, and so may be added to salads for a vivid contrast to other greens.

All amaranths love heat and high humidity, and are probably at their very best in sections of the deep and middle South. Because of these preferences, they should not be hurried on by an early seeding, as they will not catch and thrive until the weather outdoors is really warm. Seed should be sown about four to six weeks before the last anticipated frost date, at temperatures of around 70°F, and young plants should be pricked out and grown on at similar temperatures, in the brightest light available. At no time should they receive a check from cold, drought, or cramping at the roots, for any of these conditions may cause them prematurely to produce flower spikes, after which they will never make good garden plants. Young plants in nurseries and garden centers that show precocious bloom should also be passed over in favor of vigorously growing specimens with no flower buds apparent.

Transplanting should be done with a minimum of root disturbance, and young plants should be well watered and fed with a half-strength water-soluble fertilizer. When they have caught, they benefit from a light dressing of granular, vegetable-garden fertilizer, 10-10-10 or the like, and another application a month or so later, just as flower buds become apparent. Though all amaranthus will survive in nitrogen-poor, exhausted soils with little water once they have become established, the finest specimens will nevertheless be grown on humus-rich, water-retentive but well-drained soils, in as much sun as possible.

AMMI MAJUS

FAMILY: *Umbelliferae* or carrot family.

CLASSIFICATION: Hardy or half-hardy biennials grown as hardy or half-hardy annuals.

COMMON NAMES: False Queen Anne's lace, bishop's flower, ammi.

HARDINESS: Withstands very light frosts.

GROWING CONDITIONS: Fertile, well-drained garden soil. Full sun. Prefers cool weather.

PROPAGATION: From seed sown indoors in early April or outdoors in place 2 weeks before last anticipated frost.

HEIGHT: To 18″.

ORNAMENTAL VALUE: Grown for flower. *A. visnaga* grown for foliage.

LEVEL OF CULTURAL DIFFICULTY: Easy.

SPECIAL PROPERTIES: Excellent cut flower.

PRONUNCIATION: A-mee MA-jus (MY-us)

Ammi majus is one of many beautiful annual and tender plants that have recently come to surprise and delight us, although it has been popular in the European cut-flower trade for decades, and anciently, the root of the plant was chewed by North African camel drivers as a protection against the sun. In this country, however, standard garden references do not mention it before 1985, and seed was rarely offered before 1990. It so closely resembles Queen Anne's lace (*Daucus carota* [DAU-cus ca-RO-ta], the wild progenitor of carrots) that most people seeing *Ammi majus* in a garden or in a bouquet would assume it to be that much-loved wild flower. From this resemblance it has been given the common name "false Queen Anne's lace," though to call it that does it an injustice, for it has many advantages over *Daucus carota*. It is much more delicate of growth, producing fragile-seeming, two-foot stems that weave in and among other plants. Being a true annual, rather than a determined biennial (as *Daucus carota* is), it can be slipped each year into the garden, never crowding out other plants as the rank, carrotlike foliage of the true Queen Anne's lace might do. Its other common name, "bishop's flower," is equally unfortunate, borrowed from the dreadful garden pest *Aegopodium podagraria*, which is almost impossible to eradicate once established. By contrast, *Ammi majus* is extremely amiable, as its genus name seems to indicate.

The flowers of *Ammi majus,* more delicately constructed than those of *Daucus carota,* are of a far purer white. They repay close study, for they are composed of thirty to fifty tensile stems, varying in length from one to three inches, the longest arranged around the outside and the shortest in the middle, to create a perfectly flat umbel. Each stem in turn terminates in a perfect miniature of the whole, a little flat, half-inch cluster of tiny, five-petaled flowers.

AMMI MAJUS

Ammi majus is of very easy culture, coming quickly from seed sown either indoors in early April or outdoors about two weeks before the last frost. It flowers through early to midsummer, melting away in August but leaving no mess behind. It can be planted in spaces between late-flowering perennials to add interest to their dull first growth, or placed among early flowering ones to create the effect of an arranged bouquet even on the ground. A superb cut flower, it has the curious capacity of remaining fresh out of water for several hours, even overnight, which makes it ideal for bridal bouquets.

Of about eight species in the genus *Ammi,* its ancient name in both Greek and Latin, only one other seems to be cultivated in gardens. *A. visnaga* (vis-NA-ga), a very pretty plant, is useful not for its flowers but for the fresh green and remarkable ferny, threadlike texture of its foliage. The bush-like plants, which remain beautiful all summer and eventually reach a height of about three feet, are under close study for pharmacological possibilities. Like so many members of the family Umbelliferae (celery, carrots, parsnips, dill, caraway, coriander, fennel, parsley, anise), *A. visnaga* is believed to contain healthful and curative properties, particularly in the fight against heart disease.

AMMI VISNAGA *'GREEN MIST'*

AMMOBIUM ALATUM

FAMILY: *Asteraceae* or aster or daisy family.

CLASSIFICATION: Tender perennial grown as half-hardy annual.

COMMON NAMES: Winged everlasting, pearly everlasting, ammobium.

HARDINESS: Withstands light frosts.

GROWING CONDITIONS: Poor to moderately fertile, well-drained soil. Full sun.

PROPAGATION: By seed, sown 8 to 10 weeks before last anticipated frost date.

HEIGHT: To 2' when staked.

ORNAMENTAL VALUE: Grown for flower.

LEVEL OF CULTURAL DIFFICULTY: Easy.

SPECIAL PROPERTIES: Valued as dried flowers. Drought tolerant.

PRONUNCIATION: a-MO-bee-um a-LAY-tum (a-LA-tum)

*I*t is the curse put on too many plants grown as annuals that they are first bred to be compact and tidy, and then to cover themselves with masses and masses of flower in ever more vivid hues and combinations. Consequently much of the plant's natural beauty—its elegance of leaf or stem or bud or seed head—is lost, and it is turned into a mere wad of color. For those who want this, *Ammobium alatum* will be of little interest.

It is true that its first parts in particular seem nothing special, for the foot-wide basal rosette of narrow leaves looks like a chewed-on dandelion. But in June, from the center of the plant, a sheaf of stems emerges, clad in four curious, continuous ripply wings. They branch as they grow, and each branch is surmounted by a tiny, pearl-like bud, white from the start, that opens first to look like a sempervivum cut from writing paper, and eventually, when fully unfolded, reveals an egg-yolk-colored button of hundreds of minute flowers. Like many composites, these buttons stay fresh for a very long time, as much as two weeks, but the showiest part of the flower continues to be its ruff of pointed white bracts surrounding the fertile parts.

The winged stems, which continue to be produced from the center of the plant throughout the summer, can reach a length of up to two feet, but unless supported will fall into a tangle. Such untidiness might be a fault in another plant but is part of the value of *Ammobium alatum,* for stems can be bent to conceal a perennial gone shabby, such as a bearded iris, or into a patch of ground left bare by a perennial that has flowered and died down, such as an oriental poppy. It can also be made to weave and bend among other plants, providing additional interest of bloom. It is also highly valued as a dried flower, though it will be the white, papery bracts that will actually count most for that purpose. For drying, whole branched stems should be cut just as the first white bracts have fully opened and then hung in a dark, dry place to cure.

Often, the botanical name of a plant provides useful clues to its culture or its appearance. Such is the case with *Ammobium alatum.* The species name comes from the Greek *ammos,* meaning sand, and *bios,* life. In its native Australia, the plant grows as a perennial on sandy soil, and though it seems willing when grown as an annual to accept most garden soils, it does best on a fairly lean diet, and is drought tolerant. *Alatum* of course acknowledges its winged stems.

Seed of ammobium should be sown indoors about eight to ten weeks before the last anticipated frost, at temperatures around 55°F. Young plants should be pricked out as soon as they may be handled, and grown on in bright, airy conditions at around 60°F. If they are well hardened off, they may be transplanted into permanent

AMMOBIUM ALATUM

positions a week or two before the last frost date. (If a severe frost is predicted, they should be covered with old sheets, towels, or sections of newspaper weighted down with stones.) A soil over-rich in nitrogen will produce rank, poorly flowered stems so a thinner, sandy or gravelly soil is preferred. If plants seem sluggish in producing flower stems, a single light sprinkling of granular fertilizer low in nitrogen but high in phosphorus and potassium will generally move them on.

ANAGALIS SPECIES

FAMILY: *Primulaceae* or primrose family.

CLASSIFICATION: Half-hardy perennials grown as hardy annuals.

COMMON NAMES: Pimpernel, anagalis (other common names vary with species).

HARDINESS: Resistant to light frosts.

GROWING CONDITIONS: Average, well-drained soil. Full sun.

PROPAGATION: From seed, sown 6 to 8 weeks before last anticipated frost. Cuttings root easily.

HEIGHT: To 8″ or less.

ORNAMENTAL VALUE: Grown for flower.

LEVEL OF CULTURAL DIFFICULTY: Easy.

SPECIAL PROPERTIES: Excellent in containers and
window boxes. Interesting cool greenhouse
plant for late winter flower.

PRONUNCIATION: a-NA-ga-lis (an-a-GA-lis)

Of the twenty or so species in the genus *Anagalis,* only two, *A. arvensis* (ar-VEN-sis) and *A. monellii* (mo-NE-lee-ee), are grown in gardens. Old botanical references are much kinder to them than modern ones, which often refer to both as "weeds, weedy, or weedlike." Certainly neither is always smothered in flowers, for though the bloom of *Anagalis monellii* can be abundant, the flowers shut tight in cloudy weather, as do those of *A. arvensis.* When a plant is called "weedlike," brisk sales are hardly going to result, and so neither *Anagalis arvensis* nor *A. monellii* are often offered in catalogues, though both come readily from seed. Too readily, some might say in the case of *A. arvensis,* which, once it has been grown—or has crept in—will reappear for years to come. In its early growth it looks exactly like chickweed, and a good bit of it is grubbed out as that plant.

But in a neglected spot, on a sunny day, its little orange flowers, scarcely a quarter-inch wide, are bound to appear, and, though many gardeners consider it a nuisance, others would be very sad if it failed to show up. Typically, the flowers are a delicate tangerine orange, and the very keen of eye will notice that each of the five petals is marked in its center by black shading to violet. Though on a sunny day enough flowers open from the leaf axils to be noticeable, it is a flower that really should be looked at with a magnifying glass, for only then is its great beauty revealed.

The actual geographic origins of *A. arvensis* are uncertain, for being a hardy annual and a prolific self-seeder, it has naturalized wherever land has been cultivated throughout the world. Its characteristic closing on cloudy days when rain threatens and as the sun begins to set has given it two of its three popular names, "poor man's weatherglass" and "shepherd's clock." Its other popular name, "scarlet pimpernel," was anciently applied to the plant, the word *pimpernel* descending from Latin through medieval French to medieval English, and much later providing the nickname for the hero of a wildly popular novel written by Baroness Orczy in 1905.

Although forms of *A. arvensis* occur naturally in white, pink, and blue, one should turn to *A. monellii* for a clear, gentian blue—rare in the natural world. Sometimes listed as *A. linifolia* (lin-i-FO-lee-a) or *A. monellii* subspecies *linifolia,* it is popularly called the "flax-leaved pimpernel" because of its inch-long, narrow leaves. Though the plants can be lax and undisciplined if not pinched frequently when young, the beauty of the flowers cannot be questioned. They reach perhaps half an

ANAGALIS MONELLII *SUBSP.* LINIFOLIA

inch across, and are very freely produced from June to frost. Each blue petal shades down in the center to a deep rose pink, setting off the prominent bright yellow stamens.

Originating in southern Europe, *A. monellii* is actually a true perennial, though it seldom survives in northern gardens over winter. In any case, it can easily be grown from seed to flower in its first year. Seed should be sown about six to eight weeks before the last anticipated frost date, and young plants should be pricked out and grown on in bright, cool conditions around 65°F or so until they may be hardened off and transplanted into their permanent positions in the garden. Almost any soil in full sun is suitable, but drainage must be perfect, as plants rot off quickly at ground level in soggy, waterlogged earth. Cuttings taken in midsummer can be grown as winter-flowering plants in greenhouses or on sunny, cool windowsills. As there is no purer blue among plants grown as annuals, *A. monellii* is also a splendid window box or container plant.

ANCHUSA CAPENSIS

FAMILY: *Boraginaceae* or borage family.

CLASSIFICATION: Tender biennial grown as tender annual.

COMMON NAMES: Cape forget-me-not, alkanet, bugloss, anchusa.

HARDINESS: Sensitive to light frosts.

GROWING CONDITIONS: Poor, dryish to moderately fertile, well-drained soils. Full sun.

PROPAGATION: From seed, sown indoors in late February or early March.

HEIGHT: From 1′ to 16″.

ORNAMENTAL VALUE: Grown for flower.

LEVEL OF CULTURAL DIFFICULTY: Moderately difficult.

SPECIAL PROPERTIES: Excellent winter-flowering plant for cool greenhouse. Several species produce henna and rouge.

PRONUNCIATION: an-KOO-sa ka-PEN-sis

The borage family is unusually rich in flowers of precious shades of blue: *Myosotis sylvestris* (the true forget-me-not), *Cynoglossom amabile* (the Chinese forget-me-not), *Omphelodes verna* (Venus' navelwort), and the herb called "borage," which gives the whole family its name. None, however, produces quite so intense a shade as plants belonging to the genus *Anchusa*.

Without doubt, the king of the group (of three or four species) is *A. azurea* (a-ZHUR-ee-a) or *A. italica* (ih-TAL-i-ca), a stout perennial grown generally as a biennial that can produce towering, five-foot-tall masses of vivid blue flowers in its second year of growth.

The only species of *Anchusa* grown as an annual, *A. capensis* lacks the authority of *A. azurea* in stature, for none of the cultivars available will ever achieve more than two feet in height, and usually are shorter, from sixteen inches to only a foot. Still for blue flowers among plants grown as annuals, *A. capensis* is hard to match. Flowers are quite small, scarcely more than one third of an inch across, but they are borne abundantly on many upright slender stems, creating a bush of skylike hue. Their curious luminosity results from the fact that the tiny, unopened flower buds are red, and the open flowers, though at their best an intense gentian blue, preserve a faint red edge to each petal and are white at their center. In references, the cultivar 'Blue Bird' is always mentioned as superior.

There is also a 'Pink Bird', a pure white form listed as *A. c.* 'Alba' and a mix of all shades of blue, lavender, pink and white called 'Dawn'.

A. capensis is a true biennial, though tender, originating in South Africa from the Cape of Good Hope, as the word *capensis* always indicates. Like many tender biennials, it may be treated as an annual if sown in mild gardens in autumn or very early spring, and elsewhere given an early start under glass. Plants flower best in rather dry, poor soils in the cool weather of early summer, but when they begin to flag, they should not be yanked out, but rather sheared back by about a third. They will then flower again in early autumn when cool weather returns. From a late summer or early autumn sowing, *A. capensis* makes a splendid pot plant for flowering in late winter or early spring in a cool greenhouse.

A. capensis is often called "forget-me-not," and, like *A. azurea,* also "alkanet" or "bugloss." Alkanet comes from an Arabic word for skin paint or henna (as does the genus name *Anchusa,* from the ancient Greek word for rouge), and bugloss is a corruption of the Greek word for the tongue of a cow, referring to the hairy, raspy, tongue-shaped leaves anchusas typically bear.

ANDROSACE SPECIES

FAMILY: *Primulaceae* or primrose family.

CLASSIFICATION: Hardy annual.

COMMON NAMES: Rock jasmine, annual androsace.

HARDINESS: Winter-hardy to Zone 5.

GROWING CONDITIONS: Thin, free-draining, gravelly soil. Full sun.

PROPAGATION: From seed, sown in place in September or early October, or as soon as ground is open in spring. Requires cool weather.

HEIGHT: 4 to 6", rarely to 1'.

ORNAMENTAL VALUE: Grown for flower.

LEVEL OF CULTURAL DIFFICULTY: Easy in cool gardens. Difficult elsewhere.

SPECIAL PROPERTIES: Excellent in troughs and miniature gardens. Superb winter-flowering plant for cool greenhouses.

PRONUNCIATION: an-DRAH-sa-kee

The genus *Androsace* contains about 125 species, mostly perennial, and all native to the high mountainous areas of the globe. Within the clan, however, two species are annuals—*A. lactiflora* (lak-ti-FLO-ra) and *A. septintrionalis* (sep-tin-tri-o-NA-lis)—and though not commonly grown, their tiny beauty will win for them a place in any gardener's heart.

The most often cultivated of these two rare treasures is *A. lactiflora,* a hardy, self-sowing plant native to Siberia. It forms a silvery-gray rosette of two-inch long, lance-shaped leaves, from which arise thin, wiry stems, each topped with an umbel of many five-petaled white flowers. They are usually described as "primrose-like," which is no surprise given the family to which the genus belongs, Primulaceae. Under the most favorable growing conditions, stems may reach a foot, though quite happy and floriferous plants may be only six inches high. The growth of the plant is fast in earliest spring (high mountain plants always make the best of their short season) and so from a late autumn sowing in September or an early spring one in March, plants will be in flower by late May or early June, persisting in cool gardens into July, and then withering away in the heat of August. Seed must be sown in place, for young plants do not transplant well and are too tiny to handle at the stage when they would have to be pricked out. But once grown in a place it really likes, *A. lactiflora* will faithfully reappear from spring to spring as self-sown plants, sometimes where it is expected, and sometimes as a surprise at the edge of a gravel path, or between the cracks of a brick terrace. It should be left alone wherever it chooses to show up, for its appearance is always a blessing.

The other annual species of cultivated androsace is *A. septintrionalis,* a native of the high mountains of Europe. An even smaller plant than *A. lactiflora,* it produces quarter-inch-wide flowers in umbels on wiry, brownish stems that may reach eight inches in height, but are typically closer to four. Flowers may be either pink or white, but both colors are engagingly marked by a yellow eye. Like *A. lactiflora,* it craves a long, cool spring, and the sort of soil one would find in a mountain scree: gritty, humus-poor, free-draining, always moist but never waterlogged.

Serious rock gardeners will need no introduction to either of these plants and will treasure their spontaneous reappearance from year to year. Outside the specialized structures of rock gardens, however, both annual species of *Androsace* will give greatest pleasure if grown in troughs or pots, as their delicacy of bloom demands close study, and they can easily be lost in a general bedding scheme. In gardens that experience quick, hot springs, both species will be failures, but they may be cultivated successfully as winter-flowering treasures in unheated greenhouses or cold frames after a late summer or autumn sowing. In cold, mountainous northern gardens, however, they may be expected to thrive.

The name for the genus *Androsace* is derived from two ancient Greek words, *aner,* signifying a man, and *sakos,* shield, and was used by the ancient Greek botanist Dioscorides to designate another plant. *Lactiflora* describes the milk-white flowers of one species, and *septintrionalis* indicates a northern location, from the seven stars of Ursa Minor, the most northern constellation

ANGELONIA ANGUSTIFOLIA

FAMILY: *Scrophulariaceae* or snapdragon family.

CLASSIFICATION: Tender evergreen perennial grown as tender annual.

COMMON NAME: Angelonia.

HARDINESS: Hardy to Zones 9 and 10. Sensitive to temperatures much below 40°F.

GROWING CONDITIONS: Moist, fertile garden soil. Perfect drainage. Full sun.

PROPAGATION: From seed, sown indoors in late winter.

HEIGHT: To 1½'.

ORNAMENTAL VALUE: Grown for flower.

LEVEL OF CULTURAL DIFFICULTY: Moderately easy.

SPECIAL PROPERTIES: Valued as container plant and for cut flowers. Excellent winter-flowering plant for cool greenhouse.

PRONUNCIATION: an-gee-LOW-nee-a an-gus-ti-FO-lee-a

*I*n the last ten years, the explosion of available plants that may be grown as annuals has presented gardeners with new and exciting choices each season. Some of them are so beautiful, so easy of culture, and so rewarding to grow that one regrets not having come to know them sooner. At the very top of this list of "new" plants

ANGELONIA ANGUSTIFOLIA

is *Angelonia angustifolia,* which in flower resembles nothing so much as shortened sprays of botanical orchids.

Everything about angelonia is beautiful, including its genus name, though it has nothing to do with angels, but is a Latinized version of the South American vernacular name for one species. Its growth is tidy and compact, the whole plant reaching about one and a half feet tall by midsummer and broadening to a width of the same dimension as new side growth is produced. Its leaves are shiny, blade shaped, slightly toothed on their margins, and of a rich, laurel green. (The species name *angustifolia* means narrow-leaved.) Two inches long at the base of the stems, they become shorter (to a half an inch) as they move upward. Flowers occur singly on spires in the axils of the leaves, each spire opening its blooms in series over a month or more. Flowers are about a half-inch wide with the two upper lobes and three lower lobes typical of most plants in the family Scrophulariaceae. Unlike the tubular form of snapdragons, however, the lobes of angelonia are flattened out and wavy, with a shallow open throat. Flower color is typically a rich purple, whitish at the lower lip and throat, though speckled over with a deeper purple inside. Bi-colors of

white and blue exist, as well as a fine, pure white form.

A native of the West Indies, angelonia is in fact not an annual, but a tender perennial or sub-shrub hardy only in USDA Zones 9 and 10. An early sowing under glass in January or February will produce bushy plants that show their first spikes of bloom by early summer and continue to flower until frost. Then they may be lifted carefully, cut back by a third, and potted for late winter flowering in a temperate greenhouse. Angelonia also roots very easily from soft-wood cuttings, and most plants offered in nurseries are produced that way, for even earlier flowering.

Though not fussy about soils, angelonias require excellent drainage at their roots, and flower best in moist but humusy, free-draining garden loam. They appreciate a light feeding with a general granular fertilizer—10-10-10 or the like—which encourages abundant flower production. They are most attractive when planted in groups of three or more, about eight inches apart, to form the effect of a single clump, or in broad elliptical drifts across the front of the border. Angelonias are superb cut flowers, lasting well over a week in water. The stature of the plant, its long blooming season, and the vividness of its flowers make it an excellent candidate for window boxes or containers.

ANISODONTEA HYPOMANDARUM

FAMILY: *Malvaceae* or mallow family.

CLASSIFICATION: Tender shrub grown as a tender annual.

COMMON NAMES: Cape mallow, African mallow, anisodontea.

HARDINESS: Uncomfortable at temperatures much below 40°F. Extremely frost sensitive.

GROWING CONDITIONS: Humus-rich, well-drained garden loam or commercial potting soil. Full sun.

PROPAGATION: Normally from cuttings, which root readily.

HEIGHT: To 6' where hardy. To about 3' when grown as an annual. Taller if grown as standard.

ORNAMENTAL VALUE: Grown for flower, and as standards.

LEVEL OF CULTURAL DIFFICULTY: Easy.

SPECIAL PROPERTIES: Excellent container plants. Attractive winter-blooming plants for cool windowsills or cool greenhouse.

PRONUNCIATION: a-nis-o-DON-tee-a hi-po-MAN-da-rum

Anisodonteas are relative newcomers among the many plants now being offered for summer beauty in gardens that experience significant frost. Natives of South Africa, they were largely unknown until about ten years ago except to gardeners living where winter lows do not drop much below 35°F. In such places, the dense, twiggy growth of anisodonteas—to six feet or taller—made them useful as quick-growing, sheared hedges. But their long, practically non-stop blooming season, their tidiness of growth, their small, evergreen leaves, and the charm of their miniature pink or plum-colored hibiscus flowers made them too nice to remain only where they are hardy. So they have joined the large number of exciting tender plants grown from cuttings (all anisodonteas root readily) that have begun to appear in those nurseries and garden centers specializing in rare and unusual annual and tender plants.

Anisodonteas belong to the Malvaceae family (about 95 genera and 1,500 species) and are recognizably mallowlike, with clear resemblance to many garden plants such as althaeas, hibiscus, lavateras, malvas, and abutilons. All typically bear flowers of five petals, distinct or overlapped, usually spread wide, saucer fashion, but sometimes, as with abutilons, borne in down-hanging bells.

Among anisodonteas, the species most commonly offered is *hypomandarum,* sometimes listed as *A.* x *hypomandarum,* though if it is a hybrid, its parentage is unknown. But within the genus of about eighteen species are other good garden subjects, though none are greatly different in appearance from *hypomandarum. A. julii* (JOO-lee-ee) is a somewhat larger plant, as tall as ten feet, with light green raspy, lobed leaves, and flowers of a darker pink, generally about two or even three inches wide. *A. scabrosa* (sca-BRO-sa) has purplish stems and half-inch-wide flowers that may range from a whitish pink to almost magenta, with three- to five-lobed figlike leaves. *A. capensis* (ka-PEN-sis) is much confused in the trade with *A. hypomandarum,* though the former's inch-wide flowers may sometimes be a deeper shade of pink, almost to purple.

Collectors of malvaceous plants, scholars, or nurserymen would care about these distinctions, but most gardeners will find in any available species of anisodontea an interesting garden plant. They thrive unusually well in containers, though their delicacy of growth and bloom makes them useful also in general bedding schemes or in the perennial garden, where they never seem anomalous as do, for example, their larger cousins, the Hawaiian hibiscus. Because they do so well in pots, they are also among those very useful plants that may be held in reserve to drop into the irritating blank spaces left in borders where early perennials have completed their flowering or where other annual or tender plants have become exhausted or have failed.

All anisodonteas are of easy culture, providing they are not allowed to dry out at the roots. They appreciate a monthly feeding with a water-soluble fertilizer (such as Rapid Gro, Miracle-Gro, or Peters 20-20-20), particularly when grown in containers. An occasional light shearing will keep the plants in balance and encourage new, free-blooming growth. As anisodonteas are woody plants that accept even heavy shearing, they are prime candidates for standards, small trees trained to a single stem with a mop of tightly clipped growth at the tops. Whether as standards or as free-growing small bushes, anisodonteas may be lifted before frost and potted up for use as winter-flowering indoor or greenhouse plants. When grown as standards, it is worth the trouble, for specimens may be saved from year to year, eventually to become thick-trunked, four- or five-foot-tall miniature trees.

The genus *Anisodontea* takes its name from the botanical adjective *anisodontus,* from the Greek prefix *aniso-,* meaning unequal, and *-odontos,* toothed, and refers to the jagged, pinked edges of the leaves. The species name *hypomandarum* is equally flat-footed, from Greek *hypo-* meaning very, and *mandaros,* signifying bald, and merely notes the fact that the seed carpels are hairless below their tips.

ANODA CRISTATA

FAMILY: *Malvaceae* or mallow family.

CLASSIFICATION: Tender perennial grown as half-hardy annual.

COMMON NAMES: Opal cups, anoda.

HARDINESS: Extremely frost sensitive. Resents cool weather. Relishes heat.

GROWING CONDITIONS: Poor to moderately fertile, well-drained soil. Abundant moisture. Full sun.

PROPAGATION: From seed, sown in place when weather is warm and settled, or indoors in peat pots about 6 weeks before last frost. Seedlings resent transplanting.

HEIGHT: To 4'.

ORNAMENTAL VALUE: Grown for flower, and for heavy, tropical-looking foliage.

LEVEL OF CULTURAL DIFFICULTY: Easy.

SPECIAL PROPERTIES: None.

PRONUNCIATION: a-NO-da cris-TA-ta

As a garden-worthy plant, *Anoda cristata* has some stiff competition even within its own family, for the Malvaceae are rich in garden plants that are either true annuals or may be grown as annuals, such as lavateras, anisodonteas, abutilons, abelmoschus, and hibiscus, all of which might well vie with it for place. Still, those who love the characteristic flower shape of malvas—an open, five-petaled flower of crepelike texture, furnished always with a prominent central column of fertile parts—will sooner or later try them all. Among them, *A. cristata,* prettily called "opal cups" for its shimmering qualities, has its charms.

Like many garden malvas, *A. cristata* is a coarse-growing plant, achieving a sturdy, bush-like growth of from two to three feet in the heart of summer, and furnished with wide, hairy, raspy leaves that may be triangular, rounded, or lobed, several shapes often occurring on the same plant. The flowers are about two inches wide, borne from the axils of the leaves, recognizably hibiscus-like, consisting of five thin, overlapping petals forming a cup, within which the fused pistil and pollen-dusted anthers sit at the center. Typically, their color is a purplish-blue, though white, lavender, and clear pink forms exist, always with thin pencilings of a darker shade down each petal. Flowers are long stemmed, much like those of *Abelmoschus manihot* or the shrubby "Hawaiian" *Hibiscus rosa-sinensis*. They have the unusual property of lasting quite a long time (up to ten days) in water.

Like most malvas grown as annuals, *A. cristata* resents both transplanting and cool, wet springs, and so it should be seeded late, in plastic cell packs, and transplanted into the garden only when the weather has become settled and warm. It does its best in hot summers, on rather poor, well-drained soils but with abundant moisture at the roots. Though flowers may appear as early as late June, they will be most plentiful in the dog days of August.

Any annual plant of strong, shrubby growth is valuable in garden schemes, particularly toward the middle of a bed, where one seems to crave a certain weight and solidity, and so *A. cristata* has its uses there. But it also thrives unusually well in pots, seeming to relish (as does its close cousin, *Gossypium hirsutum,* the cotton of commerce) a certain amount of baking at the roots. It might therefore supply an interesting textural contrast to other annuals and tender perennials grown in large pots or containers.

The genus *Anoda* contains about ten species, all of New World origin, and occurring over a wide geographic range from southwestern North America through Mexico, the West Indies, Central and South America. Nevertheless, it takes its name from a Sinhalese word for a species of *Abutilon* native to Sri Lanka. The pretty-sounding species name *cristata* actually only indicates the crested and pollen-fringed fertile parts at the center of each flower.

ANODA CRISTATA

ANTIGONON LEPTOPUS

FAMILY: *Polygonaceae* or buckwheat family.

CLASSIFICATION: Tender perennial vine grown as tender annual vine.

COMMON NAMES: Coral vine, confederate vine, rosa de montana, queen's wreath, queen's jewels, corallita, chain of love, sweetheart vine, antigonon.

HARDINESS: Hardy in Zones 9 and 10; in 8 with protection. Leaf sensitive to light frosts.

GROWING CONDITIONS: Poor, dryish, well-drained soil. Full sun. Relishes heat and humidity.

PROPAGATION: Usually from cuttings, taken of nonflowering shoots in autumn.

HEIGHT: To 25' where hardy. To 10' when grown as an annual vine.

ORNAMENTAL VALUE: Grown for flower.

LEVEL OF CULTURAL DIFFICULTY: Easy in warmer gardens. Difficult in cool ones.

SPECIAL PROPERTIES: Rapid cover for arbors, trellises, or warm walls.

PRONUNCIATION: an-ti-GO-non (an-TI-go-non) LEP-toe-puss

Almost always the number of common names attached to a plant indicates the length of its history in gardens and the degree to which it has been treasured. *Antigonon leptopus* is remarkable in its accumulation, indicating that wherever it has thrived it has been much loved. A perennial vine native to Mexico, *A. leptopus* is a child of heat—never so happy as when temperatures are almost unbearable to human beings. Where winter temperatures do not drop below 25°F, it dies to the ground in winter but persists from year to year. And even where it is not winter hardy, it can have incredibly rapid growth in gardens where summers are hot and sultry. This makes it worth cultivating as an annual vine. Grown from seed or cuttings, *A. leptopus* may reach ten feet or more by summer's end, clad in coarse arrow- or heart-shaped dark green leaves from one to three inches long, the largest toward the base of the plant. Flowers appear in the hotter sections of the middle and upper South by July, later in cooler gardens. It is not actually the flowers that are showy, however, but the heart-shaped calyxes about one and a half inches long, and typically colored a warm, rich pink. Borne from the axils of the leaves in huge numbers, they occur in trailing, chainlike sprays between six and fifteen inches long and—as with other flowers cultivated for their calyxes or bracts—persist over a very long time. At its best, *A. leptopus,* though its bracts are much smaller, can be as showy as a bougainvillea.

A. leptopus thrives in poor, dryish soil, which promotes early and abundant flowering. It must be given the hottest and sunniest place in the garden and trained upward on strings or some other support. In gardens that are not positively scorching, best results will occur from plants taken as cuttings in autumn (they root readily) and carried over winter in a warm greenhouse or on a sunny windowsill. Among quick-growing vines that may be treated as annuals, *A. leptopus* should be a wonderful candidate for sunny, baking roof gardens as far north as New York City.

The genus name *Antigonon* is derived from Greek *anti,* meaning instead of, and *polygonon,* which acknowledges the close relationship of the two genera within the family Polygonaceae (i.e., it is "not polygonum"). Its species name, *leptopus,* means thin-stalked and refers to the slender stems on which it bears its colored bracts and flower.

ANTIRRHINUM SPECIES

FAMILY: *Scrophulariaceae* or snapdragon family.

CLASSIFICATION: Half-hardy perennials grown as half-hardy annuals.

COMMON NAMES: Snapdragon, antirrhinum.

HARDINESS: Root-hardy perhaps to Zone 7. Tolerant of light frosts.

GROWING CONDITIONS: Humus-rich, fertile, well-drained soil. Abundant moisture. Full sun in cooler gardens, afternoon shade in warmer ones. Flowers best in cool weather.

PROPAGATION: From seed, sown indoors in late February or early March. Cuttings root easily.

HEIGHT: Usually from 2 to 3′. Dwarves have been bred.

ORNAMENTAL VALUE: Grown for its spiked flowers.

LEVEL OF CULTURAL DIFFICULTY: Easy.

SPECIAL PROPERTIES: Excellent cut flower. Superb cool greenhouse plant for winter flower.

PRONUNCIATION: an-ti-RIN-um

Antirrhinum majus (MA-jus or MAY-us), "snapdragons," are one of the ten most popular plants grown as annuals in North America, presenting a singular case where the most sophisticated and the most naïve gardeners join hands in admiration. The plants have always been treasured for their pouchlike flowers that may be made to snap open and closed by a gentle squeeze at their cheeks, but even more because in the garden their spirelike scapes are a valuable vertical counterpoint to the predominately mounded or bushlike growth of other flowers. Their colors, too, are clear and vivid, ranging from bronze and red through purple-red almost to black, rich and pale pink, lemon and primrose yellow, cream and white. Most shades are marked by an orange to yellow stain at the throat, which gives them vibrancy, as one color laid over another often does. Snapdragons are also among the best flowers for cutting, and acres of glasshouses are devoted to their production for the florist trade—both here and in Europe—often as magnificent rods with stems three feet long.

All that having been said, snapdragons have been the recipient of many insults from modern plant breeders. By nature they are stately plants, as the species name *majus* implies. (It means tall and suggests the English word *majestic.*) They naturally assume a height of between two and three feet, but they can be as tall as four in full flower under good culture. Many modern strains, however, now make a mockery of their species name, for the plant has been bred to dwarf—and more dwarf—bushy forms. Blossoms have even been doubled to create "Azalea-flowered" strains, all robbing snapdragons of their most valuable characteristic, which is a stately simplicity. It is doubtless true that these dwarfer forms (such as 'Floral Carpet', to eight inches tall, or 'Magic Carpet', which is almost prostrate) have their uses in complex carpet bedding schemes, in drifts at the front of the peren-

ANTIRRHINUM MAJUS

nial border, at the edge of a path, or perhaps as container plants.

But to those who love snapdragons for what they should be, only those strains that retain the natural characteristics of the plant will serve. Open-pollinated strains come closest to the ideal, though the Rocket Series that is available as seed in separate colors is a satisfactory substitute. Outside the cutting garden also, separate colors are much to be preferred over a number of unrelated shades all in a jumble.

Snapdragons are technically half-hardy perennials, and in warmer gardens they will sometimes persist for several years if lightly mulched with evergreen boughs in winter. (It is always worth the try.) But more than almost any other member of the class of half-hardy perennials generally grown as annuals, snapdragons should be planted as one would plant most hardy perennials, in large clumps or drifts, spacing the taller varieties about eight to ten inches apart, and in separate colors. Plants flower best if they are given a long, cool growing season, and as they are slightly resistant to frost, they should be established in the garden early, but not so early that they might experience a hard freeze. They flower best when summer nights are cool, and so are apt to give their finest performance in early summer, and again, if spent flower heads are promptly removed and the plants kept in lusty growth, in early autumn.

Even when not in flower, snapdragons are handsome plants, with dark green, shiny, lance-shaped leaves about three inches long, which may be bronze or reddish in darker-flowered forms. But as with another preeminent cottage garden plant, hollyhocks, they have their bane, which is rust. Rust-resistant varieties are generally offered, though resistance in a plant is only that, and not total exemption from the problem. Rust can be minimized by keeping plants well watered, though never splashing them from above, and well nourished. Infections can be recognized by dusty, brownish spots on the undersides of leaves, and should be treated organically with powdered sulphur, or with chemical sprays. If possible, it is also always wise to rotate plantings of snapdragons, locating them in different parts of the border each year.

The genus *Antirrhinum* takes its name from Greek *anti,* meaning in place of, and *rhis,* snout or nose—an attempt to describe the snouted face the flowers suggest. Within its genus of about forty species, *A. majus* is the one most frequently grown in gardens. The expanding interest among American gardeners in annual and tender plants will, however, almost certainly make other species available. Two species native to Spain and Portugal are worth seeking out. *A. braun-blanquettii* (BRAWN-blan-KET-ee-ee) grows to about two feet and produces inch-long flowers with a yellow throat. *A. glutinosum* (glu-ti-NO-sum) is sticky-leaved, as its species name indicates, and though its stems can reach a height of fourteen inches, they tend to fall over, becoming decumbent. Flowers are about one inch long, yellowish white, with a red stripe at the lip, and quite showy. *A. molle* (MO-lee), a native of southern France, is similar, though it lacks stickiness in its leaves, which are powdered over with a light down, giving them a silvery appearance. Finally there is *Antirrhinum orontium* (o-ron-TEE-um), which, though a native to Europe and Asia, is widely naturalized throughout North America. It is popularly called "weasel snout," which is actually close to what the Greek name for the genus means. It is a somewhat weedy little plant to about a foot tall, bearing charming, solitary rose to purple half-inch flowers in the axils of its narrow, inch-long leaves.

Most antirrhinums will be acquired from nurseries and garden centers in spring as stocky, healthy young plants, ready to set out into the garden around the last anticipated frost date. Seed germinates readily, however, at temperatures around 60°F. As with many other perennials cultivated as annuals, and particularly those that relish long, cool growing conditions, antirrhinums should be seeded early, in late February or early March. Young plants transplant readily, and should be pricked out and grown on in bright, sunny conditions at temperatures around 70°F in the daytime and 10° cooler at night. When they reach about five inches tall, they should be pinched to encourage bushiness, and pinched again if their transplanting into the garden is delayed. In cooler gardens, full sun is preferred, though in warmer ones light afternoon shade will prolong flowering. Antirrhinums prefer deep, humus-rich, water-retentive but well-drained soil, and they respond well to monthly feedings with general water-soluble fertilizer (such as Rapid Gro, Miracle-Gro, or Peters 20-20-20), particularly after bloom stems have been cut back.

Snapdragons are also superb cool greenhouse plants for flower from late winter to spring. For this purpose, seed should be sown in mid-July, or tip cuttings, which root readily, may be taken from nonflowering shoots. Young plants should be grown on singly in five- or six-inch pots, kept vigorous by frequent fertilizing, and pinched to encourage bushiness and to delay flower. They should be brought under glass a week or two before the first anticipated frost of the season, and placed in the brightest and best-ventilated section of the greenhouse. Plants should be allowed to dry out slightly between waterings, though never to the point that they wilt or shrivel, and care should be taken to keep excess water off their leaves. Fertilizers should be withheld until flower buds begin to form in late winter, at which point a fertilizer low in nitrogen but high in phosphorus and potassium should be applied, and frequency of watering may be increased.

AQUILEGIA HYBRIDS

FAMILY: *Ranunculaceae* or buttercup family.

CLASSIFICATION: Biennial or short-lived perennial sometimes grown as hardy annual.

COMMON NAMES: Columbine, granny's bonnet, aquilegia.

HARDINESS: Withstands frosts.

GROWING CONDITIONS: Humus-rich, free-draining, alkaline soil. Full sun to part shade. Prefers cool weather.

PROPAGATION: From seed, sown in site in late September or early October, or in very early spring. Young plants transplant easily.

HEIGHT: To 2'.

ORNAMENTAL VALUE: Grown for flower.

LEVEL OF CULTURAL DIFFICULTY: Easy.

SPECIAL PROPERTIES: None.

PRONUNCIATION: a-ki-LEE-gee-a

With hollyhocks, foxgloves, and forget-me-nots, columbines are among that group of plants considered quintessential cottage garden flowers. Although their blossoms are complex rather than simple—five outfacing or cupped petals that elongate into inch-long spurs—they still carry an air of old-fashioned charm, as their popular name, granny's bonnet, suggests, always resonating of quiet summer mornings in the country.

The genus *Aquilegia* takes its name from nothing so gentle, but rather, from the Latin word for eagle, *aquila,* a fanciful comparison of the colored tepals and down-hanging spurred petals to an eagle in flight. The English popular name for the plant, columbine, also compares it to a bird, a dove, from Latin *columba*. Though within the genus exist many exquisite pure species treasured by alpine and woodland gardeners, the long-spurred hybrids mingle the blood of several species, chiefly *canadensis* (ca-na-DEN-sis), *vulgaris* (vul-GAR-is), *longissima* (lon-JI-si-ma), and *chrysantha* (kry-SAN-tha). They may be had in many shades of blue, pink, yellow, and creamy white, and as bi-colors.

Columbines are one of several garden plants that waver uneasily among the classifications of hardy annual, biennial, and perennial. Most will give their best flowers in spring and summer following a mid- to late summer sowing the previous year. But some seem to hurry up matters by flowering the first season from an early spring sowing. The long-spurred hybrids are particularly precocious, and so it is worth considering them as annuals. As they are quite hardy, they may be sown either in September or in very early spring, in prepared beds outdoors. They transplant easily, and so a row or out-of-the-way patch may be seeded for plants to move into gaps in the garden as they occur. They prefer a moist, humus-rich, free-draining loam on the alkaline side, though they are not fussy plants and will put up with less than their ideal. They may be grown in full sun, though where summers are hot and dry, partial shade suits them better. Care must be taken, however, especially in dry shade, to keep them well irrigated throughout their growing period. For the finest plants with rosettes of leaf a foot across and many flower scapes as much as two feet tall, young plants should be established between a foot and eighteen inches apart. Aquilegias are notoriously promiscuous plants, freely intercrossing one with another, but still seed should be saved of any particularly beautiful color for sowing the following autumn or spring. One may not get a plant identical to the parent, but still it will be pretty. Stored in a cool, dry place, such as in an airtight mason jar in the refrigerator, the seed of aquilegia has a viability of five years or more. Once aquilegias have been made happy in a garden, they will also self-seed abundantly, though never to the point of becoming a nuisance.

ARAUJIA SERICOFERA

FAMILY: *Asclepiadaceae* or milkweed family.

CLASSIFICATION: Half-hardy perennial vine grown as half-hardy annual vine.

COMMON NAMES: White bladder vine, araujia.

HARDINESS: Root-hardy to Zones 8 and 9. Frost sensitive in cooler gardens.

GROWING CONDITIONS: Any well-drained soil. Full sun. Relishes heat and humidity.

PROPAGATION: From seed, sown indoors in February. Tip cuttings root easily in spring or summer.

HEIGHT: To 20′ in one season.

ORNAMENTAL VALUE: Grown for vining coverage.

LEVEL OF CULTURAL DIFFICULTY: Easy in warm gardens. Difficult elsewhere.

SPECIAL PROPERTIES: Quick-growing, covering vine in warm gardens. Useful for arbors, porches, any unsightly object.

PRONUNCIATION: a-RAW-gee-a ser-i-COFF-e-ra

*O*f the five or so species in the obscure genus *Araujia,* only one, *Araujia sericofera* (sometimes "*sericifera*"), is in cultivation. A native of southern Brazil, it is a vigorous, twining vine that sometimes appears spontaneously where it is hardy, in USDA Zones 8 and 9. Elsewhere it is occasionally grown from seed or cuttings taken from fresh shoots in early March under greenhouse conditions. Of extremely rapid growth, it can achieve as much as twenty feet in a single season, and in just the right hot, steamy summer, it will flower in July from cutting-grown plants, and in autumn from seed germinated in a warm greenhouse in February.

The flowers of *Araujia sericofera,* however, are not the main point. They are pretty enough, sparsely borne in clusters from upper leaf axils and consisting of tiny, inch-wide white or pale pink bells, sometimes prominently striped with maroon and very fragrant. The leaves of the vine, however, are rich and bold, a smoothed-out triangle about four inches long, glossy dark green on the upper surface and silvery white beneath. Where summers are long enough for the plant to form seeds, they are a curiosity in themselves, consisting of flattened, milkweedlike pods full of silky seed, hence the common name, bladder vine.

Araujia sericofera grows in any soil, poor or rich, moist or dry. In gardens north of Zone 8, plants may be dug at the end of summer, reduced to convenient height, and the lateral growths cut back to two or three buds, potted up, and stored in a cool but frost-free greenhouse, to be planted out the following spring for an even lustier, earlier-flowering specimen the following summer.

The genus *Araujia* takes its name from the native Brazilian word for the plant, and *sericofera* indicates the silken seed within a ripe pod.

ARCTOTIS SPECIES

FAMILY: *Asteraceae* or aster or daisy family.

CLASSIFICATION: Tender perennial grown as tender annual.

COMMON NAMES: African daisy, arctotis.

HARDINESS: Root-hardy to Zones 9 and 10. Sensitive to light frosts elsewhere.

GROWING CONDITIONS: Sandy, fertile, well-drained loam. Cool nights. Full sun.

PROPAGATION: From seed, sown indoors in late winter or very early spring. Plants resent root disturbance.

HEIGHT: To 1'.

ORNAMENTAL VALUE: Grown for flower.

LEVEL OF CULTURAL DIFFICULTY: Difficult in most American gardens.

SPECIAL PROPERTIES: Superb winter greenhouse plants.

PRONUNCIATION: ark-TO-tis

Among plants, no greater proof exists of the chaos resulting from the use of common names than African daisy. It has been variously applied to dimorpothecas, gazanias, gerberas, mesembryanthemums, osteospermums, tripteris, venidiums, and the genus under discussion here, *Arctotis*. All are daisies (and look like daisies, which not all daisies do), all are very beautiful, and all—superficially or strongly—resemble one another.

In the case of *Arctotis,* the confusion hardly stops there, for many of the approximately fifty species in the genus will freely intercross, making precise botanical identification difficult, if not impossible. Nevertheless, these crosses, all grouped for convenience under the label of x *hybridus* (HI-bri-dus), produce flowers of extraordinary beauty, three-inch-wide daisies colored cream, pale or warm pink, primrose or deep yellow, apricot, dark rose, plum, or brownish red. The disk flowers at the center will be some shade of bronze or burgundy or a brown so deep as to seem black. Ray flowers, the "petals" of a daisy, are generally twenty-six in number, seeming to guarantee "she loves me" as a conclusion, though there are treacherously sometimes more ray

ARCTOTIS STOECHADIFOLIA

(bre-vi-SCAR-pa) and *A. acaulis* (a-CAW-lis) are similar in appearance, differing essentially in that the first achieves a height of about a foot, and the second is shorter by half. Both bear two- to three-inch-wide daisies, black at the center, with ray petals that are some shade of orange or yellow above, and copper or bronze red beneath. The two species are much mixed in the trade, and have probably freely intercrossed. They have also been bred with other species in the genus, especially with *A. stoechadifolia,* and bred back again, to create a swarm of beautiful plants, some named cultivars, some offered simply as color strains or mixtures.

Arctotis are not of the easiest culture in many American gardens. They thrive best in full sun in sandy soil with perfect and rapid drainage, but it is a mistake to assume that they will flourish in hot, baking conditions with little water at the roots. Like so many South African perennials grown as annuals, arctotis perform best where the days are warm and sunny but the nights are cool and moist. In such conditions, they will give abundant flower all summer long, provided spent blooms are removed promptly to prevent seed formation. But in gardens that experience both heat and drought by midsummer, they are apt to burn off, and so should be thought of as early summer flowers, quite gone by the arrival of the hot days of July. However, the very conditions that make arctotis difficult in many American gardens make them superb winter-flowering greenhouse or sun-porch plants. Cuttings root easily in late summer, or fresh seed may be sown in late August, eventually to be potted as single plants in five-inch pots of sandy, humus-rich, free-draining soil. Through autumn and early winter, plants should be kept evenly moist but not over-watered, and fertilized lightly with a water-soluble plant food. Bloom will appear in late January and continue through spring to early summer.

petals, sometimes fewer. The flowers merit the closest examination, however, for they are usually of a lighter tint brushed over with a deeper one, and where the rays meet the disk, there is a beautiful halo of a contrasting or complementary color, and sometimes several. The popular cultivar 'Zulu Prince', for example, possesses a central disk of blackest maroon, and the base of each ray petal is marked first with burnt sienna and then with chestnut red, giving way abruptly to a snowy white.

Arctotis species are all perennials of South African origin, and in those gardens that approximate their homeland in climate, namely the moister and cooler sections of USDA Zones 9 and 10, they may be perennial, though the best flowers are generally produced by treating them as biennials, establishing young plants in autumn for spring and summer bloom the following year. *Arctotis stoechadifolia* (sto-chad-i-FO-lee-a) in its selected cultivar 'Grandis' is a two-foot tall, bushy plant bearing large white daisies with a steel blue eye, their ray petals attractively brushed with lavender beneath. The leaves are deeply cut, giving the plant a lacy appearance, and they are of a fine, silvery gray-green, a characteristic the best of its hybrid progeny inherit. *Arctotis breviscarpa*

Arctotis much resemble venediums, another "African daisy" and a close South African cousin that is, if anything, even more beautiful in its flowers. From a bi-generic marriage of the two another race has arisen, classed botanically as *Arctotis* X *Venedium* (vi-ni-DEE-um). The plants, which flower in splendid shades of red, copper, burgundy, orange, and pink, are all sterile "mules," unable to be reproduced from seed. If one is lucky enough to procure stock of the cross, cuttings should be taken in late summer and carried over in a cool greenhouse or on a sunny windowsill.

Most arctotis, whether true species or hybrids, will be acquired as young plants from nurseries that specialize in unusual annuals. They bloom precociously, and so young plants may already be showing their first flower, dashingly large against small rosettes of green leaves. Where seed is available, it should be sown in late winter or very early spring at temperatures around 60°F, and young plants should be pricked out into flexible plastic six-packs to minimize root disturbance when transplanted.

ARGEMONE SPECIES

FAMILY: *Papaveraceae* or poppy family.

CLASSIFICATION: Half-hardy biennials or half-hardy perennials grown as hardy annuals.

COMMON NAMES: Devil's fig, Mexican prickly poppy, argemone.

HARDINESS: Resistant to light frosts.

GROWING CONDITIONS: Light, sandy, moderately fertile soil. Perfect drainage. Full sun.

PROPAGATION: From seed, sown in site in late autumn or very early spring, or indoors in peat pots 6 to 8 weeks before last anticipated frost date. Plants resent root disturbance.

HEIGHT: To 2'.

ORNAMENTAL VALUE: Grown for flower.

LEVEL OF CULTURAL DIFFICULTY: Easy.

SPECIAL PROPERTIES: None.

PRONUNCIATION: ar-GEM-o-nee (ar-JEM-o-nee)

Much recommends the family Papaveraceae, to which argemones belong. All of its members bear flowers of ephemeral beauty, polished like thin sheets of ivory or crinkled like the finest silk. Typically, those we recognize as poppies shake out their pleated petals from a split calyx just as butterflies shake out their wings, expanding in early morning sunlight to a full, five-petaled flower, and passing off in a day or two. As a rule, those commonly grown as annuals in gardens, such as *Papaver rhoeas* or *Papaver somniferum,* have a short but beautiful life, becoming shabby by mid-July or earlier, but scattering their seed copiously for plants the following year.

In flower, the fragile beauty of argemones is as fine as any member of the family. They are appropriately poppylike, the flowers consisting of a two- or three-inch-wide blossom of five petals— so delicate that one can see through their pleated and crinkled texture. The flower opens first as a cup and later spreads flat, the edges of each petal curving gracefully downward. In the center of each flower is a boss of yellow stamens, usually tinted purple, and so rich in pollen that sometimes as many as a dozen bees will cluster inside, causing it to tremble with their energy. In only two days, the flowers shed their petals, leaving behind a lime-green capsule topped with a little cap of mulberry red. No matter how many seeds are produced, however, the plant continues to bear fresh flowers from late June until September. In their long flower production, argemones are thus unusual among poppies.

ARGEMONE GRANDIFLORA

As with all poppies, one longs to touch the flowers of argemones or even pick them, but most are fiercely armed with sharp spines and prickles on the unopened seed calyx, the stem, and the leaf. Leaves are deeply lobed and cut, blue-green or sea-green according to species, and very beautiful, suggesting the stylized acanthus foliage on the capitals of Corinthian columns. All are marked along the veins with a tracery of pale, glaucous gray and are abundantly produced on sprawling plants from one to three feet tall, which should never be staked, as new stems and flowers emerge from the bent stalk, creating graceful, bushlike plants.

The genus *Argemone* bears a name transferred to it from an ancient Greek word for a plant believed to cure cataracts of the eye, though none of the thirty or so species within the genus have any known medicinal properties. But four, at least, are in general cultivation as ornamental plants, and they are sufficiently similar in appearance (and may intermarry freely) that only a trained botanist can distinguish among them. *A. grandiflora* (gran-di-FLO-ra), the most frequently offered, is an annual or short-lived perennial native to Mexico. Its prettiest flowers are chalk white stained maroon at the base of each petal, though a pale yellow form is listed. *A. hispida* (HI-spi-da) is a perennial from the lower Rocky Mountains, white-flowered with a yellow center, with fiercely prickly seed capsules, as its species name, *hispida* (spiny), indicates. *A. mexicana* (mex-i-CA-na) is an annual native to Central America but has naturalized widely in the southernmost parts of the United States. It has very glaucous leaves beautifully marked along the veins with a light blue wash. Flowers are typically a primrose yellow, though a white form ('Alba') and one with flowers of blood orange ('Sanguinea'—san-GWIN-ee-a) are also offered. *A. polyanthus* (po-lee-AN-thus), native to the western plains from South Dakota and eastern Wyoming south to Texas, is a biennial that in its natural range can produce a taproot three or even four feet long. It is the least prickly of the four, and bears white flowers up to four inches across. Despite its provenance, it seldom persists over winter in gardens.

Whether annual, perennial, or biennial, argemones are best treated as hardy annuals, seeded in late autumn or very early spring where they are to grow. Like all members of the poppy family, they are extremely sensitive to root disturbance, and if they are seeded in thin-walled plastic cell packs, they should be transplanted early and gently. Plants should be thinned to stand four to six inches apart. All natives to poor, dry soils in sun-baked conditions, they demand full sun and are drought tolerant, flowering most abundantly when summers become hot and dry. Still, they appreciate a dressing of fertilizer rich in phosphorus and potassium but low in nitrogen, which mimics the gravelly, mineral-laden soils in which they naturally grow. Because of the boldness of their foliage and their need for dry air about their leaves, they look and grow best with free space around them, perhaps in the rock garden or at the edge of a gravel drive. They will both look and be wretched when crowded among other bedding plants.

ARTEMISIA SPECIES

FAMILY: *Asteraceae* or aster or daisy family.

CLASSIFICATION: Hardy or half-hardy biennials or shrubs grown as hardy annuals.

COMMON NAME: Artemisia (other names vary with species).

HARDINESS: 'Powis Castle' is hardy to Zone 7. *A. annua* and *A. gmelinii* withstand light frosts.

GROWING CONDITIONS: Any moderately fertile, well-drained garden loam. Full sun.

PROPAGATION: 'Powis Castle' is grown from cuttings, which root easily at any time. *A. annua* and *A. gmelinii* may be sown in place in autumn or very early spring, or seeded indoors 6 to 8 weeks before last anticipated frost.

HEIGHT: Varies according to species.

ORNAMENTAL VALUE: Grown for attractive and scented foliage.

LEVEL OF CULTURAL DIFFICULTY: Easy.

SPECIAL PROPERTIES: Leaves retain fragrance when dried. Drought tolerant. 'Powis Castle' is superb as a standard.

PRONUNCIATION: ar-ti-MEE-si-a

*O*f the 200 or so species in the genus *Artemisia,* about two dozen are grown in gardens as hardy perennials, shrubs, or sub-shrubs, and mostly for their attractive green or silver, finely cut aromatic foliage. Many have important medicinal uses, and one, *Artemisia dracunculus* (dra-CUN-cu-lus), French tarragon, is an important culinary herb. Among perennials, only one—*Artemisia lactiflora* (lak-ti-FLO-ra)—is grown for its showy panicles of feathery white flowers on four-foot stems.

Three other artemisias are commonly grown as annuals, of which one, *Artemisia* x 'Powis (PO-is) Castle', has in the last ten years proven itself to be an almost indispensable garden plant. Raised only as recently as 1978 and named for a famous garden in Wales, 'Powis Castle' has become widely available in nurseries and garden centers. Of undocumented parentage, 'Powis Castle' is probably a cross between *A. absinthium* (ab-sin-THEE-um), a hardy perennial once used to flavor absinthe, and the tender, Mediterranean *A. arborescens* (ar-bor-ESS-ens). It inherits some of the cold tolerance of *A. absinthium,* but gardeners north of USDA Zone 6 will get better results from it when it is started as cuttings planted each spring. (It rarely flowers and is presumed not to come true from seed.) Technically a shrub and quick of growth, as are most artemisias, it rapidly builds up sprawling, woody plants about two feet tall and as much as six feet across. It branches freely, even when cut back hard to old wood, and may be encouraged to remain compact and tidy by frequent pinching.

'Powis Castle' thrives in almost any garden soil, and is drought tolerant. It may be cut back hard, severely root pruned, and potted at almost any age to be carried over in a cool greenhouse or even a frost-free shed. Cuttings root very readily and may be taken in autumn for transplants the following spring. Since half its parentage is the sturdy, woody *A. arborescens* (*arborescens* means treelike), 'Powis Castle' also makes a splendid standard when grown on a single stem to about four feet and then allowed to branch freely at the top.

Among true annuals, the only artemisia cultivated in gardens is *A. annua* (AN-u-a), a charming, old-fashioned plant once very popular under the names "sweet Annie," "sweet wormwood," or "ambrosia plant." Native to southeastern Europe as far west as Iran, it has been cultivated by the Chinese as a medicinal plant and is still valuable for treating strains of malaria that are resistant to quinine. Once widely grown in gardens, it is now seldom seen, though the new interest in old-fashioned and heirloom plants will probably return it to favor. It is valuable in gardens first for its form, a well-branched, graceful bushlike plant from four to six feet tall, with one- to three-inch fresh, light green leaves that are soft and feathery in effect. Its bloom is also attractive—consisting of minute, half-inch-wide yellow flowers borne in profuse, loose, nodding clusters—but *A. annua* is most treasured for its scent. The leaves of all garden artemisias are fragrant and, to greater or lesser degree, pungent or sweet. But *A. annua* carries the nicest fragrance of all, fresh and light and clear. It remains when the leaves are dried, and so the plant is particularly valued for making potpourri or scented wreaths.

The third artemisia commonly grown as an annual, though technically a biennial native to Siberia and northeastern Asia, is *Artemisia saccrorum* (sa-KRO-rum)—now technically *A. gmelinii* (me-LIN-nee-ee) in its selected form, 'Viridis' (vi-RI-dis). It may grow as tall as nine feet, furnished with finely cut, feathery foliage of a fine, dark green (as the cultivar name 'Viridis' suggests). Flowers are minute and insignificant, the plant being most useful as a quiet screen at the back of a border, or as an occasional cooling green accent among brashly colored flowers.

Both *Artemisia annua* and *A. gmelinii* 'Viridis', being very hardy plants, can be seeded either in late autumn or in very early spring. The finest specimens will occur from a direct seeding in the place they are to grow, though good plants may be had from an early start indoors in plastic cell packs. Young plants grown on in bright, cool conditions will be tender when raised under glass and so should be hardened off carefully and transplanted into the garden after all danger of frost is past. Both plants should stand about three feet apart. Though they accept most garden soils provided they are given full sun, they are particularly useful in gardens made on poor, dryish, sandy soil, where they will flourish.

ASARINA SPECIES (*MAURANDYA* SPECIES)

FAMILY: *Scrophulariaceae* or snapdragon family.

CLASSIFICATION: Tender perennial vine grown as tender annual vine.

COMMON NAMES: Chickabiddy, climbing gloxinia, creeping gloxinia, hummingbird vine, asarina.

HARDINESS: Sensitive to light frosts. *A. procumbens* is root-hardy to Zone 7.

GROWING CONDITIONS: Humus-rich, well-drained soil. Abundant moisture. Full sun in cool gardens; afternoon shade in warmer ones. Relish heat.

PROPAGATION: From seed, sown indoors 6 to 8 weeks before last anticipated frost.

HEIGHT: Varies with species.

ORNAMENTAL VALUE: Grown for vining habit and for flower.

LEVEL OF CULTURAL DIFFICULTY: Easy.

SPECIAL PROPERTIES: None.

PRONUNCIATION: a-sa-REE-na (mo-RAN-dee-a)

*T*wice in its botanical classification, the modest but delicately beautiful *Asarina procumbens* (pro-CUM-bens) was in good company. Once it was listed among the antirrhinums or snapdragons (*asarina* is Spanish for snapdragon) because its inch-long, primrose-yellow flowers with deeper yellow shading at the throat resemble them. Its flowers differ from true snapdragons, however, in that they occur not in spires, but are borne singly from the axils of rounded, felty, two-inch-long grayish leaves. *A. procumbens* was later transferred into a separate genus, which took its name, and included fourteen other very attractive garden plants, all bearing tubed, one- to two-inch flowers. It was a distinguished company. But one by one they were all detached, however, first into the genus *Maurandya,* from which several were then shifted into *Maurandella* (mo-ran DEL-a) and *Lophospermum* (lo-pho-SPER-mum), and one back into *Antirrhinum,* leaving *Asarina procumbens* the lone species in its genus. Botanically, chaos seems to reign, but nomenclatural confusions hardly matter, for all the plants within what once was the genus *Asarina* are beautiful and worthy of a place in gardens. They have a grace and delicacy that belie their sturdy constitution, and their capacity to grow with incredible vigor and flower with great profusion in warm, humid weather makes them valuable in gardens where summer comes soon and is hot.

As the species name *procumbens* indicates, *Asarina procumbens* does not climb, but rather creeps along the ground, or over a stone, or into the crevices of a wall, achieving a length of perhaps two to three feet in a season. It cannot be called a showy plant, but its beautiful, furred, celadon-green leaves and its charming, tubed flowers have their own distinct, quiet beauty. They last a surprisingly long time when fully developed, up to a month. *A. procumbens* is a true perennial native to the Iberian Peninsula, said to be hardy only to Zone 7, though when properly sited—against a foundation or in the protection of a large, heat-storing rock—it will reappear in gardens as cold as Zone 4, and may self-seed amiably. It prefers a sunless but open position and rather poor, dryish soil. Where it self-seeds—and it generally does—it seems able to find the position it likes best, where it should, if possible, be left alone. From an early seeding, it will flower the first year, be-

ASARINA PROCUMBENS

coming perennial south of Philadelphia, and possibly much farther north.

Of the seven or so other asarinas offered in seed catalogues, *A. barclaiana* (bar-clay-AN-a)—now *Maurandya barclaiana*—is much more dramatic. A native of Mexico, it is a delicate-looking vine that will rapidly achieve up to ten feet, twining upward by means of its leaf tendrils that twirl around supports in the manner of clematis. As it grows, it branches freely from the main stem, secondary stems hanging down gracefully around the plant and eventually finding their way upward. Leaves at the tips of stems are fully formed practically from the first, though they mature eventually to about two inches in length. They are English-ivy shaped, but of a fresh light green, and flowers are borne singly where the petiole of a mature leaf joins the stem. Flowers, dangling from fragile-seeming wiry stems that may be as long as four inches, are almost two inches long and velvety in texture, with the characteristic two lower and three upper lobes of snapdragons—though the mouth is flared open to reveal a lighter throat. Colors range from rose to purple, even a rich, royal purple in some of the finest cultivars. There is also a pure white form. Though plants may be made to scramble in, over, and among large shrubs, they display themselves best when trained to an eight-foot tripod of bamboo stakes or on a fence or trellis. Like all asarinas, they are very attractive to hummingbirds.

The other asarina still within the genus *Maurandya* (at least for the moment) is *M. scandens* (SCAN-dens), a shorter-stemmed, looser-growing plant most commonly offered for use in hanging baskets or to tumble down walls. Its flowers resemble those of *M. barclaiana* but come in a wide range of colors, from rose pink, violet, pale and deep indigo blue to white. In all shades there are named forms of superior colors propagated from cuttings. Many of the plants offered as *M. scandens,* however, may be *Asarina erubescens* (er-u-BES-ens)—now *Lophospermum erubescens*—into which genus *M. scandens* may soon also migrate. It would hardly matter to the gardener, though the flowers of *M. erubescens* are slightly larger and typically a rich, rose pink.

Whatever the genus in which they are now technically lodged, however, seed catalogues still offer most plants under asarina. All should be sown indoors from six to eight weeks before the last anticipated frost date, either in plastic six-packs or in peat pots, for root disturbance inhibits their growth. Young seedlings of all but *Asarina procumbens* will begin to twine around any support, or around each other, practically from the beginning. So support must be provided early, for young plants are filmy and fragile, and tear easily when one attempts to separate them at transplant time.

ASCLEPIAS CURASSAVICA

FAMILY: *Asclepiadaceae* or milkweed family.

CLASSIFICATION: Tender perennial grown as half-hardy annual.

COMMON NAMES: Blood flower, Indian wort, swallow wort, asclepias.

HARDINESS: Hardy to Zone 8. Foliage is sensitive to light frosts.

GROWING CONDITIONS: Ordinary, well-drained garden loam. Full sun.

PROPAGATION: From seed, sown indoors in peat pots in late February or early March. Resents root disturbance.

HEIGHT: To 3′.

ORNAMENTAL VALUE: Grown for flower.

LEVEL OF CULTURAL DIFFICULTY: Moderately easy.

SPECIAL PROPERTIES: Excellent container plant. May be made to flower in winter in cool greenhouse conditions.

PRONUNCIATION: as-KLEE-pee-as kur-a-SA-vi-ka

Flowers in shades of orange and red can often be painfully over-assertive, as ribbons of marigolds around gas stations amply illustrate. *Asclepias curassavica,* a tender plant grown as an annual, is one of the most vivid in those shades, but its effect is cooled down by its structure and its foliage: upright to about three feet and liberally furnished with four-inch-long, narrow grayish-green leaves. Its flowers—scarcely a quarter-inch wide but borne numerously in umbels atop the stems—are also cunningly crafted. They begin as tiny brilliant red beads and open into clear scarlet, five-lobed stars surrounding prominent, fused fertile parts of strong yellow. The effect is never garish, but curiously vibrant, just what may be needed to enliven a dull garden scheme.

Asclepias curassavica is a close relative of our native butterfly weed, *A. tuberosa* (tu-be-RO-sa), and is, like it, a true perennial though winter-hardy only to USDA Zone 8 and south. Like *A. tuberosa, A. curassavica* attracts butterflies, particularly monarchs, but is easier to grow, accepting ordinary garden soil in full sun and not the barren, dryish soils its cousin demands.

Like most tender perennials that may be grown as annuals, *A. curassavica* requires seeding in late February or early March, at temperatures around 60°F. Young plants should be grown on in bright, cool conditions, around 70°F, until transplanted into the garden after all danger of frost is past. Plants may be expected to flower about five months from seeding and continue until frost. Like most other milkweeds, *A. curassavica* resents root disturbance and so should be seeded into peat pots or thin-walled plastic cell packs. Pinching out the first terminal growth will result in bushier, more free-flowering plants.

A. curassavica makes a very appealing container plant, and when grown in single pots, may be cut back, regrown, and forced into late winter flowering. The species also makes a superb cut flower, and a clear completely yellow form has become a staple of the Dutch cut-flower market in winter.

The genus name *Asclepias* derives from the Greek god of healing, Asclepios, the son of Apollo, and attests to the fact that Native Americans believed the roots of several North American species had healing properties. The species

name *curassavica* attributes the origin of the plant to the Caribbean island of Curaçao.

ASPERULA ORIENTALIS
(A. AZUREA VAR. SETOSA)

FAMILY: *Rubiaceae* or gardenia family.

CLASSIFICATION: Hardy annual.

COMMON NAMES: Annual sweet woodruff, annual asperula.

HARDINESS: Withstands light frosts.

GROWING CONDITIONS: Humus-rich, well-drained soil. Abundant moisture. Part shade. Requires cool conditions.

PROPAGATION: From seed, sown in place as soon as ground may be worked in spring.

HEIGHT: To 1'.

ORNAMENTAL VALUE: Grown for flower.

LEVEL OF CULTURAL DIFFICULTY: Moderately easy.

SPECIAL PROPERTIES: Excellent late-winter-flowering plant for cool greenhouses. Fragrant.

PRONUNCIATION: as-per-OO-la o-ree-en-TA-lis

Several plants considered noxious weeds by Old World grain farmers, such as the Flanders field poppy (*Papaver rhoeas*), corn cockles (*Agrostemma githago*), or bachelor's buttons (*Centaurea cyanus*), are among the most treasured flowers grown in gardens for their winsome beauty. All are transitory pleasures, for they are plants equipped to compete with agricultural crops by maturing quickly, flowering briefly, then disappearing as their cultivated companions expand in growth. Among the most beautiful and ephemeral of these plants is *Asperula orientalis,* the annual sweet woodruff, still often listed under its previous species name, *A. azurea* var. *Setosa*. A plant delicate in all parts, it forms airy, foot-high mounds with narrow, inch-long leaves borne in whirls or ruffs of six to eight along its square stems. Each stem is surmounted by branched umbels of tiny three-eighths-inch-long tubular four-petaled flowers that open a deep blue, fade to lavender, and are sweetly fragrant.

Gardeners will recognize in the genus name *Asperula* a close relative, the perennial sweet woodruff, *Asperula odorata* (o-do-RA-ta, now transferred into the genus *Gallium* [ga-LEE-um]). Though it is a thicker, denser plant, the family resemblances are clear in the whorled leaves and the tiny flowers of both. Like *A. odorata, Asperula orientalis* prefers to grow in cool, woodsy soil in part shade. In such sites it is prettiest, forming brief clouds of blue, but it will accept full sun and flourish, though its colors may fade more quickly and its brief flowering life of only a month or so may be even shorter.

Like other common grain field annuals, *A. orientalis* should be sown in place on cold ground in early spring, or started in a cool greenhouse and transplanted carefully into the garden. It may be expected to flower about two months after seeding, achieving its peak of bloom usually in June and disappearing by mid-July. As it is very light and delicate of texture, it may be seeded among other permanent plants—irises or clumping ferns—without harming them. The best plants result from thinning to stand about six inches apart. Because the light, sweet but penetrating fragrance of *A. orientalis* is one of its most remarkable characteristics, single plants might be established in eight-inch pots to bring that pleasure indoors at night. From an autumn sowing, gardeners with cool greenhouses will find *A. orientalis* a delightful late-winter-flowering plant.

ATRIPLEX HORTENSIS

ATRIPLEX HORTENSIS

FAMILY: *Chenopodiaceae* or goosefoot family.

CLASSIFICATION: Hardy annual.

COMMON NAMES: Orach, mountain spinach, salt bush, sea purslane, atriplex.

HARDINESS: Withstands light frost.

GROWING CONDITIONS: Ordinary, fertile, well-drained garden loam. Full sun. Prefers cool weather.

PROPAGATION: From seed, sown in place in autumn or very early spring. Young plants transplant readily.

HEIGHT: To 5'.

ORNAMENTAL VALUE: Grown for attractively colored leaves and stems.

LEVEL OF CULTURAL DIFFICULTY: Easy.

SPECIAL PROPERTIES: Valued as a salad and cooked green. Self-seeds freely.

PRONUNCIATION: A-TRIH-plex hor-TEN-sis

*A*mong crops grown for food, *Atriplex hortensis* has as old a history as any. Of Asian origin, it was cultivated by both the Greeks and Romans for salads and as a cooked green. Seed, brought by the first colonists to North America, thrived and was passed on to Native American tribes, for whom it became a staple crop. Its curious property of adding savor to soups and stews was always recognized, hence its popular name, "salt bush."

A stately plant, *A. hortensis* reaches a height of as much as five feet under good cultivation. It is furnished with five- to eight-inch-long, arrow-shaped, wavy leaves (the largest always at the base of the plant) that clasp the stems and, when young, are covered with a silvery substance that makes them appear opaline. Plants grow naturally into handsome spires, topped with seed heads made up of hundreds of insignificant flowers (and later seed) encased in papery, persistent bracts. Though as a substitute for spinach the green form is preferred, many natural variants in leaf color occur, and selections have been made that may be copper, violet, or rose, with deep purple or maroon stems, or with butter yellow or almost white leaves and stems. It is, of course, the colored selections that are most valued in flower gardens, to the back of the border or even as an annual hedge.

Possessed of so many virtues, it is hard to understand why *A. hortensis* passed out of favor as a garden crop. Only those few gardeners who grew old things—plants that have now come to be called "heirloom vegetables"—kept it going. In the last ten years, however, it has returned to popularity, promoted on the one hand by a new interest in exotic greens and on the other by ornamental vegetable gardening. In certain red-leaved forms, *A. hortensis* can be very beautiful, and so is among those plants—along with bull's blood beets, ruby chard, ornamental kale, and many amaranths—that have passed freely back and forth from the kitchen to the flower garden.

The genus name *Atriplex* is Latin, taken from the ancient Greek word for the plant, and its common English name, orach, derives from medieval French. *A. hortensis* is very easy to grow in ordinary, fertile garden soil in full sun. As it is seed-hardy well into Zone 4, it may be sown outdoors either in late autumn or in spring around

ATRIPLEX HORTENSIS

the last anticipated frost date. It grows rapidly in the cool, fresh weather of spring and early summer, and it is attractive at every stage of its life. Once successfully grown, if mature plants are allowed to set seed, orach will faithfully reappear from spring to spring, even in the coldest parts of New England. Young plants that appear here and there about the garden can be left to mature as the spontaneous blessings they are, or when they have formed two or three sets of leaves, they may be transplanted. Unwanted seedlings are always welcome in the salad bowl. (Coarser growth can be harvested and cooked like spinach, serving as a substitute during hot summer weather in which spinach will not thrive.) Once one has grown orach and let a few plants go to seed, one need never plant it again. There will always be enough.

BAILEYA MULTIRADIATA

FAMILY: *Asteraceae* or aster or daisy family.

CLASSIFICATION: Annual or weak perennial grown as half-hardy annual.

COMMON NAMES: Desert marigold, baileya.

HARDINESS: Hardy to Zone 6, with perfect drainage.

GROWING CONDITIONS: Sandy, well-drained moderately fertile soil. Abundant moisture. Cool nights. Full sun.

PROPAGATION: From seed, sown in site in warmer gardens in autumn and in cooler ones as soon as the soil may be worked in spring.

HEIGHT: To 20″.

ORNAMENTAL VALUE: Grown for flower.

LEVEL OF CULTURAL DIFFICULTY: Difficult outside native range.

SPECIAL PROPERTIES: Excellent dried flower.

PRONUNCIATION: BAY-lee-a mul-ti-ra-dee-A-ta

That the beauty of a plant sometimes seems in direct ratio to the exacting difficulty of its culture is hard for gardeners. The fabled Himalayan blue poppies, *Meconopsis betonicifolia* and *M. grandis,* are cases in point. Where summer nights are cold and summer days are either drizzly or bright and fresh, they are easy to grow, but where those conditions are lacking, both plants are positive heartbreakers. Though not quite as cranky as the aristocratic meconopsis, *Baileya multiradiata,* the desert marigold, can carry its own frustrations. In gardens where it is happy, it can be a splendid summer annual, blooming from early summer to frost, or even through the winter where there is no frost. Otherwise, it is hardly worth the trouble.

B. multiradiata, a native of the deserts of western North America, flourishes in sandy, free-draining soil, not over-rich in nitrogen, where nights are crisp, days are bright, and rainfall occurs after periods of drought, falling once in the night every three weeks or so. In such conditions, it freely produces its elegant basal growth, consisting of many silvery, fine-cut gray leaves—their beauty enough for a "garden-worthy" plant. The great glory of *B. multiradiata,* however, are its elegant flowers, on single stems to twenty inches high. Recognizably daisylike, they are about two inches across, consisting of twenty to fifty overlapped ray flowers and a tight cushion of disk flowers in the center. Like many daisies, each single flower has a very long life, the ray flowers remaining attractive as the disc flowers open from the outside over a month or so. And like others in its tribe—helychrisums or *Ammobium alatum*—the ray flowers turn papery as the disk flowers mature, making *B. multiradiata* a wonderful flower for dried arrangements.

B. multiradiata is an annual or weak perennial across its natural range of desert Zones 7 to 10, where young plants freely seed and bloom beneath their parents, making it hard to know whether the parent plant has endured or simply been replaced. In Zones 6 and south, *B. multiradiata* may be treated essentially as a biennial—sown in patches in early fall for bloom the following summer. In colder gardens, seed should be sown in place—with a prayer—in early spring, and thinned for best bloom when young plants develop, to stand about a foot apart. But like many free-seeding meadow and desert plants, *B. multiradiata* can be sown to stand more thickly, a trade-off that produces fewer flowers per plant but that mimics the thick masses of bloom occurring in the deserts where it is native.

In gardens that experience hot, hazy, humid weather in summer *B. multiradiata* will probably not be a success, for its felty, fine-cut leaves will quickly melt away and its flowers will be scarce and transitory. In such muggy climates it will probably do best in a large clay pot, where its leaves and roots can dry out sufficiently.

While any plant bearing the name "Bailey" may commemorate one of four distinguished botanists and plant collectors, *B. multiradiata* probably honors Vernon Bailey, a major in the U.S. Army who studied desert flora in the early years of the last century. The species name *multiradiata* indicates the arrangement of several petals radiating outward from a center—a characteristic of most daisies.

BALLOTA SPECIES

FAMILY: *Lamiaceae* (*Labiatae*) or mint family.

CLASSIFICATION: Tender perennial grown as half-hardy annual.

COMMON NAMES: False dittany, ballota.

HARDINESS: Hardy to Zone 8. Leaf-sensitive to light frosts.

GROWING CONDITIONS: Average, moderately fertile, well-drained garden loam. Full sun.

PROPAGATION: From specialty nurseries as young plants. Seed is seldom available. Cuttings root with difficulty.

HEIGHT: To 2′.

ORNAMENTAL VALUE: Grown for attractive foliage and plant form.

LEVEL OF CULTURAL DIFFICULTY: Easy.

SPECIAL PROPERTIES: Drought tolerant.

PRONUNCIATION: ba-LOT-a

Ballota pseudodictamnus (sue-do-dik-TAM-nus) could be easily dismissed as merely a foliage plant useful for contrast—not a main player, but one that merely enhances its neighbors. Still it deserves close study, for it is possessed of its own subtle beauty. It is also sufficiently rapid of growth that small, potted specimens set out in spring after all danger of frost is past become valuable garden subjects by midsummer and into autumn, even in gardens four zones colder than its native Crete.

The flowers of *B. pseudodictamnus*—insignificant tubes of whitish-blue a half-inch long borne in the axils of the leaves—are not its main point. But the leaves are very beautiful, fitted closely all around the stems, rounded and crinkled and woolly white over an olive-green base, each an inch-long spoon. Stems ascend from the base of the plant to form dense, rounded shrublike growth to two feet. Stems are also fleeced between the leaves, making them look like pipe cleaners.

A native of Crete and a true perennial, *B. pseudodictamnus* is hardy only to Zone 8 and then only with the perfect winter drainage typical of its rocky homeland, for moisture at its dormant roots will surely cause it to rot away. Where it *is* hardy, *B. pseudodictamnus* will build up handsome clumps quickly, producing many stems from short, underground stolons. Where it is tender, however, three or more plants should be established close together, about six to eight inches from one another, to create in one season a clumped effect. Because *B. pseudodictamnus* is a Mediterranean plant accustomed to heat and drought, it also makes an excellent container plant, either potted alone where its subtle beauty can be most appreciated or in mixed container plantings as an alternative to dusty millers. Those gardeners who have cool greenhouses will find it an easy plant to dig, pot, over-winter under glass, and plant the following spring for even fuller growth. Another ballota, *B. acetabulosa* (a-see-tab-you-LO-sa), is also sometimes offered by nurseries that specialize in unusual annual and tender plants. A native of Greece and a close cousin of *B. pseudodictamnus,* it would not in any way be a poor substitute.

The genus *Ballota* takes its name from the ancient Greek word for black horehound, *Ballota nigra* (NI-gra), a native of North Africa hardy to Zone 7. The species name *pseudodictamnus* recognizes the resemblance of the plant to a popular garden perennial, *Dictamnus albus* (AL-bus), the gas plant or dittany, which is also a Mediterranean native.

BARBAREA SPECIES

FAMILY: *Cruciferae* or mustard family.

CLASSIFICATION: Hardy biennial.

COMMON NAMES: St. Barbara's herb, St. Barbara's weed, upland cress, mountain cress, barbarea.

HARDINESS: Winter-hardy to Zone 5. Withstands frosts.

GROWING CONDITIONS: Average to rich, damp soils. Full sun to part shade.

PROPAGATION: By seed, sown in place in autumn or in very early spring.

HEIGHT: To 2′.

ORNAMENTAL VALUE: Grown for attractive foliage and flowers.

LEVEL OF CUTURAL DIFFICULTY: Easy.

SPECIAL PROPERTIES: Treasured as salad green.

PRONUNCIATION: bar-BAR-ee-a

For reasons unclear in hagiography, Saint Barbara, beheaded in 225 by her own father because she had converted to Christianity and refused to marry the man of his choice, is the patron saint of all who work with violent materials—gunsmiths, miners, artillerymen, and those who handle dynamite—and her protection is particularly sought against lightning, tornadoes, and violent thunder storms. Beyond these distinctions, her name is commemorated in the genus *Barbarea,* two species of which were anciently cultivated in the Old World and are now widely naturalized as "weeds" throughout North America. Both species are edible, as their several common names suggest. Both were also once much treasured because their leafy rosettes persist throughout the coldest winters, and so were one of the very few green things one could find to eat near the Feast of Saint Barbara, which occurs on December 4.

Whether one thinks of *Barbarea verna* (VER-na) and *B. vulgaris* (vul-GAR-is) as food, flowers, or simply as weeds depends on his or her attitude. Foragers of wild greens always pause to gather the leaves for their pungent, cresslike flavor, and the recent fashionable interest in mesclun and misticanza salads has returned both species to a certain prominence as a cultivated crop. The flowers of both are also modestly pretty in a wild mustard sort of way, borne on one- to two-foot, much-branched stalks and—as with many mustards—colored chrome to egg-yolk yellow. Flowering stems arise from handsome basal rosettes of lobed, leathery, dark green leaves—as many as ten lobes in *B. verna,* fewer and larger in *B. vulgaris.* In both species, the lobes become progressively larger along the stems until they terminate in one large lobe at the end.

Barbareas defy the traditional classifications of annual, biennial, and perennial. Given the circumstances, they may be all three. Sown in late August, both will germinate rapidly and produce rosettes of leaf in cold autumn weather, blooming the following spring. *Barbarea verna* is first, flowering in early April in Zone 5, making it one of the earliest-blooming of meadow plants. *B. vulgaris* follows with its flowers about a month later, but it makes up for its tardiness with larger, showier blooms. (Both are valuable in the vegetable garden, since even in cold gardens they may be sown after the autumn crops are cleared away and harvested in earliest spring.)

For the flower garden, two cultivars are of special interest. *B. vulgaris* 'Variegata' (var-ee-GA-ta) is grown for its foliage—rosettes of lettuce-green leaves liberally splashed with white—and best treated as a hardy annual, sown in late autumn or in quite early spring. Not all seed will show variegation, however, and so those that are plain green should be tossed into the salad bowl. A particularly good variegated form can be divided in late summer, thus being treated as a perennial.

The other cultivar of *B. vulgaris* grown primarily for its flowers is *B. v.* 'Flore pleno' (FLO-reh PLE-no), the thickly petaled cobs of which can be very showy. It is a true "cottage garden" plant, much praised by earlier garden writers though it is very scarce now, waiting to be rediscovered.

Except for the choicer forms, most barbareas will simply appear, and if they sprout in pleasant places they should be left to grow, for both their attractive and edible leaves and the wild flower charm of their bloom, which may itself be added to a spring salad as an accent of daffodil yellow with a pleasant, watercress pungency.

BASELLA ALBA

FAMILY: *Basellaceae* or Malabar spinach family.

CLASSIFICATION: Tender perennial grown as tender annual.

COMMON NAMES: Malabar spinach, Indian spinach, basella.

HARDINESS: Discouraged by temperatures much below 40°F. Extremely frost sensitive.

GROWING CONDITIONS: Humus-rich, well-drained garden soil. Full sun. Relishes heat and humidity.

PROPAGATION: From seed, sown indoors 6 to 8 weeks before last anticipated frost. Cuttings root easily.

HEIGHT: To 8' when grown as an annual.

ORNAMENTAL VALUE: Attractive, fast-growing vine.

LEVEL OF CULTURAL DIFFICULTY: Very easy in warm gardens; difficult in cool ones.

SPECIAL PROPERTIES: Valued as both salad and cooked green.

PRONUNCIATION: ba-SEL-a AL-ba

There are as many unusual edible garden plants that are said to taste like spinach as there are strange meats reported to taste like chicken. One might wonder, then, why not simply grow spinach, until one has tried. For spinach requires an unusually limey soil, and in most parts of North America is strictly a cool-weather crop, quickly going to seed as late spring turns to summer. Of the several plants grown as a summer substitute for spinach, the most successful is *Basella alba.* It bears oblong

BASELLA ALBA

coastal regions of India, where people hardly wear clothes at all in the summer.

Basella is a Latinized version of an Indian vernacular word for the plant. A true child of the tropics, it performs poorly in gardens north of USDA Zone 6 when sown directly in the ground. Rather, seed should be started early indoors, at room temperature, about the time one would start tomatoes, to produce sturdy, six- to eight-inch-high plants for transplanting when all danger of frost is past. Even so, young transplants may simply sit and stare reproachfully in the cool weather of June, only to explode into growth with the arrival of warmer weather. Beyond full sun and plenty of warmth, basella has no particular growing needs; indeed, it is one of the thriftiest and most drought-tolerant ornamental vines one can grow.

BEGONIA SPECIES

FAMILY: *Begoniaceae* or begonia family.

CLASSIFICATION: Tender perennials grown as tender annuals.

COMMON NAME: Begonia.

HARDINESS: Sensitive to light frosts.

GROWING CONDITIONS: Humus-rich, water-retentive soil. Part shade.

PROPAGATION: Rarely grown from seed. Usually acquired as plants. Cuttings of many species root easily.

HEIGHT: From 6″ to 3′, depending on species.

ORNAMENTAL VALUE: Grown for flower and sometimes for attractive foliage.

LEVEL OF CULTURAL DIFFICULTY: Easy to difficult, depending on species.

SPECIAL PROPERTIES: Some species make attractive winter houseplants.

PRONUNCIATION: buh-GO-nee-a

to heart-shaped leaves, six to eight inches long, slightly ruffled along the edges and succulent in texture. A far more beautiful plant, however, is the cultivar 'Rubra' (RU-bra). Its stems are a deep violet, and its leaves, smaller by about a third than the straight species, are dark greenish-violet tinged with magenta on the undersides. Also edible, it is handsome enough to include in the flower garden, scrambling up a post or along a fence.

Love of heat is the clue to *Basella alba*'s most important cultural requirement; the hotter and steamier the weather, the more quickly it grows, reaching, in really saunalike climates, a height of thirty feet. Though now naturalized over the whole tropical world, *Basella alba* is probably of southeastern Asian origin, and takes its popular name, Malabar spinach, from one of the hottest

The family Begoniaceae, with its 1,000 species, hardly weighs in among the largest in botany. Orchidaceae, for example, comprises some 8,000 genera and as many as 30,000 species. Asteraceae, with only about 1,000 genera, includes somewhere around 20,000 species. Still, the dimensions of Begoniaceae are unusual, for it contains only three genera, but of its 1,000 species, all but fifteen belong to the genus *Begonia*. (Those fifteen, in *Hillebrandia* and *Symbegonia,* are seldom cultivated.)

Relatively modest as the number of species is, however, begonias hybridize naturally among all of them, and have done so in greenhouses and gardens practically since their first introduction into Europe in 1577. The result is more than 10,000 registered cultivars. Garden references once cut through this mass by discussing briefly a few houseplants, and devoting most of their texts to two popular hybrids grown for outdoor summer flowers: wax begonias, which are fibrous-rooted, and tuberous begonias, which sprout from large underground storage organs much as do potatoes and dahlias. These are still the best places to start.

The plant known as wax begonia, or often as *Begonia semperflorens* (sem-per-FLO-rens), is not actually a true species, but rather a complex intermingling of several species native to South and Central America and should probably be correctly called *Begonia* x *semperflorens cultorum* (cul-TOR-um). Few plants have been more popular; certainly few have been more abused. Wax begonias have been planted by the thousands in park bedding schemes and in front of filling stations, with little attention paid to their actual beauty. Sensitive gardeners might well turn away with a shudder—because as they are generally used, they might as well be plastic.

Still, they are excellent plants. Tender perennials grown as annuals, they accept a wide range of

BEGONIA SUTHERLANDII

cultural conditions from full sun to part shade, and they are among the few plants grown as annuals that will brighten the shaded retreats of high summer. With minimal attention they bloom nonstop, from tiny, three-inch-tall infants in a six-pack until frost cuts them down. Their abundant flowers may be pure white, pale pink, coral, vivid pink, or red, and though generally single, double forms exist that resemble miniature roses. Their leaves, which clasp the stems thickly, are as shiny as if freshly varnished, and their juiciness makes it difficult to resist the impulse to squeeze them for the cool liquid they would exude. Leaf color can be a bright, lettuce green, olive-maroon, or a pale green liberally splashed with white. A well-grown specimen in a five-inch clay pot can be very beautiful on a patio table, and bedded out they may be fine too, but they must be planted in the right way—not in prison-camp fences of boxwood or as rigid lines edging flower beds, but in natural-looking clumps, preferably all of one leaf and flower color.

Wax begonias are far easier to buy than to grow from seed. Raising one's own plants used to be necessary, because nurseries offered only mixes that could turn up a white-, a pink-, and a red-flowered form, two perhaps with brown leaves and the rest green, all in the same six-pack. Now that seed-grown strains, uniform in leaf and flower color, are offered, starting plants from seed seems hardly worth the bother. Still, if one must, several stern realities should be faced. First, the seed is very tiny, hardly a pinch of snuff, and one sneeze can blow away the whole crop before it ever gets going. Second, seedlings are equally tiny, needing to be pricked out with tweezers and grown on in a warm, humid atmosphere hovering around 70°F, which is also just the perfect condition for various fungus diseases fatal to young plants.

By contrast, tuberous begonias are easy to start at home from mail-order tubers, which are much cheaper than nursery-grown plants. In late March or early April, dormant tubers are placed in a shallow flat on a bed of barely moist peat, with more peat pressed between them, but with the indented tops left uncovered. Tubers sprout best when kept around 70°F. When new growth is two to three inches long and good roots have begun to form, individual tubers should be potted in four- or five-inch pots, in a peat-based compost lightened with perlite or sharp sand for perfect drainage. When roots have filled the pots, the young plants should be moved up to seven- or eight-inch pots, and fed weekly with a water-soluble plant food high in nitrogen at half the strength recommended on the package. Plants develop best in fairly cool temperatures hovering around 60°F, and the first blooms should be pinched out when buds show, to encourage rapid and full growth. Plants should be repotted into outdoor containers or bedded out only after all danger of frost is past.

Tuberous begonias are complex hybrids of several Andean species, and breeding work over the years has concentrated on larger flower size (to as much as six inches across) and on flower form,

which may be fringed like a carnation, may resemble a double camellia, or even a rose. Colors range from white and ivory to pale and deep yellow, clear to intense pink, coral, orange, light and dark red, indeed, almost every color and shade but blue. Forms have also been developed for specific purposes: some stocky and upright with abundant, smaller flowers appropriate to bedding out; others with giant flowers for specimen pot culture; and still others with pendulous growth appropriate to hanging baskets. Culture is the same for all, however, and consists of establishing plants in rich, free-draining compost, a weekly schedule of fertilizing with a water-soluble plant food at half strength, and a fresh, moist, partly shaded atmosphere. Generally, the best plants develop in bright, dappled light, or in morning sun and afternoon shade, though in cool, northern gardens tuberous begonias will flourish in full sun. At the end of the season, water is withdrawn from potted plants to induce dormancy, and bedded plants should be lifted and set in boxes in a shaded place without water until top growth has withered. Earth is then carefully cleaned away, the tubers air-dried for half a day, and then packed in boxes and stored at around 40°F, to be started into growth the following spring.

Wax and tuberous begonias hardly exhaust the possibilities, for within the genus are many other species that are as free-flowering, as easy to reproduce, as beautiful, and often far more interesting. But *Begonia sutherlandii* (su-ther-LAN-dee-ee), for example, is a plant of strikingly different effect. It quickly forms a fresh mound of two-inch-long, lettuce-green winged leaves on lax, red stems, and freely produces panicles of inch-wide, pale orange flowers throughout summer until frost. It thrives in moist, semi-shaded positions in the garden and is especially pretty grown among hostas. Though small-flowered, it is actually a tuberous begonia, and so can be lifted and stored before frost. Equally delicate, though taller and more upright, is *Begonia* x *richmondensis* (rich-mon-DEN-sis), an old hybrid of questionable parentage, but probably a cross between *B. fuchsioides* (fuchs-OY-des) and a cultivar of *B.* x *semperflorens cultorum*. If so, it has inherited from the first parent great delicacy of form, and from the second the capacity to bloom freely from spring to fall. Stems sprout from a fibrous root system, eventually reaching about two feet in height and arching over gracefully as they mature. They are slightly zigzag, and the two-inch-long, wing-shaped leaves are spaced attractively along them, not bunched tight as with wax begonias. The leaves are a fresh, varnished green above, and an attractive reddish-maroon beneath, as are the stems. Flower color varies from pale to bold pink, and each tiny, half-inch single flower is set off by an eye of bright gold stamens.

Far bolder in effect are several tall cane-growing begonias, the "Angel Wing" sorts familiar as houseplants. Young plants started from cuttings taken in winter make superb bedding plants, producing several canes that may reach a height of two to three feet by summer's end. There are many forms, not all of the same parentage, but two old cultivars are still among the most beautiful, 'President Carnot' and 'Irene Nuss'. The first bears heavy, drooping clusters of deep pink flowers, and the second, though similar in habit, bears flowers of a beautiful coral pink nicely set off by dark green leaves with a reddish cast, maroon beneath. Cane-growing begonias thrive in bright shade, and they may be expected to bloom all summer. As they build up heavy top growth, however, they must be carefully staked to prevent them from toppling over in their pots or being snapped by heavy wind and rain. They may be lifted before frost, cut back as necessary, and carried over the winter indoors in an east or west window, where they will continue to grow and bloom, offering a supply of fresh cuttings in late winter for the following summer.

In the last few years, the distinction has broken down for many gardeners between plants used for outdoor summer bedding and houseplants, thus releasing many beautiful species from the confinement of the parlor window to the freedom of the outdoor garden. A visit to any good greenhouse specializing in rare and unusual houseplants will turn up sturdy, easily grown, beautiful summer-flowering begonias, all of which should root easily for additional plants. When bedding out into the summer garden they also will look their best nestled among hardy plants of lush appearance, particularly hostas and ferns, as single specimens or in seemingly natural clumps or drifts.

BELLIS PERENNIS

FAMILY: *Asteraceae* or aster or daisy family.

CLASSIFICATION: Hardy or half-hardy perennials grown as hardy annuals.

COMMON NAMES: English daisy, lawn daisy, bellis.

HARDINESS: Wild forms hardy to Zone 4. Cultivated forms withstand frost.

GROWING CONDITIONS: Any garden soil. Abundant moisture. Full sun. Cool conditions.

PROPAGATION: From seed, sown in pots outdoors in warmer gardens in late summer, and in very early spring in cooler ones. May be sown indoors in cool temperatures 6 to 8 weeks before last anticipated frost.

HEIGHT: To 8".

ORNAMENTAL VALUE: Grown for flower.

LEVEL OF CULTURAL DIFFICULTY: Easy.

SPECIAL PROPERTIES: May be grown as a winter-
   flowering cool greenhouse plant.

PRONUNCIATION: BELL-is per-IN-is

*I*t is hard to think of the beautiful little English daisy as a nuisance, but the English often do, for in its unimproved forms it freely colonizes lawns, and is to the British what dandelions are to Americans. It was Chaucer's favorite flower, however, and is called "eye of the day" (from the Old English *daeges eage* and the Middle English *dayes' eye*) because its minute, half-inch flowers of pale pink or white open only on sunny days and close at night. The wild form is a true perennial, hardy in America from Zones 4 to 10, colonizing

BELLIS PERENNIS

healthy lawns and producing crops of flowers between mowings. (Easy to establish, it should, however, be started in moister and richer parts of a lawn, in a slight hollow or dip so it takes hold without shearing from the lawn mower.)

Much less sturdy than their wild progenitor are improved forms of the English daisy, selected for larger flowers, semi-double or doubled into tight buttons, or quilled like miniature pincushions, with colors to coral, crimson, true red, and pristine white. Even the largest forms of *Bellis perennis* hardly reach eight inches in height, and the flowers, borne singly on naked stems above tufts of two-inch-long leaves, are proportionately tiny, usually less than an inch across. They are traditional for bedding among tulips, whose rigid bearing they help to soften, but they are worth studying up close in a window box or lining a path in spontaneous-looking clusters.

All improved forms are treated in warmer gardens as hardy biennials, and in colder gardens as half-hardy or even tender annuals. Where winters are mild, English daisies may be seeded directly into the garden in August for late winter and early spring bloom. But as the seed is very tiny, it is usually more convenient to plant it in pots, pricking out the young seedlings and growing them in nursery rows or in larger pots until they are big enough to put in place. (They transplant with great ease, even when in full bloom.) In colder gardens, young plants are usually bought at the garden center in early spring, but they can also be seeded in a cool greenhouse (50°F in late winter) and grown on and planted out when danger of frost is past. English daisies will bloom as long as the weather remains cool if spent flowers are removed, but it is worth leaving a few blooms to ripen into seed. When plants cease to flower at the onset of hot weather, they should still be left in place, for they may re-bloom when the weather cools. Possibly they will become perennial, and if they should seed into the lawn they should be treasured—they are always most delightful there.

BETA VULGARIS

FAMILY: *Chenopodiaceae* or goosefoot family.

CLASSIFICATION: Half-hardy biennial grown as hardy annual.

COMMON NAMES: Beet, beet green, beet root, Swiss chard.

HARDINESS: Withstands frosts.

GROWING CONDITIONS: Humus-rich, well-drained garden loam. Full sun.

PROPAGATION: From seed, sown in site after last frosts, or indoors 6 to 8 weeks before last anticipated frost.

HEIGHT: To 18" under good culture.

ORNAMENTAL VALUE: Grown for foliage.

LEVEL OF CULTURAL DIFFICULTY: Easy.

SPECIAL PROPERTIES: Valued as salad and cooked green, and for edible roots.

PRONUNCIATION: BAY-ta vul-GAR-is

*T*hough very few vegetables are pretty in flower, many have beautiful leaves, none more so perhaps than certain cultivars of the common beet, *Beta vulgaris*. A plant of coastal European origins, it was cultivated by the ancient Celts as early as 2000 B.C. In Roman gardens, the plant became divided into two races, those grown primarily for their edible roots (beets) and those grown for their leaves (chard). This distinction has passed down through the ages, and though the resemblance between beets and chard is apparent, most modern gardeners do not realize that they are merely variants of one genetic prototype. In both groups are plants of striking ornamental value, worth growing as much for their beauty as for their culinary uses.

Among the cultivars of *Beta vulgaris* that form knobby roots, all are handsome, with rich green, red-veined, crinkled leaves borne on burgundy or beet-red stems, but two are valued as ornamental plants. Generally the sophisticated gardener's vote goes to 'MacGregor's Favorite', which produces a graceful rosette of narrow, nine-inch-long, inch-wide leaves of a glossy, burgundy red. (It may be very similar to, if not the same as, the cultivar listed in old catalogues as *Beta vulgaris* 'Dracaenifolia', now apparently no longer in commerce under that name.) But the cultivar dramatically christened 'Bull's Blood' also has its admirers, growing half a foot taller, with wavy-margined leaves of triple the width of 'MacGregor's Favorite', looking more like the familiar foliage of garden beets, but colored a deep, brooding purple-red. As cooked greens, both have fine value if one can bear to rip them out of the bed when they are young and succulent. Otherwise, young leaves may be robbed here and there to add vibrant color and delicious flavor to a bowl of mixed salad.

The familiar Swiss chard of gardens is merely an ancient selection of the common garden beet, grown not for its roots but for its leaves, and served in Elizabethan times not as a green vegetable, but as the principal component of a tart sweetened with raisins and honey. Any random patch of it in a vegetable garden will be pretty enough, particularly in the rainbow strain, which combines plants with handsome petioles of translucent red, orange, and white, and thick, rippled, lettuce-green leaves veined in the same colors. But selections have been made that seem almost as varied as coleus, producing leaves that are coppery with pink veins, rust-purple with metallic splashes, pumpkin-colored with orange veins, merlot-colored through and through, and some that are curled and crinkled almost like kale. All are as good to eat as to look at, so it will not much matter whether they are grown in the vegetable or the flower garden, as a few mature leaves may be taken from single plants without marring their beauty.

In whatever form, beets are among the easiest of garden plants to grow, flourishing in any reasonable soil, but appreciating supplementary doses of granular fertilizer, or better, composted seaweed or fish emulsion, which reminds them of their maritime origins. All forms may be sown as early in spring as the soil can be worked. It is important to know, however, that a beet seed is actually a fruit, containing as many as four separate seeds, all of which may germinate. For plants of the greatest ornamental value, therefore, young seedlings should be carefully separated when they achieve two or three true leaves, and established at a distance of six to eight inches apart. Chards are sown in the same way, but as they form relatively large plants, when grown in rows they should be spaced about eight inches apart for full development.

Forms of chard with ornamental stems and leaves are becoming more common in catalogues, but the most vibrant forms of true beets are still very scarce. So if one is lucky enough to obtain stock of 'MacGregor's Favorite' or 'Bull's Blood', it is worth digging six or so roots in autumn, storing them in sand in a quite cool but frost-free place over the winter, and planting them out in spring. As they are true biennials, they will form flower stalks as tall as three or four feet in their second year, from which one may harvest, in midsummer, enough seed to carry on the race another year, and to share with other gardeners.

BIDENS FERULIFOLIA

FAMILY: *Asteraceae* or aster or daisy family.

CLASSIFICATION: Tender biennial or short-lived tender perennial grown as tender annual.

COMMON NAMES: Beggar's tick, burr marigold, pitchforks, Spanish needles, sticktights, boot jacks, bidens.

HARDINESS: Dislikes temperatures much below 40°F. Extremely frost sensitive.

GROWING CONDITIONS: Moist, well-drained, fertile soil. Full sun.

PROPAGATION: From seed, sown indoors 6 to 8 weeks before last anticipated frost.

HEIGHT: Procumbent, to 1'.

ORNAMENTAL VALUE: Grown for flower and for attractive foliage.

LEVEL OF CULTURAL DIFFICULTY: Easy.

SPECIAL PROPERTIES: Excellent for hanging baskets and window boxes.

PRONUNCIATION: BI-denz fe-roo-li-FO-lee-a

As its numerous common names indicate, the seed of the genus *Bidens* has attracted far more attention than its flowers. Even the Latin name—*bis,* twice, and *dens,* tooth—acknowledges the fact. Its seed are not quite burrs (wasting no effort on surrounding themselves with bristles), but consist of a fruit encased in two sharp spurs. For dispersal, they are very efficient, piggybacking on almost anything, especially anything nappy, woolly, or furry. One will be picking these seeds off the family cat or dog, or one's own favorite sweater, after an autumn walk through the fields.

Almost all members of the genus—about 200 species distributed worldwide—are noxious weeds with mostly inconsequential flowers. But one species, *Bidens ferulifolia,* is garden worthy, as much for its leaves as for its flowers. The leaves of fine, lacy, fernlike consistency give the species its name because they resemble those of the ornamental giant fennel, *Ferula communis.* But the flowers are also pretty, consisting of inch-wide daisies of a clear egg-yolk yellow with darker centers, borne from midsummer until frost. Though plants may achieve a height of two to three feet, they will actually flop over, lying gracefully supine and presenting their flowers at a height of about a foot. Rather than staking the plants, their graceful floppy habit should be exploited to cover bare spots left by early-flowering perennials of ephemeral habit, such as Oriental poppies, or to bend and weave gracefully among and in front of sturdy clumps of summer-flowering perennials,

such as phlox and asters. Like many other composites—notably tall zinnias and marigolds—flowers will be much more numerous when the main stems of the plant are grown horizontally.

B. ferulifolia is of very easy culture although as a native of southern Arizona and Mexico it is tender and should not be sown in the garden or transplanted until the weather warms. Despite its origins, however, it is not a desert plant, doing best in moist, well-drained fertile soil in full sun. Given these conditions, plants grow quickly in summer heat, and flowers will appear from midsummer until frost, the slightest whisper of which ends the show. Seed of *B. ferulifolia* is scarce, and so a few ripened seed heads should be saved to plant again for another season of bloom and to share with other gardeners.

BIDENS FERULIFOLIA

BORAGO OFFICINALIS

FAMILY: *Boraginaceae* or borage family.

CLASSIFICATION: Hardy annual.

COMMON NAMES: Cool tankard, alewort, borage.

HARDINESS: Withstands frosts.

GROWING CONDITIONS: Well-drained, moderately fertile soil. Full sun.

PROPAGATION: From seed, sown in very early spring. Seedlings resent transplanting.

HEIGHT: To 2'.

ORNAMENTAL VALUE: Grown for attractive blue flowers.

LEVEL OF CULTURAL DIFFICULTY: Easy

SPECIAL PROPERTIES: Flowers and young leaves used in salads and in cooling drinks. Candied flowers used to decorate pastries.

PRONUNCIATION: bo-RA-go o-fi-shi-NA-lis

*T*he true borage, *Borago officinalis,* is of antique cultivation, grown by both the ancient Greeks and Romans as an edible herb and for its medicinal properties. It belongs to a small genus of three species and is the signature plant for the family Boraginaceae, which includes 100 genera and some 2,000 species, many of garden importance and most of which are characterized by raspy or bristly leaves. (The name "borage" comes from the Latin *burra,* signifying a woolly or hairy texture in a garment.) The species name *officinalis* indicates the importance of the plant in the medieval pharmacopoeia, for it was dispersed from the "offices" of ancient monasteries to cure troubles of the heart, improve the circulation of the blood, and stimulate the urinary tract. Modern herbalists still believe it valuable as a poultice on inflamed veins of the foot and ankle, and in popular lore, it has been believed to induce bravery, from which comes the old folk saying, "Borage for courage."

Besides these virtues, fanciful or possibly real, *B. officinalis* is a very pretty plant. Native to Mediterranean Europe, Asia Minor, and North Africa, it has naturalized throughout the world, proving hardy and self-seeding almost wherever gardening occurs. In good soil, the plant produces bushy growth up to two feet tall, clad in crinkly, hairy leaves about a foot long and a little less than half that in width. When crushed, the leaves omit a strong but pleasant cucumber scent, and may be used in salads when quite young (but still chopped fine to prevent their hairy texture from catching on the tongue). Older leaves are often used to flavor ale, claret cups, punches, or other cooling summer drinks, from which the plant takes its most venerable common name, "cool tankard."

The star or wheel-shaped flowers of *B. officinalis* are each quite tiny, no more than three-fourths of an inch wide, borne in loose, leafy clusters, but so numerous as to be quite showy. They open a rosy, pinkish blue and mature to a clear, sky blue, contributing their bit to the family heritage, which contains some of the most beautifully blue flowers a gardener can grow. Beyond that, the prominent stamens, extending as much as a fourth of an inch beyond the petals and so deep a blue as to be almost black, add to the beauty of each individual flower. Like its leaves, the flowers of *B. officinalis* are also said to be healthful, and so are often included in punches and summer drinks, in salads, and, when crystallized, as a garnish for frozen desserts and sugar-glazed or iced pastries. In the Middle Ages and the Renaissance, flowers that were both healthful and lovely were especially treasured, and so the blossoms of *B. officinalis* occur frequently in embroidery and in paintings that feature flowery meadows.

Most "borages" grown in gardens are actually stout perennial species of a closely related genus,

Symphytum, the comfrey of herbalists. *Borago officinalis,* by contrast, is a true annual of rapid growth, flowering in early to midsummer from an early spring sowing. In all gardens it will self-seed freely, so much so that once planted, it may never need planting again. Unwanted seedlings may easily be eliminated, however, as the plant accepts transplanting very hesitantly. But unless one's gardening style is very relaxed, volunteers may not appear exactly where they are wanted, and so fresh seed should be sown each spring. Any soil or climate will do, and though *B. officinalis* will grow in part shade, the finest plants will occur in full sun. A rare white form—should one wish any flower white that is so pretty in blue—is available, under the cultivar name 'Alba'.

BOUVARDIA SPECIES

FAMILY: *Rubiaceae* or coffee family.

CLASSIFICATION: Tender shrubs grown as tender annuals.

COMMON NAMES: Scarlet trompetilla, bouvardia.

HARDINESS: Hardy to Zones 9 and 10. Intolerant of temperatures much below 40°F. Extremely frost sensitive.

GROWING CONDITIONS: Humus-rich, moisture-retentive soil. Perfect drainage. Full sun. Relishes heat.

PROPAGATION: From tip cuttings, taken in late winter.

HEIGHT: To 6' where hardy. To 2' when grown as an annual.

ORNAMENTAL VALUE: Grown for flower.

LEVEL OF CULTURAL DIFFICULTY: Moderately difficult.

SPECIAL PROPERTIES: None.

PRONUNCIATION: boo-VAR-dee-a

*D*uring the Edwardian period, bouvardias enjoyed a sort of heyday. Properties of consequence were equipped with ranks of heated greenhouses devoted to the propagation of flowering plants for brief moments of glory in conservatories and in elaborate bedding schemes. Bouvardias were darlings, migrating from their native homes in Mexico and western Texas to elaborately heated stove houses throughout Europe. But with the collapse of the great estates and the consequent shrinking of accommodations for exotic flowering shrubs, bouvardias got crowded out by many other plants. The new increased interest in tender flowering plants for summer display, however, and the development of a greenhouse industry that supports it, seem to promise bouvardias a second wave of popularity.

Only two of the thirty or so species in the genus have been important in floriculture, though at one time many named hybrids and selected cultivars existed (and may be re-discovered), such as 'President Garfield', 'President Cleveland', 'Dazzler', 'Princess of Wales', and 'Albatross'. At this point, however, modern gardeners will be offered one of two species, either *Bouvardia longifolia* (lon-ji-FO-lee-a) or *B. ternifolia* (ter-ni-FO-lee-a). Both are fine plants, and neither is to be scorned in the absence of lost hybrids and cultivars.

Bouvardia longifolia is primarily a fall- to winter-flowering shrub, though with careful pruning it can be made to delay its bloom until early summer, when its jasmine-scented clusters of three-inch-long, tubular flowers flared into four oval, pointed petals at the end become an important component of brides' bouquets. As a conservatory or greenhouse plant, it is also valuable, thriving in nighttime temperatures around 55°F, and freely producing new growth and fragrant flowers throughout the winter. Sprays of bloom, with or without their glossy two-inch-long leaves, are

BOUVARDIA TERNIFOLIA

own distinct presence, and so it is hard to imagine them in general bedding schemes. Their branches are also extremely brittle, breaking at the lightest pressure of a hose or careless weeding hand. They are best when they may be studied alone, either as single potted specimens or in a large container of three or more plants.

The soil in which bouvardias are grown should be a humus-rich, free-draining compost liberally laced with sharp sand or perlite. The finest flowers are produced at the ends of young shoots, and so stems should be cut close to the woody base of the plant just as blossoms fade. A weekly drench of water-soluble fertilizer at half strength will encourage abundant blooms. As with most flowering shrubs from the southeastern United States and Mexico, bouvardias relish full sun in the hottest corner of the garden, and so flourish magnificently in containers on hot stone terraces.

Though their introduction into Europe probably occurred well after his death, the genus *Bouvardia* is named for Dr. Charles Bouvard (1572–1658), head gardener at the Jardin du Roi during the reign of Louis XIV.

often offered by sophisticated florists throughout the winter months.

For flower in the summer garden, however, a second species, *Bouvardia ternifolia,* is much more important. Where it is hardy (USDA Zones 9 and 10), it will build up into a congested shrub of arching branches as much as six feet tall. In colder gardens, young plants rooted from fresh growth or propagated from root cuttings in late winter will make graceful specimens to about two feet tall, each arching branch terminating in a loose cluster of two-inch-long, tubular flowers flattened into crosses at the end. They are generally of a fiery scarlet red, though select forms may veer either to orange-yellow or to rose. A dwarf albino form, 'Alba', also is listed, though at present it is rare in commerce.

In its native habitat, *Bouvardia ternifolia* blooms more or less continuously, and so in gardens where it is not hardy, it may be had in bloom from late June, when the weather has settled into summer warmth, until early frosts put an end to its show. At the end of the season, plants may be cut back hard and carried over in a cool greenhouse, where they will regrow and produce flowers beginning in late winter.

Bouvardias are very elegant plants with their

BRACHYCOME (SOMETIMES *BRACHYSCOME*) SPECIES

FAMILY: *Asteraceae* or aster or daisy family.

CLASSIFICATION: Annuals or tender perennials grown as tender annuals.

COMMON NAMES: Swan River daisy, brachycome.

HARDINESS: Sensitive to light frost.

GROWING CONDITIONS: Average fertile garden loam. Perfect drainage. Full sun.

PROPAGATION: From seed, sown indoors in late March or early April. Perennial and shrubby species from rooted cuttings.

HEIGHT: To 9″.

ORNAMENTAL VALUE: Grown for flower and fine-textured foliage.

LEVEL OF CULTURAL DIFFICULTY: Moderately difficult.

SPECIAL PROPERTIES: Superb in containers and window boxes. Excellent winter-flowering plants for cool greenhouses.

PRONUNCIATION: brak-ee-KO-mee (brak-is-KO-mee)

Botanical names often pass over the most important characteristics of a plant, at least from a gardener's point of view. That has certainly been the case with the Swan River daisy, whose winsome, inch-wide flowers of blue, lavender, mauve, pink, or white ought to be its main point. The common name suggests its real beauty as one imagines the gently flowing Swan River in Australia, with stately white birds nestling amid clouds of ferny foliage and tiny, enamel-bright blue daisies. The genus name, however, is derived from two ancient Greek words, *brachys,* short, and *kome,* hair, and refers merely to the tiny, bristly parachute of each seed, provided to aid its dispersal like dandelions and milkweeds.

The species within the genus most commonly cultivated is a true annual, called *iberidifolia* (i-ber-i-di-FO-lee-a) through some perceived resemblance to the foliage of *Iberis,* the candytuft of gardens. But the fine light green foliage of *Brachycome iberidifolia* does not resemble the sturdy dark green oval leaves of that plant at all. We must assume that the botanist who named it was working from a dried specimen and made a descriptive error.

Native to the moister parts of Australia and New Zealand, *Brachycome iberidifolia* entered European cultivation only in the nineteenth century, but its tidy, nine-inch mounds of filigreed foliage and its abundant flower over a long period of time made it treasured from the beginning as a "fringe" plant, good for the edges of Edwardian carpet bedding schemes. When that style of horticulture passed out of fashion, the twenty or so named varieties available from seed shrank to two or three, 'Purple Splendor' being the one most generally offered. But if so gentle and modest a flower can be described as having a renaissance, then the Swan River daisy is. Seed strains are now available with ray flowers of clear blue, purple, lilac, mauve, pink, and white, usually with yellow eyes, though sometimes, quite strikingly, with black ones. For those who still like edging plants, the Swan River daisy has a far softer, gentler look than dwarf ageratums, zinnias, or French marigolds. And when placed along the front of a border in natural-seeming patches rather than a straight row, or along a stone path or seeded into the cracks of pavement laid on sand, it can be even more beautiful. Mostly, however, one sees *B. iberidifolia* in mixed container plantings or window boxes, where its froth of ferny green leaves and abundant tiny daisies spills over and softens the edges.

Young plants of *B. iberidifolia,* perhaps already in flower, can be bought from nurseries after all

BRACHYCOME IBERIDIFOLIA

danger of frost is past. Seed also germinates easily in a cool greenhouse with nighttime temperatures around 55°F, where it should be sown in late March or early April for summer bloom. As the Swan River daisy loves cool temperatures, it may also be sown in mid-September, pricked out into five-inch pots of standard greenhouse potting mix, and carried through the winter in a cool greenhouse or sunny heated sun porch for beautiful late winter or early spring flowering plants.

Although a true annual, *B. iberidiflora* belongs to a genus of about seventy species, many of which are perennials or sub-shrubs, and all of which are hardy to Zones 8 to 10. They much resemble the Swan River daisy, making superb plants for summer containers, but being perennial, they may be transferred to a cool greenhouse, where they will bloom again in late winter or early spring. Gardeners with such greenhouses should look for the four species *melanocarpa* (me-lan-o-CAR-pa) *multifida* (mul-TI-fi-da), *nivalis* (ni-VA-lis) var. *alpina* (al-PEE-na) 'Pink Mist', or *tadgellii* (ta-JELL-ee-ee) 'Tinkerbell'. All will produce delicate, misty foliage, surmounted by inch-wide daisies—on single stems or in loose clusters—rounded, star-shaped, or engagingly ragged, according to species and variety.

BRASSICA OLERACEA

FAMILY: *Cruciferae* or mustard family.
CLASSIFICATION: Hardy biennial grown as hardy annual.
COMMON NAMES: Flowering cabbage, ornamental cabbage, and ornamental kale.
HARDINESS: Withstands significant frost. Winter-hardy to Zone 8 and warmer.

GROWING CONDITIONS: Average, well-drained garden loam. Cool temperatures. Full sun.
PROPAGATION: From seed, sown in rows or flats outdoors in May. Young plants transplant readily.
HEIGHT: To 1'.
ORNAMENTAL VALUE: Grown for colored leaves.
LEVEL OF CULTURAL DIFFICULTY: Easy.
SPECIAL PROPERTIES: Valued for extreme cold tolerance.
PRONUNCIATION: BRASS-i-ka o-ler-A-cee-a

*M*ost American gardeners cannot remember when they saw their first ornamental cabbage or kale, but it must have been about fifteen years ago. Of course, all cabbages are beautiful, their glaucous, wax-coated leaves of gray-green or brooding purple folding out like a rose and catching drops of dew into beads that glisten like mercury. Kales are beautiful, too, especially the crinkled forms in dark green or purple, and though adventurous gardeners sometimes planted both in beds of flowers, they were primarily pleasures of the vegetable garden. No longer. The development of so-called flowering kales and flowering cabbages has caused them to become as ubiquitous as mums, a sort of sturdy reliable after all the pretty things of summer have passed.

The cabbages and kales grown primarily as garden ornaments suffer from several confusions. First, though often called flowering, the colorful center leaves that look like giant peonies or roses are not flowers at all, but merely leaves. Second, there is no botanical distinction between ornamental cabbages and kales. Like their more homely vegetable-garden counterparts, they are both direct descendants from one wild progenitor, *Brassica oleracea,* a ragged, foot-high plant native to both sides of the English Channel and first cultivated by the ancient Celts. (Interestingly, broccoli, broccoli rabe, cauliflower, kohlrabi, and Brussels sprouts are also merely selections of the same plant, and not individual species.) Strictly as garden terms, however, the word *cabbage* applies to round-leaved forms of the plant, and *kale* to those with curled or fringed leaves.

Finally, ornamental cabbages and kales are as edible as any other cabbage or kale with one caveat: When cooked their flavor will not be of the best, for they were not bred for that, and purple leaves are apt to turn an unattractive brownish shade, white leaves a muddy gray. Their best kitchen use is as a garnish or as colorful bits in mixed salads.

Ornamental cabbages and kales are as easy to grow as any other member of the brassica group. Seed is sown either in the open ground or in flats, spaced about an inch apart. When young seedlings have formed two true leaves, they are thinned to stand a foot to eighteen inches apart, or transplanted into five-inch pots, later to be placed in the garden or in containers, or moved to eight-inch pots for single specimens. Leaf color develops best in autumn, and is at its finest after the first frosts or when night temperatures remain consistently below 50°F. Since plants are therefore not much use in the summer garden, there is no value in starting seed early; late May or early June is soon enough. Specimens grown in rows may be transplanted with care, though pot-grown plants are obviously easier and, with their smaller root masses, more flexible. All forms are extremely hardy, withstanding temperatures of 29°F or even lower, and are more apt to be discarded in favor of Christmas greens than to perish from the cold. One old variety of vegetable garden kale, now no longer available, was in fact called "the Hungry Gap," because its extreme hardiness made it the only vegetable crop available from the garden in the depths of winter. Or-

BRASSICA OLERACEA

namental cabbages and kales might themselves be called "the Floral Gap," for the way they furnish planters and flower beds at a time when no other bedding plants will survive.

Ornamental cabbages also make striking cut flowers. A single, perfectly formed head placed in a low bowl can be magnificent, perhaps much more so than in the frost-hardened earth of a half whiskey barrel. Recently, stylish urban florists have also been offering bunches of cabbage "roses," particularly the relatively small, tight-cupped Japanese forms, such as 'Osaka Mix'. They are both novel and very pretty, though their vase life is relatively short, since, like any cabbage, their thick stems will begin to smell rank after a week or so, hardly of roses. Changing the water daily will somewhat impede this unfortunate side effect.

BREYNIA NIVOSA

FAMILY: *Euphorbiaceae* or spurge family.

CLASSIFICATION: Tender shrub grown as tender annual.

COMMON NAMES: Hawaiian snowbush, leaf-flower, breynia.

HARDINESS: Hardy in Zones 9 and 10. Uncomfortable at temperatures much below 40°F. Extremely frost sensitive.

GROWING CONDITIONS: Average, well-drained garden loam. Abundant moisture. Full sun.

PROPAGATION: From tip cuttings, taken in late winter.

HEIGHT: To 4'.

ORNAMENTAL VALUE: Grown for ornamental leaves.

LEVEL OF CULTURAL DIFFICULTY: Moderately easy.

SPECIAL PROPERTIES: Excellent cool greenhouse plant.

PRONUNCIATION: BRAY-nee-a ni-VO-sa

The genus *Breynia* includes between twenty and thirty species of shrubs and trees native to the South Sea Islands, southeastern Asia, and Australia. Only one, *Breynia nivosa*—often *B. disticha* (dis-TI-ca)—is cultivated in gardens and greenhouses, and even so, must still be classed among rare and little-known plants. Still, it is very charming and has begun to show up as a novelty in mixed containers of annuals and tender plants for summer decoration.

A native of the South Sea Islands and hardy only in the warmest parts of the country (USDA Zones 9 and 10), at full maturity it scarcely reaches four feet and maintains throughout its life a fragile, delicate appearance. Its slender, wiry stems are a pronounced reddish purple, somewhat pendant, carrying nickel-sized rounded to oval papery leaves on petioles of a brighter red. In the species, the leaves are liberally splashed with white, giving it the popular name "Hawaiian snowbush." The most commonly cultivated form, however, is the selected cultivar 'Rosea Picta', which adds splashes of pink to the mottling of green and white on the leaves, causing it to be popularly called "leaf-flower." There is also a cultivar with maroon leaves, 'Atropurpurea'.

Breynia is of very easy culture, asking little more than reasonably good soil, good drainage, full sun, and moisture at its roots. Its delicate, ferny texture blends well with other plants in containers, and because of root competition in confined spaces, the colors of its stems and foliage are apt to be even more brilliant than when it grows freely in the ground. At season's end, plants are easily carried over in a cool greenhouse or sunny windowsill with a minimum nighttime temperature of 55°F for larger specimens the following year. Tip cuttings taken in late winter, inserted in half peat and half sharp sand, root readily in a closed environment.

The genus name *Breynia* commemorates Jacob Breyne (1637–1697), a merchant in Danzig, and his son, Johann Phillip Breyne (1680–1764), a physician also of that city, both of whom were amateur botanists specializing in the study of rare and little-known plants. The species name *nivosa* signifies snow, and refers to the white tip growths of the plant, a phenomenon nicely picked up in its common name as well.

BROWALLIA SPECIES

FAMILY: *Solanaceae* or deadly nightshade family.

CLASSIFICATION: Tender perennials or annuals grown as half-hardy or tender annuals.

COMMON NAMES: Bush violet, amethyst flower, baby-blue-eyes, browallia.

HARDINESS: Sensitive to temperatures much below 40°F. Foliage is extremely frost sensitive.

GROWING CONDITIONS: Humus-rich, water-retentive but well-drained soil. Full sun in cooler gardens, part-shade in warmer ones.

PROPAGATION: From seed, sown indoors 8 weeks before last anticipated frost. Cuttings root readily.

HEIGHT: From 1 to 2′ depending on species.

ORNAMENTAL VALUE: Grown for flower.

LEVEL OF CULTURAL DIFFICULTY: Easy.

SPECIAL PROPERTIES: All species valued as winter-flowering house and greenhouse plants.

PRONUNCIATION: bro-WA-lee-a

*I*n late spring and early summer, nursery owners are maddened by the repeated question, "What can I plant that will bloom in shade all summer?" Sadly, most long-flowering annual and tender plants are children of light, preferring full sun or at least demanding half a day of it. *Browallia speciosa* (spee-see-O-sa) is therefore a treasure, since it does its best in warm, dappled shade. (Its flowers fade quickly in full sun.) And though the blue and lavender forms are splendid, for once the white-flowered cultivars are equally valuable, bringing light and coolness to shadowy places.

The showiest species in the genus (as "speciosus" always indicates), *Browallia speciosa* bears tubular one-inch-long flowers flattened into a five-lobed face about one-and-a-half inches across. Once cultivated mostly in the lavender-blue form, 'Major', it has now been bred in several shades of pinkish-blue, mauve, deep blue, purple, and white, most of which preserve the large flower form of that cultivar. In all but the palest colors, the white at the center is brushed outward, creating a starry, surprised look to each flower that is entirely engaging. Flowers are borne in profusion throughout the summer on sturdy, bushlike plants about a foot tall, forming in the axils of the leaves as the stems mature. The leaves are also very pleasing, consisting of two-inch-long pointed ovals puckered at the veins to display a quilted effect.

Very sensitive to cold, *B. speciosa,* a native of the tropical portions of Columbia, suffers when temperatures fall to 40°F. Though it germinates readily from seed, which should be sown about eight weeks before the last expected frost, most plants are acquired ready-grown and already showing flower from nurseries and garden centers. Neither homegrown seedlings nor bought plants should be transplanted into the garden, however, until the weather is settled and warm. Though not particular as to soil, *B. speciosa* should never dry out at the roots, and so, if it is used in hanging baskets, containers, or window boxes—for all of which uses it is an excellent choice—adequate water must be supplied. The species is actually a tender perennial, and, at season's end, makes a pleasing houseplant for a cool, bright window or the greenhouse. Cuttings also root easily.

BROWALLIA AMERICANA

Though *Browallia speciosa* is the most popular in a genus of eight or so members, it is not the only one worth growing. Two other species, *B. americana* (a-mer-i-CA-na)—sometimes offered as *B. elata* (e-LA-ta), and *B. viscosa* (vis-CO-sa), which is similar to it in appearance, have great charm. They are both true annuals that come quickly from seed and, though also South American natives, will self-seed in all but the coldest gardens. Both bear flowers in profusion, each about a half inch long and as wide or slightly wider, little blue "eyes" prominently marked with white in *B. viscosa* and with pale yellow in *B. americana*. *B. americana* may be expected to reach about two feet, with small raspy or hairy leaves borne alternately along the stems. As plants mature, however, they are apt to tumble over, producing additional stems from the axils of their leaves, eventually creating a full, bushy effect. *B. viscosa* is shorter, about a foot tall, with clammy or viscid leaves, as its species name indicates. Both are airy, engaging plants, substituting a winsome delicacy for the sturdy, showy beauty of *Browallia speciosa*.

Seed of all three species of *Browallia* (the genus name commemorates John Browall, 1707–1755, a Swedish bishop, amateur botanist, and friend of Linnaeus) may be sown in July, and young plants grown on singly in five-inch pots for superb flower through winter and into spring for a cool, bright window, the greenhouse, or a heated sun porch. Alternatively, cuttings can be taken at the same time, preferably from nonflowering shoots, rooted in half peat, half sharp sand, and grown on for the same purpose. For though *B. speciosa* is a true perennial, and *B. americana* and *B. viscosa* are annuals, the latter two root as easily as the former and, when given a bright, frost-free environment

BROWALLIA SPECIOSA 'AMETHYST'

in which to grow, seem not to realize that they should fulfill the destiny of true annuals and die at season's end.

BRUGMANSIA SPECIES

FAMILY: *Solanaceae* or deadly nightshade family.

CLASSIFICATION: Tender shrub grown as tender annual.

COMMON NAMES: Angels' trumpets, brugmansia.

HARDINESS: Hardy in Zones 9 and 10. Displeased by temperatures much below 40°F. Extremely frost sensitive.

GROWING CONDITIONS: Humus, very rich, free-draining soil, with extra fertilizer.

PROPAGATION: From cuttings taken in early summer.

HEIGHT: To 10′ where hardy. To 6′ in one season when grown as an annual.

ORNAMENTAL VALUE: Grown for flower and for coarse, shrublike growth.

LEVEL OF CULTURAL DIFFICULTY: Moderately easy.

SPECIAL PROPERTIES: Flowers are powerfully night-scented.

PRONUNCIATION: brug-man-SEE-a

*U*ntil recently, species of *Brugmansia* were included in the genus *Datura*. Now, however, they have been firmly detached, giving Sebald Justin Brugmans (1763–1819), an otherwise obscure professor of natural history at Leyden, the recognition he was intended to have. Even to the most botanically naïve gardener, however, the differences between the two genuses will be clear. All species of *Brugmansia* are stout, treelike plants, whereas daturas are coarse, sprawling annual or perennial herbs. The blooms are similar, consisting of flared tubes of five fused petals, but those borne by brugmansias are more-or-less down-hanging, whereas flowers of daturas are borne laterally or up-facing.

Though both genuses are cultivated for bold effect, few plants are as assertive in the summer garden as a well-grown brugmansia. Flowers, from ten to fifteen inches long, are abundantly produced throughout the summer months and are usually hauntingly scented at twilight and through the night. A perfect specimen, hung with dozens of foot-long trumpets, is unforgettable.

The genus *Brugmansia* is quite small, consisting of only five species, mostly native to the moist tropical regions of South America. They are reliably hardy only in the warmest parts of North America, retaining both their leaves and their pulpy, woody growth over winter only in USDA Zones 9 and 10. Although in colder gardens they are sometimes planted in the ground as part of a summer bedding scheme, generally they are featured as very large tubbed or potted specimens on terraces or decks. That is perhaps their best use, for they can easily look peculiar in a northern flower border lacking the companionship of other bold plants that would surround them in tropical gardens.

BRUGMANSIA *X* CANDIDA *'GRAND MARNIER'*

BRUGMANSIA VERSICOLOR

Though all species of *Brugmansia* are of quick and lusty growth (a rooted cutting can grow easily to six feet in one season), their very exuberance can make successful culture a little difficult. Like many tropical plants, their fleshy root systems are not as large as one might suppose for so large a plant. Still, a twelve-foot, heavily wooded, large-leaved, and huge-flowered plant will need some room. So as young plants develop, they should be moved frequently into larger and larger containers until they come to occupy the largest pot, tub, or box one can conveniently manage. (After that, an annual spring pruning should attempt to keep plant and container in aesthetic balance.) Containers must also be stabilized, for a mature brugmansia in full sail can easily blow over. Protection from wind is necessary also, because the plants require abundant water—sometimes twice a day in dry summer heat—and dessicating winds compound the problem. When their need for water is denied, brugmansias will shrivel and wilt almost immediately, often shedding immature flower buds and even leaves in a premature preparation for winter dormancy. As one would expect from such a vigorous plant, brugmansias are also voracious feeders, requiring the richest, free-draining compost, and then supplementary feedings of water-soluble plant food throughout the summer. A commercially prepared food specifically formulated for tomatoes works wonders when applied at half strength every week throughout the summer months.

Brugmansias may be expected to produce some flower from young cuttings in their first season if started early or bought from a nursery. But the most spectacular results will occur in subsequent years from older plants. If their requirements for winter dormancy can be met, they are fairly easy to carry over. In autumn, flower production will decrease and leaves will begin to yellow and drop, signaling that the plant is entering a winter dormancy. Before the slightest touch of frost, however, plants should be taken into a cool, frost-free place for winter storage. Temperatures that hover around 45°F are ideal, and very little light is needed. Only so much water should be given as is needed to keep the youngest, most succulent shoots from shriveling, and no supplementary food should be applied.

The hardest part of overwintering brugmansias will occur around late March, when the plants finally become impatient of their winter confinement and break dormancy. As they are extremely frost tender, a place must be found indoors for them to begin growth, such as a heated sun porch or a cool, sunny guest bedroom. When plants first show new growth, they may be pruned to convenient size, generally by shortening lateral branches by a third or even by half. They should also then be repotted into fresh compost. If they have reached the largest container that is manageable, they may also be root-pruned, by turning them out of their pots, teasing away an inch or two of soil around and at the base of their roots, and trimming straggly exposed roots even with the reduced root ball. They may then be replanted into the same pots they previ-

BRUGMANSIA X CANDIDA

ously occupied, with an inch or two of fresh compost about and below their roots. Plants should be returned to their positions outdoors only when all danger of frost is past and should be accustomed gradually to bright light by first being put in a partly shaded spot for two or three days. (Frequent wetting of the new foliage and stems will also help them.) New growth will be rapid, and the first flowers should appear by early summer.

Though brugmansia comprises only species, it is currently enjoying such a vogue among gardeners that a surprising number of cultivars have recently become available for so small a genus. Species appear freely to intermarry, and so the brugmansia most frequently offered previously has been *B.* x *candida* (CAN-di-da), a naturally occurring hybrid between two Peruvian natives, *B. aurea* (AU-ree-a) and *B. versicolor* (ver-SI-color). As the botanical name "candida" always indicates, naturally produced hybrids are a pure, shining white, and occur either in graceful single or dramatically congested double forms. But pale yellow and bluish-white flowers also naturally occur, and so by careful selection, breeders have created single and double forms that are lemon or melon colored. The very popular cultivar called 'Grand Marnier' also probably belongs to this group, with single flowers of a pale orange tan. So sumptuous have cultivars of x *candida* become that its chaste name seems now no longer to apply.

Additional melon and pink shades can be had from *Brugmansia* x *insignis* (in-SIG-nis), and white, cream, peach, melon, and buff from one of its parents, *B. versicolor.* From the other, *B. suaveolens* (swa-vee-O-lens), one gets a flower of pristine white, much like that of a single white x *candida,* but shorter by two or so inches, more flared at the mouth, and of a strikingly delicate poise and texture. For shades of true red, scarlet,

deep orange, and even a lemon-lime combination of yellow with green veins, one must turn to *B. suaveolens.* Its tubular flowers are the smallest of all the species, at six to eight inches.

All brugmansias are lovely, but unless one is intent on making a large collection of them (which would amount to a herd of pet elephants in the backyard), perhaps the pure white forms *B.* x *candida* or *suaveolens* are the best choice for their powerful fragrance and their eerie, lantern-like glow on summer nights.

BUPLEURUM ROTUNDIFOLIUM

FAMILY: *Umbelliferae* or Queen Anne's lace family.

CLASSIFICATION: Hardy annual or short-lived perennial grown as hardy annual.

COMMON NAMES: Hare's ears, thorow-wax, bupleurum.

HARDINESS: Withstands light frost.

GROWING CONDITIONS: Dry, moderately fertile to poor soil. Perfect drainage. Full sun.

PROPAGATION: From seed, sown indoors in peat pots 8 weeks before last anticipated frost. Young plants resent root disturbance. Will self-seed in Zone 4 and warmer.

HEIGHT: To 2'.

ORNAMENTAL VALUE: Grown for ornamental foliage and for flower.

LEVEL OF CULTURAL DIFFICULTY: Moderately easy.

SPECIAL PROPERTIES: None.

PRONUNCIATION: boo-PLU-rum ro-tun-di-FO-lee-um

*M*ost gardeners would probably mis-identify *Bupleurum rotundifolium.* Its grayish, two-inch leaves neatly clasping the stems as if pierced by them look very like the fragrant branches of eucalyptus sold by florists. And its flowers, tiny tufts of golden yellow brushes nestled in four-pointed, lime-green bracts, closely resemble the flowers of certain euphorbias. All appearances belie the fact that *B. rotundifolium* belongs to the vast family Umbelliferae, which includes parsley, celery, dill, Queen Anne's lace, *Ammi majus,* and many other important garden plants.

But the botanists who first classified *B. rotundifolium,* working presumably from dried specimens, miscalled it as well. The genus name originates from two ancient Greek words that signify the rib of an ox, though none of the 100 or so species in the genus seem to resemble the anatomy of that animal. And *rotundifolium* should suggest leaves as round as a silver dollar, though in fact the species bears elliptical leaves, somewhat pointed.

This confusion about *B. rotundifolium's* botanical name should not stop anyone from planting it in the garden. If seeded in early spring, plants should form sturdy, stiff-branched bushes by midsummer, about two feet tall, surmounted by many cupped bracts holding bunches of egg-yolk yellow umbels. The effect is certainly not showy but is always a pleasant surprise when planted in a generous drift among more vivid annuals or perennials, or in a sunny bay of the shrubbery border, or along a path. Its interestingly crafted leaves and flowers justify planting a row or two in the cutting garden, where generous stems could be freely taken. It is also very beautiful as a dried flower, as the small bracts turn the color of old ivory and firmly hold in their centers small, almost black seed.

A hardy annual or sometimes weak perennial, *B. rotundifolium* is native to southern Europe and North Africa. Despite the mild climates of these habitats, however, it will self-seed pleasantly in gardens as cold as Zone 4. It relishes dryish, rather poor soils, though—like many lean-living annuals and tender perennials—it is grateful in youth for an extra ration of granular fertilizer weak in nitrogen but stronger in phosphorus and potassium, such as 5-10-10. Like most members of the family Umbelliferae, it resents transplanting, but it may be started in plastic cell packs about eight weeks before the last expected frost and transplanted carefully, with minimal root disturbance, into the garden around the last anticipated frost date. It may also be seeded where it is to grow as early in spring as the soil is workable, and later thinned to stand about eight inches apart.

CALANDRINIA SPECIES

FAMILY: *Portulacaceae* or purslane family.

CLASSIFICATION: Tender perennials or half-hardy annuals grown as tender annuals.

COMMON NAMES: Rock purslane, calandrinia.

HARDINESS: Discouraged by temperatures much below 40°F. Frost sensitive.

GROWING CONDITIONS: Well-drained, fertile sandy loam. Cool temperatures. Full sun.

PROPAGATION: By seed, sown in site in very early spring. Cuttings may also be taken.

HEIGHT: From 6 to 18", depending on species.

ORNAMENTAL VALUE: Grown for flower.

LEVEL OF CULTURAL DIFFICULTY: Difficult except under ideal conditions.

SPECIAL PROPERTIES: *Calandrinia cilliata* is used as a salad or cooked green in its native Peru and Ecuador.

PRONUNCIATION: cal-an-DRIN-ee-a

No one questions the beauty of calandrinias. The flowers open only on bright, sunny days, but they match the splendor of fine Indian silks, their shiny petals generally colored some improbable shade of violet-crimson, hot rose, or magenta. Of

CALANDRINIA UMBELLATA

the 150 or so species in the genus, however, only five are grown in gardens, and those but seldom, because calandrinias make a poor show where their exacting needs are not met. Natives to cool, dryish regions of the world, chiefly parts of South America and western North America, they do best in atmospheric conditions that mimic their homelands. Above all, they insist on very well-drained, dry, fertile sandy loam.

All calandrinias grown in gardens are either annuals or are best treated as annuals, flowering from seed sown in very early spring. Of the two species of *Calandrinia* most frequently grown, *C. umbellata* (um-be-LA-ta) is quite tiny, scarcely reaching six inches in height. Its succulent, needle-like, hairy, blue-gray leaves grow in a basal tuft, above which rise loose clusters of as many as thirty flowers that, though only three-quarter inch across, seem surprisingly large for so small a plant. They are generally five petaled, though individual blossoms may have as few as three or as many as seven petals, formed typically into a flat cup of satiny crimson or magenta. Flowers last only a day or two but are abundantly produced from June to September.

The second garden favorite, *C. grandiflora* (gran-di-FLO-ra), is a much larger plant in all its

parts with succulent, maroon-red stems reaching a height between twelve and eighteen inches. The oval, pointed, fleshy, grass-green leaves are between five and seven inches long, and the flowers—rose to light purple—may be two or more inches across. A tender perennial native to Chile, it will flower all summer from a late winter or very early spring sowing under glass at temperatures between 45 and 50°F.

Three other species of *Calandrinia* (named in honor of Jean-Louis Calandrini, an eighteenth-century professor of mathematics and philosophy in Geneva) are also sometimes grown in gardens. *C. discolor* (DI-co-lor) reaches about a foot in height, with bright rose flowers shaded a pronounced yellow in the center, as its species name indicates. *C. nitida* (NI-ti-da), similar to *C. umbellata,* is about six inches in height and bears rose-colored flowers throughout July and August. *C. cilliata* (si-li-A-ta), in the typical form native to Peru and Ecuador, is a hardy annual sprawling a foot and a half tall and bearing pale purple to almost white flowers about half an inch across. It is far showier in the variety *menziesii* (men-ZEE-see-ee), which occurs as a natural variant in western North America, with fleshy leaves that are said to be edible in salads or as cooked greens, much like purslane, a near cousin. Both *Calandrinia cilliata* and *C. cilliata* var. *menziesii* are sometimes listed as *C. speciosa* (spee-see-O-sa).

CALCEOLARIA SPECIES

FAMILY: *Scrophulariaceae* or snapdragon family.

CLASSIFICATION: Perennials, true annuals, or tender shrubs grown as tender annuals.

COMMON NAMES: Slipperwort, lady's slippers, pocket book plant, pouch flower, calceolaria.

HARDINESS: Varies with species. None hardy much
  below 40°F.
GROWING CONDITIONS: Humus-rich, well-drained
  garden loam. Abundant moisture. Cool temperatures. Full sun in cool gardens, dappled shade
  in warmer ones.
PROPAGATION: By seed. Cuttings of shrubby species
  root easily.
HEIGHT: Varies with species. Generally under 2′.
ORNAMENTAL VALUE: Grown for flower.
LEVEL OF CULTURAL DIFFICULTY: Very difficult to
  moderately easy, depending on species and
  growing conditions.
SPECIAL PROPERTIES: None.
PRONUNCIATION: cal-see-o-LAR-ee-a

The calceolaria most familiar to gardeners are probably those found in a florist's shop. From late winter to spring, they are offered by greenhouses as single plants with masses of improbably shaped pouched flowers an inch long and half as wide, surmounting rich cushions of rough, dark green leaves. The flowers, often comically ruffled or puckered at the upper edge of the pouch, are of sumptuous colors—many shades of pink, apricot, brick red, yellow, orange, or brown, usually fantastically freckled or marbled with deeper tints or contrasting colors.

These plants represent months of hovering care, beginning the previous May with the sowing of tiny seed, so minute that it must first be shaken out on white paper and distributed onto flats of fibrous, sphagnum-enriched earth with tweezers and a magnifying glass. Germination is very slow, and the infant plants must be pricked out with a pointed stick in one hand and a notched one in the other. Plants are first established in tiny rows in another flat, and then moved progressively into larger and larger pots until they come to settle in the eight-inch ones in which they will flower. Eventually, after a year of careful growing, buds form and the heavy masses of bloom develop.

Not everyone admires the results. Graham Rice, the English garden writer, has compared them to "the beloved bedroom slippers of 1950s seaside landladies." (The genus name refers to the signature shape of the flower, from the Latin *calceolus,* a slipper, since all species bear blooms with a shortened upper lip and an enlarged pouch or slipper-shaped lower lip.) Still, for cool greenhouses and heated sun porches, they make interesting and beautiful plants. And if one is lucky enough to live in those parts of North America that enjoy moist, frost-free winters and long, cool springs, cultivars of the x *hybrida* (HI-bri-da) or *crenatiflora* (cre-na-ti-FLO-ra) group are superb for winter bedding.

There would not be much more to say to general gardeners about calceolaria were it not for the fact that in the large genus—about 500 species—several are far less exacting in their needs. Other annual species of *Calceolaria* are sometimes grown, and will be more frequently grown as what might be called the "easy" calceolaria become more popular. Among the true annuals, by

CALCEOLARIA MEXICANA

far the easiest is *Calceolaria mexicana* (mex-i-CA-na). One should not, however, be misled by its species name into assuming it will flourish in arid soils under broiling sun. It requires in fact just the opposite conditions, and will achieve its full foot of bushy growth only in a fertile, porous soil with some shade from the hot, midday sun. The feet of no fat landlady could be imagined fitting into its delicate, lemon-yellow flowers, for they are only about half an inch long, though they are borne in profusion all summer, well above rough, dark green, deeply lobed three-inch leaves.

Similar in most ways to *C. mexicana* is *C. scabiosaefolia* (sca-bee-o-si-FO-lee-a), a native to Chile and Ecuador. It is taller, to about two feet, but its small purses of flower are about the size of those of *C. mexicana* and seem to dance above its deeply indented, heavily lobed five- to eight-inch-long leaves. Another annual species, *C. tripartita* (tri-par-TI-ta), is a much-branched, bushy plant with darker, bluish-green leaves and the recognizable, half-inch pouched flowers of the group, borne from late June to frost. It is a highly variable species, some forms giving relatively few flowers for a great deal of leaf, and others producing ample sprays. All this group suggests work for breeders, especially as their more modest flowers may cross with larger-flowered, greenhouse varieties, producing plants almost as sturdy and as variable perhaps as marigolds. In all but the very coldest gardens, annual calceolaria will self-seed pleasantly, usually returning year after year once they have been grown for a season.

Among the shrubby sorts of *Calceolaria*, *C. integrifolia* (in-te-gre-FO-lee-a) is the most frequently cultivated. Sometimes listed as *C. rugosa* (ru-GO-sa), it is very popular in Europe as a summer bedding plant, for it produces its graceful sprays of yellow to reddish-brown flowers from spring to autumn, persisting even after light frosts. A native of Mexico, it is reliably winter-hardy only to Zone 9, where it can build up into a woody shrub as much as six feet tall. Though it can be grown from seed, most plants are raised from cuttings taken in autumn and early winter and inserted in damp sand in a moist environment. The species is seldom seen in American gardens, though as more and more gardeners become interested in tender woody plants for summer bedding, it is apt to be more commonly offered. Crosses between it and other shrubby calceolarias should yield a wide range of colors, particularly in dusky pink, terra cotta, and orange. From this mixture of races, the resulting group may perhaps properly be known under the clumsy name *Calceolaria fruitocohybrida* (fru-ti-co-HY-bri-da). But however named, new crosses of calceolaria are apt to be fine plants for the summer garden, as they are equally resistant to heat and light frost, and the shape of their pouched flowers is unmatched by any others, save some rare orchids.

CALENDULA SPECIES

FAMILY: *Asteraceae* or aster or daisy family.

CLASSIFICATION: Half-hardy to hardy annual.

COMMON NAMES: English marigold, pot marigold, calendula.

HARDINESS: Withstands light frosts.

GROWING CONDITIONS: Fertile, well-drained, humusy soil. Full sun.

PROPAGATION: By seed. Will self-sow in most gardens.

HEIGHT: From 8 to 30″, depending on cultivar.

ORNAMENTAL VALUE: Blooms from spring to frost, and throughout winter in mild climates.

LEVEL OF CULTURAL DIFFICULTY: Easy.

SPECIAL PROPERTIES: Used to thicken and flavor soups and stews, in salads, and to color butter.

PRONUNCIATION: ka-lin-DEW-la

Though cheerful plants of sunny disposition, calendulas draw their genus name from the Calends, the depressing first day of each ancient Roman month on which rents, interests, tributes, tithes, and taxes were due. It was not their fault, however, that where they are native, they bloom every month out of the year. The genus is a small one, of about fifteen species growing throughout the Mediterranean region, only three of which are frequently grown in gardens. The most familiar of them is *Calendula officinalis* (o-fi-shi-NA-lis), the pot marigold, so-called because it was anciently cultivated as a culinary herb used to flavor and thicken soups and to color butter. It might still have those uses, though in soups experimentation should be cautious, as a single fresh flower head, or even half of one, will be enough. Single petals also make an attractive gold or yellow garnish for salads, though they should be sprinkled over the salad after it is dressed and tossed, as otherwise they will become muddy and tint the whole mass a dull mustard yellow.

In its wild form, *C. officinalis,* a sprawling, branched plant, bearing two-inch-wide, single orange daisies, is somewhat ragged looking, although it possesses its own wild, meadow-weed charm. Modern forms are much prettier, varying in height from eight to thirty inches, and thickly furnished with medium to gray-green, two- to three-inch-long oval leaves. In single forms, the number of ray petals (those one plucks as a test of true love) has been increased to produce a perfectly circular, flat daisy, often with a contrasting eye of black or green disk flowers. Semi-double and full doubles have also been bred, as well as forms with quilled petals. Colors may be any shade of ivory white to primrose or deep yellow, light or vivid tangerine, orange-pink, true orange, or a chestnut red so deep as to approach bronze. Bi-colored forms are also becoming popular, with ray petals of light shades backed by deeper,

CALENDULA OFFICINALIS

complementary colors. Some varieties have come so close to true pink or true red as to suggest that those colors will also eventually occur.

Calendula officinalis is classed as a hardy annual, and in gardens where temperatures do not dip much below 30°F, plants may bloom all winter. Elsewhere, seed should be sown in late fall (where winters are mild) or in very early spring outdoors, or indoors about six weeks before the last frost. They develop quickly from seed and flower most abundantly in cool weather.

Calendula are thrifty plants, performing well in average to poor soils. In climates where air conditioners are largely pointless, they will bloom nonstop from early summer until autumn, withstanding even light frosts and snows. Frequent dead-heading will increase flower production and size, and the stockiest, most attractive plants are produced by pinching out the first flower bud. In warmer gardens, calendula may flag in midsummer heat, either taking a rest until the cooler weather of autumn arrives, or dying outright. In all but the coldest gardens, young seedlings will volunteer for years once plants have been grown, though they will revert to the simpler, rangier form of the wild plant. Young plants grown from a midsummer seeding and lifted and potted before frost make superb winter-flowering plants for the cool greenhouse or heated sun porch.

Of the two other species of *Calendula* commonly cultivated in gardens, neither competes with modern forms of *C. officinalis* in beauty, though they are useful as components of a wildflower meadow into which annual plants are seeded. *C. maderensis* (ma-der-EN-sis)—or *C. incana* (in-KAH-na) subsp. *maderensis*—called the "Madeira marigold," grows erect to two feet and bears light orange, cup-shaped simple daisies of ten to twenty ray petals surrounding a darker disk. *C. arvensis* (ar-VEN-sis), the field calendula bearing flowers of clear yellow, is a common grain-field weed throughout central Europe and the Mediterranean and is now widely naturalized in neglected ground throughout California.

CALLIRHOE SPECIES

FAMILY: *Malvaceae* or mallow family.

CLASSIFICATION: Hardy perennial or hardy annual grown as hardy annual.

COMMON NAMES: Poppy mallow, wine cups, callirhoe.

HARDINESS: Depends on species. Hardy to light frosts when grown as annuals.

GROWING CONDITIONS: Loose, sandy soil of moderate fertility. Perfect drainage. Full sun.

PROPAGATION: From seed, sown indoors in late winter in peat pots or plastic cell packs. Plants resent root disturbance.

HEIGHT: To 2–3′.

ORNAMENTAL VALUE: Grown for flower.

LEVEL OF CULTURAL DIFFICULTY: Difficult.

SPECIAL PROPERTIES: None.

PRONUNCIATION: ka-LI-ro-ee

One can only guess why the English botanist Thomas Nuttall (1786–1859) chose *Callirhoe* as the name for a small North American genus of plants whose flowers closely resemble miniature single hollyhocks. Perhaps the vibrant violet-red color of the flowers suggested to Nuttall the self-destructive avarice of Callirhoë, the daughter of an ancient Greek river god. Her passionate desire for the baleful necklace of Harmonia caused the death of her husband, herself, and indeed of all who came to possess it. Whatever Nuttall's intention, he saddled gardeners with a botanical name easy to stumble over. (It is correctly pronounced ka-LI-ro-ee.) And for once, even the most botanically minded of gardeners might prefer the popular name "wine cups," which is both pretty and accurate for the vivid two-inch flowers with five delicate, crepelike petals overlapping to form a single cup.

Of the eight species in the genus, *Callirhoe involucrata* (in-vo-lu-CRA-ta) has the widest distribution, from Wyoming to southern Texas, and because of its northern range, is the most reliably perennial in cold gardens. All others have a more southern distribution and will become persistently or weakly perennial in the climates that approximate their native ranges.

C. *digitata* (di-ji-TA-ta), for example, with a natural range extending into Missouri, will persist
in Zone 5 gardens if given dryish, not over-rich
soil. But *C. papaver* (pa-PA-ver), native from
Florida through southern Texas, will last only
one season in most American gardens. Since all
species bloom their first year from seed, however, they are often treated as annuals, and some
are often classified as such in garden references
and in seed catalogues.

All callirhoes form carrotlike taproots and resent root disturbance, so, whatever the species,
two or three seed should be sown in peat pots or
in individual cells of plastic cell packs, with the
intention of clipping out all but the strongest.
Like all perennials or biennials grown as annuals,
seeding should occur in late winter or very early
spring, preferably by late February or early
March, in this case at temperatures around 60°F.
Care should also be taken to disturb the fleshy
roots as little as possible when young plants are
established in their permanent positions. The
soil should be perfectly drained, loose, and
sandy, and for abundant bloom, lean and dry.
Full sun is an absolute requirement. Given these
conditions, plants of all species should develop
quickly into two- to three-foot, loosely
branched, lax-stemmed bushes, and two-inch
flowers will be borne in profusion from late June
until frost.

Differences among species exist largely in the
height of the plants and the shape of their leaves,
not so much in their flowers. Flower color will
vary slightly from species to species, but most
would be described as deep rose, violet-rose, violet-red, purple-red, or (if one is not afraid of the
word) magenta. White forms exist, but they have
trouble competing with the vividness of typically
colored plants, all of which bear the popular
name "wine cups."

CALLISTEPHUS CHINENSIS

FAMILY: *Asteraceae* or daisy family.

CLASSIFICATION: Hardy annual.

COMMON NAMES: China aster, callistephus.

HARDINESS: Withstands light frosts once established.

GROWING CONDITIONS: Fertile, well-drained soil.
Full sun.

PROPAGATION: From seed, sown in place in early
May, or indoors in March or early April.

HEIGHT: From 6″ to 3′, depending on cultivar.

ORNAMENTAL VALUE: Grown for flower.

LEVEL OF CULTURAL DIFFICULTY: Difficult.

SPECIAL PROPERTIES: Excellent as cut flowers.

PRONUNCIATION: kal-i-STEF-us chi-NEN-sis

When well grown and free of diseases, *Callistephus chinensis,* popularly called the "China
aster," is among the most beautiful of all annual
flowers. Perhaps a hundred varieties are available
to gardeners, ranging in height from six inches to
three feet, forming tightly bunched cushions or
angular, airy scaffolds according to variety. Flowers may be as small as an inch across or as large as
five. Colors are sumptuous, ranging from chalk
white through old ivory and primrose yellow,
pale or deep lavender blue, every shade of pink to
wine, crimson, and deep red, deep purple-blue,
and magenta. All China asters descend from one
wild progenitor, the only species in its genus, a
simple daisy with one or two rows of ray flowers
and a flattened button of yellow disk flowers.
From it forms have developed as variable as any
among annuals, including singles, semi-doubles,
doubles with petals curved inward or outward,
powder puffs, pom-poms, and spider forms with
thin, threadlike petals, sometimes whorled into a

CALLISTEPHUS CHINENSIS

ball in the center. Well-grown plants amply earn the genus name made up of two ancient Greek words, *kalli,* meaning beautiful, and *stephos,* a crown. Were it not for myriad diseases that can strike the plant, China asters would be among the most popular of all plants grown as annuals, for they can be incomparably pretty, both in the garden and in the vase.

In the plant world, however, too often the beauty of a flower seems in direct ratio to the difficulty of its cultivation. For all but the very lucky, China asters may prove challenging. Classed as hardy annuals, they do best when seeded directly in the garden, and thinned to stand from nine to twelve inches apart. Bloom will occur about eight weeks from seeding, and if all goes well, seed sown in May will produce flowering plants by midsummer, just in time for the August slump, when early summer perennials and annuals are done and the great autumn show has not yet begun. (Earlier bloom may be had by seeding China asters indoors in late March or early April, but seeds germinate slowly and young plants are extremely susceptible to the fungal disease called "damping off" and also to aphids.)

Once a good stand of China asters is growing in the garden, however, and even budding up for bloom, troubles are not over. The plant is susceptible at any point to two other fungus diseases. The first, aster yellows, may be recognized by sickly, pale growth, small or deformed flowers, and a stunted look to the plants. The fungus is spread by leaf hoppers, and frequent precautionary spraying, on the assumption that they might appear, is the best safeguard. As the fungus appears to have a short but active life underground, annual rotation of the areas in which China asters are grown will also help prevent the disease.

For the second fungal disease, aster wilt, there is no safeguard at all, for it enters the roots of plants directly and is invariably fatal. It also remains dormant in the soil for long periods of time, and so where it is prevalent, the growing of China asters should simply be given up. Wilt-resistant varieties are sometimes offered, though resistance does not mean immunity, and gardeners who have once been struck by aster wilt may find resistant varieties also susceptible.

Still, China asters can be so beautiful, particularly in the rich, deep purple and plush-red shades, that one may feel one has to grow them, at least occasionally. If so, one can follow the suggestion of the great English gardener Christopher Lloyd, and grow them only in pots, in sterilized soil mix. They accept pot culture very well, and they may be carefully watered and fed frequently with water-soluble fertilizer to achieve magnificent results. The length a plant will be in bloom, either in a pot or in the garden, is relatively brief, no more than five weeks or so, and unlike most other true annuals, picking or dead-heading actually seems to inhibit bloom. But one could have a sequence of potted specimens in bloom throughout the summer, and in the case of some of the more compact varieties that cover themselves with flower all at once, each pot would be a living bouquet.

CAPSICUM ANNUUM

FAMILY: *Solanaceae* or deadly nightshade family.

CLASSIFICATION: Tender annual, short-lived perennial, or shrub grown as a tender annual.

COMMON NAMES: Ornamental pepper, bird's eye pepper, capsicum.

HARDINESS: Hardy to Zone 10. Damaged elsewhere by temperatures below 40°F. Leaves extremely frost sensitive.

GROWING CONDITIONS: Moist, well-drained, fertile soil. Full sun.

PROPAGATION: By seed, sown 8 to 10 weeks before last expected frost. Cuttings may be taken of choice varieties.

HEIGHT: From 1 to 5', depending on variety.

ORNAMENTAL VALUE: Valued for ornamental fruit, borne from midsummer to frost.

LEVEL OF CULTURAL DIFFICULTY: Easy.

SPECIAL PROPERTIES: Fruit used as a pungent seasoning.

PRONUNCIATION: kap-SI-cum an-NUE-um

*A*ll peppers are of tropical American origin, where they have been cultivated for at least 9,000 years. So long an association with humanity inevitably results in significant modifications in a plant, and so, from a botanical point of view, peppers represent a confused race. Whether there are several distinct species and many hybrids in the genus or one single species from which hundreds of varieties have descended is uncertain. Most botanists believe, however, that widely different forms were developed out of a single ancestor, *Capsicum annuum,* a stout, shrubby plant that grows as an annual or sometimes a short-lived perennial or shrub, and that is capable of achieving as much as eight feet of growth in its native habitat. It bears small, yellow or red, pungent,

inch-round fruit, quite similar to those ornamental varieties of pepper called bird's eyes. Though most of the world's peppers are in fact grown as annuals, "annuum" seems hardly appropriate for a shrub that can persist from year to year in warm climates (USDA Zone 10), and so some botanists prefer the species name *frutescens* (fru-TES-ens), meaning bushy. The genus name *Capsicum* originates either from the ancient Greek word *kapto,* meaning to bite, or the Latin *capsa,* signifying a box or chest, a logical allusion to the hollow, several-chambered fruits in which seed is encased.

As with other food crops that seem to have diversified remarkably from a single wild progenitor (the brassicas, for example), cultivars are grouped by type, in this case of fruit. Five general categories are recognized: *cerasiforme* (se-ra-see-FOR-muh), the cherry peppers with small, rounded fruit; *conoides* (co-NOI-des), with erect, one- to two-inch, cone-shaped fruit; *fasciculatum* (fa-si-cu-LA-tum), the cluster peppers with multiple, erect, three-inch-long fruit; *grossum* (GROW-sum), the familiar "bell" peppers; and *longum* (LON-gum), with down-hanging fruit as much as a foot in length. Though all peppers are attractive plants, it is from the first three categories of small-fruited forms that those grown for ornamental value have been drawn. Within these categories, however, are many varieties prized in Southeast Asian cooking for their fiery heat, and also for their natural antibacterial properties. A recent increased interest both in Southeast Asian and in authentic Mexican and Central American cooking has made many highly decorative peppers newly available to American gardeners through specialty seed companies, to the extent that anyone inordinately fond of peppers could have a whole garden, just of them.

Generally, small-fruited peppers are borne profusely on dense, twiggy, pleasantly rounded bushes that mature at a height of a foot or slightly taller. The small, smooth leaves are typically laurel-green, though in some varieties they may be purple-veined, or all purple, or purplish-brown splashed and marbled with cream or white. Fruits, which are prominently displayed across the top of the plant, may be round or cone shaped, according to variety. Young fruits will generally be white, ivory, or pale yellow, deepening in tint to red, purple-red, purple, or almost black as they mature. Peppers remain in attractive condition on the plant for a long period of time, so quite impressive displays can build up over the summer. (One should always wear gloves when working around ornamental peppers and certainly when harvesting and preparing the fruit for cooking because its juice can burn sensitive skin tissue under fingernails or around the eyes.)

Both for ornamental and culinary uses, the culture of all peppers is the same. Seed is started indoors or under glass eight to ten weeks before the last expected frost. Germination occurs best at temperatures around 70°F, and young plants should be grown on in the brightest possible light at similar temperatures, then be set out into the garden or established in containers outdoors about two weeks after the last frost. Because peppers relish warm conditions—developing best when daytime temperatures remain well above 70°F—there is little point in rushing to plant them early. They also need a longer period to mature than tomatoes, and they are greedy feeders, relishing supplemental fertilizer, in either granular or liquid form. Phosphorus, particularly, is required for abundant flower and fruit set. (Old-time gardeners used to bury two or three kitchen matches under the roots of each transplant.) Soils should be humus-rich and water-retentive, but well drained. Plants require irrigation during

CAPSICUM ANNUUM

periods of drought, and as much sun as they can possibly receive.

Though ornamental peppers are attractive in both the vegetable and the flower garden, many are also grown as single potted specimens for indoor decoration in autumn and winter. Like another Central American plant, the poinsettia, they have become associated with Christmas, though they are equally attractive in early and late autumn. When cultivated in pots for indoor decoration, they should never experience a check in their growth by being pot-bound or underwatered. Also, they must be protected from chills and drafts. Any of these conditions will cause ornamental peppers to drop their leaves. Once a plant is in decline, it is very difficult to restore it to full health indoors.

CARDIOSPERMUM HALICACABUM

FAMILY: *Sapindaceae* or golden rain tree family.

CLASSIFICATION. Tender perennial vine grown as tender annual vine.

COMMON NAMES: Balloon vine, heartsease, heartseed, love-in-a-puff, cardiospermum.

HARDINESS: Root-hardy to Zone 7. Uncomfortable at temperatures below 40°F.

GROWING CONDITIONS: Moderately fertile, well-drained soil. Full sun.

PROPAGATION: By seed, sown in peat pots 6 weeks before last expected frost. Resents root disturbance.

HEIGHT: To 10', more where root-hardy.

ORNAMENTAL VALUE: Grown for vining habit and for attractive seed pods.

LEVEL OF CULTURAL DIFFICULTY: Easy.

SPECIAL PROPERTIES: None.

PRONUNCIATION: kar-dee-o-SPER-mum ha-li-KA-ka-bum

Sometimes plants are cultivated not because they are edible for humans or beasts, or possess medicinal value, or are just simply pretty, but because they carry some association or have some trick in them that amuses or intrigues us. *Cardiospermum halicacabum* is such a plant. As a modest vine its leaves are pretty enough—a trident of deeply toothed leaflets in fresh, medium green, the central one about three inches long and the flanking ones slightly shorter—but the flowers, minute white specks, usually bloom completely without notice. The seeds, however, are the reason gardeners cultivate *C. halicacabum*. Jet black, hardly the size of a pea, each is marked with a tiny, chalk-white heart. They are encased in light green, three-sided papery globes, about an inch and a half across, inflated like small balloons that dance on long stems among the leaves. By summer's end, when the globes turn buff brown, they are ready to open to reveal their secret.

Assuming that all characteristics of plants and animals have some evolutionary purpose, some edge in the scramble for survival, it is hard to know why "heartseed" (a literal translation of the genus name, from the ancient Greek *kardia,* meaning heart, and *sperma,* a seed) is marked as it is. Except, of course, that gardeners continue to plant it just for its tiny valentines. It may be that plants are cleverer than we suppose at exploiting us for their survival.

A perennial herbaceous vine, *C. halicacabum* is presumed to be native to southern Texas and Florida to Bermuda, but it's naturalized throughout the warmer regions of the world. It is able to regrow from winter-dormant rootstock each spring in Zone 7 gardens and warmer (Zone 6 with protection). Elsewhere, it is grown as an annual vine that will form seed from a late spring sowing by autumn, or earlier if sown in peat pots about six weeks before the last frost date, and

CARDIOSPERMUM HALICACABUM

transplanted with great care when the weather becomes warm and settled. The seed is quite hard, and so germination is more rapid if it is soaked overnight in water, filed lightly, or rubbed between two pieces of sandpaper as one would with morning glory seed.

Though the growth of cardiospermum is rapid in warm weather, it may not be described as rampant. It will scramble by means of tendrils over any support to a length of about ten feet, forming a pleasant drapery over spring-blooming shrubs—supplying an extra season of interest—and a splendid covering for chain-link fences. When grown to cover walls, board fences, or the sides of outbuildings, it will need a trellis or a grid of strings to cling to.

CARPANTHEA POMERIDIANA

FAMILY: *Aizoaceae* or ice plant family.

CLASSIFICATION: Half-hardy annual.

COMMON NAMES: Ice plant, carpanthea.

HARDINESS: Not hardy much below 40°F.

GROWING CONDITIONS: Perfectly drained, gravelly soil of moderate fertility. Cool nights and bright warm days. Full sun.

PROPAGATION: By seed, sown indoors 6 to 8 weeks before last frost date.

HEIGHT: 6″ to 1′.

ORNAMENTAL VALUE: Blooms mid- to late summer. Succulent leaves also attractive.

LEVEL OF CULTURAL DIFFICULTY: Easy where growing conditions are ideal. Difficult elsewhere.

SPECIAL PROPERTIES: None.

PRONUNCIATION: kar-pan-THEE-a pom-uh-RI-dee-ana

CARPANTHEA POMERIDIANA

*I*n the last twenty years or so, gardeners have become steadily more interested in the flora of South Africa as a neglected source of interesting annual and tender plants. *Carpanthea pomeridiana,* an unusual and beautiful garden plant, is a prime example. A native of the Cape Province and a true annual, it is a succulent, which is to say that it has modified its leaves and stems to store water, but also that it has a fragile, juicy look, which cacti seldom do. It forms a much-branched, erect plant to about a foot in height, clad with four-inch-long, flattish, blade-shaped leaves about an inch in width. Plants appear silver from a thick coating of downy white hair on leaves and stems, a device that presumably protects them against scorching sun, and also possibly traps condensation and dew.

Flowers develop on terminal growths, and as with many succulents, they are surprisingly large for the size of the plant, as much as three inches across, borne singly on inch-long hairy stems. They are quite showy, consisting of many thin, fringy petals complexly shaded from straw at the tips to golden yellow and then to greenish lemon-yellow at the center. The outer petals face down, and inner layers are carried erect or curved inward, creating a cupped effect. As the Latin species name *pomeridiana* (the middle of the day) indicates, the flowers open at midday.

Because carpanthea is a succulent, it will be easy for some gardeners, and hard-to-perhaps-impossible for others. It requires a perfectly well-drained gritty soil, but one also that is reasonably fertile and moisture-retentive. Heavy, sour, or soggy soils will be fatal, causing plants to rot off at the roots. Carpanthea will also require a high proportion of hot, bright, sunny days during the summer, and ideally, cool, fresh nights like the "Mediterranean climate" of southern California. Because of both its cultural needs and its appearance, it would be best suited—and look best—in a rock garden, perhaps with the companionship of the white-flowered Mexican prickly poppy, *Argemone grandiflora,* or the California poppy, *Eschscholzia californica,* both of which share its needs.

For early flower, carpanthea should be seeded indoors on sterilized potting medium to which sharp sand or perlite has been liberally added to ensure perfect drainage. After seedlings germinate, flats should be kept in a fresh, airy environment and the medium should be allowed to dry out slightly between waterings and never become waterlogged, as a deterrent to the fungal disease called "damping off." Plants should not be established outdoors until the weather has become quite warm and settled, which in most American gardens is somewhere around the second week of June. Though flowers may not appear until late August, carpanthea can also be direct seeded in the garden after danger of frost has passed. Damping off is never a serious problem in the open air, though where spring rains are heavy, a pane of glass might be propped over the seed bed to prevent the soil from becoming saturated.

CARTHAMUS TINCTORIUS

FAMILY: *Asteraceae* or aster or daisy family.

CLASSIFICATION: Hardy annual.

COMMON NAMES: Safflower, false saffron, bastard saffron, distaff thistle, carthamus.

HARDINESS: Frost-hardy.

GROWING CONDITIONS: Moderately fertile, moist, well-drained soil. Full sun.

PROPAGATION: By seed, sown in place just after last frost.

HEIGHT: To 4′.

ORNAMENTAL VALUE: Flowers mid- to late summer.

LEVEL OF CULTURAL DIFFICULTY: Easy.

SPECIAL PROPERTIES: Used as a dye plant and in cosmetics. Seed valued for cooking oil.

PRONUNCIATION: KAR-tha-mus tink-TOR-ee-us

*A*lthough the date of its first cultivation is lost to history, *Carthamus tinctorius* was used to tint silks in ancient times. The flowers of the plant—variously yellow, pink, purple, or violet—yield a dye that may be rendered into any shade of pink, rose, or clear red as its species name *tinctorius,* meaning a plant valued for dyeing, indicates. And for centuries Arabic women have used the powdered flower heads as rouge, lip coloring, and a tinting for palms and the soles of feet. (The name of the genus is a Latinized version of an ancient Arabic word, *quartom,* meaning to paint.) By the medieval period, the dried flowers were also used in Europe as a substitute, albeit an inferior one, for saffron, hence the modern name "safflower," which descends through the Middle English *saffleur* from the Old Italian *safflore.* The pearly, four-sided seed of the safflower, extremely rich in oil, is now of enormous dietary importance, since it is the highest in polyunsaturated fats of all oils suitable for cooking and is an excellent source of Vitamin E.

Carthamus tinctorius belongs to the family Asteraceae (formerly Compositae), a family so vast that it has been divided into twelve tribes. The genus *Carthamus* is placed in the Carduus tribe, which contains all thistles, since it shares with them more-or-less spiny leaves, a prominent row of leaflike bracts surrounding the flower heads, and blooms composed entirely of disk flowers (the fertile center of a daisy) with no ray flowers or petals. Blooms are about an inch long and wide, and consist of a gathering of hair-fine, fringy flowers, a form that is typical of most thistles. They may be variously colored orange-red, bright orange, lemon or primrose yellow, and more rarely violet to purple. Unlike many other annuals, which are to be preferred in single colors, all shades are attractive in a mix. When cut, flowers last an unusually long time in water, and they may also be dried for winter arrangements.

Like most thistles carthamus is of very easy culture, developing well in almost any soil. Seed may be sown in March indoors but is usually sown directly in the garden after all danger of frost is past. Little is gained by starting seed for early bloom, as safflowers may become shabby after their midsummer flowering, a condition that should be delayed as long as possible.

Safflowers are stout of growth and remain erect without staking, achieving a height of as much as four feet before coming into flower. Leaves are broadly oval, dark green, and spiny, decreasing up the stem until they modify as bracts forming a stiff ruff around the flowers. As the plants are somewhat coarse in texture, their best use is perhaps in the wilder parts of the garden, at the edge of a meadow, or in open places along a hedgerow.

CATHARANTHUS ROSEUS (SYN. *VINCA ROSEA*)

FAMILY: *Apocynaceae* or vinca family.

CLASSIFICATION: Tender perennial grown as half-hardy annual.

COMMON NAMES: Annual periwinkle, bush periwinkle, Madagascar periwinkle, old maid, catharanthus.

HARDINESS: Hardy in Zones 9 and 10. Not hardy much below 40°F.

GROWING CONDITIONS: Moderately fertile, moist, well-drained soil. Full to part sun. Heat.

PROPAGATION: By seed, sown in late February. Cuttings root easily.

HEIGHT: From 8″ to 2′, depending on cultivar.

ORNAMENTAL VALUE: Flowers late spring to frost.

LEVEL OF CULTURAL DIFFICULTY: Easy.

SPECIAL PROPERTIES: Superb container plant. Excellent winter-flowering houseplant for sunny windowsill.

PRONUNCIATION: ka-tha-RAN-thus ROS-ee-us (VIN-ca RO-see-a)

*M*any people are given their first hint that an "annual" is not always an annual by seeing masses of *Catharanthus roseus* naturalized in southern Florida. The two-foot-high, ragged bushes are clearly not of one single season's growth. Like so many plants treated as annuals, it is actually a tender perennial, native to the Old World Tropics, chiefly to Madagascar (hence one common name) and to India. It was first cultivated in the Jardin du Roi in Paris in the eighteenth century, when Madagascar was under French control, and has for many years been a staple "annual" for the summer garden, particularly where summers are very hot. For most of its botanical history, it has

CATHARANTHUS ROSEUS

been classified as *Vinca rosea,* and is still often listed under that name in botanical references.

The original Madagascar periwinkle is a much-branched but somewhat rangy shrublike plant—up to two feet tall—bearing at the tips of branches inch-wide flowers consisting of a fused tube and five rounded lobes. Each lobe (the "petals" of the flower) slightly overlaps its neighbor on the left side, creating a pinwheel effect. *Catharanthus* is taken from two ancient Greek words, *katharos,* meaning pure, and *anthos,* flower. The name seems more than merely fanciful, for there is a certain innocence to the winsome, staring blossoms of the plant, and they have a faintly bitter, antiseptic smell of cleanliness. The name *roseus* recognizes the deep pink flowers of the species, though a white form was early known.

The Madagascar periwinkle has been much improved by modern breeding, first made more compact to about ten inches (though even dwarfer forms exist), and of a thicker, more fully branched structure. Colors have been purified, eliminating the trace of lavender in the pink of the species, to create plants bearing flowers of pale and deep pink shading into violet, and warmer pinks veering toward apricot. A clear carmine red with a white eye represents a color breakthrough, as do whites and light pinks with an eye approaching yellow. All

these improved forms should be available at most good nurseries, where healthy young plants, often showing their first precocious bloom in the six-pack (for they bloom young and then continuously), can be found in spring.

Although plants are not difficult to grow from seed, they are very slow. Seed should be sown in late February for plants that may be set out in the garden only after frosts are over. Seed germinates readily in one to two weeks, and the young plants must be grown on under bright conditions around 70°F. They transplant easily, and indeed, may be moved as mature young plants if taken up with a generous root ball, watered well, and shaded until they adjust.

Except in the hottest climates, where afternoon shade will be appreciated, the Madagascar periwinkle thrives best in full sun. It requires moderately rich, well-drained soil, and should not be allowed to dry out completely at any time. It is of particular value where summers are very warm, for it flowers most profusely then, providing color under conditions that cause other perennials, annuals, and tender plants to fail. Its love of heat and its capacity to bloom nonstop under difficult conditions make the Madagascar periwinkle particularly valuable in containers and hanging baskets. Since each plant is of an attractive bushy shape and well furnished with handsome leaves and flowers, single specimens are also beautiful in eight-inch clay pots as decorations for terraces, decks, or balconies. Grown this way, the plants may be brought indoors for winter flowering on a sunny windowsill, sun porch, or in a heated greenhouse. Cuttings root easily and may be taken in late winter from stock plants for summer flowering. The handsome, variegated form of the plant, which is very useful in containers and hanging baskets, does not come true from seed, and so may only be carried over from year to year in this way. It is, however, a treasure that is worth the trouble, such as it is.

CELOSIA SPECIES

FAMILY: *Amaranthaceae* or amaranth family.

CLASSIFICATION: Tender perennials grown as half-hardy annuals.

COMMON NAMES: Cockscomb, wool flower, prince's feathers, celosia.

HARDINESS: Not hardy much below 40°F.

GROWING CONDITIONS: Rich, moist, well-drained soil. Full sun. Heat.

PROPAGATION: By seed, sown indoors in April or outdoors in mid-May.

HEIGHT: 6″ to 6′, depending on cultivar.

ORNAMENTAL VALUE: Grown for flower.

LEVEL OF CULTURAL DIFFICULTY: Easy, if grown on without a check.

SPECIAL PROPERTIES: Valued as dried flowers for wreaths and dried arrangements. Excellent plants for containers.

PRONUNCIATION: sel-O-see-a

The only trouble with good taste is that it can so easily become boring. Now that many gardeners have had their fill of the English-inspired, misty, pastel borders, they find themselves turning to brighter colors, more arresting leaf shapes, and botanical oddities. Celosia, in all these regards, have been waiting in the wings. Whether bred as four-foot giants or six-inch midgets, they are always stout, stocky, coarse-leaved plants. Their inflorescences are usually the brashest shades of pumpkin orange, taxi yellow, or flaming scarlet, sometime with bronze foliage thrown in for good measure. The shapes of the flowering structures, though often a tolerably familiar bunched cob of spires, can also be fantastically twisted and lobed, looking, as is often remarked, like a brain. It is true that plant breeders have created forms with arrow leaves and elegant single spires of bloom—

what one might call "well-bred" celosia—in delicate shades of pink and white. But the celosia that are currently exciting to many gardeners are precisely those that are uncompromisingly celosia-like.

Three species of *Celosia* are often listed in catalogues: *Celosia argentea* (ar-GEN-tee-a), *C. cristata* (cris-TA-ta), and *C. plumosa* (plu-MO-sa). In fact, all garden celosia appear to be selections from *C. argentea,* a pan-tropical weed that can grow to as much as nine feet in a single season, bearing coarse, narrow leaves and oblong, silvery white inflorescences about four inches long. Flowers are inconspicuous, nestled in chaffy structures that remain in good condition as seed matures. A close relative of the garden amaranths, celosia have some importance in the Orient as a leafy vegetable, though they entered European gardens in the sixteenth century purely as ornamentals. In its original form, *C. argentea* still has its admirers, though most celosia now grown are far different in appearance and much more vividly colored. (The genus name *Celosia* is drawn from the ancient Greek *keleos,* meaning burning.)

Celosia are divided into two groups (formerly species): the cockscombs (*cristata*) and the prince's feathers (*plumosa*). In the former group are those with fantastically shaped, generally lobed or fanned inflorescences, in many colors, from white, straw yellow, deep yellow to orange, pink, scarlet, deep red, and bronze. Plants may be six inches to two feet in height, depending on variety. Though their odd appearance makes them difficult to combine with less eccentric garden flowers, they can be attractive against other bold shapes (such as ornamental cabbages) in self-conscious, carpet bedding designs or in containers. They are valued for dried arrangements, and particularly for making tight plush wreaths.

CELOSIA SPICATA

Plumosa forms, by contrast, though still borne on rather rigid plants, bear softer inflorescences that may be very attractive in informal bedding schemes, particularly when grouped by color. Colors, also, are often softer, including rose and melon shades, silvery pinks and whites, though the full range of violent scarlets, oranges, and yellow also exists. In this group, too, are the most vivid of all celosias, those with dark, purplish foliage and scarlet or deep red flowers. Plumosa forms are also valued for dried arrangements, looking particularly fine among tawny brown and wheat-colored grasses.

Because celosias flower about two months from germination, plants grown from seed outdoors in late spring will produce flowers in August and September, at which time perhaps their strong colors look best. Earlier flower may be had by sowing seed indoors about five weeks from the last anticipated frost date, a desirable practice if plants are wanted for pots or containers. However, any check experienced by young plants will force them into premature flower, even when tiny, and once they have formed bloom structures, they will never develop into good specimens. Therefore, plants grown indoors should be seeded in peat pots, never allowed to dry out, and transplanted to the garden with great care after all danger of frost is past. (Obviously, young plants in bloom at the nursery, cute as they may be, should be passed over.) For best development, celosias require a rich, moist, well-drained soil and plenty of heat. Feeding with granular fertilizer may, however, cause the cockscomb sorts to crack or split, and so they should be fed with water-soluble fertilizer at half the strength but twice as often as the regimen suggested on the package. Celosias are at their best in hot, humid conditions where no one would venture out into the garden at midday.

Recently, another species of *Celosia* has become popular, *C. spicata,* particularly in the selected strain marketed as 'Flamingo'. Plants form upright, well-branched clumps to about a foot tall, and flowers are produced in narrow, pointed spires at the tips of branches. The chaffy inflorescence in which they are borne—the showy part of the plant—displays a cool lavender-pink from first formation, shading down to silver at the base as the minute, inconspicuous flowers come into bloom and form seed. In effect, bloom spikes are rather like ears of grain, with which they are often combined in winter arrangements, as they preserve their color for several years when dried. For this purpose, a row or two of plants might be grown in the cutting or vegetable garden, since whole plants should be uprooted when flowering stems are well developed, and hung upside down in a dark, airy place to dry.

All celosias make excellent container plants, since they enjoy heat, particularly at their roots. Some of the most vividly colored cultivars and those with crinkled or crimped inflorescences look even better in pots or containers than in the open garden, where their sometimes stodgy growth and single, fantastic "bloom" make them difficult to compose with other garden flowers.

CENTAUREA SPECIES

FAMILY: *Asteraceae* or aster or daisy family.

CLASSIFICATION: Hardy annuals.

COMMON NAMES: Knapweed, bachelor's buttons, cornflower, ragged robin, ragged sailors, blue bonnets, bluebottle, hardheads, centaurea.

HARDINESS: Withstand light frosts.

GROWING CONDITIONS: Well-drained, moderately fertile, limey soils. Full sun.

PROPAGATION: By seed, sown indoors in peat pots in late April or outdoors just after frost. May be sown in autumn in Zone 6 gardens and warmer.

HEIGHT: 15″ to 4′, depending on cultivar.

ORNAMENTAL VALUE: Grown for flower. *C. cineraria* valued for silvery-gray foliage.

LEVEL OF CULTURAL DIFFICULTY: Easy.

SPECIAL PROPERTIES: Leaves used as poultices and for treatment of rheumatism.

PRONUNCIATION: sin-TOH-ree-ah

Centaurea cyanus (si-AN-us) carries an impressive string of common names, indicating both its long history in gardens and the degree to which it has been cherished. Its limpid blue, ragged blossoms once made glorious the wheat fields of Europe and England, along with the rose corn cockle (*Agrostemma githago*) and the scarlet corn poppy (*Papaver rhoeas*). To the grain farmer, however, it was merely an unproductive weed, a nuisance to be tolerated until modern selective herbicides virtually eliminated it from cultivated ground. But its place in gardens has been firmly established since the sixteenth century, first as a medicinal herb and later for its floral beauty. The most frequently grown annual species within its genus, *Centaurea cyanus* is widely cultivated in Holland for the world cut-flower market, particularly in winter, since plants may be easily forced into bloom under relatively cool temperature, and the blooms last well in water.

In its wild form, *C. cyanus* is a sprawling, somewhat rangy, much-branched plant growing about a foot and a half tall, with narrow, five-inch-long leaves, abundant in a basal tuft and sparser along the stems. Both stems and leaves are covered with minute silver hairs, giving them a grayish cast. Flowers are borne in profusion at the tips of the stems, appearing first as cunningly crafted buds covered over with scaly bracts and looking like tiny artichokes. Bloom consists of a tight bunch of disk flowers surrounded by a single row of fringy petals of clear, light blue, though darker blue, white, and violet forms occur in wild populations. Modern breeding work has created more compact plants from fifteen inches to four feet in height, depending on variety, and has extended the color range to pale pink, deep purple, and wine red. Flowers have also been generally doubled to form fluffy heads, the darker forms displaying an almost black center.

Of easy culture, *C. cyanus* thrives in well-drained, moderately fertile, limey soil. As it resents root disturbance, it is best sown where it is to grow in very early spring, as soon as the ground is workable. In gardens south of Zone 5, however, the finest plants will be produced by treating it as a biennial, sowing seed in early October to produce rosettes of growth before the arrival of winter. Technically a hardy annual,

C. cyanus blooms best in cool weather, flowering about six weeks from seed germination. Where summers are hot and muggy, it may be subject to powdery mildew, best minimized by not allowing the plants to experience drought. *C. cyanus* is an essential component of an annual flowering meadow, which would be almost unthinkable without it.

The genus *Centaurea* draws its name from the Greek *centaur,* Chiron, who used the leaves of *C. cyanus* to cure a wound inflicted by the arrow of Hercules. Modern herbalists still use infusions of the flowers and leaves as treatment for scrapes and to alleviate the pain of rheumatism.

In addition to *C. cyanus,* two other members of the genus may be grown as annuals. *Centaurea americana* (a-mer-i-CA-na), the basket flower native to the central United States and Mexico, grows to as much as six feet in height, bearing four-inch-wide, recognizably centaurea-like flowers: a single row of delicate, threadlike pink to rose-lavender petals surrounding a pincushion of fertile, yellow disk flowers. Unopened buds are covered with fringed, webbed bracts that later spread out, forming the basket in which the flower sits. Named forms exist in pure white and in a richer lilac pink. In culture, *C. americana* is identical to *C. cyanus,* though being such a large plant, it will require more space.

Though technically a half-hardy perennial persisting over winter in Zone 7 gardens and warmer, *Centaurea cineraria* (sin-uh-RA-ree-a) is often grown as an annual for its fine, lacy silver foliage. It takes its species name from the Latin adjective *cinereus,* meaning ash-colored, and is popularly called dusty miller, though that name is shared with *Senecio cineraria* and with several artemisias. Generally propagated from cuttings or bought as young plants, it is at its best in summer heat, becoming silverest in full, broiling sun. Its preference for heat makes it a valuable container plant.

CENTRADENIA SPECIES

FAMILY: *Melastomataceae* or melastoma family.

CLASSIFICATION: Tender shrub grown as tender annual.

COMMON NAME: Centradenia.

HARDINESS: Sensitive to temperatures below 50°F. Killed by light frost.

GROWING CONDITIONS: Moist, very rich, well-drained soil. Filtered sun. Must not be allowed to dry out.

PROPAGATION: From cuttings taken of terminal shoots when in active growth.

HEIGHT: Cascading to 2' or upright to 5', depending on species.

ORNAMENTAL VALUE: Grown for colored foliage.

LEVEL OF CULTURAL DIFFICULTY: Easy.

SPECIAL PROPERTIES: Excellent plant for pots and containers.

PRONUNCIATION: sin-tra-DEEN-ee-a

*I*t is always pleasant when a botanical name tells a story, offers a vivid description of a plant, or signals some important attribute it possesses. The genus designation of *Centradenia,* however, does none of these things, signifying merely a spurlike gland on the anthers of the flowers (from ancient Greek *kentron,* meaning spur, and *aden,* gland). The genus comprises only five species and is at present probably unfamiliar to most gardeners. (With equal probability, so is the family to which it belongs, the Melastomataceae, comprising some 240 genera and 3,000 species of Old and New World tropical trees and shrubs.) But the search for tender annuals and perennials has begun to make centradenia popular, particularly as it thrives in containers.

Two species of *Centradenia* are currently offered by nurseries specializing in unusual annual and tender plants. The first, *C. inaequilateralis* (in-ay-qwi-la-ter-A-lis), takes its curious species name from the fact that its paired leaves are unequal in length. Leaves are pointed, about four inches long (more or less), and tinted purple. Stems are lax and cascading to about two feet in length, making the plant an attractive subject for window boxes, hanging baskets, or the edges of large containers of mixed annual and tender plants. Flowers of a vivid rose pink bloom in profusion all summer, and consist of dense clusters of four-lobed tubes an inch and a half long by half an inch wide.

The other species of *Centradenia* sometimes offered is *C. grandiflora* (gran-di-FLO-ra), with upright, shrubby growth to five feet, also with purple-tinted leaves, but bright red on the undersides. It flowers most profusely in spring and early summer, producing terminal clusters of rose-pink flowers on thin stems, and for flower, is best grown in a conservatory, greenhouse, or heated sun porch. (Flowering branches last well when cut, and occasionally are offered by sophisticated florists as winter and early spring cut flowers.) The tinted leaves of *C. grandiflora* continue to make it an attractive and interesting plant throughout the summer, even when not in flower.

Centradenia may be expected to thrive anywhere that fuchsias do well. Natives of tropical Mexico and Guatemala, they grow in moist, fertile conditions at the verges of forests. As potted plants, they require a soil rich in compost, water-retentive but very well drained. Both complete drying out and excess water at the roots will be fatal. As with fuchsias, cuttings taken from non-flowering shoots root easily at any time. Young plants should be pinched occasionally to promote branching, and older plants are pruned to maintain full, abundant growth. Centradenia are very sensitive to frost, and also dislike cold, raw weather. They should therefore not be established outdoors until the weather is warm and

CENTRADENIA GRANDIFLORA

settled, usually the second week of June for most American gardens.

CERINTHE MAJOR

FAMILY: *Boraginaceae* or borage family.

CLASSIFICATION: Hardy annual.

COMMON NAMES: Honeywort, cerinthe.

HARDINESS: Hardy to light frosts.

GROWING CONDITIONS: Moderately fertile to poor but moist soil. Cool temperatures. Full sun.

PROPAGATION: By seed, sown in peat pots about 6 weeks before last frost, or in place just after last frost. Resents root disturbance.

HEIGHT: To 2′.

ORNAMENTAL VALUE: Valued for leaves, bracts, and flowers.

LEVEL OF CULTURAL DIFFICULTY: Easy.

SPECIAL PROPERTIES: Grown as a bee plant since ancient times.

PRONUNCIATION: ser-IN-thee MA-jer

The words *aristocratic, subtle,* and *refined* are often applied to *Cerinthe major,* indicating, as they generally do, a plant to be grown more for the pleasures of close study than for masses of high-impact color. The plant is beautiful in all its parts, but none carries the forceful assertiveness typical of the most popular annuals for summer bedding. *C. major* is native to Greece and the Mediterranean, where, as its common name indicates, it has always been an important bee plant, but only in the last five years or so has it begun to appear in American gardens. This is partly because gardeners are actively seeking a wider range of annual and tender plants, and partly because they have begun to value those of quiet charm, realizing that not everything in the summer garden should create vivid waves of color.

C. major grows as an open plant with few branches, creating an airy scaffold for the display of the leaves, bracts, and flowers. Leaves at the base of the plant are oval, with down-turned spooned edges, and are about six to eight inches long. At one time, the waxy, gray-green foliage was believed to be a source of beeswax. (*Kerinos,* the ancient Greek word from which the species takes its name, means waxen.) The leaves decrease in size as they spiral up the stems until they modify into bracts clasping the flowers and unopened buds. In the typical species, leaves are occasionally spotted or freckled with white, and the bracts at the ends of the stems may be tinged gold, olive drab, or purple. Flowers are down-hanging three-quarter-inch-long tubes, colored maroon red for the first third of their length, and then, without any shading or modification, turning chrome yellow. Each small bell is slightly pinched at the end, creating a mouth, and the inside of each bell is a lighter yellow fading almost to cream.

Though the typical form of *Cerinthe major* is charming, many gardeners consider a naturally occurring variant, *Cerinthe major* var. *purpurescens* (pur-pur-ES-ens), so superior as to displace it altogether. Its upper leaves are a deeper gray-green, carrying a tinge of blue that intensifies to bluish-purple in the clasping bracts. Flowers are also blue tending to purple (which the Latin adjective *purpurescens* means) and though only three fourths of an inch long, they can be quite vivid. There is no color of flower that is not made more beautiful by the companionship of the plant, its gray-green and blue complementing both hot, vibrant shades of red, orange, and yellow, and also gentler shades of white, silver, pink, mauve, and blue.

Cerinthe major should either be sown in place in the garden in early spring, or seeded in peat pots or plastic cell packs about six weeks before the last frost-free date. Care should be taken in transplanting young plants into garden soil, as they resent root disturbance. Too much fertility will cause the plants to grow rank, flop over, and color poorly. Color is best in cool weather, and if plants become shabby in the heat of high summer, they should be pulled and replaced, as cutting them to the ground produces next to nothing. Cerinthe is a hardy annual that will self-seed in all but the coldest gardens. In warm gardens seedlings may appear in late summer and develop through the autumn to flower the fol-

CERINTHE MAJOR

lowing spring, behaving essentially as biennials or weak perennials.

CHENOPODIUM SPECIES

FAMILY: *Chenopodiaceae* or goosefoot family.

CLASSIFICATION: Hardy annuals.

COMMON NAMES: Goosefoot, chenopodium (other common names vary with species).

HARDINESS: Withstands light frost.

GROWING CONDITIONS: Any soil.

PROPAGATION: By seed, usually sown in place; abundant self-seeders.

HEIGHT: From 1 to 8', depending on species.

ORNAMENTAL VALUE: Grown for moderately attractive leaves. *C. amaranticolor* is useful as quick-growing hedge or screen.

LEVEL OF CULTURAL DIFFICULTY: Easy.

SPECIAL PROPERTIES: Several species anciently treasured as grain, seasoning herbs, and as salad or cooked greens.

PRONUNCIATION: chin-o-PO-dee-um

Of the 250 or so species in the genus *Chenopodium,* several have for centuries been significant sources of food for people throughout the world. The protein-rich seed of *Chenopodium quinoa* (ki-NO-a, qwi-NO-a), for example, was a staple grain of the Aztecs, though its culture was suppressed by Christian missionaries because it was mixed with human blood for ritual consumption. *C. ambrosioides* (am-bro-zee-OY-des) is epazote, an herb favored in the cooking of Central and South American countries. Both *Chenopodium album* (AL-bum), lambs quarters, and *C. bonus-henricus* (BO-nus HEN-ree-cus), good King Henry, allgood, or wild spinach, have been gathered since ancient times as greens, the

first to use in salads and the second to cook as a substitute for spinach. The edible-leaved forms of chenopodium have anciently been called "goosefoot" from the shape of their foliage, that being a literal translation of the ancient Greek words from which the genus and family draw their names, from *chen,* a goose, and *podion,* small foot.

Many species of *Chenopodium* have naturalized around the globe, occurring as rank weeds bearing trident- or arrow-shaped leaves on stout, woody stems. All are abundant self-seeders, adapted to poor soils and relative drought, though thriving better in the rich soils of roadside ditches and at the edges of midden heaps. They are usually among the first weedy species to move into disturbed or degraded land, as those who gather *Chenopodium album* or *C. bonus-henricus* for greens know well. (Diana Kennedy, the great authority on Mexican cooking, happily found a naturalized stand of epazote growing in Central Park.)

When healthy and well grown, all species of *Chenopodium* seem to have a certain attractiveness born of forceful vigor, but only a single species in the genus is cultivated as an ornamental. *Chenopodium amaranticolor* (am-a-ran-TI-co-lor) can grow as tall as eight feet, becoming a stout, branching, pyramidal plant. Though a true annual, the impression it creates in the garden is of a large woody shrub, liberally furnished with toothed, broadly arrow-shaped light green leaves. At the growing tips of each branch, newly forming and half-grown leaves are splashed at their base with magenta, lending the plant a certain modest appeal. (The unusual species name *amaranticolor* means the color of globe amaranth— a deep magenta purple.) The plant is, however, of uncertain origin, and whether its leaves are edible or not is unclear. *C. amaranticolor* is of such rapid growth that little would be gained by sowing it early indoors; it is much easier to sow it in place in early spring where it is to grow. Young, self-seeded plants transplant easily. Though *C. amaranticolor* may be grown as a curiosity or as a cover plant for disturbed ground, it might be most useful as a quick-growing dense screen or annual hedge, in which case plants should be thinned to stand about a foot and a half apart, and fertilized for unusually heavy, leafy growth.

CHRYSANTHEMUM (DENDRANTHEMUM) SPECIES

FAMILY: *Asteraceae* or aster or daisy family.

CLASSIFICATION: Hardy and half-hardy perennials and shrubs grown as half-hardy annuals.

COMMON NAME: Chrysanthemum (other hardy names vary according to species).

HARDINESS: Most species withstand light frosts.

GROWING CONDITIONS: Moderately rich, well-drained soil. Full sun.

PROPAGATION: By seed, sown in place; rooted cuttings or divisions in some species.

HEIGHT: From 6" to 3', depending on species.

ORNAMENTAL VALUE: Most species grown for abundant flower.

LEVEL OF CULTURAL DIFFICULTY: Easy.

SPECIAL PROPERTIES: The flowers and leaves of some species are used in salads.

PRONUNCIATION: kris-AN-thuh-mum (din-DRAN-thuh-mum)

*C*hrysanthemum is a pretty name for a flower, made up of two ancient Greek words, *chrysos,* meaning gold, and *anthemon,* a blossom. Though *Chrysanthemum* is the botanical name for a once-large genus, it was also comfortably used by most gardeners as a popular name for many lovely and familiar garden plants. Now, however, the genus has been broken up—all but two of its approximately 150 species have been shifted among ten other genera—and for gardeners, this shift in botanical nomenclature has been hard. Some have simply balked at the change, as have catalogues and nurseries, which still list many species and varieties under *Chrysanthemum*—shasta daisies, for example, now relocated into *Leucanthemum* (loo-KAN-thuh-mum), or marguerites, now in *Argyranthemum* (ar-guh-RAN-thuh-mum). To gardeners, by far the most familiar plant that once was a chrysanthemum is the garden or florist's mum, now *Dendranthema grandiflora* (gran-di-FLO-ra).

Cultivated in China and Japan for more than 3,000 years, its hundreds of varieties represent a complex mixing of five or more wild species. Probably more of these plants are sold than any other, both as cut flowers and in pots. Naturally fall-blooming, their appearance at roadside stands in autumn signals what one wit has called the "Mummification of North America." (One may have chrysanthemums on any day of the year, however, because, being light sensitive, they can be forced into bloom at any time by altering day lengths through shading in greenhouses.) Their life as cut flowers is long, and so they are florists' darlings, as apt to appear in bouquets with daffodils in spring or roses in high summer as in autumn. Chrysanthemums also seem to be essential components of funeral wreaths at any season, so, though in the garden their pungent leaves smell of autumn, out of the florist's refrigerator they may only smell of death.

Few of the potted mums bought in autumn can be expected to survive over winter in most American gardens. Though technically classed as hardy perennials, resistance to winter cold varies from cultivar to cultivar, and most plants sold in flower have been selected for floral form or color, or abundance and uniformity of bloom rather than for cold hardiness. In any case, they have been force-fed into large, bushy plants with root systems inadequate to support them through the winter. So they are best considered annuals, bought in bud and dropped into gaps in the perennial garden for late season color, and then discarded. More success with hardiness will result from starting out in spring, taking rooted cuttings of a cultivar with proven winter hardiness, perhaps from a neighbor's plants, or from an old-fashioned nursery that grows its own stock. They can then be established in place in the garden, with results that will be looser and far more beautiful than the wads of dropped-in color one generally sees.

Only two species now remain firmly in the genus *Chrysanthemum,* both annuals native to Europe, and both cultivated since ancient times. The first is *Chrysanthemum segetum* (se-JE-tum). The species name means bristly, though its leaves are not spined, but only mildly raspy. Its common name is corn marigold because its bright yellow daisies once were a much-loved weed in European and English wheat fields. It forms a stout, well-branched shrubby plant, to three feet, composed of fleshy blue-green stems clad with somewhat succulent, rich green leaves of crinkly texture, not divided or fringed as are many annual "chrysanthemums." In its native form, it produces many two-inch daisies that develop from prominent buds, first a felty white, but later showing the yellow of the flowers while still unopened. Modern forms have been selected that are white, cream, and primrose yellow. *C. segetum* is also wonderful in annual wildflower meadows, where it adds its bright yellow to the blue of cornflowers, the rose-pink of corn cockles, and the brilliant scarlet of corn poppies.

The other chrysanthemum one might call "legitimate," for the moment at least, is *C. coronar-ium* (kar-i-NAY-ree-um), the crown daisy or garland flower, so-called because from ancient times it was woven into festive crowns or wreaths. A native of southern Europe and North Africa, it forms two-foot-tall, dense, rounded shrubby plants with fingery, deeply divided leaves. Flowers are typically an inch and a half wide, with yellow disks and golden ray petals, though cultivars exist in primrose yellow, ivory, buff, orange, and red. Darker shades have an almost black center. Though the petals of most "chrysanthemums" are edible, and may be used in salads for their bright colors or to garnish sandwiches and platters of cold meat, *C. coronarium* is the only species cultivated for its pungent, edible leaves. The young shoots, called *shungiku* in Japanese, are employed in oriental cooking, particularly in stir fries, fish, and chicken dishes.

Several other annuals once considered chrysanthemums are worth growing, and though they have been shifted to other genera, they are still usually listed by seed catalogues and nurseries as chrysanthemums. Among the loveliest of them all is *C. carinatum* (kar-i-NAY-tum), the tricolor chrysanthemum or painted daisy. A native of Morocco, though now widely naturalized in southern California, it grows from one to three feet tall, forming a lightly branched bush clad in fresh green leaves so deeply cut as to appear ferny, though they are thick of texture and somewhat succulent. Its flowers can be glorious, as much as two and a half inches wide, with deep purple disk flowers and almost overlapping ray flowers of yellow, pink, salmon, crimson, maroon, or bronze, but marked by a single (or sometimes double) band of contrasting color.

C. frutescens (fru-TES-ens), now *Argyranthemum frutescens,* is the familiar Marguerite or Paris daisy. A native of the Canary Islands, it is not actually a true annual, but rather a persistent, woody sub-shrub as the Latin word *frutescens* always indicates. Hardy only to Zone 9, it is treated as an annual, valued for its clean, bright green, coarsely divided foliage and its abundantly produced daisies, as much as four inches across, typically with yellow disks and white ray petals, but occurring also in deep yellow, lemon yellow, and recently, pink. There is an anemone-flowered cultivar with a large pincushion in the center surrounded by white ray petals, and a form with silvery gray-green leaves and smaller, inch-wide white daisies. *C. frutescens* is capable of blooming continuously throughout the summer, though occasional light shearing across the top or patient dead-heading of the spent flowers will produce more abundant bloom. Container-grown plants, or plants lifted from the garden and potted, may be cut back lightly (never into old wood) and carried through the winter on a sunny windowsill or in a cool greenhouse.

Chrysanthemum multicaule (mul-ti-CAW-lee), now *Coleostephus* (ko-lee-OS-tee-pus) *myconis* (MI-co-nis), is a small, sprawling plant that forms a mat of clean, medium green leaves around six or eight inches wide. In the species, it produces little bright gold daisies about an inch across, though selected forms have larger flowers, to as much as two and a half inches wide, that look both comical and beautiful dancing on single stems above so small a plant. Colors vary from a rich, deep golden yellow through paler lemon and primrose shades. *Chrysanthemum multicaule* blooms best in cool weather, and makes an interesting companion to pansies and violas as an early planting for window boxes.

Chrysanthemum paludosum (pa-loo-DO-sum), now *Leucanthemum paludosum,* is grouped in the same genus with shasta daisies, now *Leucanthemum* x *superbum* (soo-PER-bum). It much resembles a miniature shasta daisy, with dark green leaves surmounted by eight- to ten-inch flower stems bearing inch-and-a-half-wide white daisies with a yellow center. Its species name means of marshes and wet places, but it thrives in any rich, moisture-retentive garden soil and, in fact, quickly becomes ill and rots away on heavy, poorly drained earth.

C. parthenium (par-THEN-ee-um) is the familiar feverfew of old-fashioned gardens, still used by herbalists to treat many maladies, particularly chronic and migraine headaches. It has traveled through an unusually large number of genera, having been listed at one time or another as *Matricaria capensis, M. parthenoides, Pyrethrum parthenium,* and *Chrysanthemum parthenium.* Now, for the moment, it has been allowed to settle in *Tanacetum* (ta-na-SEE-tum) as *T. parthenium.* A native of Europe and Asia and anciently cultivated, it is a highly variable species, producing plants anywhere from eight inches to three feet tall, clad in roughly arrow-shaped, chamomile-scented leaves that may be broadly lobed or cut almost into filaments. Some cultivars are reliably perennial, returning year after year to the garden and susceptible to increase by cuttings and divisions. Others behave as weak perennials or biennials, flourishing for a year or two and then fading away. Still others are best grown as annuals, seeded each year in late autumn or very early spring. Flower form is also variable, consisting either of half-inch-wide chamomile-like buttons in white or yellow, yellow-centered daisies with white ray petals, and double forms that may be either fluffy masses of white petals or anemone-flowered, with a high cushion of modified disk flowers surrounded by a single row of ray petals. A very fine gold-leaved form exists, suitable for planting in some shade and more valued for its foliage than for its sparse flowers. But whatever the leaf or flower form or color, there is a curious purity about feverfew, a freshness that justifies the species name it has tended to retain through several genera, from the ancient Greek *parthenos,* meaning virgin.

Chrysanthemum ptarmiciflorum (tar-mi-si-FLO-rum) is now also listed in *Tanacetum,* a genus that contains many pungently scented plants, such as tansy. The genus name *Tanacetum* descends through the Latin *tanazita,* a word still in use in parts of southern Europe, from the ancient Greek *athanasia,* signifying immortality. The curious species name *ptarmiciflorum* is from the ancient Greek *ptarmike,* signifying a flower that causes one to sneeze. *Chrysanthemum ptarmiciflorum* is not grown for its flowers, however, but for its finely cut, silvery white leaves. It—along with many other plants in the genera *Artemisia, Centaurea, Cineraria,* and *Senecio*—is called "dusty miller," and sometimes "silver lace," for its foliage is more finely cut than any of the other plants employed to provide the "silver note" in mixed plantings.

All forms of *Chrysanthemum* except *C. frutescens* and possibly *C. parthenium* may be direct-seeded in the garden or started indoors about eight weeks before the last expected frost. All are open-meadow plants that relish full sun. Average garden soil is sufficient, and too much richness will cause abundant, leafy growth at the expense of flower. Generally, annual chrysanthemums grown for flower look best in generous patches and in fairly dense stands, each plant approximately eight inches from its neighbor. Grown this way, staking is seldom necessary, though if plants are inclined to flop they may be kept upright by twiggy brush inserted unobtrusively into the planting. *C. frutescens* is technically a tender shrub, and is usually purchased as started plants grown from cuttings, often already in flower. Though feverfew, *C. parthenium,* may easily be grown from seed, plants of good form, such as some of the doubles, are easily rooted from cuttings acquired from another gardener, or transplanted as young, self-seeded

plants that will generally occur wherever it has been grown.

CIRSIUM JAPONICUM

FAMILY: *Asteraceae* or aster or daisy family.

CLASSIFICATION: Half-hardy biennial grown as half-hardy annual.

COMMON NAMES: Rose thistle, plume thistle, Japanese thistle, cirsium japonicum.

HARDINESS: Withstands light frosts once established.

GROWING CONDITIONS: Moderately fertile, well-drained soil.

PROPAGATION: By seed, preferably sown in place in early spring. Seedlings may be started indoors in peat pots six weeks before last anticipated frost. Seedlings resent root disturbance.

HEIGHT: 2 to 3'.

ORNAMENTAL VALUE: Grown for attractive, thistle-like flowers.

LEVEL OF CULTURAL DIFFICULTY: Easy.

SPECIAL PROPERTIES: Excellent cut flower.

PRONUNCIATION: SEER-si-um ja-PON-i-cum

The daisy family Asteraceae is so vast that botanists have divided it into twelve "tribes," like the ancient nation of Israel. While the Carduus tribe, which takes its name from the classical Latin word for thistle, contains two delicious esculents, artichokes and cardoons, and a number of fine annual and perennial garden plants, its 150 to 200 species also include some of the most vicious weeds known to farmers and gardeners alike. The bits of root from a single plant of *Cirsium arvense* (ar-VEN-see), the Canada thistle, if dragged through a field by a cultivator, can sprout into an army of fiercely spined, ineradicable dev-

CIRSIUM JAPONICUM

much-branched stem terminates in an almost rounded puff of shaving brush flowers. Like all members of the Carduus tribe, buds are encased in beautifully crafted bracts that show a bright spot of color practically from first formation. Flowers, which are in fact a dense bundle of fertile parts, the disk of a daisy without ray petals, open over a long period of time, lasting in good condition on the plant for as long as three weeks. Flower color is typically a vibrant rose-red, though softer colors of dusty rose and pale pink have been bred, as well as clear whites. Mixed shades look beautiful together, both in the garden and also in a vase, for *Cirsium japonicum* is a superb cut flower.

C. japonicum, a native of Japan as its species name indicates, is technically a biennial, or sometimes (as with the case of most biennials) a short-lived perennial. In gardens warmer than Zone 5, it will often appear as a self-sown plant, forming a rosette of beautiful leaves in autumn, persisting over winter to flower early the following summer. Even in colder gardens, once it has been grown for a season, it will reappear here and there though its seedlings will tend to germinate and flower all in one season. Generally, the best plants result from seed sown in place as early in spring as the soil may be worked, though they may also be sown indoors about six weeks from the last frost date for earlier-flowering plants.

Cirsium japonicum appears to be indifferent to soil quality, accepting rich and poor alike, as long as it has good drainage. Full sun is a necessity, and if young plants appear thriftless, a single application of vegetable garden fertilizer rich in phosphorus and potassium will encourage them to develop into strong plants. *C. japonicum* is particularly attractive in an annual wildflower meadow, where its gently thistly nature seems at home.

ils, and the bull thistle produces thousands of silky, airborne seed—the delight of children who love to see them blowing in the wind until they step, barefoot, on the resulting thorny weeds.

If plants, like people, are often judged by their family connections, then *Cirsium japonicum* is much to be pitied, but, in fact, it displays all the virtues of its clan and none of their damning faults. The leaves of all thistles are actually quite beautiful, once one sees beyond their painful spines, and those of *C. japonicum* are especially pretty. They form a basal tuft of deeply lobed, dark green leaves veined with silver, each as much as a foot long, becoming smaller near the top of upright stems that grow to about three feet in height. Though distinctly thistly in appearance, they threaten more than they can do, for the spines are not needle-like, but soft. Each

CLADANTHUS ARABICUS

FAMILY: *Asteraceae* or aster or daisy family.

CLASSIFICATION: Hardy annual.

COMMON NAMES: Palm Springs daisy, cladanthus.

HARDINESS: Withstands light frosts.

GROWING CONDITIONS: Well-drained, ordinary garden soil. Full sun.

PROPAGATION: By seed, sown in place in very early spring. Seed may be started indoors about 8 weeks before last frost.

HEIGHT: 2 to 3'.

ORNAMENTAL VALUE: Grown for flower and for attractive form.

LEVEL OF CULTURAL DIFFICULTY: Easy.

SPECIAL PROPERTIES: May be grown in cool greenhouses for early spring flower indoors.

PRONUNCIATION: kla-DAN-thus a-RA-bi-cus

*T*here are plenty of bright yellow daisies available to gardeners, and *Cladanthus arabicus* would simply be one more of them, were it not for the engaging way its flowers form on a very pretty two- to three-foot bush richly furnished with feathery, bluish-green leaves. (They give off a strong but pleasant fragrance when crushed.) About three months after germination, the first flowers appear, nestled singly in the very tips of developing stems. As they expand into two-inch-wide daisies, three or four short branches develop immediately beneath them, each with its own terminal bud, and eventually its own whorl of branches bearing yet more buds. Individual flowers remain fresh over a long period of time, so eventually the entire plant is covered with daisies and buds, all borne like exploding fireworks.

Cladanthus arabicus is a hardy annual native to southern Spain and North Africa, from where it draws the species name *arabicus,* meaning of Arabia. (The genus takes its name from two ancient Greek words, *klados,* meaning branch, and *anthos,* flower.) Of very easy culture, it requires only ordinary garden soil, full sun, and good drainage. Seed may be sown directly where it is to bloom in the garden as early in spring as the soil may be worked, or it may be sown indoors about eight weeks before the last expected frost date. Flowering best in the cool weather of early summer, it generally takes a rest in high summer and then flowers again in autumn. It withstands light frosts, though autumn flowers may be smaller than early summer ones.

Those gardeners who have cool greenhouses will enjoy experimenting with *C. arabicus* for early spring bloom. Seed should be sown in September, and young plants moved into progressively larger pots until they occupy those of five or six inches, in which they will flower. The best specimens will develop at temperatures of around 50° to 60°F with good ventilation and may be had in flower in mid-March, when their golden daisies seem especially cheerful.

CLARKIA SPECIES

FAMILY: *Onagraceae* or evening primrose family.

CLASSIFICATION: Hardy annual.

COMMON NAMES: Satin flower, garland flower, farewell to spring, clarkia, godetia.

HARDINESS: Withstand light frosts once established.

GROWING CONDITIONS: Moderately fertile, well-drained soil. Cool temperature. Full sun, afternoon shade in warmer gardens.

PROPAGATION: From seed, preferably sown in place in very early spring. May be started indoors in peat pots 8 weeks before last frost. Seedlings resent root disturbance.

HEIGHT: Variable, from 1 to 4'.

ORNAMENTAL VALUE: Grown for flower.

LEVEL OF CULTURAL DIFFICULTY: Easy in suitable conditions; difficult elsewhere.

SPECIAL PROPERTIES: Excellent cool greenhouse plants for early spring flower.

PRONUNCIATION: klar-KEE-a

So beautiful are clarkias that they would be in every summer garden except for their demanding cultural requirement for fresh, cool nights and mild, sunny days. Like many plants native to the western coast of North America, they perform superbly where these conditions are met, but may be miserable failures where hot, humid summers arrive early, and where soils are heavy clay. Still, in gardening as in life, when confronted with something so supremely desirable as clarkias, no one should give up without a try. Where they may be made to thrive, clarkias are splendid, producing sumptuous sherbet-colored flowers borne on wiry stems of purplish red from early July into October.

Both as a genus and in its individual species, *Clarkia* is highly variable, to the extent that the

CLARKIA *SPECIES*

genus was once broken into two, *Clarkia* (commemorating Captain William Clark, who, with Captain Meriwether Lewis, completed the first transcontinental crossing of North America) and *Godetia* (go-DEE-shee-a), with many species and subspecies. The genus *Godetia* is now retired, though it still exists in catalogues and as a popular name for *Clarkia amoena* (a-MEE-na) (*Godetia amoena, G. grandiflora*), popularly called "farewell to spring" for its rich bloom in early summer. It can produce a beautiful, two-foot-tall bushy plant with two-inch-wide cup-shaped flowers ranging from satiny pinkish-lavender to clear and coral pink, often blotched or streaked with crimson. They are borne in spires, and when combined with any flower that blooms in blue at the same time—larkspurs or certain campanulas—they make an unforgettable combination.

Gardeners who are interested in western native American wildflowers (one or more of the thirty-three species in the genus is native from the Rocky Mountains to British Columbia and south to California, and in southern South America) and who live where clarkia perform well would want to search out sources for species *Clarkia*. Others will be content with packets offered by good commercial seed companies, which will include complex hybrids of *Clarkia unguiculata* (un-gee-cu-LA-ta), or *C. elegans,* or *Clarkia pulchella* (pul-CHEL-a) and possibly other species.

Clarkias grown from commercial seed will vary in height from a foot to as much as four feet, depending on variety. Whether dwarf or tall, plants are lax at first but then produce many ascending, wiry stems that will not require staking in full sun. Leaves are oval, of a pleasing dark green with a prominent central vein, and measure about two inches long at the base of the plant, becoming smaller as they ascend up the stems. Flowers are borne in the axils of the leaves in great abundance, usually starting in early July and continuing well into autumn where summers are mild. Plants will attempt to set enormous numbers of seed, however, in long, slender, pointed pea-pods, and patient dead-heading will be necessary to prolong bloom. But as clarkia are superb for indoor arrangements, frequent cutting will take care of some of this chore.

The two species from which garden *Clarkia* are principally bred are both single-flowered, consisting of four-inch-long, paddle-shaped petals, with the lower third of each petal pinched into a narrow stem, called a "claw" by botanists. In native populations, colors are generally some shade of white, rose, red, or pink. Modern hybrids are usually double, with several sets of petals creating an effect like miniature carnations. Colors are both sumptuous and subtle, in a range from clear and dark pink through old rose, deep salmon, carmine, light and dark red, and purple. Seed is occasionally offered in individual colors, making possible exciting combinations with other perennial and annual plants, but general mixes also produce beautiful results, since no color seems to clash with any other.

Clarkias may be expected to bloom in about three months from seed. Where summers are hot and early summer plants are needed, seed should be sown indoors in early March, or outdoors at the same time if the soil is workable. Though young seedlings may be transplanted, the work must be done with care. Indoors, peat pots or plastic cell packs should be used, and outdoors quite small plants should be taken with an ample ball of earth. The best results will be had, however, if plants are seeded where they are to grow, which, in the warm gardens of Zones 8 to 10, may be done in late September. Plants should be spaced closely together, about nine inches apart for finest flower. Soil should be well drained and not over-rich. In northern gardens, full sun is required, though farther south some afternoon shade will prolong bloom.

From a late August or early September sowing, clarkia will make splendid bloom in greenhouses, beginning in late winter and lasting to late spring with dead-heading. Flower buds will only form, however, when nighttime temperatures rise to about 50°F, and so extra heat would have to be supplied in January. Such exacting cultural requirements were once routine on great estates where both the rarest and the most common flowers were raised to perfection throughout the winter and early spring months for indoor decoration. It is a skill still to be mastered by those who have the facilities and the will to experiment.

CLEOME HASSLERIANA
(C. SPINOSA)

FAMILY: *Capparidaceae* or caper family.

CLASSIFICATION: Hardy annual.

COMMON NAMES: Spider flower, cleome.

HARDINESS: Withstands light frosts once established.

GROWING CONDITIONS: Moderately fertile to poor soils. Full sun to part shade.

PROPAGATION: By seed, sown in place 2 weeks before last frost, or indoors 8 to 10 weeks before last frost.

HEIGHT: To 6'.

ORNAMENTAL VALUE: Grown for flower.

LEVEL OF CULTURAL DIFFICULTY: Easy.

SPECIAL PROPERTIES: Excellent cut flower.

PRONUNCIATION: klee-O-me hass-ler-i-AN-a (spi-NO-sa)

The name "spider flower" is not the only burden *Cleome hassleriana* must bear. As a plant, it is usually described as "coarse," an adjective that fits its rank,

CLEOME HASSLERIANA

woody, shrublike growth. Its leaves are composed of five to seven slender fingers arranged in a palm, superficially resembling those of *Cannabis sativa,* from which marijuana and hashish are derived. (Indeed, cleome has had a vogue as a camouflage plant, used in an attempt to shelter cannabis from unwanted gaze.) Like cannabis, the leaves of cleome are sticky or clammy to the touch, a quality that gives some gardeners the shudders. At the base of each leaf there is generally a pair of cruel, hooked green spines that can inflict considerable pain on the unwary. All parts of the plant possess a rank odor that some gardeners charitably call "not entirely unpleasant," and others call foul.

But still, *Cleome hassleriana* is the star of both its extended and its immediate family. (It belongs to the family Capparidaceae, comprising some thirty-seven genera, but is the only member of its own genus, *Cleome*—some 200 species—that is grown in gardens.) It quickly achieves five or six feet in height under good culture, making it a fine subject for the back of deep borders. Flowering begins in July and continues until frost. The flowers are formed in dense cobs at the tips of branches, each cob about six inches across and composed of a thick cluster of colored buds at the tip and fully opened flowers in various stages of

maturity below. Each flower consists of four-inch-long, paddle-shaped petals and six prominent stamens that protrude outward about three inches, something like the whiskers of a cat. Seed forms quickly and consists of a thin, string-bean-like pod borne outward on a rigid but filament-fine two-inch-long stem. The entire structure—of bud, flower, and seed pod—creates a distinctly fringy effect. Most attractively, unopened buds and freshly opened flowers are of a generally stronger color than fully opened and fading flowers, creating a pleasing, many-toned effect. Blooms on the naturally occurring species are a deep rose-magenta, and self-seeded plants will eventually revert to this hue. Selected seed strains are far superior, both in color and in size of flower, and may be had in deep or pale rose-pink, in purple, lavender, or mauve, and in a splendid white, the latter being almost indispensable where white flowers are required over a long season.

Cleome may be seeded indoors about eight to ten weeks before the last anticipated frost date, though it is so rapid of growth that direct seeding in the garden a week or two before the last frosts is equally effective. Young plants transplant successfully only when less than eight inches tall. Any reasonably good garden soil suits *Cleome hassleriana,* which seems to tolerate heavy clay and dryish sandy ones alike, though the finest and tallest plants are grown in good, loamy, well-drained garden soil, and are improved by a feeding of general vegetable garden fertilizer in granulated form—10-10-10 or the like—when plants are about eight inches tall. Full sun is appreciated, though cleome will perform well either in afternoon or in morning shade (not both). Flower cobs are attractive when cut, continuing to open for a week in water, though for the most attractive effect seed pods should be removed and faded flowers picked off daily.

Cleome is attractive either in rich masses or as

occasional accent plants throughout the border, but except in the wild or meadow garden, volunteer seedlings should be discouraged by removing mature plants after frosts have ended the display of flowers or earlier in warm gardens, when pods begin to split and scatter their seed. Without this precaution, a thatch of self-seeded plants will occur the following spring. Though native to tropical America and the West Indies, the seed of *Cleome hassleriana* possesses considerable hardiness, enough to make its prolific self-seeding a nuisance in gardens as cold as Zone 5.

COBAEA SCANDENS

FAMILY: *Polemoniaceae* or phlox family.

CLASSIFICATION: Tender perennial vine grown as tender annual vine.

COMMON NAMES: Cup-and-saucer vine, cobaea.

HARDINESS: Root-hardy to 30°F. Sensitive to light frosts. Resents cool weather.

GROWING CONDITIONS: Rich, well-drained garden loam. Full sun to part shade.

PROPAGATION: By seed, sown indoors in peat pots 8 to 10 weeks before last frost. Seedlings resent root disturbance.

HEIGHT: To 20′ when grown as an annual. To 40′ where hardy.

ORNAMENTAL VALUE: Grown for quick, screening growth and for flower.

LEVEL OF CULTURAL DIFFICULTY: Easy to moderately difficult, depending on climate.

SPECIAL PROPERTIES: Useful as quick cover for arbors, porches, or buildings.

PRONUNCIATION: ko-BAY-a (KO-bey-a) SCAN-dens

No garden ever has enough vines. Beyond camouflaging structures that are unsightly or embellishing surfaces that are irritatingly blank, vines perform other functions. They relate buildings to the garden, they soften and smooth edges, and in trained form (like espaliers) or as embowering drapery, they always seem to carry an air of softness, abundance, and romance. But few annual vines except for the ubiquitous 'Heavenly Blue' morning glories and perhaps sweet peas are ever seen, perhaps because the space that might support them is given over to permanent woody vines or to espaliers made of shrubs.

However, the choice of vines grown as annuals should include *Cobaea scandens,* the cup-and-saucer vine. A native of Mexico, the genus was named for an early Jesuit missionary, Fr. Bernado Cobo (1575–1659), and within its perhaps twenty member species, *C. scandens* is the only one cultivated in gardens. Actually a persistent woody vine, it is hardy in gardens where temperatures do not dip much below 40°F. In such conditions, it can eventually build up a scrambling growth to forty feet, enough to swallow a small house. But even in colder gardens, when treated as an annual, it can achieve as much as twenty feet of growth in a single season.

For so rampant a plant, however, it never creates the feeling that it is a bully. Its leaves are delicately fashioned, consisting of three or four pairs of oval, dark green four-inch leaflets, widely spaced along the stem and held gracefully at an angle to it. Each leaf terminates in a single tendril. These tendrils are astonishingly sensitive and tenacious, able to find any rough surface and cling to it, allowing the vine to scramble upward and often even sideways along the edge of a roof or the side members of a pergola without a grid of wires or guiding strings. In fact, the vine, which branches lightly, is more beautiful when allowed to find its own pattern.

Flowers are borne in the axils of the leaves, on drooping or outfacing foot-long stems. They are

COBAEA SCANDENS

a light green when they first appear, changing as they mature to greenish violet and then to purple. Their shape is striking, consisting of a two-inch-wide cup of fused petals (technically a corolla, such as daffodils possess) resting on a prominent, flattened calyx. Hence, the popular name, cup-and-saucer vine. Within the corolla the anthers are very prominent, extending beyond its edges and then crooking curiously back on themselves. Mature flowers have a wonderful satiny sheen and make splendid cut flowers, either on their long stems or as cups and saucers floating in a bowl of water. A white form, 'Alba', looks very pretty either grown alone or with the purple, and a rare variegated form also exists, though it does not come true from seed and must be carried over the winter by cuttings taken in autumn.

Where *Cobaea scandens* is hardy, it blooms continuously from June to October. When grown as an annual, however, flowers can be expected about three months from seeding, and as young plants are frost sensitive, seed must be germinated indoors in March to produce flowering vines for most gardens. Because the large, flat seeds are sensitive to rot they should be inserted edgewise in well-drained, fibrous potting compost. Young vines resent root disturbance, and so seed should be established in peat pots, or in small plastic pots from which they must be transplanted with great care. About three seeds should be planted in each pot, with the firm determination of nipping out all but the strongest. Seed viability can be poor so one should hedge against failures in germination by seeding twice the number of plants one wants. (Other gardeners will gratefully accept any surplus.)

Over the long period in which young vines will be grown indoors, they should receive as much sun as possible and be frequently pinched both to control their growth and to promote branching. At a certain point, sticks or small trellises should be provided for the developing vines. They should also not be grown within tendril reach of one another, else they may twine into an inseparable mass at planting time. Young plants may not be established in the garden until after all danger of frost is past, though it is interesting that mature vines will endure a few degrees of frost at season's end without perishing. Any moderately rich, well-drained soil is adequate, though quickest development and flowering can be encouraged by a single application of granular vegetable garden fertilizer, such as 10-10-10, about two weeks after transplanting. In Zone 5 gardens and colder, plants should be given a warm, sunny southern exposure for best development. In warmer gardens, an east or west exposure is adequate, providing it is in full light.

COLEUS × HYBRIDUS (SOLENOSTEMON SCUTELLARIOIDES)

FAMILY: *Lamiaceae* (*Labiatae*) or mint family.

CLASSIFICATION: Tender shrubs grown as tender annuals.

COMMON NAME: Coleus.

HARDINESS: Sensitive to light frosts. Resent cool weather.

GROWING CONDITIONS: Humus-rich, well-drained garden soil. Part shade.

PROPAGATION: From seed, sown in warm conditions 6 to 8 weeks before last frost. Easy from cuttings.

HEIGHT: From 1 to 4', depending on cultivar.

ORNAMENTAL VALUE: Grown for decorative leaves.

LEVEL OF CULTURAL DIFFICULTY: Easy.

SPECIAL PROPERTIES: Excellent indoor winter or cool greenhouse plants.

PRONUNCIATION: KO-lee-us HI-bri-dus (so-li-NOS-tuh-mun scoo-tel-uh-ROY-i-dees)

*I*f one commented on a fine plant of *Solenostemon scutellarioides* in a neighbor's garden or asked for it in a nursery, one would probably be met with a blank stare. Botanically, however, that is the cumbersome name under which coleus, the very familiar nettle-like plant grown for its brilliantly colored leaves, must now travel. It will be a long time before such awkward syllables flow off most gardeners' tongues, and in fact they need be in no hurry, for further shifting is likely to occur among the closely related genera of *Coleus* (retired for the moment), *Solenostemon,* and *Plectranthus* (plek-TRAN-thus).

Like most annual plants that are easy to grow, are bright in color, and do steady, hard work in the garden, coleus have experienced distinct highs and lows of popularity. In the Victorian period, they were treasured for their ease of cultivation, their vividly colored leaves (particularly in that Victorian favorite, deep velvet maroon), and their usefulness in rigidly patterned bedding schemes. When the looser, more natural planting styles championed by William Robinson and Gertrude Jekyll came into fashion, coleus were largely banished from sophisticated gardens, but as is always the case with good plants that fall from fashionable regard, they were still cultivated by simple unstylish gardeners. In the late 1940s and 50s, coleus had a resurgence in popularity, in part because they present a starched, crisp tidiness that appealed to the Betty Crocker era. A subsequent decline occurred in the late 60s, when a certain dishevelment in the garden became fashionable, and again in the mid-70s, when if a plant was not perennial it had no chance of interesting gardeners. Now, however, coleus are gardeners' darlings, returned to favor, one supposes, by people who evaluate a plant for the deftness with which it is used, and not with a prejudiced memory of how it has been misused. Many good plants, such as amaranths, cannas, impatiens, petunias, salvias, and zinnias, could, if they had tongues, tell the same story.

The coleus of gardens is not actually a species, but rather a complex intermarriage of several species and repeated backcrosses, so the old designation, × *hybridus,* seems more accurate than the current descriptive species name, *scutellarioides.* But the variability of *Coleus* cultivars, chiefly in color but also in shape of leaf, is not so much the result of cross-hybridization as of patient selection over two centuries of garden history. In Japan, particularly, where complex variegation has always been treasured, coleus of great beauty have been developed, some of which are now available to American gardeners.

Ease of cultivation in any ornamental plant is generally a characteristic in its favor, and coleus

COLEUS X HYBRIDUS

ranks among the easiest of the easy to grow. Seed germinates readily in soils warmed to rather high temperatures (around 75°F) on top of the basement furnace, over an old-fashioned radiator, or by use of electric, bottom-heat pads sold by greenhouse supply companies. At such high temperatures, young seedlings appear within five or six days, and, like baby chicks, are cute from the beginning. The first pair of true leaves, though tiny, will display pretty much everything an individual plant will show its whole life long. Generally, the largest, most vigorous seedlings will have the least vivid leaf color, and the old advice was to exterminate them in the seed pan by a firm pinch. But now that larger-growing, plain-leaved coleus have become fashionable, particularly in single colors of chartreuse, lime-green, and dull purple, the life of the rankest seedlings should perhaps be spared. Their very unassertiveness may make them serviceable candidates in the perennial border, particularly in the semi-shaded end where good filler plants may be hard to come by. Young plants, which transplant easily, may be pricked out into individual pots or plastic cell packs when they have formed two or three sets of true leaves and are easy to handle. They thrive on a bright windowsill until the weather outdoors is warm

and settled, at which point they may be hardened off and located in the garden.

Though generally grown as annuals, coleus are actually tender sub-shrubs native to the Old World tropics and are hardy in the warmest parts of North America. Their bushy growth, semi-woody at the base, varies typically from about ten inches to as much as four feet in height, though there are many procumbent forms that may actually be only as tall as a single lax stem. Older cultivars generally sported leaves with one or sometimes two colors in the center, surrounded by a toothed border of green at the edges. Such forms will still occur from modern seed strains and are likely to be the plants, also seed-grown, offered in mixed colors at roadside stands in plastic six-packs.

In the last ten years, however, magnificent coleus have become available, chiefly propagated from plants imported from Europe or Japan. Many have leaves all of one rich color, gold or amber, or chartreuse green, sometimes with a contrasting underside of purple or yellow. Others have leaves marked by two complementary colors, such as deep russet with a border of gold, or contrasting colors, such as maroon with a chartreuse edge. There are also forms with fantastic splashes, streaks, or marblings of one color over another. All these special forms must be carried on by cuttings, as they do not come true from seed. But among gardeners the expression "It roots like a coleus" designates a plant that may be propagated with absurd ease. Cuttings are best taken from terminal shoots that have not formed flower buds, and will root in almost any moist medium or, as one's grandmother did, in a glass of water on the windowsill. Old plants may be cut back hard and forced into fresh growth as winter houseplants, where they will thrive in an east or west window. Generally, however, the strongest and most attractive plants will result from fresh cuttings taken during late summer.

Coleus are extremely sensitive to frosts, and they also resent chills even above freezing, so they should not be planted in the garden until the weather has warmed. They require fertile, humus-rich, well-drained soil for best development, and plenty of moisture. No plant more quickly shows its need for supplementary water than coleus, which will wilt dramatically when it is dry at the roots, a sort of fake suicide attempt that, if prolonged, can result in the real thing. It is assumed about coleus that because they are shade-tolerant, and in fact require some protection from full sun in warm gardens, they will thrive in deep shade. In fact, however, they may make a miserable show in such conditions. Leaf color and general vigor are always best with bright overhead light or, in cool gardens, with half a day of sun.

Though coleus may be used as bedding plants, random combinations of different colors and possibly different growth habits always look messy. Better results come from segregating individual colors, either in drifts of one color or as single specimens. Perhaps the best way to enjoy coleus, however, is as container plants, either for foliage color in combination with flowering plants, or (and particularly with the choicest cultivars) as single potted specimens arranged in a collection of fine clay pots.

COLLINSIA SPECIES

FAMILY: *Scrophulariaceae* or snapdragon family.

CLASSIFICATION: Half-hardy annual.

COMMON NAMES: Chinese houses, pagoda flower, collinsia.

HARDINESS: Withstand light frost.

GROWING CONDITIONS: Rich, moist, well-drained soil. Full sun; afternoon shade in warmer gardens.

PROPAGATION: Preferably from seed sown in place about 2 weeks before last frost. May be sown indoors in peat pots 8 weeks before last frost. Seedlings resent root disturbance.

HEIGHT: To 2'.

ORNAMENTAL VALUE: Grown for flower.

LEVEL OF CULTURAL DIFFICULTY: Moderately easy to difficult, depending on location.

SPECIAL PROPERTIES: Excellent cut flowers. May be grown for early spring bloom in cool greenhouses.

PRONUNCIATION: ko-LIN-see-a

The western United States, and particularly coastal California, is as rich in beautiful native annual plants as any region of the world, yet few of them are seen in American gardens. They require some careful handling, it is true, as most do not transplant with great readiness, but more to the point, they tend to flower best in moist and pleasantly cool summer conditions, requiring, particularly, cool, buoyant nights. The hot, muggy August weather of most American gardens puts an end to their bloom, and often their life. Where those conditions arrive even earlier, their beauty is at best ephemeral. But it is good, sometimes, to experiment with beauty that is ephemeral, for not all garden pleasures ought to be as sturdily nonstop as those provided by impatiens, marigolds, and the like.

Among the loveliest of West Coast wild flowers are the *Collinsia*, whose genus name commemorates Zacheus Collins (1764–1831), an important Philadelphia naturalist. There are about twenty species in the genus, all of which inherit a birthright of winsome beauty. But for gardens, perhaps the best is *Collinsia bicolor* (BI-co-lor), often listed as *C. heterophylla* (he-te-ro-

PHI-la). It forms a loose, wiry plant to two feet tall, with oblong, toothed leaves of shiny green borne opposite each other low on the plant, and then in threes as flower stems develop. Leaves vary from one to two inches in length, the larger ones tending to be low on the plant, but not always. The species name *heterophylla* (meaning diverse-leaved) acknowledges this fact, while the current species name *bicolor* is far more descriptive, since the inch-long tubular flowers are generally of two colors, violet and white. (A dainty, all-white form, var. *candidissima* [kan-di-DIS-i-ma] occurs in the wild and has been isolated to come true from seed.)

Collinsia belong to the family Scrophulariaceae. The signature plant is *Scrophularia acquatica,* a ditch and streamside plant once believed to be a cure for scrofula, but the family includes many charming members, such as snapdragons, monkey flowers, mask flowers, wishbone flowers, and toadflax, all of which bear winsome blossoms suggestive—as their common names suggest—of something else. In *Collinsia heterophylla,* the lower part of the flower consists of two lobes or liplike structures, generally colored rose-purple or violet, and an upper, fanciful forehead of white, rakishly slanted backward as if the inch-long individual blossoms meant to kiss a close inspector. Flowers are borne in whorls, the lowest of which remain in good condition as upper ones develop, hence the popular names "Chinese houses" or "pagoda flowers."

Another species sometimes grown, *Collinsia grandiflora* (gran-di-FLO-ra), is very similar to *C. heterophylla* in effect, though its flowers, not significantly larger for all its species name, are borne on outfacing green threads about half an inch long instead of snugly clustered against the stems. It is also native to the California coast and British Columbia, and bears the slightly embarrassing but predictable popular name "blue lips."

Collinsia do best when sown directly in the garden where they are to grow, a week or so before the last frost, though in order to secure flowering plants before hot summer weather arrives, they may also be started indoors in peat pots or plastic cell packs about eight weeks earlier. They require a rich, moist but well-drained soil, and they appreciate some protection from the hot midday sun in all but the coolest gardens. Flowering should begin about two months from germination, and either will cease with the advent of hot weather, or the plants will take a rest and resume flowering in the cool weather of early autumn. A good show of autumn flowers can also sometimes be had by a mid-July sowing in partial shade. In all but the coldest gardens, collinsia will reappear as self-sown seedlings, though those that appear in autumn will seldom outlive the winter. Collinsia make superb winter-grown pot plants for spring flowering in cool greenhouses (developing best with a minimum nighttime temperature of around 50°) and also make very fine cut flowers.

Though collinsia are chiefly western American natives, one, *Collinsia verna* (VER-na), has a native range from New York to Kentucky and westward to Kansas and Wisconsin. It thrives in shade in moist, rich woodland soils, achieving a height of about two feet and bearing flowers a third of an inch long on stems the same length, clustered at the top of wiry branches. The upper lip of each flower is white, and the lower lip blue. Sometimes cultivated in the wild garden, it should be grown more frequently, not only for its pretty flowers but also for the two popular names it has carried since colonial times, "blue-eyed Mary" and "innocence."

CONSOLIDA SPECIES

FAMILY: *Ranunculaceae* or buttercup family.

CLASSIFICATION: Hardy annuals, biennials, or weak perennials grown as hardy annuals.

COMMON NAMES: Larkspur, consolida.

HARDINESS: Withstand light frost.

GROWING CONDITIONS: Very rich, well-drained, moisture-retentive soils. Cool weather.

PROPAGATION: By seed, sown in place in September or very early spring, or in peat pots, indoors or out, 2 weeks before last frost. Seedlings resent root disturbance.

HEIGHT: 15" to 4', depending on culture.

ORNAMENTAL VALUE: Grown for flower.

LEVEL OF CULTURAL DIFFICULTY: Easy in cool climates, difficult in warmer ones.

SPECIAL PROPERTIES: Superb cut flower. Useful as dried flower.

PRONUNCIATION: kon·SA·li·da

*A*ll garden larkspurs once belonged to the genus *Delphinium,* which is a botanist's nightmare. After detaching the thirty or so species with joined upper petals into the separate genus *Consolida* (from Latin *consolido,* meaning whole or unified), more than 300 species still exist within the genus *Delphinium,* many of which are so beautiful that they have been treasured in gardens for centuries. Species of delphinium were cultivated both in ancient Egypt and in ancient Greece. (The name "delphinium" is a near transcription of the Greek word *delphinion,* from *delphis,* a dolphin, since the unopened buds of some species resemble that amiable sea mammal.) Though such early cultivation might have been for the beautiful flowers of delphiniums—most often in some shade of celestial blue—probably more plants were grown for their seed, which was used as a purge of intestinal worms and as a deterrent to scorpions.

Species of delphinium were cultivated in England as early as were any plants grown for the beauty of their flowers rather than for their purely medicinal properties. Serious breeding work began in the early Victorian period, using *Delphinium elatum* (ee-LAY-tum), a native of central Europe to Siberia as a primary parent, but crossing it with other species to produce the ancestors of the magnificent, towering garden delphinium we now know. Further significant breeding work was done in America by Frank Reinelt in 1925, producing the first of the Pacific Giant series, and by the great German nurseryman Karl Foerster, who, over a sixty-year career as a plant hybridizer, bred and named more than 600 cultivars of garden delphiniums. Breeding work continued on other species as well, producing fine garden plants of a gentle and more modest demeanor, such as the popular 'Connecticut Yankees' series, bred by the photographer Edward Steichen. So tangled is the genealogy of most delphiniums that even gardeners who insist on knowing the

CONSOLIDA *SPECIES*

botany of their plants will soon be over their heads.

It is all a welter, though gardeners seeking information solely on plants that might be grown as annuals have a simple time of it. The genus *Consolida* includes only annual species, among the forty or so of which are the familiar and much-loved garden larkspurs. (In catalogues, they may still be listed among *Delphiniums,* the genus to which they once belonged, though the popular name "larkspur" is always reserved for them.) The most familiar used to be listed (and often still is) as *Consolida ambigua* (am-BI-gew-a), or sometimes as *C. orientalis,* and sometimes catalogues will list both. But properly (for the moment at least) they should all be listed as *C. ajacis* (ay-JA-sis) after Ajax, the Greek warrior who killed himself for shame at the fury he showed when the armor of the dead Achilles was bestowed on Odysseus.

Seed companies are generally clear enough about the form the plants will take. The leaves of all cultivars of *Consolida* are very finely divided, generally fringy, and most plants branch freely to produce many flower spikes in very beautiful shades of pink, rose, purplish red, lavender, white, and—best of all—every tint of blue from skim milk to deep indigo. Separate color strains are often offered, and when that is the case, one would of course go for the bluest blue available. Plant height will range from about fifteen inches to four feet, depending often as much on culture as on variety, though tight-bunched dwarf strains are offered, for reasons that will be unclear to gardeners who know larkspurs at their elegant, airy best. As cut flowers and for use as dried flowers in winter arrangements (for which they are superb), gardeners often prefer the double forms, called "stock" or "hyacinth" flowered, with blooms crowded tightly up and down the stems, though in beds and in annual wildflower meadows, the lighter, more delicate single forms are much to be preferred.

Even more refined is another species in the genus *Consolida, C. regalis* (ree-GA-lis), which grows to two and a half feet or so, and produces wiry, dark green stems on which single, five-petaled flowers float like tiny, inch-wide butterflies. It comes in a splendid deep blue, a paler blue, and a pristine white, and so delicate is its growth that it may be planted among late-flowering perennial plants for early summer bloom without crowding their development.

Larkspurs are classed as hardy annuals, which means that in all but the coldest gardens, or gardens with heavy clay soils that remain sodden in winter, seed may be sown in place in September for superb flower the following summer. Indeed, the best plants are always grown this way, though care must be taken to thin them in spring after winter losses are clear, so that they have room to develop and plenty of air circulation, as they are prone to mildew in mid- to late summer. Even in favored gardens, however, it is often more convenient to transplant started plants, especially where elaborate bedding schemes are developed, and so larkspurs may also be sown in plastic cell packs or in peat pots in very early spring, even outdoors with no extra warmth. Young seedlings are extremely resentful of root disturbance, however, and so great care should be taken in establishing them in the beds where they are to grow. Few annual plants respond more dramatically to the best growing conditions—full sun, deep, humus-rich soil, and supplementary fertilizer—and few will be as disappointing with compromises. In most gardens, once larkspurs have been grown, they will reappear here and there as self-seeded plants, and though garden references often say that such volunteers will be inferior in color and form, they have in fact a simple, faded charm that is in its own way endearing.

CONVOLVULUS TRICOLOR

FAMILY: *Convolvulaceae* or morning glory family.

CLASSIFICATION: Half-hardy annual or short-lived perennial grown as half-hardy annual.

COMMON NAMES: Dwarf morning glory, bush morning glory, convolvulus.

HARDINESS: Hardy to Zones 9 and 10. Frost sensitive elsewhere.

GROWING CONDITIONS: Well-drained, sandy soil of moderate fertility. Full sun. Enjoys summer heat.

PROPAGATION: By seed, sown in place in warmer gardens or in peat pots 6 to 8 weeks before last frost. Seedlings resent root disturbance.

HEIGHT: Lax, to 2' length.

ORNAMENTAL VALUE: Grown for flower.

LEVEL OF CULTURAL DIFFICULTY: Moderately easy.

SPECIAL PROPERTIES: Useful in hanging baskets and window boxes. Excellent cool greenhouse plant for late winter flower.

PRONUNCIATION: kon-VOL-vew-lus TRI-co-lor

William Robinson, the great nineteenth- and early-twentieth-century garden authority, called *Convolvulus tricolor* "one of the most beautiful of the hardy annuals." He was referring, of course, to the flowers, borne singly or in pairs or threes from the axils of its leaves. The blooms, five petals fused into an almost perfect circle about two inches across, create in miniature the familiar, flattened funnel shape of morning glories, though happily, these remain open most of the day. Flowers may be primarily white, pink, dusty rose, garnet red, lavender, or pale or deep purple-blue, though each will have a prominent yellow throat and a feathery brushing of white halfway up the petals. The effect is curiously animated, as if a tiny explosion had just occurred in the heart of each flower. Though the garnet red is intense and handsome, most other shades have a chloroxed look, charming in its way, but no competition for the deepest purple-blue, which is in fact closest to the wild form. (Fortunately, it can be had in a separate seed strain called 'Royal Ensign' or sometimes 'Royal Blue'.)

A native of southern Europe cultivated since the early seventeenth century, convolvulus was once a common and much-loved garden plant. But like other species that transplant only with great care, it fell out of favor, superceded by plants such as marigolds and zinnias, which can be torn from a flat and may even benefit from some root disturbance. The development of thin-walled flexible plastic cell packs, however, is returning to favor many unwilling transplanters. A gentle pinch or poke at the bottom of the cell will free the soil block intact, like a cube of ice, leaving the roots of young plants undisturbed. Still, if one buys young plants of *C. tricolor*, one must take them on faith at first, for the splendidly colored inch- to two-inch-wide flowers will not show their pretty faces in the sixpack, but will only appear with the onset of warm weather—early July in most American gardens.

CONVOLVULUS TRICOLOR

Convolvulus tricolor belongs to the signature genus of the family Convolvulaceae to which morning glories and sweet potatoes also belong. Both family and genus names are taken from the Latin *convolvo,* meaning to twine around, and in the case of some members, such as the dreadful bindweed, *Convolvulus arvensis* (ar-VEN-sis), no name could be more apt. Once established, bindweed's deep roots are almost ineradicable, and its twining stems must be patiently unwound from desirable plants, since an impatient yank will bring away everything on which it has wrapped.

Fortunately, *C. tricolor* is no such menace. A true annual, native to Portugal, Greece, and North Africa, it may survive over winter, like many other true annuals, in the warm gardens of Zones 9 and 10, becoming weakly perennial. Elsewhere, it is treated as an annual. It forms a bushy little mound about a foot tall and twice as broad, made of many erect or slightly lax branched stems. In the axils of its oval, two-inch-long leaves, wavy at the margins and of a leathery texture, the flowers are borne.

Seed of *C. tricolor,* like that of most members of the family, is covered by a thick shell that must be filed lightly on one side, nicked, or softened by an overnight soak in water. The seed is also coated with wax—an extra protection against premature germination in autumn—which should be removed by rubbing it between soapy hands. Seed should be sown in cell packs about six weeks before the last expected frost. Though William Robinson described the plant as a hardy annual, it is in fact half-hardy for North American gardeners, and so should not be transplanted outdoors until all danger of frost is past. In gardens warmer than Zone 5, seed may also be sown in late autumn directly in the garden where the plants are to grow, and the young plants thinned to stand about a foot apart. Sandy,

well-drained soil and full sun are required, and fertilizing should not be liberal, or else plants will go to leaf and will flower poorly. *C. tricolor* blooms best in hot weather, and makes a very fine plant for a container, window box, or hanging basket. Seed sown in September and established in five-inch pots will produce wonderful flowers in late winter and spring in a cool greenhouse.

COREOPSIS SPECIES

FAMILY: *Asteraceae* or aster or daisy family.

CLASSIFICATION: Hardy or half-hardy annuals.

COMMON NAME: Tickseed (other popular names vary with species).

HARDINESS: Variable, depending on geographic distribution.

GROWING CONDITIONS: Ordinary to sandy, well-drained soil. Full sun.

PROPAGATION: By seed. Tender species sown indoors 8 to 12 weeks before last frost. Hardy species sown in place in late autumn or very early spring.

HEIGHT: 8″ to 2½′, depending on species and cultivar.

ORNAMENTAL VALUE: Grown for flower.

LEVEL OF CULTURAL DIFFICULTY: Easy to moderately difficult, depending on species.

SPECIAL PROPERTIES: *C. tinctoria* valued as dye plant.

PRONUNCIATION: kor-ee-OP-sis

*I*t is no etymological accident that our modern word *daisy* comes from the Old English metaphoric name for the sun, the "day's eye," for most daisies have an innate cheerfulness that gives a sensation of sunlight even on a cloudy day. One thinks of zinnias and marigolds, of calendulas and sunflowers. And certainly of coreopsis. Of the hundred or so members of the genus, twelve or more are cultivated. All are North American wild flowers, and all are easy to grow, as happy in the garden as in their native habitats.

Among the species in cultivation, the best-known is *Coreopsis grandiflora* (gran-di-FLO-ra), a native of the central and southern United States from Kansas and Missouri south to Georgia, Louisiana, and northern Florida. A true perennial with the unpleasant name "tickseed" (a translation of its genus name from ancient Greek *koris,* meaning bug, and *opsis,* meaning like), it forms a plant familiar to most gardeners: about two feet tall—three feet in robust varieties—with narrow, three- to five-lobed dark green leaves, surmounted by abundant, clear yellow daisies on long, wiry stems, in bloom from early summer until the end of August. Each broad, blunt ray petal is notched or "pinked" at its end, creating an appearance that remains constant through the genus, somehow ragged and orderly at once. Though listed as a perennial hardy to Zone 4, *C. grandiflora* may in fact be short-lived in colder and damper gardens, requiring frequent replacement. But it comes very easily from seed, and has the happy capacity of blooming in its first year, behaving essentially as an annual. Seed should be sown directly in the garden in early spring, and young plants may be thinned or transplanted to stand about nine inches apart. (More generous spacing is required where the species is reliably perennial.) Alternatively, seed may be sown under glass in February or early March, at temperatures around 60°F, and young plants grown on in bright, airy conditions until they can be hardened off and transplanted around the last expected frost. Ordinary garden soils, even on

COREOPSIS TINCTORIA

the lean side, produce the best plants, though perfect drainage is required.

C. grandiflora is often a component of seed mixes for flower meadows, and its ease of cultivation and its quick growth have made it a valuable roadside plant where enlightened highway departments are replacing swaths of mown turf with wild flowers. As a species, its close relationship to the very similar *C. lanceolata* (lan-see-o-LA-ta) causes botanists considerable discomfort, especially those concerned with the accurate classification of named cultivars. The gardener, however, will achieve quite similar results from seed offered as either species, at least as annual plants.

Another perennial species of *Coreopsis* often grown as an annual is *C. maritima* (mah-RIT-i-ma), a native of southern California and hardy only to Zone 9. Although it bears the popular name "sea dahlia," its succulent, bright green, ferny leaves look more like those of a cosmos than a dahlia. *C. maritima* would be attractive enough to grow merely for this foliage on a much-branched shrubby plant to three feet tall, but its four-inch-wide, clear butter-yellow daisies appear above the leaves on long stems from midsummer until frost. *C. maritima* should be seeded indoors about eight to twelve weeks before the last expected frost, and as it is native to a very warm climate, young plants should not be transplanted until the weather is quite settled. Its flowers and foliage make it a fine container plant, though it must never be allowed to dry out.

The true annual species of *Coreopsis* were once placed in a separate genus, *Calliopsis* (kal-ee-OP-sis), and though it is now retired, some still bear it as a common name. Among annual coreopsis, the easiest and most rewarding to grow is *Coreopsis tinctoria* (tink-TOR-ee-a), the dyer's coreopsis, so-called because its fresh flower heads yield dyes in shades of rust orange to bright yellow. It has a wide natural range across the central and western United States from North Dakota south to Louisiana and west to British Columbia and California, and is among the sturdiest and most easily grown of North American wild flowers. Plants typically reach a height of about thirty inches, though compact dwarf forms have been selected that are only about eight inches tall. Leaves are very finely cut, divided into narrow segments, providing an attractive foil for the long-stemmed, inch-and-a-half- to two-inch-wide flowers. In wild stands, flowers will typically be single bright yellow daisies with eight or so broad ray petals, notched across the outer edge, shaded a deep mahogany where they join the dark brown central disk. In horticultural forms, the shading may extend halfway up the petals, forming a prominent eye, or the entire flower may be suffused with rust red, brown, mahogany, or crimson. All these colorations are pleasing when massed together. The rather more baroque tigered, striped, or mottled forms—yellow on a crimson or brown base—probably deserve to be grown alone.

Because *Coreopsis tinctoria* is quick of growth, flowering in about seventy days from seeding, little is gained from starting seed indoors. A hardy annual, it may be sown as soon as the ground is workable in spring. South of Zone 5, it may also be seeded in late autumn for very strong plants the following spring. Ordinary well-drained garden soil in full sun produces the best plants. Like many other annuals native to open prairies and savannas, *C. tinctoria* looks best when somewhat crowded, and so should be thinned to stand as close as six inches from plant to plant. Although it flowers over a long period of time, from July to October, spent blossoms must be picked to prevent seed formation, which brings an end to flower production. Early in the season, this is fairly easy to do, but as flowers become more numerous, it can be tedious. Some relief is offered from the fact that *C. tinctoria*, like all coreopsis, is a superb cut flower. But when mature seed heads begin to outnumber unopened buds and flowers, a radical approach is to gather whole sheaves of flowering stems for a terminal snip of the garden shears. Generally, fresh buds and flowers will soon appear.

Coreopsis tinctoria is so hardy and so easy to grow that most American gardeners may have little interest in several other annual species native to the southwestern United States, chiefly Texas, all of which are tender annuals and so require special care in Zone 5 gardens and colder. Still, enthusiasts of American wild flowers will want to grow them, and where they are hardy they are very beautiful in annual flowering meadows. *C. drummondii* (dru-MON-dee-eye), often listed as *C. basalis* (BA-sa-lis), bears the irresistible popular name "golden wave" and is generally a foot-tall plant with narrow, lobed leaves and two-inch-wide yellow daisies shading to brownish-purple in the center. As with *C. tinctoria*, orange, crimson, and mahogany forms occur, and wildflower specialists in the warmer parts of North America might build up over time their own distinct color strains.

COSMOS SPECIES

FAMILY: *Asteraceae* or aster or daisy family.

CLASSIFICATION: Hardy or half-hardy annuals.

COMMON NAME: Cosmos.

HARDINESS: Sensitive to light frosts.

GROWING CONDITIONS: Well-drained, average to poor soil. Full sun.

PROPAGATION: By seed, sown indoors, 6 to 8 weeks before last frost.

HEIGHT: 2 to 5', depending on cultivar and culture.

ORNAMENTAL VALUE: Grown for flower.

LEVEL OF CULTURAL DIFFICULTY: Easy.

SPECIAL PROPERTIES: Excellent cut flowers.

PRONUNCIATION: KOZ-mus

Cosmos shares its name with the universe, from the ancient Greek word *kosmos,* signifying an ordered and harmonious beauty. Whether or not those assumptions remain true in the eyes of modern astronomers, most gardeners would agree that they suit the plant, and the name is so pretty that the two cultivated species in the genus have never attracted any vernacular name. They are known simply as "cosmos," a noun both singular and plural, though to avoid confusion, *Cosmos bipinnatus* (bi-pi-NAY-tus), the elder in cultivation, bears the name unmodified by an adjective, while *C. sulphureus* (sul-FUR-ee-us) is known as the "orange cosmos."

Both are true annuals native to Mexico, and both relish warm weather, seeming to be most encouraged by the worst heat summer has to offer. But in garden effect, the two species are very different plants. *Cosmos bipinnatus* grows into an open-branched, shrubby plant, whereas *C. sulphureus* always remains congested, crisscrossed in its branches and flowering stems. The foliage of *C. bipinnatus* is cut into fine, fringy segments, so

that a number of plants grown together look like a misty green cloud. The leaves of *C. sulphureus* are much coarser, divided into lobes and as long as nine inches at the base of the plant. It is in the color of the flowers, however, that the greatest difference between the two species lies. Those of *C. bipinnatus* are all in shades of white, pale or dark pink, rose-red, or magenta, and *C. sulphureus* bears flowers of clear yellow, orange, reddish orange, or scarlet. In the garden they rarely look good together.

The cultural requirements of the two species are for the most part the same. They flower best on average to fairly lean, well-drained soil in full sun. When pampered, the taller varieties can reach impressive heights of five to seven feet, though flowers will be delayed almost until frost. Flowering is most abundant in mid- to late summer and in early autumn, when the weather is generally settled and hot. Patient dead-heading of spent blossoms prolongs the production of bloom, but where many plants are grown, it can be tedious work. Both species make superb cut flowers, however, and knowing that can help with the task.

Of the two species, *C. bipinnatus* has received the most modification from breeders. The old-fashioned plant, generally with flowers in shades of magenta, white, and muddied pink, grew quite tall and bloomed late in the season, sometimes producing only a few flowers in colder gardens before frosts cut it down. All modern varieties are much earlier flowering, sometimes showing a button of bud in the six-pack. (It should be pinched out at transplant time to encourage fuller branching.) They tend as well to be more compact, though one can buy tall and dwarf varieties in most colors, the tall reaching a height of about five feet and the dwarfs closer to two or three feet. Colors have been improved, and now range from pure white through soft pinks to deep, rich dusty rose and purple. Some cultivars also pos-

COSMOS SULPHUREUS

of the plant are also quite brittle, and it is easy to snap one off when working around them. *C. bipinnatus* often self-seeds, though volunteer plants will generally be of inferior colors and slower to flower than named cultivars.

Few alterations have been made to *Cosmos sulphureus* beyond selecting more compact forms, which now range from a foot to thirty inches in height, and purifying and segregating color forms. The orange cosmos may now be had in clear lemon and deeper yellow, in a rich, clear orange, and in orange-red shaded with rust. Though each color has a special impact when grown alone, the colors are also quite beautiful when blended together. Each individual two-inch-wide flower resembles a single dahlia, making clear the close relationship between the two genera.

C. sulphureus is somewhat more tender than *C. bipinnatus* and slower to develop into flowering size from seed. It should be seeded indoors about eight weeks before frost and planted in the garden when the weather is quite warm and settled. Unlike *C. bipinnatus,* it requires care in transplanting. Young plants established in the garden should be moved with a generous ball of earth, and transplants from cell packs should never be disturbed at the roots.

Recently, a third species of *Cosmos* has attracted considerable attention, particularly among gardeners who love chocolate. The "chocolate cosmos," *Cosmos atrosanguineus* (a-tro-san-GWIN-ee-us), bears dark, brownish-maroon, two-inch-wide flowers richly scented of bitter chocolate. Sometimes listed under the closely related genus *Bidens* as *B. atrosanguineus,* chocolate cosmos is actually a tender perennial native to Mexico and hardy only in warm gardens in Zones 8 to 10. Elsewhere, it may be expected to flower abundantly from midsummer to autumn, particularly when grown in a pot or other container, for it loves a baking heat at

sess a shading, or eye, of a complementary color around the central yellow disk. Flower form has also been modified, into semi-doubles that produce several circles of somewhat ragged petals around the disk, and anemone-flowered forms, where disk flowers have been modified into a tight pincushion of petals surrounded by the larger ray petals. The most radical alteration has been to create "quilled" or "shelled" flowers, in which the ray petals are curled on themselves to make eight tidy little horns or deep cups, pale on the outside and more deeply tinted within. All these modifications of flower form are quite pretty, until one remembers the simple, winsome elegance of the original.

Cosmos bipinnatus can be expected to flower about two months from seeding. For earliest bloom, seed should be sown about six weeks before the last frost, and young plants moved to their permanent homes when the weather becomes settled. Good but later-flowering plants may be had by seeding directly in the garden after heavy frost, usually around late April or early May. Young plants transplant with great ease—even when a foot or so tall—if they are shaded for a day or two and watered well. Taller varieties may need a single stake to keep them upright. The branches its roots. Plants grow to about a foot in height, with three- to six-inch-long divided leaves clustered at the base. Flowers are born singly on slender, eight-inch stems that rise well above the foliage, as if presenting themselves to nose level. *C. atrosanguineus* is tuberous-rooted, much like its close relative, dahlias, and when grown in a pot, it is easy to carry over from year to year. When the foliage dies down in late summer or autumn, the pot is allowed to become dry and is then stored in cool but frost-free conditions, just such as suit dahlias, gladiolus, cannas, and other tender perennials that grow from corms or tubers. Somewhere around March, pots are taken from storage, barely moistened, and placed in warmer conditions at temperatures around 65 to 70°F. Shoots of new growth will soon appear, at which time the pots should be placed in bright, sunny conditions at daytime temperatures around 75°F. Watering should be increased and a light, water-soluble fertilizer should be applied at weekly intervals to encourage growth. The first flowers should appear by the end of June, and if they are promptly removed as they fade, others will follow until frost.

CRASPEDIA SPECIES

FAMILY: *Asteraceae* or aster or daisy family.

CLASSIFICATION: Tender perennial grown as half-hardy annual.

COMMON NAMES: Drumsticks, yellow bachelor's buttons, billy buttons, craspedia.

HARDINESS: Sensitive to light frosts.

GROWING CONDITIONS: Well-drained sandy soil of moderate fertility. Full sun.

PROPAGATION: By seed, sown indoors 8 to 10 weeks before last frost.

HEIGHT: 10 to 12", occasionally taller.

ORNAMENTAL VALUE: Grown for flower.

LEVEL OF CULTURAL DIFFICULTY: Moderately difficult.

SPECIAL PROPERTIES: Excellent cut flower. Useful as dried flower.

PRONUNCIATION: kras-pee-DEE-a

The genus *Craspedia,* with about seven species native to Australia and New Zealand, takes its name from the ancient Greek word *kraspedon,* meaning a fringe, which refers not to the flower but to the milkweedlike parachute that disperses individual seeds by wind. The popular name "drumsticks" is much more suggestive of the real distinction of the species most grown, *Craspedia globosa* (glo-BO-sa), which bears inch-round, tightly packed globes of petals in brilliant taxi-cab yellow. Each globe is borne on a wiry ten-inch stem much like drumsticks and making them excellent cut flowers. They retain their color when dried and are valuable for winter arrangements, wreaths, and other decorations.

Craspedia globosa is actually a true perennial, persisting from year to year in dryer gardens in USDA Zones 9 and 10. But it begins to flower in about four months from seed, and so an early April sowing indoors at temperatures around 60°F will produce flowering plants by midsummer. If spent blossoms are removed, plants that have begun to flower will continue until frost. Flower stems rise about basal mounds of foot-long, oval leaves densely covered with tiny hairs, giving them a silvery appearance. Flowers are attractive, however, only so long as they remain upright, and so plants should be grown in a position sheltered from wind and on rather lean, dryish soils. Once stems have toppled, it is best to cut them and wait for a new crop, since bundling them together against a stake ruins their beauty.

Very rarely seed is also offered of *Craspedia glauca* (GLAW-ka), a highly variable species—or perhaps several species—with a wide natural range across all states of Australia and New Zealand. It forms a basal rosette of oblong leaves, each up to ten inches long, and in most plants covered with woolly hairs. The tightly packed drumsticks of flower are more oval than spherical, borne on thin stems that vary in height from plant to plant, within a range of ten inches to two feet. Flower color may be white, ivory, pale yellow, or yellow-orange. Sometimes listed as *C. uniflora* (u-ni-FLO-ra), *C. alpina* (al-PEE-na), or *C. richea* (RICH-ee-a), *Craspedia glauca* is even more insistent on a gritty, perfectly drained soil, moisture at the crown being certain to cause rotting off. In all other ways, its culture is identical to that of *Craspedia globosa*.

CREPIS RUBRA

FAMILY: *Asteraceae* or aster or daisy family.

CLASSIFICATION: Hardy or half-hardy annual.

COMMON NAMES: Hawkweed, hawk's beard, annual hawkbit, crepis.

HARDINESS: Withstands light frosts when well established.

GROWING CONDITIONS: Well-drained, poor, dryish soil. Full sun. Prefers cool weather.

PROPAGATION: From seed, sown in place in very early spring, or indoors 6 to 8 weeks before last frost.

HEIGHT: To 1′.

ORNAMENTAL VALUE: Grown for flower.

LEVEL OF CULTURAL DIFFICULTY: Easy in cool gardens. Moderately easy in warm ones.

SPECIAL PROPERTIES: Useful as late-winter-flowering cool greenhouse plant.

PRONUNCIATION: KREY-pis RU-bra

Crepis rubra much resembles a dandelion in all particulars except flower color. Those who like dandelions will find it a wonderful little plant, and even those who don't might be won over by its delicate, porcelain-pink flowers. A native of Greece and southern Italy, it is one of only two species in its genus (of about 200) that is much grown in gardens, the other being the similar *Crepis incana* (in-KAH-na), a somewhat fickle perennial reliably hardy only to Zone 6 and then only on very well-drained, gritty soils. The genus name comes from the ancient Greek word for a laced boot, *krepis,* and seems to have no application to any part of any plant in the genus, and the species name, *rubra,* signifies red rather than pink. Still, it is a very pretty little plant with many distinctions beyond the confusion in its names.

C. rubra flowers in about two months from seed, and as it is a hardy annual, it may be seeded directly in the garden as soon as the soil can be worked, in expectation of flowers in early July. Alternatively, for even earlier bloom, it may be seeded indoors six to eight weeks before the last anticipated frost date. The plants themselves are nothing remarkable in appearance, consisting of a basal rosette of toothed, dandelion-like leaves from which branching growth ascends upward a foot or so. But the inch- to inch-and-a-half-wide flowers, borne in profusion on single stems, are very beautiful, consisting of daisies a little more ragged and loosely formed than those of dandelions, and the prettier for it. The white form, var. *alba,* looks wonderful alone, or blended with the paler and deeper pinks. Spent blossoms are followed by attractive, fluffy seed heads, but if they are prevented from forming by dead-heading, new flowers will be produced well into the autumn, even after fairly heavy frosts. In fact, *Crepis rubra* is at its best in cool weather and will cease flowering in gardens that experience hot, steamy summers, perhaps resuming when the cool weather of late summer arrives.

C. rubra flowers most freely on poor, dryish soils, and is an excellent candidate for naturalizing on dry, gravelly banks or fresh cuts into subsoil. In gardens warmer than Zone 5, it will generally reseed itself on undisturbed ground. A little fresh seed, gathered and sown in mid- to late summer, pricked out and grown on in five-inch pots in a cool, sunny greenhouse, produces flowering plants in late winter and early spring.

CRYPTOTAENIA JAPONICA

FAMILY: *Umbelliferae* or Queen Anne's lace family.

CLASSIFICATION: Hardy annual, biennial, or hardy perennial grown as hardy annual.

COMMON NAME: Cryptotaenia.

HARDINESS: Withstands light frost.

GROWING CONDITIONS: Full sun to full shade. Shade required in warmer gardens.

PROPAGATION: From seed, sown indoors 8 to 10 weeks before last frost. Self-seeds abundantly once grown.

HEIGHT: 12 to 18".

ORNAMENTAL VALUE: Valued for purple foliage.

LEVEL OF CULTURAL DIFFICULTY: Easy.

SPECIAL PROPERTIES: None.

PRONUNCIATION: krip-to-TAY-nee-a ja-PON-i-ca

*I*n the short time it has been available to American gardeners—no more than five years or so—*Cryptotaenia japonica* has already entered the ranks of plants treasured for purple foliage, joining such stalwarts as *Perilla frutescens, Atriplex hortensis,* and *Haloragis erecta.* All four occur in mousy, dull green forms, but they also possess glamorous plum-, chocolate-, or chestnut-leaved varieties that come true from seed. None bear flowers of any particular importance, though the small, pale pink to white umbels of cryptotaenia are the prettiest of the lot. But the dark leaves are invaluable in borders because they seem to enhance any flower color, whether on the hot side—chrome yellow, orange, and red—or the cool—rose, purple, blue, mauve, and white.

Cryptotaenia grows from twelve to eighteen inches tall, producing leaves composed of three broadly arrow-shaped leaflets joined at the base into a graceful, outfacing triad. The leaflets are attractively puckered and may be deeply toothed along their edges or merely fringed as if cut with pinking shears. When newly produced, they are a beautiful, rich plum color with lead-gray overtones, though they age down to olive green. Plants are unbranched, but each leaf is carried on a long, brownish-maroon petiole that forms a V with the central stem, and from which an additional, smaller leaf is often borne. A single stem with leaves suggests an Art Deco elegance, though sadly, it will slump miserably after a few hours in a vase.

Cryptotaenia is rare at present, and so it is apt to be acquired from nurseries specializing in unusual annual and tender plants. If seed is available, however, it is easy to germinate and grow on. It should be started about eight to ten weeks before the last anticipated frost date, at temperatures of around 60°F. Unlike many Umbellifers, cryptotaenia transplants with reasonable ease and so may be sown in pots and pricked out as soon as young plants can be handled. They should then be grown on in cool, bright conditions until hardened off for transplanting after all danger of frost is past. When newly grown in gardens, individual specimens are attractive, especially when they poke through the embracing foliage and flower of other plants. But better effects are often achieved by establishing several plants about five inches one from another, to grow together and create a graceful, bushlike effect, which is usually more attractive than single plants standing alone. In all but the coldest gardens, self-seeded plants are apt to occur in abundance, often proving to be something of a nuisance, though they are easy to grub out.

Cryptotaenia is native to moist, fertile meadows and woodland edge in Japan, where it is a familiar "ditch" plant along the damp verges of country roads. Its preference is therefore for a rather heavy, moisture-retentive soil in full sun or part shade, though in gardens it seems to accept any reasonably fertile soil, provided adequate moisture is supplied, for it is intolerant of drought. In the hottest gardens, it prefers part to full shade, though elsewhere it seems to grow equally well in any light conditions from full sun to full shade. Its relative willingness to accept rather gloomy growing conditions makes it invaluable for furnishing dim areas underneath large shrubs or shaded bays in shrubbery borders. And though a large pot planted only with cryptotaenia makes an interesting foliage display for a patio, its best use seems to be as a "dot" plant, established in closely planted groups at intervals in a border to create a subtle rhythm of foliage and an enhancement to brighter, flowering plants.

CUPHEA SPECIES

FAMILY: *Lythraceae* or lythrum family.
CLASSIFICATION: Tender perennials or woody shrubs grown as tender annuals.
COMMON NAMES: Mexican cigar plant, firecracker plant, cuphea.
HARDINESS: Hardy in Zones 9 and 10. Sensitive to light frosts elsewhere.

GROWING CONDITIONS: Humus-rich, well-drained moist soil. Full sun in cooler gardens, part shade or filtered sun in warmer ones.
PROPAGATION: By seed, sown about 12 weeks before last frost. Cuttings taken at any time root readily.
HEIGHT: 12 to 18".
ORNAMENTAL VALUE: Grown for flower and for neat, shrubby appearance.
LEVEL OF CULTURAL DIFFICULTY: Easy.
SPECIAL PROPERTIES: Excellent windowsill or cool greenhouse plant. May be trained into standards.
PRONUNCIATION: KEW-fee-a (kew-FAY-a)

*U*ntil recently, it did not occur to many gardeners that cuphea, long valued as houseplants and in greenhouses and conservatories, also make superb outdoor bedding plants in the summer garden. *Cuphea* are an entirely New World genus of about 250 species, the showiest of which are natives of tropical Central America, chiefly Mexico and Guatemala. Though actually tender woody perennials and sub-shrubs hardy to Zones 9 and 10, they will flower in about three months from seed, and so may be had in bloom in June from an early March sowing indoors. Cuttings, taken at almost any time of the year, will root easily when inserted in damp sand or in half peat, half perlite and kept moist. Like many other plants native to the rich jungles of Central America, such as fuchsia, cuphea require a well-drained, humus-rich, and water-retentive soil. They are greedy feeders and benefit by an application of water-soluble plant food every two weeks during the growing season. Given these attentions, they will thrive in full sun in cool gardens, and in bright shade where summers are hot. With some midday protection, they will tolerate high heat and humidity, flowering continuously from early summer until frost, and even producing seedlings beneath the mother plant that will flower as well by late summer. Young plants may be lifted at season's end, potted into six-inch pots, and grown on for winter flower in a bright window or cool greenhouse. Though interesting and useful as bedding plants, cuphea are also superb in containers, hanging baskets, and window boxes. They may also be trained as standards— small, mop-headed miniature trees on a single trunk.

The most commonly offered *Cuphea* is *C. ignea* (IG-nee-a), popularly called the "Mexican cigar plant" or "firecracker plant." It forms a neat, many-branched shrublet about a foot tall and as wide, with lance-shaped one- to two-inch-long leaves of a fresh laurel green, prominently marked with a white central vein. Flowers are

borne in the axils of the leaves and consist of tiny, three-quarter-inch-long tubes of burning orange, marked by a red band near the end and terminating in a flared, ash-blue mouth, from which a fringe of prominent stamens protrudes. Flowers almost outnumber leaves, creating the effect of a haze of scarlet red. A beautiful form with variegated leaves exists, and also pretty forms with white or rose flowers.

Cuphea micropetala (mi-cro-PET-a-la) is larger than *C. ignea* in all its parts, sacrificing some of the dainty charm of that species for perhaps a greater—or at least more obvious—showiness. It can grow into an erect, shrubby plant as tall as four feet, with oblong leaves as much as five inches wide. The tubular flowers, borne in leafy terminal clusters, are as much as two inches long and are a vibrant yellow-orange shading to yellow-green with scarlet at the base. This combination of colors

CUPHEA IGNEA

occurs elsewhere in the flower kingdom, in *Fuchsia splendens* and in *Alstroemeria psittacina,* and it is always wonderful. In culture and in general garden uses, *Cuphea micropetala* is identical to *C. ignea,* though the two might best not be grown side by side, as comparisons would be invidious to both.

Cupheas are such excellent and easy garden plants that other species are bound to surface in the next few years. At present, however, one other is commonly available, *Cuphea hysopifolia* (hih-so-pi-FO-lee-a), appropriately called the "elfin shrub." Hardy only to Zone 10, it forms a wiry, much-branched shrublet with half-inch, downy leaves crowded along its stems, creating a look something like garden hyssop (*Hyssopus officinalis*), from which it draws its species name, or like heath or heather, from which it takes two other common names, false or Mexican heather. Its flowers, however, are nothing heatherlike, consisting of six paddle-shaped, starry petals, violet or rose-red or white, only one-quarter-inch long and scarcely wider. But they are borne in great abundance in the axils of the leaves whenever the plant is in active growth. Though all color forms are attractive, the snow white one is perhaps most useful, as a crisp and clean edging plant in borders or window boxes, or in large containers.

The genus name, *Cuphea,* is taken from the ancient Greek word *kyphos,* meaning curved, and refers either to the shape of the seed capsule, or perhaps to the hornlike curve of the fused petals of some species.

CYNARA SPECIES

FAMILY: *Asteraceae* or aster or daisy family.
CLASSIFICATION: Half-hardy perennials grown as half-hardy annuals.
COMMON NAMES: Cardoon, artichoke.
HARDINESS: Winter-hardy to Zone 7 with protection. Grown as annuals in cooler gardens.
GROWING CONDITIONS: Extremely rich, well-drained moist soils. Full sun.
PROPAGATION: By seed, sown in late February.
HEIGHT: 3 to 5' in leaf.
ORNAMENTAL VALUE: Valued for dramatic, architectural form of the leaves.
LEVEL OF CULTURAL DIFFICULTY: Difficult from seed. Easy from purchased young plants.
SPECIAL PROPERTIES: Both species valued as edible plants.
PRONUNCIATION: si-NA-ra

*A*lthough many Americans still cling to the notion that flower and vegetable gardens are separate domains, the fact is that keeping the plots separate is detrimental to both. Flowers look very beautiful among edible crops, and on the other side, some vegetables make wonderful additions to the flower garden, adding a boldness of leaf often missing in many border perennials and annuals. One thinks particularly of red and Savoy cabbage, ornamental cabbage and kale, Bull's Blood and MacGregor's beets, purple-leaved basil, orach and amaranths, scarlet runner beans, and sweet corn with purple or variegated leaves.

Of all the vegetables that might be included in ornamental gardens, none are more splendidly architectural than two species in the genus *Cynara:* cardoons and artichokes. Both have been cultivated since ancient times: artichokes for their succulent, fully formed but unopened flower buds, and cardoons for the fleshy, esculent midrib of their leaves.

Though the gastronomic value of the two plants differs, their effect in the garden is similar.

Both produce magnificent fountains of upward growing and outward facing gray-green leaves in their first year from seed. Cardoons are taller, to as much as five feet, with coarser leaves showing a prominent watery midrib and deeply lobed sides, silvery-green above and woolly white beneath. The lobes of the leaves terminate in spines that, though they must be paid attention to, are not deadly. Artichokes form smaller fountains of leaf, to three feet or so in their first year, with greener, less furry leaves, and few spines. When grown for ornamental purposes, both plants are best used singly, so that their strong architectural form has greatest value, though a rhythm of them repeated down a long border can also be effective. Both, also, are especially fine grown among other plants valued for their leaves or their structure, such as ornamental grasses, castor beans, or cannas.

Whether artichokes and cardoons are different species or merely variants of one is in doubt. As is often the case with agricultural crops of ancient cultivation, no natural progenitor of the artichoke has ever been found. It is assumed, then, that it is a selection made centuries ago from *Cynara cardunculus* (kar-DUN-cu-lus), the cardoon, of a form with unopened flower buds as edible as the leaves. The first selection must have been small, fibrous, and spiny, though subsequent selections resulted in fatter buds with thicker, more meaty petals (actually bracts) and eventually established artichokes as aristocrats among vegetables, a status they have enjoyed since Roman times. By contrast, cardoons are seldom eaten in this country, requiring as they do patient blanching in the garden and elaborate preparation. (Cardoons are given the species name *cardunculus,* meaning little thistle. Artichokes borrow their species name, *scolymus* [sko-LEE-mus], from the genus designation of another plant seldom but occasionally grown for its edible taproot, *Scoly-*

mus hispanicus [hi-SPAN-i-cus], the Spanish oyster plant.)

Artichokes and cardoons are both perennial plants native to the Mediterranean region. Cardoons are hardier, surviving over winter in Zone 7 gardens with the protection of a thick mulch, and producing in their second year eight-foot-tall, coarse stalks terminating in a candelabrum of several two- to three-inch, rounded bluish-rose thistle flowers. Many gardeners think the flowering plants less beautiful than those in leaf and cut out the flower buds just as they begin to form to encourage richer leaves. Artichokes may persist as far north as Zone 7, though winter wet is a greater enemy than cold, causing the crowns to rot. In colder gardens where they have a chance of being hardy, the crowns should be cut down to six inches after frosts, covered with wooden boxes and then with a thick insulating blanket of hay.

Like many half-hardy or tender perennials or biennials grown as annuals, artichokes and cardoons should be sown very early indoors, no later than the end of February, in order to produce decorative plants for the summer garden. Germination occurs within a week or two at temperatures around 65° to 70°F, and the infant

CYNARA CARDUNCULUS

plants are beautiful almost from their first appearance. Unless one has a sunny greenhouse, however, steady growth so early in the year is best achieved under fluorescent light units. Both artichokes and cardoons are very greedy feeders, and young plants develop best with weekly applications of half-strength liquid plant food. Young plants may be hardened off and transplanted into the garden at about the time it is safe to transplant tomatoes. Soils should be well drained, but as deep and rich as possible, with perhaps as much as a bushel of rotted manure or compost incorporated into each planting hole. Though individual plants will be small at transplant time, their eventual girth should not be overestimated, for with the arrival of summer's heat they will quickly expand into plants three or four feet wide and at least as tall. Gardeners in colder regions who have never grown either plant for ornamental purposes will be perhaps intimidated, surprised, and delighted by their size and beauty. Once grown, they are apt to become essential components of the summer border, treasured for the fine textural contrast they offer to the somewhat fiddly nature of most annual and perennial plants.

CYNOGLOSSUM AMABILE

CYNOGLOSSUM AMABILE

FAMILY: *Boraginaceae* or borage family.

CLASSIFICATION: Half-hardy biennial grown as half-hardy annual.

COMMON NAMES: Chinese forget-me-not, hound's tongue, cynoglossum.

HARDINESS: Resistant to light frosts.

GROWING CONDITIONS: Ordinary, well-drained garden soil. Full to part sun.

PROPAGATION: From seed, sown in place in autumn in Zone 7 gardens or warmer, in early spring in colder gardens, or indoors 8 weeks before last frost. Self-seeds in all but coldest gardens.

HEIGHT: 12 to 15".

ORNAMENTAL VALUE: Grown for flower.

LEVEL OF CULTURAL DIFFICULTY: Easy.

SPECIAL PROPERTIES: Excellent cut flower.

PRONUNCIATION: si-no-GLOS-um a-MA-bi-lee

Flowers of an intense, clear blue, with no muddying of mauve or red, can be among the most difficult of all to grow. It is a surprise, then, to find a flower of a good, clear blue that is easy to grow under ordinary garden conditions and sufficiently abundant with its flowers to be really showy. *Cynoglossum amabile,* the Chinese forget-me-not, is such a plant, and it is hard to understand why it is not grown more frequently. There is no other flower color—red, orange, yellow, purple, mauve, rose, or white—that is not made more beautiful by its abundant sprays of marine blue, in bloom from early July until October. Most unusual among blue flowers also, it is excellent for cutting.

The Chinese forget-me-not is amiable in other ways as well. Though technically a biennial that may be sown in Zone 7 gardens (and warmer) in September, in colder gardens it is treated as an annual, flowering in two months from sowing outdoors after frosts have passed in May. Alternatively, seed may be sown indoors in March at temperatures of around 60°F. Young seedlings should be pricked out as soon as they are large enough to handle and grown on in bright, cool conditions until they may be hardened off and established in the garden.

Cynoglossum is not particular as to soils, flourishing even in hot, dry locations, in full or part sun. In most gardens, once it has been grown for a season it will self-seed, and seedlings, when quite young, can be transplanted with care.

Plants of *Cynoglossum amabile* may be expected to reach as much as two feet under good culture, though fifteen inches is more typical. They are bushy and upright, with two- to three-inch-long, attractive gray-green, tongue-shaped leaves of a soft, velvety texture, giving the genus both its Latin and one of its popular names, from ancient Greek *kyon,* meaning dog, and *glossa,* tongue. Flower stems are numerous, creating a brushy effect, and each is thickly crowded on one side with tiny, half-inch-wide, five-lobed forget-me-not flowers. Both light and turquoise-blue forms exist, the best perhaps being the cultivar 'Blue Showers' bred by the Dutch for the world cut-flower market. There are also pink and white forms, pretty enough, but hardly competitive with the blues.

Cynoglossum amabile is largely untroubled by insects, though its downy leaves can fall prey to powdery mildew where humid, hot, rainy weather follows a prolonged period of drought. Deep watering in dry weather helps prevent the disease, which may also be treated with a dusting of horticultural sulphur or with synthetic chemical sprays.

DAHLIA X HORTENSIS

FAMILY: *Asteraceae* or aster or daisy family.

CLASSIFICATION: Tender tuberous perennial grown as tender perennial or tender annual.

COMMON NAME: Dahlia.

HARDINESS: Leaves sensitive to light frosts. Appreciates summer heat.

GROWING CONDITIONS: Very rich, humusy, well-drained soil. Abundant moisture. Full sun.

PROPAGATION: From individual tubers or from seed sown indoors 12 weeks before frost.

HEIGHT: Variable, from 6" to 4', according to variety.

ORNAMENTAL VALUE: Grown for flower.

LEVEL OF CULTURAL DIFFICULTY: Moderately easy.

SPECIAL PROPERTIES: Dwarf forms make excellent window box and container plants.

PRONUNCIATION: DA-lee-a (DAY-lee-a) hor-TEN-sis

*F*ew gardeners would know how to cook a dahlia, but the first two species to enter Europe, *Dahlia coccinea* (co-CHIN-ee-a) and *D. pinnata* (pi-NA-ta), were taken from Mexico to Spain in the hope of finding a food as nutritious and palatable as the potato. In that, dahlias were a disappointment, though stock was maintained at the Royal Botanic Garden in Madrid, and imported into England by the Marchioness of Bute in 1789. Both species were native to the high plains of Central America, the first bearing yellow-centered, single scarlet flowers and the second, single flowers of a pale lavender purple. They freely intercrossed, producing a color range interesting enough to create a significant vogue in the early nineteenth century, abetted by the Empress Josephine, who grew them enthusiastically in her garden at Malmaison. Like many Central

DAHLIA 'BISHOP OF LLANDAFF'

American natives, however, early dahlias were short-day plants, blooming only from October to November. But by 1870 forms had been bred that would flower in late June and continue well into autumn, and the popularity of the dahlia was ensured.

Certainly no other garden flower has been bred from so limited a genetic stock into so many forms and colors. Although the genus contains about twenty-five species, modern dahlias are descendant from only four modest-flowered wild progenitors. Plants now range in height from a foot to eight feet, with foliage that may be olive or bronze green or deep brownish-maroon. Flowers, measuring from two to twelve inches in diameter, occur in almost every color except true blue: white and yellow, orange, pink, red and purple to bronze, with many bi-colors. The American Dahlia Society recognizes eighteen flower forms, and the International Register of Dahlias currently lists 20,000 distinct cultivars.

Until fairly recently, only breeders who wanted to secure new cultivars bothered to grow dahlias from seed, and seed-grown plants generally did not flower until their second year of growth. Seed strains now exist, however, that will flower in about twelve weeks from sowing, sup-

plying blooming plants in late June from an April seeding indoors. Seed-grown dahlias are generally less than four feet in height, many forming compact, bushy plants hardly a foot tall and useful for pots and containers. Though the first dahlias developed to be grown from seed were singles, strains are now offered that are fully double, cactus-flowered with needle-like petals, ball-shaped pom-pom forms, and "collarette" with a second row of short ray petals surrounding the disk.

Seed of dahlias germinates very readily at temperatures around 70°F, and seedlings transplant easily. As dahlias are extremely frost-sensitive, however, young plants should not be established in the garden until the weather is settled and warm. Soils should be deep and fertile, though extra nitrogen in the form of animal manures should be avoided, as it will promote soft, leafy growth at the expense of flowers, and may impair the storage capacity of the tuberous roots. Fertilizers rich in phosphorus and potassium will encourage the strongest growth and most abundant flowering. Taller forms may require staking, though if plants are pinched after they have produced three sets of leaves they will become bushy and may stand alone. Bloom time is extended by dead-heading spent blossoms, though one must be careful not to disturb bumblebees that often fall asleep within the flowers.

Modern seed strains are fairly uniform, producing the same or at least a similar blossom type and color from one seed packet, though mixes will offer a variety of colors, some of which may be particularly pretty. Roots of those plants should be dug after frost has withered the top growth, left in a dry, airy place for a day or two, freed of soil, and stored in bags of dry vermiculite at temperatures of 38° to 50°F. Bags should be checked periodically throughout the winter, and the vermiculite barely moistened if tubers show any signs of shriveling. Roots may be divided in the spring, though new plants sprout from the juncture of the stem and tubers, and tubers without at least one "eye," or growing point, will never sprout. Division is easiest if clusters of tubers are placed in moist peat in a warm room until they have barely sprouted, showing where cuts can be made with a sharp knife. Tubers can then be started indoors in pots for early flower, or planted outdoors in June about the time it is safe to plant corn.

DATURA SPECIES

FAMILY: *Solanaceae* or deadly nightshade family.

CLASSIFICATION: Annuals or half-hardy perennials grown as tender annuals.

COMMON NAMES: Devil's apple, thorn apple, stinkweed, mad apple, angels' trumpets.

HARDINESS: Root-hardy to Zone 6. Leaves damaged by light frosts.

GROWING CONDITIONS: Humus-rich, well-drained garden soil. Full sun.

PROPAGATION: By seed, sown indoors 8 to 10 weeks before last frost.

HEIGHT: From 3 to 5', depending on available support.

ORNAMENTAL VALUE: Grown for flowers.

LEVEL OF CULTURAL DIFFICULTY: Easy.

SPECIAL PROPERTIES: All species contain hallucinogenic substances that are highly toxic.

PRONUNCIATION: da-TUR-a

*I*n Nathaniel Hawthorne's tale "Rappaccini's Daughter," a jealous magician is so possessive of his beautiful only child that he encourages her to cultivate poisonous flowers in her garden. Bit by bit, she becomes so imbued with poison that she is deadly to the touch. She might well have cultivated daturas, not only for their sinister, night-borne beauty, but also because, like so many other members of the nightshade family, parts of the plants are saturated with deadly toxins. It has been said, in fact, that the genus *Datura* has been responsible for more deaths than any other, putting aside mushrooms. But those who choose to grow its various showy species and hybrids will find startling and beautiful additions to the summer garden.

Daturas bear blooms consisting of flared tubes of five fused petals. The first of these enormous trumpets appears when the stout stem of the plant divides, revealing a single bud sheaf in its cleft that matures into a tightly furled umbrella of a dull purplish green. The bud gradually elongates to eight or ten inches, at which point, just at twilight, it unfurls into a single trumpet six to eight inches across with a throat almost a foot deep. (This process is actually visual to the very patient observer.) Like most flowers pollinated by night-flying moths, these are intensely perfumed, with a fragrance close to that of *Lilium speciosum.* Flowers last only for a single night, after which they hang limp and exhausted for a day, and then drop off as the spiny, seed-bearing fruit develop. Stems continue to divide, producing more buds and blossoms until, by mid-August, perhaps as many as fifty flowers will open on a single plant at twilight. Garden daturas generally produce lax, sprawling plants as much as five feet tall, clad in felty gray-green, broadly arrow-shaped leaves about six inches long. When crushed, the leaves omit a slightly unpleasant odor, accounting for one common name, "stinkweed."

To greater or lesser degree all species of *Datura* contain potent alkaloids, most significantly hyoscyamine, a powerful hallucinogen that induces insanity in large doses and may be fatal. Wherever species occurred natively, in both

DATURA METELOIDES

Datura may yet prove of enormous utility in the treatment of nervous disorders, lung disease, and rheumatism.

The genus *Datura,* from an Indian vernacular word, *dhatura,* once contained about thirteen species of true annuals, weak or persistent perennials, and stout, sometimes treelike, shrubs. The latter have been detached into the genus *Brugmansia,* which now contains five species, leaving datura with eight, all of which bear up- or outfacing flowers, as opposed to brugmansia, the flowers of which hang downward. Individual species of *Datura* waver between being persistently or weakly perennial or annual, with climate and other conditions often making the difference between whether a plant will persist for a year or two or perish after its first season of bloom. But like other members of the family Solanaceae (peppers, tomatoes, and eggplant), all species will flower in about twelve weeks from seeding, blooming in early July and continuing until frost from an early April sowing indoors. Though all daturas are native to mild or tropical regions of the world, their seed is surprisingly winter-hardy, so that several species are naturalized throughout Europe and in North America as far north as Zone 5.

Most daturas grown in gardens travel under the name of either *Datura metel* (ME-tel) or *Datura meteloides* (me-tel-OY-dees). The two species are very similar, if not hopelessly intermarried, for all daturas grown in gardens appear to hybridize among themselves. Over centuries of selection in its native India and in China, however, *D. metel,* which generally bears rich white trumpets, occurs in other colors, of cream and yellow, white-flushed lavender to purple, and even red. But in its simpler, single form, *D. metel* is generally confused with the southwestern American and Mexican species *D. meteloides,* which, in typical form, bears flowers of white flushed at the

hemispheres, they have found their way into religious and mystic rituals, and were most probably the drug used to induce trances in the priestesses of the Oracle at Delphi. The narcotic properties of *Datura* species were anciently recognized in both India and China, where it was also used to treat a wide range of medical disorders and as a topical anesthetic. By the early Renaissance, Italian apothecaries had learned to distill poison from its leaves and seeds. One New World species, Jimson weed, *Datura stramonium* (stra-MO-nee-um), grows naturally along roadsides throughout the southern tier of the United States. It is the plant once used in shamanistic rituals by Native Americans, and the one that killed soldiers at Jamestown, Virginia, who ate it boiled. (Hence the popular name, "Jimson," a corruption of Jamestown.) Despite all this, species of edges with an almost unearthly lavender, and with which *Datura metel* may well have mated. To further complicate matters, most material offered as *Datura meteloides* may in fact be another southwestern native—*Datura inoxia* (in-OX-ee-a) in either of two subspecies: *D. inoxia* subsp. *inoxia,* or subsp. *quinquecuspidata* (quin-ku-cus-pi-DA-ta).

So startling and beautiful are the simple, uncomplicated flowers of these species and their progeny, however, that more baroque colors and forms, particularly the "hose in hose" types with one or two additional blossoms squeezed into the original funnel, might well be avoided except as garden oddities.

Whatever form of datura one may have, whether from packets or seed collected from a friend's garden or along the roadside, treatment of young plants will be identical to that of other garden solanums such as tomatoes or peppers. Seed is sown indoors about eight to ten weeks before the last frost. Germination occurs best at warm temperatures, somewhere around 70°F, under which conditions seedlings will appear within two weeks. Just as with peppers, tomatoes, and eggplants, the goal is to produce sturdy young plants about six inches high by last frost, when they may be transplanted to the garden. One need not be in a hurry, however, for daturas—particularly those started indoors—will be sensitive to raw, rainy weather, and would do better held a week or so indoors rather than exposed to shivering outdoor conditions. Though young seedlings may be transplanted, they do not like their roots disturbed, and so should be slipped carefully from six-packs or grown in peat pots, and volunteers, which may occur in gardens in Zone 5 and warmer, should be transplanted with a generous ball of earth while quite young. Even at transplant time, one will note swollen root below the growing plant, indicating a sort of modified tuber that will form and that may be lifted at season's end and stored over winter for another season of growth, as one would store dahlias.

DIANTHUS SPECIES

FAMILY: *Caryophyllaceae* or carnation family.

CLASSIFICATION: Half-hardy annuals, biennials, or perennials grown as half-hardy annuals.

COMMON NAMES: Annual pinks, annual carnations, annual dianthus.

HARDINESS: Hardy to light frosts.

GROWING CONDITIONS: Well-drained, moderately fertile, limey garden soil.

PROPAGATION: From seed, sown indoors 12 weeks before last frost, outdoors in September in warm gardens.

HEIGHT: To 12″.

ORNAMENTAL VALUE: Grown for flower.

LEVEL OF CULTURAL DIFFICULTY: Moderately difficult.

SPECIAL PROPERTIES: Excellent cut flower.

PRONUNCIATION: di-AN-thus

From the Middle Ages until late in the sixteenth century, very few plants were grown in gardens merely because they were pretty. But the monks of the Middle Ages and prudent housewives in the Renaissance must have treasured certain plants in their gardens not only because they promised remedies to illnesses, but also because they were beautiful. Indeed, one suspects sometimes that uses were invented for pretty plants simply to justify their presence in the limited space of cloister gardens or the tight confines of Renaissance manor houses. Dianthus belong in this category, for no part of the plant has any

DIANTHUS CHINENSIS

proven therapeutic efficacy. Still, it was early recognized that the bracing fragrance of dianthus produced a lightening of the heart and a sense of contentment. In Chaucer's day, the petals of dianthus were added to wines and to sweet courses as a tonic believed to strengthen the heart and lungs and to improve courage. All species of *Dianthus* are edible, and some, particularly the old-fashioned perennial "clove pink," are still used in pastries, sorbets, jellies, and salads, where they impart a mild, spicy fragrance and a decorative effect.

There are more than 300 species in the genus *Dianthus,* many grown at least since the twelfth century. (The genus takes its name from ancient Greek *Di,* of Zeus, and *anthos,* a flower.) Most are worthy of space in gardens, and several have naturalized throughout eastern North America. When they do not have the pedigree of high alpine species suitable for rock gardens, however, they are a very confused race. Most gardeners recognize three sorts: the carnations of florists and sometimes of summer gardens (*Dianthus caryophyllus* [ca-ree-o-PHIL-us]); the old-fashioned clove pink or hardy carnation, generally either *D. plumarius* (plu-ma-REE-us) or *D.* x *alwoodii* (all-WOOD-ee-ee), which is a complex cross

between *D. caryophyllus* and *D. plumarius;* and sweet William, *D. barbatus* (bar-BA-tus). Clove pinks, many of which are persistently perennial well into USDA Zone 4, will not flower in one season no matter how early one sows the seed indoors, though both the florist's carnation, a tender perennial, and sweet William, generally classed as a biennial, may well flower their first summer in the garden from an indoor seeding in late February or early March. (Seed catalogues often recommend special varieties for this purpose.)

One could easily imagine attempting to grow the florist's carnation as an annual, for it is native to southern France, and so is really only hardy to Zone 8 or so. Though its narrow, glaucous, gray-green blade-shaped leaves are attractive, clasping the jointed stems in pairs, it is—at least in its splendid modern forms—a plant strictly to grow for its flowers, the heavy heads of which require elaborate support throughout their entire development. Those bought in shops are generally grown—one might actually say "produced"—in vast numbers in temperature-controlled greenhouses throughout the year, where developing stems and flowers poke through supporting grids of wire or string until they are cut for market. In the privileged gardens where they are hardy, or where they are grown from an early seeding as annuals, their floppy character seldom makes them attractive in mixed borders. Since they are such splendid cut flowers, however, a few might be grown in the vegetable or cutting gardens, in rows supported by thickets of twiggy branches or grids of string.

Dianthus barbatus, the sweet William, probably takes its popular name from St. William of Acquitaine, and not for the Conqueror, who was hardly known for the mildness of his disposition. It has been cultivated at least since the twelfth century and is among the best-loved of old-fashioned cottage garden flowers. It is also one of those plants that make nonsense of the tidy classifications of annual, biennial, and perennial, for it may be any of those, or all three. It is in any case short-lived, seldom flowering over two seasons, though one's chances of that are best if its abundant heads of flower are removed promptly before they set seed. Only the very impatient would grow sweet William as an annual, for it is a native of Russia and is perfectly winter-hardy to Zone 4 at least. Also, by far the finest plants and prettiest colors—in white, pale or carmine pink, rose, red, light or black purple, and banded or "eyed" forms, called "auriculas" from their resemblance to the flowers of auricula primroses—are to be had from a mid-summer sowing for flowers early the following summer. The species has, however, lent itself to hybridization with others, producing excellent, summer-flowering plants, of which the 'Telstar' series, in typical dianthus colors and picotees, is (for the moment) the best.

As the genus *Dianthus* is fairly promiscuous, and as the race to develop more and more annual forms of familiar and treasured biennials and perennials continues, other superb pinks and carnations that flower in one season from seed are bound to appear. At present, however, the most reliable of all annual carnations are cultivars of *D. chinensis* (chi-NEN-sis), a native of eastern Asia that once bore only single, five-petaled inch-wide flowers over a short period of time, but that now has been doubled and sometimes fringed, with a color range extending from white, pale and deep pink to carmine, blood and crimson red, lilac and deep purple, often with a contrasting eye, or with bi-colored petals, most dramatic in the cultivar called 'Black and White Minstrels', with fringed petals of deep purple black on top and white beneath. The fanciest forms are often offered as *Dianthus heddewigii* (hed-WIG-ee-ee), after Carl Heddewig, who

grew *D. chinensis* for the first time in Europe at St. Petersburg from seed sent him from Japan. Catalogues often promise strains of *D. chinensis* that are strongly fragrant, and that is a characteristic much to be desired. It seems true at present, however, that all cultivars and crosses of the species are faintly fragrant at best, smelling most often simply of cleanliness, like fresh air-dried laundry.

All dianthus grow best in well-drained, moderately fertile, neutral to alkaline soils in full sun. Where blueberries and rhododendrons flourish, they will appreciate the addition of lime. They relish cool weather, and so may be treated as hardy annuals, set out at about the time one would plant pansies, usually sometime in April in most American gardens. South of Zone 7, where winters are mild, the dianthus that are generally grown as annuals may be treated as biennials, by sowing seed in August or September for bloom the following season. Frequent dead-heading will prolong flowering, and shearing plants back by about a third when bloom flags in hot weather may produce a second flush of bloom in autumn.

DIASCIA SPECIES

FAMILY: *Scrophulariaceae* or snapdragon family.

CLASSIFICATION: Half-hardy or tender perennials grown as half-hardy annuals.

COMMON NAMES: Twinspur, diascia.

HARDINESS: Hardy under ideal soil conditions to Zones 7 and warmer. Plants are frost resistant when well established.

GROWING CONDITIONS: Deep, fertile, perfectly drained but moisture-retentive loam. Full sun in cooler gardens, afternoon shade in warmer ones.

PROPAGATION: From seed, sown indoors 10 to 12 weeks before last frost. Cuttings root easily.

HEIGHT: From 8 to 15", depending on cultivar.

ORNAMENTAL VALUE: Grown for flower.

LEVEL OF CULTURAL DIFFICULTY: Easy in ideal climates, moderately difficult to difficult in others.

SPECIAL PROPERTIES: Excellent hanging-basket or window-box plants in cool climates.

PRONUNCIATION: di-AS-she-a (di-AYE-she-a, di-AYE-ski-a)

*U*ntil the early 1980s, only the most sophisticated specialists in rock garden plants grew diascia. But so assured is their popularity now that they may sometimes be found outside supermarkets at curbside sales of annual and tender plants. They will almost certainly be among the offerings of any good garden center now that seed, once extremely rare, is offered by several major seed companies. In fact, diascia provide one of the very best examples of the hundreds of annuals and tender plants that have leapt from obscurity to popularity in the last twenty years in response to the demands of American gardeners for beautiful new plants.

Certainly, diascia deserve this popularity, for their dainty, open, or slightly cupped faces, each scarcely half an inch wide, lay claim to the charm that seems the birthright of all the members of their family, the Scrophulariaceae or snapdragon family. Their individual flowers have two lips, the upper divided again into two up-facing, rounded lobes, and the lower into three, the center lobe being the largest. Unlike snapdragons, however, the flowers are not tubed, and a gentle pressure on either side with thumb and forefinger will not cause them to snap open and shut like a tiny dragon's mouth, but just to squish.

Behind each flower and extending downward are two nectar-bearing spurs, each marked with a yellowish, translucent patch called a "window." (These spurs or pouches give the genus its common name, "twinspur," and its botanical one, from ancient Greek *di,* meaning two, and *anthos,* a sack.) Again depending on species and hybrid, flowers are borne above the plants either in loose, rather ragged terminal racemes, or—as is most pronounced in the species *D. rigescens* (ri-GEH-shins), meaning rigid—in tight, well-organized terminal spires. Flowers are apt to be of some melting shade of shell, coral, melon, apricot, or rose-pink, always one of the most beautiful ranges of garden color. Even those varieties bred to deeper, brick red shades, or toward lilac or violet, will still have an underlay of warm pink.

Diascia make dense, matlike, wiry growth of many ascending stems from a central crown, reaching a height of eight to fifteen inches depending on species and hybrid, and usually tumbling one upon the other. The tiny, three-quarter-inch-long leaves are borne in pairs along the stem, and range from broadly pointed, toothed ovals to almost needles.

The genus *Diascia* contains as many as fifty species of South African origin, and though botanical manuals assert that some are true annuals, all species and hybrids under cultivation at present appear to be tender or half-hardy perennials. But precisely *how* perennial is a subject of much learned debate. Reference works on perennial plants—and those specialty catalogues that make a point of extending no false hopes—generally list all species and hybrids as hardy to Zones 8 and 9, possibly to Zone 7 under ideal conditions. From time to time, claims are put forth for the hardiness of one species over others. This much is certain: Winter survival appears to depend much more on other variables than cold, for with very sharp drainage and a deep snow cover, gardeners report survival of plants well into Zone 4, whereas gardeners in heavy clay soils in Zone 8 will almost certainly lose all their plants over the winter. But most gardeners will find a ready supply of well-grown diascia, in an ever-lengthening list of cultivars, to add each spring as annuals, much as one adds their cousins of dubious perennial standing, such as snapdragons themselves, nemesias, angelonias, and alonsoas.

Under ideal conditions, a diascia should be in flower from late spring until frost, progressively enlarging in girth and producing a greater and greater abundance of flower. But as all diascia relish cool nights and bright, sunny days, they will tend to flag in the hot, humid weather of many American gardens, ceasing to bloom or even melting away altogether. The soil conditions they relish—a deep, fertile, perfectly drained loam that never dries out—will do much to prolong their flowering, and the farther south they are grown, the more they will appreciate some protection from the hot afternoon sun. Clipping away spent flower stems will at least usually produce fresh vegetative growth, which may be kept vigorous by weekly applications of dilute liquid fertilizer, and which may sport a crop of flowers as the weather cools toward autumn. Treat them as one will, however, even in the coolest gardens of New England and the upper West Coast, diascia may produce sheets of bloom all summer in one year and nothing but leaf in another. As with other desirable plants of erratic performance, one hopes for the good year, and keeps planting.

Until fairly recently, diascia were propagated vegetatively, either from division (from nodal cuttings taken just below a swollen leaf joint) or, where plants proved somewhat stoloniferous, from side shoots emerging from the central crown. They are not impossible plants to grow from seed, however, though seed retains viability only briefly and should be sown as fresh as possible. None of it will be of common garden origin, however, for diascia depend on highly evolved insects native to their homeland for pollination and to set seed, and so will always be barren elsewhere. Seed should be sown on sterilized compost and kept at around 60°F until germination occurs. It will be erratic, taking anywhere from two weeks to a month, but once young seedlings have appeared, they are easy to grow on in very bright light and at slightly warmer temperatures around 65° to 70°F, until they may be hardened off and transplanted into the garden. They bloom when quite small, but for sizeable plants ready to flower in the cool weather of late spring seed should be sown early in the new year.

A drift of diascia, say five, seven, or more plants allowed to knit together, will always add distinction anywhere plants of low growth and abundant, unusual flower are wanted. They are therefore excellent at the front of a perennial border, in patches in the rock garden, or along the stepping stones of a path. They seem generally to associate well with stonework, perhaps in memory of their craggy mountain homes, and they are never finer than when allowed to tumble from

DIASCIA RIGESCENS

the top of a low stone retaining wall. Where weather conditions are to their liking, diascia also make superb plants for containers and hanging baskets, though it should always be remembered that being allowed to dry out at their roots will at the least terminate flowering and at the worst kill them outright.

DICHONDRA SPECIES

FAMILY: *Convolulaceae* or morning glory family.

CLASSIFICATION: Tender perennials grown as half-hardy annuals.

COMMON NAMES: Colt's foot, lawn leaf, dichondra.

HARDINESS: Not hardy much below 25°F.

GROWING CONDITIONS: Any well-drained soil, preferably moderately rich, water-retentive garden loam. Part shade to full sun.

PROPAGATION: By seed, sown indoors 6 to 8 weeks before last frost. Tip cuttings root easily.

HEIGHT: To 6" or less, but trailing to 2' in a season.

ORNAMENTAL VALUE: Grown for foliage and delicate structure.

LEVEL OF CULTURAL DIFFICULTY: Easy.

SPECIAL PROPERTIES: Useful in window boxes and hanging baskets. May be carried over as a winter houseplant.

PRONUNCIATION: di-KON-dra

Dichondra are tough little plants, actually tiny vines that root as they go and produce half-inch-wide, rounded leaves, cleft in the middle where they join lax petioles and looking something like the leaves of a minute water lily. Well-grown stands can produce sheets of leaves no more than six inches high, shorter in sun or poor soil, above an interlaced network of wiry stems so dense that it smothers out all other vegetation. Very fast of growth once it gets its roots beneath it, dichondra produces complete groundcover within six weeks from seed spaced about eight inches apart.

Gardeners in southern California or the dryer parts of the Southwest or along the Gulf Coast might wince at the name "dichondra," for in the 1950s and 60s several species were celebrated as a solution to the difficulties of growing lawns in those areas. Where winter temperatures did not drop much below 25°F, the idea was to seed over a prepared space in March or October when moisture would be abundant or when irrigation was permitted by local authorities. The result would be a dense, green "lawn" that would then endure summer drought and heat.

Like many such horticultural promises, dichondra proved too good to be true. Gardeners experienced difficulties within the first year of the experiment. The western flea beetle found dense stands of it irresistible and chewed away blissfully at the leaves until all were gone. Fungus and mildew set in, requiring frequent spraying. Though stands developed amazingly quickly and were satisfying at first, rapid growth required both irrigation and fertilizer. Maintenance therefore became almost as elaborate as for lawn grass, and though a well-maintained stand of dichondra looked wonderful, a really vigorous game of Frisbee reduced it to unattractive mush.

Still, with maintenance, dichondra can look splendid where it is not too much trod upon, and the charm of its tiny, cunningly formed leaves makes it useful as an annual for northern gardens. Plants will quickly form sheets of dark green, uniform growth, suitable perhaps as a rim-high planting in a large terra rosa pot, where growth would quickly drip down the edges. Dichondra might also be used to create tiny "lawns" in city window boxes or in wooden frames on roof gardens, where it would relish the heat, and where it might be sheared tight with scissors. It is also very attractive creeping between the cracks of paving or stepping stones.

There are only nine species in the *Dichondra* genus, if so many, for even highly trained botanists have difficulty distinguishing one from another. All are native to the warmest parts of the globe in both hemispheres and are quite tender, being reliably hardy only where few degrees of frost are experienced in winter. The three species generally offered are *Dichondra repens* (RE-pens), *D. micrantha* (my-KRAN-tha), and *D. carolinensis* (ka-ro-LIN-en-sis), though all three are generally mixed up in the trade and perhaps in nature also. Some botanists speculate that they may all be variants of one species, which is generally listed as *D. micrantha*. A very beautiful form of dichondra has recently appeared in good nurseries and in some mail order catalogues, under the name *D. argentea* (ar-GEN-tee-a), though its actual species is in doubt. It displays somewhat crinkled leaves covered over with tiny hairs, as are the stems, giving the plant a dusty, silver look. It makes a fine felty-white groundcover at the front of the summer border, though it also thrives in pots, where it is invaluable either as a component of a mixed planting or all alone.

Dichondra is easily grown from seed, which should be sown indoors about six to eight weeks before the last anticipated frost date. All dichondra can be carried over the winter easily in a cool greenhouse or on a sunny windowsill, and a well-grown plant can be carved up into chunks for use in the garden when all danger of frost is past. Tip cuttings of all forms root with great ease in early spring, and *D. argentea* must be propagated that way, as seed is not available.

DICHRANOSTIGMA SPECIES

FAMILY: *Papaveraceae* or poppy family.

CLASSIFICATION: Hardy annual.

COMMON NAME: Dichranostigma.

HARDINESS: Hardy to frosts. Seed-hardy well into USDA Zone 7.

GROWING CONDITIONS: Light, free-draining, moderately fertile sandy soil. Full sun.

PROPAGATION: By seed, sown in late autumn or very early spring in place, or indoors in peat pots in late April or early May. Seedlings resent root disturbance.

HEIGHT: To 2'.

ORNAMENTAL VALUE: Grown for flower.

LEVEL OF CULTURAL DIFFICULTY: Difficult.

SPECIAL PROPERTIES: None.

PRONUNCIATION: di-kran-O-stig-ma (di-kran-o-STIG-ma)

Those gardeners who love a poppy above all things will find a rich field to cultivate beyond the familiar plants in the genus *Papaver*. Although it contains about fifty species, the genus belongs to a much larger family, the Papaveraceae, which contains twenty-four other genera and approximately 200 species. Most of the plants within that splendid botanical realm are garden-worthy, among them three species in the genus *Dichranostigma*, which have yet to be discovered by even the most adventurous gardeners—*D. franchetianum* (fran-che-tee-A-num), *D. leptopodum* (lep-TOP-o-dum), and *D. lactuoides* (lak-too-OY-des). All are native to western and central China, the latter provenance usually ensuring that an annual plant is hardy. All three are much confused in trade, and in fact also in botany, since all three appear to be highly variable and may simply be geographic variants of a single species. Never mind, for whatever the specific botanical identity, any dichranostigma will be beautiful.

Dichranostigma produce splendid rosettes of leaf in spring, from seed sown either in autumn or very early in the year, even before the ground is thawed. Then, in early summer, they produce a branched candelabrum of stems that will reach a height of two feet or more, each branch terminating in a panicle where many open, one-and-a-half- to two-inch-wide poppies bloom—all of some shade of yellow from palest primrose to richest egg yolk. Though each individual flower lasts only a day, they open in succession from late June until well into August, offering a length of flowering time unusual in the poppy family. Where dichranostigma have been previously grown, self-seeded individuals germinating later may well continue the show into September and even October, depending on the arrival of frost. Where summers are hot and dry, however, the handsome basal rosette of leaves may yellow and wither away, leaving the flowering stems looking gaunt and naked, even though fresh poppies may still open daily for several weeks. Where that is likely to be the case, a fluffy cloak of another annual or perennial plant might provide a reasonable decency.

Dichranostigma, seed-hardy well into USDA Zone 4 and possibly Zone 3, are best sown thinly in place in late September or as early in spring as is possible, on light, sandy, well-drained soil in full sun. Like almost all members of the family Papaveraceae, dichranostigma are very impatient of transplanting, which is seldom successful, no matter how deeply one digs and how large an earth ball one takes. Young seedlings may, however, be successfully established in the garden if sown in early May in peat pots or flexible plastic cell packs, grown on in bright, cool, airy condi-tions, and transplanted with minimal root disturbance after all danger of frost is past. Plants should be thinned or planted to stand about a foot apart, or used singly as dramatic accents. Watering in dry weather will tend to prevent the basal rosettes of leaves from turning shabby, though as plants mature, they are generally more attractive at their tops than at their bases. Seed, which is scarce, should be gathered when it is ripe to share with other gardeners and to establish a population of seedlings in years to come.

The name of so glamorous a genus is fairly dull when translated, deriving from the ancient Greek *dikranos,* meaning branched into two, and *stigma,* signifying the female part of the flower which receives pollen. The species name *franchetianum,* however, commemorates Adrien René Franchet (1834–1900), one of the first botanists to work systematically on the incredible trove of Chinese species introduced into European gardens in the nineteenth century.

DICLIPTERA SUBERECTA

FAMILY: *Acanthaceae* or acanthus family.

CLASSIFICATION: Tender or half-hardy perennial grown as tender annual.

COMMON NAMES: King's crown, dicliptera.

HARDINESS: Possibly hardy to Zone 7. Grown as an annual elsewhere. Frost-sensitive when first planted.

GROWING CONDITIONS: Well-drained, dryish, fertile sandy loam. Full sun.

PROPAGATION: From cuttings taken from nonflowering tips in spring or early summer.

HEIGHT: To 1', but trailing to up to 3' in a season.

ORNAMENTAL VALUE: Grown for flower and for attractive leaves.

LEVEL OF CULTURAL DIFFICULTY: Moderately easy.

SPECIAL PROPERTIES: Excellent in containers, hanging baskets, and window boxes.

PRONUNCIATION: di-CLIP-ter-a sub-ee-REC-ta

A native of Uruguay, *Dicliptera suberecta* is a tender perennial that may be hardy well into Zone 7, especially where soils are light and well drained and some winter protection, in the form of evergreen boughs, may be provided. There it will make handsome clumps of out-arching (suberect) three-foot-long stems, clad in attractive oval leaves of velvety silver-gray two and a half inches long. In mid- to late summer each stem will be surmounted by a cluster of coral to brick-red tubular flowers about two inches long. The popular name "king's crown" probably describes the rounded growth of a well-grown clump, ornamented with its jewel flowers at the tips of each stem.

Where *Dicliptera suberecta* is not hardy, it is still valuable as a quick-growing annual, planted in the garden or in containers as young rooted cuttings bought from nurseries or mail order catalogues specializing in tender plants. A very easy plant to grow, *D. suberecta* appreciates well-drained, somewhat dryish but fertile soil, such as is easy to provide in hanging wire baskets lined with sphagnum or sheet moss. It is impatient of soggy conditions at its roots and thrives best in full sun. A water-soluble fertilizer rich in potassium and phosphorus, such as that formulated for tomatoes, will produce early and abundant flowering. Like most tender perennials, it may be cut back in autumn before frost, repotted in sandy, fertile soil, and carried over the winter in a cool greenhouse or on a sunny windowsill. Tip cuttings taken from nonflowering shoots root easily in spring and early summer, though, like fuchsias and other tender flowering perennials and shrubs, they may be difficult once flower bud has been initiated.

D. suberecta is particularly treasured for use in mixed plantings in hanging baskets, where its lax stems will droop over the edges gracefully and soon produce their clusters of flowers, and for its irresistible appeal to hummingbirds. They will visit it at regular intervals all summer long, and because their minute size is matched only by their fearlessness, one may sit near a hanging basket and admire them while they buzz over the flowers.

D. suberecta takes its genus name from the ancient Greek words *diklis,* meaning folded, and *pteron,* wing, attesting to its double folded seed. Once located in the now extinct genus *Jacobinia,* all of its kin were reassigned into the important genus *Justicia,* where several species have since cut a significant figure as the beautiful "shrimp plants" of gardens. *D. suberecta* went alone into the genus *Dicliptera,* which comprises approximately 150 species of trees and shrubs native to the tropical and temperate parts of the globe. Within that genus it seems to be the only one ever offered for sale outside the mildest parts of Zones 8 to 10 in North America.

DICLIPTERA SUBERECTA

DIGITALIS PURPUREA

FAMILY: *Scrophulariaceae* or snapdragon family.

CLASSIFICATION: Hardy bienniel sometimes grown as a hardy annual.

COMMON NAMES: Foxgloves, digitalis.

HARDINESS: Winter-hardy to USDA Zone 4. Young transplants withstand light frosts.

GROWING CONDITIONS: Humus-rich, moisture-retentive, well-drained soil. Full sun to part shade in cool gardens, part shade to filtered sun in warmer ones.

PROPAGATION: From seed, sown indoors in late March or early April, or in place as soon as soil may be worked in spring.

HEIGHT: To 4′.

ORNAMENTAL VALUE: Grown for flower.

LEVEL OF CULTURAL DIFFICULTY: Easy.

SPECIAL PROPERTIES: Medicinal plant used in treatment of heart disease.

PRONUNCIATION: di-jee-TA-lis pur-PUR-ee-a

*S*everal flowering plants are so associated with quiet old rural gardens that they seem redolent of fresh country mornings wherever they are grown: china-blue forget-me-nots (*Myosotis sylvestris*), sweetly fragrant dame's rocket (*Hesperis matronalis*), towering, crepe-petaled hollyhocks (*Alcea rosea*), and foxgloves (*Digitalis purpurea*). Curiously, many of them are by natural preference biennial plants. Though all will thrive in city gardens—even in rather dank, sour-soiled ones—they are associated with the country for good reasons. Splendid in flower, they take space to mature, occupying ground in their first vegetative season of growth that might otherwise be given over to other flowering plants, either annuals that bloom in their first season or perennials that flower reliably, year after year. In country

gardens, space is not at a premium, and there are always odd corners where biennial plants may self-seed, either to be thinned for the best display or to be transplanted as year-old rosettes into blank spaces in autumn. As all the plants named above prefer part shade, they often naturalize in areas that cannot quite be said to be cultivated, but that are a midway zone between the garden itself and the surrounding fields and woods. There the inevitable untidiness that follows while the seed develops is not the distraction it might be in small suburban or city gardens, where every corner must be kept trim.

So desirable are these plants, however, that breeders have made every attempt to convert them into annuals that will flower reliably in the first year from seed. With foxgloves—their spires of flower so valuable for the contrast they make among plants that are generally dome- or table-shaped—their efforts have met with some success. Old estate gardeners always knew that a very early seeding under glass would produce some plants that flowered in their first season. Now, however, species have been carefully selected and intercrossed to produce reliably flowering plants in their first season of growth from a late March or early April seeding indoors.

Among foxgloves, *Digitalis purpurea* 'Foxy', an All-American Award winner, is the first to be developed, though others are sure to follow. Gardeners should understand, however, that no biennial treated as an annual will ever attain the magnificence it can offer when grown according to its innate natural preferences. 'Foxy', for example, is a low little thing, hardly reaching three feet under the best culture, and might be a letdown to gardeners who expect the glorious six-foot-tall spires that biennial foxgloves can achieve at their best. It must be said, however, that it is very attractive in the garden, and also in an eight-inch clay pot, and that it may be grown as either a cut flower or a pot plant from a late summer seeding to blossom approximately five months later under cool greenhouse conditions. One may therefore actually have it on the table in the January doldrums, when poinsettias and paper-whites have ceased to please.

All foxgloves enjoy deep, humus-rich soil that is well drained but never dries out. Their natural preference is for bright shade or half a day of sun, such as might be found at the edges of a woodland rich with decayed leaves. Here they are superb. In cool northern gardens on either coast, however, they can be magnificently grown in full sun. When cultivated as annuals, they develop best with a rich supplementary feeding of granular fertilizer, or general water-soluble fertilizer if they are grown in pots, though plants treated as biennials should not be heavily fertilized in their first year of growth, as it may make them what the old gardeners called "winter proud," by producing heavy rosettes of fleshy growth that are too soft to endure the cold of the darkest part of the year.

Native to open British woodlands and roadside verges, foxgloves were seemingly transported almost on the boot soles of English settlers wherever they went and are now naturalized in temperate areas across the globe. It is not unusual in many parts of North America to come upon lusty stands of them, apparently far from where anyone has ever gardened. The genus name *Digitalis* originates from the Latin *digitus,* meaning finger, and attests to the almost irresistible urge to slip one's own fingers into the soft tube of a single blossom. *Purpurea* always signifies the color purple and describes the natural shades of flowers growing in the wild, though paler and darker variants and creams and pure whites were early noted as occurring in wild stands. These have all been bred into seed strains with a blend of many fine colors, and the gardener can, by eliminating less preferred shades among deliberately seeded or self-seeded plants, eventually build up a color selection of his own.

The popular name "foxglove" is of very confused etymology. As it stands in modern English, it describes a glove or sock a wily fox might slip over his toes to muffle the sound of his tread as he goes about his stealthy business. That was good enough for Chaucer, though an older etymology suggests that the popular folk name is anciently derived from a musical instrument, a "gleow," which consisted of a series of graduated bells on an arch of wood, which, when struck, would produce music up and down the scale. That essentially describes the shape of the native English wild flower, which bears all its blossoms on one side. English purists consider that America messed up this form about forty years ago, when a single specimen was discovered in this country that bore its bells evenly spaced around the stem, and not down-hanging in a single row. Rather than some shade of purple, it was pure white as well. From this single progenitor, the modern 'Excelsior' strain has been bred, and also the annual forms. So the other ancient etymology of the popular name—*faux gleow,* false bells—seems to apply to American hybrids of the last

DIGITALIS PURPUREA

thirty years in quite another sense, the so-called annuals included.

Foxgloves, though grown in gardens for their flowers, are the source of the chemical *digitalin,* an important cardiac medicine that is extracted from all parts of the plant, and that has never been successfully synthesized in the laboratory. Gardeners should know, however, that though species of *Digitalis* have been important in saving human life since at least 1780, all parts of the plant are poisonous.

DIMORPHOTHECA SPECIES (*OSTEOSPERMUM* SPECIES)

FAMILY: *Asteraceae* or aster or daisy family.

CLASSIFICATION: Tender perennial grown as half-hardy annual.

COMMON NAMES: Star of the Veldt, African daisy, cape marigold.

HARDINESS: Slightly frost hardy when established.

GROWING CONDITIONS: Sandy, perfectly drained loam of moderate fertility. Full sun.

PROPAGATION: By seed, sown 6 to 8 weeks indoors before last frost, outdoors in warmer gardens when weather is settled.

HEIGHT: 8″ to 1′.

ORNAMENTAL VALUE: Grown for flower.

LEVEL OF CULTURAL DIFFICULTY: Easy in ideal conditions, difficult elsewhere.

SPECIAL PROPERTIES: None.

PRONUNCIATION: di-mor-PO-the-ka (os-te-o-SPER-mum)

*E*ven highly trained botanists boggle over the classification of species in the genus *Dimorphotheca,* if indeed they even agree that it is a separate genus and not a subdivision of *Osteospermum*

or vice versa. In botanical references, a species listed under one is often followed by parentheses listing it under the other, as, for example *Dimorphotheca ecklonis* (eck-LO-nis) (*Osteospermum ecklonis*). To complicate matters further, species themselves often resemble each other so closely as to be considered minor variants of the one or the other, as with the white-flowered, faintly purple-tinged *Dimorphotheca annua* (AN-u-a) with pointy ray petals, and the similarly white-flowered *D. pluvialis* (plu-vi-A-lis), which tends to put its purple tinge on the underside of its blunt petals.

To most gardeners, these botanical distinctions will matter far less than the flowers, which are always beautiful where they may be grown well. They might simply be called "daisies" though most daisies tend to make up for whatever they lack in grace with a cheerful, open-faced simplicity. Not these, for most forms have an unusual grace with flowers borne singly on long, thin stems, facing upward at first and then nodding gently with age. Their ray petals, usually in a single row, cup slightly at the center and then flare out at the edges like a shallow bowl. Generally narrow, they overlap where they join the darker, central disk but separate eventually into a multipointed star. They would make beautiful cut flowers except that many forms close at night or in dim weather.

Among the twenty or so species of *Dimorphotheca* usually grown in gardens, the most common is *D. aurantiaca* (au-ran-TI-a-ca), which bears daisies of various shades of yellow and orange with a contrasting darker eye. Through natural selection other tints were added, of apricot, salmon, buff, cream, and white. Crosses were also made with other species to produce flowers of pale pink, rose, deep pink, or red, and also violets, deep lavenders, and purples. The natural tendency of some species to have ray flowers tinted violet or purple beneath has further broadened the range of possibilities, and some varieties have been bred that shade gently from darker to lighter (or lighter to darker) hues from the center outward. There are also forms with quilled petals, and of course, unfortunately, some double forms.

All members of the genus (or genuses) are daisy-flowered annuals, perennials, or sub-shrubs native to South Africa, but almost all species grown in gardens may be treated as annuals or, where winters are very mild, as biennials. All seem freely to intercross, to the extent that Norman Taylor, in *Taylor's Encyclopedia of Gardening* (1936), rightly observed that "there are many fine, showy garden forms, but their identity or parentage is very doubtful."

When treated as an annual, seed of dimorphotheca may be sowed indoors about six to eight weeks before the last anticipated frost, or outdoors when the weather is settled and warm. Young plants should be spaced about a foot apart, and though the first bloom may be expected about six weeks from germination, depending on the weather, it is good to pinch out the growing tip of each plant after three or four true sets of leaves have formed, to encourage basal branching. Dimorphothecas thrive best in ordinary, well-drained soil in full sun, and are miserably intolerant of heavy clay soils, excessive moisture, or even partial shade. Like most native South African plants, they perform best when night temperatures are slightly above 50°F and days are warm, dry, and sunny. Where these conditions may be met, they will flower with impressive abundance from early summer until frost, though an occasional removal of spent flowers encourages bloom.

DIMORPHOTHECA (OSTEOSPERMUM) *X* HYBRIDA

Dimorphothecas make excellent winter- and early spring–flowering pot plants for the cool greenhouse or heated sun porch, developing well when nighttime temperatures are kept at around 50°F. For this purpose, seed should be sown from September to November, and seedlings transplanted singly, first into two-inch pots and then into five-inch pots, in which they will flower from January until late spring. The potting medium should be a sandy, free-draining loam, and care should be taken in the darker months not to over-water, which will cause rotting off.

Species of *Dimorphotheca* (seven used to be listed) bear flowers capable of producing viable seed from both the ray petals and the disk florets that form the center of the daisy. Hence the genus name, from ancient Greek *dimorphos,* meaning of two forms, and *theka,* fruit. Both forms of seed are viable, though a gardener who shakes a pack of them out into the palm of his hand might be legitimately confused, for those borne by the disk florets are round and flat, and those borne by the ray petals are rodlike and slightly corrugated. By contrast, *Osteospermum* (from *osteo,* bone, and *spermum,* seed) produce viable seed only from the ray petals. A third genus, *Tripteris,* once contained all the species that bear three-winged seed (from ancient Greek *tri,* three, and *pteron,* wing), but is now extinct, its species having been assigned either to *Dimorphotheca* or *Osteospermum.*

This botanical welter might for once justify the simple use of a common name, though alas, the one most persistently used for these plants, "African daisy," is shared with at least four other South African genera, namely *Gazania, Gerbera, Mezembrianthemum,* and *Venedium,* and (illogically) with one North American native, *Echinacea purpurea.*

DIPLADENIA (*MANDEVILLA*) SPECIES

FAMILY: *Apocynaceae* or periwinkle family.

CLASSIFICATION: Tender woody vines grown as tender annual vines.

COMMON NAMES: Dipladenia, mandevilla.

HARDINESS: Sensitive to light frosts.

GROWING CONDITIONS: Rich, moisture-retentive, well-drained soil. Full sun. Best in hot weather.

PROPAGATION: By tip cuttings.

HEIGHT: 6 to 8′ in a growing season.

ORNAMENTAL VALUE: Grown for flowers and for vining growth.

LEVEL OF CULTURAL DIFFICULTY: Easy.

SPECIAL PROPERTIES: None.

PRONUNCIATION: di-pla-DEEN-ee-a (man-da-VILL-a)

*U*ntil about ten years ago, most American gardeners would have encountered dipladenia only on a vacation to Florida or in greenhouses attached to large public botanical gardens. But today many are grown, for the current interest in annuals and tender plants has particularly favored vines, among the most splendid of which are several species known as dipladenia.

Dipladenia are either twining vines or shrubs, though some species waver between the two categories, choosing to be shrubby in youth and climbing later on in life. Flowers are very showy, borne profusely whenever the weather is warm, generally from April to November, and consisting of flattened trumpets of five fused petals, each blossom from two to five inches across according to species. Usually flowers are some shade of white, silvery or rich pink, rose or cherry red, often with a contrasting throat of a deeper hue than the petals or of yellow. Though, like camellias, the beauty of most species seems to be bought at the expense of fragrance, *Dipladenia suaveolens* (swa-vee-O-lens) bears two-inch-wide funnels of ivory- to pinkish-white that are intensely perfumed with the scent of gardenias, most strongly at night.

Dipladenia leaves are generally of a fresh, glossy laurel green, rather thick of texture, carried in fairly widely spaced pairs along the stems. They range from three to eight inches in length, are heart- or arrow-shaped, and tend to be evergreen and leathery in texture in most species.

The most commonly cultivated dipladenia is 'Alice Dupont', bred at Longwood Gardens from a complex and uncertain back-crossing of several species, and generally listed as *D.* x *amabilis* (a-MA-bi-lis), a Latin adjective designating the species—accurately—as "delightful." When 'Alice Dupont' was first encountered in good garden centers about ten years ago as rooted cuttings, already precociously flowering and reaching out for something to climb on, it seemed merely another pretty houseplant. Then one began to see it in gardens, as a tubbed specimen trained on a pyramid of bamboo stakes, or even bedded out to scramble over fences or stone walls, where its profuse, silvery-pink salvers of bloom opened one at a time on six-inch-long graceful petioles in the axils of each pair of leaves.

The popularity of *Dipladenia* 'Alice Dupont' seems to have blazed a trail on which other dipladenias have followed, for now one can have them in paler or richer pink and even in pure white. Some, such as the deep, pinkish-red called 'Red Riding Hood', perhaps a cultivar of *D. splendens* (SPLEN-dens), are determined to be shrubby, and so are best used at the edges of large containers or in hanging baskets. But even in the nursery, one can usually tell which plants will be compact of growth and which will want to as-

cend upward, for would-be climbers will bear questing stems even when quite young, and may already have been trained to bamboo stakes or small redwood trellises by the nursery owner. Even climbers, however, should be pinched after two sets of leaves have formed on a stem, to encourage branching. It is also wise to detach upward-twining stems very carefully and train them sideways on a support or trellis so they will clothe it evenly, rather than ending up in a flowering mass at the top with naked shanks below.

Dipladenia are native chiefly to the moist, humus-rich forests of Brazil and Argentina, and so will require fertile, well-drained, fibrous soil that never dries out. They also enjoy as much heat as possible, which in northern gardens will usually

DIPLADENIA (MANDEVILLA) BOULIVIENSE

be supplied by the baking sides of clay pots or the reflected heat of house walls, and the paving of patios or pool aprons. They are greedy feeders, and so when they are in active summer growth, they appreciate a weekly dose of water-soluble plant food applied at half the strength recommended on the carton. The soil in which they grow should be sweetened from time to time by a sprinkling of charcoal from the barbecue grill (real charcoal and not the remains of charcoal briquettes) or a dusting of wood ash from a fireplace.

Dipladenia are perfectly hardy in Zones 9 and 10, but most American gardeners will treat them as annual climbers, bought each year anew as vigorous, well-rooted cuttings. It is not, however, difficult to carry over plants from year to year, provided one has a home greenhouse or glassed-in sun porch heated to a minimum of 55°F. Container-grown plants should be placed under cover before frost, and each shoot should be cut back to two or so green leaves on a scaffold of old wood. Plants grown in the open ground should be lifted carefully before heavy frosts, cut back, and potted up in fresh potting compost. It is a bit of an art to dig plants established in the ground, for a mass of swollen tubers, rather like those of dahlias, will lie just below the surface, and care must be taken to break off as few as possible. Should one break away, however, it is no use to pot it up singly in the hope that it will sprout, for the tubers are merely underground storage mechanisms, and cannot regenerate growth as can a potato, for example.

Plants lifted from the garden or carried on in pots can be expected to give abundant growth and flower for two, perhaps three, years. Eventually, however, they begin to decline, and new plants should be secured. Cuttings root readily if taken with two pairs of mature leaves in March, inserted in half-peat, half-perlite, or sharp sand, and kept in a humid environment, preferably

with some bottom heat. Fortunately, however, vigorous new plants are now available each spring in good garden centers and in an ever-widening range of colors.

DOLICHOS LABLAB (DIPOGON LABLAB, LABLAB PURPUREUS)

FAMILY: *Leguminosae* or bean family.

CLASSIFICATION: Tender perennial vine grown as tender annual vine.

COMMON NAMES: Hyacinth bean, Egyptian bean, bonavist, zarandaja, dolichos lablab.

HARDINESS: Sensitive to light frosts. Prefers warm weather.

GROWING CONDITIONS: Deep, very fertile, humus-rich soil. Abundant moisture. Full sun. Prefers heat.

PROPAGATION: From seed, sown in place when weather is warm and settled, or indoors in peat pots 6 weeks before last anticipated frost. Seedlings resent root disturbance.

HEIGHT: To 12' in one season.

ORNAMENTAL VALUE: Valued for flower, ornamental seed pods, and as a quick-growing cover for trellises, arbors, and small buildings.

LEVEL OF CULTURAL DIFFICULTY: Easy.

SPECIAL PROPERTIES: When young, beans are sometimes eaten, after elaborate soaking and boiling in several changes of water. Toxic otherwise.

PRONUNCIATION: do-LI-kos la-BLAB (di-PO-gon, pur-PUR-e-us)

Though *Dolichos lablab* is now grown in American gardens as an ornamental plant, it has a long history as a food crop. First cultivated in ancient

Egypt, it spread throughout Africa and the Asian Tropics to India. By the late eighteenth century, it had made its way to the New World, probably as a quick-growing, protein-rich food for African slaves, who knew how to cook its fat bean seeds in several changes of water, to rid them of bitterness. From Haiti and Santa Domingo it entered North America through Florida and Louisiana, where it still springs up gorgeously as a weed with its twining bean-leaved stems and abundant purple to whitish-pink pea flowers followed by large, deep, purplish-black pods.

The popular names of *Dolichos lablab* attest to its rich history: "Egyptian bean" recognizes its ancient origins, "hyacinth bean" attempts to describe its beautiful, scented panicles of flower, "bonavist" is an old Haitian word for a welcomed arrival, and "zarandaja" is the name it travels under in parts of India.

A tender perennial climber, *Dolichos lablab* is probably root-hardy in Zones 9 and 10 of North America or anywhere that winter temperatures do not fall much below 25°F. In such places, it makes an impressive annual growth of as much as thirty feet, ornamenting itself richly with its three-part, broad, and pointed leaves up to five inches long, producing from their axils abundant pea flowers. Flowers are borne from late May to November on stiff, up-facing stems standing well away from the leaves and are followed by broad pods varnished with magenta or deep purple—almost more decorative than the flowers themselves.

Farther north, hyacinth beans are best treated as annuals, and they are most successful where summers are very hot and humid. There they should be sown in place in spring, as soon as the weather has warmed, each bean inserted with its

DOLICHOS LABLAB

eye facing downward, in moderately rich garden soil and in full sun. Two or three beans are capable of clothing a good section of picket fence or trellis, since growth is rapid in warm weather and vines may reach as much as twelve feet in length in a single season. Nevertheless, several seed should be sown about six inches apart, and the seedlings later thinned to stand from one to three feet apart. Thinning should be done only after several true leaves have developed, for then one can distinguish the dull, olive-green seedlings from those suffused with purple, eliminating the former to give space to the latter, which will produce the richest-colored flowers and pods.

Gardeners in Zones 6 and colder may germinate seedlings of hyacinth beans indoors, about six weeks before the last anticipated frost date. Like all legumes, however, they are unwilling to be transplanted, so two or three beans should be sown to a single peat pot, with the firm resolution of clipping out all but the strongest—or purplest—as the case may be. There is no need to hurry them on, for they should not be transplanted until the weather is quite settled and warm. Seedlings that are stunted from being held indoors too long, or that flower precociously in their pots, may never make vigorous, free-flowering plants outdoors. Fortunately, however, hyacinth beans may be the last tender seed sown indoors and will still flower and pod magnificently in their brief season.

Botanically there is much confusion surrounding this plant. It is usually listed as *Dolichos lablab, dolichos* being ancient Greek for long, referring either to the five- or six-inch pods or to its twining tendrils, and *lablab,* an ancient African or possibly Indian vernacular word for a pea or bean. In botanical references, however, it sometimes shows up as *Dipogon lablab,* from *di,* meaning two, and *pogon,* a beard, which describes the two lower lobes of the typically pea-shaped flower, or as *Lablab purpureus,* taking its species name from the Latin adjective meaning purple for the flower and the richly colored pod that follows.

DOROTHEANTHUS BELLIDIFORMIS (MESEMBRYANTHEMUM CRINIFLORUM)

FAMILY: *Aizoaceae* or ice plant family.

CLASSIFICATION: Tender annual.

COMMON NAMES: Livingstone daisy, ice plant, mesembryanthemum.

HARDINESS: Slightly frost-hardy when established.

GROWING CONDITIONS: Dry, gravelly, or sandy soil. Prefer daytime heat and cool nights.

PROPAGATION: From seed, sown 10 to 12 weeks before last frost.

HEIGHT: To 6".

ORNAMENTAL VALUE: Grown for flower.

LEVEL OF CULTURAL DIFFICULTY: Easy where preferred conditions can be met; difficult elsewhere.

SPECIAL PROPERTIES: None.

PRONUNCIATION: do-ro-thee-AN-thus bel-lid-i-FORM-is (me-sem-bri-AN-thee-mum cry-ni-FLO-rum)

*M*esembryanthemum was once a vast genus with many species of South African annuals and perennials that have now been divided among twelve or more smaller ones. Instrumental in this botanical partitioning was the German authority on succulent plants, Dr. Martin Henrich Schwantes (1881–1960), who honored his mother, Dorothea Schwantes, in the genus *Dorotheanthus.* Of its approximately ten species, two—*D. bellidiformis* and *D. gramineus* (gra-min-EE-us)—are grown as annuals. To both, however, the popular name "mesembryanthemum" has clung, perhaps because, as the British garden writer Graham Rice points out, the word is such fun to say.

The species name of *Dorotheanthus bellidiformis* means daisylike, implying a resemblance of its upturned, one-and-a-half-inch-wide flowers to the English lawn daisy, *Bellis perennis*. *D. bellidiformis* grows into a neat rosette about six inches across and almost as tall. Each thick, tubular leaf, two inches long and a fourth of an inch wide, is a fresh dark green dusted over with tiny, translucent spots that shimmer like minute flakes of ice, giving rise to another common name, "ice plant." Flowers are borne across the tops of plants, sometimes in such profusion that they become cushions of bloom, the leaves all but hidden except on cloudy days, when the flowers do not open. Flower color can range from white to pale or deep pink, orange, yellow, apricot, biscuit tan, red, purple, and magenta. Usually seed is sold in mixed rather than single colors, though a fine yellow cultivar with unusually large, fringy-petaled flowers and chocolate centers, called 'Yellow Ice'—and sometimes 'Lunette'—is offered. When mixes are grown, all the colors accord beautifully except the stronger magenta shades, which may predominate in inferior blends or where the plant self-seeds.

The other commonly grown species, *D. gramineus*, a lower, denser, smaller-leaved plant, draws its name from its three-inch-tall tufts of dense, small, grasslike leaves, the tufts about eight inches across and as tall. When well grown, its vivid pink, rose, red, or white daisies cover the plant, sometimes displaying a beautiful center of dark red or deep blue, often surrounded by a zone of white. Gardeners who specialize in suc-

DOROTHEANTHUS BELLIDIFORMIS

culent and South African plants usually consider it the more beautiful of the two species, though seed is seldom offered.

Where either species of *Dorotheanthus* grow well, they are interesting additions to the front of a flower border or along a path. Though plants may be bedded out in drifts or colonies (*D. bellidiformis* is often treated this way), they seem to look best as rather spontaneous, seemingly self-seeded surprises. Both species are handsome in rock gardens, where they relish the heat of stones and the gravelly or sandy soils that prevail there. Because both enjoy a baking at the roots and a period of relative drought before watering, they are excellent subjects for pots and containers, though their jewel-box quality suggests that they would be nicest when grown alone, and not as components of a mixed planting. Both may be grown to perfection in home greenhouses over the summer while the usual occupants enjoy an outdoor vacation. There, they may be protected from excess moisture, and they relish the daytime heat that builds up in glass houses.

Like most other mesembryanthemums, species of *Dorotheanthus* are native to the poor soils of arid South African deserts, and that is the princi-

DOROTHEANTHUS BELLIDIFORMIS

pal clue to their successful culture in gardens. When over-fed, crowded together, or kept even moderately well watered, they are apt to suffer from fungal diseases, causing them, in the gardener's phrase, to "mug off," either as tiny seedlings, promising young plants, or even in full flower. They thrive in relatively infertile soil, in full sun, and always look their best in gardens where days are hot and bright and nights are cool. With both species, flowers begin to occur about ten to twelve weeks from seed, which may be sown thinly indoors in March or April for flowers from July to frost.

Seed germinates best when lightly pressed into a sandy, free-draining sterile soil mix, and covered with a sheet of cardboard or black plastic until sprouting occurs, usually within one to two weeks at temperatures around 65°F. Young seedlings must be kept in a fresh, airy environment and watered only when the soil of the seed flat becomes dry, preferably by standing the seed pans in water until the soil is saturated. Though mature plants may resist a few degrees of frost in autumn, young seedlings are sensitive to cold and damp and should not be transplanted into the garden until the weather is warm and settled. Alternatively, where summers are long, seed may be

sown directly into the garden, and young plants thinned to stand about eight inches apart.

DOWNINGIA SPECIES

FAMILY: *Lobeliaceae* or lobelia family.

CLASSIFICATION: Half-hardy annual.

COMMON NAMES: Blue calico flower, downingia.

HARDINESS: Sensitive to frost.

GROWING CONDITIONS: Humus-rich, fertile, moisture-retentive soil. Filtered light or part shade.

PROPAGATION: By seed sown 6 to 8 weeks before last frost date.

HEIGHT: To 1'.

ORNAMENTAL VALUE: Grown for flower.

LEVEL OF CULTURAL DIFFICULTY: Easy.

SPECIAL PROPERTIES: None.

PRONUNCIATION: dow-NIN-gee-a

*E*xcepting possibly the Cape Province of South Africa, no region of the world is richer in beautiful annual plants than the western coast of North America, from middle California up to Washington, Oregon, and British Columbia. Many botanists—particularly English botanists—early recognized that fact, and scarcely a single splendid American West Coast native that could be grown from seed escaped the notice of William Robinson (1838–1935), who revolutionized Edwardian garden practices in *The English Flower Garden* (1883). As the introduction to the 1984 Sagapress edition of that great book, with its startling emphasis on pure species and naturalistic planting, points out, Robinson "reinvented gardening as we (the civilized) know it." He singled out *Downingia elegans* (EL-uh-gans) and *D. pulchella* (pul-CHEL-a) for special praise, as "charming little half-hardy California annuals." Since then, however, only those gardeners who specialize in native western American plants have grown downingia, and outside those rarefied circles, seed sources are scarce.

This is a great pity, for unlike many other splendid West Coast native annual plants, downingia are easy to grow, requiring (as do most members of Lobeliaceae, the lobelia family) only abundant moisture, a little shade, and some coolness on summer nights. They are small plants, *Downingia elegans* scarcely reaching a foot in height, and *D. pulchella* growing about as tall, but becoming lax, even trailing, as it grows along. The leaves of both species are alternate, about an inch long at the base of the plant, but becoming smaller as they ascend up the stems. The flowers, which are approximately an inch wide, are borne in the leaf axils and possess three lower petals and two upper ones, with an extended, lobed central lip, giving them the look of tiny cattleya orchids. The flower color of both is typically a limpid blue, though deeper blue and pure white forms occur in both species.

Both species come readily from seed, which should be sown indoors in late April or early May in moist but free-draining compost and covered lightly with a sprinkling of sharp sand. Germination should occur within a week, and flowers may be expected in about ten weeks from sprouting. Young plants should be established in the garden after all danger of frost is past and may be expected to flower from early July to September, or until frost cuts them down. Seed, which is scarce, should always be saved for the following year's plants.

The genus name *Downingia* commemorates Andrew Jackson Downing, whose landmark work *A Treatise on the Theory and Practice of Landscape Gardening Applied to North America* was first published in 1841 but remained in print well into the twentieth century. Downing, a passionate egalitarian, argued that the beauty of the landscape was held in common by all people, and therefore, barriers that excluded the public view or that sequestered property were fundamentally undemocratic, and by extension, un-American. Some of the happy results of his widely accepted beliefs are the National Parks system and the magnificent public parks designed by Frederick Law Olmsted (among others), including Central Park in New York, Golden Gate Park in San Francisco, Boston's "Green Necklace," the splendid chain of public parks that extends through the center of Philadelphia, and major public parks in Chicago, Cincinnati, Louisville, and other American cities.

The names of both species of *Downingia* attest to their charm, *pulchella* signifying pretty and *elegans,* elegant.

DRACOCEPHALUM MOLDAVICUM

FAMILY: *Lamiaceae (Labiatae)* or mint family.

CLASSIFICATION: Hardy annual.

COMMON NAMES: Moldavian dragonhead, Moldavian balm, dracocephalum.

HARDINESS: Sensitive to light frosts until well established.

GROWING CONDITIONS: Fertile, moisture-retentive soil. Part shade.

PROPAGATION: By seed, sown indoors 6 to 8 weeks before last frost.

HEIGHT: 12 to 20".

ORNAMENTAL VALUE: Grown for flower.

LEVEL OF CULTURAL DIFFICULTY: Easy.

SPECIAL PROPERTIES: Leaves mildly fragrant when crushed. Excellent bee plant. May be grown in cool greenhouses for late winter flower.

PRONUNCIATION: dra-co-SE-fa-lum mol-DAV-i-cum

The genus *Dracocephalum* takes its name from the fanciful resemblance of its lipped, hooded flowers to the head of a dragon, from ancient Greek *draco,* dragon, and *cephala,* head. Most of the forty-five species in the genus are perennials, but one cultivated species, the Moldavian dragonhead, is a true annual, native to the Danube River basin but widely naturalized throughout the temperate world. An old-fashioned plant of a gentle charm, it was once frequently grown in gardens but is now rarely seen, except possibly by wildflower enthusiasts who may find the whorls of small violet or blue flowers on tall stems flourishing in damp ditches along shaded country roads.

Dracocephalum forms a neat bush from twelve to twenty inches high, nicely furnished with the typical lance-shaped, toothed leaves of the mint family, each leaf about an inch or an inch and a half long. The pretty, soft gray-green of the leaves effectively sets off the violet-blue, inch-long flowers that are borne above the plant in tall, leafy spikes. The flowers deserve close study, for they are cunningly composed of an arched upper lip and a puckered lower one, furnished even with teeth, and each looking like a tiny, gentle dragon. All parts of the plant possess a mild, balmlike fragrance, and the flowers are adored by bees.

Seed of dracocephalum may be sown indoors in late March or early April for plants that will flower in July and August. Though classed as a hardy annual, seedlings raised indoors should be carefully hardened off and transplanted into the garden only after danger of frost has passed. Once it has been grown in temperate gardens, however, a ready supply of young seedlings should volunteer each year. They may be thinned to stand six to twelve inches apart or transplanted elsewhere in the garden.

Dracocephalum moldavicum is also lovely when single plants are established in eight-inch clay pots, which shows off the symmetry of their form and the subtle beauty of their flowers. Seed may be sown for this purpose in early February for early summer flowering, or an August seeding may be made for flowering plants in a cool greenhouse in winter.

Though the best flower color of *D. moldavicum* is a rich violet blue, a white cultivar exists ('Album'), which for once is as pretty as the blue. *D. moldavicum* deserves to be reintroduced into gardens, not only for its quiet beauty but also because, like many members of the mint family, it grows well in damp, semi-shaded positions where showier annuals will not thrive.

DRACOPSIS AMPLEXICAULIS

FAMILY: *Asteraceae* or aster or daisy family.

CLASSIFICATION: Hardy annual.

COMMON NAMES: Cone flower, dracopsis.

HARDINESS: Slightly frost-hardy when established.

GROWING CONDITIONS: Moderately fertile, well-drained soil. Full sun.

PROPAGATION: By seed, sown 8 to 10 weeks indoors before last frost, or in site outdoors with the arrival of warm weather.

HEIGHT: To 15".

ORNAMENTAL VALUE: Grown for flower.

LEVEL OF CULTURAL DIFFICULTY: Easy.

SPECIAL PROPERTIES: Used as an arresting cut flower when petals are stripped away, leaving only disk flowers.

PRONUNCIATION: dra-KOP-sis am-plex-i-CAUL-is

*M*ost gardeners would assume *Dracopsis amplexicaulis* to be a rudbeckia, but because of minute botanical differences it occupies a genus of its own and is the sole species within it. Generally, rudbeckias, which are perennial or biennial, have overshadowed it to the extent that few botanical references exist and seed is very seldom offered. Still, it is a sturdy and beautiful American wild flower, native from Kansas to Texas and eastward to Georgia, and enthusiasts of native plants or gardeners interested in subtle differences among plants might well grow it.

Dracopsis amplexicaulis takes its name from the ancient Greek *draco,* meaning dragon, and a suffix meaning resembles. There is nothing at all particularly dragonlike about its flowers, however, which are cheerful, two-inch-wide daisies with deep, chrome-yellow ray flowers stained purple-brown at their base, and a central, inch-high cone of fertile flowers in the center. As the flowers age, the ray petals tend to droop downward, and the central cone becomes quite prominent and thickened, tapering at its top to a point, and colored a rich, deep brown. It is at that stage, perhaps, that *D. amplexicaulis* cuts its finest figure, not on the plant but in stylish florists' shops where bunches of cones, stripped of their ray petals, are offered on long stems for autumn arrangements.

D. amplexicaulis may be sown indoors from mid-March to early April, and transplanted after frosts have passed. Alternatively, seed may be sown outdoors about two weeks before the last frost date where the plants are to grow. Dracopsis thrives in ordinary, moderately fertile, well-drained soil in full sun. Plants should be spaced about a foot apart to leave room for the development of their graceful candelabra of blooming stems, clad at the base in two-inch, leathery blue-green leaves. (The species name *amplexicaulis* means stem-clasping.) Bloom should occur about two months after seed germination and will continue for about six weeks. Plants started indoors will flower in early to midsummer but may be cut back after blooming for another flow-ering in autumn. Seed sown directly into the garden will produce plants that flower from late summer to autumn. *Dracopsis amplexicaulis,* like many daisies, lasts well when cut, and so a row or two might be grown for fresh arrangements or as a component of dried autumn arrangements or wreaths.

DYSSODIA TENUILOBA (CHRYSANTHEMUM TENUILOBUM, THYMOPHYLLA TENUILOBA)

FAMILY: *Asteraceae* or aster or daisy family.

CLASSIFICATION: Tender perennial treated as half-hardy annual.

COMMON NAMES: Dahlberg daisy, golden fleece, dyssodia.

HARDINESS: Withstands light frost once established.

GROWING CONDITIONS: Sandy, perfectly drained soil of moderate fertility. Full sun.

PROPAGATION: From seed, sown indoors, 6 to 8 weeks before last anticipated frost.

HEIGHT: 8" to 1'.

ORNAMENTAL VALUE: Grown for flower.

LEVEL OF CULTURAL DIFFICULTY: Easy.

SPECIAL PROPERTIES: None.

PRONUNCIATION: dy-SO-dee-a ten-yew-i-LO-ba (kri-san-THE-mum ten-yew-i-LO-bum, ti-MA-fil-a *or* ti-ma-FIL-a)

*I*t is a pity that so pretty and winsome a plant as the Dahlberg daisy suffers from so much name confusion. Once comfortably lodged in the genus *Chrysanthemum* as *C. tenuilobum* (from the Latin *tenuis,* meaning slender or thin, and referring to its finely divided threadlike leaves), it was shifted first into the now-extinct genus *Thymophylla* (from a fanciful resemblance of its leaves to thyme) and then into the genus *Dyssodia* (meaning bad smelling), which includes a number of odiferous weeds of the southwestern United States and northern Mexico collectively called "dogweeds" or "fetid marigolds."

That does it an injustice, for its leaves are pleasantly aromatic and fresh-smelling, and so a more pleasant common name was required. Someone christened it "golden fleece," which, though certainly more pleasant than "dogweed" or "fetid marigold," misses the mark, as it is the three-quarter-inch-long leaves, each fringed into seven to ten green threads, that cause the plant to look fleecelike, and not its half-inch-wide, butter yellow daisies with orange-yellow centers, each of which stands out perkily above the plant like a tiny marguerite.

Though dyssodia is native to Texas and Mexico, it does not seem to do its best in heat, where its life will be brief, though often seedlings will appear after the demise of the mother plant, growing to maturity and blooming the same season. In cooler gardens, however, dyssodia will come into bloom in June from an indoor sowing six to eight weeks before the last anticipated frost and remain effective well into August, when, if it becomes shabby, it can be lightly sheared back for fresh bloom in autumn.

Dyssodia is at least true to its origins in preferring a sandy, well-drained soil of moderate fertility, and full sun. Where it may be grown well, it makes an excellent hanging basket or container plant.

ECCREMOCARPUS SCABER

FAMILY: *Bignonaceae* or trumpet vine family.
CLASSIFICATION: Tender woody vine grown as half-hardy annual.

COMMON NAMES: Chilean glory flower, eccremocarpus.
HARDINESS: Hardy to USDA Zone 7 on light, well-drained soils. Slightly frost-hardy elsewhere when established.
GROWING CONDITIONS: Fertile, well-drained, moisture-retentive soil. Full sun. Heat.
PROPAGATION: By seed, sown indoors in peat pots 8 to 12 weeks before last frost. Seedlings resent root disturbance.
HEIGHT: From 8 to 12' in a season.
ORNAMENTAL VALUE: Grown for flower and for quick vining cover on pergolas, arbors, fences, etc.
LEVEL OF CULTURAL DIFFICULTY: Easy.
SPECIAL PROPERTIES: Excellent cut flowers.
PRONUNCIATION: ek-re-mo-KAR-pus SKAY-ber

*U*ntil recently—except perhaps for a lamppost against which morning glory seed were planted each year—few American gardens possessed places to grow vines at all, never mind annual ones. But with the recent increase in sophistication among American gardeners, structures such as trellises, arbors, pergolas, and internal fences are being included as crucial design elements in the garden, and the wealth of true annual vines—and tender vines that may be treated as annuals—is beginning to be discovered.

Eccremocarpus scaber, the magnificent Chilean glory flower, is one such vine. A woody, scandent perennial native to the Andes of Chile and Peru, it is hardy as far north as Zone 7, though in its northernmost range it will be killed back to old wood or even to the ground in winter. Still, it is of very rapid growth, sprouting quickly when cut back hard. Further north, it may be treated as an annual, sown in late April for flowers in mid- to late summer and well into autumn, often remaining unscathed by the first light frosts. Seed should be sown at temperatures around 60°F, and it may take as long as three weeks to germinate. But much like *Cobaea scandens,* the cup-and-saucer vine, it does no good to sow the seed too early, as seedling vines may quickly become an unmanageable tangle, and in any case will not begin to develop rapidly outdoors until the weather is settled and warm. Young seedlings resent root disturbance, which may permanently set them back, and so three or four seed should be sown to an individual peat pot, and all but the strongest clipped out when two full sets of leaves have developed.

Even without its splendid flowers, *E. scaber* is quite a pretty vine, clothed in delicate-seeming leaves made up of many dark green, heavily veined oval leaflets each about an inch long, the entire compound leaf terminating in a tendril at the end. Vines develop best in fertile, well-drained soil with abundant moisture, in full sun, and in colder gardens, earlier flowers may be had if the vines are trained to a south-facing support, preferably a fence or wall that will reflect the sun's warmth. Growth may reach eight to twelve feet in the first summer, and as the vines resent crowding, they should be given plenty of room by being established no closer than eight to ten feet apart.

The flowers of *E. scaber* are borne in clusters of as many as fifteen individual blooms at a time, on reddish, waxy stems about eight inches long that either stand straight up from the vine or curve gracefully down and upward. Each individual flower is about an inch long, and consists of a narrow tube, slightly pouched beneath into a sort of belly and pinched at the end into lips. The flowers resemble nothing so much as a school of tiny goldfish, and it is remarkable that the plant has escaped the popular name "goldfish vine," which seems so apt. The naturally occurring species typically bears flowers of a clear, fiery orange, shading to a paler orange that is almost yellow at the mouth, though variants have been selected that range from cream through golden yellow to scarlet and crimson. 'Tresco Crimson' and 'Tresco Cream' isolate two of these colors, which are attractive, but hardly improvements on the vividness of the species.

Eccremocarpus scaber is the only member of its genus of three or four species commonly grown in gardens. The genus name is taken from its abundantly produced, slender, two-inch-long down-hanging seed pods, from ancient Greek *ekkremes,* hanging, and *karpos,* a fruit. The species name *scaber* is Latin for rough, a description of the slightly raspy texture of the leaves. Even where the vine is not hardy, the flat, shiny black seed

ECCREMOCARPUS SCABER

may survive the winter to sprout the following spring. When such volunteers occur where they are wanted, the resulting plants will always be stronger and earlier-flowering than those started indoors and transplanted into the garden. Where flowers are abundantly produced and may be spared from the garden, whole clusters also make interesting and long-lasting additions to summer and autumn bouquets.

ECHINOCYSTIS LOBATA

FAMILY: *Cucurbitaceae* or cucumber family.

CLASSIFICATION: Hardy annual vine.

COMMON NAMES: Wild cucumber, mock cucumber, echinocystus.

HARDINESS: Sensitive to light frosts.

GROWING CONDITIONS: Any reasonably fertile soil. Abundant moisture. Heat.

PROPAGATION: From seed, sown indoors in peat pots 4 to 6 weeks before last anticipated frost. Seedlings resent root disturbance.

HEIGHT: To 20' in a season.

ORNAMENTAL VALUE: Grown for quick cover.

LEVEL OF CULTURAL DIFFICULTY: Easy.

SPECIAL PROPERTIES: None.

PRONUNCIATION: eh-kin-o-SIS-tus lo-BA-ta

For camouflaging unsightly features in the landscape—large piles of brush or abandoned hen houses, for example—*Echinocystis lobata* is ideal. Rapid of growth, the annual vine reaches as much as twenty feet in a single season, thriving especially in the eastern half of North America where it is native, from New Brunswick to central Canada, and southward to Florida and Texas. It climbs by tendrils, throwing swags of angled stems and flowers over roadside bushes and forest-edge shrubs, and producing creamy panicles of male flowers and solitary female ones from late July to mid-September. Each individual flower is minute, hardly a quarter-inch long, but male flowers are produced in profusion, creating a greenish-white foam above the broad leaves. Closely allied to garden cucumbers, from which the plant draws its popular name, it has a look like no other native vine, perennial or annual, and so is easy to identify. Its leaves are light green and coarse, roughly heart-shaped, from three to five inches across and up to eight inches long, scalloped at the edges with three to seven broad lobes and raspy to the touch.

Seed of *Echinocystis lobata* is seldom offered and so must be acquired from natural stands along the roadside in autumn. Although seeds are hardy well into Zone 3, quick coverage in the garden is best procured by sowing the seed indoors about four to six weeks before the last anticipated frost, and transplanting young seedlings into the garden where they are to grow when the weather is settled and warm. Like all members of the family Cucurbitaceae, *E. lobata* resents root disturbance and so should be sown in peat pots, three seeds to a pot, all of which may be allowed to develop. Slow to germinate, seed is dependent outdoors on the softening effects of a long winter. To speed germination, it should be soaked for a day or two in water before being sown. Once the vine has been grown in gardens, it is apt to reappear each year, though its intolerance to root disturbance makes it fairly easy to eradicate and keeps it from becoming a nuisance. All soils seem to suit echinocystis equally, though it grows best when it receives plenty of water.

Echinocystis lobata is the single species in its genus, the name of which is composed of two ancient Greek nouns that describe its papery, inflated, somewhat spiny seed pod, *echinos,* meaning hedgehog, and *kystis,* a bladder. The species name *lobata* describes its broadly lobed leaves.

ECHIUM LYCOPSIS
(E. PLANTAGINEUM)

FAMILY: *Boraginaceae* or borage family.

CLASSIFICATION: Hardy biennial grown as hardy annual.

COMMON NAMES: Viper's bugloss, annual echium.

HARDINESS: Withstands frosts.

GROWING CONDITIONS: Any soil. Full sun.

PROPAGATION: By seed, sown in autumn in site in warmer gardens, in very early spring in colder ones. May be started indoors 6 to 8 weeks before last frost.

HEIGHT: From 1 to 3', depending on cultivar and cultural conditions.

ORNAMENTAL VALUE: Grown for flower.

LEVEL OF CULTURAL DIFFICULTY: Easy.

SPECIAL PROPERTIES: None.

PRONUNCIATION: EK-ee-um lye-KOP-sis (plan-ta-gi-NEE-um)

*E*chium is an Old World genus of approximately thirty-five species, some of which are grown in the most privileged gardens of North America, in Zones 9 and 10, for their towers of reddish, violet, or blue flowers, sometimes more than twelve feet tall. The most treasured are the reddish-violet *E. pininana* (pi-ni-NA-na), called "tower of jewels," *E. fastuosum* (fas-tu-O-sum), the "pride of Madeira" with its giant cobs of violet-blue flowers, and crosses between it and *E. wildprettii* (wild-PRET-ee-ee), which bear thousands of powder-blue to sky-blue flowers in spires up to fourteen feet tall. Gardeners who have seen them in California in their full magnificence are tempted, at least once, to cultivate them as large potted plants, though the attempt generally seems to end in failure, as they require vast amounts of space to overwinter and just the right

fresh, buoyant atmosphere to survive and flower.

Those who live in colder or more arid climates must be content, then, with two much more modest species, both biennials native throughout Europe and into England. Of the two species, *Echium vulgare* (vul-GAR-ee) is by far the more common, having naturalized throughout the eastern half of North America to the extent that many people assume it to be a native wild flower. Stubbornly biennial, it waits for its second year to send up three- or four-foot-high spikes of minute flowers that open pink and fade to lavender blue.

The other commonly grown hardy biennial species is *Echium lycopsis* (sometimes listed under the synonym *E. plantagineum*), which, in addition to being showier in flower, may easily be grown as an annual. *Echium lycopsis* forms a generally bushier plant than *E. vulgare,* producing many arching, one-sided flower spikes to as much as three feet tall, crowded with half-inch-wide flowers over a long period of time. In most cultivars, the flowers open pink and quickly change to purplish blue, though close study reveals that each small flower takes its color from brushings or veining of deep purple over a lavender ground. Forms also exist that are a paler grayish lavender, rose-pink, or white, and they are sometimes offered in a dwarf mix that grows only twelve inches tall. Though those are certainly very pretty, both the height and the flower color of the naturally occurring species can hardly be improved upon. Almost any garden soil of moderate fertility will suit either plant, both of which are excellent for meadow gardens, bank cuts, or any waste places where grass is thin.

Echium lycopsis may be grown from an autumn sowing outdoors in Zone 7 gardens and warmer, or from a very early spring sowing in colder gardens. Plants sown directly into the garden will flower from late July until well into autumn, though earlier-flowering plants may be had by sowing seed indoors about six to eight weeks before the last anticipated frost date, after which they may be transplanted into the garden to stand about a foot apart.

Unfortunately, *E. lycopsis* is often offered (even by quite reliable seed companies) as *E. vulgare,* resulting in considerable confusion. If the seed listed is designated as a hardy annual, one may take one's chances, with the understanding that the plants may flower in their first year or may simply make wide rosettes of leaves, narrow, warted, and bristly dark green, then flowering magnificently the following season.

Both species bear the common name "viper's bugloss" because they were once believed to ward off poisonous serpents, and an infusion of the roots was used in ancient Greek medicine to treat snakebite. The curious old English word *bugloss* descends also from the ancient Greek through Latin and medieval French, from *bous,* meaning cow's head, and *glossa,* tongue, a description of the raspy, oblong green leaves of both plants.

EMMENANTHE PENDULIFLORA

FAMILY: *Hydrophyllaceae* or waterleaf family.

CLASSIFICATION: Half-hardy annual.

COMMON NAMES: California golden bells, whispering bells, emmenanthe.

HARDINESS: Sensitive to frost.

GROWING CONDITIONS: Sandy, well-drained, mineral-rich soils. Abundant moisture.

PROPAGATION: From seed, sown indoors in peat pots about 5 weeks before last frost.

HEIGHT: From 5 to 18", depending on culture.

ORNAMENTAL VALUE: Grown for flower.

LEVEL OF CULTURAL DIFFICULTY: Easy when conditions approach its natural range; difficult elsewhere.

SPECIAL PROPERTIES: None.

PRONUNCIATION: em-uh-NAN-thee pen-du-li-FLO-ra

*T*o find a large stand of *Emmenanthe penduliflora* in full bloom somewhere in the deserts of California or New Mexico must be tremendously exciting. Sadly, one is apt to see it no place else. Seed is seldom offered, and its culture as an ornamental is limited to the gardens of wildflower enthusiasts close to its natural range, from the lower half of California to northern Mexico and eastward to southern Utah.

Under the best growing conditions, which is to say a sandy, well-drained soil rich in minerals, moist from vernal rains and in full sun, *Emmenanthe penduliflora* forms a bushy plant as much as eighteen inches tall. It is a peculiarity of the species, the only member of its genus, that its flowers—loose, many-branched clusters of lemon to cream-yellow, campanula-like bells—last a surprisingly long time when open. (This gives the genus its name, from ancient Greek *emmenes,* meaning enduring, and *anthos,* a flower.) As they age, the inch-long flowers become somewhat papery in texture, accounting for one of the plant's two lovely popular names, "whispering bells." Even in its chosen home, however, plants may be only a few inches high, though still nicely furnished with bloom and with leaves finely cut into segments.

E. penduliflora flourishes best when nights are cool and days fresh and bright, flowering most freely at the end of spring and into early summer, and then melting away without a trace, leaving room for sturdier, heat-loving annuals and perennials. It should be started indoors, about five weeks before the last anticipated frost date, and transplanted into the garden after all danger of frost is past. Young seedlings must be grown on healthily, in a buoyant atmosphere, and should not receive a check either from drying out or from transplanting, else they will never develop into vigorous, full-flowering plants. Alternatively, in those gardens that enjoy a long, cool but sunny late spring and early summer, seed may be sown in place and young plants thinned to stand about a foot apart. In such gardens, emmenanthe is likely to self-sow on undisturbed soil. Seed might also be sown in early August for winter-flowering plants in a cool greenhouse.

EMILIA COCCINEA
(E. JAVANICA, E. FLAMMEA, CACALIA COCCINEA)

FAMILY: *Asteraceae* or aster or daisy family.

CLASSIFICATION: Half-hardy annual.

COMMON NAMES: Tassel flower, Flora's paintbrush, emilia.

HARDINESS: Withstands light frost once established.

GROWING CONDITIONS: Well-drained garden loam of moderate fertility. Full sun.

PROPAGATION: By seed, sown indoors in peat pots about 8 weeks before last frost, or in place 2 weeks before last frost.

HEIGHT: To 18".

ORNAMENTAL VALUE: Grown for flower.

LEVEL OF CULTURAL DIFFICULTY: Easy.

SPECIAL PROPERTIES: None.

PRONUNCIATION: eh-MEE-lee-a co-CHIN-ee-a (ja-VAN-i-ca, FLA-mee-a, ka-KA-lee-a)

There are mysteries about *Emilia coccinea*—where the genus name came from, what its original native habitat was—but none about its charms. From basal rosettes of smooth, lance-shaped, gray-green leaves rise many slender stems, eighteen inches tall, each of which branches freely and bears tiny flowers typically a clear scarlet, though orange, yellow, and pinkish-orange forms occur. Some seed mixes may include them all, in very beautiful blends, all the colors of which accord well together. For a brief time the descriptive species name *flammea* was attached to the plant, from the Latin adjective meaning flame-like, an apt metaphor for its vivid flowers that glow like tiny, half-inch brush piles. The wiry stems and minute dancing flowers are excellent when cut, and enhance almost any other flower color, but particularly shades of blue. Because of its delicacy *Emilia coccinea* is best studied up close, and so groups might be established along a path, in the rock garden, or in a sequestered but sunny patch in the shrubbery.

The genus *Emilia* bears a pretty name, one that was surely meant to pay a compliment to a wife, daughter, or sweetheart dear to the namer. But because her precise identity remains unknown, the compliment falls a little flat. Of the twenty species contained in the genus, most of which occur in the Old World tropics, the one most commonly grown in gardens was originally located in the genus *Cacalia*, as *C. coccinea*. The subsequent placement of the plant in *Emilia* added to that genus its principal ornament, but, sadly, detracted from *Cacalia*, whose fifty remaining species possess no horticultural interest whatsoever. The plant cultivated in gardens came to be called *Emilia javanica* from its assumed Javanese origins, and though its precise prehistoric birthplace has in fact proven to be mysterious, that species name has stuck, perhaps because it is so evocative of a romantic, faraway place. For the moment, the rules of nomenclature demand that the correct botanical designation of the plant is *Emilia coccinea*, the species name deriving from a Latin adjective that means orange-red.

Emilia coccinea is of very easy culture, flowering from late June until frost from a seeding indoors in late April or outdoors about two weeks before the last anticipated frost date. Because seedlings are impatient of transplanting, peat pots or flexible cell packs should be used for indoor sowing, and young plants should not be moved once they are established. Plants flourish in free-draining, moderately fertile garden loam, in full sun. Frequent removal of flowering stems encourages bloom over a long period of time so one can cut freely without robbing the plants of all their effect in the garden. Much like dandelions, which it somewhat resembles, *E. coccinea* has seeds equipped with silken parachutes that, once aloft, can travel great distances, and so it has naturalized wherever conditions are congenial.

A closely related species, *Emilia sonchifolia* (son-chi-FO-lee-a), named for the resemblance of its leaves to *Sonchus,* the sow thistle, is sometimes offered. It resembles *Emilia coccinea* in every way, except that it bears reddish-purple or magenta flowers. A pretty enough plant, it might be more highly thought of were it not in competition with its vibrant cousin.

ERIGERON KARVINSKIANUS

FAMILY: *Asteraceae* or aster or daisy family.

CLASSIFICATION: Tender perennial grown as half-hardy annual.

COMMON NAMES: Mexican fleabane, bonytip, Mexican daisy, vittadinai, annual erigeron.

HARDINESS: Frost-sensitive until established.

GROWING CONDITIONS: Perfectly drained, lean soils. Full sun.

PROPAGATION: By seed, sown indoors 6 to 8 weeks before last frost.

EMILIA COCCINEA

HEIGHT: To 1' or less.

ORNAMENTAL VALUE: Valued for flower and for creeping, matted growth habit.

LEVEL OF CULTURAL DIFFICULTY: Easy.

SPECIAL PROPERTIES: Excellent in hanging baskets, window boxes, and containers.

PRONUNCIATION: eh-REE-ger-on kar-vin-ski-AN-us

*M*ost American gardeners know the fleabanes as sturdy, reliable perennials that generally bloom in early to midsummer, providing beautiful daisies of clear or violet blue, mauve or pink, always with perky yellow centers. They are splendid for cutting, and in the garden they look like flowers that might be painted on fine porcelain. Although often described as resembling Michaelmas daisies, the comparison is hardly fair to them because they have their own special charm, one of which is to flower in the freshness of the gardening season. (The precocity of their flowering is recognized in the first part of their genus name, the ancient Greek adjective *eri,* which means early; the noun *geron* signifies an old man and refers to the downy, silvery leaves of some species.)

But tucked in among the many good perennial fleabanes is one, *Erigeron karvinskianus,* that can be grown quite successfully as an annual. A native of northern Mexico to Venezuela, it is in fact a true perennial, hardy to Zone 9, but it has the amiable characteristic of flowering in three months from seed. A sowing indoors under glass in late March or early April will produce flowers by midsummer. A small, creeping plant that hardly achieves a height of a foot, it has tiny three-quarter-inch-wide daisies borne in profusion throughout the summer and practically all year where it is hardy. Each flower opens a pale, pinkish white, and then changes first to deeper pink and then to reddish-purple, resulting in an attractive blend of colors. Leaves are an inch long, toothed, and slightly hairy.

The charms of *E. karvinskianus* are considerable, but they are more modest than showy. It thrives in dryish, rather lean soils, which produce compact and abundantly flowering plants. It looks its best when associated with stone paving and old mortared walls, such as one sees it in the southwest of England, where, rather surprisingly for a plant of Mexican origins, it has happily naturalized. Where it must be treated as an annual and planted anew each year, the effect might be copied by tucking it among the paving stones of a terrace or establishing it along a path or in the rock garden. *E. karvinskianus* also makes a superb container plant, seeming to relish some dryness at the roots.

Erigeron karvinskianus is very easy from seed, which should be sown indoors about six to eight weeks before the last anticipated frost date, at temperatures of around 55°F. Young plants should be pricked out and grown on as soon as they may be handled, at similarly cool temperatures, in bright, airy conditions. They may be transferred to their

ERIGERON KARVINSKIANUS

permanent garden positions as soon as frost is not a danger, and they tend to develop best in the cool conditions of spring. The cultivar most frequently offered is 'Profusion', which bears large numbers of pink daisies shading to white, and which is especially fine in hanging baskets, window boxes, or at the edges of large containers of mixed annuals and tender perennials.

It is uncertain whether various species of *Erigeron* actually deter fleas, since no scientifically verifiable tests appear to have been conducted. Still, the common name "fleabane" has adhered to the entire genus and has certainly added an extra value to the considerable charms of the many garden-worthy species within it.

ERYSIMUM SPECIES

FAMILY: *Cruciferae* or mustard family.

CLASSIFICATION: Hardy perennials, biennials, or subshrubs grown as half-hardy annuals.

COMMON NAMES: Blister cress, wallflower, cheirianthus, erysimum.

HARDINESS: Hardy to Zone 7 under ideal conditions. Frost-hardy elsewhere when established.

GROWING CONDITIONS: Well-drained, gritty, fertile soil. Full sun. Cool temperatures.

PROPAGATION: By seed, sown in late winter. Some species carried over by tip cuttings.

HEIGHT: From 8″ to 2½′, depending on cultivar.

ORNAMENTAL VALUE: Grown for flower.

LEVEL OF CULTURAL DIFFICULTY: Easy under ideal conditions; moderately difficult elsewhere.

SPECIAL PROPERTIES: None.

PRONUNCIATION: e-RIH-sih-mum

To English gardeners, wallflowers of all sorts are readily available as started plants, and can even be bought in village markets in bundles, bare rooted and wrapped up in damp newspaper. They are almost obligatory in the spring garden, clothing the shanks of tulips or filling the floral gap between the primroses and the first bedding plants of earliest summer. An English garden would not be what it is without the sharp, sweet scent of wallflowers after a spring shower. But they are little grown in the United States, and the principal explanation is not hard to locate. Most American gardens do not enjoy the brief mild winters and cool moist springs and early summers typical of many parts of the British Isles, where nighttime temperatures hover around 50°F, bright, sunny days reach temperatures near 75°F, and 80°F is considered "very warm."

It is true, however, that a few erysimum might be considered good bets for most American gardeners and, in a lucky season, can offer a wonderful display of neat bushes clad in linear foliage and topped with spikes of fragrant, nearly inch-wide four-petaled flowers. Two species are sometimes offered, both of which can be brought to flower as annuals. The first is *Erysimum linifolium* (lin-i-FO-lee-um) (sometimes offered as *Cheiranthus linifolius*), the alpine or flax-leaved wallflower, a native of Spain and Portugal. It is a true but short-lived perennial, hardy to Zone 7 or possibly Zone 6 if soils are very well drained and if plants are protected by evergreen boughs in winter. It is best grown, however, as a hardy annual from an autumn sowing in a cold frame or an early February sowing under glass. Young plants may be transplanted into the garden as soon as the soil dries out in spring, where they will form loose, procumbent mounds of growth as much as a foot high and wide, topped with spikes of lilac or grayish-purple flowers, sometimes opening to a wonderful biscuit tan and then fading to mauve. Several named forms exist, and there is one with beautiful silvery leaves bordered in cream, pretty enough to grow even if no flowers ever occurred, and very effective in winter where it is hardy.

The second erysimum occasionally offered is *E. perofskianum* (per-of-SKEE-a-num), the Siberian wallflower, which is remarkable for its plurality of names. It is sold as *Cheiranthus allionii* (all-ee-ON-ee-ee), *Erysimum allionii, E. perofskianum, E. murale* (mur-AY-lee), *E. hieracifolium* (hi-er-a-ci-FO-lee-um), and *E. alpinum* (al-PEE-num). Not a Siberian native, for all its common name, it occurs naturally in Pakistan and Afghanistan but was named for the Russian general V. A. Perovski (1794–1850), who is also remembered in the genus name of *Perovskia atriplicifolia,* the elegant hardy perennial called Russian sage. *E. perofskianum* is a biennial or sometimes weakly perennial, plant that is best treated as a hardy annual, seed being sown in early autumn for flowers the following summer. Alternatively, seed may be sown in February in a cool greenhouse, and the young plants potted on until they can be hardened off and established in the garden in early spring.

Recently, another fine erysimum has appeared in the American nursery trade, called 'Bowles Mauve' after the great British plantsman Edward Augustus Bowles (1865–1954). Its exact botanical placement is uncertain, though it has been offered as a cultivar of *Erysimum linifolium* or as *Cheiranthus linifolius.* It may be a hybrid of two or several species, but for the moment at least, it is placed in the North American species, *Erysimum arkansanum* (ar-kan-SA-num), synonymous with *E. asperum* (AS-per-um). It forms an essentially shrublike, billowy plant to three feet tall, with much-branched stems, corky at their bases and clothed in narrow, silvery-gray, inch-long leaves. Simply as a foliage plant, *Erysimum* 'Bowles Mauve' is useful in the garden, but in just the right cool, somewhat dryish summer, flowers

will be borne abundantly on elongated spikes about eight inches tall, from mid-July until frost. They are of a beautiful grayish purple that accords perfectly with the pewter-colored leaves below, and the whole plant—shape, leaf, flower—offers a wonderful structure and a quietly dignified foil to brighter flowers in the border. Though persistent for a year or two in very favored gardens in Zones 6 and warmer, the best display to be gotten from *Erysimum* 'Bowles Mauve' is with new young plants each spring. Cuttings of nonflowering stems, which root very readily, should be taken in late summer or early autumn, and rooted plants should be grown on through the winter in a cool greenhouse or heated sun porch and pinched frequently to produce stocky, well-branched transplants after all danger of frost has passed. The growth of young plants is very rapid, and substantial foot-high bushes should occur by late June or early July.

All erysimum flourish best in rich but well-drained, somewhat dryish, alkaline soils, such as would occur at the base of very old mortared walls or even in crevices of decayed cement where leaves have collected and rotted. This accounts for their popular name "wallflower." Success is also to be had—given appropriate climatic conditions—in old gardens that have been faithfully manured and sanded for a century or more, to produce deep, fertile soils with a distinct "grit" to them. When these conditions cannot be met, or at least approximated, most species are seldom successful, though *Erysimum* 'Bowles Mauve' can be surprisingly splendid on the heavy clay soils of the middle and upper South of North America.

The common name "wallflower" properly belongs to species in the genus *Cheiranthus,* but it is completely uncertain exactly where, botanically speaking, the genus *Cheiranthus* belongs. It differs from the genus *Erysimum* only in the minutest particulars of seed formation, and in both genuses there are garden-worthy cultivars that do not set seed at all. Species in either genus therefore tend to slosh back and forth and among themselves. References are uncertain, also, as to whether species grown under either genus name are annuals, biennials, perennials, sub-shrubs, or "all of the above."

The genus name *Erysimum* is of ancient origin, from the Greek *eryo,* meaning to draw, and attesting to the belief that a paste of the pounded leaves of the plant could pull toxins from boils and painful blisters, much as the membranous skin of an egg is believed to do.

ESCHSCHOLZIA CALIFORNICA

FAMILY: *Papaveraceae* or poppy family.

CLASSIFICATION: Short-lived perennial grown as hardy or half-hardy annual.

COMMON NAMES: California poppy, eschscholzia.

HARDINESS: Slightly frost resistant when well established.

GROWING CONDITIONS: Perfectly drained, sandy or gravelly soil. Abundant moisture. Full sun.

PROPAGATION: By seed, sown in late autumn or in very early spring.

HEIGHT: From 1 to 2'.

ORNAMENTAL VALUE: Valued for flower.

LEVEL OF CULTURAL DIFFICULTY: Easy.

SPECIAL PROPERTIES: None.

PRONUNCIATION: esh-OLT-zee-a ca-li-FOR-ni-ca

California poppies are among America's best-loved wild flowers. They once grew in such abundance in their native state that during his voyage up the Pacific coast in 1572, Sir Francis Drake reported that they tinted the sky with reflected gold, leading him to believe he had found the golden realm. In a sense, perhaps for gardeners, he had, for within the family Papaveraceae, which contains so many splendid garden plants, they are still worth gold. From an orange-sapped taproot grows a busy plant about two feet wide and almost as high, with stems and much-divided, ferny leaves of a soft, dusty bluish-gray. Flowers are borne well above the leaves on single stems, beginning as tiny, furled umbrellas and opening to two-inch-wide, graceful cups of four overlapping petals with a wonderful sheeny texture. In species occurring in the wild, the color of the flowers is a deep, burnished orange, though forms have been selected that range from burgundy through cinnabar-red to orange, apricot, pink, cream, and near-white. In almost every color, however, there is a curious luminescence to each flower, made up of washes of a deeper tint on a paler one. In some cultivars, also, the inside of the flower cup is a paler shade than the outside, creating an effect at once fragile and beautiful.

Most references on California poppies comment that though they self-seed freely (and nicely) along gravel drives and on slopes of poor, thin soil, or in the carefully cultivated rock garden, volunteer plants will quickly revert to their original burnished gold. In fact, however, when populations of any color are kept separate, they seem to seed true, and if the odd bright gold or yellow plant occurs within them, it can be eliminated before it influences the preferred color of the line. Particularly persistent are shades of ivory and primrose-white, and they are always cool and beautiful.

California poppies are weakly perennial plants that are almost always grown as annuals from a late autumn or very early spring sowing where they are to bloom. Such sowings will produce attractive plants full of flower by midsummer. Though natives of coastal California, they are seed-hardy well into most areas of Zone 4, provided their most important need is met—good drainage. And as they are difficult to transplant (though not impossible when flexible plastic six-packs or peat pots are used), little is gained by starting them early indoors, especially as they require warm, settled weather to develop. Self-seeded plants or seed sprinkled by the gardener's hand on cultivated ground always, in any case, makes the best show. As with all poppies, however, care must be taken not to sow the seed too thickly. Mixing the seed with fine sand (baked in the oven until it is dry) and sprinkling the mixture over the ground with a salt or pepper shaker will prevent the waste that may occur when young plants must be thinned to stand six or so inches apart.

Almost any garden soil is suitable for California poppies, though it must be well drained and in full sun. The most compact and full-flowered plants develop on moderately fertile, dryish, gravelly soil, rich in potassium and phosphorus but relatively low in nitrogen. Where conditions are ideal, or even moderately suitable, California poppies will provide more than two months of beauty, starting with ferny, delicate plants that are pretty in themselves and then are quickly covered with flowers. Dead-heading of spent blossoms prolongs flower production to some extent, though sooner or later—sometimes sooner than one would wish—the whole plant turns straw-colored, sheds its seed, and dies. Where summers are very dry, deep irrigation will go some way toward keeping plants alive and flowering, but like many desert plants of western North American origin, California poppies seem to have some internal wisdom that tells them when to pack up and be off, whatever intentions the gardener may have for them.

For this reason, California poppies are not suited to bedding schemes where a full summer

ESCHSCHOLZIA CALIFORNICA

and an early autumn of beauty must be guaranteed, or for window boxes or containers, unless one is sure that replacements are ready at hand or that other plants that burgeon in the heat of high summer will fill the gaps they leave. They are best enjoyed in more natural situations, along a drive or in a meadow, or perhaps in a rock garden, where their delicate, lacy growth never smothers out more permanent plants and they will not be greatly missed when they go. They are a very important component to annual wildflower meadows, where the rich orange color typical of the species shows beautifully with blue ragged robins, larkspurs, and the vibrant red of corn poppies. Cultivars exist with a double row of petals, and true doubles are on the way. Whether that will be an improvement on the elegance of the single form remains to be seen.

Even those gardeners who are accustomed to botanical Latin and take pleasure in using it have a problem with the genus *Eschscholzia*. The difficulty of pronouncing such a name is vastly compounded when one comes to know several very desirable hardy perennials and shrubs in the genus *Elsholtzia*. The two genera are very far apart, however, not only botanically—for one is a poppy, and one is a mint—but historically.

The latter is named for Sigismund Elscholts (1623–1688), a Prussian physician, amateur horticulturist, and garden writer. Johan Frederich Eschscholtz (1793–1831), whose name is represented by the California poppy, had the distinction of accompanying Otto van Kotzebue on his first voyage around the world (1815–1818).

EUPHORBIA SPECIES

FAMILY: *Euphorbiaceae* or spurge family.

CLASSIFICATION: Hardy or half-hardy annuals or biennials grown as half-hardy annuals.

COMMON NAMES: Spurge, euphorbia (other common names vary according to species).

HARDINESS: Varies with species.

GROWING CONDITIONS: Moderately fertile, dryish sandy soil. Full sun.

PROPAGATION: By seed, sown in place after last frosts. May be seeded indoors in peat pots 6 to 8 weeks before last frost.

HEIGHT: 1 to 3'.

ORNAMENTAL VALUE: Valued for ornamental leaves.

LEVEL OF CULTURAL DIFFICULTY: Easy.

SPECIAL PROPERTIES: Used medicinally in ancient medicine.

PRONUNCIATION: yew-FOR-bee-a

Within the huge family Euphorbiaceae, which contains somewhere around 7,000 genera, are many plants that have been useful to humanity, providing rubber, varnish, natural insecticides, medicinal drugs, important fruits, and foodstuffs over many centuries. Few are cultivated on a large scale outside tropical climes, although there are many familiar greenhouse and household plants, several hardy perennials, and a few garden annuals within the genus.

The three euphorbias grown as annuals were once much enjoyed in gardens when subtle shadings of leaf and plant form were considered as valuable over a long season as masses of bloom. Particularly in country gardens—those old-fashioned, rather spontaneous plots where pretty, self-seeding "weeds" were allowed to flourish—annual euphorbia generally ended up growing next to the dahlias, one or two in the cabbage row, a few perhaps by the fence. As that style, fashionably called "cottage gardening," continues to gain in popularity, so will these euphorbias.

Euphorbia cyathophora (si-a-THO-for-a), called the "hardy poinsettia," may be a bit of a letdown to those who like the most familiar of all ornamental euphorbias—*Euphorbia pulcherrima* (pul-CHER-i-ma), the Christmas poinsettia. Still, *E. cyathophora,* a half-hardy annual native to Mexico and Central America, forms a neat, tidy little bush about two feet tall, with leaves of variable form, mostly blade or eggshaped, but occasionally with a shape like a fiddle. In mid- to late summer, upper leaves will begin to show oval markings of clear scarlet at their bases, and smaller leaves surrounding the flower bracts will be all scarlet. The flowers themselves, insignificant and without petals, consist of yellowish-green, fuzzy bunches. Taken all together, it is a quaint, old-fashioned plant, once much grown in southern country gardens and still occurring there as a volunteer. Color is best on moderately fertile, dryish soils, and seed should be sown where the plants are to grow in spring after danger of frost is past.

A much showier plant is *Euphorbia marginata* (mar-ji-NA-ta), called "snow on the mountain" or "snow in summer," because its one- to three-inch-long oval leaves begin at the base of the plant a cool, bluish green and become progressively more marginated with white as the plant grows upward. They become almost all white as they modify into bracts with only a blade of green down the center. A prairie plant native across central North America from the Dakotas to Texas, it seems nowhere to occur in large stands. But once grown in gardens, it faithfully reappears even after the gardens are long abandoned. Unlike *E. cyathophora,* however, the color of which develops only after the plant has almost completed its growth and is ready to flower, the margination begins to develop on snow in summer when it is about half grown, usually in mid- to late June from an outdoor sowing in early spring, though it is finest in the hottest days of August, when the combination of cool green and white is a sort of visual glass of ice water. Unfortunately, however, as the plant matures, it becomes a little bare at its shanks and so is perhaps best used at the back of a border or anywhere lower plants may be grown around it. Its dramatic leaves make it valuable in almost any garden color scheme, though it seems to be as effective singly as when planted in drifts. It can look very fine in an annual wildflower meadow, where its cool elegance is striking among tawny grasses and the withering growth of early-flowered annuals. Well-marked branches are popular with flower arrangers, although care should be taken not to let the milky sap come in contact with the skin and especially the eyes, as severe burns may result. Also, cut stems should be dipped immediately in boiling water for a second or two, or scorched briefly with a candle or pocket lighter, so they will not turn the water in the vase milky and then wither prematurely.

The third euphorbia commonly grown as an annual is *Euphorbia lathyris* (la-THI-ris), popularly called the "gopher plant," or "mole plant," from its supposed ability to discourage underground burrowing rodents. Alas, those who have tested the supposition have found whole rows of young plants tossed out of the ground as readily as any others, but the plant is still very handsome and worth growing where its rigidity of form can be exploited. A biennial native to northern Europe, it forms a single-stemmed, unbranched plant to about three feet, with narrow, prominently veined leaves of purple-tinted olive green. The principal charm of the plant is that those leaves are arranged in fours, each neatly aligned opposite the ones below and the ones above, creating a quartered effect. In the first season of growth, the shape of the plant is handsomely architectural, but the effect can be somewhat military-looking when several plants are evenly spaced down a border. Plants gain in beauty by occurring in more spontaneous patterns and even by being different heights.

Euphorbia lathyris is surprisingly cold-resistant, and even where it is not hardy (Zones 7 and warmer) it will stand in the garden well into late November, its leaves and stems becoming beautifully burnished with copper and dull red. Where it does overwinter, in the following season it will produce small, insignificant, yellow-green flowers in clusters at the top of the stem, each one interestingly clad in a hood (actually a bract) formed of two pointed leaves. When the first seed ripens, however, the plants will generally become shabby and should be removed to the compost heap, from the edges of which one can probably transplant fine young seedlings the following spring.

The genus name *Euphorbia* commemorates Euphorbus, personal physician to Juba II, king of Mauretania around the beginning of the first century A.D. Little is known about Euphorbus, but Juba II appears to have ruled Mauretania in great prosperity until his death somewhere between A.D. 19 and 24. During his life, he wrote learned texts on geography and on botanical and historical subjects. Juba was given credit for first discovering that some of 1,500 species in the vast, pan-global genus *Euphorbia* could be used to pro-

EUPHORBIA MARGINATA

duce violent activity in the human body, in the hope of ridding it of desperate maladies. The maladies must have been desperate indeed, for the sap of many euphorbia can create severe dermatitis in susceptible people, and when ingested, can cause violent and prolonged vomiting. Hence the popular name "spurge," from the Latin verb *expurgare* meaning to rid by violent means. Some New World peoples knew that the milky sap of *Euphorbia* species familiar to them, when added to streams or ponds, could stun or even kill fish, thus causing them to rise to the surface of the water for an easy catch.

EUSTOMA GRANDIFLORUM

FAMILY: *Gentianaceae* or gentian family.

CLASSIFICATION: Biennial grown as half-hardy annual.

COMMON NAMES: Prairie gentian, Texas bluebell, lisianthus, eustoma.

HARDINESS: Modern forms are sensitive to light frosts.

GROWING CONDITIONS: Rich, light, well-drained but moisture-retentive soil.

PROPAGATION: By seed, sown early in the year.

HEIGHT: 1 to 3'.

ORNAMENTAL VALUE: Grown for flower.

LEVEL OF CULTURAL DIFFICULTY: Difficult.

SPECIAL PROPERTIES: Superior cut flower.

PRONUNCIATION: yew-STO-ma gran-di-FLO-rum

The cornucopia of splendid native American wild flowers is deep, but among its many splendors, none is more gorgeous than *Eustoma grandiflorum*. The sheer lusciousness of its two- to three-inch-wide bell-shaped flowers, carried elegantly on celadon green stems clasped by oval, bluish-green leaves, causes many gardeners to turn away from it with puzzlement. Perfection, in plants as in people, can sometimes be intimidating, and though *E. grandiflorum* lacks fragrance, it still seems to be perfect. It comes in meltingly beautiful colors, of ivory white, shell pink, many shades of rose, violet, pale and deep purple, and now, even in red and primrose yellow. There are picoteed forms, in which a deeper complementary shade is brushed along the edges of the flower, and there are doubles so thickly crowded with petals that they look almost like roses. In texture, the flowers seem not to be made of living plant tissue, but rather of fine silk, or wax, or even perhaps of cake icing. The flower buds are very graceful, resembling perfectly furled umbrellas, and they open slowly to full-blown flowers that will last three weeks or more, either in the garden or in a vase.

Within its native range, which extends from Nebraska and Colorado south to Texas, *E. grandiflorum* is so abundant as to be considered a pest in cultivated fields. There, it behaves as a biennial, developing a rosette of glaucous, oval leaves its first season, and two-foot-tall flowering stems the following summer. The typical color of the species is a pale purple, with a darker stain in the center. The cup-shaped flowers, consisting of five or six overlapping lobes fused in the center, are seldom more than two inches wide and deep, and usually smaller. *Eustoma grandiflorum* was seldom grown in gardens (except occasionally by wildflower enthusiasts) until about fifteen years ago, when stock of it went to Japan and returned improved into larger flowers, fantastically beautiful colors, doubles, picotees, and dwarfs.

Like many native American wild flowers, however (and like many gentians in the family to which it belongs), *Eustoma grandiflorum* can be very difficult to grow from seed, so much so that experienced growers often wince at its name, and most gardeners prefer to purchase well-grown plants in late spring. It is a true biennial, and like many other biennials grown as annuals, it must be started very early, usually no later than the end of January, for flowers in July. The dust-fine seeds, which resemble snuff, must lie on the surface of rich, fibrous but well-drained potting compost, and the pots should be watered from below so as not to bury the seeds. Pots are then covered with a pane of glass or plastic film, and stood in a moderately cool greenhouse at temperatures around 55°F until germination occurs, usually within two to three weeks. The seedlings are so minute that they must develop three or even four sets of true leaves before they may be transplanted, and they must not be hurried on by applications of fertilizer, which will burn their sensitive roots. Watering must at all times be very carefully applied, usually from below, as waterlogged soil or dampness on the leaves will result first in yellowed foliage and then in death.

When plants are about six inches high, they may be pinched to encourage multiple flower stems, and young plants may be transplanted carefully into the garden after all danger of frost is past. They require a rich, light, well-drained soil, and though in hot climates light afternoon shade prolongs their bloom, in most gardens they should be grown in full sun. Frequent dead-heading or cutting for flower arrangements will encourage the continuation of bloom well into autumn, but it is an odd thing about *Eustoma grandiflorum* that though its natural range lies well within Zones 4 and 5, it does not seem able to persist over winter in eastern gardens or to self-sow there.

If, as should be, one's aim is to plant the garden so that one mass of flowers blends harmoniously into another, the placement of *Eustoma grandiflorum* can pose problems, for it always seems to call attention to itself. More than other annuals, its dramatic appearance requires a prop, a large stone perhaps, a gatepost, or the frame of a surrounding mass of neutral foliage. The usual recommendation is to place plants approximately a foot apart, but a more natural effect will occur if three plants are placed close together, as if a clump springing from one root. Both single and double eustoma come in mixed colors, but drifts of single colors, or darker and lighter shades of one color, always appear more natural—or as

EUSTOMA GRANDIFLORUM

natural as this plant ever can look. Because of its elaborately crafted appearance, *Eustoma grandiflorum* never shows better than when grown in clay pots. Or when cut for a vase. There, it has the remarkable property of lasting up to a month in water, which makes it a florist's darling.

Eustoma is a pretty genus name, composed of the ancient Greek word *eu,* meaning good, and *stoma,* mouth, but by extension, denoting a beautiful face or pleasing countenance. As with "petunia" or "impatiens," it may come to serve both as the genus and the popular name, though the name of another genus into which *Eustoma grandiflorum* was mistakenly once put, *Lisianthus,* still clings to it like lint.

EVOLVULUS GLOMERATUS
(*E. PILOSUS*)

FAMILY: *Convolvulaceae* or morning glory family.

CLASSIFICATION: Tender or half-hardy perennial grown as half-hardy annual.

COMMON NAMES: Blue daze, evolvulus.

HARDINESS: Commercial stock is sensitive to light frosts.

GROWING CONDITIONS: Moderately fertile, perfectly drained, dryish soil. Full sun.

PROPAGATION: By tip cuttings taken in late winter.

HEIGHT: To 8″, but spreading to up to 2′ in a growing season.

ORNAMENTAL VALUE: Valued for flower and attractive, matted growth.

LEVEL OF CULTURAL DIFFICULTY: Easy.

SPECIAL PROPERTIES: Excellent in hanging baskets, containers, and window boxes.

PRONUNCIATION: ee-VOL-vew-lus glo-mer-AH-tus (pi-LO-sus)

*U*ntil as recently as five years ago, only sophisticated authorities on native American plants were aware of evolvulus, a mat-forming, shy little subshrub or creeping vine with pretty, nickel-sized blue flowers borne along its stems in the axils of its scarcely inch-wide oval leaves. But those large wholesale nurseries that supply local garden centers with new and desirable plants were preparing evolvulus for a grand entrance. As a market strategy the popular name "blue daze" was coined. It is, of course, a pun, though neither meaning quite fits the innate modesty of the plant. Nevertheless, there it was, suddenly, in hanging pots, showing off its tidy, procumbent growth and endearingly limpid blossoms, ready to be bought in full bloom and to bloom all summer long.

Because of its recent prominence, general garden references are very scarce on evolvulus. The genus contains around 100 species, though only one (or possibly two) appear to be in cultivation. The genus name is amusing, based on the Latin word *evolvo,* meaning untwisted or unraveled, and refers to the fact that this small member of the morning glory family does not climb upward but lies flat on the ground. This makes it, of course, a wonderful candidate for hanging baskets, window boxes, or the tops of stone walls since, lacking solid ground to creep across, it will tumble over the sides of any container. Though at least two members of the genus are Old World plants, the evolvulus widely offered in nurseries at present is a native American, with an extraordinarily wide geographic distribution, extending north to Montana and South Dakota, east to Arkansas and Tennessee, and south to Arizona and New Mexico. Precise species designations are in doubt, for the plant sold in a white plastic hanging pot may be *E. glomeratus,* a species name generally signifying flowers clustered into rounded heads, or it may be *E. nuttalianus* (new-ta-lee-AN-us), commemorating Thomas Nuttall (1786–1839), the great English botanist who catalogued American plant species in the years between 1811 and 1834. Many botanists now believe the two species to be synonymous, in which case, one hopes Thomas Nuttall will win out, for *glomeratus* is neither an attractive nor an accurate species designation, since flowers are apt to be borne in the axils of the leaves as much as in tightened clusters at the ends of growing stems.

Species of *Evolvulus,* whatever they may be, are seldom grown from seed except by botanists, researchers in floriculture, and wildflower enthusiasts. The plants purchased by gardeners in late spring are all produced from cuttings struck in late winter and grown on for spring sales. Those cuttings have been taken from the most floriferous plants, whatever their geographic distribution. Generally, it appears that the plants that flower most abundantly occur in the southern range of the species, and so are hardy only in North American gardens in Zones 9 and 10, where they make splendid groundcover and flower virtually all year long. Elsewhere, they must be treated as tender annuals that cannot be expected to survive even light frost especially in elevated positions. But those gardeners who have the facilities to overwinter plants in cool greenhouses or heated sun porches can salvage specimens of evolvulus and even expect them to bloom sparingly throughout the winter.

Wherever evolvulus grow naturally, they seem to require a sandy, well-drained soil of moderate fertility. In the most northern occurring examples of the species, winter survival seems to depend on perfect drainage and ample snow coverage. Both can be supplied in eastern gardens, the first by the incorporation of coarse sand and gravel into the planting medium, and the second by a covering of spruce or fir branches in late autumn, where win-

EVOLVULUS GLOMERATUS

ter snows are late to arrive. Cuttings taken from specimens of evolvulus in its northernmost range might easily survive in eastern gardens in Zones 4 and 5. In that event, evolvulus would join an interesting group of plants generally treated as annuals—diascias, gladiolus, phacellias, and even some antirrhinums—that are capable of surviving the winter in cold damp gardens and reappearing in spring as perennial plants.

EXACUM AFFINE

FAMILY: *Gentianaceae* or gentian family.

CLASSIFICATION: Sub-shrub grown as a tender annual.

COMMON NAMES: Persian violet, Arabian violet, German violet, tiddly winks, exacum.

HARDINESS: Extremely cold sensitive.

GROWING CONDITIONS: Rich, fibrous, well-drained loam. Even moisture. Part shade. Prefers warm, humid weather.

PROPAGATION: Usually from tip cuttings, taken in late winter.

HEIGHT: 6" to 2'.

ORNAMENTAL VALUE: Grown for flowers and for neat, bushy growth.

LEVEL OF CULTURAL DIFFICULTY: Moderately easy if requirements are met; difficult otherwise.

SPECIAL PROPERTIES: Useful container plant. Excellent winter houseplant or cool greenhouse plant where preferred conditions can be supplied.

PRONUNCIATION: EX-uh-cum ah-FIN-ay

Exacum affine is a little plant amiable in all its parts. It forms a neat, low bush of succulent stems from six inches to two feet tall (depending on age), thickly covered with shiny, heart-shaped, dark green leaves, each about an inch and a half long at maturity and perfectly creased down the middle. If it were grown only for its laurel-like foliage, it would be an interesting plant, but healthy specimens are studded with a constant display of flowers borne in the axils of the leaves, each about three-quarters of an inch across, of a vibrant royal purple, richest at the center, and set off by a bunch of orange-yellow anthers and a curious, curved pistil. The flowers are sweetly fragrant, a characteristic that, with their color, justifies the popular names "Persian violet," "Arabian violet," and "German violet."

The actual origin of *Exacum affine* is neither Persia, Arabia, nor Germany, however, but the island of Socotra in the Indian Ocean. This offers a clue to its culture, for the plant requires a minimum temperature of 60°F to flower, and as much atmospheric humidity as possible. Where these conditions obtain, it seems to flower constantly, never requiring a rest.

Like many other plants recently introduced as annuals, *Exacum affine* began its career at the florist's. It has been particularly treasured throughout central Europe and Scandinavia as a winter-blooming plant, bought in full flower and discarded when it succumbs to the conditions of overheated rooms. It is still serviceable for that, though where its real needs can be met, in a moderately heated, humid greenhouse or perhaps on the windowsill above the kitchen sink, it may thrive all winter and longer. Outdoors in the summer garden it is both useful and pretty, particularly as it relishes light shade where few other blooming plants perform well.

Only plant breeders or those gardeners who grow everything from seed would bother to germinate *Exacum affine*. That it belongs to the family Gentianaceae, as its gentian-blue flowers attest, should be a warning. Like so many plants in its family, the seed is dust-fine and slow to germinate. The seedlings are minute and fragile in the infant stages, susceptible to any number of childhood illnesses, the worst being those fungal diseases collectively called "damping off," which will carry off a whole pot of six-week-old babies in one night. As it is actually a sub-shrub, seed must also be sown very early, about five months before flowering plants may be secured. Those gardeners who wish to try, and who can secure seed, should follow the instructions offered for *Eustoma grandiflorum*, a relative in the family, adding a precautionary dose of fungicide in the form of benomyl, every two weeks from the point at which the seedlings are visible until they may be transplanted into the garden. Transplanting should occur in mid- to late June, after the weather has become warm and settled and well beyond the point usually specified for planting annuals, which is after all danger of frost is past.

Fortunately, in the last five years or so, *Exacum affine* has become readily available from nurseries specializing in unusual summer-blooming plants and from urban florists. Both sources offer plants in June as small, well-grown bushes, six or eight inches high, studded with flower, and ready either to transplant into the garden or to plant in patio containers or window boxes. Plants grown in five- or six-inch clay pots may also be brought inside before frost, for flowering, brief or prolonged, according to conditions. Cuttings taken from the tips of vigorous shoots also root readily in damp perlite and are an easy source of increase for those gardeners who have greenhouse facilities heated at night to around 50°F.

Exacum affine has demanding growing conditions, but—like African violets—once they are understood they are not difficult to arrange. Cool, light shade suits the plant best, as does a humid atmosphere, which can be supplied either by a daily spritz bath or by locating pots or plantings close to a lightly shaded patio pool or fountain. The two most important requirements for successful culture are a fibrous, well-drained potting mix or planting bed and plenty of richness. Moist peat or well-decayed leaf mold should be incorporated into the planting mix, along with sharp sand, gravel, or perlite to insure perfect drainage. Supplementary feeding, in the form of water-soluble fertilizer applied to the foliage and soil at half the strength recommended on the package, but twice as often, will work wonders.

Exacum affine is so recent an addition to the summer garden that breeders have hardly begun to work on it. Nevertheless, there are already rather smug, compact forms, though the species itself is always trim and tidy, and can easily be snipped to shape. There are also white cultivars, which might possibly be an addition to cool, shaded patios, and there are pinks. Most certainly, there will soon be other colors, variegated leaf forms, and possibly even doubles.

The Latinized genus name *Exacum* is ancient Gallic (from *exacon*) for some other plant that was believed to drive out evil spirits, and the species name *affine* means looks like or closely resembles. Few gardeners who grow *E. affine* will have seen the plant it closely resembles and so will be unable to test its capacities to drive out evil spirits. But pretty as it is, there is good promise.

FEDIA CORNUCOPIA

FAMILY: *Valerianaceae* or valerian family.

CLASSIFICATION: Hardy annual.

COMMON NAMES: African valerian, horn of plenty, fedia.

HARDINESS: Withstands frost.

GROWING CONDITIONS: Average, moderately fertile garden loam. Full sun.

PROPAGATION: From seed, sown in place in autumn or very early spring. May be started indoors 4 weeks before last frost.

HEIGHT: To 1'.

ORNAMENTAL VALUE: Grown for small, bright pink flowers.

LEVEL OF CULTURAL DIFFICULTY: Easy.

SPECIAL PROPERTIES: All parts of plants are edible in salads.

PRONUNCIATION: FAY-dee-a kor-nu-KOP-ee-a

Fedia cornucopia is a plant of Mediterranean origin, anciently cultivated as a salad crop though now rarely grown. Most general garden references pass over it, and seed is only occasionally offered. Nevertheless, the present interest in unusual salad greens and especially in mesclun or misticanza may well bring *Fedia cornucopia* to prominence. Italian gourmets declare that a proper misticanza must contain at least twenty-one separate species, and so *Fedia cornucopia* may well follow orach and puntarelle, both virtually unknown as salad greens in America ten years ago but now on the menus of expensive restaurants.

As an ornamental plant, however, *Fedia cornucopia* is also well worth growing. Its charms are hardly showy, but it possesses a modest beauty that many gardeners weary of great displays of color might enjoy. It forms a stout, branching, shrublike plant about a foot tall, with reddish-purple stems and two- to four-inch-long, light green, shiny oval leaves arranged closely in pairs along the stems. By midsummer, the tips of stems will show clusters of small tubular flowers, each about an eighth-inch long, of a clear fuchsia pink, and numerous enough to attract attention.

Fedia cornucopia is a hardy annual, able to self-seed and reappear from year to year in gardens as cold as Zones 4 and 5. Seed should be scattered on moderately fertile, well-drained soil, either in late autumn or, where winters are unusually severe, in very early spring where the plants are to grow. Seed may also be sown indoors, about four weeks from the last anticipated frost date, though little is gained by an early start, especially when the plants are grown primarily as ornamentals. Any good vegetable garden soil will suit fedia, and like most garden plants of Mediterranean origin, it requires full sun. Plants should be thinned to stand eight inches to a foot apart. Though the flowering stems, bearing clusters of small but vividly colored flowers, are valuable in arrangements and an interesting addition to salads, a few should always be left to produce seed for the following year.

Fedia cornucopia is the only cultivated member of an obscure genus of perhaps three species. The genus name, of unknown origin, offers not the slightest clue about its meaning. The species name *cornucopia* might in itself lure a gardener into growing the plant, since it attests to the utility of the species and supplies its nicest popular name, "horn of plenty." Young leaves, tips of shoots, and even the minute flowers may be eaten and are a rich source of Vitamin C.

FELICIA AMELLOIDES

FAMILY: *Asteraceae* or aster or daisy family.

CLASSIFICATION: Half-hardy sub-shrub grown as half-hardy annual.

COMMON NAMES: Blue daisy, blue marguerite, felicia.

HARDINESS: Withstands very light frosts once established.

GROWING CONDITIONS: Humus-rich, water-retentive soil. Sun in cool gardens, afternoon shade in warmer ones.

PROPAGATION: From seed, sown 3 months before last frost. Cuttings root readily at any time.

HEIGHT: To 3' where hardy, but more usually 1' or less when grown as an annual.

ORNAMENTAL VALUE: Grown for flower.

LEVEL OF CULTURAL DIFFICULTY: Moderately easy.

SPECIAL PROPERTIES: None.

PRONUNCIATION: feh-LI-shuh a-muh-LOY-deez

Felicias are such charming plants that few gardeners can resist them, especially in mid-spring when they are offered in nurseries with their clean, shrubby growth, their dark green, spoon-shaped, inch-long leaves, and perky, inch-wide, kingfisher-blue daisies on long stems. In their four-inch pots they are already wonderfully pretty and seem to promise more prettiness to come. Alas, in most places in North America this is a false promise, for felicias are South African natives and require cool nights and bright, airy days to flower well. As outdoor plants, they seem to do their best in a climate like San Francisco's, where they are hardy all year round even in containers. In those privileged conditions, plants reach a height of up to three feet and as much across, and they seem never to lack daisies—fully open with more to come if spent flowers are removed.

But in most other North American gardens, though felicias are fine in June as started plants, they tend to cease producing flowers in the heat of midsummer, resuming only when nighttime temperatures fall to around 50°F. Then they may have a brilliant month before heavy frosts cut them down, usually sometime in October. They can, however, have a wonderful second career indoors, flowering through the dull days of winter, if they are lifted, cut back lightly, planted in well-drained potting compost, and brought indoors to a sunny windowsill, a heated sun porch, or a cool greenhouse.

The most familiar felicia is *Felicia amelloides.* *Amelloides* means closely resembling *Amellus,* a genus name of other South African plants with little horticultural interest. Some gardeners might recognize the name *amellus* as a species designation for one of the few Old World hardy asters, *Aster amellus.* Its beautiful violet flowers with yellow centers do in fact resemble those of *F. amelloides.*

Felicia amelloides is an attractive, bushy plant generally about a foot tall, gracefully composed of many angular branches. It takes only a few of its rich blue, inch-wide daisies to make it look well furnished, though more is always better. Its delicate, polished charm seems more suited to pots, window boxes, or other containers than to the open ground. It thrives in rich, well-drained compost, and the application of a water-soluble fertilizer high in phosphorus and potassium but low in nitrogen, such as is fabricated specifically for tomatoes, encourages bloom. At least one cultivar has variegated foliage, which is an attraction where the plant flowers shyly, though certainly a distraction where it flowers well. There is also a white-flowered cultivar, 'Read's White', which looks fresh and sparkling above its mid-green leaves, and a pink one with a shy, painted china sort of charm.

Felicia amelloides is easy to grow from seed if it is started indoors in early March at temperatures of around 60°F. The young seedlings should be grown on in bright, cool conditions, and pinched frequently after they have formed two sets of leaves to encourage fullness of growth. Flowering should occur about fifteen weeks from germination. But cuttings taken at any time root easily in moist perlite, and so the plant is generally propagated that way, supplying larger, fuller plants for transplanting into the garden or into outdoor containers after all danger of frost is past. Stock plants are easily lifted in autumn, cut back lightly, and potted up into six-inch pots. Grown under bright conditions with a minimum nighttime temperature of around 50°F, they will generally flower all winter, provide cuttings for additional plants, and serve as ornaments outdoors the following season.

FELICIA AMELLOIDES

FELICIA AMELLOIDES

The nomenclature of felicia is very confused, and plants offered under several different names often turn out to be either *F. amelloides,* which is a sub-shrub, or *F. bergeriana* (ber-ger-ee-A-na), one of several true annuals in the genus, both of South African origin. *F. bergeriana* is popularly called the "kingfisher daisy," a pretty and promising name, but its flowers are generally a rather pale blue, less vivid by many shades than the finest forms of *F. amelloides.* Classed as a half-hardy annual, it may be expected to flower in mid- to late summer from a sowing outdoors around the date of the last anticipated frost. Alternatively, it may be seeded indoors six to eight weeks earlier and grown on in bright, airy conditions until it may be transplanted.

Felicia bergeriana is a little plant, hardly reaching eight inches in height, with pleasant, grasslike, gray-green foliage and winsome, pale blue daisies, each about half an inch wide with perky yellow centers. These daisies only open in the morning, however, and only on days that are bright and clear.

Felicia belong to a genus of perhaps eighty species, many of which are cultivated in climates where they perform well. The genus name is meant to commemorate a certain Herr Felix, though little more is known of him than that he served his state in some official capacity and died at Regensburg in Germany in 1846. The name of the genus is very pretty, and for gardeners who can grow felicias to perfection, Herr Felix requires no further distinctions.

FERULA COMMUNIS

FAMILY: *Umbelliferae* or Queen Anne's lace family.

CLASSIFICATION: Tender perennial grown as half-hardy annual.

COMMON NAMES: Giant fennel, ferula.

HARDINESS: Hardy to Zone 7 with protection. Frost-hardy elsewhere.

GROWING CONDITIONS: Rich, well-drained, moisture-retentive soil. Full sun.

PROPAGATION: From seed, sown in site or in flats in autumn and exposed to winter freezing.

HEIGHT: To 8' or more where hardy. To 5' when grown as an annual.

ORNAMENTAL VALUE: Grown for filmy, threadlike foliage.

LEVEL OF CULTURAL DIFFICULTY: Moderately easy.

SPECIAL PROPERTIES: None.

PRONUNCIATION: feh-RU-la co-MU-nis

*A*lthough *Ferula communis* has no aromatic properties, and no culinary uses, it remains confused with its close cousin, *Foeniculum vulgare,* the true fennel used as a salad or cooked vegetable or to impart a faint anise or licorice flavoring. *Ferula communis,* by contrast, is only for show, though its beauty has been appreciated since ancient times. A native of the Mediterranean, the genus still bears the classical Latin name that Pliny employed, deriving from *ferule,* a rod or cane used to punish juveniles and adult dependents. Simply the threat of the broomstick-thick, flower-bearing rods would be enough to encourage re-form in any child or slave. But in mythology the rods had a happier use, for the slow-burning pith within the outer fibrous walls of the stems served Prometheus as the cane with which he secretly transferred fire from the gods to men. (The species name *communis* comes from the clusters of individual growing points bunched together on the thick, fleshy roots; each point will, in time, produce its own rod of flower.)

Ferula communis is a magnificent plant, one of the tallest and stateliest of perennials where it is hardy. Sadly, in North America, that means only gardens in Zones 7 to 9, though in rich, well-drained soil, particularly near lakes, streams, or large ponds, it may sometimes survive milder winters in Zone 6. A true perennial, it takes several years from seed to build up enough strength to produce its towering rods of flower, which may be as much as twelve feet tall and are crowded with flattened Queen Anne's lace um-bels, each as much as a foot across and containing hundreds of tiny, lime-green blossoms.

Outside the range where it is root-hardy, *Ferula communis* is sometimes grown as an annual for the beauty of its delicate foliage. If seed can be procured from a friend or a garden correspon-dent in a warmer climate, it should be sown in autumn and left in a place that experiences light frosts until spring, when seedlings should appear. They may then be treated as hardy annuals and transplanted where they are to grow as soon as they are large enough to be handled and the ground is workable. Alternatively, seed ordered from the few companies that offer *Ferula commu-nis* should be sown as early in the spring as possi-ble—outdoors in flats or in the open ground where the plant is to grow—and later trans-planted or thinned to stand about a foot apart.

The only effect that gardeners in Zones 4 and 5 will get from *Ferula communis* is its filigreed fo-liage, in single fans to about a foot tall, composed of delicate, filmy leaves, much divided into threadlike filaments. Some day, however, seed may be offered or selected (as it is with artichokes and cardoons) from the plant's northernmost range, resulting in strains that might prove hardy at least in Zone 5 with protection.

Within the genus *Ferula* one other important plant exists, although most American gardeners would not think of growing it. That is *Ferula assa-foetida* (ass-a-FEH-ti-da), cultivated since ancient times as a medicinal herb, as a culinary spice, and for its properties in warding off evil spirits. A native of Iran, it is not so handsome a plant as *F. communis,* being generally shorter in stature and with coarser, more carrotlike leaves. *Assa-foetida* is still used, though sparingly, in In-dian cookery, and is one of the important flavor-ing ingredients in Worcestershire sauce. More important, a vile-smelling paste exuded from wounds made in the growing crowns of the plant is still used in satanic rituals and is tied in a tiny cloth bag around the necks of infant chil-dren throughout the Caribbean nations and the deep South of the United States.

FOENICULUM VULGARE

FAMILY: *Umbelliferae* or Queen Anne's lace family.

CLASSIFICATION: Hardy perennial or biennial grown as hardy annual.

COMMON NAME: Common fennel.

HARDINESS: Hardy to Zone 7 with perfect drainage. Grown as an annual in colder gardens.

GROWING CONDITIONS: Moderately fertile, perfectly drained soil. Full sun.

PROPAGATION: From seed, sown indoors 4 to 6
   weeks before last frost, or in place in very early
   spring.
HEIGHT: To 5'.
ORNAMENTAL VALUE: Grown for finely divided,
   threadlike leaves.
LEVEL OF CULTURAL DIFFICULTY: Easy.
SPECIAL PROPERTIES: Used as a vegetable and for
   flavorings.
PRONUNCIATION: fo-NI-cue-lum vul-GAR-ay

*A*s a culinary and medicinal herb, fennel has an almost unbroken association with humanity from ancient times to the present. The Romans learned the value of *Foeniculum vulgare,* a Mediterranean native, from the Greeks, and the genus name is classical Latin, a diminutive meaning little hay, from the use of its dried stems as a flavoring bed on which whole fish were steamed. The species name, *vulgare,* which never indicates any invidious judgment, occurs often in botany and means common, frequently available, or frequently occurring. One of only three species in its genus, and the only one of any horticultural interest, the plant continues to be an important source of food and flavorings. The thickened bulbs of one variety, *Foeniculum vulgare* 'Azoricum' (ah-ZOR-i-cum), called "Florence fennel" from the region in which it thrives, provides an excellent winter salad when sliced thin and dressed with oil and vinegar. Another variety, generally offered as *F. vulgare* 'Dulce' (DUL-chay), produces succulent stems that taste like celery and also have a faint but wonderful aftertaste of licorice or anise. This flavor is typical of all parts of the plant, the seeds of which are employed to disguise the vile taste of some medicines and, more pleasantly, in fish

dishes, pastries, and even in toothpaste. To these gustatory lusters *F. vulgare* adds ornamental qualities, for in all forms it is a beautiful vegetable and in one particularly, the bronze-leaved fennel, it is a very valuable addition to the flower garden.

The *Foeniculum vulgare* grown for ornament is a tall plant, reaching perhaps five feet from an early spring sowing, and producing strong stems clad in much-divided, fernlike leaves, each filament of which is hardly thicker than a common sewing thread. The effect of the plant is of strength and delicacy at once, making it an interesting contrast to plants with more predictable leaves. The umbels of tiny, greenish-yellow flowers borne in late summer are a bonus and last well when cut for flower arrangements.

As a wild plant within its native range, which corresponds to USDA Zones 7 to 10, *Foeniculum vulgare* is perennial, persisting from year to year on barren, stony soils with little summer moisture. Within that climatic range, it has naturalized widely and is a familiar roadside weed, providing an important source of food for good bugs, such as hover flies, lacewings, ladybirds, paper wasps, and soldier bugs—all insects that in other times of the year provide natural protection against aphids and sap-sucking mites.

For garden purposes, however, all forms of *F. vulgare* are generally grown as annuals, either for a succulent harvest of bulbs and stems in late autumn or as ornamentals. The most frequent cultivars in flower gardens are the brown- or maroon-leaved forms, variously listed as 'Purpureum', 'Rubrum', 'Bronze', 'Giant Bronze', or 'Smokey'. Though they may vary in depth of hue, one suspects that they are all progeny of a single variant, a common fennel selected for maroon or bronzish-green foliage, and grown as an ornamental annual since Victorian times. The finely divided leaves of the bronze-leaved fennels may also be used in the kitchen as an interesting garnish to fish dishes or salads.

Generally, where bronze-leaved forms of *F. vulgare* are allowed to self-seed, the gardener is usually instructed to weed out their mint-green progeny, leaving only seedlings with darker leaves for eventual transplanting. The paler green forms, however, are very pleasing in themselves when planted as clumps that contrast nicely with the late-summer yellow daisies, purple or pink asters, blue monkshoods, and goldenrods.

All forms of *Foeniculum vulgare* respond to the same culture, whether grown as vegetables or as ornamentals. Seed is sown indoors four to six

FOENICULUM VULGARE

weeks before the last anticipated frost date, or it may be sown in place in the garden when soils are workable in early spring. Quite young seedlings transplant readily, though after they have formed their thick, carrotlike roots and are approaching maturity, they cannot be moved with any hope of success. Moderately fertile soils with perfect drainage suit them best, and full sun is required. Cultivars grown for kitchen use should be spaced about a foot apart in the row, though forms of *F. vulgare* grown in flower borders—whether bronze or green-leafed—should be planted with three to five seedlings close together, giving a clumped effect their first year. When mature plants have blossomed, a prompt removal of the seed heads may ensure perenniality, at least for a year or two. Alternatively, seed may be allowed to form, which will occur in plenty, and those not carried off by birds, which adore them, will fall to the ground for an abundant crop of seedlings the following spring, even in the cold gardens of Zone 4.

Any gardener who grows *Foeniculum vulgare* in any form will sooner or later be confronted with evil-looking, black- and green-striped hairless caterpillars, intent on stripping off the fernlike foliage, leaving only the ugly bare stems and stalks behind. These unattractive marauders can be pulled off by hand and exterminated, or one can apply sprays of *Bacillus thuringiensis* (Bt to gardeners), a bacterium harmless to the environment. But the problem is this: Those vile-looking caterpillars represent the first stages of the glorious swallowtail butterflies, several species of which were cultivated by Sir Winston Churchill in specially designed cages planted with common fennels. As with so many other things in gardening, therefore, one must make a difficult choice, in this case between fennel and butterfly.

FUCHSIA SPECIES

FAMILY: *Onagraceae* or evening primrose family.

CLASSIFICATION: Tender shrub.

COMMON NAMES: Fuchsia, ladies' eardrops.

HARDINESS: Sensitive to light frosts. *Fuchsia magellanica* is hardy to Zone 7 with careful winter protection.

GROWING CONDITIONS: Rich, fibrous, moisture-retentive soil. Perfect drainage. Full sun to part shade in cooler gardens, afternoon shade in warmer ones.

PROPAGATION: From cuttings taken from nonflowering shoots.

HEIGHT: Variable, depending on cultivar, age, and cultural conditions.

ORNAMENTAL VALUE: Grown for flower.

LEVEL OF CULTURAL DIFFICULTY: Easy in cooler gardens, difficult in warmer ones.

SPECIAL PROPERTIES: Useful as standards.

PRONUNCIATION: FEW-sha

The fuchsia most commonly cultivated in modern gardens are complex crosses of several species, chiefly *F. fulgens* (FUL-gens) and *F. magellanica* (ma-juh-LAN-i-ca), and back-crosses of their progeny, with the result that most can have no more accurate designation than *Fuchsia* x *hybrida* (HI-bri-da). That group, of an estimated 5,000 cultivars, includes plants that are stubbornly upright in growth, some that are gracefully arching, and even some that are almost vinelike. Leaves may be as dark as a privet's and the same size, or almost as tiny and pale as chickweed, some veined in purple, and many splashed with cream or white. Flowers may be as large as a wine cork or smaller than a pencil eraser, slim or chubby, with upturned or down-hanging sepals (the upper row of "petals" on a fuchsia flower), and corollas (the bell-shaped, lower petals) may be either tightly cupped or flared. Corollas may be sublimely single, with only four petals, semi-double with eight, or doubled with petals as thickly packed in as a rose. Flower color can be any tint except true red, yellow, or blue, though some hybrids inch so close to orange or crimson, or to bluish purple, as almost to approach those primary colors. And because a fuchsia flower has two distinct parts, the sepal and corolla, each can be separately colored to make practically infinite combinations.

Though forms of *Fuchsia* x *hybrida* account for the largest number by far of fuchsias grown in American gardens, great interest is currently being shown in some of the pure species within the genus. There are more than a hundred, all of which are more-or-less showy in flower. Collectors search out rare treasures within the genus, but gardeners interested in only a few plants for summer decoration will have little trouble finding *Fuchsia triphylla* (tri-PHIL-a), called the "honeysuckle fuchsia" from its fringes of narrow, down-hanging tubular flowers borne throughout the summer, and indeed, throughout the year where it is hardy (Zones 8 to 10) or in a moderately heated greenhouse or sun porch. Handsomest among the several cultivars available is the old form, 'Gartenmeister Bonstedt', a sturdy, upright plant to about three feet, with abundant, dark green leaves veined in burgundy, and with panicles of scarlet, tubular flowers thickly produced at the ends of growing stems. Selected cultivars and hybrids of *F. triphylla* now also exist in every shade of red, rose, purple, coral and cameo pink, and an almost pure white. *F. triphylla* is also much more heat-resistant than forms of *Fuchsia* x *hybrida,* making it an excellent choice for gardens in the middle and upper South.

Probably the species of *Fuchsia* that has created the most excitement among gardeners in recent years is *F. magellanica,* which occurs in many variations across its extensive range in Argentina and southern Chile. It forms a lax, mounded shrub that may sometimes build up to eight feet where its top growth is not damaged by winter (such as in the warmer parts of Ireland, where it is a popular hedging plant), with slender, red-tinted stems, and narrow, half-inch- to inch-long leaves. Though typically a fresh green, the leaves of some cultivars may be all gold or splashed with silver. Healthy plants seem always to be abundantly furnished with flowers, which are tiny but hang gracefully from threadlike peduncles an inch or more long. The color of the sepals is typically a rich red and the corolla is purple, though cultivars have been selected that are all white, or shades of pink, or with contrasting parts in deeper and paler reds or purples.

Because of its wide natural range, which includes some of the colder parts of South America, there was hope that *F. magellanica* might prove hardy, at least in Zone 7 and possibly 6. Though cut to the ground by frost, plants may survive in that range if carefully mounded up with earth around their crowns and given some protection in the form of evergreen boughs or other covering. However, the plant is of such rapid growth as to make overwintering unnecessary except by those gardeners who enjoy such experiments. Because of its dainty flowers and its very rapid, shrubby growth, *F. magellanica* is perhaps more useful in flower borders than *F.* x *hybrida,* most forms of which will generally look odd when planted in the open ground, suggesting more of the florist than the flower garden.

In most American gardens, fuchsias are largely grown for summer decoration on porches, terraces, or decks, or in window boxes on the shadier sides of houses. The cultural requirements of fuchsias are simple but strict. The first necessity is a fibrous and moisture-retentive soil that is also very free draining—most growers prefer a good, peat-based soilless potting mix such as Pro-Mix. More than usual care should be taken in placing bits of broken crockery in the bottom of the pot, as perfect drainage is an absolute requirement of all fuchsias.

Where drainage is perfect, one can almost never overwater a fuchsia, and plants also benefit hugely from frequent wetting of the foliage, which discourages spider mites and also raises atmospheric humidity, mimicking their foggy mountain homelands. Like many plants that crave moisture, fuchsias are also greedy feeders and nourishment is best supplied by a water-soluble plant food, at half the strength recommended on the package but twice as often. When well potted and well nourished, a fuchsia will respond almost before one's eyes with vigorous healthy growth,

FUCHSIA *'ISIS'*

FUCHSIA TRIPHYLLA *'GARTENMEISTER BONSTEDT'*

rich abundant leaves, and flowers produced from every leaf axil from late May to the end of August. Plants that are not flourishing should be checked for spider mites and white fly, and steps should be taken to eliminate them. Otherwise, if plants fail it will be from poor drainage, inadequate watering, or excessive atmospheric heat or dryness.

Though many fuchsias are discarded at summer's end, they are in fact tender shrubs and are very easy to overwinter for another season of bloom. When flowering ceases in late summer, plants should be cut back quite hard to a woody scaffold of branches, taken from their pots, and repotted in fresh, well-draining compost. They should then be placed in bright but cool conditions (a 50°F nighttime temperature is ideal) and watered sparingly until new growth appears. Young shoots should be pinched after they form their second set of leaves to encourage bushiness, and liquid fertilizer should be given when plants resume vigorous growth. Pinching should cease about four weeks before the last frost-free date, after which the plants should be hardened off in a shady, protected place for a week or so outdoors and then put into their permanent places in the garden. Temperatures should be watched carefully, however, for even a degree or two of frost will kill plants still tender from being grown indoors.

In cool, northern latitudes on the east and west coasts of North America, fuchsias will thrive in full sun, though farther south they will require part shade. In gardens that experience very hot, dry conditions in midsummer, they may cease to bloom, in which case they should be cut back lightly, and they will resume flowering in autumn when temperatures are cooler.

Fuchsia were brought into cultivation in Europe in 1788, where they have remained popular for more than 200 years. The genus name was an honor bestowed on Leonhart Fuchs in 1703 by

FUCHSIA TRIPHYLLA

the French botanist Plumier, who was the first to describe the plant we now know as *Fuchsia triphylla*. Fuchs himself, professor of medicine at the University of Tübingen, would have had no opportunity to examine even a dried specimen of the more than 100 species in the genus that bears his name. For he was born in 1501, and they inhabited lands from Mexico to Patagonia (with three isolated species in New Zealand)—all largely unguessed at in the sixteenth century.

FUMARIA OFFICINALIS

FAMILY: *Fumariaceae* or fumitory family (sometimes *Papaveraceae* or poppy family).

CLASSIFICATION: Hardy annual.

COMMON NAMES: Earth smoke, fumitory, hedge dolls, drug fumitory, cure all, fumaria.

HARDINESS: Withstands light frosts.

GROWING CONDITIONS: Any moist soils. Light shade to full sun.

PROPAGATION: By seed, sown in place in late autumn or early spring, or started indoors 4 weeks before last frost.

HEIGHT: 12″ or less.

ORNAMENTAL VALUE: Grown for flower and for attractive foliage.

LEVEL OF CULTURAL DIFFICULTY: Easy.

SPECIAL PROPERTIES: Anciently assumed to have many medicinal values.

PRONUNCIATION: fu-MA-ree-a o-fi-shi-NA-lis

Fumaria officinalis is now seldom grown in gardens except as a pretty weed. Indeed modern gardeners who are not sophisticated in the ancient lore of plants will hardly know of its existence, but in the fifteenth or sixteenth century no garden would have been complete without it. It is an attractive plant that achieves an erect height of about twelve inches, though with many branching stems to all sides, creating a slender bush. All parts of the plant above ground are delicate. The leaves and stems are colored a glaucous blue-green or powdery gray, and each leaf, divided into fragile, fernlike segments, much resembles the foliage of California poppies except that the leaflets are a little broader, looking something like small hands. The flowers, borne at the tips of growing stems, are tiny, each made up of four fused petals, coral pink for most of their length, though a bright fuchsia pink at the tips. Although each flower is scarcely half an inch long, its vivid colors contrast beautifully with the watery green-blue texture of stem and leaf. Bloom continues over a long period of time from June to August, the first flowers in a raceme setting seed before the last have opened.

Not a plant for large masses of color or any of the uses to which typical bedding annuals are generally put, *F. officinalis* is nevertheless worth treasuring wherever it appears in the garden, and worth encouraging, in rich open woodlands, in flower borders or rock gardens. When grown in a five-inch clay pot, a single plant is interesting not only for the beauty with which it is crafted but also as a reminder of the hopes it once extended to people suffering from dire maladies.

The only one of twenty or so species in its genus that has ever been cultivated, *F. officinalis* was anciently singled out for many medicinal uses, as its species name *officinalis* indicates, from the *officina,* or office, first of the Roman pharmacists and later of the medieval monasteries that prescribed medicinal curatives to the poor. Still sometimes popularly called "cure all," the plant was considered therapeutic for a host of ailments. Taken internally, an infusion of its stems and roots might be prescribed to treat gall bladder diseases, to stimulate the liver, to clear toxins from the blood, and as a purgative or laxative. Externally, lotions and poultices could be applied to treat eczema, to clear severe acne and boils, to bleach freckles and aid in the removal of skin blemishes. Beyond their medicinal uses, the flowers, leaves, and stems of *Fumaria officinalis* were also employed to yield a fine, mustard-yellow dye for woolen cloths and rugs, until the development of chemical dyes in the early nineteenth century made that use obsolete.

F. officinalis will be hard to procure from seed, though some nurseries specializing in rare annuals have begun to offer it as started plants. Most gardeners encounter it by surprise as a lovely little volunteer that has sprouted unaccountably in the rock garden or in a flower bed. Wherever it has been grown, it appears to naturalize, and, as with most poppylike plants, its seed has a surprisingly long life underground—up to fifty years or more—until the spade or the family cat or a burrowing rodent turns it up. Where it appears, if left to flower, it will spread itself about without ever becoming a nuisance, since, as with all members of the vast poppy clan, it hates disturbance at the roots and so is easy to grub out.

If seed of *F. officinalis* is available, it should be

sown in place in late autumn or very early spring, and young seedlings should be thinned after two or three sets of leaves have developed so that mature plants will stand about eight inches apart. Alternatively, seed may be sown indoors, about four weeks before the last anticipated frost date, in peat pots or plastic cell packs so that minimal root disturbance will occur when plants are transplanted into the garden.

The genus name derives from the classical Latin *fumus terrae,* meaning smoke of the earth. An exact translation of that Latin phrase still adheres to it as a popular name in parts of England, aptly descriptive of its pale, gray-green, ferny leaves and stems, borne on plants that can sprout in such abundance on sandy waste ground that the earth seems to be burning.

GAILLARDIA SPECIES

FAMILY: *Asteraceae* or aster or daisy family.

CLASSIFICATION: Biennials or perennials grown as half-hardy annuals.

COMMON NAMES: Blanket flower, Indian blanket, gaillardia.

HARDINESS: Withstands light frost once established.

GROWING CONDITIONS: Sandy, well-drained dryish soil of moderate fertility.

PROPAGATION: From seed, sown 10 to 12 weeks before last frost.

HEIGHT: Plants to 12″, bloom stems to 2′.

ORNAMENTAL VALUE: Grown for flower.

LEVEL OF CULTURAL DIFFICULTY: Moderately difficult.

SPECIAL PROPERTIES: None.

PRONUNCIATION: gayh-AR-dee-a

Gaillardias are American wild flowers that occupy a wide native range from the plains of Colorado and New Mexico east in some species to Virginia and south to Texas and New Mexico. Though they have many competitors of easier culture, such as marigolds, zinnias, and calendulas, for example, extensive manipulation of the genus began in the nineteenth century, when they bore the designation "florist's flowers," a label that did not indicate—as it does today—flowers forced in greenhouses in Holland in the dead of winter and shipped within two days of their picking to expensive shops in New York and elsewhere. The older use of the phrase meant flowers that could be hybridized into fantastic colors, sizes, and forms to win prizes on the show benches of local competitions for amateur flower growers—then called "florists." Several species of *Gaillardia* were interbred for this purpose, using as a base the natively perennial species, *G. aristata* (a-ri-STA-ta), but intermarrying it with other species, including the annual *G. pulchella* (pul-CHEL-a), to produce plants now generally classified as *G.* x *grandiflora* (gran-di-FLO-ra). Seed is offered of many of these named hybrids, particularly by English seed houses, and they may all be grown satisfactorily as annuals.

In leaf and stem structure gaillardia plants vary little, all consisting of basal tuffets of lance-shaped, rough, hairy gray-green leaves up to about ten inches long, from which flowering stems extend to as much as two feet. Each stem bears a single daisy, with many ray petals and a central disk of fertile flowers. The flowers within the disk begin opening when the ray petals are merely a promise and continue to open toward the center after the ray petals are fully formed. This gives individual blossoms a very long life on the plants and in a vase, making them superb cut flowers. If they are not picked, spent blossoms should be snapped off to prolong bloom when they turn brown and are setting seed.

The structure of the plant may not vary, but

GAILLARDIA PULCHELLA

the flowers do, although color stays within a range of yellow to brown and purplish mahogany. In their simplest form, blossoms are typical daisies, two to three inches wide. Those closest to naturally occurring species will present a single layer of ray petals around a central disk, generally with the outer edges of the rays notched or "pinked" and with bands or zones of color, usually proceeding from bright yellow at the edges of the petals through warm brown to deep mahogany at the center. Cultivars exist, however, that are a clear egg-yolk yellow throughout or that are deep, purplish brown, and hybrids and selected cultivars may display a double row of ray petals, or may be so doubled as to resemble the autumn-blooming florists' chrysanthemums. There is even one hybrid in which the ray petals have been eliminated or modified entirely, to create a spherical fluffy ball something like an orange-brown powder puff.

Although some gaillardias are listed as true perennials, they will not perform as such except in the western half of the United States and on very well-drained, poorish soils in Zones 6 to 9—conditions that approach their native habitats. If, in other gardens located in the Northeast, Mid-

west, or Northwest, forms of gaillardia return for a year or two, so much the better. Then one would be wise to take basal cuttings in midsummer (so-called Irish cuttings—a fan of growth with a bit of root tissue at the end), plant them in damp sand and peat or perlite, overwinter them in cold frames, and plant them out in May for additional flower.

Seed of named hybrids may be grown satisfactorily from an early start in March under glass, pricked out when they form two true sets of leaves into single pots or rows in flats, hardened off, and transplanted into the garden after all danger of frost is past. Treated this way, they will be half-hardy annuals, whatever their species and however mixed their blood might be. It is as such that they can be bought from nurseries specializing in started plants of unusual annuals or from sophisticated seed companies.

All gaillardias require the same culture, which—all their life from tiny seedlings to fully grown flowering plants—consists mostly of sandy, well-drained soil, full sun, dryness, and heat in the atmosphere. Although species of *Gaillardia,* particularly *G. pulchella,* are often included in wildflower mixes, little can be expected of them except an occasional flower or two here and there when seed is sown on heavy, moist ground of clay consistency, particularly if the ground has not been cleared of pasture grasses, tilled, and rolled. However, in their native places they form rich fields of flower, almost mono-specific, consisting of vast expanses of brown, yellow, and mahogany red, all together. Images of such fields have led many people to expend considerable sums on seed of this plant with little success because, like many American wild flowers, it grows best where it is native.

The popular names of all gaillardias, "Indian

blanket" or "blanket flower," are supposedly derived from the resemblance of their warm and varied colors to the superb productions of Native American weavers, chiefly the Hopi and the Navaho. The genus name commemorates a French magistrate of the late eighteenth century, Monsieur Gaillard de Charentonneau.

GAURA LINDHEIMERI

FAMILY: *Onagraceae* or evening primrose family.

CLASSIFICATION: Hardy or half-hardy perennial often grown as half-hardy annual.

COMMON NAME: Gaura.

HARDINESS: Root-hardy to Zone 4 on perfectly drained soil and with protection. When grown as an annual, plants withstand light frost once established.

GROWING CONDITIONS: Moderately fertile to poor, dryish, well-drained soils.

PROPAGATION: From seed, sown 12 weeks from last frost. Select forms propagated by basal cuttings.

HEIGHT: From 2 to 3'.

ORNAMENTAL VALUE: Grown for flower.

LEVEL OF CULTURAL DIFFICULTY: Moderately easy.

SPECIAL PROPERTIES: None.

PRONUNCIATION: GAUH-ra lind-HIME-er-eye

The current enthusiasm for *Gaura lindheimeri* reflects, as clearly as anything could, a radical shift in attitudes among American gardeners about annuals and even perennial plants. For gauras possesses a gentle beauty far from plants that may be counted on to create waves of color. In its first year from seed, *Gaura lindheimeri* will produce three or four upright stems from a fleshy carrotlike taproot, each sparsely furnished with green to gray-green, hairy, willowlike leaves, each between one and three inches long and usually raggedly "pinked" or cut into notches. The stems may reach three feet eventually and, in the top half, furled buds of coral pink will be produced from vestigial leaf axils opening to flowers of pure white (in typical forms) that age to rust pink before forming seed. More thin wands will be produced from plants that survive their first winter, or their second, to form impressive clumps of many flowering stems with hundreds of flowers bearing them down almost to the ground over a season that begins in late June or early July and extends to frost. The flowering parts of the plant are surprisingly frost-hardy and will continue producing blossoms well into October in Zones 6 to 9—and where autumns are mild, even in Zone 5.

Flowers are about an inch wide, composed of four petals of usually uneven length, "clawed" in botanical language, which means that each one is pinched into a sort of stem where it meets the calyx. A delicate but prominent boss of stamens and pistil emerges from the center of each flower, giving it a fragile look. Few flowers open at any one time—appearing here and there but never in bunches—and are often compared to flights of butterflies or small white moths settled on the wiry stems.

Until about ten years ago *Gaura lindheimeri* was both much underrated and much misunderstood. A native American wild flower, its natural range is limited to the dryer parts of eastern Louisiana and the southern third of Texas and into northern Mexico. Because of this range, it was assumed to be hardy not much beyond Zone 7, or possibly Zone 6, if planted in well-drained gravelly soil and given some protection. But as it is capable of flowering the first year from an early

GAURA LINDHEIMERI

March seeding, the general advice was to grow it as an annual. It was, however, usually designated as "for the wild garden," or "of interest chiefly to wildflower enthusiasts." None of these recommendations would be understood as positively encouraging to gardeners who might think of growing the plant outside its native range, even as an annual.

But *Gaura lindheimeri,* despite its southern origins, has proven to be a surprisingly hardy perennial, capable of surviving for several years as far north as Zone 4, assuming the cultural conditions it requires wherever it might be grown. Those are for well-drained, poorish soils in full sun, and some winter protection in the form of snow cover or evergreen boughs or both. Given these conditions, plants may persist for two years or three. But they are not long-lived perennials in the sense that Siberian iris are, or peonies, which, when well suited in their needs are practically forever. Plants of *G. lindheimeri* will weaken after three or so years in the garden, and then they are best restarted from seed.

Fortunately, plants grown from seed are very easy, whether they are discarded at season's end as annuals or left in place for one or two more seasons of beauty. As with most true perennials that may be grown for flower in their first season, seed should be sown quite early, in March at least, for plants that will flower from early July until frost. Seed should be sown in free-draining compost, even with sharp sand or perlite added to a third of its volume, and young plants should be pricked out and grown on in sunny indoor or greenhouse conditions until they may be hardened off gradually and planted outdoors after all danger of frost is past.

As usually happens with garden plants that achieve sudden prominence, several selected forms of *Gaura lindheimeri* have become available, each with its own remarkable characteristic. There is a golden-leaved form and one with a thin variegation of cream on the margins of the leaves, which is very pretty up close but rather dusty from a distance. More significant, forms have been selected with blossoms of a richer, deeper pink, not actually prettier than the delicate, pale shell pink of the typical species but more effective when viewed from a distance. These select forms of the plant are propagated as cuttings taken in summer and are available from mail order nurseries that specialize in rare and unusual perennials.

Gaura lindheimeri is the only member of its genus—perhaps twenty species of New World annuals and perennials—that is currently grown in gardens. Its genus name is taken from the classical Greek adjective *gauros,* meaning splendid or superb, which gardeners will realize might be applied to a plant of the subtle beauty it possesses. The species name *lindheimeri* commemorates Ferdinand Jacob Lindheimer (1801–1879), about whom little is known except that he was a political exile from Germany who spent the bulk of his mature life on an extensive study of native Texas flora.

GAZANIA SPECIES

FAMILY: *Asteraceae* or aster or daisy family.

CLASSIFICATION: Tender perennials or half-hardy annuals grown as tender annuals.

COMMON NAMES: Treasure flower, pied daisy, African daisy, gazania.

HARDINESS: Frost sensitive.

GROWING CONDITIONS: Dryish, moderately fertile to poor, sandy soil. Perfect drainage. Warm days and cool nights.

PROPAGATION: By seed, sown 12 weeks before last frost, or by basal cuttings.

HEIGHT: 6 to 12″.

ORNAMENTAL VALUE: Grown for flower.

LEVEL OF CULTURAL DIFFICULTY: Difficult except in dryer parts of Zones 9 and 10.

SPECIAL PROPERTIES: Drought tolerant.

PRONUNCIATION: ga-ZAY-nee-a

The genus *Gazania* includes perhaps as many as two dozen separate species, all of which are of South African origin and most of which are very pretty. Where they are hardy—the dryer gardens of southern California and other parts of the world with a similar Mediterranean climate—cultivars of *Gazania* x *hybrida* (as all are now accurately listed) make splendid, almost indispensable plants, both for use in the flower garden and also as vividly flowered groundcover along freeways and in awkward patches on domestic grounds.

Where they are not hardy, however, plants are of limited use, for flowers tend to close in dark or damp weather, as a response not so much to the absence of the sun as to sudden drops of temperature. Although gazania have been bred—and the breeding program continues briskly—to produce flowers that will remain open, or at least grace-fully cupped, in cloudy weather, the genus is still apt to be far more important to gardeners in the West, where flowers stay open most frequently, than to those in the East.

All gazania are daisies, belonging to the vast family Asteraceae, the composites. As such, they bear flowers composed of two parts, a furry disk of fertile flowers in their centers, surrounded by a showy ruff of ray petals around the outside. The flowers are frankly splendid, often so elaborately crafted as to seem like flowers of the imagination. The ray petals are brilliant, not just from their predominate colors—various shades of pink, rose, or mulberry red, white, primrose yellow, gold, bronze, tarnished or freshly polished copper, deep brown, and mahogany—but because in the center of each daisy will be a band of color where the ray flowers meet the disk. It may occupy as much as a third of the flower, sometimes less, in a neat ring, and may be any one of several strange colors: tan or khaki, olive or metallic green, or deep brown approaching inky black. Also where the ray petals join the disk, there may be a small dot of white, tan, black, or some indescribable but always harmonious color, put there for heaven-knows-what purpose.

The predominant shape of the flowers, borne singly on long stalks, is typically daisylike, but petals curve outward or inward into a cup, depending on the cultivar and the state of the weather. There are also doubles, though no one knows why, since a daisy of perfect proportions is really good enough. Unlike many members of the family Asteraceae, individual flowers last a relatively brief time on the plant, so spent flowers should be snapped off to prevent the formation of seed, thus encouraging the production of new flowers.

Both in the wild and in gardens, the two dozen species in the genus freely intercross among

GAZANIA 'SUNDROP'

for hot, dryish soils makes them ideal—particularly in the trailing kinds—in individual pots, containers, window boxes, and in hanging baskets.

As most gazania, and certainly the prettiest, are hybrids, few are propagated by seed; they are rather started by basal cuttings that may be taken from nonflowering shoots at almost any time but are easiest to manage in the dryer parts of late spring or early summer.

The plants are called "gazania" after the medieval scholar Theodore of Gaza (1398–1478), who, during a life extraordinarily long for his time, translated the botanical works of Theophrastus from Greek to Latin. In his wildest imagination, however, he could not have pictured the flowers produced from modern hybrids, most of which were not cultivated in Europe or in America until the nineteenth century.

themselves, making precise identification a matter for learned conjecture at best. Whatever their specific parentage, the gazania grown in gardens are divided into two rough groups: those that form clumps and those that form runners along the ground. It is among the clumping forms that the most splendid flowers are to be found. They are very complex hybrids that produce a mound of evergreen leaves, generally dark green above and white and furry beneath, though there are forms that are silvery-white all over. Variegated forms also exist, banded either with gold or with silver, a plus in climates where flowers tend to remain closed most of the time. Leaves are usually strap- or bladelike, though there are filigreed forms, with leaves that are notched or cut into lobes.

In the hotter and dryer parts of Zones 8 to 10, gazania are very serviceable plants, often recommended as groundcover along freeways and in front of service stations in California, both for months of color from bloom and also because plants are unusually drought-tolerant. Elsewhere they are treasured plants, perhaps grown in the flower border, but more likely in pots or containers, even for a few of their remarkable, exotic colored daisies, and even if they are fully open only on the finest days of the summer. Their preference

GERBERA JAMESONII

FAMILY: *Asteraceae* or aster or daisy family.

CLASSIFICATION: Tender perennial grown as tender annual.

COMMON NAMES: Transvaal daisy, Barberton daisy, veldt daisy, African daisy, gerbera.

HARDINESS: Sensitive to frosts.

GROWING CONDITIONS: Humus-rich but perfectly drained, sandy soils. Full sun.

PROPAGATION: By seed, sown indoors in late autumn or early winter, and by basal cuttings taken in late spring or early summer.

HEIGHT: Leaves to 8", flower stems to 12".

ORNAMENTAL VALUE: Grown for flower.

LEVEL OF CULTURAL DIFFICULTY: Difficult.

SPECIAL PROPERTIES: Best in pots, containers, and window boxes.

PRONUNCIATION: GUR-bu-ra jaym-SON-ee-ee

Most American gardeners will know gerbera best as cut flowers, for they are offered by florists throughout the year, in sumptuous colors of white, pink, violet, yellow, salmon, and flamered, and often in almost improbable shades of coral orange or grayish purple—colors that sometimes suggest something painted or dyed rather than borne naturally on any living plant.

One may say of gerberas that in the vast daisy clan that possesses so many distinguished members, they are among the most elegant, with four- or five-inch-wide flowers, always beautifully colored, poised gracefully on long stems. Sadly, however, the gerbera daisy is a very tricky plant to grow. Where it is hardy—which is to say the dryer parts of Zones 8 to 10 in North America—it may, with proper attention, settle down to become a short-lived perennial, forming tufts of eight-inch-long, hairy but shiny dark green leaves, generally lobed and very gracefully borne. Peak bloom is in early summer and in autumn, and spent flowers should be removed to prolong flowering. When plants begin to deteriorate, they should be re-propagated by basal cuttings taken from old clumps, or fresh young plants should be purchased. Because gerbera form deep taproots and resent disturbance, they will be slow to settle down to new plants if divisions are attempted, and losses may be heavy.

Where they are not hardy, gerberas are to be treated as potted annuals, sometimes depressingly short-lived, lasting only a week or two, hardly longer than they would as cut flowers. They are, it is true, almost irresistible, grown as single, compact plants in four- or six-inch clay pots, surmounted by one or two brilliant flowers, and showing buds to come. But once removed from controlled greenhouse conditions, gerberas are extremely subject to root and crown rot, and most plants succumb quickly, either from overwatering or from excessive atmospheric humidity. If kept in cool, airy, sunny conditions, watered only when moderately dry, fed occasionally with water-soluble plant food (for despite their need for well-drained soils, they are surprisingly greedy feeders), one may have luck with them, and then they will be very rewarding plants.

Though technically tender perennials, the gerberas generally seen as single, potted specimens in garden centers are usually grown as tender annuals. They will flower in about six months from seed under controlled conditions, and seed should be sown quite early, in October or November, to provide flowering plants the following April or May. Seed should be sown in extremely well-drained potting compost, and the seed flat covered with a sheet of glass until germination, which occurs best at temperatures around 60°F. The glass should then be immediately removed. When moderately dry, pots should be placed in a pan of water until the surface soil is moist. Pricking out can occur as soon as the plants are large enough to handle, and young plants should be grown on in temperatures between 50° and 60°F at night and about ten degrees warmer in the daytime. Whenever they are repotted, or when they are transplanted into the garden, the crowns of plants should be elevated about a half inch above the surrounding soil, to minimize crown rot. Where soils are heavy or remain damp for long periods of time, gerberas should be grown either in pots or in raised beds of extremely fast-draining, sandy but humus-rich soil.

The most elegant gerberas are single, either with long, fringy petals such as the naturally occurring wild species shows, or slightly broader and more substantial ones, such as most florists' forms possess. There are also semi-double forms, called "duplexes," in which a smaller, second row of petals is superimposed upon the first. Sadly, there are also doubles, in which all the natural grace and beauty of the flowers have been completely bred out.

Gerberas belong to a surprisingly large genus of about forty species, named for the German naturalist Traugott Gerber (1710–1743). The only species in general cultivation, however, is *jamesonii,* sometimes listed as x *jamesonii,* or even as x *hybrida,* though all the richly colored flowers in cultivation are probably crossings and recrossings of the single species.

GILIA SPECIES

FAMILY: *Polemoniaceae* or phlox family.

CLASSIFICATION: Hardy annuals or biennials grown as hardy annuals.

COMMON NAMES: Queen Anne's thimbles, gilia.

HARDINESS: Resistant to light frosts.

GROWING CONDITIONS: Moderately fertile, well-drained, moisture-retentive soil. Full sun.

PROPAGATION: By seed, sown in place in warmer gardens in early fall, and in early spring in cooler ones. Plants resent root disturbance.

HEIGHT: 12 to 20", depending on culture.

ORNAMENTAL VALUE: Grown for flower.

LEVEL OF CULTURAL DIFFICULTY: Moderately difficult outside native range.

SPECIAL PROPERTIES: None.

PRONUNCIATION: GIL-ee-a

Gilia is chiefly a North American—and chiefly Pacific coast—genus that reflects at present huge botanical confusion. It was once quite large, including as many as 100 species, though many contained in it have been shifted into related genuses, shrinking *Gilia* to only thirty species, more or less (and for the moment) most of which are quite pretty, of fairly easy culture as hardy annuals, and worth a place in North American gardens.

Still, seed of only two species of *Gilia* are generally available (except from wildflower societies and seed companies specializing in native American flora), and neither could be called commonly grown, though both make fine contributions to the summer garden. *Gilia capitata* (ka-pi-TA-ta) is, of the two, more frequently offered. It is popularly called "blue thimble flower," "globe gilia," or more frequently, "Queen Anne's thimbles," thus commemorating in yet another American wild flower the unfortunate Queen Anne of England (1665–1774), who suffered ten miscarriages and lost five children.

At maturity, plants of *Gilia capitata* form slender bushes eighteen to twenty-four inches tall, furnished with toothed and congested, chrysanthemum-like leaves, sometimes more finely cut and filimented, but of a dark, bluish green. In gardens where sowing occurs in early spring, bloom may be expected about six to eight weeks after germination, depending on weather. Plants are hurried into precocious bloom by sudden warmth in early summer, but they flower later and longest where they have been established in the garden in early spring and where summers are cool, continuing to flower sometimes well into October. Little is gained therefore by starting plants indoors. *G. capitata* makes an excellent cut flower, its wiry grace and its blue "thimbles" of tubular flowers contributing to arrangements a delicate, unusual charm.

The other gilia available from some seed companies and nurseries that specialize in unusual annual and tender plants is *Gilia tricolor* (TRI-color), which forms a plant ten to twenty inches tall, though usually it falls over from its own weight. One could stake it with twiggy branchlets and prunings to stay upright, but in some circumstances its tendency to flop may make it useful, both as a plant that can bend and weave among annuals and sturdy perennials, and also as a gracefully draping sheet of bloom over the edges of pots, window boxes, and hanging baskets. Its foliage is grayish green, finely cut, and in warmer gardens, the whole plant is said to smell faintly of chocolate. It takes its popular name, "birds' eyes," from the coloration of its half-inch-wide tubular flowers, borne in clusters of two to five, and sometimes singly. They are colored a deep violet-purple, fading to lilac at the tips, and yellow at the base of each petal, the whole flower clasping anthers coated with blue pollen. The effect is perky and entirely charming, and in cool bright gardens, flowers may be had from June to September.

A native of the Pacific coast from Washington to California, gilia often behaves as a biennial where it grows naturally, and so, in warmer gardens, seed should be sown in late summer or early autumn where the plants are to grow. Seedlings will appear one or two weeks after sowing, and if soils are well drained and winters do not fall much below 0°F, young plants will survive to flower in early summer, continuing as long as the weather remains reasonably cool. In colder gardens, however, *Gilia capitata* must be cultivated as a hardy annual, seeded where it is to grow in early spring, and seedlings thinned to stand about six to ten inches apart. Gilias prefer full sun, and soil should be of moderate fertility, well drained but reasonably moisture retentive.

All gilias make interesting and attractive plants for those who have cool greenhouses and have mastered their management, and who also like to experiment with unusual annuals and tender plants that may be brought into flower in late winter and very early spring. Seed of most species should be sown in midsummer, potted on until they occupy five- to six-inch pots, and grown in bright, cool conditions. As with any other plant expected to flower out of season and early in the year, watering and fertilizing should be very carefully monitored because an excess of both will cause rotting at the crowns just when the plants are most promising with bloom.

The genus name is assumed by some horticulturists to commemorate the Roman astronomer Filippo Luigi Gili (1756–1821), who lived at a time when all science was a common pursuit and scientists paid compliments to one another across the lines of specific disciplines. Other experts believe it memorializes Philip Salvador Gil, a Spanish botanist whose specific dates and accomplishments have not been otherwise recorded.

GLAUCIUM SPECIES

FAMILY: *Papaveraceae* or poppy family.

CLASSIFICATION: Hardy or half-hardy perennial or biennial grown as hardy annual.

COMMON NAMES: Horned poppy, sea poppy, glaucium.

HARDINESS: Resistant to light frosts when well established.

GROWING CONDITIONS: Poor, gravelly, perfectly drained soil. Full sun.

PROPAGATION: By seed, sown in place in autumn in warmer gardens and in very early spring in colder ones. May be seeded indoors in peat pots 6 to 8 weeks before last frost.

HEIGHT: 1 to 2'.

ORNAMENTAL VALUE: Grown for flower.

LEVEL OF CULTURAL DIFFICULTY: Moderately difficult.

SPECIAL PROPERTIES: None.

PRONUNCIATION: GLOW-kee-um

Where they grow wild on sandy, shingly beaches and windswept dunes, various species of *Glaucium* are always a pleasant surprise, handsome even as youthful unflowered rosettes of lobed leaves. Though in some species the leaves may be a powdery white, usually they are a cool bluish gray, their color giving the genus its name (from the ancient Greek adjective *glaukos,* meaning gray-green). From the rosettes, branching stems emerge, clad sparsely with leaves, creating a loose bush, each stem terminating in a single, poppy-like flower, about two inches across and possessed of a splendid, satiny sheen.

All that is well enough in their native habitats, one species or another occurring from southern England to the Mediterranean and as far east as Afghanistan. In gardens, however, the young plants and the blossoms (produced freely in cooler gardens from late June to August) are very beautiful, but the species of *Glaucium* under cultivation are rather sloppy plants, developing an angularity at best and sometimes a disorderly tangle of stems, not thrown out evenly like a wheel, but hither and yon, creating a distinctly lopsided effect. For this reason, they look best when planted in the craggy terrain of a rock garden that mimics their native places and also provides the lean, fast-draining soil they require to perform best.

Of the twenty or so species in the genus, only two are cultivated as ornamental plants. The more common is the yellow horned poppy, *Glaucium flavum* (FLA-vum), which forms a ragged, bushy plant to three feet, with charming, cup-shaped flowers made up of four overlapping petals, slightly crinkled at their edges. Though

GLAUCIUM FLAVUM

the typical flower color is a clear, egg-yolk yellow, the variety *aurantiacum* (o-ran-ti-AH-cum) bears flowers of a brilliant shining orange.

The other species under cultivation is the red horned poppy, *Glaucium corniculatum* (kor-ni-cu-LA-tum), which derives its species name from the Latin word for horn. It forms a somewhat smaller plant than *G. flavum,* to about two feet tall, and its flowers, generally shades of red sometimes with a black or yellow spot at the base of each petal, are less graceful, as they generally do not overlap, but stand outward. Inferior forms bear small, inch-wide flowers often hidden by the leaves; superior ones produce flowers two or more inches across, borne well above the foliage. At one time, the larger-flowering forms were given independent species status as *Glaucium grandiflorum* (gran-di-FLO-rum), and seed is still sometimes offered under that name.

Whether horned poppies are true perennials, biennials, or annuals is uncertain, since they may behave as all three. However, both species can be brought to flower in their first year from seed sown in very early spring, or, in warmer gardens, in late autumn. Like most members of the family Papaveraceae, they will not tolerate disturbance at the roots, and so they are best either sown where they are to grow, and later thinned to stand about a foot apart, or seeded indoors six to eight weeks before the last anticipated frost, in peat pots or plastic cell packs, and transplanted into the garden very carefully after all danger of frost is past. They demand full sun and perfect drainage, and they are most compact of growth in rather barren soils, poor in nitrogen but rich in potassium and phosphorus. Where their needs are perfectly suited and winters are relatively mild, plants may appear again, for a year or two, from a thick, gnarled, woody root stock.

The horned poppies take their popular name—and indeed, in *G. corniculatum,* the species

GLAUCIUM FLAVUM

name—from their long, thin, pointed seed pods, which, in *G. flavum,* may reach as much as a foot in length. In all but the coldest gardens, seedlings may appear from year to year once plants have been grown. Such volunteers should be left in place, if they are in the right place, for they will generally make better plants than any sown by the gardener outdoors or carefully transplanted. If they are in the wrong place they must simply be weeded out. *G. flavum* has naturalized in North America on both the East and West Coasts and so may appear spontaneously in gardens where it was never planted.

GOMPHRENA SPECIES

FAMILY: *Amaranthaceae* or amaranth family.

CLASSIFICATION: Half-hardy annuals.

COMMON NAMES: Globe amaranth, life-in-death, gomphrena.

HARDINESS: Sensitive to light frosts. Prefer hot weather.

GROWING CONDITIONS: Ordinary fertile, well-drained garden soil.

PROPAGATION: From seed, started indoors 6 to 8
weeks before last frost. May be seeded in place
in spring in warmer gardens.

HEIGHT: 1 to 2'.

ORNAMENTAL VALUE: Grown for flower.

LEVEL OF CULTURAL DIFFICULTY: Easy.

SPECIAL PROPERTIES: Excellent cut or dried flower.

PRONUNCIATION: gom-FREY-na (gom-FREE-na)

The genus *Gomphrena* contains about 100 species of both Old and New World origins, only two of which, *Gomphrena globosa* (glo-BO-sa) and *G. haagiana* (hay-GEE-a-na), are much grown in gardens. *G. globosa,* which has been cultivated in European gardens since at least the early eighteenth century, is by far the more familiar. It is a plant of very easy culture, particularly in warm gardens where it thrives in summer heat, producing much-branched bushes about two feet tall, well furnished with oval, light green, disease-free, raspy leaves from two to four inches long. Its cloverlike flower heads begin to appear when plants are quite small, hardly six inches high, and show color even as tiny buttons clasped by the leaves. The individual flowers are actually chaffy, paperlike bracts in which the true flowers—tiny yellowish white, starry tubes a quarter-inch long—are borne over a long period of time, sometimes a whole summer as the bracts elongate. Thus, an individual plant may be furnished with dozens of blossoming heads, ranging from tiny ones just formed to mature spheres an inch across and as long.

Until about fifteen years ago, *G. globosa* was of limited use in the summer garden, because the typical color of the species is a strong, uncompromising magenta, a color not then in favor with many gardeners. But the species has now been bred into a wide range of beautiful colors, from white and palest pink to lavender, deep rose, plush red, and dark purple. There are also some fine bi-colors, actually forms in which the immature bracts in the center of the flower head begin whitish-rose and deepen as they mature. Seed is offered that comes true to individual colors, but the plant is perhaps never so pretty as when grown in a large planting with all the colors blended. Dwarf, compact forms have also been developed that make smug little bushes about eight inches tall, useful to those gardeners who like a tidy edge of one species for their borders.

The other species of *Gomphrena* grown in gardens is *G. haagiana,* commemorating a great German seedsman of the nineteenth century, J. N. Haage (1826–1878). It is most familiar to gardeners in the superb cultivar called 'Strawberry Fields', until recently assumed by most to be a color breakthrough in the predominantly rose to purple shades of *G. globosa*. It is probable, however, that it is a selected form of *G. haagiana,* a species that typically bears flowers of yellow-orange to scarlet, but which in 'Strawberry Fields' are a splendid crimson-red. Plants of *G. haagiana* are a little taller than those of *G. globosa,* rangier and longer of stem, and the leaves are narrower and more bladelike. It makes its best appearance (as indeed does *G. globosa*) when plants are established no farther than six or so inches apart and in generous blocks—closer together than one would normally plant an annual that will ultimately achieve a height of two feet. Like *G. globosa,* forms of *G. haagiana* and particularly 'Strawberry Fields' make splendid dried flowers because of their papery bracts. Hence one popular name, "life-in-death." Whole bushes may be harvested when full of flower heads, hung upside down in a dry, airy place, and later stripped of withered leaves for use

GOMPHRENA HAAGIANA *'STRAWBERRY FIELDS'*

tropical Southeast Asia and *G. haagiana* native to southern Texas and northern Mexico. They therefore perform best when summer heat arrives. In gardens that experience significant early summer warmth, they may be sown outdoors where they are to grow, or seeded in rows and later transplanted. In cooler gardens, they are best started indoors about six to eight weeks before the last anticipated frost, hardened off, and transplanted outdoors when the weather is settled and warm. The cottony seed may be slow to germinate, requiring as much as three weeks, though germination may be hastened by soaking seed for a day or two or by bathing it for a minute in boiling water. In any case, germination will not be successful at soil temperatures much below 70°F, and young plants must be grown on in full sun and watered carefully to avoid root rot.

At all times in their lives, plants of gomphrena will require full sun and will deteriorate quickly in heavy, water-logged soils or if over-irrigated. One should not make the mistake, however, of assuming that they prefer poor, sandy soils, for they grow best in soils that are fertile and humus-rich but well drained. Like many other annuals that enjoy warm dryish soils, they are excellent when grown in pots or containers, in which they may be planted quite close together, as many as six to a ten-inch pot. Single specimens in five-inch pots may also be grown in an out-of-the-way place to drop into gaps that appear in the border in mid- to late summer.

The genus name *Gomphrena* is a corruption of the classical Latin *gromphaena,* signifying a member of the amaranth family (though not necessarily this plant) that retains its color when dried. Thus, we are told in Homer that the dead body of Achilles was covered with "gomphrena" to signify his immortality.

in winter bouquets. The stems of gomphrena are quite stiff and woody when dry and so are easily inserted into arrangements.

One other species of *Gomphrena* has recently made an appearance in catalogues and nurseries specializing in rare and unusual annuals—*Gomphrena dispersa* (dis-PER-sa), marketed as "pink pinheads" and suggested as annual groundcover. Its lax, foot-high bushes produce large numbers of tiny, rose-colored bracts, each about one-eighth-inch long. Possessed of a charm that would have to be called modest, *G. dispersa* is best when viewed up close, in a container, in a hanging basket, or in the rock garden.

All gomphrenas originate in quite warm or tropical environments. *G. globosa* is native to

GYNURA AURANTIACA

FAMILY: *Asteraceae* or aster or daisy family.

CLASSIFICATION: Tender annual.

COMMON NAMES: Purple velvet plant, purple passion, gynura.

HARDINESS: Extremely sensitive to light frosts. Resents cool weather. Relishes heat.

GROWING CONDITIONS: Humus-rich, moist but well-drained soil. Full sun in cooler gardens, afternoon shade in warmer ones.

PROPAGATION: By cuttings, taken in spring or summer.

HEIGHT: Variable, from 1 to 4′.

ORNAMENTAL VALUE: Grown for purple-downed foliage.

LEVEL OF CULTURAL DIFFICULTY: Easy.

SPECIAL PROPERTIES: None.

PRONUNCIATION: GNUR-a o-ran-tee-A-ca

*A*lmost no plant in cultivation is more suggestive of overheated Victorian drawing rooms than *Gynura aurantiaca,* the purple passion or purple velvet plant. A native of the steamy tropical jungles of Indonesia, it has been in continuous cultivation as a parlor plant for more than 150 years. It is of very easy culture, asking only a moderately rich, loamy soil, adequate water, and reasonably bright light. But, it must be confessed, it generally looks fairly dreary in most indoor conditions, producing long, lanky stems, depressingly down-curved leaves, and little bunches of dull yellow flowers that look like the center of a ragged daisy from which all the ray petals have been stripped away.

But gynura is one of many tender houseplants that has jumped its confines from the parlor windowsill to the summer garden in recent years, and as an outdoor plant in semishade it can look quite splendid. Though still an upright or some-what sprawling shrubby plant to three feet, its alternate leaves can reach a length of as much as eight inches, rather than the modest two or three it achieves indoors. They are broadly oval in shape, somewhat fleshy in texture, pointed at the ends, and with toothed margins that turn downward, giving each leaf the shape of an inverted spoon. Their base color is a shiny, olive green, but they are made remarkable by being thickly covered with soft, downy hairs of a vivid purple violet. These hairs become unusually dense and bright in the strong light of the outdoor garden, justifying the two popular names, "purple passion" and "purple velvet plant."

Actually, however, the name "purple velvet plant" should be reserved for the taller growing form of gynura, which attempts to be upright as long as it can, though its branches are eventually borne sideways and down by the weight of its leaves. A second form is much more procumbent and ivylike, with branches that always trail and bear smaller leaves than those of purple velvet. The two plants are sufficiently different in character that nineteenth-century botanists assigned the trailing form its own botanical designation, *G. sarmentosa* (sar-men-TO-sa), which means having running branches. It then acquired its own popular name, "purple passion." Though the two plants are now considered to be merely genetic variants of one species, gardeners can still choose one over the other according to its use. Purple velvet is best to the middle or even back of a wide border furnished with tender foliage plants, whereas purple passion makes a very fine container or hanging basket plant.

The culture of gynura is very simple, though it is a plant that will only look its best if some efforts are made to please it. The best growth is produced from deep, humus-rich, evenly moist soils, and like all jungle plants, it is a greedy feeder, relishing a generous application of time-release fertilizer such as Osmacote at planting, and biweekly foliar feedings of water-soluble fertilizer thereafter. It will accept quite deep shade and is often planted there simply because it will live under such difficult conditions, though its leaves then lose much of their vividly colored down and become an uninteresting olive green. In brighter light the coloring becomes much stronger, and in full sun the whole plant can almost seem to glow. However, where summers are blisteringly hot, protection from afternoon sun will be required.

Gynura is never propagated from seed, but rather from soft tip cuttings taken in spring, or from semi-ripe cuttings in summer, both of which root readily, though as with all cuttings of downy-leaved plants, care must be taken to keep the leaf surface dry during the rooting period in order to prevent rot. After cuttings are well rooted and potted up, they should be pinched frequently to encourage branching. Rooted cuttings are easy to carry over the winter on a bright windowsill, where they will often flower. Only curiosity would justify not pinching out the buds as soon as they appear, for flowers are not the plant's most attractive asset.

The genus Gynura is surprisingly large, containing about fifty species, all native to the tropical forests of Africa and southern Asia, where some species are used both as a cooked green and for medicinal purposes. The curious name of the genus, which one would suppose to be a vernacular word, in fact comes from ancient Greek *gyne,* meaning female, and *oura,* a tail, and is an attempt to describe nothing more exciting than the rough extended stigma of the flower. Only *Gynura aurantiaca,* the species name of which means colored orange and describes the flowers, is commonly cultivated. Whether because of its appearance, its popular names, or some unperceived quality, *G. aurantiaca* seems to possess a strong fascination for men who otherwise may have little interest in gardening.

GYPSOPHILA ELEGANS

FAMILY: *Caryophyllaceae* or carnation family.

CLASSIFICATION: Hardy annual.

COMMON NAMES: Annual baby's breath, annual gypsophila.

HARDINESS: Withstands light frost.

GROWING CONDITIONS: Moderately rich, well-drained, limey garden soil. Full sun.

PROPAGATION: Sown in place in autumn in warmer gardens, in very early spring in cooler ones. May be sown indoors 6 weeks from frost. Intolerant of root disturbance.

HEIGHT: 6 to 18", depending on cultivar.

ORNAMENTAL VALUE: Grown for flower.

LEVEL OF CULTURAL DIFFICULTY: Moderately difficult.

SPECIAL PROPERTIES: None.

PRONUNCIATION: jip-SO-fi-la EL-uh-gans

Gypsophila elegans is delicate in all its parts, offering an effect that may be had from no other annual plant. Its thin, wiry stems, slightly swollen or knobbed at their joints, reach a height of twelve to eighteen inches, forking and branching freely in the top half of their growth. The sparse leaves are a waxy gray-green, up to three inches in length, tapered at both ends and somewhat fleshy. Tiny flowers, each hardly a quarter-inch across, are composed of five petals fused together at the center and curving outward gracefully, making a bowl or salver for a golden drop of nectar at the center. Whole plants come into bloom at one time, producing clouds of flower over a short span of three or four weeks. Usually the flowers are a startling chalk white in the variety *grandiflora* (gran-di-FLO-ra) or its selected cultivar 'Covent Garden', which bears larger flowers, up to half an inch across. Forms of the plant exist, however, that produce flowers of rose, deep pink, crimson, or purple. Seed of individual colors is offered, but a mix of all of them is most beautiful.

Gypsophila elegans is prized as a cut flower, adding lightness and delicacy to summer bouquets. In fact, however, its perennial cousin, *G. paniculata* (pa-ni-cu-LA-ta), the "baby's breath" of florists, is better for that as its sprays of flower last very much longer in water and retain their color and form even when dried. *G. elegans* is best thought of as a garden or annual flowering meadow plant, and it would be very fine if its bloom period—and indeed its whole life as a plant—were not so brief. It still has value, for like other ephemeral annuals such as *Ammi majus,* the annual Queen Anne's lace, or *Nigella damascena,* love in a mist, seed may be sprinkled among perennials or other annuals for a quick and brief display of flower while they are still developing. All three plants are so delicate of leaf and stem that they cause no harm by crowding their neighbors, and they quietly melt away when their bloom is over. Alternatively, an out-of-the-way patch of the garden can be sown thickly with *G. elegans,* perhaps in all its lovely colors together, enjoyed for its brief period of flower, then repeat seeded with gypsophila or turned to some other use.

Gypsophila elegans will bloom in about eight weeks from seed, and often a second generation of plants will occur at the end of the summer from seed scattered by others at its beginning. Because it is so rapid of development, and because it resents root disturbance, little is really gained by starting it indoors. However, gardeners who are for some reason in a hurry to have it can sow seed about six weeks before the last frost date. It should be sown in plastic cell packs and transplanted after frost with great care. *G. elegans* is a hardy annual originating in the Caucasus, and so the correct time for seeding it outdoors is while the weather is still quite cool, just around the last frost date—sometime in April in most American gardens. In warm climates it may also be seeded in late autumn for strong plants the following spring. Seedlings should be thinned to stand fairly close together, about four inches apart, for mutual support. For a steady supply of flowers in the cutting garden, seed may also be sown at intervals of two to three weeks from early spring until midsummer.

In addition to *Gypsophila elegans,* another annual species, *G. muralis* (mew-RA-lis), is sometimes offered by nurseries specializing in unusual annual and tender plants. Called "cushion baby's breath," it makes a low, sprawling mound to about a foot tall and across, covered with hundreds of tiny one-eighth-inch-wide dusty pink flowers from June to October. A native of Europe, it grows naturally on limestone outcroppings and decayed mortared walls from which it draws its species name *muralis,* meaning of walls. Because of its delicacy of texture, its growth habit, and its preference for warm conditions and sharp drainage, it is a perfect subject for containers or for hanging baskets, where it lightens mixed plantings and where the beauty of its tiny flowers may be appreciated up close. Recently a form that produces double and semi-double flowers has appeared and is to be preferred over the species form, since the doubling adds more substance to the plant that otherwise can tend to fade away in a mist when viewed at some distance.

As the genus name suggests (from ancient Greek *gypsos,* meaning gypsum or lime, and *philos,* love), all gypsophila grow best on sweet soils, and so where soils are very acidic they will appreciate a dressing of powdered or pelleted lime. Though bloom in very hot gardens may be prolonged a bit by afternoon shade, for the most part all members of the genus demand full sun.

HALORAGIS ERECTA

FAMILY: *Haloragaceae* (*Haloradigaceae*) or water milfoil family.

CLASSIFICATION: Tender perennial grown as tender annual.

COMMON NAMES: Toatoa, haloragis.

HARDINESS: Possibly root-hardy to Zone 8; leaves are sensitive to light frosts.

GROWING CONDITIONS: Rich, evenly moist, well-drained soil. Full sun to afternoon shade.

PROPAGATION: By seed, sown indoors 6 to 8 weeks before frost. Tip cuttings root easily.

HEIGHT: To 2'.

ORNAMENTAL VALUE: Grown for richly colored leaves.

LEVEL OF CULTURAL DIFFICULTY: Easy.

SPECIAL PROPERTIES: Excellent container plant. Performs well as a winter houseplant.

PRONUNCIATION: ha-lo-RA-gis ee-REC-ta

Familial relationships among plants, just as those among people, can sometimes be odd. No clearer example exists than in the family Haloragaceae (sometimes Haloradigaceae), which contains two completely dissimilar plants: *Myriophyllum aquaticum* (miri-o-PHIL-um a-QUA-ti-cim), the ferny-leaved milfoil or parrot's feather sometimes cultivated in aquariums and ponds for its diaphanous growth, and *Gunnera manicata* (GUN-uh-ra man-i-CA-ta), a plant possessed of the largest leaves of any perennial, huge, raspy, lobed palms sometimes as wide as nine feet across.

Recently, another genus within the family Haloragaceae that resembles neither of its cousins has begun to appear in gardens—*Haloragis* in the bronze-leaved selection of the species *erecta* (ee-REC-ta). The most desirable form of the plant is the cultivar 'Rubra' with shiny leaves of olive-drab overlaid with shades of maroon and brownish purple. Spikes of greenish-yellow flowers, charitably described as interesting, develop in mid- to late summer, though they are not the reason for growing the plant, which is of value solely for its attractive foliage. A true perennial, *H. erecta* quickly develops from seed or from rooted cuttings into a branched mound as much as two feet tall, thick with inch-long, oval, alternate leaves, toothed along their margins like the blade of a saw.

A native of New Zealand, *Haloragis erecta* has been under cultivation for so short a time that few references to it exist and even the spelling of the name (sometimes *Halorages*) is confused. Its exact hardiness is uncertain, though one would guess from its origins that it would be root-hardy probably into warm Zone 8 and would be one of many plants gardeners in that zone would choose to leave in the ground with a little extra winter protection.

Seed of *Haloragis erecta* 'Rubra' is offered and should be sown six to eight weeks indoors before the last anticipated frost date. The plant is usually cultivated, however, from tip cuttings, which root readily. Well-developed, youthful specimens can be acquired from nurseries or mail order catalogues specializing in unusual tender plants. Haloragis prefers a rich, fibrous, well-drained soil though it demands abundant moisture and will flag quickly when its roots dry out. The best coloration occurs when it is grown in full sun, but in warmer gardens it will appreciate afternoon shade. The bronze tints of its foliage make it a useful and attractive foil for plants grown for flowers. It makes a superb container plant, whether grown alone or in combination with other plants with similar cultural needs. At summer's end, plants may be lifted, potted, and cut back, or cuttings may be taken for plants that will remain attractive in the greenhouse or on a sunny windowsill all winter, and that can be returned to the garden the following summer.

HELIANTHUS ANNUUS

FAMILY: *Asteraceae* or aster or daisy family.

CLASSIFICATION: Hardy annual.

COMMON NAMES: Sunflower, annual helianthus.

HARDINESS: Withstands light frosts.

GROWING CONDITIONS: Any well-drained, moderately fertile soil. Full sun.

PROPAGATION: From seed sown in spring, preferably in place. May be sown indoors 4 weeks before frost.

HEIGHT: Variable from 15″ to 15′, depending on cultivar.

ORNAMENTAL VALUE: Grown principally for flower, but useful as annual hedges.

LEVEL OF CULTURAL DIFFICULTY: Easy.

SPECIAL PROPERTIES: Valued for its oil-rich seed. Drought tolerant.

PRONUNCIATION: he-li-AN-thus AN-u-us

*I*t is probably true that no annual has received such affection as have sunflowers, which are routinely described by garden writers as "friendly," "cheerful," and "undemanding." All they ask to flourish, apparently, is sunshine, for they accept all soils and have naturalized in sour vacant lots and neglected waste places in inner cities as willingly as in the more salubrious environments of field edges and country roadsides. Their amiability and ease of culture is matched only by their economic value, for their seed contains as much as 30 percent its own weight in oil, which is healthful and easy to extract. From agricultural land too poor for corn and other cereal crops, and without costly irrigation, 200 bushels of seed can be produced from a sowing of about three quarts, providing nourishment for people, for livestock, for domestic poultry, and for wild birds.

Occurring naturally in the western half of North America from Minnesota to California, *Helianthus annuus* was recognized as a valuable crop by Native Americans, and harvested seed has been found in archeological remains dating from 3000 B.C. By the time Europeans arrived in the New World, the cultivation of sunflowers extended throughout North America and into much of South America, where the Incas developed the first large-seeded cultivars. The history of sunflowers as ornamental plants, by comparison, is very brief, for the beautiful forms accessible to us are essentially twentieth-century creations, and the last ten years have seen the greatest advance in their breeding.

Easily the most familiar sunflower is still the one chiefly grown for its seed, the cultivar called 'Russian Giant'. It produces a single, huge, twelve- to fourteen-inch-wide flower on a straight-up pole as tall as fourteen feet, making it both the tallest and the widest-flowered of all annuals. Whether it has any ornamental value depends, perhaps, on the wit with which it is planted, for it is at best a funny-looking thing, seeming to nod its head in shame at its gawky extent, but in fact bending downward under the sheer weight of its seed, which are arranged with fantastic symmetry, a quality known as "phyllotaxy" by botanists. Probably no plant is more frequently recommended for introducing children to gardening, for the seeds are large and comfortable in a small hand. It is satisfying to children to press them, one by one, edge-wise, into moist ground; germination occurs speedily (within a week if the soil is warm and frosts are over), and growth is very rapid.

Some children are destined to be gardeners no matter how they start, however, and for them growing something that is genuinely pretty might be more satisfying than growing something that is simply very big and very odd. Fortunately, many cultivars of *Helianthus annuus* exist that are beautiful in the eyes of all gardeners. In 1910, a chestnut-red form of *H. annuus*—or perhaps of *H. debilis* (DEH-bi-lis), another annual species, or perhaps a cross between the two—occurred spontaneously in a field in California. From that chance variant or hybrid, many beautifully colored sunflowers have descended, adding tints of copper and bronze, maroon red, and lately, almost pink to the original egg-yolk yellow of the species. *H. debilis,* worth growing on its own for its clear yellow flowers with burgundy red centers and shadings, also contributed a branching, bushy growth to modern hybrids, and in its subspecies *cucumerifolius* (kew-kew-mer-i-FO-lee-us), the cucumber-leaf sunflower, the dwarf habit of many modern forms that are less than fifteen inches tall. A naturally occurring double form of *H. debilis,* the cultivar 'Flore-Pleno' (FLO-reh-PLAY-no), has also helped to increase the ray petals in the blossoms of some sunflowers. Breeding work has also extended to softer colors of primrose yellow and near-white on freely branching plants with small flowers that seem at home in the mixed border. There are even pollen-free forms that will not shed on table tops when picked for indoor decoration.

No annual plant is easier to grow than sunflowers, which seem intolerant only of shade, a fact made abundantly clear by both their popular and genus name (from ancient Greek *helios,* signifying

HELIANTHUS ANNUUS

sun, and *anthos,* flower). In fact, sunflowers follow the sun in its progress across the sky, turning their blooms from east to west like sunbathers in deck chairs. Because of their love of the sun and their rapidity of growth, little is probably gained by starting them early indoors, as it is hard to give them enough light to develop well, and they quickly become spindly and weak. Better results are had by sowing the seed outdoors after the soil has warmed and all danger of frost is past, though if it is more convenient to establish plants than seed—in a grassy meadow, for example—seed should be started no earlier than three weeks before the last anticipated frost date. Taller varieties may topple over in windy summer rainstorms, but they will topple at ground level, and so individual stakes need not be more than two feet tall.

Helianthus annuus are at once so naïve and so wonderful that a fistful of them crammed into a mason jar cannot be anything but beautiful. It is also possible to buy huge single blossoms on three-foot stems from street florists throughout most of the winter. Such gawky rods, each with a single flower at the top, would be much harder to integrate tactfully into the summer garden than smaller-flowered, much-branched plants such as the pale yellow 'Stella', or the even paler 'Italian

White', but indoors they brighten the first months of the year.

Sunflowers are hardy annuals, and once grown may reappear from year to year though they will generally revert to the original yellow of *Helianthus annuus.* Even seed scattered from feeders by birds may germinate, but the seed and husks of sunflowers possess a quality known as "phytotoxicity," which inhibits or prevents the growth of other plants, even lawn grass. It is a clever mechanism to eliminate competition possessed by other cunning plants such as the English lawn daisy (*Bellis perennis*), foxgloves (*Digitalis purpurea*), and the American black walnut (*Juglans nigra*). Where bird feeders are stocked with sunflower seed, therefore, the husks and fallen seed should be carefully scraped away.

HELICHRYSUM SPECIES

FAMILY: *Asteraceae* or aster or daisy family.

CLASSIFICATION: Tender annual, perennial, or shrub grown as half-hardy annual.

COMMON NAMES: Strawflower, everlasting, paper daisy, immortelle, helichrysum.

HARDINESS: Hardy in Zones 9 and 10. Frost-sensitive elsewhere.

GROWING CONDITIONS: Moderately fertile, well-drained soil. Full sun.

PROPAGATION: By seed sown indoors 6 to 8 weeks before last frost. Nursery stock is grown from tip cuttings.

HEIGHT: Variable from 1 to 3', depending on cultural conditions.

ORNAMENTAL VALUE: Principally for flowers, which retain their color when dried. *H. petiolare* is grown for silver, chartreuse, or white-splashed leaves.

LEVEL OF CULTURAL DIFFICULTY: Easy in suitable climates, moderately difficult elsewhere.

SPECIAL PROPERTIES: Valued as a dried flower.

PRONUNCIATION: he-lee-KRI-sum

The familiar strawflower of old-fashioned gardens is still listed in most catalogues and garden references as *Helichrysum bracteatum* (brac-tee-A-tum) and is treated here under that name. Its new name, however, *Bracteantha bracteata,* acknowledges in both genus and species its most salient floral characteristic, as well as that of most helichrysums: The blossoms possess no real petals, but rather papery or chaffy bracts that surround the disk of true flowers in the center. As with other everlasting flowers—*Amobium alatum, Gomphrena globosa, Salvia horminum*—it is these bracts that make the plant so desirable for winter bouquets since they hold their color when dried. Indeed, the popular name of *H. bracteatum,* "immortelle," attests to the popularity its flowers once had when used in winter funeral wreaths when fresh flowers were not available.

Because of its popularity in the florists' trade as a dried flower—and lately a fresh flower, for it lasts a very long time in a vase—much work has been done on it, particularly in Germany, to produce plants with a fantastic color range. So one may now have helichrysums in white and all the warm colors of the spectrum, from ivory to lemon and egg-yolk yellow to orange, scarlet, light and deep pink, crimson, an almost true red, tan, bronze, and mahogany. Many of these colors are available separately, which is useful to the gardener concerned with specific color schemes, though generally, strawflowers, like zinnias, have a warm bright beauty when planted all together in many shades.

Since the naturally occurring form of the plant called "Monstrosum" (mon-STROW-sum), with flowers up to an inch wide, has chiefly been used as a base for breeding, modern cultivars bear flowers as much as two and a half inches wide, consisting of many layers of varnished, pointed bracts surrounding a central disk. The bracts, borne terminally on strong stems, show color even when they are very small, tightly clasped buds. About halfway through their process of unfolding, flowers wanted for winter bouquets should be cut and hung upside down in an airy place to dry, and their leaves stripped away. Even when fully dried, however, flowers may be weak at the neck, a problem florists solve by inserting a thin wire through the stem and out through the blossom, bending it into a tiny hook, and drawing it back through the center. But this takes a strong sense of purpose, because the flowers are particularly pretty as they unfold with a cone of immature bracts surrounded by a ruff of open ones, and fully opened flowers are equally pretty, showing an inner row of bracts curving upward, cupping the disk of true flowers that unfold very slowly. Individual blossoms may last almost a month, depending on the weather, so many gardeners tend to leave them in the garden.

Helichrysum bracteatum is a very variable species, so much so that it must be tempting to graduate students in botany as a possible Ph.D. dissertation. Whether it is annual, perennial, or a shrub depends in part on where seed was gathered, and in part on how it has been hybridized and selected.

Weather seems to be everything to strawflowers. They appear to perform best in warm, dry gardens, especially where soils are not over-rich or over-moist. But wherever they are grown, it is obvious that they, like any plant with the name of the sun in it (from ancient Greek *helios,* for sun, and *chrysos,* golden), need as much sunlight as they can have. They will fail miserably when even a few hours of shade fall across them. Also,

HELICHRYSUM BRACTEATUM (BRACTEANTHA BRACTEATA)

helichrysums detest heavy clay soils, muggy, humid days, or frequent summer rains. Although flower production can be increased by humus-rich soils or biweekly feeding with water-soluble fertilizers, color and keeping-quality will be poorer and the lower leaves of plants may shrivel away. Where helichrysums grow well, however, they are invaluable for summer decoration, and in the dryer parts of Zones 9 and 10, where they are hardy, they will be either perennial or shrubby, blooming virtually all the year.

H. bracteatum may be started indoors about four to six weeks before the last anticipated frost date, and grown on in bright, cool conditions, kept only moderately watered until plants can be hardened off, and transplanted into the garden after all danger of frost is past. Alternatively, sturdy young plants, already showing bloom and identifying their colors, can be bought from nurseries or garden centers specializing in unusual annuals and tender plants.

Though forms of strawflower most frequently offered by nurseries will probably be *H. bracteatum,* another helichrysum, *H. petiolare* (pey-tee-o-LA-ray) (sometimes incorrectly *petiolatum*), is also very often available. In Zones 9 and 10, where it is perennial, it will produce, in winter, chaffy white flowers that make its kinship to other helichrysums recognizable, but in most gardens it is essentially grown as a foliage plant. It is popularly called "licorice plant" from the fact that under certain rare conditions its leaves will give off a very faint scent of licorice. (The licorice of commerce is produced by quite another plant, *Glycyrrhiza glabra* [glie-sir-EYE-za GLA-bra].) A true perennial, *H. petiolare* typically bears downy, silvery leaves about three-quarters of an inch long on thin, wiry stems that weave in and out of other plants, nicely knitting mixed plantings in containers together.

Its silver form is splendid, but it has been almost overshadowed by a chartreuse-yellow cultivar, 'Limelight', which brings brightness to any combination of plants grown in containers. Also attractive is a subtle, silver- and white-leaved cultivar, 'Variegatum' (var-ee-uh-GA-tum), though it is a less vigorous grower than either the silver or chartreuse forms. No form of licorice plant is grown from seed, though it could be. Plants are generally produced from tip cuttings, which root readily, and which quickly produce attractive, youthful specimens for planting in the garden, or in window boxes, pots, or other containers, after all danger of frost is past.

HELICHRYSUM PETIOLARE

Even after botanists detached *Helichrysum bracteatum* and placed it in the much smaller genus *Bracteantha,* dozens of garden-worthy species and cultivars remain. Indeed, there are astonishing riches in the genus *Helichrysum* with 300 to 500 species. The numbers suggest an unusually wide margin for botanical miscounting and rearrangement. In fact, the genus has been poorly studied, and many species in the wild remain undescribed, chiefly in the most southern parts of the Eastern Hemisphere, particularly in South Africa and Australia.

Where the species grows well, gardeners will want to be alert to other helichrysums sure to become available. Notable among them is *H. cassianum* (cas-SEE-a-num), the tiny, quarter-inch-wide, starry dried flowers in pink or white that are familiar in tight bunches at florists' and crafts shops. It makes an excellent garden plant, producing a shrubby bush to about a foot tall and flowering abundantly throughout the summer. Worth considering also are *H. davenportii* (da-vin-POR-tee-ee), a true annual about a foot tall bearing pink, typically papery flower heads about an inch across, and *H. elatum* (ee-LAY-tum), a perennial usually grown as an annual, which achieves a height of about three feet, with attractive, whitish, hairy leaves and two-inch-wide flower heads of papery bracts and a yellow disk.

HELIOPHILA LONGIFOLIA

FAMILY: *Brassicaceae* or cabbage family.
CLASSIFICATION: Half-hardy annual.
COMMON NAMES: Cape stock, heliophila.
HARDINESS: Damaged by light frosts.
GROWING CONDITIONS: Fertile, well-drained, evenly moist soil. Full sun. Cool weather.

PROPAGATION: By seed, sown indoors 6 to 8 weeks
    before last frost, or in place in the garden
    when conditions become warm and settled.

HEIGHT: 8 to 12″.

ORNAMENTAL VALUE: Valued for flowers.

LEVEL OF CULTURAL DIFFICULTY: Moderately easy in
    cool moist gardens, difficult elsewhere.

SPECIAL PROPERTIES: None.

PRONUNCIATION: he-lee-o-PHIL-a lon-ji-FOL-ee-a

*T*hose who feel compelled to give common names to unusual garden plants often display an extraordinary lack of imagination. This is never more true than when a vernacular name is borrowed from one plant to apply to another. Stock, the common name for *Mattiola incana* (matt-ee-O-la in-KA-na), suits their tight-crowded clubs of flower. The word is drawn from Old High German into medieval English and applies to wooden uprights and beams, brood cows and sheep, extending from that sense of animals as wealth eventually to the very basis of modern commerce.

By contrast, the two or possibly three species of *Heliophila* grown in gardens, though popularly called "cape stocks," are remarkable for their unsubstantial delicacy and airy grace. The species most often cultivated is *Heliophila longifolia,* the long-leaved cape stock, a true annual that produces a tidy but delicate plant to about a foot tall, with many wandlike stems furnished with narrow, bladelike blue-green leaves about two inches long. The stems terminate in racemes of widely spaced, half-inch-wide flowers, composed of four rounded petals (typical of most members of the family Brassicaceae [bra-see-A-see-aye]) of a clear, sky blue. At the center of the flower, the petals are pinched up into a white corolla like the cup of a miniature daffodil, giv-

ing each flower a winsome eye. Quite similar in effect is *H. leptophylla* (lep-toe-FILL-a), though its flowers are yellow-centered. A shrubby form of *Heliophila*—*H. linearifolia* (lin-ee-ah-ri-FOL-ee-a)—is also sometimes grown, particularly in cool greenhouses, where it blooms as single plants in five-inch pots in late spring from seed sown in September. It forms a compact, bushy plant from one to two feet tall, and bears abundant powder-blue flowers, the petals of which are pinched into slender, yellow stems where each meets the center of the blossom, an effect botanists call "clawed." Oddly, for a plant bearing the name of the sun, its flowers tend to close at midday, making it of limited use as a summer bedding plant.

The genus, composed entirely of plants native to South Africa, is moderately large, containing perhaps 100 species, all lovers of the sun, as the genus name (from ancient Greek *helios,* meaning sun, and *philein,* to love) attests. Heliophilas come quickly into bloom, but they remain in flower fairly briefly, about six weeks or so, and therefore might be grown for attractive, early bloom among developing perennials or other annuals. For early flower, seed should be started indoors about six weeks before the last anticipated frost date and young plants grown on in full sun, hardened off, and transplanted into permanent positions when all danger of frost is past. They are impatient of transplanting, and so should be grown in peat pots or plastic cell packs, and disturbed as little as possible at the roots when put into their permanent positions. Because of their delicacy of form, plants should be established rather closely, about six to eight inches apart. Good garden soil is preferred—fertile and well drained—and of course full sun. Successive sowings for continuing flower may be made every four weeks or so directly where the plants are to grow, though heliophilas bloom best in cool

HELIOPHILA LONGIFOLIA

SPECIAL PROPERTIES: Powerful scent. May be grown
   as a houseplant or cool greenhouse plant in
   winter. Drought tolerant.
PRONUNCIATION: he-lee-o-TRO-pee-um ar-bor-ESS-
   ens

summer weather, tending to flag in the hot, steamy conditions that obtain in most American gardens in late July and August. Where they grow well, they make invaluable cut flowers.

HELIOTROPIUM ARBORESCENS

FAMILY: *Boraginaceae* or borage family.

CLASSIFICATION: Tender shrub grown as a tender
   annual.

COMMON NAMES: Cherry pie, heliotrope.

HARDINESS: Damaged at temperatures below 40°F
   and killed by frost. Sensitive to cold, damp
   weather.

GROWING CONDITIONS: Very rich, well-drained soil.
   Moderate water. Full sun. Prefers heat.

PROPAGATION: Usually by cuttings, particularly of
   desirable forms, or from seed, started indoors 6
   to 8 weeks before frost.

HEIGHT: Up to 12′ where hardy. Variable in gardens, depending on training, from 1 to 6′.

ORNAMENTAL VALUE: Valued for flower.

LEVEL OF CULTURAL DIFFICULTY: Moderately difficult.

$\mathcal{A}$ powerful fragrance is not among the gifts of most annuals and tender plants. Where scent is present, it is generally mild and gentle (petunias, annual phlox, violas, sweet alyssum) or occasion-ally sharp and pungent (marigolds and certain an-nual chrysanthemums). Heliotrope is an exception to this rule, for in the right cultivars the fragrance is very strong, giving the impression, as one bends toward its blossoms, of a perfume bottle unstopped.

That is not the end of its charms, however, for though the naturally occurring species, a native of the Peruvian Andes, produce flowers of pale pink-ish violet, the most popular garden heliotropes have been bred into deep and sumptuous shades of purple, a color seeming almost a visual repre-sentation of their scent. And though heliotropes may be grown from seed started indoors about ten or twelve weeks before the last anticipated frost date, those with the richest colors and finest scents are generally propagated from cuttings.

Though there are as many as 200 species in the genus *Heliotropium,* only *H. arborescens* is under general cultivation. It is sometimes offered under the synonyms *H. peruvianum* (pe-ru-vee-AN-um) and *H. corymbosum* (kor-im-BO-sum), but its proper species name, *arborescens,* attests to the fact that it is a plant of stout, woody, shrublike growth, reaching a height of as much as twelve feet where it is hardy in Zones 9 and 10, useful there even for hedges. It commends itself to this purpose not only by its shrubby, compact habit of growth and its fragrant flowers, but also by its leaves, which are pointed ovals about three inches long, heavily quilted where the prominent veins cause the surrounding leaf tissue to pucker, and of a rich dark green often overcast with purple. Where heliotrope is not hardy, however, it is a valuable plant for summer bedding and for use in containers, particularly around terraces, decks, and swimming pools, or wherever its remarkable fragrance may be especially enjoyed. The woody character of the plant also makes it an ideal candidate for training into standards: small, mop-headed trees that lift the scent closer to nose level.

Heliotrope is extremely frost-sensitive, but at the end of summer it may be lifted from beds, cut back hard, and regrown on a warm windowsill with the hope of some flower during the darkest months of the year. Potted specimens need only to be kept moderately dry in sunny conditions around 50°F until new growth appears. They should then be given dilute doses of liquid plant food to encourage leaf growth and flower.

Heliotrope is of easy culture, though its needs are particular and must be met. It thrives in rich, well-drained, humusy soil, though unlike most plants with those preferences, it is sensitive to over-watering, which will quickly cause blackening of the leaves, root rot, and perhaps even the death of the plant. Full sun is required, and it flowers best in warmer gardens, sometimes proving sulky in those with cool, moist nights. Such requirements make it suitable for container culture, of course, and so many gardeners grow plants in pots to drop into gaps in the border created by the passing of early-flowering annuals and biennials, such as opium poppies, foxgloves, and hesperus.

Heliotropium is a famous botanical misnomer, for it means turning with the sun, from ancient Greek *helios,* signifying sun, and *trope,* to turn. Certain plants like the common sunflower do that, but heliotropes budge not an inch. An old-

HELIOTROPIUM ARBORESCENS

fashioned name for heliotrope, now not much used, is "cherry pie," from the cooked sugar and fruit smell of its flowers. Though the Incas are said to have used an infusion of the leaves to reduce fevers, all parts of the plant are toxic.

HIBISCUS SPECIES

FAMILY: *Malvaceae* or mallow family.

CLASSIFICATION: Shrubs, shrubby perennials, and tender annuals cultivated as half-hardy or tender shrubs.

COMMON NAME: Hibiscus (other common names vary with species).

HARDINESS: Extremely frost sensitive.

GROWING CONDITIONS: Light, fertile, well-drained soil. Shrubby species require abundant moisture, but perfect drainage. Full sun.

PROPAGATION: By seed for annual species, sown 6 to 8 weeks before last frost date. Rooted cuttings for shrubby species. Annual species resent root disturbance.

HEIGHT: Variable. Shrubby species may reach 12′
where hardy. True annuals vary from 1 to 4′, according to species.

ORNAMENTAL VALUE: Grown principally for flower,
or, in some species, for leaf color.

LEVEL OF CULTURAL DIFFICULTY: Easy.

SPECIAL PROPERTIES: Some species are used in per-
fumery, as salad greens, or as preserved fruits,
and for strong stem fiber that may be woven
into ropes or baskets.

PRONUNCIATION: hi-BIS-cus

The genus *Hibiscus* contains between 150 and 200 species, ranging from stout, woody, treelike plants through shrubby and clumping perennials to true annuals. The genus name descends directly from the ancient Greek word for mallows, species of which have been cultivated for more than 3,000 years for many uses, including perfumes and medicines, dye-stuffs and cosmetics, fiber and vegetables. Far-flung and diverse, the genus occurs throughout tropical, subtropical, and warm-temperate regions of the globe, and in habitats ranging from arid gravelly hillsides and dry open scrub land to bogs, streamsides, and deep, fecund jungles.

As one might expect from so varied a genus, it is in constant botanical flux. Indeed, many species formerly listed in *Hibiscus* have migrated to *Abelmoschus*. Left behind, however, are many plants frequently cultivated, all of which differ from *Abelmoschus* merely in possessing a calyx that is not split.

The two species in the genus *Hibiscus* most familiar to gardeners are probably *H. rosa-sinensis* (RO-sa sin-EN-sis) and *H. syriacus* (si-ree-A-cus). The former, a tender woody shrub, produces magnificent six- to eight-inch-wide flowers all summer long in colors that range from white through primrose yellow to scarlet, orange, and deep red. It will be the flower tucked behind the ear of the prototypical Hawaiian maiden, since its blooms have the peculiar property of remaining fresh a full day out of water (and for a much shorter time when put in a vase). *Hibiscus syriacus,* by contrast, though a native of eastern Asia, is the much-beloved althaea or rose of Sharon of American gardens, where it thrives in almost all zones, enlivening the August slump with its four-inch-wide single or double flowers of white, pink, and lavender blue. Both species are enduring shrubs, sometimes attaining great age, though gardeners without facilities for overwintering *H. rosa-sinensis* often treat nursery-grown plants as annuals, enjoying them in pots and containers through the summer and discarding them when frost blackens their leaves.

One very desirable plant still in the genus *Hibiscus* is a true annual that deserves more attention than it generally gets. That is *Hibiscus trionum* (tri-O-num), whose common name, "flower of an hour," has probably hurt its chances in gardens, though the flowers of most hibiscus last hardly a day. *H. trionum,* however, will only flower in sunny weather, and closes when clouds spread over summer skies. Still, it is a charming plant, producing small, sturdy bushes to about two feet tall, decorated by beautiful, three-fingered lobed leaves of a green so dark as almost to be black. Flowers are borne in profusion from July to frost on plants started indoors in early March or about six weeks before the last anticipated frost date. Each flower is about two and a half inches across, of a gentle primrose yellow shading at the center to burgundy, the rich color of which nicely sets off the orange pollen-laden stamens that surround the turkey-red pistil. Any garden soil seems to suit the plant, but flowers

HIBISCUS ROSA-SINENSIS

HIBISCUS TRIONUM

will be most abundantly produced in light, fertile but dryish conditions.

Though a native of central Africa, *Hibiscus trionum* is surprisingly seed-hardy, often reappearing even in cold Zone 4 gardens as a volunteer for many years after the plant has been grown. Seedlings often appear where they look best, along a path or in an uncultivated corner of the garden, in accidental places that suit their shy, somehow antique beauty. But once recognized they may be transplanted, always with a generous ball of earth, for they resent root disturbance.

One species of *Hibiscus* not grown for its flowers but for its leaves is *H. acetosella* (a-see-tow-SELL-a), a shrubby perennial native to central East Africa. It has been cultivated for centuries both as a salad crop and cooked greens. In the species form, its handsome, maplelike leaves are a dark, burnished green overcast with maroon, and are borne on stout, shrublike bushes as tall as five feet. Plants are useful at the back of the perennial or annual border for weight and substance or to create a hedge. Recently an even better, burgundy-leaved cultivar has appeared in seed catalogues—

marketed as 'Coppertone' or 'Red Shield'—that may become an invaluable, almost indispensable border plant when grown as a tender annual. Plants of either the bronze- or burgundy-leaved form should be started indoors about eight weeks before the last anticipated frost date. Young plants should be hardened off and transplanted into their permanent positions when the weather is settled and warm. Care should be taken in transplanting as plants may be permanently stunted from too much disturbance at their roots. *H. acetosella* relishes a deep, fertile, well-drained soil and plenty of moisture and heat. In frost-free gardens, attractive, typically mallowlike flowers, yellow with a maroon center or purplish red, will be borne singly in the axils of the leaves in about ten months from seed germination.

One other annual hibiscus, *H. sabdariffa* (sab-DAR-ih-fa), is occasionally grown more as an oddity than for any practical purposes, though where it really thrives—in the warmest parts of Zones 9 and 10—it was once an important garden vegetable. Called "roselle," "Jamaica sorrel," or "India sorrel," it is probably a native of tropical Africa, though it is now widely naturalized from cultivated stock throughout the tropical world. It is perennial, in the sense that many plants may be perennial where frost never occurs, but it is generally cultivated as an annual, making a tall, upright bush to five feet or more in its first season and producing abundant, five-fingered, handlike, dark green leaves about four inches across. They are sometimes added to curries and salads when small, to impart a sharp acid flavor something like that of true garden sorrel, *Rumex acetosa* (ROO-mex a-ce-TO-sa). Flowering begins when the days shorten in late summer, but the typical mallowlike blossoms last briefly, no more than a day, dropping off to make way for quickly enlarging, fruitlike calyxes of dull purple. These are harvested when barely mature and are used to impart a pleasant acid flavor to summer drinks and teas, jellies, jams, and sauces. At one time, the plant was of considerable importance in the Tropics as a substitute for cranberries or currants, neither of which thrives in very warm climates. But as it requires a long and hot growing season, and as the smallest touch of frost inhibits flowering, it is of little value except in those American gardens where poinsettias flourish outdoors. In the Tropics, it is still cultivated for the strong, pliable fibers of its inner stems, which may be woven into ropes or fabrics much like jute or hemp.

HIBISCUS ACETOSELLA

HUMULUS JAPONICUS

FAMILY: *Cannabinaceae* or marijuana family.

CLASSIFICATION: Tender perennial vine grown as half-hardy annual vine.

COMMON NAMES: Japanese hop, annual hop.

HARDINESS: Root-hardy to Zone 9. Leaves damaged by light frosts.

GROWING CONDITIONS: Rich, fertile, well-drained soil. Full sun to part shade.

PROPAGATION: From seed, sown indoors 8 to 10 weeks before last frost.

HEIGHT: Vining, to 20′ in a season.

ORNAMENTAL VALUE: Quick-growing vine with attractive cream- and white-splashed leaves.

LEVEL OF CULTURAL DIFFICULTY: Easy.

SPECIAL PROPERTIES: Valuable for covering porches, arbors, old tractors, or anything else over which a scrambling vine is needed.

PRONUNCIATION: HU-mu-lus ja-PON-i-cus

The hop grown to flavor, clarify, and preserve beer is *Humulus lupulus* (loo-PU-lus). A hardy perennial vine, it is quite pretty in a wild, rampant sort of way, and the strobiles—scaly cones the size of an acorn, borne by female vines—are both curious and beautiful. They are also rich with a liquid alkaloid called "lupulin," the substance that gives the hop flavor to beer. For decorative purposes, a very fine golden-leaved male form of the commercial hop exists, as well as a deep maroon-leaved female vine.

The Japanese hop is as pretty as either of these, though it has no commercial uses in brewing. Like its European cousin, *Humulus japonicus* is also a perennial vine, dying to the ground each year and re-sprouting in spring from its roots. It

HUMULUS JAPONICUS

is not root-hardy much north of USDA Zone 9, however, but its growth is so rapid that it is often planted as an annual. A single plant may reach a height of twenty feet in a season, branching freely and draping itself over any support its questing, hairy stems can find. It is thus grown to shade porches or pergolas, on trellises against buildings, or to conceal unsightly objects in the summer. Its maplelike, lobed leaves are about four inches long and as wide, and are borne opposite each other on petioles about five inches long. Leaves, stems, and petioles are raspy to the touch, covered with tiny, stiff hairs hooked at their ends, somewhat like Velcro. Though the typical form bears attractive, medium-green leaves, it is the variegated form, with leaves of light green attractively splashed with white or cream, that is usually cultivated.

Japanese hops should be sown indoors about eight to ten weeks before the last anticipated frost date or outdoors after all danger of frost is past. An early start is advisable, however, because it may take as long as a month to germinate, though the seed may be hastened a little by nicking and soaking them overnight before sowing. Because young plants resent root disturbance, seed should be sown in peat pots, three to a pot. Not all the seedlings will show desirable variegation, however, and so those with less vivid markings should be clipped away with scissors as soon as their leaves can be evaluated. For this reason it is well to sow at least six or more peat pots, later giving away well-colored unwanted extras to gardening friends. Young plants should be hardened off carefully and planted outdoors when the weather becomes mild and settled, as they are sensitive to frost.

The supports provided for the vines must be very sturdy. It is easy to underestimate their rampant growth and their resulting weight. They will also quickly smother any other plants with which they come in contact, and so should not be planted at the base of spring-flowering shrubs. The stems of the vine twine from left to right, and the first shoot may need some help in finding the support provided for it. Stems are quite brittle at their tips, however, and should be handled gently. There is no way to determine the sex of an individual vine until it flowers, but with luck, one will have both a male and a female, in which case the female will bear attractive fruit in late summer, quite similar in appearance to the female beer hop. Fertilization from a male vine will provide seed for successive generations in the garden and to share with other gardeners.

HUNNEMANNIA FUMARIIFOLIA

FAMILY: *Papaveraceae* or poppy family.
CLASSIFICATION: Tender perennial grown as half-hardy annual.
COMMON NAMES: Mexican tulip poppy, gold cups, hunnemannia.

HARDINESS: Sensitive to light frosts.

GROWING CONDITIONS: Lean, gravelly, perfectly drained soil. Full sun.

PROPAGATION: By seed, preferably sown in place in mid-spring. Seed may be started indoors 8 weeks before last frost. Seedlings are intolerant of root disturbance.

HEIGHT: 12 to 15".

ORNAMENTAL VALUE: Grown for flower.

LEVEL OF CULTURAL DIFFICULTY: Difficult.

SPECIAL PROPERTIES: May be grown in cool greenhouses for early spring flower.

PRONUNCIATION: hun-uh-MANE-ee-a fu-mah-ri-FO-lee-a

As an example of the color yellow in its clearest and most beautiful shade, nothing can match *Hunnemannia fumariifolia,* the Mexican tulip poppy. Any lemon would be dingy by comparison. Borne singly on long, graceful stems, poised well above the fringy, gray-green filigree of leaves, the poppies are typically four crepelike petals surrounding a fringe of golden anthers. The petals are held in a graceful, goblet shape very like tulips, and at their edges they sometimes look pleated, like Fortuny silk. Plants in flourishing good health may attain a height of as much as two feet, though twelve to fifteen inches is more typical, and they remain in bloom from July until frost. Unlike most poppies, which shatter after only a day or two in a vase, flowers of hunnemannia stay fresh for as much as a week if they are cut just as the buds are ready to open and the ends of the stems are seared briefly by holding them over a flame.

One might wonder why a plant with so many assets is so seldom grown. The answer, alas, is that it is difficult unless its particular needs can be met. A lean, sandy soil suits it best, and it de-mands full sun. But above everything, it requires absolutely perfect drainage. Even prolonged periods of rain or damp, muggy summer weather will cause it to rot at its roots—not surprising, because hunnemannia is a native of the drier mountains of Mexico. In gardens that experience no frost (USDA Zones 9 and 10), hunnemannia will behave as a perennial, persisting for several years from its fleshy, brittle rootstock and self-seeding abundantly. Elsewhere, it is grown as an annual, since it flowers very quickly from seed in its first year, as rapidly as five weeks from germination under good growing conditions. Though seed may be started indoors about eight weeks from the last anticipated frost date, the young seedlings often fare badly in indoor conditions. Water must be carefully applied to avoid fungus diseases and rot. Full sun is an absolute necessity. Finally, even in a family known for its difficulty in transplanting (the Papaveraceae), hunnemannia is unusually sensitive, and so plants should be seeded in peat pots and handled gently at transplant time.

For all these reasons—and given its precocity in flowering—little is probably gained by starting hunnemannia indoors, as plants may be had

HUNNEMANNIA FUMARIIFOLIA

in flower by early July from a late May sowing directly where they are to grow. Seedlings should be thinned to stand about a foot apart, and no supplementary irrigation should be supplied except in near-desert conditions. Hunnemannia's need for perfect drainage makes it suitable to grow at the top of retaining walls or in gravelly sections of the rock garden. Where soils are heavy and water retentive, it will thrive best in pots in a lean soil made up of half Pro-Mix or some other soilless potting compost and half very coarse, gravelly sand, with a generous sprinkling of lime. Pots made of unglazed clay should be used since they allow soil to dry out quickly and provide warmth at the roots that tulip poppies enjoy.

Gardeners with greenhouses who are skilled in growing tender plants for late winter and early spring bloom will find hunnemannia challenging but beautiful. Seed should be sown directly into pots in the dry weather of September, with the young plants grown outdoors until frost and then moved into a bright, airy greenhouse heated to a minimum of 50°F. If watered carefully, plants may begin flowering in late February and continue into spring.

Normally, when a flower possesses an innate grace, to double its petals is to insult its beauty; but hunnemannia is an exception. A double form called 'Sunlite', with eight rather than four petals, arranged in two layers, the lower one held flat and the upper one cupped, is, if anything, even more beautiful than the single-petaled form.

The only species in its genus, *Hunnemannia fumariifolia* commemorates John Hunneman (?–1839), a British amateur botanist. The species name, correctly *fumariifolia* but sometimes spelled *fumariaefolia,* acknowledges the resemblance of the plant's leaves to another member of the poppy family, *Fumaria officinalis.*

HYPOESTES PHYLLOSTACHYA

FAMILY: *Acanthaceae* or acanthus family.

CLASSIFICATION: Sub-shrub grown as a tender annual.

COMMON NAMES: Polka-dot plant, freckleface, measles plant, flamingo plant, baby's tears, hypoestes.

HARDINESS: Sensitive to light frosts.

GROWING CONDITIONS: Rich, well-drained, humusy soil. Moderate moisture. Part shade.

PROPAGATION: Easy from seed, sown 3 months before last frost. Select forms are grown from tip cuttings.

HEIGHT: 3' where hardy. Less than 10" when grown as an annual.

ORNAMENTAL VALUE: Grown for colorful foliage.

LEVEL OF CULTURAL DIFFICULTY: Easy.

SPECIAL PROPERTIES: Excellent for containers, particularly in light shade. Good winter houseplant or cool greenhouse plant.

PRONUNCIATION: hy-po-ES-teez fi-lo-STA-kee-a

In less than ten years, *Hypoestes phyllostachya* has gone from being a rare novelty to the darling of supermarket florists. Its appeal is immediate, consisting of numerous Pepto-Bismol-pink spots splashed on narrowly heart-shaped leaves about three inches long. The leaves begin a medium green but darken with age, making the spotted markings even more vivid. A tender sub-shrub hardy to frost-free USDA Zones 9 and 10, it can attain a height of as much as three feet, though it is generally sold as a juvenile plant, spreading low in its pot with three or four short branches shingled over with vivid leaves, and looking, to those who like it, very cute. It has an unusually large number of popular names, which in a plant usually attests to a long history in gardens, but in the case of hypoestes, it merely suggests instant popularity. It is also an easy plant, unfussy in its requirements and loving shade. In cooler gardens it will flourish as well with half a day of sun.

Whether its charm endures for most gardeners, however, is an open question, for one plant looks remarkably like the next, suggesting something made of plastic rather than something living. Most nurseries dealing in unusual annual and tender plants have ceased to offer it, but its fortunes may be improving, for selections have recently been made with white- or cream-colored spots, creating plants with a much less assertive look that are much easier to combine with other container plants or to use in bedding schemes. These new, somewhat muted selections look cool and fresh in shady parts of the garden, on terraces or decks, and particularly in combination with ferns. As the number of annual and tender plants that will accept shade is limited, new forms of hypoestes with gentler markings may prove valuable.

Most gardeners will acquire young plants of hypoestes from nurseries or perhaps from the supermarket, but it can easily be grown from seed, which germinates readily. To produce plants of significant size, however, the seed should be sown three months before the last anticipated frost. Fortunately young plants are very easy to manage, developing well on windowsills that do not receive full sun or in the shadier parts of greenhouses. They should be pinched when about six inches tall to encourage branching low on the plant. As their markings are obvious from the second set of true leaves, they can be very charming when quite small, and appealing to children, particularly under the least attractive of their common names, "measles plant."

At all stages of growth, hypoestes will require rich, fertile, well-drained soil and moderate moisture. Heavy or poorly drained soils will result in rotting at the roots and the death of the plants. Their cultural requirements are much the same as those for fuchsias, coleus, wax begonias, and tender ferns. Therefore, they can be expected to flourish in combination with these plants, assuming the typical coloration is pleasing or the white-freckled cultivar is used.

Except where it is hardy, or in gardens that experience long, frost-free autumns, hypoestes will seldom bloom, though both its genus and species names allude to its flower characteristics. *Hypoestes* is made up of two Greek words, *hypo,* signifying under, and *estia,* house or shelter, referring to the bracts that cover the calyx, a group of modified leaves that shelter the flower bud as it forms. *Phyllostachya* means leafy spike, though it is not particularly descriptive of the flowers of the plant, which are sprinkled among its leaves and consist of tiny, deep violet, half-inch tubes divided into two lips, the lower one smooth and the upper one three-lobed.

Though usually used as a summer bedding plant or in containers outdoors, hypoestes is of very easy culture as a houseplant. It requires bright light, such as might be found in an east or west window, and no direct sun. During winter, when the plant may be growing little, water should be applied only when the soil is moderately dry, approximately halfway through saturated and parched. Drainage must be perfect, and as plants resent water poured over their leaves in winter, watering should occur by standing the pots in water for an hour or two.

IBERIS SPECIES

FAMILY: *Cruciferae* or mustard family.
CLASSIFICATION: Hardy annual.
COMMON NAMES: Annual candytuft, annual iberis.

HARDINESS: Withstands light frosts.

GROWING CONDITIONS: Sandy, moderately rich,
    free-draining soil. Full sun.

PROPAGATION: From seed, sown in early spring.

HEIGHT: 16" to 2', varying with species.

ORNAMENTAL VALUE: Valued for flower and for
    scent.

LEVEL OF CULTURAL DIFFICULTY: Easy.

SPECIAL PROPERTIES: Excellent late-winter-flowering
    plant for cool greenhouses.

PRONUNCIATION: i-BER-is

"Candytuft" is a pretty word in English, seeming to compare the sugar-white or pastel colors of the often fragrant flowers of iberis to confections. In fact, however, though "tuft" describes the bush-like habit of most species grown in gardens, "candy" is a corruption of *Candia,* the Latin word for the Greek island of Crete, where certain species grow wild. All iberis are native to southern Europe, western Asia, and the Mediterranean islands, and the genus draws its name from the Latin word for Spain, Iberia. By far its most familiar species is *Iberis sempervirens* (sim-per-VIR-ens), the perennial, shrubby, evergreen plant with shiny, small green leaves and umbels of chalk-white flowers, which seems an almost obligatory companion to tulips in spring.

The annual species of *Iberis,* by comparison, are not frequently grown, though they are among the easiest of all hardy annuals. The seed of *I. umbellata* (um-be-LA-ta), the globe candytuft, germinates rapidly in a little more than a week, and it begins to flower as early as six weeks later. Because of this precocity, and also because it is capable of enduring some frost, it is most often sown directly in the garden, as early in spring as the soil may be worked, and later thinned to stand from six inches to a foot apart. It grows into a dense little bush that branches freely from the ground, but its stems are wiry and its two- to three-inch-long leaves are narrow blades, so it always preserves a look of delicacy. The flowers, as the species name indicates, are flat-topped umbels about two inches across, densely packed with tiny, four-petaled flowers in colors that range from white through pale and deep pink, lilac, violet, and purplish red. The slender branches of the plants are apt to interweave, creating a pretty effect at the front of a border with blended shades in a harmonious color range. (A scarlet red, recently developed form tends to throw the whole blend off, but it is a shy seeder so flowers in this color will be few.)

I. umbellata possesses no fragrance worth recording, but it makes up for that lack by an abundance of flower, which, in cool, moist gardens, will begin in June and continue until well after the first frosts. In hotter, dryer gardens, plants are apt to set seed after a month or so and cease flowering. It is then worth the effort of shearing them back by about a third of their height and watering them well, in the hope that a second flush of growth and flower will be produced in late summer. Plants bloom best in full sun, in well-drained but only moderately fertile soils. Soils rich in nitrogen will produce growth at the expense of flower, although supplementary phosphorus and potassium are appreciated where those elements are deficient.

The culture of other annual *Iberis* follows that of *I. umbellata.* A particularly desirable species is *I. amara* (ah-MA-ra), from the Greek *amarakos,* meaning marjoram. Popularly called "rocket candytuft" or "hyacinth-flowered candytuft," it produces handsome rods of fragrant white flowers each about half an inch wide. Though it might fancifully be said to resemble a hyacinth, in fact the flower rods seem shingled and gradually elongate into handsome, pagoda-like cobs. The entire plant, flower stems included, will be about twelve to fifteen inches tall.

Two other annual *Iberis* sometimes grown are *I. affinis* (ah-FIN-is), meaning similar, though to what has not been recorded, and *I. pinnata* (pi-NA-ta), so named from its compound or "pinnate" leaves. *I. affinis* is a tiny plant, hardly reaching six inches in height, with delicate, whitish-gray to pale lilac flowers. Though pretty enough, especially when grown at the edges of a path or between stepping stones, its chief distinction is its fragrance, which smells strongly of honey and carries powerfully on any breeze. *I. pinnata* produces a plant to about a foot tall with dark, almost black-green, delicate leaves. Its umbels show color even when they contain quite tiny, unopened buds of soft lilac. Individual flowers open from the edges of the umbels inward, fading to white as they fully expand, though the unopened buds in the center remain lilac. At various stages, umbels of flower are scattered over the plants like dainty little stars.

All annual *Iberis* make superb late-winter-flowering plants for the cool greenhouse, and *I. amara* possesses the extra advantage of being an excellent cut flower for winter bouquets. Seed should be sown in September for plants that will begin flowering in January and last until early spring, if spent flowers are promptly removed to prevent seed-set. A nighttime temperature between 45° and 50°F should be maintained, with no more than a ten- or fifteen-degree rise in the daytime. Full sun and a sandy, well-draining soil are required, and only very dilute liquid fertilizer low in nitrogen should be applied while the plants are making vegetative growth.

IMPATIENS SPECIES

FAMILY: *Balsaminaceae* or touch-me-not family.

CLASSIFICATION: Tender shrubs, perennials, or annuals grown as tender annuals. *I. glandulifera* is a hardy annual.

COMMON NAME: Impatiens (other common names vary with species).

HARDINESS: Sensitive to light frosts.

GROWING CONDITIONS: Average to good, well-drained but moisture-retentive soil. Part shade to full sun.

PROPAGATION: By seed. Cuttings of many shrubby species root easily.

HEIGHT: From 8″ to 6′, varying with species.

ORNAMENTAL VALUE: Grown for flower.

LEVEL OF CULTURAL DIFFICULTY: Easy.

SPECIAL PROPERTIES: None.

PRONUNCIATION: im-PAY-shins

The genus *Impatiens* takes its name directly from the Latin *impatiens*, referring to the fact that the pods of most species, when ripe, will explode impatiently at the slightest touch, propelling individual seed as far as twenty feet away from the mother plant. Most gardeners will know only *I. walleriana* (wa-ler-EE-a-na), given the irritating name "busy Lizzy" many years ago but called by most gardeners simply by the genus name, *Impatiens*, though they may also be familiar with the recently popular New Guinea hybrids. The genus is surprisingly large, however, containing at least 500 species, many of them both beautiful and garden-worthy. Some of these species are slowly making their way into seed catalogues and nurseries that market unusual annuals and tender plants, and more are sure to follow.

All species of *Impatiens* possess certain characteristics in common. Their stems are juicy, and their leaves are almost always oval, pointed at the end, prominently veined, toothed along each side, and generally of a fresh, lustrous color. Leaf color varies from species to species, but it is generally deep green, shading to olive and from there possibly to maroon. Flowers will always be showy, either in the wheeled way of *I. walleriana,* or as curiously pouched forms, such as *I. glandulifera* (glan-doo-LI-feh-ra). All will carry the family signature of a nectar-bearing organ behind each flower, pronounced or relatively inconspicuous. None will be plants for parched places and dry soils, since the places in which they evolved—primarily the tropics and subtropics of Asia and Africa—are apt always to be moist, whether jungle or deep temperate forest, meadow streamsides, sunny wetlands fed by melting snow, or slippery, sun-drenched rocks. The genus is rich with beauty, and as the way into gardens has been forged by "busy Lizzy," all gardeners know what an impatiens is, or thought they did—till now.

Until about 1960, *I. walleriana* was known, if at all, as a pleasant houseplant, taken out in summer to decorate the terrace or patio and get a little fresh air to revive it for its primary purpose, indoor growth. Surprisingly it was seldom used as a

IMPATIENS GLANDULIFERA

bedding plant. A native of tropical East Africa, it was grown as a greenhouse staple by the middle of the nineteenth century, and named for Horace Waller, a missionary to East Africa about whom little else is known. In its natural form—and in all forms known before 1960—it is a somewhat upright, rangy plant, with succulent, branching stems bearing oval, pointed leaves of light green, and flowers of deep or light pink, grape purple, and a rather dingy white.

In less than twenty years, however, the popularity of *Impatiens walleriana* has exploded to the extent that it now accounts for the largest number of sales in nurseries, surpassing all other summer bedding annuals. Over these years, its demeanor was improved by being made more compact, more freely branching, and more richly clothed with leaves of a good, medium to dark green, though variegated forms quickly became popular as well. Now there are semi-doubles and doubles, the latter bearing flowers like miniature roses, though they are far less vigorous than the single forms. Impatiens are not particular about soils, and so with little more than warmth and water they quickly make mounded, densely leaved bushes to about fifteen inches tall and wide. Without doubt, their ease of culture has done almost as much as their appearance to account for their remarkable popularity.

Modern forms may be said almost to smother themselves with inch-wide, five-petaled flowers in a bewildering range of shaded variations of red, orange, pink, purple, and white. Some forms possess petals streaked with a white "star," and others are brushed with white over a darker color. Few other annual plants have proven themselves more malleable in the hands of breeders, except possibly petunias, and in mixed plantings the result may be a riotously lurid effect. Their wide range of bloom color, however, also makes possible very sophisticated combinations if beds are limited to complex shadings of one dominant tint.

There is no doubt that the modern impatiens are good, serviceable plants, particularly for shaded spots, though in all but the warmest gardens they do as well in full sun if kept adequately watered. There is also no doubt that their popularity has ultimately worked against them, as always happens when a plant behaves so well that it is grossly overused. Still, they are of easy culture, certainly rewarding in the bloom they produce from June to frost, and unless neglected and allowed to dry out, they are always neat in appearance and never require dead-heading.

Interestingly, however, for so popular a plant, impatiens can be very difficult to raise from seed. Therefore, it seems far more sensible to buy seedlings from nurseries. There will certainly be no shortage of them, for impatiens are the nurseryman's darling. As precocious bloomers, they sell themselves by showing their cute first flower when only four inches tall.

And soon, one imagines, there will be no shortage of the New Guinea hybrid impatiens either. Though they are crosses and selections of two species native to New Guinea—*I. hawkeri* (HAWker-eye) and *I. linearifolia* (lin-ee-ah-ri-FOL-ee-a)—the new hybrids most closely resemble the former in their appearance and are often botanically listed under it. (*I. hawkeri* was named for a Lieutenant Hawker, who collected plants in the South Sea Islands early in the nineteenth century, but about whom little else is known.) In the 1980s, the New Guinea impatiens began to appear in nurseries, generally as plants grown from cuttings, and since then they have steadily gained in popularity. Larger in all their parts than *I. walleriana,* and therefore even more vivid, they produce sturdy, much-branched bushy plants as tall as two feet. Their leaves, up to eight inches long, may be dark green, olive, bronze, or maroon, and many

plants show striking variegation, generally in the form of a blazed pattern of yellow that follows the veins of the leaf, shading to scarlet and then to dark green. Foliage like this is enough to justify growing any plant, but the New Guinea impatiens stud their branch tips with flowers less abundantly produced than those of *I. walleriana,* but larger, to as much as two and a half inches across. Colors may be a clear white, pink, lilac, purple, orange, or red, sometimes shaded or blotched with a deeper color on a lighter ground. Seed of New Guinea impatiens has only recently begun to be offered, first as mixes, and now in individual colors of flower and leaf. Cuttings also root easily. Plants accept less shade than *I. walleriana* and so should not be expected to lighten up the darkest corners of the garden.

Both *Impatiens walleriana* and the New Guinea hybrids are actually tender perennials, though they will not regrow from their roots if hit by frost. But several other impatiens grown in gardens are true annuals, and one, *Impatiens balsaminea* (bal-sa-mi-NEY-a), has been cultivated in Western gardens for at least 400 years. Its species name means balsam-bearing, and it has always carried the popular name "balsam," though no part of the plant is fragrant. A native of subtropical India and China, it was once among the most treasured of annual garden plants, but it is not often seen in gardens today. That is a pity, for it is very easy to grow, and its appearance is quite distinctive in a gentle sort of way. The plants achieve an ultimate height of around two feet, and are stiff and upright in character, for which reason they always look best in drifts of plants spaced about eight inches apart. Flowers are borne in the axils of the light green leaves along the top half of the plant, and are about an inch wide, in various shades of red, pink, white, yellow, and purple, often with deeper shadings in the center. Seeds in furry, olive-shaped pods will explode at a slight touch when ripe. Generally, the most popular forms have been "camellia flowered," an accurate description of the appearance of their many-petaled, inch-wide, waxy flowers. Single forms often possess more grace and beauty, however, and the nectar-bearing spur behind each flower is more prominent. It is hard to buy seed of single forms, but fortunately balsam self-seeds abundantly. Once grown in all but the coldest gardens, it will generally reappear in following years, and reversions to the simpler single form will inevitably occur, in many pretty shades. Balsam requires full sun to flourish and bloom well and, like all impatiens, insists on a humus-rich soil and abundant moisture. Very quick of growth, it is generally sown directly in the garden, but for earlier-flowered plants, it is easily raised from seed sown indoors about six to eight weeks before the last expected frost date.

Another annual, *Impatiens glandulifera,* is currently rare in gardens, though one suspects not for long. The stately Himalayan balsam or Himalayan jewelweed grows from seed to a height of as much as ten feet in six weeks, producing a thick, hollow stem swollen at the joints. Its flowers begin to appear in early July and continue until September, by which time the plant has produced many narrow pods of seed that are among the most explosive in the genus. Flowers are produced in clusters on thin, delicate stems from the axils of the upper leaves. Their color is generally either a rich, burgundy red or a silver pink, colors that go wonderfully together. (A pure white form, 'Candida', also exists.) The structure of the blossoms makes clear the extreme complexity of the flowers of all impatiens, for they are composed of an upper, flared petal, and two smaller, lower ones, forming a mouth. But the flower also possesses a prominent nectar-bearing pouch from which it takes its species name, Latin for gland bearing. *I. glandulifera* may

be grown either in part shade or in full sun, and will tolerate, even flourish in, very wet, boggy soils. Of ingenious construction, the plants are given enormous strength by their thick, tubular central stems and are further buttressed by aerial roots that burrow into the earth in the manner of a corn stalk. Nevertheless, when they achieve full height they may be blown over by summer winds if they are grown too closely together or in too much shade. Spacing between plants of about a foot and a half will make them stockier and stronger, but seedlings should not be pinched to encourage bushiness.

Because *Impatiens glandulifera* is so rapid of growth, little is gained by starting plants in the garden. It is classed as a hardy annual, which means that seed may be sown outdoors as soon as the soil may be worked in spring, or even in autumn. The seed is capable of surviving over winter even in cold Zone 4, and tiny seedlings possess resistance to light frosts. In that fact exists a warning, for seed is produced in great abundance and is propelled a significant distance from each plant in all directions. Every individual seed will germinate the following spring, creating a carpet of seedlings. Although they must be exterminated where they are not wanted and laboriously thinned where they are to grow, they are not difficult to eliminate, since they pull up easily by handfuls. Although stunning in full growth and bloom, the plants should not be grown in gardens that are not tended frequently, and probably never near wetlands, into which they could escape and thrive.

Similar in growth to the Himalayan jewelweed is *Impatiens noli-me-tangere* (NO-lee mee TAN-ger-ee), which bears a Latin species name, touch-me-not, that has been extended to many members of the genus. It is also a very handsome plant, though shorter in stature than *I. glandulifera,* achieving only perhaps five feet of growth. Its

IMPATIENS BALFOURII

leaves are a much darker green, and its flowers, borne at the top of mature growth, are a clear butter yellow. It is equally invasive. For some reason, Japanese beetles, which ignore other species of impatiens, find it particularly attractive and will shred the leaves before the plant comes into flower.

The very charming *Impatiens auricoma* (o-ri-CO-ma), its species name rather bafflingly describing it in Greek as golden-haired, has only begun to appear in catalogues and nurseries in the last two years. Probably a tender perennial, and similar in culture to the New Guinea hybrids, it bears numerous, bright gold half-inch-long tubular flowers shaded to deep orange in their throats, each flower looking like the face and open mouth of a goldfish. Several selections have been made of softer yellow, peach, and tangerine, and all look beautiful together. Like the New Guinea impatiens, *I. auricoma* will require bright light to achieve its best growth and flower.

Perhaps more a curiosity than a staple garden flower, *Impatiens niamniamensis* (nyam-nee-a-MEN-sis) is a tender perennial species native to the most tropical parts of Africa, where it generally grows in deep shade and produces oddly shaped flowers throughout the year. They are borne singly on thin stems from the axils of the leaves, and consist of greenish petals, reduced almost to the point of being vestigial, and a three-quarter-inch-long swollen nectary pouch of brilliant orange, terminating in a long spur curving upward. The flowers look like nothing so much as exotic, brightly colored insects, but they are weirdly beautiful, especially when a ray of light shines through them, making them translucent. Like all other perennial species of *Impatiens*, *I. niamniamensis* could be expected to be hardy only in the warmest, most tropical parts of USDA Zone 10. Elsewhere it may be cultivated as an annual, seeded indoors about eight to ten weeks before the last anticipated frost. It is more than usually sensitive to cold, and certainly to frost. It is probably best grown in a pot, as an attractive and interesting oddity.

Finally, another tender *Impatiens, I. balfourii* (bal-FOUR-ee-ee), can sometimes be found in catalogues that specialize in rare and unusual seed. A native of the western Himalayas, it commemorates Sir Isaac Bayley Balfour (1853–1922), Regius Keeper of the Royal Botanic Garden at Edinburgh. Though perennial, it behaves much like *I. glandulifera,* in that seedlings will appear in mid-spring, grow rapidly, and flower in their first year, allowing it to be treated as an annual, even a self-seeding one. But its seed-borne progeny, while not pestiferously numerous as is that of *I. glandulifera* or even *I. noli-me-tangere,* is at least plentiful. It is of fairly small stature, however, and delicate, achieving a modest, congested growth of about three feet. Flowers are small, half an inch wide and long, borne on slender stems in clusters from the axils of the lettuce-green leaves. They have a winsome beauty, consisting of a delicate blend of orchid pink, pale pink, and white, most vividly colored on their prominent upper lobe. So subtle is the plant that a drift of it might be a bit of a letdown, though an occasional specimen, peeping out shyly here or there, is very charming.

INCARVILLEA SINENSIS SUBSP. *VARIABILIS*

FAMILY: *Bignonaceae* or trumpet vine family.

CLASSIFICATION: Half-hardy perennial grown as half-hardy annual.

COMMON NAMES: Summer gloxinia, incarvillea.

HARDINESS: Exact root-hardiness unknown. Leaves are frost sensitive. Pots may be overwintered in cool, frost-free conditions.

GROWING CONDITIONS: Humus-rich, well-drained
   soil. Full sun. Afternoon shade in warm gardens.
PROPAGATION: By seed, sown in mid-April indoors.
HEIGHT: To 2'.
ORNAMENTAL VALUE: Grown for flower and for at-
   tractive, ferny foliage.
LEVEL OF CULTURAL DIFFICULTY: Moderately diffi-
   cult.
SPECIAL PROPERTIES: Excellent for pot culture.
PRONUNCIATION: in-car-VIL-ee-a sye-NIN-sis *sub-
   species* va-ree-A-bi-lis

The genus *Incarvillea* contains between twelve and fourteen perennial species, the best known of which is *Incarvillea delavayi* (de-la-VI-ee), the so-called hardy gloxinia. It bears coarse basal leaves about a foot long divided into toothed leaflets and produces bold spikes of five-lobed, trumpet-shaped flowers, rose-pink with a yellow throat in the species. Though it can be brought into flower in ten months from seed, it is classed as a hardy perennial.

Recently, however, another incarvillea has begun to appear in some seed catalogues and nurseries, *I. sinensis*, which, though a true perennial that will also begin flowering in ten weeks from seed, is not hardy north of USDA Zone 8, and so must be grown in most gardens as a half-hardy annual. In appearance, it is very different from *I. delavayi*, branching low from the ground and being almost shrublike in appearance. Typically, it will achieve a height of two feet in its first year of growth, with leaves that are very finely divided into threads, creating a delicate, ferny effect. The flowers are borne two to three or more on terminal, lightly leafed stems and will appear by July from a mid-April seeding under glass. They are smaller than those of *I. delavayi*, consisting of narrow tubes about an inch long and three-quarters of an inch wide at their mouths. The flower color of the species is a rather coarse reddish purple, but in the subspecies *variabilis* they are a lilac pink faintly tinged with yellow. A beautiful naturally occurring variant of the subspecies also exists with creamy white flowers, marketed under the name 'Cheron' but properly 'Alba'.

Plants of *Incarvillea sinensis*, native to China as the adjective *sinensis* always indicates, thrive in well-drained, humus-rich soil and respond well to weak, liquid fertilizer when just coming into flower. They bloom best in full sun, though they will be grateful for some afternoon shade in very warm gardens. Because the plant has only become available to American gardeners in the last three years or so, its exact hardiness is unknown. But like other incarvilleas, its survival over winter anywhere will probably depend on perfect drainage and a covering of straw or evergreen boughs for insulation. Potted plants are easily overwintered in a dormant state, kept in a cold but frost-free environment, and started back into growth in April or when they show quickening in the form of small fresh shoots. As the delicate beauty of the plant suits it for pot culture, that may be the best way both to grow and to preserve it from season to season.

INCARVILLEA SINENSIS

IONOPSIDIUM ACAULE

FAMILY: *Cruciferae* or mustard family.

CLASSIFICATION: Hardy annual.

COMMON NAMES: Diamond flower, violet cress, ionopsidium.

HARDINESS: Withstands light frosts.

GROWING CONDITIONS: Moist, humus-rich, well-drained soil. Full sun to part shade.

PROPAGATION: By seed, sown in place in autumn or spring.

HEIGHT: To 2″.

ORNAMENTAL VALUE: Grown for diminutive flowers.

LEVEL OF CULTURAL DIFFICULTY: Easy.

SPECIAL PROPERTIES: Excellent in cracks of pavement or in walls. Good for cool winter greenhouse. May be used in salads.

PRONUNCIATION: eye-o-nop-SIH-dee-um a-KAU-lee

*T*hose gardeners who insist on waves and waves of brilliant color from their annual and tender plants will pass over *Ionopsidium acaule* without a second thought. Although not the tiniest annual that exists, it is certainly very small, achieving in its short life a height of perhaps two inches and a width of possibly three. Still, garden references describe it using words such as "dainty," "modest," "gentle," and "delightful." It is all those things, and it responds with compliant amiability to most climates and situations, presenting its neat domes of leaf and its tiny flowers at many unexpected times of the year. *Ionopsidium acaule* is popularly called "diamond flower" or "violet cress," both of which names suit it to perfection. The genus name is built of two ancient Greek words, *ion,* meaning violet, and *opsis,* like. (Most botanists consider it to be the only member of its genus.) It is an accurate description, for though diamond flower is a member of the vast mustard family, and so possesses the typical, four-petaled flowers of all Cruciferae, each flower is cupped, one rounded petal overlapping the other, making them look very like tiny violets. They are also sweetly fragrant, if one goes down on one's hands and knees to determine that.

Violet cress is surprisingly tough for such a shy thing and from such a temperate origin—Portugal. It may be sown in place in the garden at almost any time of the year. Even in the coldest gardens, seed sown in early spring will produce flowers by midsummer. Seed sown in midsummer will produce flowers in autumn, and seed sown in autumn may produce flowers in early spring or even in mild spells during late winter. It appreciates a moist, humus-rich soil abundant with moisture in part shade to full sun, but it will put up with less. Indeed, the best plants may occur in places they were never intended to be and shouldn't grow well in, though they chose to volunteer there. For violet cress, once it is established in gardens, will reappear year after year, almost always in places that give it protection from drying winds, its only seeming intolerance. And though the general advice is to thin seedlings so the plants stand an inch apart, few gardeners get out the tweezers to guarantee that appropriate spacing.

In most gardens, perhaps the greatest usefulness of violet cress is between the pavers of a terrace or a path laid on sand or in the decayed joints of old, mortared walls. There it will be very happy, in either part shade or full sun, creating tiny, creeping tuffets of rounded leaves, half an inch long and as wide, on stems that seem extensions of the leaves themselves. (*Acaule* means stemless or nearly so.)

As *Ionopsidium acaule* is a very hardy annual, there is little value in starting seed indoors. Rather, it should be sown in the garden where the plants are to grow. It is also a favorite of those gardeners who have cold greenhouses and who grow annuals for flower in winter and very early spring. Grown this way, the minute beauty and the fragrance of *I. acaule* can be appreciated, for the potted plants can be held up to eye and nose level. For this purpose, seed should be sown in August or September. Individual seedlings should be established singly in three- or four-inch clay pots, in humus-rich, well-drained soil, and grown on at nighttime temperatures around 45°F. Once the plants begin flowering, the pots may be mulched with fine gravel or pea stone, which nicely sets off their attractive flowers and leaves. Unless seed is wanted, flowering is protracted by removing spent blooms.

The leaves of violet cress, and the flowers too, possess a pleasant, peppery taste. If one can bear to rob so tiny a plant of any of its upper parts, they are an agreeable addition to salads, particularly in early spring.

IPOMOEA SPECIES

FAMILY: *Convolvulaceae* or morning glory family.

CLASSIFICATION: Tender annual or perennial vine grown as tender annual.

COMMON NAME: Ipomoea (other popular names vary with species).

HARDINESS: Sensitive to frost.

GROWING CONDITIONS: Rich, well-drained, fertile soil. Abundant moisture. Full sun.

PROPAGATION: By seed, sown indoors in peat pots in mid-April. Nick, soak, or sandpaper seed to hasten germination. Seedlings resent root disturbance.

HEIGHT: Climbing, to 20′.

ORNAMENTAL VALUE: Grown for flowers and for quick annual cover to arbors and fences.

LEVEL OF CULTURAL DIFFICULTY: Easy to moderately difficult.

SPECIAL PROPERTIES: Interesting winter-flowering plants for cool greenhouse.

PRONUNCIATION: i-po-MEE-a (i-PO-mee-a)

To most gardeners, morning glories are synonymous with 'Heavenly Blue', the most popular of all the morning glories and indeed the most popular of all annual vines. Many gardeners would say that its funnel-shaped blossoms, four to five inches long and up to four inches wide, possess—on first opening in the very early morning—the finest shade that blue can come in, set off attractively by white to yellow shadings, deep in their throats.

In fact, however, the genus *Ipomoea* contains 400 to 500 species widespread throughout the tropical parts of the globe, and a few originating from temperate climes. Among these species are many garden-worthy plants, to the extent that a monograph would be required to treat them all. Catalogues and nurseries that list unusual annual and tender plants seem to include a new species each year. All are worth a try. Most—not all—will be variants in leaf and flower color of the morning glory one remembers from childhood—probably 'Heavenly Blue'. They will generally be vigorously climbing vines, for the genus takes its name from two ancient Greek words, *ips,* meaning worm, and *homios,* similar to or resembling, and describes the terminal growths of most species, which climb by twining their growing tips around whatever slender support they come in contact with. They will also generally bear trumpet-shaped flowers with flaring mouths made up of five fused petals, usually with a darker stripe or pleat where petals join. Each flower is of very brief duration, typically lasting

IPOMOEA BATATAS 'ACE OF SPADES'

only a single morning, or sometimes a single evening. The colors of the flowers are usually shades of blue, purple, pink, crimson, or white, though rare Mexican forms may be yellow.

Within so large a genus, there will of course be many exceptions to this general description. Among ipomoeas in cultivation, the greatest of exceptions will perhaps be *Ipomoea batatas* (ba-TA-tas), the sweet potato that is of enormous importance as a food crop throughout tropical regions of the world. (The species name *batatas* is the Carib word for the plant, still in common usage in the Caribbean Islands.) As it grows in fields as an agricultural crop, the sweet potato is handsome enough, producing lax, coarse vines that sprawl rather than climb, leaves that are heart- or sometimes maple-leaf shaped with three lobes and of a rich dark green color. Few

gardeners would choose to grow the common sweet potato strictly as an ornamental, however, since its flowers are almost never produced except in the very deep South.

But within the last five years or so, several decorative-leaved sweet potatoes have appeared that promise, even in so short a time, to become almost ubiquitous in large containers of mixed annuals and tender plants. The first was one with deep maroon—almost black—foliage. It was soon followed by a form with bright chartreuse leaves, and then by a variegated-leaf form with cream markings over a pale green ground. Now there has come one with rainbow markings of cream and green and white, and quite recently, a particularly handsome one with translucent bronze leaves. The ornamental-leaf sweet potatoes achieved almost instant popularity because, like most *Ipomoea,* they thrive when their root run is restricted, and they enjoy the heated-up soil of containers standing in the sun. One now sees their coarse but attractive growth spilling over the edges of cement planters onto the sidewalks of many major cities. New plants are most often propagated by cuttings taken from the tips of shoots, which root with extreme ease.

Perhaps as much dissimilar to the typical morning glory as sweet potatoes is a group of vines with scarlet, red, or orange flowers. The most familiar is the cypress vine, *I. quamoclit* (KWA-mo-clit). The derivation of its curious species name is obscure, but it may be a corruption of a native dialect in Mexico, where it originates. It is a vigorous climber, able to reach as much as twenty feet in a season, covering a surface with a mantle of much-divided, ferny, two-inch leaves that, from a distance, *do* look like the foliage of cypress or junipers. The flowers, vivid scarlet tubes with yellow throats and prominent white anthers, are each about an inch and a half long and as wide, flaring at their mouths into five-pointed stars. They are borne in great profusion practically from the time the vines are set out until frost (to which they are extremely susceptible), though it is probably best to remove the first flowers to give the vines extra strength. Forms exist with both white- and salmon-pink flowers. Cypress vine may be grown on any fence, trellis, or sturdy support in full sun, but it is particularly attractive when grown on grape arbors, where its ferny leaves are a nice contrast to the coarse leaves of grapes and its vivid flowers provide summer interest.

With another orange-flowered species of *Ipomoea*, *I. hederifolia* (heh-der-i-FO-lee-a), a hybrid has been created, *I.* x *multifida* (mul-TI-fi-da), bearing much-divided leaves (which its species name signifies) and an even greater abundance of scarlet, starry tubes than either of its parents. Often listed incorrectly as *Ipomoea* x *sloteri* (SLOW-tuh-ri), it is among the best plants to attract hummingbirds to the garden. Where it is grown to shield a porch or cover an arbor, one can sit and watch their fearless, tiny bodies suspended in air as they probe the inch-long throats of each flower.

Finally, a third atypical morning glory that has recently appeared in seed catalogues and nurseries is *I. lobata* (lo-BA-ta), previously listed as *Mina lobata* and sometimes still appearing under that name. It draws its species name from its three-lobed, light green leaves, though in fact its flowers are by far its most distinctive characteristic. They are inch-long tubes, borne sometimes as many as twelve in one-sided spikes, of graduated size, from largest at the bottom to tiny buds at the top. The buds start out crimson, open to scarlet red, and then fade to orange and finally pale yellow. At any one time, there will be flowers in all stages of fading, giving the spikes an interesting and beautiful multicolored appearance, if unsettlingly a little like the candy corn popular at Hallowe'en. As with other morning glories, *Ipomoea lobata* may be grown on strings or any support, but it is particularly attractive when trained to a tripod of tall bamboo stakes, as it tends to flower when young and continues until frost. One should not, however, underestimate its height, for it can reach up to twelve feet in warm gardens though it seems quite dainty at first.

After these atypical morning glories are put aside, one turns to a welter of confused or uncertain species, all of which—when offered—should probably be tried at least once. Some may be annual indispensables, such as 'Heavenly Blue', the most celebrated of the cultivars of *Ipomoea tricolor* (TRI-co-lor), though by no means the only one. The species in fact takes its name from the wild form, which shows a red tip on its furled umbrella bud and opens to purplish blue with a white throat. Flowers, in both it and its selected forms, are about four inches wide, borne in clusters on stems in the axils of its leaves, though only one flower opens at a time. The leaves are generally four to five inches long, oval or heart-shaped, and of a clear, medium green. In addition to 'Heavenly Blue', there are forms in deep purple, crimson, and pink, and all these colors are apt to occur in a mixed swarm of seedlings

IPOMOEA BATATAS 'MARGARITA'

IPOMOEA NIL (IPOMOEA X IMPERIALIS)

white, or purple, some showing pronounced stripes of a darker color where the petals are fused. In gardens, the species is most valuable for an almost black cultivar that bears the name of the man who found it on an abandoned Indiana farm, 'Kniola's Purple-black'. It comes true from seed, and its flowers, of typical morning glory form, though a little smaller than 'Heavenly Blue', are the deepest purple, appearing actually black in the early morning just after they have opened.

Ipomoea nil, sometimes listed as *I.* x *imperialis* (im-per-i-A-lis), is actually a tender perennial, though it may be treated as an annual. It is the parent of the fantastic Japanese imperial morning glories that are cultivated by the Japanese almost with frenzy. Though vines may reach a height of as much as ten feet, in Japan they are carefully pinched and cramped in their pots, thus trained into much smaller plants that bear flowers sometimes of fantastic size. Individual blooms may be as much as six inches across—in shades of blue, purple, red, or rose, or even strange, unclassifiable colors—among hairy, heart-shaped four- to six-inch-wide, lobed leaves. There are ruffled, scalloped, striped, fringed, and mottled forms, and of course, doubles. Many, as one might assume, have variegated leaves splotched with silver or white. Until recently, the only form of imperial morning glory available in America was the cultivar 'Chocolate', with five-inch-wide flowers of a very dusty, beige rose.

Morning glories grow extremely well in pots or containers, seeming to enjoy being somewhat constricted at their roots. Larger vines, however, which can achieve a length of ten feet or more, can be awkward except in very large containers or in halved whiskey barrels where they can climb upward on tall bamboo tripods. Even there, they are apt to travel quickly to the top of the poles and create a wad of tangled stems, leaves, and blooms, destroying the architectural shape of the

that may volunteer from year to year after 'Heavenly Blue' has been grown. They are generally inferior to any named form, however, and so, except in wilder parts of the garden, they should probably be eliminated in favor of freshly acquired seed of named cultivars.

Similar to *Ipomoea tricolor* is *I. purpurea* (pur-PUR-ee-a), called the "common morning glory" because, though many morning glories self-seed from year to year, it has been most successful in naturalizing, and appears all along the eastern seaboard, generally growing as a tangled mass in fields or even in the vacant lots of major cities, glorifying rubble and chain-link fences. It can climb to as much as fifteen feet in a season, clothing its stems with four- to five-inch-long heart-shaped leaves and producing flowers three inches long and across, in many shades of pink, blue, support. Recently, however, "dwarf" morning glories have been developed that produce vines scarcely six feet long, with abundant though rather smaller flowers. The first of these was a cultivar of the species *I. hirta* (HIR-ta), called the "hairy morning glory" from its species name, though many other species possess leaves and stems that are also downy. The cultivar was called 'Mini-Sky Blue', perhaps to capitalize on the popularity of 'Heavenly Blue', though its flowers tend more to a pale lavender with typical shadings of white at the throat. The fused petals do not seem to follow the typical circular, pleated form of most morning glory flowers, but tend rather to divide into five sharp points at the edges. The result is actually quite charming, and it is very handy to have a small-growing morning glory suitable for planting in smaller containers or window boxes.

It could be argued that the noblest member of the many garden-worthy ipomoeas is the moon vine, *Ipomoea alba* (AL-ba), previously listed as a separate genus and species, *Calonyction aculeatum* (ka-lo-NIK-tee-on ac-yew-lee-A-tum), and sometimes appearing as *Ipomoea noctiflora* (nok-ti-FLO-ra). Whichever Latin name it carries, however, the popular name "moon vine" suits it perfectly. It is a rampant grower, to twenty feet or more in a hot summer, and it has brought down more than one support that seemed adequate to it as a small, newly transplanted vine. Its stems are hairy, and its heart-shaped leaves can be quite large, up to eight inches wide and as long, though four to six inches is more typical. Flowers are trumpets four inches long and as much as five or six inches across. Unlike many typical ipomoea flowers, which seem fragile, even diaphanous, the flowers of moon vines are quite substantial, thick and somewhat waxy-looking in their texture. Cream-white is a word that fits, especially as the throats of the flowers deepen down almost to

IPOMOEA PURPUREA

butter yellow, though some will show an unearthly band of green around their edges. Individual flowers, borne one at a time from clusters of buds in the axils of the leaves, unfold at sunset so rapidly that the process is visible. Shortly thereafter, they become sweetly fragrant, substituting, as so many white and nocturnal flowers do, fragrance for color as a way of attracting night-flying insects to pollinate them. Flowers close at dawn, but fresh flowers will open nightly from midsummer until frost. Because of their nocturnal habits and their rich fragrance, they should be planted near where one sits at night, by a porch, deck, or pool, or perhaps on a stout trellis by one's bedroom window.

For such popular vines, morning glories are not of the easiest culture. To begin with, seeds are coated with a thick, shiny black shell, which gives them incredible viability. Fifty-year-old herbarium specimens have sprouted as successfully as seed produced the year before. But this thick rind makes germination very slow, taking as much as forty days. The general advice is to soak the seed for up to two days in tepid water. (Constantly tepid water is hard to secure for two days, but it may be contrived with a home heating pad set at low or by placing the container of water and seed on several thicknesses of newspaper on top of the household furnace or an old-fashioned radiator.) After two days, seeds that swell visibly should be planted, and the others nicked with a small file and soaked for another day. Alternatively, if one is handy and has a very small file, all the seeds can be nicked, soaked for a day, and planted. This

IPOMOEA (MINA) LOBATA

process is called "scarification" and is employed with other seed that is similarly protected, such as that of cannas.

Successful germination will only occur at temperatures around 70° to 80°F, which, in colder houses, may again be achieved by the furnace trick. All ipomoeas are extremely adverse to root disturbance as seedlings or as young plants, however, and so two or three seed should be sown to a single peat pot, the two less vigorous clipped away with scissors after two true sets of leaves have formed. Little is gained by sowing the seed much before mid-April for most American gardens, since the young seedlings must be grown on in full sun and a warm atmosphere (one at least comfortable to humans), and it is difficult to keep their wayward shoots from tangling among one another or into other indoor or greenhouse plants. In any case, all ipomoea love the warmth, and if they are transplanted too early into the garden, even though frost is past, they may be permanently stunted, or at the least, they will sit still and turn yellow and sickly until settled warm weather occurs. Sudden changes in temperature will also discourage them greatly— even permanently—and so they must be carefully hardened off before being planted in their permanent quarters. In climates warmer than USDA Zone 5, the best results may be had by sowing seed directly in the garden, later thinning them to stand six inches to a foot apart for they seem to enjoy growing close together.

The ipomoeas most commonly grown in American gardens may be either true annuals or tender perennials, though those generally offered in catalogues, even if perennial, will flower their first year from seed. It is useful to know, however, that the perennial sorts, which include *Ipomoea alba, batatas, nil, setosa,* and *tricolor,* may be preserved from year to year either by lifting their fleshy roots and storing them in a frost-free place, potted but reasonably dry, or by taking cuttings in autumn, generally of mature stems with a leaf or two, and growing them on as living plants in a cool greenhouse. Either from dormant roots or cuttings, twining stems may be produced early in the year, but shoots can be pinched to keep plants compact and to prevent them from overwhelming their neighbors.

All ipomeas commonly grown in gardens also make pleasant plants for the cool greenhouse or sun porch heated to around 55°F at night, but 15° or so warmer during the day. Seed should be sown in early September, or cuttings taken then, for flowers in late February and into early spring. The vines may be trained on wires or grown on tripods of bamboo stakes. Flowers will remain open for a full day in the wan light of late winter. As winter-flowering plants, ipomoea have been particularly popular in the dim windows of weather stations above the Arctic Circle. There, spider mite, which is their bane in most enclosed conditions, does not seem to have naturally occurred.

IPOMOPSIS RUBRA (PREVIOUSLY *GILIA RUBRA*)

FAMILY: *Polemoniaceae* or phlox family.

CLASSIFICATION: Half-hardy biennial or sometimes short-lived perennial grown as hardy annual.

COMMON NAMES: Standing cypress, Texas plume, ipomopsis.

HARDINESS: Withstands light frosts.

GROWING CONDITIONS: Light, rich, well-drained soil. Full sun.

PROPAGATION: By seed, sown in place in autumn or early spring, or indoors 6 to 8 weeks before last anticipated frost. Seedlings resent root disturbance.

HEIGHT: To 3′ or taller, depending on growing conditions.

ORNAMENTAL VALUE: Grown for flower.

LEVEL OF CULTURAL DIFFICULTY: Easy to moderately difficult.

SPECIAL PROPERTIES: Superb as cut flower.

PRONUNCIATION: ih-po-MOP-sis RU-bra GIL-ee-uh

*D*espite its beautiful rods of flower and its ease of culture, *Ipomopsis rubra* is not often seen in gardens. Its rigidity of form may be the reason, for each plant produces a single stem of growth that stands determinedly upright without staking. That stem may reach a height of six feet throughout its natural range—the southern third of the United States from South Carolina to Florida and Texas—though something like three feet is more common in gardens. The somewhat gawky impression made by the single stems can be avoided by planting them in drifts of eight or a dozen, fairly close together at about four inches apart. Alternatively, three plants may be established in one hole, creating the impression of a clump. These planting devices are worth the effort, to achieve the one splendid feature of the plant—its elongated panicle of two-inch tubular flowers, five lobed and flaring like a trumpet. If color could be sound, their hue would be trumpetlike as well, for the outside color is the clearest, most vibrant scarlet. Those who look inside will find tints of creamy white, heavily freckled with red. The stem is closely furnished with attractive, much-divided ferny leaves, each about two inches long, which give *I. rubra* its popular name, "standing cypress."

Another species of *Ipomopsis*—*I. aggregata* (ah-gree-GA-ta), also sometimes offered by specialty seed companies, is probably the western equivalent of *I. rubra*. It occurs naturally from British Columbia south to California and east to the

Rocky Mountains. It is a little crankier than *I. rubra* because it insists on cool summer weather, and so it is seldom satisfactory in gardens outside the upper East Coast and sections of the West Coast where it is native. Similar in carriage and in leaf to *I. rubra,* though a little shorter, at two feet, its flowers are only an inch long and are bunched at the tips of the stem in thick (aggregate) clusters. They vary in color from scarlet through gold and yellow to pink and almost white. A particularly attractive form occurs naturally with internal yellow speckling over a clear red ground. The petals are narrow, pointed, and starlike, giving the plant its popular name, "skyrocket," for each head of flowers resembles a firework explosion of shooting stars.

Both species of *Ipomopsis,* though they behave as biennials or even weak perennials within their native ranges, can be cultivated as summer-blooming annuals. Classed in seed catalogues as hardy annuals, they are quick to germinate and may be seeded in place in September where winters are mild and elsewhere in early April. Alternatively, they may be sown indoors about six weeks before the last anticipated frost, though they should be planted three to a peat pot or plastic cell pack and all but the strongest clipped away as they resent root disturbance. Growth is best in light, rich, well-drained soil, and, once established, plants are tolerant of drought. Heat is another matter, however, for both species resent hot weather and are apt to finish their bloom prematurely where it occurs. In cool gardens, however, plants will remain in flower from June until frost.

IPOMOPSIS RUBRA

IPOMOPSIS RUBRA

GROWING CONDITIONS: Rich, well-drained soil. Abundant moisture. Full sun to part shade.

PROPAGATION: By cuttings, which root easily at any time.

HEIGHT: Where hardy, to 5′. To 2′ when grown as an annual.

ORNAMENTAL VALUE: Grown for vividly colored leaves.

LEVEL OF CULTURAL DIFFICULTY: Easy.

SPECIAL PROPERTIES: Excellent conservatory or cool greenhouse plants.

PRONUNCIATION: eh-ri-SEE-nay (ir-IH-see-nee)

Neither species is effective as a container plant though they make excellent cut flowers, if one can bear to decapitate the whole plant for its single stem of bloom.

IRESINE SPECIES

FAMILY: *Amaranthaceae* or amaranth family.

CLASSIFICATION: Tender shrub grown as tender annual.

COMMON NAME: Iresine (other popular names vary with species).

HARDINESS: Extremely sensitive to frost. Resents cool weather.

*I*resines belong to a family rich in colored-leaved plants, the Amaranthaceae, but though many are cultivated both for leaf and for inflorescence, iresines are grown solely for their vividly colored leaves. They seldom flower outside the frost-free gardens of Zone 10, but the woolly, chaffy, whitish-gray flowers that give the genus its name (from ancient Greek *eiros,* meaning wool) are not their most appealing feature. It is strictly for foliage that they are grown. One cannot look at iresines without thinking of nineteenth-century bedding schemes, where they were so much used to create elaborate patterns and even floral clocks. Of very easy culture, they are currently sharing the renewed vogue for colored-leaved plants, along with coleus, acalyphas, *Amaranthus tricolor,* alternantheras, plectranthus, and the like.

Iresine lendenii (lin-DIN-ee-ee) commemorates Jean Jules Linden (1817–1898), a native of Luxemburg who made extensive botanical explorations in South America and later became a celebrated nurseryman in Belgium. It is popularly called "blood leaf" for its oval to broadly lance-shaped, three- or four-inch pointed leaves that show prominent veins of bright red on a maroon-red background. The leaves appear to be folded along the central vein and then to bend in an arch, with the tip pointing downward. They have a waxed or varnished effect both on top and underneath that greatly contributes to their beauty. All other visible parts of the plants—stems and leaf petioles—are also red, adding to their vividness. A very beautiful cultivar with red stems but yellow leaf markings like broad smears over a dark green ground, called 'Formosa', is also often cultivated. Though plants attain a height of as much as five feet in their native Ecuador, they are much smaller here, hardly more than two feet. Frequent pinching of tip growth creates bushy plants and renewed crops of fresh, brightly colored leaves.

Iresine herbstii (AERBST-ee-ee) (from the German *herbst,* meaning autumn) is native to southern Brazil, and is an equally brilliant plant, with four- to five-inch leaves broadly veined in red on a purplish-red or almost chocolate ground. Its darker hue accounts for its usual popular names, "beef plant" or "beefsteak plant." A much more vivid, almost iridescent cultivar exists that is appropriately named 'Brilliantissima' (bril-ian-TISS-i-ma), and another with bright yellow veins on an all-green ground named 'Aureoreticulata' (o-re-o-ree-ti-cu-LA-ta).

All the iresines under cultivation have been selected for pronounced leaf coloration, and so the plant is seldom grown from seed. Rather, it is propagated from cuttings, which root with extreme ease. Plants are lifted or cuttings taken before the slightest hint of frost, for iresines are among the most frost-sensitive of all summer bedding plants. Stock plants or rooted cuttings are carried through the winter indoors, where they make attractive and easily managed houseplants. Fresh cuttings are then taken in April, for, as the cuttings both root and grow rapidly, size-able plants can be had by June when the weather becomes settled and warm. Nothing is gained by earlier planting, as an unexpected spring frost will wipe out all the young plants.

In cool, northern gardens, iresines will flourish in full sun, though they appreciate some shade where summers are hot. They require a rich, fibrous, well-drained soil, and they respond well to supplementary feeding with a water-soluble fertilizer. They thrive in containers of mixed annual and tender plants, and are effective also as single potted specimens, one or more of which can be taken indoors or into the greenhouse over the winter to provide cuttings for plants the following year.

JUSTICIA BRANDEGEEANA (J. GUTTATA)

FAMILY: *Acanthaceae* or acanthus family.

CLASSIFICATION: Tender perennial or shrub grown as tender annual.

COMMON NAMES: Shrimp plant, false hop, justicia.

HARDINESS: Hardy in Zones 9 and 10. Very frost-sensitive elsewhere.

GROWING CONDITIONS: Humus-rich, fertile soil. Abundant moisture. Full sun in cool gardens, part shade in warmer ones.

PROPAGATION: Named forms are propagated from tip cuttings, which root easily.

HEIGHT: To 2′.

ORNAMENTAL VALUE: Grown for ornamental bracts.

LEVEL OF CULTURAL DIFFICULTY: Easy.

SPECIAL PROPERTIES: Often grown as a warm greenhouse plant.

PRONUNCIATION: joos-TEE-si-a bran-duh-GEE-ay-na (gu-TA-ta)

The genus *Justicia* commemorates James Justice (1730?–1763), a celebrated Scottish horticulturist, and contains more than 400 species, making it by far the largest member of the acanthus family. Its showiest members are all native to the Tropics and subtropics of both hemispheres, and where they are hardy, in the more moist, privileged gardens of USDA Zones 9 and 10, large collections could be made of them alone. Beyond these zones, however, only one species—*Justicia brandegeeana*—is grown with any frequency, both as a houseplant and as a container or bedding plant for semi-shaded areas of the garden during summer. It takes its current species name from Townsend Stith Brandegee (1843–1925), an American civil engineer who botanized extensively in California and Mexico, to which it is native.

The vegetative growth of *Justicia brandegeeana* is nothing much to speak of, consisting of oval, light green leaves borne on weak, square stems that may reach two and a half feet. But the odd inflorescences of a well-grown specimen make it a rewarding and curious plant to grow. It will smother itself with inch-long, heart-shaped, coppery-red bracts, laid one over another quite precisely, to create a long, arching structure that does somewhat resemble the tail of a shrimp, giving it its popular name, "shrimp plant." The showiest part of the plant is these structured bracts, which, because they are modified leaves, last a long time, a month or more before turning black. The actual flowers, borne among them, are by comparison insignificant, consisting of narrow, inch-long, whitish tubes that divide into two lobes at the mouth, the lower one freckled with reddish-purple spots. In addition to various shades of rust or coppery-red, forms also exist with yellow and chartreuse bracts.

The shrimp plant flourishes in part shade and enjoys summer heat. It likes a rich, fibrous, well-drained soil, and responds almost visibly to weekly drenchings with water-soluble fertilizer at half strength. If allowed to dry out, however, or if kept too wet, it will shed its leaves and quickly become shabby. Young plants should be frequently pinched to encourage branching, as otherwise, long, gangly stems will be produced, with fewer inflorescences.

Select forms of the shrimp plant are propagated from nonflowering tip cuttings, which root easily. Given enough sunlight and warmth, potted specimens will also continue to create bracts and flower throughout the winter, making them valuable as houseplants and for the heated conservatory or greenhouse.

JUSTICIA BRANDEGEEANA

KOCHIA SCOPARIA
(BASSIA SCOPARIA)

FAMILY: *Chenopodiaceae* or pigweed family.

CLASSIFICATION: Half-hardy to hardy annual.

COMMON NAMES: Summer cypress, burning bush, Belvedere cypress, firebush, kochia.

HARDINESS: Withstands moderate frosts once established.

GROWING CONDITIONS: Well-drained, humus-rich soils. Full sun. Resents drought. Prefers heat.

PROPAGATION: From seed sown in site after frost. Start in peat pots indoors 6 weeks before frost. Seedlings resent root disturbance.

HEIGHT: From 2 to 3'. Up to 5' under good cultural conditions.

ORNAMENTAL VALUE: Grown for fine-leaved shrub-like form and for vivid autumn color.

LEVEL OF CULTURAL DIFFICULTY: Moderately difficult.

SPECIAL PROPERTIES: Useful for dried arrangements.

PRONUNCIATION: KO-kee-a (KO-chee-a) sco-PA-ree-a (BA-see-a)

Kochia scoparia, the charming summer cypress or burning bush, offers a clear example of how plant names sometimes shift about, often to the frustration of gardeners. In 1800, the German botanist Albrecht Wilhelm Roth (1757–1834) noted the genus *Kochia,* giving Wilhelm Daniel Josef Koch (1771–1849), professor of botany at Erlangen, the honors due to him. But in 1766, a relatively obscure Italian botanist, Allioni, had published a description of the plant under the genus name *Bassia,* honoring the director of the Bologna Botanic Garden, Ferdinando Bassi (1714–1774). According to the *International Code of Botanical Nomenclature,* the first published name of a genus or species takes precedent over all other subsequent published names. So the plant familiarly known as *Kochia* is correctly *Bassia.* All but the most botanically sophisticated gardeners, however, and certainly all seed catalogues, still list it under the previous name, offering Bassi an obscure triumph at best. Throughout this shifting, however, the Latin adjective *scoparia,* meaning broomlike, accurately descriptive of the only member of the genus cultivated in gardens, has stuck.

Under whatever name, summer cypress is a valuable addition to gardens, possessing a look like no other plant grown as an annual. It is generally cultivated in the form *trychophylla* (try-co-PHIL-a), meaning hairlike, and referring to the thread-fine, two-inch leaves, which so densely clothe the numerous ascending branches that one cannot see through the plant. (The form *trychophylla* also differs from the straight species in possessing a broadly oval to almost spherical, rather than a spirelike, pointed habit.) Though references list yellow-leaved forms, only the green and a weakly variegated form covered with white speckles seem to be cultivated. The green is in any case best, for it is a fresh, light green, complementary to all flowering annuals and perennials, particularly to those that bloom in shades of yellow. Complementary, that is, until autumn approaches, when the entire plant turns a firey purplish red (some would say magenta) from top to bottom, accounting for two other popular names, "firebush" and "burning bush." (Cut at this stage, the leaves will retain their color when dried.)

Though *Kochia scoparia* may form a bush as tall as five feet, two to three feet is more typical. It is often recommended for use in forming an annual hedge along paths or in the front of beds. But used this way, it can look dreadful for most of the summer, while gaps remain between the rounded forms of individual plants, causing the whole to look like ill-formed teeth. It is far more successful when used singly in smaller gardens as a solitary accent, or in drifts in larger ones, some to the fore, some behind, with their rounded shapes eventually interlocking. The cypress plant is also very attractive when grown as single specimens in ten-inch clay pots. (One waits for the most fashionable New York florists to discover this fact.)

Generally, plants are most successful when seeded directly in the garden after all danger of frost has passed, and later thinned to stand about a foot apart. Germination and growth are very rapid in warm weather, which the plant generally prefers. Alternatively, seed may be started indoors about six weeks before the last anticipated frost date, though young seedlings dislike root disturbance, and so should be sown in peat pots, eliminating all but the strongest seedling, or in plastic cell packs, the roots being very gently slipped out in a cube at transplant time. (The seed is very small, as many as 500 to 1,000 seeds in a pack.) *Kochia scoparia* requires full sun, and a rich, well-drained humusy soil. If at any point—whether as seedlings waiting to be transplanted into pots or into the garden—plants experience drought or any root disturbance, they will fail to develop, remaining stunted and often coloring prematurely.

The flowers of *Kochia scoparia* are tiny and insignificant, though they are borne in great numbers when plants reach maturity and shortly before they assume their autumn coloration. And here lie two cautions: People who are susceptible to hay fever may find the pollen of the flowers as irritating as that of ragweed. Also, volunteer seedlings may occur in warmer gardens in such numbers as to constitute a significant nuisance. (In parts of the South and the Midwest, the plant is a pernicious weed in agricultural fields.) But as *Kochia scoparia* is a plant that resents root distur-

KOCHIA SCOPARIA

bance, unwanted seedlings can be easily eliminated by hoeing the soil, unless they have germinated in the center of clumps of perennials, in which case they will have to be pulled, one by one. Even with these liabilities, *Kochia scoparia* can be a wonderful addition to the summer border.

LANTANA SPECIES

FAMILY: *Verbenaceae* or verbena family.

CLASSIFICATION: Tender shrub grown as tender annual.

COMMON NAMES: Lantana, shrub verbena.

HARDINESS: Sensitive to frosts.

GROWING CONDITIONS: Almost any soil. Full sun.

PROPAGATION: By cuttings of selected forms. Seed may be sown about 8 weeks before the last anticipated frost date.

HEIGHT: From 2 to 6'.

ORNAMENTAL VALUE: Grown for flower.

LEVEL OF CULTURAL DIFFICULTY: Easy.

SPECIAL PROPERTIES: Excellent where summers are quite hot. Drought tolerant.

PRONUNCIATION: lan-TAN-a

Gardeners who live in Zones 8 to 10 need no description of lantana and indeed might resent praise of it, for the plant, although originally native to tropical South America, has naturalized wherever it is hardy. In the deep South, Texas, and southern California, it is a rank and pestiferous roadside and garden weed, and in Hawaii it is a serious menace, where large stands of it have replaced native vegetation much as lythrum has in the wetlands of the Northeast. But wild forms are quite beautiful, never weedy, and a joy—to tourists at least. Even where the species form has naturalized widely, many fine selections and hybrids justify the cultivation of lantana.

One of the loveliest of these, *Lantana camara* (KA-muh-ra), forms a woody bush reaching a height of up to six feet where happy, but typically three feet in gardens north of Zone 7, unless plants are carried over the winter in a cool greenhouse. Dwarf forms also exist, which reach only two feet and are useful for certain bedding schemes. In frost-free areas, plants will bloom almost throughout the year, and in cooler gardens from early summer to frost. In the very hottest weather, they will smother themselves with domed, two-inch-wide umbels of tightly packed tiny, one-third-inch-long tubular flowers flared into four- or five-lobed stars at the ends. Individual blossoms in the cluster open from the outer edges to the center and have the endearing habit of beginning as pale yellow and then turning deeper as they age—to bright orange and copper red in the oldest flowers. Since the individual flowers last a long time, a single cluster may show several colors at once, the darker at the edges shading to the palest in the center. Raspy, dark green, oval to heart-shaped leaves, two to four inches long, give off a strong, pungent odor when crushed. The flowers are very popular with bees and butterflies, and birds love the black, fleshy

LANTANA CAMARA

fruits that follow, thus continuing the dispersal of lantana in areas where they are hardy. These fruits, closely resembling blackberries, pose a danger to children, however, as they are toxic.

Even in unimproved form, the flowers of *Lantana camara* are quite pretty, in a brash, summery sort of way. But the plant has been both hybridized and selected for forms that may be pure white, pink or lavender, coppery or pinkish orange, melon, or a fading blend of several of these colors, usually with a primrose-yellow eye in the center of each tiny flower. Many named forms exist, and new varieties are constantly appearing.

Many modern forms of *Lantana camara* are hybrids with another species in the genus, *L. montividensis* (mon-ti-vi-DEN-sis), popularly called "weeping lantana" for its vinelike, trailing stems that may reach a length of four feet and that interlace to form dense mats. This growth habit makes it popular as a flowering groundcover or to form a drapery when grown at the top of walls or to spill over the edges of large containers of mixed annuals and tender plants. In its typical form, the tightly clustered flowers are a strong pinkish lilac, retaining that color throughout the life of the cluster but fading a bit to a paler pink at the edges of the oldest flowers. Through crosses with *L. camara* and back-crosses of their progeny, weeping lantana exists in both strong and pale yellow and white, some cultivars having inherited *L. camara*'s capacity to open in paler shades and fade to darker ones with age.

Usually lantana come into gardens from nurseries as cutting-grown plants, but they are also easy from seed, which is generally offered as a blend of many colors. It should be sown about eight weeks before the last anticipated frost date, and young plants should be pricked out and grown in bright light, and transplanted into the garden after all danger of frost is past. Seedlings can show their first flowers as early as six weeks after germination when the colors one likes can be saved and the rest given away. But all the colors harmonize with each other because of their undercast of yellow, and none is ever ugly.

Lantana are of very easy culture, flourishing in almost any soil, provided it is well drained, but they produce the most abundant flowers in fairly lean, sandy soil on the dry side. In containers, however, plants must not be allowed to dry out to the point of withering, which will set them back and may kill them outright. If they are grown in hanging baskets, therefore, they may require almost daily watering, and they respond well to feeding with water-soluble fertilizer every two weeks, though excess feeding in the open ground will produce leaves and rank growth at the expense of flower. Full sun is an absolute requirement, and plants will reach their peak of flower in the very warmest months of the year.

At summer's end and before frost occurs, plants may be lifted and potted into well-draining compost, cut back hard, and brought indoors or into the cool greenhouse to regrow and possibly bloom during the winter. Alternatively, softwood cuttings may be taken at the end of August, rooted in a shady place, and potted up for vigorous young plants. Lantana make excellent houseplants on sunny windowsills where humidity is kept within the comfort range of people, and temperatures do not exceed 70°F during the day, with a ten-degree drop at night. Dry, overheated household air will quickly cause them to flag, and so the best results may occur in a less heated guest room, on a frost-free sun porch, or in the cool greenhouse. During the darkest months of the year, indoor or greenhouse plants should be kept moderately dry, though watering may be increased when the days begin to lengthen, and water-soluble fertilizer will then encourage growth and flower. Stock plants or young rooted cuttings should be frequently pinched when vigorous growth begins, to make well-branched, bushy plants. Great care should be taken to eliminate white fly as soon as it appears, for all lantana seem to be the McDonald's for that pest, which, once well established, is very difficult to eliminate.

The genus name *Lantana* is post-classical Latin for the shrubby genus *Viburnum*. It is not hard to see how the tight-packed umbels of lantana must have struck some botanist as resembling the similar but much larger umbels on some garden viburnum, though the two genera are completely unrelated. *L. camara* takes its species name from a vernacular South American word for this plant.

LASTHENIA SPECIES

FAMILY: *Asteraceae* or aster or daisy family.

CLASSIFICATION: Half-hardy to hardy annual.

COMMON NAMES: Goldfield, lasthenia.

HARDINESS: Sensitive to light frost.

GROWING CONDITIONS: Light, fertile, well-drained but moisture-retentive soil. Full sun.

PROPAGATION: From seed, sown in place in early spring.

HEIGHT: Up to 18", depending on culture.

ORNAMENTAL VALUE: Grown for flower.

LEVEL OF CULTURAL DIFFICULTY: Moderately easy.

SPECIAL PROPERTIES: None.

PRONUNCIATION: las-THIN-ee-a

*O*ften, when ornithologists train their binoculars on a bird that proves to be uninteresting, they refer to it dismissively as an LGB, a little gray bird. Gardeners could refer to many pleasant annuals as LYD's, little yellow daisies, for there are so many of them. Two charming California natives in the genus *Lasthenia* might be described this way. Both are very pretty, however, very easy to grow, and bloom over a long period from late June until September. When grown well, and paid close attention, they might well justify their culture, seeming more than just another LYD.

The genus name *Lasthenia* derives from one of two female pupils in Plato's Academy, an Athenian girl named Lasthenia, who is said to have disguised herself as a boy to obtain the privilege of studying with the master. Her name aptly fits the two species cultivated in gardens—*Lasthenia chrysostoma* (kri-SOS-toe-ma) and *L. glabrata* (gla-BRA-ta)—for the inch-wide flowers of each make an impression at once delicately pretty and assertively bold.

Both species (in a genus of about sixteen) are true annuals and both bear the common name "goldfield," from the masses of bright yellow daisies they produce where they are native. They are plants of vernal pools, depressions in open fields retaining water over winter that slowly evaporates in spring and early summer, encouraging successive rings of plants—usually distinct species—ending with those that finally germinate in the moist clay soil at the bottom. The two species of *Lasthenia* grown in gardens flourish best in light, moist but well-drained, fertile soil, a seeming contradiction until one realizes that the edges of vernal pools become precisely that as the water retreats.

Seed of either species is seldom offered in general catalogues, though it may be obtained from several seed companies specializing in California native wild flowers. Of the two, *Lasthenia chrysostoma* (the species name means with golden pores) is the rarer in gardens. It produces much-branched plants to sixteen inches, though individual plants will generally topple over, producing upright secondary stems and flowers from the procumbent growth. Flowers are of typical daisy form, about an inch in diameter and a clear golden yellow. The leaves are somewhat fleshy, to about three inches long, bright green but covered with fine hairs. *L. glabrata* differs from *L. chrysostoma* principally in the fact that it usually holds its twelve- to eighteen-inch bushy growth upright, and its narrow, two- to four-inch-long leaves are relatively hairless. (The species name *glabrata* means becoming hairless.) Its inch-wide daisies are a rich, egg-yolk yellow.

Both plants are classed as hardy annuals and perform best when they are grown in light, fertile but moist soil in full sun. The seed is sown in place and covered with a light dusting of fine soil, generally in early spring, though in gardens that experience mild winters seed may be sown in autumn. Young plants should be thinned to stand about six inches apart. Flowering should begin eight or so weeks after germination and is prolonged by faithful dead-heading and by deep watering in dry spells. Blooms should continue from the end of June until autumn frosts. If flower production seems to flag in mid- to late summer, plants should be sheared down by half their height and given a drenching with water-soluble fertilizer. So treated, they will generally rally to produce fresh growth and another sequence of bloom. Lasthenia make attractive cut flowers, lasting well in water.

LATHYRUS ODORATUS

FAMILY: *Leguminaceae* or pea family.

CLASSIFICATION: Hardy annual vine.

COMMON NAMES: Sweet pea, lathyrus.

HARDINESS: Resistant to mild frosts.

GROWING CONDITIONS: Rich, heavy soil. Abundant moisture but good drainage. Full sun.

PROPAGATION: From seed, sown as early in spring as ground is workable. In warmer gardens, autumn sowing is preferred.

HEIGHT: To 10', with support.

ORNAMENTAL VALUE: Grown for flower.

LEVEL OF CULTURAL DIFFICULTY: Difficult except in gardens where exacting cultural difficulties may be met.

SPECIAL PROPERTIES: Excellent cut flower. Intense fragrance in selected varieties.

PRONUNCIATION: la-THI-rus o-do-RA-tus

More than one garden writer has confessed the need to take a deep breath before plunging into the subject of sweet peas. The history of the plant is long and interesting, and the elaborate efforts by which finer and finer forms have been developed are probably unparalleled among annual flowers. Where they thrive, they are, as the great English gardener William Robinson (1838–1935) asserted, "perhaps the most precious annual plant grown." Of course he meant the adjective "precious" to apply in its usual sense of something greatly valued, though the secondary meaning of the word—of something over-elaborated or excessively cultivated—might also apply. For in the quest to grow perfect sweet peas, a great deal of lore, useful information, and sheer lunacy have accumulated around the plant.

All sweet peas in cultivation are descendants from one wild species, *Lathyrus odoratus,* which produces flowers that are rich purple on the upper part (the hooded petal called the "banner" or "standard"), and lighter purple on the lower part (the two "wings") and on the two large lower petals fused together in a boat shape, called the "keel."

The sweet pea entered England in 1699 as seed sent from Malta by the monk Franciscus Cupani. This unimproved species is still cultivated under the name 'Cupani', and though its flowers are small, some sweet pea enthusiasts declare that it has the richest fragrance of all. For the next hundred years, only five color variants appeared in English gardens, including, in 1726, the still popular bi-color 'Painted Lady', with a bright pink banner and paler pink wings and keel.

Up to 1870, the sweet pea was considered a pleasant but not terribly important garden plant. But in that year, Henry Eckford began his incredible breeding program, which eventually resulted in more than 300 fixed color forms, many with larger flowers than the species but retaining much of its fragrance. This race came to be known as 'Grandiflora' (gran-di-FLO-ra) from their relatively large flowers, and, though soon eclipsed by finer floral forms, they have recently had a renaissance in modern gardens, largely because of their intoxicating scent.

The next milestone in the development of sweet peas occurred in 1901 when a variation (or "sport") of Eckford's 'Prima Donna' appeared simultaneously in three places: his own garden, in the cut-flower fields of the venerable firm of Unwin's, near Cambridge, and in the garden of Countess Spencer at Althorp House, in Northamptonshire. All three possessed the wide, frilled petals that have since become typical of most cultivated sweet peas, and which represent the form of a sweet pea in most people's minds, gardeners and nongardeners alike. Silas Cole, head gardener at Althorp House, introduced this variant under the cultivar name 'Countess Spencer', and William Unwin introduced his under 'Gladys Unwin'. The Unwin form, with slightly smaller flowers but stable recurrence from seed, provided the basis for the modern sweet pea, though the name Spencer is firmly fixed to the race, which are called "Spencer Sweet Peas."

From that point on, the breeding of sweet peas was incredibly brisk, resulting in an estimated 3,000 named cultivars, all stable, though perhaps only a tenth of that number are still grown. The color range of sweet peas was continuously expanded to include eventually every color, tint, and shade except true blue and chrome yellow, although the most modern purples and primrose yellows move close enough to be practically there. Bi-colors, streaked forms, and forms splotched or freckled with deeper colors were soon developed. Breeders concentrated also on very early-blooming forms that could be grown in winter in glass houses for the cut-flower market, and on heat-resistant forms of which the best known are the Cuthbertson types. In 1894 a major breakthrough came about in California when a dwarf plant occurred spontaneously, forming a fat little bush to two feet tall, bearing flowers with a rose-pink banner and pale pink wings and keel. It was christened 'Cupid' and is still grown as a more-or-less self-supporting bedding plant. Other dwarf forms soon were developed, ranging from eight inches to two feet, making the sweet pea appropriate for pots, containers, and window boxes.

Along the way in this incredible development of sweet peas their most precious attribute, that of fragrance, was partially or entirely lost. The sweet pea on the show bench was evaluated according to its length of stem, number and poise of blossoms, its size, and the subtlety or vibrancy of its colors. But to most gardeners, a sweet pea without fragrance is no sweet pea at all, and so, understandably, many of Eckford's grandifloras have been recovered and are either grown under their original cultivar names or used in breeding programs to return to sweet peas the magical fragrance they should possess.

For all the romance that clings to them, sweet peas are, to say the least, demanding plants, and though a handful of blossoms may be grown almost anywhere except in very hot and arid gardens, the best success will depend on climate. Sweet peas—like their culinary cousins, the garden pea *Pisum sativum* (PY-sum sa-TI-vum)— only really reach perfection in climates enjoying long springs and summers, cool sometimes to the point of being uncomfortable to those who garden there. Parts of England suit them to perfection. William Robinson, for example, in his garden at Gravetye Manor, grew sweet peas that reached a height of ten feet and flowered top to bottom (by means of judicious pruning and doses of manure tea) on the same spring-sown plants, from late June until October. (There is actually a photograph of him next to them, to prove the point to doubters.) No such success is possible anywhere in North America, though on the upper East Coast and in the Pacific Northwest good plants may be grown, and bloom will be abundant from early June until perhaps mid-July. In the mildest climates, they may be successfully grown as winter-flowering annuals. Elsewhere, they will be either a fleeting pleasure or a total failure.

Perhaps no other annual flowering plant depends more on general culture—careful soil preparation, timely sowing, successful germination, and subsequent after-care—than do sweet peas. They are extremely greedy feeders, but they are sensitive to the slightest overdose of chemical fertilizers, and so most of their nourishment should be supplied by digging quantities of aged manure or compost into the soil to a depth of at least eighteen inches. They also prefer a sweet soil, and so a generous sprinkling of lime should be dug in where soils are acid, along with a few handfuls of superphosphate to encourage strong root and stem growth. Preparations for their culture should actually begin in autumn, when the soil should be prepared so that it will settle over the winter and be firm, for sweet peas are peculiar in their preference for a relatively firm but extremely fertile soil, and not the fluffy, devil's-food cake that is ideal for many other flowering plants.

The sowing of sweet peas is also a rather exacting process. In most climates, they may be sown directly where they are to grow as soon in spring as the ground is thawed, at intervals of about two inches, and later thinned to stand four to six inches apart. Young seedlings will be resistant to mild frosts but not to heavy ones, which, if they can be anticipated, require a light covering over the newly germinated seed. Where winters are not severe but still frosty, one might also take the gamble of sowing them in late autumn, in the hope that they will germinate but not sprout above ground before heavy frost, in which case the seed bed should be covered with salt marsh hay or some other insulating material to prevent heaving and thawing. Many American gardeners have the best success by sowing sweet peas in peat pots indoors, for like most legumes they deeply resent root disturbance and great care must be taken in transplanting them. Three seeds are sown to a pot, about four to six weeks before the last anticipated frost date. There is no point whatsoever in hurrying the process, as young seedlings quickly become drawn and stunted under indoor conditions. Seed germinates best at about 60°F, and stocky young plants develop best at ten degrees lower still, in the brightest light that can be given them. Such conditions are rare in American homes but may exist in an unheated, south-facing guest bedroom, a sun porch, or a small greenhouse kept very cool. In mild climates

LATHYRUS ODORATUS

that have what could still be called a real winter, peat pots of seed sown in early winter could be kept in cold frames for germination and growing on in very early spring.

But no matter when or how the seed is sown, most—not all—of it should be soaked for two or three days (changing the water daily to prevent putrefaction) and the seeds that swell up should be promptly sown. Some gardeners actually have good results by placing the swollen seed between two damp dish towels until germination occurs and then carefully sowing it without breaking the questing taproot. If the seed does not swell, it should then be carefully nicked with a sharp knife until the pale flesh shows beneath, but always opposite the prominent "eye" where the taproot will emerge. The seed should then be promptly sown in peat pots, in rich but well-drained humusy soil, or in a soilless, peat-based potting compost such as Pro-Mix.

The exceptions to this process are seed that are white or cream colored. It is a peculiarity of *Lathyrus odoratus* that white and cream-colored flower forms will emerge from white seed, lavender and pale pink forms from mottled seed, and the darker purple and red forms from black seed. It is this characteristic, of course, that made *L. odoratus* so convenient to Frederick Mendel in exploring genetics when he formulated Mendel's Law. (It is also convenient to the gardener when sowing strains of mixed colors in peat pots, for three seed of one color can be put in each, thereby ensuring that when the weakest two are eliminated one will not be discarding all the pale or dark colors.) The darkest seed possess the hardest seed coat, and so are slowest to germinate. They require soaking, nicking, or rubbing lightly between two pieces of sandpaper. Mottled seed will generally respond to soaking alone, but white seed, which germinate most easily, may rot if treated before sowing, and so should be sown directly into pots or the garden.

When sown in peat pots, seed should be inserted about half an inch deep. It is convenient to make the holes with the end of a pencil or chopstick, as soaked seed may already have thrown out a minute taproot, which, if damaged, will cause failure in germination. When seed is sown directly in the garden it should be more deeply covered, to two inches, and should be protected against slugs, snails, and especially birds, which relish it just when it emerges. When the young seedlings have produced three or four leaves, they should be pinched to encourage branching, which will produce several flower-bearing stems. If they are grown indoors or in the greenhouse, they should be carefully hardened off and transplanted into the garden as soon as the frost is out of the soil. The entire peat pot should be buried and the earth firmed around it. Nothing is better than a bare foot to do this, though if the weather is really chilly one will have to use the palms of one's hands.

With the exception of the dwarf bush sweet peas, about which many committed sweet pea lovers remain dubious, the next great effort in growing sweet peas is providing adequate supports for them to climb on. Each plant should produce two or more stems, which ideally will scramble upward to a height of six feet or more, clinging to the supports provided by means of branched tendrils at the ends of compound leaves with two or more sets of oval leaflets. Though these tendrils are remarkably efficient at grabbing anything nearby (including their neighbors), they are sometimes not sufficient to hold up the heavy mature vine, which will also perversely show a tendency to grow *away* from its support, toward greater light. So whatever staking method one uses, it should be very strong, and the vines may need to be tied into it, individually or in bunches, to keep them from falling off or sliding down.

Exhibition growers use a very strict system in training the vines, called the "cordon" method. Each vine is tied to its own tall bamboo stake, and no more than two laterals are allowed to develop, the rest being pinched away as soon as they show in the axils of the leaves. Under this method—and given ideal weather, careful soil preparation, and judicious fertilizing—elegantly straight flower stems are produced as much as eighteen inches long, bearing huge, perfect flowers, suitable for the show bench. Growing sweet peas this way is not so much gardening as a sort of competitive sport, and most home gardeners will be better pleased by plants with several lateral growths that produce abundant, if smaller, flowers on shorter stems.

Staking is still an issue, however, and there are many opinions about it. In a letter written by Henry Eckford to William Robinson, an ideal method is described, which consists of growing sweet peas not in rows, but in clumps of several plants, trained on twiggy branches inserted firmly into the earth and tied together at the top into a cone. The sweet peas grow up and through the twigs, obtaining support and eventually producing a cone of flowers. This method might still be useful in the perennial border, where a tepee of sweet peas, flowering from base to top, could be splendid for as long as it lasted. Most sweet peas, however, are grown not for ornamentation in the flower garden, but strictly for cutting, and so are grown in efficient rows, much as are culinary peas. By far the most elegant staking is provided by thickly twigged branches, inserted close together into the earth to form a sort of fence or screen, with at least one wire, strung between two posts, running through them and to which they are tied for support. The method is redolent of both the cottager's careful gardening and the exacting standards demanded by head gardeners on large nineteenth-century estates. Its only problem, aside from intensive labor, is that it is difficult for most American gardeners to obtain enough twiggy branches eight feet tall to make such a support. Where it may be done, however, it is certainly the way to do it.

The usual alternative to branches is to plant rows on either side of a panel of six-foot-tall chicken wire, supported at either end and along the middle by sturdy posts driven deep into the ground. The results are fairly homely, for chicken wire eventually bows and bends outward, no matter how well supported and stapled in, and the vines must still be tied into the wire to prevent them from falling away in sheets. A far more attractive and efficient method is to use black plastic bird netting, which is almost invisible, provides many opportunities for clinging tendrils, and can be tied to towers or rows of ten-foot bamboo stakes inserted three feet into the ground. The stakes may be in tepee form, or in two long rows four feet apart, each pair of stakes bent together and tied to a central ridgepole running down the center. The netting is then tied to the poles, stretched, for neatness, as taut as possible.

Once young sweet pea vines have germinated or been transplanted, growth should be rapid in cool, moist weather and in well-prepared ground. The vines themselves are very attractive, with deep green, winged stems, alternate, compound leaves, and clinging tendrils. The first flowers should occur in most gardens in early June and continue until hot weather terminates production. A cooling mulch of hay, decomposed grass clippings, or extremely well-rotted manure will protect the roots of vines from heat and extend flowering. At no point should the vines be allowed to become even moderately dry at the roots, and supplementary water should penetrate very deep into the soil as the roots of the vines may quest as much as three feet downward. Nourishment is best provided by well-prepared soil, but if supplementary fertilizer is applied it should be water-soluble at half strength or less, as even slight amounts of excess fertilizer will cause vines to drop their buds. Most important, flowers should be picked every morning, for once seed begins to set on the lower part of a vine, all flower production will cease. As sweet peas are treasured and long-lived cut flowers, this is not a terribly hard discipline, though if one must be away from home for several days, it is wise to remove all but the smallest flower buds before they open. When one has been given a rare or heirloom variety that is not available in seed catalogues, one or two vines must be designated as seed bearers, their flowers allowed to ripen for next year's seed, and the cessation of flower production accepted. In this way, antique varieties that are often far superior to modern cultivars, in fragrance at least, can be preserved.

The genus *Lathyrus* takes its name from the ancient Greek *lathyros*, used by Theophrastus to designate some form of pea or pulse. *Odoratus* of course means fragrant. The genus contains 130 to 160 species, and though *Lathyrus odoratus* is the undisputed queen, there are several valuable perennial species within the genus, and at least two other annual species that are worthy of space, even in the most crowded gardens. The first is *L. chloranthus* (klo-RAN-thus), a native of Turkey, called the "green-flowered sweet pea," more for the resemblance of its large flowers to *L. odoratus* than for any perceptible fragrance. As both its species and popular names indicate, it bears pea-shaped flowers of a clear yellow over-stained with green. The effect is startling and quite lovely, though garden visitors will always bend toward its flowers and then wrinkle their noses in disappointment. It produces loose vines to eight feet, which may effectively be grown through and over spring-blooming shrubs such as forsythias or flowering quinces without doing harm. It may also be grown on trellises or standing supports. Though it ideally requires the same careful soil preparation as *Lathyrus odoratus*, its bloom season in cool gardens is very long, from June to frost, provided spent flowers are promptly removed.

A second annual species worth notice is *Lathyrus tingitanus* (tin-ji-TAN-us), named for its place of origin, the ancient Roman Tingis. In the typical species form, it produces large, purplish-red flowers on eight-foot-long vines, though pink-flowered forms with darker streaks have been bred, as well as bi-colors and a very beautiful cultivar with salmon pink flowers. It is of very easy culture and, like *Lathyrus chloranthus*, is a pleasant surprise threaded through shrubs that have exchanged their spring glory for a dull summer greenness. Even more than other lathyrus, however, its spent blossoms must be promptly removed, for at the first seed set it will cease flowering. One plant, obviously, must be allowed to go off in that way, as seed is scarce and once grown, one would want it for subsequent seasons as might all one's gardening friends.

Finally, it should be noted that all species of *Lathyrus*, despite the delicious fragrance of some and the close resemblance of their flowers to culinary peas, are toxic, and so, though the temptation might be strong, they should never be used as decorations for pastries and cakes or as garnishes in salads.

LAURENTIA SPECIES

FAMILY: *Lobeliaceae* or lobelia family.

CLASSIFICATION: Tender or half-hardy annuals grown as half-hardy annuals.

COMMON NAMES: Blue star, laurentia.

HARDINESS: Hardy to light frosts. May persist in Zone 5 gardens if well sited.

GROWING CONDITIONS: Humus-rich, fertile, well-drained soil. Abundant moisture. Sun to part shade. Cool growing conditions.

PROPAGATION: By seed sown 6 to 8 weeks before last frost, or by cuttings or self-rooted bits.

HEIGHT: From 3″ to 2′, depending on species.

ORNAMENTAL VALUE: Grown for flower and for low, hummock-forming mats.

LEVEL OF CULTURAL DIFFICULTY: Moderately easy to difficult, depending on conditions.

SPECIAL PROPERTIES: Good container plant. Interesting winter houseplant.

PRONUNCIATION: lo-REN-tee-a (lo-REN-si-a)

*B*otanists have had much trouble placing the several plants known as "blue star." Two (or possibly three) species are cultivated under that popular name, though botanically they have been shifted (and may still be listed) under four genera: *Pratia* (PRA-ti-a), *Laurentia*, *Isotoma* (eye-so-TO-ma), and *Solenopsis* (so-lee-NOP-sis). Of the four, the latter is probably the correct name, although nurseries and mail order catalogues specializing in rare and unusual tender plants are apt still to employ *Isotoma* or more frequently *Laurentia*. Therefore, with apologies to gardeners current in their botany, these charming plants are discussed here under the letter *L*. In the face of such botanical confusion, it is obviously impossible to list the numbers in the genus or their geographical distribution with any shadow of accuracy. Nevertheless, of the twenty-five or thirty species that show marked resemblance to one another, representatives occur in temperate areas of North and South America, southern Europe, and Africa. Those usually cultivated in gardens, however, are all native to the moister parts of Australia.

Of these, by far the most common is *Laurentia*

fluviatilis (floo-vi-A-ti-lis), an extremely charming, vigorous plant that seldom reaches a more impressive height than three inches. In favorable ground, it produces low green mounds, its creeping stems acting as a scaffold over which to throw out others, one atop another, to as much as a foot across. With luck and accurate spacing, individual plants may, by summer's end, create a ground-cover of stems and tiny, oval, lettuce-green leaves scarcely a quarter-inch long and broad. The plants very much resemble colonies of baby's tears, *Soleirolia soleirolii* (so-lee-ih-RO-lee-a so-lee-i-RO-lee-ee), with the exception that *L. fluviatilis* will be sprinkled with tiny quarter-inch-wide flowers, consisting of a tube and five starlike petals or lobes. It seems hardly to matter whether flowers are thick enough to cover the mats of leaves or sparse enough to offer a spangle here and there. Either way, they succeed in stopping viewers in their progress from one vivid flowering plant to the other, just to admire how amazingly quiet such beauty can be.

The exact hardiness of *Laurentia fluviatilis* is in great doubt. Conflicting reports exist in references as well as among gardeners who have grown it. It is generally listed as hardy to USDA Zone 8, but if plants are carefully sited and pro-

LAURENTIA AXILLARIS

tected by the warmth of a cellar foundation or a heavy coat of snow, or by a snug covering of evergreen boughs, they may survive in gardens as cold as USDA Zone 5. For so winsomely beautiful and charming a plant, there is every reason to experiment.

But in fact, *Laurentia fluviatilis* is of such easy propagation and such rapid growth that one should not fear losing it to a bitter winter. One need only take up a plug of growth and roots, pot it in rich, well-drained, humusy soil, and keep it on a moderately sunny windowsill or in bright light in a cool greenhouse through the winter. About five weeks before the last anticipated frost, pots may be divided in turn, grown on indoors, and reestablished in the garden after all danger of frost is past. They may join sturdy outdoor survivors (if any exist) when the weather warms, with never a difference in their growth.

Laurentia fluviatilis is not properly a groundcover, whatever references say, for its filmy structure of stem and leaf supplies a comfortable mulch for vigorous weeds and grasses that must then be laboriously tweezered or hand-plucked from its tuffets. It should therefore be established in very clean ground, in rich, fertile, humusy, seed-free soil that will encourage rapid and thick growth. At all times it requires abundant moisture, as its current species name *fluviatilis*—Latin for of rivers or running waters—indicates. But unlike baby's tears, it will not reach perfection when planted in a clay pot that stands in a saucer of water; it requires a moist soil but one that has abundant oxygen at the roots supplied by good drainage. It is splendid as a mat across the top of a clay pot, and, because it accepts part shade, it makes a splendid covering for the sides of moss-lined hanging baskets planted with begonias, impatiens, or the like.

Two other laurentia, now correctly listed in the genus *Solenopsis*—*Laurentia axillaris* (ax-i-LAR-is) and *L. petraea* (pe-TRAY-uh)—have begun to be offered by nurseries that specialize in unusual annuals and tender plants. Closely related to *L. fluviatilis,* they are quite different in appearance, forming foot-high tuffets of stems clothed in spiky, lobed leaves that look like miniature thistles (though their points are not sharp) or like the dark green veins of leaves after the tender tissue has been chewed away by some insect. Both are tender perennials hardy to USDA Zones 9 and 10, but elsewhere they are classed as tender annuals, transplanted outdoors from cutting-grown stock after all danger of frost is past.

L. axillaris (*Solenopsis axillaris*) produces plants as tall as twelve inches, abundantly furnished with thin, five-petaled, starlike flowers of purplish blue. A pink form exists, and flowers are often freckled over with spots of darker color. *L. petraea* (*Solenopsis petraea*) is taller, to as much as eighteen inches, forming a thick, rounded bush clothed with thicker though lobed and pointy leaves to two and a half inches long. Its abundant flowers, borne from June to frost, also consist of an inch-long tube terminating in a slender, five-pointed star that may be pale blue, lilac, or white. *S. axillaris* and *S. petraea* cross readily in gardens and in the wild, however, so many intermediate forms exist, making precise identification difficult.

Cultural requirements are constant for both species and their hybrids, and, indeed, for all members of this confused botanical group. They consist of humus-rich, well-drained soil, abundant moisture, and buoyant summer conditions: cool nights and mild, bright summer days. They are not apt to be successful in hot, arid gardens or in those experiencing muggy, late-summer days that encourage fungal diseases.

LAVATERA SPECIES

FAMILY: *Malvaceae* or mallow family.

CLASSIFICATION: Tender shrubs or annuals grown as half-hardy annuals.

COMMON NAMES: Tree mallow, rose mallow, lavatera.

HARDINESS: Sensitive to light frosts.

GROWING CONDITIONS: Rich, fertile, perfectly drained soils. Full sun to late afternoon shade.

PROPAGATION: From seed, sown indoors 6 to 8 weeks before last frost. Woody forms propagated from tip cuttings.

HEIGHT: From 3 to 6'.

ORNAMENTAL VALUE: Grown for flower. Some species grown for ornamental leaves.

LEVEL OF CULTURAL DIFFICULTY: Moderately easy to difficult.

SPECIAL PROPERTIES: None.

PRONUNCIATION: la-va-TER-a

*P*lant breeders have only just gotten to work on species of *Lavatera.* The genus, named after two distinguished seventeenth-century Swiss men of science, the brothers J. R. and M. M. Lavater, contains about twenty-five species though only three or four are cultivated widely in temperate gardens. By far the best known is *L. trimestris* (tri-MES-tris), which takes its species name from the fact that it will flower nonstop for three months, from late June to early September. A true annual native to southern Europe, it has been grown in gardens for more than a century as a modest plant of easy culture, valued as much for its shrublike growth—to six feet in a season—and handsome, broad, maple-like leaves as for its mallow-like flowers, five-petaled and of a strong rose red.

Lavatera trimestris exploded into popularity, however, with the first improved selection, a cultivar that bears the puzzling name 'Silver Cups', for it is in fact a bright true rose engagingly marked, as are most lavateras, with darker veins. Though the growth of the species is somewhat gangly, that of 'Silver Cups' is more compact, at approximately three feet. Further, it smothers itself in flowers with five broad petals overlapping into flared cups, borne on slender stems from the axils of the leaves, and possessing a startling grace.

'Silver Cups' was soon followed by another extraordinarily beautiful cultivar of purest white shading to ivory yellow at the throat. It was christened 'Mont Blanc' and differed from 'Silver Cups' not only in the pristine quality of its flowers, but in much darker, light-reflecting leaves that admirably set off its blossoms. 'Mont Rose' arrived next, with flowers of a far softer shade than 'Silver Cups' and one much easier to integrate into subtle color schemes in the garden. 'Ruby Regis', by contrast, produces a powerful splash of rose pink, most useful away from other flowering annuals, perhaps in bays of dark shrubbery. 'Pink Beauty' is almost lavender in effect, gentle wherever it is grown. Soon warm pink and salmon forms will be offered, as well as color mixes that will harmonize beautifully one with another.

The excitement over *Lavatera trimestris* is due only partly to its beautiful flowers and to their abundance, which continues well into autumn if spent flowers are removed. The plant is most valuable because no other flowering annual produces such a shrublike presence in the garden. Given enough room, the sturdy, much-branched, bushy plants with woody, corky lower stems are full and graceful, with no pinching or staking required, and from a distance they create the effect of a well-grown, full-flowered single shrub rose.

LAVATERA TRIMESTRIS

All these virtues would make *Lavatera trimestris* an ideal annual except for one problem. In the last ten years, a fungus has appeared among the once easy-to-grow species. Most reliable seed companies now treat seed against the disease, but still it may strike, causing an apparently healthy plant to collapse in full growth, wilting as if it needed water. Watering, actually, only exacerbates the disease, which is without cure. But the plants are so valuable that precautions should be taken before the fungus strikes. Seed might be treated with a fungicide if the supplier has not already done so, and sown directly in the garden after all danger of frost is past. Alternatively, seed might be sown indoors six to eight weeks before the last anticipated frost, in peat pots in a perfectly sterile, peat-based potting compost such as Pro-Mix and not pricked out or moved on as root disturbance seems to invite the disease. Seedlings should be grown in bright, airy conditions and not watered until the soil in their pots has become moderately dry. When all danger of frost is past, well-grown seedlings should be transplanted into the garden to stand approximately eighteen to twenty-four inches apart. Well-drained, rich soil in full sun suits *L. trimestris* best, and plants are surprisingly drought tolerant once established. Over-watered

or poorly drained soil will surely be fatal. If the fungus occurs, one is pushing one's luck to plant lavateras where they grew the previous season, for the disease, which is soil-borne, will likely prove fatal the second year, if it has not the first.

Unlike many plants in the family Malvaceae, successfully cultured lavateras make superb cut flowers if whole branches are taken. They last a reasonably long time in a vase, but if tip branches are inserted into an opaque vase filled with wet sand, the clusters of immature buds may open successively over the length of a whole month.

Lavatera trimestris is the only annual species of the genus grown in most gardens, though several other species are often treated as annuals where they are not hardy. *L. arborea* (ar-BOR-ee-a), the tree mallow, is also native to southern Europe, though it may be hardy in America as far north as Washington, D.C. It is actually a tender biennial or short-lived perennial, with magnificent, velvety, round-lobed leaves as much as nine inches long and as broad. Flowers, which appear only in the most privileged gardens and then only in the second year after seeding, are about two inches wide, and may be variously colored purple, pink, or deep red, but always with deeper veins striping each petal. In most American gardens, however, *L. arborea* will be grown as an annual plant strictly for its foliage. In species form, the foliage is handsome enough, but selected forms that come true from seed are yellow-leaved or magnificently mottled with white on a bright green ground.

Another tender shrublike species of *Lavatera, L. assurgentiflora* (a-sur-gen-ti-FLO-ra), is also often grown in temperate gardens as an annual. Its foliage is handsome, in a rank sort of way, each leaf about six inches wide and as broad, made up of five to seven triangular, coarsely toothed lobes. It quickly forms a shrublike plant from five to eight feet tall in its first season. Toward the end of summer, abundant, two-inch-wide, five-petaled mallow flowers will be produced at the ends of its branches, of a rich rose purple and veined with a deeper tint. Its species name *assurgentiflora* means tip-flowering, though in that it is not different from other species of *Lavatera,* all of which produce thick clusters of bud at the tips of growing branches. *L. assurgentiflora* is native only to the Channel Islands off the coast of southern California and, as such, is one of the very few members of the genus indigenous to North America. Seed started indoors in late April may be expected to flower in late July or early August, and continue until frost. Like all garden lavatera, it flourishes best in dryish, fertile soils and is particularly to be treasured in seaside gardens because its sturdy growth is resistant to wind and to salt spray.

One other species of *Lavatera* deserves special mention—*L. thuringiaca* (thur-in-GUY-a-ca), particularly in its selected form, 'Barnsley'. Native to southern Europe and hardy from Zone 9 to perhaps Zone 6 with winter protection, *L. thuringiaca* is quite lovely and has for many years been valued as a cottage garden plant, forming a sturdy shrub five feet tall or more in a single season, with stout ascending branches clothed with felty, maple-like lobed leaves, and bearing three-inch-wide, rose-red flowers throughout the summer and into autumn. Some years ago the distinguished English gardener Rosemary Verey discovered a lovely form with pale pink flowers fading to almost white in the center and named it after her family home, Barnsley House. Though it is a semi-hardy shrub or shrubby perennial, it roots very easily from tip cuttings and so has become popular throughout North America as a summer-flowering annual. Where it is not reliably hardy, tip cuttings may be taken in midsummer, stripped of their flower buds but not their leaves, inserted into damp sand, and rooted for stock plants to carry over the winter. Bloom occurs precociously, so rooted cuttings, if potted in rich, free-draining compost and grown on a sunny windowsill or in a cool greenhouse, will flower throughout the winter months, and may be cut back hard and transplanted back into the garden after all danger of frost is past. It is ironic that the straight species, previously neglected, now has been catapulted into favor, to the extent that gardeners vaunt themselves on possessing the "non-Barnsley" form. For some undetermined reason, however, both the species and selected form will occasionally make rank, thick-leaved plants and produce not a single flower. Over-feeding with fertilizer or compost rich in nitrogen is probably the explanation. If plants are to be fertilized, they should be given feedings high in phosphorus and potassium but low in nitrogen, such as is specifically formulated for tomatoes.

LAYIA ELEGANS (L. PLATYGLOSSA)

FAMILY: *Asteraceae* or aster or daisy family.

CLASSIFICATION: Hardy annual.

COMMON NAMES: Tidy tips, layia.

HARDINESS: Withstands very light frosts.

GROWING CONDITIONS: Light, sandy, well-drained loam. Full sun.

PROPAGATION: By seed, sown in place in very early spring. Will not transplant.

HEIGHT: From 12 to 18" tall.

ORNAMENTAL VALUE: Grown for flower.

LEVEL OF CULTURAL DIFFICULTY: Easy within native range, moderately difficult elsewhere.

SPECIAL PROPERTIES: None.

PRONUNCIATION: LAY-ee-a EL-e-gans (pla-ti-GLOSS-a)

The popular name "tidy tips" avoids being excessively cute only because it is so descriptive of the flowers of *Layia elegans*. A California native and a much-loved wild flower along roadsides and the edges of cultivated fields, it bears numerous, inch- to two-inch-wide daisies with eight to twenty broad, overlapping ray petals, each notched or pinked at the end. Many tubular ray flowers are packed into the heart of the bloom. The daisy's great charm is that the center of each, disk and ray petals alike, is a pretty butter yellow that shades abruptly to creamy white, as if the yellow had been painted in a neat circle over a white ground. The species name *elegans* appropriately applies to the color pattern; the genus *Layia* commemorates George Tradescant Lay (?–1841), a British naturalist.

Where layia is native, it is a spring and early-summer-blooming ephemeral, largely disappearing with the onset of summer drought. In gardens that experience relatively cool summers, however, it has a long blooming period, from late June until frost, from seed sown in April or as soon as the soil is dry enough to work. Its preference for cool, moist weather has made it a very popular summer annual in England, though in America, outside its native range, it offers its best only in the Northeast, the Pacific Northwest, and parts of the East Coast and mountainous areas that enjoy cool summers. It requires full sun and accepts almost any soil that is not heavy or waterlogged, though it prefers a light, sandy, well-drained loam a little on the dry side. Seed is always sown where the plants are to grow, for seedlings may not be transplanted with success. The seed is sprinkled thinly on prepared ground and barely covered with a dusting of soil rubbed between one's hands, as it requires light to germinate. Seed germinates within ten to fifteen days, and young plants grow rapidly in the cool outdoor weather of early spring, catching up with and surpassing seed sown indoors in peat pots. Young plants should be thinned to stand about eight inches apart, and if seed has been scattered too thickly, the strongest plants should be left behind where possible. The soil around each of these should be pressed by the first two fingers of one's hand—held in a narrow V—so as not to disturb the earth while the others are pulled.

The vegetative growth of *L. elegans* is not its most attractive characteristic, for it tends to be somewhat straggling, forming a loose bush from a foot to eighteen inches tall. It is more pleasing if one goes to the trouble of inserting brushy twigs firmly into the ground among the plants, each extending about a foot above the soil. Other annual or perennial plants would also provide some support. Leaves are very narrow, deep green with a grayish cast, larger and lobed at the base of the plant, smaller and lance-shaped where flower stems are produced. Each two-inch-wide daisy is delicately poised on a wiry stem that seems almost too slender to bear its weight. The blooms make excellent, long-lasting cut flowers, if one can bear to rob the garden of their charm. Dead-heading prolongs flowering though this also is hard to do, for the fertilized disk flowers form charming and persistent buttons as the ray flowers curl away beneath them. Supplementary watering should be provided in very dry spells, as complete drying out at the roots will signal to the plants that their season is over and they will wither away.

There is a white form of *Layia,* var. *Alba,* but it hardly competes with the perky beauty of the species type. Another species, *L. glandulosa* (glandew-LO-sa), is sometimes offered by seed companies specializing in American wild flowers. Native from British Columbia south to Mexico and east to Idaho, it is popularly called simply "white daisies." Its vegetative growth is not as branched as that of *L. elegans,* and all parts are covered with clammy hairs, especially the lance-shaped, inch- to inch-and-a-half-long leaves. (Hence the species name *glandulosa,* indicating glands that produce viscous material.) *L. glandulosa* bears daisies about an inch and a half wide, made up of fresh white ray petals and a central yellow disk. Though perhaps easier to grow in warmer gardens, *L. glandulosa* lacks the cunning coloration of the flowers of *L. elegans* and is not much cultivated except in wildflower mixes or by gardeners who specialize in native flora.

LEONOTIS LEONURUS

FAMILY: *Lamiacea (Labiatae)* or mint family.

CLASSIFICATION: Shrubby tender perennial grown as a tender annual.

COMMON NAMES. Lion's ears, lion's tail, leonotis.

HARDINESS: Hardy to Zones 9 and 10; root-hardy in Zone 8. Damaged by light frost.

GROWING CONDITIONS: Well-drained, moist sandy loam. Full sun. Relishes heat.

PROPAGATION: From seed, sown indoors in late February or early March.

HEIGHT: To 6′ where hardy. Typically to 3′ when grown as an annual.

ORNAMENTAL VALUE: Grown for flowers.

LEVEL OF CULTURAL DIFFICULTY: Difficult.

SPECIAL PROPERTIES: None.

PRONUNCIATION: lee-o-NO-tis lee-o-NUR-us

Whether one considers leonotis a plant of angular grace or merely an oddity depends in part on one's attitude but more on where and how well the plant is grown. A tender perennial behaving as a shrub, it possesses the moisture-loving nature of most mints and is hardy in North America only in those parts of Zones 8 to 10 that receive ample summer rain or that can be irrigated. (In its native South Africa it flourishes along the edges of moist ditches and seeps.) Until quite recently, it was encountered rarely in colder climates, but now, as part of the growing interest in bold and tropical outdoor bedding schemes, it has a small vogue among cool climate gardeners. It belongs to a genus of thirty or so species but is probably the only one much grown in gardens.

In those climates where it can grow freely over several seasons, leonotis forms a bushy plant to six feet with many ascending upright stems clad in coarse, grass-green lance-shaped leaves from one to two inches long, toothed at their edges, often slightly curled or cupped, and prominently veined. The leaves are borne alternately along thick, squared stems, fairly close together for the first two thirds of the plant's growth, then more widely spaced. Above each pair of leaves in the top third or so of the stems, thick, disklike whorls of many buds form in tiers, showing color as they expand and opening over a long period of time. Each individual flower is about two inches long at maturity, composed of two lips, the lower one divided into three small lobes, and the upper, which is densely downed, curving over it. The color of both newly formed buds and mature blooms is a fiery yellowish orange.

Outside the climatic range where leonotis is happy, however, it is sometimes difficult to make it look good. Even with the best of conditions, plants may wait to bloom until late August or early September, producing a single, gaunt stem with only coarse leaves at the bottom and widely separated bracts of flower at the top. *Leonotis leonurus* appears to be a variable plant in the wild, with shorter forms growing to only two feet, branched from the base, and producing whorls of flower more closely spaced together. Two have been listed as separate species, *L. dysophylla* (di-SO-fi-la) and *L. dubia* (DEW-bee-a). Both are actually dubious, from a botanical point of view, because they may simply be variants of the species. But as garden plants, especially for cool gardens, they may be more desirable than the six-foot-tall familiar form, for there is much more flower in the top third of the plant, creating an effect of more scarlet-orange and less gauntness of stem and leaf. There is also a rare white-flowered form, *L. leonurus* var. *albiflora* (al-bi-FLO-ra), which carries the cultivar name 'Harrismith White'.

Leonotis is not a plant that is easy to grow outside the climatic conditions that approximate its South African homeland. Generally young plants, either cutting-grown or raised from seed sown in late February or early March under glass, can be acquired from specialty nurseries in spring. But they should be grown on carefully and not transplanted into the garden until the weather is warm and settled, for they are extremely sensitive to frost and resent cold, damp weather. While they are waiting to be transplanted, over-watering of the pots or shaded conditions and stagnant air at any point will almost always cause mildew and other fungal diseases that may be fatal. Out in the garden, full sun and a well-drained but moist sandy loam are absolute requisites, and plants will develop best in the hottest part of the garden against the heat-reflecting wall of a garage or other building.

To an observer with a vivid imagination, the bloom whorls of leonotis *might* look like the ears of a lion, giving the genus its name, from ancient Greek *leon,* lion, and *otis,* ear. The species name, however, attempts to refine this fuzzy perception and refers to the flower structures with *leon* and *oura,* meaning tail. It is true that a whorl of bloom more closely resembles the puff of fur on a lion's tail than its ears.

LIMNANTHES DOUGLASII

FAMILY: *Limnanthaceae* or meadow foam family.

CLASSIFICATION: Hardy annual.

COMMON NAMES: Fried egg flower, poached egg flower, meadow foam, limnanthes.

HARDINESS: Withstands light frosts.

GROWING CONDITIONS: Moist, fertile, well-drained soil. Cool growing conditions. Fails in summer heat.

PROPAGATION: From seed, sown in place in autumn in warmer gardens, in very early spring elsewhere. Seedlings will not transplant.

HEIGHT: From 6 to 8".

ORNAMENTAL VALUE: Grown for flowers.

LEVEL OF CULTURAL DIFFICULTY: Moderately difficult to difficult, depending on region.

SPECIAL PROPERTIES: Superb winter-flowering plant for cool greenhouses.

PRONUNCIATION: lim-NAN-thees doug-LASS-ee-ee

Though seldom more than six or eight inches high, *Limnanthes douglasii* is among the greatest treasures in the rich American West Coast flora. Native from Oregon to central California and the foothills of the Sierra Nevada, it forms sheets of flower from March to May in wet meadows and edges of vernal pools. The seed sprouts after winter rains, and plants quickly grow into lax-stemmed, sprawling little bushes with attractive chartreuse-green pinnate leaves of eight or so leaflets arranged feather fashion on the stems. As the meadows and vernal pools begin to dry, flowers appear in great profusion, smothering the little plants. Perhaps no other native American wild flower is as charming in bloom, for each inch-wide flower is composed of five notched petals and carries a circular zone of bright yellow that gives way abruptly to white. Attractive, prominent veins of reddish brown mark the yellow zone of each petal. Ten stamens, each about a quarter-inch long, radiate out from the center, adding to the delicacy of the flower. Flowers are sweetly fragrant and seldom without visiting bees.

Limnanthes is a variable plant, with cultivars that differ in flower color from the typical species. There are completely yellow forms, or completely white, and one with pale pink, heavily veined flowers. Though all are lovely in their own way, they scarcely compete in charm with the yellow-centered form, and they distract from its elegance when grown among it.

In general garden references there is great confusion about the sowing, culture, and bloom time of limnanthes. The plant is said to require moist to wet soils or well-drained ones; seed is to be sown in autumn or in early spring; bloom time is said to be in spring and early summer, or in mid- to late summer or sometimes late June until after light frosts. All this contradictory information may be true or false, depending on where one lives. All authorities agree, however, that limnanthes reaches perfection only in cool periods and will cease flowering after only a brief period when the weather warms, or will prove to be a complete failure in gardens that experience hot, humid weather.

As a hardy annual, limnanthes may be sown where it is to grow in autumn in gardens warmer than Zone 5. Soils, however, should be well drained for optimum winter survival as cold, heavy wet soils will cause many young plants to perish. Flowers will begin bloom in early to mid-spring (depending on how early spring comes) and continue through June or whenever the weather becomes hot. In colder gardens, however, seed is best sown in early spring as soon as the soil may be worked, and plants will flower from late July until after light frosts, assuming late summer nights remain fresh and cool.

Limnanthes, like many annuals native to California, is extremely intolerant of transplanting, and though others in its category can sometimes be successfully started indoors, in peat pots or in plastic cell packs, and shifted to the garden with minimal root disturbance, limnanthes, when so treated, will never grow into strong, well-flowered plants. It is therefore always sown in place, in full sun, and the young plants are thinned to stand about five inches apart as soon as possible. As with poppies, care must be taken not to sow seed too thickly, as those plants that are to remain can be damaged by pulling those that are to be discarded. Though a true annual, once grown in most gardens limnanthes is apt to be there forever, as volunteers will generally appear for years after the first sowing. Where conditions are to its liking, spring-flowering plants from an autumn sowing may produce a second crop of plants that will flower shyly but attractively in late summer and autumn, and if winters are mild, again with great abundance in spring.

Those gardeners who possess the luxury of a cool greenhouse will find limnanthes a superb winter-flowering plant. In late August or early September, pinches of seed should be distributed

LIMNANTHES DOUGLASII

across the top of six-inch pots (filled to within an inch of their rims with moisture-retentive but well-drained compost) and then covered with about an eighth of an inch of fine soil or sand. After germination, seedlings should be thinned so that five remain, evenly spaced. Plants must be grown on in cool but bright conditions, a night-time temperature of about 50°F being ideal, and growth may be encouraged by weak applications of water-soluble fertilizer. Flowering should begin in late winter, creating a dome of bloom across the top of the pot.

Limnanthes douglasii is the signature species—and the only one grown in gardens—in the family Limnanthaceae, which contains two genera and six other species. The genus name originates from two ancient Greek words, *limne,* meaning marsh, and *anthos,* flower, describing the conditions of its native West Coast habitat. The species name *douglasii* commemorates the brilliant Scottish plant explorer David Douglas (1798–1834), who on two expeditions sponsored by the Royal Horticultural Society discovered many important native American plants and introduced them into European gardens.

LIMONIUM SINUATUM

FAMILY: *Plumbaginaceae* or plumbago family.

CLASSIFICATION: Half-hardy biennials grown as half-hardy annuals.

COMMON NAMES: Statice, sea lavender, sea pink, limonium.

HARDINESS: Sensitive to frost.

GROWING CONDITIONS: Moderately fertile, well-drained soil. Full sun.

PROPAGATION: By seed, sown indoors 6 to 8 weeks before last frost.

HEIGHT: To 2'.

ORNAMENTAL VALUE: Grown for flowers.

LEVEL OF CULTURAL DIFFICULTY: Easy.

SPECIAL PROPERTIES: Valued for dried flowers.

PRONUNCIATION: li-MO-nee-um sin-yew-A-tum

Gardeners are often hostile to botanical names, but *statice,* the ancient Greek word for several seaside plants, has clung to members of the genus *Limonium.* Even though it has been discarded by botanists, it is firmly fixed as a vernacular name along with "sea lavender" and "sea pink," which have been stretched to cover the forms of limonium grown as annuals. (Both names properly apply to the perennial species, beautiful, deep-lavender-flowered *Limonium latifolium* [la-ti-FO-lee-um], which reaches perfection only in warm, sandy, seaside gardens.) One sometimes also hears the annual forms called "German statice," though it is hard to know why, as they are mostly native to the Mediterranean region and southeastern Europe.

The most frequently grown of several annual statices is *Limonium sinuatum,* a tender biennial in its native Mediterranean habitat but easily grown as an annual in almost all American gardens. The genus name derives from the ancient Greek word for meadow, *leimon,* and refers to the thick stands that form in salt marshes in southern Europe. It forms a tight, ground-hugging rosette of lyre-shaped, dark green leathery leaves, each about six or seven inches long. They are wavy or rippled along their edges, supplying the species name *sinuatum,* meaning sinuous or curving. Several stiff, self-supporting flowering stems are produced from the center of the plant, each surmounted by a much-branched cluster of flowers. The blossoms are quite tiny, scarcely three eighths of an inch across, each one cupped by a chaffy calyx only slightly larger. The true flowers—clusters of tiny white or cream-colored stars—have a very brief life, but the calyxes stay in good condition for a very long time, retaining their form and color practically forever when dried. In the wild species form, the calyxes are a soft lavender, though modern limoniums are generally much improved, particularly in their range of color, which extends through many shades of lavender, dark and pale pink, deep and light purple, red, apricot, strong and pale yellow, cream, and pristine white. Newer varieties have also been selected for greater sturdiness, for more lasting color when dried, and for shatter resistance, since *L. sinuatum* is perhaps more popular as a dried flower than in the garden.

Other species of *Limonium* that may be grown as annuals are also popular, and more are soon likely to appear. One, *L. suworowi* (soo-WOE-ro-ee), a native of Turkestan, is so different from other limoniums both in its appearance and its botanical characteristics that it has recently been assigned to a separate genus, *Psylliostachys* (si-lee-o-STAY-kis). Popularly, it is called "pink pokers" from the form of its flower spikes, consisting of dense, narrow cones of calyxes crowded along the tips of stems.

LINARIA SPECIES

FAMILY: *Scrophulariaceae* or snapdragon family.

CLASSIFICATION: Hardy annuals and sometimes hardy perennials grown as hardy annuals.

COMMON NAMES: Toadflax, linaria.

HARDINESS: Withstands light frosts.

GROWING CONDITIONS: Well-drained loamy soil of moderate fertility. Full sun.

PROPAGATION: Sow seed in place in early spring. Start indoors 6 weeks before last frost.

HEIGHT: From 6" to 2', depending on cultivar and culture.

ORNAMENTAL VALUE: Grown for flowers.

LEVEL OF CULTURAL DIFFICULTY: Easy.

SPECIAL PROPERTIES: None.

PRONUNCIATION: li-NA-ree-a

LIMONIUM SINUATUM

Linaria takes its name from the signature of the genus: needle-like leaves that resemble those of *Linum,* the genus to which flax belongs. Where the toad part comes in is hard to say, for toads do not weave, nor do they wear linen shirts, at least not before reverting to princes. Perhaps the name originated from the fact that all linaria bear a nectar-rich spur that makes them very attractive to many insects, and therefore, as a convenient bait to any toad that might crouch among them.

The genus contains between seventy-five and a hundred species, and fully a third of those are garden-worthy, though most gardeners will be familiar with only one or two. By far the most commonly grown annual species is *Linaria maroccana* (mar-o-KA-na), a native of North Africa as its species name indicates, though widely naturalized in the eastern parts of North America along roadsides and in fields of thin grass. It produces a much-branched, bushy little plant to about a foot tall, bearing thin, narrow leaves of a fresh lettuce green. Its flowers resemble miniature snapdragons, as do all species of *Linaria*. The individual, half-inch-long flowers are borne numerously in spikes, and each has a prominent yellow or orange spot on its lower petals, which fuse with the upper ones to form a long, nectar-bearing spur containing a forked pistil and four pollen-laden anthers. The color of the wild plant is a reddish violet with a yellow spot, but modern garden forms have been selected for a wide range of colors, including white, lilac, mauve, pale and strong pink, red, blue, purple, copper, and light brown. Seed is never offered in single colors, but in mixes that may contain all these shades, though purples, reds, and strong pinks will be in the majority. This multicolored offering of flow-

LINARIA MAROCCANA

ers makes linaria inappropriate for sophisticated bedding schemes, though if plants are spaced about six to eight inches apart, they soon interweave to form a blended patch of color that is merry and pleasing.

Linaria maroccana blooms so rapidly from seed that there is little point in starting it early indoors, though where summer heat comes early, it might be seeded about six weeks before the last anticipated frost date, to produce plants that would flower shortly after they were transplanted into the garden. Otherwise, it should be sown in place either in late September or as soon in spring as the soil can be worked, which is about the time one would plant peas. Care must be taken to sow the seed thinly in ground that is as free of weed seeds as possible, for the young seedlings are very tiny—hardly more than green hairs on the ground—and weeding can be difficult. Full sun is an absolute requirement, though almost any soil will do as long as it is porous and free draining.

Though the most frequently grown, *Linaria maroccana* is not the only true annual toadflax worthy of garden space. All are native to southern Europe, chiefly Spain and Portugal, though the range of several extends into North Africa, and so they may all be expected to require full sun and well-drained, somewhat lean soils. *L. amethystea* (a-muh-THIS-tee-a) grows into a branched plant up to fourteen inches tall, producing three-quarter-inch-long flowers of blue, violet, yellow, cream, or white, all freckled with purple. Spikes are borne well above the narrow, gray-green leaves, and may contain between two and ten flowers each. *L. broussonetti* (bru-so-NET-ee), which commemorates the eighteenth-century French botanist Pierre Broussonet (1761–1807), is sometimes offered as a separate species, though it is probably synonymous with, or a subspecies of, *L. amethystea*. Plants offered under that name are generally smaller than those of *L. amethystea*, bearing tiny yellow snapdragons with deep orange throats.

Linaria bipartita (bi-par-TI-ta) takes its species name from its deeply cleft upper lobes. It grows to about a foot tall, with narrow, whorled, gray-green leaves each about an inch long, and its one-and-a-half-inch flowers with curved spurs may be violet, deep and light purple to white, but always with an orange-yellow throat. If sown in place in the garden in early April, *L. bipartita* will flower over a long period of time from late June until autumn.

Though several *Linaria,* both annual and perennial, have naturalized in North America, *L. canadensis* (ca-na-DEN-sis) is the only native American species cultivated in gardens. It is called "the oldfield toadflax" from its preference for thin exhausted pasture land, and it possesses a natural range from southern Canada through the eastern United States, south to Texas and west to South Dakota. Its upright, slender plants may reach a height of as much as two feet, bearing whorls of narrow leaves and loose clusters of violet-blue flowers with a yellow-spotted lip. In parts of its range or in milder gardens, it may behave as a biennial, blooming the second year after germination; such plants always grow tallest and produce the finest flowers. In most gardens, however, it will behave as a pleasantly flowered annual.

Linaria reticulata (ri-ti-cu-LA-ta) generally grows to about a foot in height in gardens, though under ideal conditions it may reach a height of as much as four feet. Its two-inch-long flowers possess spurs as long as its corolla, typically of a light purple with a yellow or orange lip, though it also appears in shades of red and maroon. The cultivar 'Aureo-purpurea' (o-RE-o pur-PUR-ree-a) bears flowers of an even deeper and richer purple.

A perennial linaria that may be grown as an annual is *L. aeruginea* (air-u-JIN-ee-a), the species name of which is taken from the Latin adjective meaning rust-colored. This is not particularly descriptive since, though some plants bear flowers of a rusty purplish brown, others may be yellow, violet, purple, cream, or almost white though always with a prominent orange spot on the lower lip shading to purple at the throat. A variety of *L. aeruginea,* var. *nevadensis* (neh-va-DEN-sis), originating from the mountains of Spain and Portugal (and not the American state), is sometimes offered as a separate species. It produces a lower, almost creeping plant with gray-green, needle-like foliage, and bears a profusion of long-spurred, horn-shaped flowers complexly shading from orange to bright scarlet.

Another species, *Linaria triornithophora* (tri-or-ni-THO-fer-a), though also a true perennial, can be made to behave as an annual, which, as it is hardy only to Zones 8 to 10, may be the only way most American gardeners can have it. It reaches a height of about three feet, with whorls of brilliant green leaves and inch-and-a-half-long, showy flowers that are pale purple above and lilac beneath the petals and along the prominent spur. The lower lobes are pinched at the opening, looking somewhat like puckered faces, and bear two pale yellow cheeks freckled over with darker purple. Flowers are borne in whorls giving the plant its curious species name, which translates as "three birds flying."

New and previously unknown linarias, both annual and perennial, appear in good seed catalogues every year, while others, previously introduced, are dropped. No one gardener could grow them all. The genus is so rich in decorative species that it deserves a monograph and even possibly a whole botanical garden all of its own. Of course linarias are not for all gardens, as they are intolerant of heat, high humidity, and heavy clay soils. But where they may be grown well, their ease of culture, the charm of their little flowers, and their jewel-like colors make them very desirable garden plants.

LINUM GRANDIFLORUM

FAMILY: *Linaceae* or linum family.

CLASSIFICATION: Hardy annual.

COMMON NAMES: Flax, linum.

HARDINESS: Withstands light frosts when established.

GROWING CONDITIONS: Moderately fertile, free-draining, moisture-retentive soil. Full sun.

PROPAGATION: By seed, sown in place in autumn in warmer gardens, and in very early spring in cooler ones.

HEIGHT: From 1 to 1½′ tall.

ORNAMENTAL VALUE: Grown for flower.

LEVEL OF CULTURAL DIFFICULTY: Moderately difficult.

SPECIAL PROPERTIES: One species is the source of linen cloth.

PRONUNCIATION: LI-num gran-di-FLO-rum

Of the two annual flax grown in gardens, *Linum grandiflorum* may be the most beautiful, but *L. usitatissimum* (u-si-ta-TISS-i-mum) has the longest association with humanity. The species name is a Latin adjective meaning most useful, and few plants more fully earn the name. *L. usitatissimum* has variously provided food, medicine, cooking oil, and, of course, clothing. After leather, it was the most important fabric for garments until the latter part of the eighteenth century, when machines for ginning, spinning, and weaving cotton were invented.

The distinction of the prettiest garden plants in the genus, however, does not belong to agricultural flax, but to two perennial flax, *Linum narbonense*

(nar-bon-EN-suh) and *L. perenne* (per-EN-ne), and to *L. grandiflorum,* a true annual. But *L. usitatissimum* is pretty enough, forming wispy, grasslike clumps of slender stems to as much as three feet tall, clad in tiny, needle-like leaves and surmounted by branched clusters of pale, sky-blue flowers. The flowers, which, like most linums, are very short-lived, lasting scarcely a day, open in great profusion, so that fields of commercially raised flax seem, on a clear day, to have drawn heaven to earth. Each bloom is about half an inch wide, with its five petals held apart but cupped by a green calyx. The texture of the petals is gossamer thin, practically translucent, though netted with prominent veins of deeper blue. A pure white form also exists, which is very lovely in itself and also when mixed with the blue.

Though it lacks economic importance or so rich a history, *Linum grandiflorum* is more beautiful for the size and vivid coloration of its flowers. It is a shorter plant than commercially grown flax—about a foot and a half tall—with slender bushy growth and gray-green, needle-like leaves surmounted by wiry, branched, and leafless bloom stems. The stems are so thin and hairlike that they seem unlikely supports for the flowers, each of which is about an inch and a half wide—a cup of overlapping petals. Flowers are delicate of texture, with the beautiful satiny sheen one sees in poppies, which they superficially resemble. Their beauty is much increased by a prominent, circular, darker zone in the center of each bloom. An individual flower lasts very briefly, scarcely more than a day, but is quickly replaced by others.

In the garden, both *Linum usitatissimum* and *L. grandiflorum* respond to the same culture. Both are hardy annuals, and as is so often the case with plants in this category, they do not respond well to transplanting, even when it is done with great care. Germination is rapid, however, taking about a week, and the first flowers are produced about eight weeks from sprouting. Seed should be

LINUM GRANDIFLORUM

broadcast on well-drained soil, as early as it can be worked in spring, and in full sun. Seedlings should stand rather close together, about six inches one from another, to provide mutual support for their thin, willowy stems. (Alternatively, they may be sown in patches among more sturdy annuals or perennials that will offer support.) No other special care is needed.

There is considerable disagreement in general garden references about the length of time that *Linum grandiflorum* will flower. English gardeners often praise its unusually long bloom period—from late June to September from an April sowing. American garden authorities, however, often suggest repeat sowings every two weeks or the shearing back of plants to about half their height when bloom flags, to encourage a repeat flowering in late summer. The explanation for the contradiction lies in the fact that *L. grandiflorum,* again like many other hardy annuals, performs best (and longest) in gardens that enjoy cool nights and bright, fresh days, even in high desert gardens where supplemental irrigation will be required. In warmer gardens, however, especially when summer weather is uncomfortably humid, linum must be treated as flowers of early summer, perhaps with a second crop in autumn from a midsummer sowing. In such gardens an autumn sowing is often possible, for even earlier and longer-blooming plants in spring.

Linum grandiflorum was once a very popular garden plant with many listed cultivars, including the still-offered 'Rubrum' with clear red flowers. Several of these listed cultivars no longer appear to be offered, though some may still be grown as heirloom varieties. Happily, a form thought to be lost, called 'Bright Eyes', with white petals and a prominent, burgundy-red central zone, has been recovered and is offered. A very beautiful white cultivar, 'Alba', sometimes also appears in catalogues. But the rich, bluish-purple form, 'Caeru-

leum' (se-RU-lee-um), seems not to have been offered for many years, which is a pity since it might be very fine in a mixed planting with 'Rubrum'. The orange-red cultivar 'Coccineum' (co-CHIN-ee-um) is also listed in references but is absent from catalogues. This shrinking of offerings, and the commensurate infrequency with which *Linum grandiflorum* is seen in gardens, is due to the fact that until recently, hardy annuals that would not accept transplanting, and that therefore could not be bought in garden centers and nurseries, quickly dropped from popularity with gardeners. The recent increased interest in unusual or little-grown annuals, however, has been followed by an increase in skill on the part of many gardeners in managing some of the more difficult or demanding ones. It may be hoped, then, that lost cultivars of *Linum grandiflorum* will be recovered, offered, and grown again.

LOASA TRIPHYLLA VAR. *VOLCANICA*

FAMILY: *Loasaceae* or loasa family.

CLASSIFICATION: Half-hardy annual.

COMMON NAMES: Chilean nettle, ortiga, loasa.

HARDINESS: Sensitive to light frosts.

GROWING CONDITIONS: Rich, well-drained soil. Full sun.

PROPAGATION: By seed, sown in site or started indoors 6 to 8 weeks before frost. Resents transplant disturbance.

HEIGHT: To 2'.

ORNAMENTAL VALUE: Grown for flowers.

LEVEL OF CULTURAL DIFFICULTY: Easy.

SPECIAL PROPERTIES: All parts cause painful skin irritation on contact.

PRONUNCIATION: lo-AH-sa tri-PHIL-a vol-KA-ni-ca

No one denies that the Chilean nettle is beautiful. From midsummer until frost, it produces curiously crafted flowers, each about an inch or an inch and a half wide, made up of five hooded, slender, chalk-white petals that hover over and protect an odd, clawed center of bright yellow streaked with red and white. Though seed is offered in catalogues with fair frequency, it is doubtful that many gardeners will choose to grow the plant except possibly once, out of curiosity, for all of its parts—the lobed dark green, three-inch-wide leaves and the flowers—are armed with stinging hairs that cause immediate pain and result in burns on the skin that may be irritating for up to three days.

Loasa, native to most of Central and South America, from Mexico to Chile and Peru, is the signature genus of its family, the Loasaceae, which contains approximately thirteen genera and as many as 230 species. Both the family and genus names are taken from a vernacular native Chilean word for this family, signifying plants that hurt. Within both the family and the signature genus, only *Loasa triphylla* var. *volcanica* is cultivated, if at all, and only by the brave. The species name "triphylla" indicates its three-lobed leaves, and "volcanica," though it technically means a plant growing "on or near volcanoes," speaks for itself.

Loasa triphylla var. *volcanica* comes into bloom in most American gardens in August from a direct seeding in rich, well-drained soil in full sun. Plants must later be thinned (with gloved hands) to stand approximately eight inches apart. Alternatively, seed may be sown in March or early April and transplanted into the garden after all danger of frost has passed. Minimal root disturbance will help young plants adjust to their place in the garden, and so peat pots or cell packs should be used. Once newly established young plants show vigorous growth in the garden, a light dressing of granular fertilizer such as 10-10-10 will encourage rich leafy growth and abundant flower.

Loasa triphylla var. *volcanica* is said to make an excellent cut flower, taken stem, leaf, bloom, and all, though it is hard to find anyone who has tried it for this purpose.

LOBELIA SPECIES

FAMILY: *Lobeliaceae* or lobelia family.

CLASSIFICATION: Tender perennials grown as half-hardy annuals.

COMMON NAME: Lobelia.

HARDINESS: Withstands light frost when established. Winter-hardy in Zones 8 to 10.

GROWING CONDITIONS: Humus-rich, well-drained soil. Full sun. Afternoon shade in warmer gardens. Prefers cool weather.

PROPAGATION: By seed, sown indoors in late winter. Cuttings root readily.

HEIGHT: To 4", but trailing forms may reach a foot or more in length.

ORNAMENTAL VALUE: Grown for flowers.

LEVEL OF CULTURAL DIFFICULTY: Easy to difficult, depending on species.

SPECIAL PROPERTIES: *Lobelia erinus* is a superb hanging basket plant. Excellent winter-flowering plants for cool windowsills or greenhouses.

PRONUNCIATION: lo-BEE-li-a

In a genus of perhaps 350 species comprising true annuals, perennials, shrubs, and even trees distributed across tropical and temperate areas of the globe, the little *Lobelia erinus* (E-ri-nus) is, for gardeners, the most important. It is one of the true indispensables in summer gardens. Its compact forms are used for edging, though it is most

LOBELIA ERINUS

There are many bi-colors as well, with lips of various shades of blue and a clear white throat. They are very pretty and become prettier when blended with entirely blue forms and with white. Many colors of *Lobelia erinus* are available in both a bunched and a trailing form, but blended plantings usually look best when they are all of one type or the other. In both forms, lobelia is also available in cultivars ranging from pale pink through rose to a purple that is almost red, the darker shades often also showing a white eye. Doubtless, they have their uses in bedding schemes limited to those colors, though the deeper shades can appear somewhat muddy when viewed from afar.

Lobelia erinus is a quite small plant, seldom reaching a height of much more than four inches, though trailing forms may extend downward from pots or hanging baskets to as much as a foot or more. Both its stems and half-inch oval notched leaves are generally an attractive, fresh green, but bronze-leaved forms are popular. Each tiny flower is scarcely more than half an inch wide, but they are cunningly fashioned, consisting of two lips—the upper one made up of two lobes that turn jauntily backward, and the lower, of three somewhat broader lobes. When the plant is grown well and is happy with its environment, it will almost cover itself with flowers. And as it is a true perennial, plants may be sheared back in early autumn, lifted carefully, and potted for indoor winter bloom on a cool, bright windowsill. Alternatively, cuttings may easily be taken, which will already show white roots on stems that touch the ground and have been kept moist by the matted foliage above. A few choice lobelias such as the exquisite, double-flowered cultivar 'Kathleen Mallard' can only be reproduced in this way and if one is lucky enough to find it, it should certainly be carried over the winter for fresh cuttings and more plants the following spring.

familiar as an essential component in mixed containers and hanging baskets, where—according to how it has been bred to behave—it forms tight, floriferous little bunches of flower or graceful, trailing cascades. It is interesting to note that even though hundreds of thousands of started plants are bought each spring, *Lobelia erinus* has never attracted to itself any common name. All gardeners, amateurs and sophisticates alike, call it by its genus name—simply "lobelia."

To many people there is no other color for a lobelia than blue, whether it is the beautiful, powdery pale shade or an intense, saturated hue rivaled only by some gentians. It is true, however, that the pure white cultivars can be crisp and fresh, though it is important to know if one sows one's own seed that roughly 10 percent of the seedlings will be some shade other than white.

Lobelia is a tender perennial native to South Africa and winter-hardy in North America in cool, frost-free climates such as that of San Francisco. In such privileged places, it achieves a vibrancy of bloom that can be stunning in the dark, damp days of winter. Elsewhere, it is generally grown as an annual, blooming most profusely in late spring and early summer, and again in autumn. It always performs best where nights are cool and days are bright and fresh, though even in hot, humid gardens it will be worth growing if it can receive a little shade from the afternoon sun.

Started plants of *Lobelia erinus* are so easily obtained that only a point of pride would justify starting them from seed, especially since the seed is dust-fine, almost invisible (there may be as many as 30,000 in a single gram), and extremely difficult to distribute evenly over the well-drained, sterile compost it will require to avoid juvenile fungus diseases. Most growers sow it in pinches. Seed should be sown early, in late February or early March, and the minute seedlings may sometimes be very slow to appear. Because it is almost impossible to prick out individual seedlings into single pots, plugs of three, four, or more are separated and potted together. Where mixes are sown, this has the advantage of blending shades evenly together.

Young plants should be set out after all danger of frost is past in rich, free-draining loam. All lobelias are intolerant of both heavy, waterlogged soil and dry, arid sand, but they demand even moisture at their roots. Complete drying out—as sometimes occurs in hanging baskets—may permanently damage the plants. Full sun always produces the most abundant flower, though in hot gardens afternoon shade is appreciated. Lobelias may grow well in shade, but few flowers will be produced.

Lobelia erinus, though by far the most important, is not the only member of its genus that may be grown as an annual. Another species, *Lobelia valida* (VA-li-da), takes its name from the Latin adjective meaning strong or muscular, acknowledging its stiff, upright form to as much as eighteen inches in height. Its leaves are narrow and somewhat succulent, of a bright, grass green, and its flowers are a magnificent deep blue. Where seed is available it is well worth a try, though cutting-grown plants are easier to manage. Compared to the relative cultural ease of *Lobelia erinus,* however, *L. valida* can be fussy, demanding rich, well-drained loam, full sun, cool conditions, and protection from drying winds.

Perhaps the most exciting lobelias that may flower from seed in their first year are the 'Compliment' series, bred in Canada by Wray Bowden and now listed botanically as *Lobelia* x *speciosa* (spee-see-O-sa). They are hardly as well known as they should be. Their parentage is entirely uncertain, consisting of crosses and back-crosses of many species, though the blood of the magnificent scarlet-flowered perennial American native *Lobelia cardinalis* (car-di-NAH-lis) is clearly predominant. From it, also, they inherit great tolerance to heat and cold, for in the conditions *Lobelia cardinalis* likes, it may be hardy in an unusually wide range of temperatures from Zones 2 to 9. Lobelias in the 'Compliment' series will flower approximately five months from seed, and so should be sown indoors in January at about 65°F and grown on in bright, sunny conditions to be transplanted when all danger of frost is past. Plants raised indoors will always be delicate and so will require hardening off and protection from frost in their first year as transplants.

For growing conditions, lobelias in this group demand full sun, protection from winds, moist soil, and as rich a diet as can be provided, preferably in the form of well-rotted animal manures, compost dug into the soil, or frequent applications of dilute liquid fertilizer. They are worth the trouble, for they now come in startling shades of blue, violet, purple, rose, pink, and blood red. They are superb for cutting, producing straight rods of bloom from two to four feet tall. Where they can be made happy, they will become perennial, though rather weakly so, unless they are divided annually in early spring and replanted in newly enriched soil. Elsewhere, they perform well as annuals and, as one would suppose, make superb, late-winter-flowering plants for the cool greenhouse. For this purpose, seed should be sown in late summer or cuttings taken from strong, non-flowering shoots. The plants should be grown on in cool, airy conditions, with nighttime temperatures hovering around 55°F and daytime temperatures perhaps ten degrees warmer. A balanced, water-soluble fertilizer such as Peters 20-20-20 should be applied every week at half the strength recommended on the package. Bloom should occur from February through early April, after which the plants can be cut back to encourage basal growth, which may be divided for transplants.

Though the pretty flowers of lobelias might seem tempting decorations for cakes or garnishes for salads, they contain—like many blue flowers or flowers that began by being blue—alkaloids that cause vomiting and may be toxic.

LOBELIA ERINUS

The name "lobelia" commemorates the eminent Flemish botanist and physician Mathias de l'Obel (1538–1616), who in the last nine years of his life had the difficult job of tending the health of King James I of England (1566–1625), who was always a sickly monarch.

LOBULARIA MARITIMA

FAMILY: *Cruciferae* or mustard family.

CLASSIFICATION: Half-hardy perennial grown as hardy annual.

COMMON NAMES: Madwort, sweet alyssum, lobularia.

HARDINESS: Withstands light frosts.

GROWING CONDITIONS: Ordinary, well-drained garden loam. Full sun. Afternoon shade in warmer gardens.

PROPAGATION: By seed, sown indoors 6 to 8 weeks before frost or sown in site in early spring. Plants resent root disturbance.

HEIGHT: From 5 to 8".

ORNAMENTAL VALUE: Grown for flowers. A popular edging plant.

LEVEL OF CULTURAL DIFFICULTY: Easy.

SPECIAL PROPERTIES: Fragrance. Charming winter-flowering annual for cool greenhouse.

PRONUNCIATION: lob-you-LA-ree-uh ma-RI-ti-ma

*I*t has been many years since botanists transferred sweet alyssum into the genus *Lobularia,* but the name of the genus to which it belonged, *Alyssum,* has clung stubbornly to it and is the popular name by which most gardeners know it. Alyssum is both a pleasant word and a meaningful one—made up of the ancient Greek negative *a-* meaning not or against, and *lyssa,* meaning madness. Since ancient times, sweet alyssum has been used as a cure for both rage and madness, which the ancient Greeks thought closely connected, the first causal to the second. Though the belief that sweet alyssum might heal the darkest reaches of the human mind rests on no scientific basis, it is not difficult to understand why it carried credence from ancient times well into the seventeenth century. A gentle little plant, modest in its demeanor, sweet alyssum possesses a calming but unassertive honey-sweet fragrance.

The individual flowers are quite tiny, hardly more than a fourth of an inch wide, though they reward close study. The four rounded petals, typical of all Cruciferae, form a little cup with a flaring rim, deep inside which are six stamens, two shorter than the other four, and four sepals. Flowers are borne in tight, dome-shaped clusters about three-quarters-inch wide, in various stages of maturity from tight buds in the center to partially opened and then mature flowers around the edge. In modern varieties tiny, paddle-shaped seed pods are hidden by the flowers until most have opened. (*Lobularia,* from the Latin *lobulus,* refers to the small, lobed pods.) Unless crowded by its neighbors, an individual specimen of sweet alyssum will form an almost perfect circle of blooming stems, so close together that the branched structure of the plant and its inch-long, lance-shaped leaves are completely hidden.

Lobularia maritima is native to southern Europe and Eurasia, and in its wild form is a somewhat rangy and sprawling plant that may reach a height of as much as a foot, though it is generally shorter. All along the coast of California, where the plant has freely naturalized, specimens of this sort may be seen, for the plant quickly reverts to its natural form, and in that climate, as in its native range, it behaves as a true perennial.

In gardens, however, sweet alyssum is usually grown as an annual, in forms that are vastly improved from the wild species, which bears flowers of a rather dingy white. Plants are much more compact, forming solid domes of flower from five to eight inches tall and spreading to as much as ten inches across. White forms, still preferred by many gardeners, are very pure, with no hint of gray, though other cultivars have been developed bearing flowers that may be cream, mauve, lavender, apricot, copper, red, purple, or biscuit tan. As is usually the case with a fragrant plant, however, this elaboration of color has occurred at the expense of scent, a lack that has been addressed by breeders, who have produced at least one white form so far that is intensely fragrant.

Sweet alyssum is an annual plant of very easy culture. It is not particular as to soils, though it will not thrive in heavy, waterlogged clay, and it prefers, as do most annual plants, a deep, rich, well-drained loam. The best plants are always produced in full sun, though in very hot gardens some afternoon shade will prolong the length of bloom. Once established, sweet alyssum is tolerant of periods of drought, though not of heat, which will usually curtail flower production or cause plants to "run to seed." When plants become shabby, with elongated stems showing seed pods and with only a few flowers at the top, bloom time may often be prolonged by shearing the plants by about a third, or just at the point where flowering stems emerge from leafy growth. One must not wait until all flowering has ceased, however, else the seed will be sufficiently ripe that the plant will not re-sprout, and one will be left with an ugly little bristle of stems. Water-soluble fertilizer applied according to the directions just after shearing will help to encourage new flower growth. Fresh seed may be sprinkled among the older plants in late June or early July to produce a crop of young flowering plants by late summer and into autumn.

Sweet alyssum may be expected to bloom about six weeks from germination, which should

LOBULARIA MARITIMA

occur about a week after seed is sown. The earliest flowering plants may be obtained by sowing the seed indoors about six to eight weeks before the last anticipated frost date, to produce small flowering plants that may be set out as soon as the weather is settled. Seedlings accept root disturbance only when very small, and so it is best to sow three seed to an individual cell pack, allowing all three to develop and planting the individual cell with minimal root disturbance. This method is particularly desirable when mixed colors are sown, as it will produce a nice, faded chintz blend of many shades. Alternatively, young plants may be obtained from most nurseries in springtime, already showing their tiny domes of bloom.

Since sweet alyssum is a hardy annual, seed may also be sprinkled outdoors as soon as the soil may be worked for flowering plants by early June. The seed is very small, however, and if it is sown too thickly, it is tedious to thin so that young seedlings stand about four to six inches apart. An even sowing without overcrowding may be achieved by mixing seed with fine canary sand, available in the pet departments of most supermarkets. For even greater assurance against overcrowding, the seed and fine sand may be put into a salt shaker and tapped out lightly where patches of plants are wanted—particularly along paths, in the cracks of brick or stone paving, over clumps of maturing daffodil foliage, or in rock gardens. Sweet alyssum is not attractive, however, when it is used in regimented lines as a strip or edging to flower beds, a practice that forfeits all the natural grace and charm of the plant.

As a hardy annual that relishes cool growing conditions, sweet alyssum makes a superb winter-flowering plant for the cool greenhouse or minimally heated sun porch. Seed should be sown at the end of summer or in early autumn in five- or six-inch pots and later thinned to stand about three inches apart. Developing seedlings will appreciate light applications of water-soluble plant food, and if spent flower stems are promptly removed, plants should flower from early winter well into spring.

LOPEZIA RACEMOSA

FAMILY: *Onagraceae* or evening primrose family.

CLASSIFICATION: Tender annual or tender sub-shrub grown as tender annual.

COMMON NAMES: Mosquito flower, lopezia.

HARDINESS: Sensitive to light frosts.

GROWING CONDITIONS: Ordinary, evenly moist loam with perfect drainage. Full sun. Relishes summer heat.

PROPAGATION: By seed, sown indoors about 8 weeks before last frost. Cuttings may be rooted.

HEIGHT: To 4' in Zones 9 and 10. Normally less than 2' when grown as an annual.

ORNAMENTAL VALUE: Grown for flowers.

Lopezia is a small genus of eighteen or so species, all native to Mexico and Central America. In American gardens that experience no frost, at least six species are valued as annuals or sub-shrubs for their delicate, bushlike growth and the clouds of flowers they produce freely through the winter months. The effect of a plant in full bloom is as if a swarm of tiny, deep pink or carmine-red winged insects had settled over it, hence the popular name "mosquito flower."

But since lopezias flower from autumn to spring and are frost-sensitive, few are important to most American gardeners except as windowsill or cool greenhouse plants. At least one *Lopezia,* however, *Lopezia racemosa,* can be coaxed into behaving as a summer-flowering annual from an indoor sowing in March, or about eight weeks from the last anticipated frost date. It germinates and grows quickly, producing delicate, much-branched small bushes with reddish stems and smooth, glossy, dark green oval leaves about an inch and a half long. Flowers may appear as soon as nine weeks from sowing and will thereafter bloom freely in clusters (hence the species name *racemosa*) from the growing tip of each small branch. "Clusters," however, gives an inaccurate idea of their appearance, for each flower is borne on a long petiole and seems to float free of the others.

The flower is very complicated, consisting of five petals, of which the larger two are lobed or heart-shaped, arranged opposite each other and tilted slightly upward, with two narrow, blade-shaped petals in between, and an abbreviated petal below, above which extends a prominent, needle-like pistil. Behind the true flower are four sepals (the protecting sheath on an unopened bud), which expand into narrow, petal-like structures as the flower opens. *Lopezia racemosa* may grow as tall as four feet where it is hardy, though when cultivated as a summer-blooming annual, it rarely reaches a height of a foot and a half. It grows best in evenly moist, ordinary garden loam, though it requires good drainage. Heavy, claylike soils will not suit it at all. Full sun is required, and it flowers best in summer heat. Because of these requirements, *Lopezia racemosa* seems to make its best appearance in a pot, hanging basket, or window box, which also allows the complexity of its inch-wide delicate flowers to be studied up close.

The genus name commemorates an obscure Spanish botanist, Tomás Lopez, who sent accounts of Mexican plants back to Spain around the year 1540.

LOTUS SPECIES

HEIGHT: Cascading to 2′ or more in a season.

ORNAMENTAL VALUE: Grown for flower and for attractive, cascading vines.

LEVEL OF CULTURAL DIFFICULTY: Moderately easy.

SPECIAL PROPERTIES: Excellent winter greenhouse plant. Useful in hanging baskets.

PRONUNCIATION: LO-tus

In the genus *Lotus,* the two plants cultivated as ornamentals have so little in common with the lotus of popular imagination that most people will say "It's a *what?*" Most likely, they will picture the beautiful Chinese holy lotus, *Nelumbium nelumbo,* though the ancient Greek word *lotos* has been attached to a number of plants from classical antiquity down to modern times. Linnaeus variously applied the word to several leguminous plants including clover, eaten by the Irish as a famine food well into the seventeenth century, and the lotus eaters of Homer's *Odyssey* probably feasted on a species of jujube, *Zizyphus lotus,* the fruit of which is very popular in China as a confection. Another fruit, the Himalayan persimmon, *Diosporus lotus,* carries the word as its species name.

The lotus grown in gardens as annuals, *Lotus berthelotii* (ber-te-LO-ti-ee) and *L. maculatus* (ma-KOO-la-tus), both have silvery, cascading stems and interesting flowers that make them popular as winter greenhouse plants and in summer for the edges of hanging baskets, window boxes, and mixed container plantings. Both are native to the Canary and Cape Verde islands, though they occur naturally with extreme rarity in their native habitats because their complex flowers are adapted to bird pollinators that appear to have vanished from the islands. Both are widely cultivated, however, and where hardy—Zones 9 and 10—are often used as groundcover.

Of the two plants, *Lotus berthelotii* commemorates Sabin Bertheolot, 1794–1880, French consul to the Canary Islands and coauthor of the first study of its fauna and flora. It is the more frequently cultivated for its trailing, branching stems that will cascade gracefully from a pot, reaching a length of as much as two feet in a single summer. Its leaves are minute needles, less than half an inch long, resembling those of a tiny conifer, though not stiff or prickly, but rather quite soft to the touch. They are borne profusely in whorls along the slender stems, and though the leaves are actually celadon green, the plant has a silvery, misty look from a distance. Its curious beak- or claw-shaped flowers, over an inch long and large for such tiny leaves, are borne in clusters all along the stems and are a vivid coral-red. Gardeners in warm climates who cultivate the plant only for summer decoration and discard it after frost will seldom see the flowers, however, for bud-set occurs only when nighttime temperatures are cool, with maximum bloom in spring or again in very late summer and autumn.

Lotus maculatus differs from *L. berthelotii* in producing slightly fleshier leaves on stringier, less-branched stems and, more notably, in bearing flowers of clear yellow-orange with scarlet-red or brownish markings. They look as if a paintbrush of the darker color had been drawn over the lighter ground, giving the plant its species name *maculatus,* meaning spotted or blotched. In truth, however, the two plants are very similar, and when not seen next to one another they are difficult to distinguish. In the trade, plants offered under either name may well be the other, and, to confuse matters further, they also cross freely, producing intermediate forms.

If seed of either species is available, it may be sown in a mixture of half standard potting compost and half sharp builder's sand in early March. Seed germinates best at room temperature, about

70° to 75°F, and young plants should be pricked out and grown on at temperatures cooler by about ten degrees until they may be potted, several to a pot. Cuttings root readily, however, and most plants are propagated in this way. They should be taken in summer just after new growth has followed the spring flush of bloom, inserted in sharp sand or in perlite and kept moist until rooting occurs, when they can then be potted in rich, humusy but well-drained potting compost to which about a third sharp sand has been added by volume. When in active growth, plants benefit from applications of water-soluble plant food, and as the long, trailing stems develop, they should be pinched to encourage branching and to produce a full veil of growth. At all times in their lives, plants of both species require full sun and sharp, quick drainage.

LUPINUS SPECIES

FAMILY: *Leguminosae* or pea family.

CLASSIFICATION: Hardy annuals or sometimes half-hardy perennials grown as hardy annuals.

COMMON NAME: Annual lupine.

HARDINESS: Most species withstand light frost once established.

GROWING CONDITIONS: Rich, fertile, well-drained soil. Full sun.

PROPAGATION: By seed, sown in site in late autumn in warmer gardens, in very early spring in cooler ones. Seed may be sown indoors in peat pots in early March. All species resent root disturbance.

HEIGHT: From 12" to 2', depending on species.

ORNAMENTAL VALUE: Grown for flower.

LEVEL OF CULTURAL DIFFICULTY: Moderately difficult.

SPECIAL PROPERTIES: None.

PRONUNCIATION: loo-PI-nus

There are perhaps as many as 200 species of lupines in the world, distributed throughout North, Central, and South America, Europe, and North Africa, with the greatest concentration of species in western North America. The name of the genus descends directly from the classical Latin word for the plant, *lupus* (meaning wolf), and reflects the ancient belief that, as southern European species were often found growing on thin, sandy soil, they were vegetable predators, consuming the richness of the earth. Their deep-questing central taproots seemed to corroborate this assumption, though in fact, quite the opposite is true. For lupines, like all other members of the family Leguminosae, are able to utilize soil-borne bacteria to draw nitrogen from the air and convert it into usable form. It is this characteristic (along with its unpalatability to cattle) that has enabled at least one annual species, *Lupinus subcarnosus* (sub-car-NO-sus), the Texas bluebonnet, to spread a glorious carpet in May over thin, overgrazed pastures throughout the American Southwest, earning it the status of the state flower of Texas. Interestingly, lupines are also among those plants that draw toxic wastes and pollutants out of the ground, and so were planted for that purpose in quantity at Chernobyl after the famous nuclear disaster there.

The genus *Lupinus* is variable in character, containing perennials, annuals, and glorious shrublike, woody plants to as tall as eight feet. The latter, known as "tree lupines," are selections of the native California *L. arboreus* (ar-BOR-ee-us), which is hardy only in the moister parts of Zone 8, and so is seen by most gardeners only while on vacation to San Francisco or to places with similar climates. The lupine most familiar to American gardeners is the hardy perennial *Lupinus polyphyllus* (po-lee-FI-lus), which is native to the western United States but is now widely naturalized in moist, cool pastures and along un-mown roadsides throughout the northern half of the continent. It served as the genetic base for the spectacular perennial lupines grown in gardens today, created by George Russell of Yorkshire, England, in the first decades of the twentieth century, through patient crossing and back-crossing of *L. polyphyllus* with other species. The annual lupines, however, of which there are many, are largely unknown to gardeners, though the great nineteenth-century English gardener William Robinson called them "among the best of the hardy annuals."

There is good reason for this neglect, even though some—such as *Lupinus mutabilis* (mu-TA-bi-lis) or *L. hartwegii* (hart-WEG-ee-ee)—are clean and tidy of growth and stunningly beautiful in flower. All annual lupines are classed as hardy annuals, and like so many in that group, they must be sown early in spring in the place where they are to grow, since they produce long taproots and are impatient of transplanting. It can be done with great care from a plastic cell pack, or individual peat pots may be used. But plants germinated and grown on in this way are never as fine as those that grow up free from any confinement and have called one spot of earth home for all their lives. So the best way to have them is the old way, by raking off patches in the border in early spring—usually in late March or early April in most American gardens—sowing the seed, marking the spot well with a little hedge of twigs, and thinning the emergent seedlings first to four or five inches apart, and then, when all are safely thriving, to approximately eight inches. Growth is very rapid in the cool weather of spring, so actually there is little to be gained by starting plants early indoors. They are in any case completely intolerant of night temperatures much above 50°F when they are making vegetative growth, and such nighttime coolness is a rare condition in most American houses in late February or early March.

Of perhaps twenty species of annual lupines that may be fairly easily grown in gardens, *L. hartwegii* is the one most often offered in seed catalogues, and arguably the most beautiful. It commemorates intrepid German plant explorer Karl Theodor Hartweg (1812–1871), who botanized in Mexico between 1836 and 1837, and in California between 1846 and 1847, sending seed back to the Royal Horticultural Society in London.

Though a native of Mexico, it requires a neutral, well-drained soil, cool night temperatures, and constant, even moisture to flourish. It produces a sturdy, bushlike plant between eighteen inches and two feet tall, with typically lupinelike leaves of seven to nine fingers, though they are quite narrow and delicate, and heavily downed. The flowers are typically a clear blue, borne in widely separated whorls on long, narrow panicles that are reminiscent more of certain elegant salvias than of the often cobby, bunched-up panicles of other members of the genus. Many other shades also exist, of deeper blue and purple, rose, and a fine white called 'New Snow' ('Bianconeve'). From a March or early April sowing in the open garden, plants will produce bloom from July to September, especially if spent flower heads are promptly removed. Though usually grown as an annual, Hartweg's lupine is actually a tender perennial and may persist over winter in warmer gardens that approximate its native habitat.

Second in popularity is *L. mutabilis,* which may appear in catalogues under several confusing listings, such as *L. cruckshanksii* (cruk-SHANX-ee-ee), *L. cruckshanksii mutabilis,* or *L. mutabilis* var. *cruckshanksii.* No record seems to exist of who Mr. Cruckshank was, but the flowers of the plant deserve the name *mutabilis,* which generally describes a complex color, often one that changes as the flower progresses from bud to seed. Each flower, borne in sturdy panicles, is of the typical pea-flower shape, but their colors are an elaborate blend of deep blue on the lower petals, shading to paler blue streaks on the upper, which transitions to pale violet, marked in the center with a yellow blaze. Older flowers at the base of the panicle take on shades of copper and bronze as they age. Well-cultured plants, in rich, moist but well-drained soil and full sun, may reach a height of three to four feet, with abundant, fresh green, fingered leaves, and from a sowing directly in the garden after frost, flowers will be produced from mid-summer until well into autumn. Their complex blend of colors makes them both interesting in themselves and a flattering companion to many other flower colors. Like most lupines, they are also excellent cut flowers if picked in the early morning just as the lower florets are opening.

The Texas bluebonnet, *Lupinus subcarnosus,* requires discussion simply because of its prominence as one of the most-loved wild flowers of the American Southwest. Outside its native range, however, it is often not an easy plant to grow well. Where it is native, it behaves essentially as a biennial, germinating in autumn, making a basal rosette of growth over the mild, cool winter, and flowering in May, while nights are still cool and moisture is abundant. Such a combination of growing conditions is not to be found in most American gardens, but seed of the plant is often included in annual "flowering meadow" mixes. It would be worth some trouble to grow, where it wishes to grow at all, for it produces stout, eight- to twelve-inch branching plants, somewhat fleshy, as the species name *subcarnosus* suggests, that are attractive in themselves, with palmate leaves of five to seven fingers, clad on both sides in silky, silvery hairs. Individual flowers are a rich, clear blue, each marked with a

prominent white or yellowish spot that makes a field in bloom seem full of watching eyes. The unopened buds at the top of the panicles are downy and grayish, adding to the attractiveness of the bloom. *L. texensis* (tex-EN-sis), considered by some to be the "true" Texas bluebonnet, is closely related, and possibly one species is simply a naturally occurring variant of the other. *L. texensis* produces flowers of an even deeper and richer blue, and is lovely for that.

About the other annual lupines William Robinson remarked that "Many other sorts are so much alike that they are not worth separating." That is not quite true, for among annual lupines, the genus contains many treasures, mostly native to the southwestern United States and Central America, and sometimes available from seed companies that specialize in native American plants. *L. densiflorus* (den-si-FLO-rus), the "gully lupine," is native to California, where it flourishes in drainage ditches, moist meadows, and vernal pools, blooming in May after a winter of vegetative growth. From an autumn sowing in warmer gardens, or a March sowing in cooler ones, it quickly forms a shrublike plant up to two feet tall, with palmate leaves of five to seven hirsute leaflets, and produces thick spikes of flower in midsummer. It is very popular in England, where many named forms are available in shades of white, yellow, and pink.

L. pubescens (pu-BES-ens), from Central America, is similar in growth and appearance, producing spikes of violet blue flowers, each marked with a white blotch. Whether it is hairier than other lupines, as its species name seems to indicate, is up to question, but it has been selected and possibly hybridized with other species into many beautiful colors of pale and deep blue, red, rose, yellow, and white.

L. nanus (NAY-nus), as its species name, from

the Latin adjective for small implies, is a little, bushy plant, achieving fifteen inches at most in height from an early spring sowing, making it—as one English catalogue suggests—"ideal for edging," assuming anyone still cares to do that sort of thing. Also a California native, it has a longer blooming period than the vernal lupines, flowering from May to July where it may be sown in autumn, and from June to September from early spring sowings in colder gardens. Called the "sky lupine" in wildflower books, it produces loose racemes on slender stalks that are typically medium blue with purple spots on the upper petals, though pretty variants exist in shades of white, cream, and pink.

Though the annual lupines seem to have their greatest center of concentration in the southwestern United States and Central America, there are several desirable species that are native to southern Europe and North Africa. *L. luteus* (LOO-tee-us), a native of southern Europe, particularly Spain, is especially desirable, producing branched plants up to two feet tall, and abundant spikes of fragrant yellow flowers. It thrives on rather poor, sandy soil, and may be the plant that classical botanists first named *lupinus*. *L. hirsutus* (hir-SOO-tus) is also native to southern Europe, growing to two feet and bearing the hairy, fingered leaves typical of most lupines grown in gardens. Its flowers are blue with white markings, though pure white, red, and pink forms have been recognized for centuries. Finally, one annual lupine from the North African coast of the Mediterranean, *L. varius* (VA-ree-us), has attracted its admirers, though it is probably best grown as a cool greenhouse plant through the winter, to be stood about in pots for summer bloom. It grows into a branched plant about two feet tall, with silver-downy fingered leaves, and from a careful sowing under glass in March or early April, produces thick cobs of rich blue flowers with a white eye, which age down to

deep black-purple (hence, the species name *varius,* meaning of different colors).

The seed of *Lupinus varius* is surprisingly large, as big as a broad bean, and it is coated with a thick, impermeable rind. In natural habitats, where seed falls to the ground in summer or early autumn, and remains in moist cool conditions for several months, this protective seed coat softens to allow the seed root and cotyledon to emerge. But where seed is received in winter through the mail, and sown in early spring, the gardener must substitute for this softening process, by "scarifying" the seed. According to the thickness of the seed rind, this may be done (carefully, with respect to one's fingers) by nicking the seed with a very sharp knife, by filing through the rind with a nail file, and sometimes by working away at each seed with a very serious carpenter's file, if the rind is really thick. The nick or groove must always be opposite the "eye," where the newly germinated taproot will emerge, and the eye can usually be recognized by an indentation and sometimes by a paler coloration, such as would be seen on an ordinary kitchen black or red bean. After scarification, seed should be soaked for a day or two in tepid water on the windowsill. Those that have been successfully scarified will swell up to about twice their size and should be sown immediately. Those that do not swell up should be filed, nicked, or hacked at again, and re-soaked until they obediently swell up and can be sown.

Given the conditions they prefer—full sun, a deep, neutral, well-drained soil, plenty of moisture, and the sort of cool night conditions that are pleasant to most people—most annual lupines are easy and beautiful plants for the summer border. They have, however, one serious pest, and that is aphids—either white or black—some of which seem specific only to lupines and will migrate first from tree lupines, where they may be grown, and then to perennial lupines, and finally to the annual sorts, which they seem to consider dessert. They colonize on bloom stems, always thick in their numbers, and they suck all the vital juices of the plant away, resulting in wizened, deformed, anemic growth. Only the most careless gardener will be able to ignore them. An immediate recourse to some pesticide, whether organic or chemical, according to one's conscience, is the only remedy.

MACHERANTHEMA TANACETIFOLIA

FAMILY: *Asteraceae* or aster or daisy family.

CLASSIFICATION: Hardy annual or biennial grown as hardy or half-hardy annual.

COMMON NAMES: Tahoka daisy, macheranthema.

HARDINESS: Will withstand light frost when well established.

GROWING CONDITIONS: Moderately fertile, alkaline soil. Perfect drainage. Full sun.

PROPAGATION: From seed sown in place in fall or very early spring. Sow indoors in March. Seed requires stratification.

HEIGHT: From 1 to 2′.

ORNAMENTAL VALUE: Grown for flower.

LEVEL OF CULTURAL DIFFICULTY: Easy within native range; difficult elsewhere.

SPECIAL PROPERTIES: Excellent cut flower.

PRONUNCIATION: ma-ku-RAN-thuh-ma tan-a-see-ti-FO-li-a

Although William Robinson (1839–1935) loved all plants and especially North American annuals, in his landmark book *The English Flower Garden,* he dismissed *Macheranthema tanacetifolia* in four quick lines, concluding with the phrase that it is "scarcely worth growing." A native of the dryer parts of western and southwestern North America, the plant could not be expected to cut much of a figure in the cold, damp climate where Robinson gardened. But where Tahoka daisy (from Tahoka, Texas) flourishes, it is a charming and serviceable annual, garnering much praise where it can be grown well.

A close relative of many garden asters (and, in old references, classed in that genus), *Macheranthema tanacetifolia* is the only member of its genus under common cultivation. It draws its genus name from the ancient Greek word for a dagger, *machaira,* which describes its seed, and its species name from the resemblance of its leaves to common tansy, *Tanacetum vulgare. M. tanacetifolia* grows into a sturdy, much-branched bushy plant from one to two feet high, very thickly furnished with grayish to dark green bristly, divided leaves made up of five or so narrow, toothed leaflets. They are sticky to the touch and emit a pleasant pine-needle smell when crushed. Flowers occur in clusters at the tips of branches, each one a perfect daisy of twenty or so narrow ray petals colored the rich, dusty violet common to so many North American asters. The petals surround an egg-yolk yellow disk. Like many composites, flowers remain in attractive condition for a month or more, as the tiny disk flowers open from the outside in. Eventually, however, fertilized disk flowers turn a silvery gray, at length producing a spherical seed head not unlike that of a dandelion.

M. tanacetifolia behaves either as an annual or as a biennial, depending on where it occurs within its extensive natural range from South Dakota and Montana to Mexico. In colder areas, it will sprout in very early spring after a long winter's dormancy, but where climate allows, it prefers to germinate in early winter and grow sturdily on, for a splendid burst of flower in spring and early summer. In either case, flowering will occur approximately three months after germination and will continue as long as nights are cool and dry. In gardens that experience a mild winter, seed may be sown in place in autumn and elsewhere it may be sown in very early spring. After germination is secure, plants should be thinned to stand about six to eight inches apart. As with so many plants that waver uncertainly between the classifications of annual and biennial, the best results will always be produced by the longest possible vegetative period before flowering begins, so if young plants are grown indoors, seeding should take place in March for midsummer flowers.

However it is sown, seed will germinate stubbornly—if at all—unless it has experienced some winter chill, outdoors in the garden or indoors in the refrigerator, where it should be mixed with several tablespoons of barely moist peat and kept for three weeks in a mason jar with a tight-fitting lid until just before sowing. (Freezing temperatures, however, are fatal.) Young seedlings are best grown in very bright light at temperatures around 50°F, and pricked out or moved on into larger pots as they enlarge. Plants raised indoors must be carefully hardened off and then transplanted after all danger of frost is past. Alternatively, they make superb potted plants, grown either as single specimens or in combination with other summer- and autumn-flowering annuals.

Absolutely perfect drainage is required, either in open beds or in pots that have an inch or so of broken pot shards or coarse gravel in their bottoms. The soil should be only moderately fertile as too much nitrogen in the form of organic material or chemical fertilizer will produce rich and abundant leaf at the expense of flowers. Soils on the acid side produce sickly and chlorotic plants, but at a pH between 6.0 and 7.0—such as produces the best spinach—macherantheras will thrive. Where climates approximate their native range, they will flower from mid-June until frost, particularly if spent blossoms are removed. Cut blossoms last a very long time in water.

MADIA SPECIES

FAMILY: *Asteraceae* or aster or daisy family.

CLASSIFICATION: Hardy or half-hardy annual.

COMMON NAMES: Tar weed, oil plant, madia.

HARDINESS: Sensitive to light frosts.

GROWING CONDITIONS: Dryish, well-drained, alkaline soil. Part shade. Prefers cool weather.

PROPAGATION: From seed, sown in place in warmer gardens, in very early spring in cooler ones. Sow indoors in March.

HEIGHT: From 1 to 2'.

ORNAMENTAL VALUE: Grown for flower.

LEVEL OF CULTURAL DIFFICULTY: Easy, where cultural preferences may be met.

SPECIAL PROPERTIES: Scented foliage. Valued for oil-rich seed.

PRONUNCIATION: MAY-dee-a

Of the eighteen or so species in the genus *Madia,* only two, *Madia elegans* (EL-uh-gans) and *M. sativa* (sa-TEE-va), are sometimes cultivated in gardens. Both plants, members of the vast composite family, bear ragged daisies of clear yellow to yellowish orange, often marked with a central zone of brown to reddish maroon, on much-branched plants that may be as tall as four feet, but are more typically two feet or less in height, and somewhat sprawling. The flowers are hardly prepossessing and may be best described in the abbreviation common to wildflower enthusiasts as a MYD (medium yellow daisy), of which there are so many, particularly in dry, grassy meadows and along roadsides in midsummer throughout North America.

But within this class, madia are unusual in several ways. First, they grow naturally and do best in most gardens where they receive some shade, for their flowers are apt to close up in the full glare of the midday sun. Second, their narrow, three- to five-inch, bladelike leaves, sticky to the touch, are scented even when they are not crushed, reminiscent of mangoes, some people say, or of pineapple or ripe berries. Catalogues simply say "of tropical fruits." Finally, both species under cultivation have been valuable plants to native foragers. The first, *M. elegans,* is a common wild flower in western North America and was eagerly sought by West Coast Native Americans for its oil-rich seed. The second, *M. sativa,* is native to Chile and is still important to the Arucana people of that country as a source of oil and of protein. (*M. sativa* has comfortably naturalized throughout the range occupied by its northern cousin—Oregon through California and west to Nevada—and hikers often find the two plants growing side by side.)

So far, however, the two cultivated species of *Madia* have cut a modest figure in American gardens because their growth and flower is—to put it kindly—rather modest. Or, as J. L. Hudson, the eminent American seedsman says, "Not showy. But nice."

Madia of both species are very easy from seed. Both are classed as hardy annuals, and so seed may be sown in place as soon as the ground may be worked in early spring or in autumn in warmer gardens. Alternatively, seed may be sown indoors in March, and the young seedlings pricked out and grown on in bright light until they may be transplanted as soon as all danger of frost is past. At all times, both species are sensitive to over-watering and grow best in dryish, well-drained alkaline soils. In the garden, one is usually told that drifts are best, which probably merely emphasizes the fact that flowers are not individually showy. In the spirit of the famous joke about the two ladies vacationing in the Poconos ("the food was terrible, and the portions were too small"), dead-heading increases flower production.

The genus name *Madia* is Latinized Chilean vernacular for the plant, and the species name *sativus* (of woods) attests to its preferred habitat at the shady edges of scrub woodland turning to pasture. *Elegans,* the species name of the most commonly grown North American native, speaks for itself.

MALCOMIA MARITIMA

FAMILY: *Cruciferae* or mustard family.

CLASSIFICATION: Hardy annual.

COMMON NAMES: Virginia stock, mahon, malcomia.

HARDINESS: Withstands frost once established.

GROWING CONDITIONS: Lean, well-drained soil. Full sun. Prefers cool weather.

PROPAGATION: From seed, sown in site in autumn or in very early spring.

HEIGHT: Between 6 and 10".

ORNAMENTAL VALUE: Grown for flower.

LEVEL OF CULTURAL DIFFICULTY: Easy.

SPECIAL PROPERTIES: Excellent winter-flowering plant for cool greenhouses.

PRONUNCIATION: mal-KO-mee-a ma-RI-ti-ma

Malcomia maritima was once a staple plant in old-fashioned flower gardens, and its disappearance would be hard to explain, except for the fact that it can only be grown well when seeded directly where it is to bloom. Its flowers, also, though undeniably pretty, are borne on individual plants for a brief time, hardly a month, though in gardens that experience summer nighttime temperatures

MALCOMIA MARITIMA

generally below 70°F, successive sowings in the last weeks of May, June, and July can ensure abundant flowers over a long period of time. Its origins are Mediterranean, as the species name *maritima* usually indicates, but it was known even by Victorian English gardeners as "Virginia stock" and encouraged to seed where it would. In English cottage gardens still, it is taken almost for granted as a companion to spring-flowering bulbs and a gentle, front-of-the-border plant at all seasons. It is, among annual plants, perhaps one of the easiest of all to grow, having no great particularity as to soils, and indeed flourishing best where they are rather poor, in full sun or part shade. And once established in congenial gardens, it will self-sow from year to year, asking only to be thinned a bit to stand four to six inches, one neighbor from another.

But, like many plants that fall into the class of "hardy annuals," Virginia stock does not transplant well and certainly cuts no figure in modern garden centers, which—for all the riches they offer—have largely favored perky, precocious, and long-blooming annuals that are easy to transplant over many old-fashioned favorites. So, though *Malcomia maritima* was once ubiquitous, it is very seldom seen in American gardens today

and seldom offered by seed companies. Its return to popularity, therefore—at least where gardeners wish to go to the very little trouble it requires—may garner them the best of all garden compliments, the question "What lovely plant is that?"

Malcomia maritima prefers to sow itself in late summer or autumn, for germination in very early spring, just as the frost is out of the ground, and most gardeners will do well to follow suit. It quickly produces much-branched, thin-stemmed plants between six and ten inches tall, which will come into flower about four to six weeks after the seed has sprouted, providing a pleasant accompaniment to the first tulips. Its flowers are typically cruciform, consisting of four petals, each shaped into a heart at its end, and all four cupping the pistil and anthers in the center. Flower color may range through white, pale and deep pink to carmine red, and even (in the cultivar 'Lutea') a pale, primrose yellow, but in all but the palest flowers, petals will be veined with a deeper color, and the center of each flower will show a darker eye.

Though it tends to flower vernally when left to its own devices, malcomia does not seem to be particular about when it blooms, so long as nights are cool and fresh. Seed sown in autumn will produce flowers in early spring, but seed sown in March or April, or as soon as the ground can be raked smooth, will produce flowers in June. Successive sowings may produce flowers throughout the summer months and into autumn, for malcomia has the happy property of flowering as soon as five weeks from germination. This makes it invaluable for seeding in clumps of ripening bulb foliage, or wherever there may be bare patches of ground.

As one might suppose, malcomia is also a very charming winter-flowering annual for the cool greenhouse, flourishing and blooming at nighttime temperatures maintained at around 40°F.

For this purpose, seed should be sown in pots of well-drained, moderately rich compost in autumn, and successive sowings made up to mid-December, for early to late winter bloom.

MALOPE TRIFIDA

FAMILY: *Malvaceae* or mallow family.

CLASSIFICATION: Half-hardy annual.

COMMON NAMES: Annual mallow, bush mallow, malope.

HARDINESS: Sensitive to frosts.

GROWING CONDITIONS: Moderately rich, well-drained soil. Good drainage. Full sun.

PROPAGATION: From seed, sown in site, or indoors in peat pots 2 to 3 weeks before last frost. Resents root disturbance.

HEIGHT: To 3′.

ORNAMENTAL VALUE: Grown for flowers.

LEVEL OF CULTURAL DIFFICULTY: Moderately difficult.

SPECIAL PROPERTIES: None.

PRONUNCIATION: mal-O-pee TRI-fi-da

*A*mong annual plants, malope would seem to have every advantage. From a late spring or early summer sowing, it quickly produces a sturdy, pyramidal plant to three feet tall, made up of a central stem and many side branches. Three-lobed leaves, from three to five inches wide, are a healthy dark green, and flowers are borne abundantly on slender, four-inch stems from late June until frost. Each flower is about three inches across with the five petals typical of all mallows; but the petals, which overlap gracefully in a cup, are clawed at the base, each petal pinched into a slender stem where it meets the apple-green calyx, empty space showing through the openings at the base of the petals as a star. Claude Monet, who grew quantities of malope at Giverny, was the first to note the resemblance of this effect to the great stained-glass rose windows in Gothic cathedrals. Flowers in shades of white, pale and deep pink, lavender, and an almost scarlet rose show a darker veining and sometimes a bold brush of deeper color over a paler ground. As with many mallows, the texture of the petals is gossamer thin but still possessed of a satiny sheen. In culture, the plant is easy, flourishing in well-drained, moderately rich to thin soils in full sun.

All these virtues once made malope popular—no Victorian garden would have been complete without it—when annual plants were sown from seed out of a packet often in the place the plant was to grow and flower. But like most mallows, malope resents root disturbance. Infant plants in the garden center look dowdy and unpromising—no precocious little blossom in sight—and their shelf life is very limited because they resent the confinement of a plastic six-pack. The whole crop is apt to go off in one single, muggy early summer day. The firmly held conviction that all annual plants should be mussed up at the roots when planted (erroneous in almost all cases) will be death to malopes and would probably result in a complaint from customers to the garden center owner that the plants simply did not "take." So, though of undeniable value in the summer landscape, malopes are largely grown only by old-fashioned cottage gardeners—who pass through modern garden centers without a twinge of temptation—or by sophisticated plantsmen who routinely cruise specialty seed catalogues for forgotten or newly discovered treasures, and seldom visit garden centers at all.

Without some special precautions, malope seed can be very stubborn in its germination. To break dormancy and sprout, it requires at least a brief simulacrum of the mild winters of the Mediterranean coast where it is native. Seed should therefore be placed in the refrigerator (never the freezer) for two to three weeks before it is sown, protected from moisture that might trigger premature germination by being enclosed in a tight-lidded mason jar. Because of its sensitivity to root disturbance, sowing the seed in peat pots is best, planting two or three seed to a pot. After successful germination has occurred, the weakest two are not clipped out with scissors (according to the usual advice) because handsome effects result from three interlaced plants that may support one another without staking. Many gardeners sow seed fresh from the packet in peat pots filled with commercial potting mix such as Pro-Mix, moist but not sopping wet, and then wrap the pots in plastic bags and refrigerate the lot.

Malope should be germinated two to three weeks before the last anticipated frost date. Hurrying things on is no good, as young plants do not grow well in indoor conditions. In any case, after transplanting, they are apt to sulk in the garden until warmth of summer causes them to explode into growth and bloom. In most gardens, direct seeding in early April—or as soon in spring as the garden can be worked—will produce results as good as, or better than, plants started indoors. Seed should be sown in hills, slightly mounded structures about four to six inches above the prevailing grade of the garden and each about a foot wide. Five to seven seed should be sown about two inches apart and barely covered with soil crumbled between one's hands. If germination is successful, all but three of the seed should be eliminated. For mass plantings, hills should be spaced about two feet apart; five to seven hills will make a splendid drift at the back of the border. As a precautionary measure, a single stake inserted about two feet into the ground and extending as far above should be supplied for each plant, the central stem of which should be tied in with a soft, non-constrictive tie of sisal, hemp, or raffia. It is useful to know that many tall, bushy annuals will tumble over just at ground level, and so the stake need not be so tall as to be visible when the plant matures.

Individual flowers on their long, slender stems are excellent for small bouquets, and when whole branches are cut for larger bouquets, immature buds will continue to open for ten days or more.

MALVA SPECIES

FAMILY: *Malvaceae* or mallow family.

CLASSIFICATION: True annuals, biennials, or tender perennials grown as hardy or half-hardy annuals.

COMMON NAME: Malva.

HARDINESS: Hardiness varies with species. Most are slightly frost-resistant.

GROWING CONDITIONS: Rich, well-drained loam. Abundant moisture. Full sun.

PROPAGATION: From seed, sown indoors 6 to 8 weeks before last frost date, in peat pots, or in place after frost. Plants resent root disturbance.

HEIGHT: From 3 to 10', depending on species and culture.

ORNAMENTAL VALUE: Grown for foliage and for flower.

LEVEL OF CULTURAL DIFFICULTY: Easy.

SPECIAL PROPERTIES: Taller forms grown as annual hedges.

PRONUNCIATION: MAL-va

The large family Malvaceae contains about ninety-five genera and includes many important garden and economic plants, most notably *Gossyp-*

ium, various species of which provide cotton, and *Abelmoschus,* which includes okra. Its signature genus, *Malva,* contains about thirty species of mostly rank and weedy annuals, biennials, or perennials. So few of these are of garden value that the genus is eclipsed by other family members, including abutilons, althaeas, hibiscus, and lavateras. Still, within the genus *Malva* are several plants—true annuals or biennials, and perennials grown as annuals—that have been treasured for centuries in dooryard gardens and are still popular.

Among true annual malvas, the one most often grown is *M. verticillata* (ver-ti-si-LA-ta), particularly in the select form 'Crispa', which merely intensifies the crimped or curled edges of the leaves typical of the species. *M. verticillata* forms a stout, almost treelike plant from three to as much as ten feet tall. Bushy, erect, and much-branched from a central woody stem, the plant is cultivated principally for its leaves—broad and dramatic, consisting of a palm of five to seven lobes, crimped along the edges, and carried on long, slender petioles. To some gardeners, there may seem to be too little flower for so great an amount of leaf, but the massive structure of the plant looks quite handsome at the back of a border, and the flowers, borne in the leaf axils on the upper third of the plant, are pretty enough, consisting of clusters of small, two-inch-wide, five-petaled blossoms of white or light rose, each petal squared off, notched, or pinked at its end, gossamer thin, but heavily creped like Fortuny silks.

M. verticillata occurs wild in southern Europe and Eurasia, and has widely naturalized both in Europe and in North America. It has been in cultivation since at least the last quarter of the sixteenth century, when it was grown not for ornament but as a salad crop and for boiled greens. *Malva* is the classical Latin name for plants in this genus, and *verticillata* means netted or woven into whorls or spider-web-like patterns

MALVA SYLVESTRIS

and may refer to the interwoven nature of the branches of the plant.

Depending on the reference one consults, another popular species of *Malva, M. sylvestris* (sil-VES-tris), may be listed as an annual, a biennial, or a perennial. It can behave as all three, though the best plants are usually grown as annuals, persisting over winter as weak perennials only in the milder parts of the country, and sometimes germinating there in autumn and overwintering to produce magnificent, early-summer-flowering plants. The species name *sylvestris* is curious, as it generally designates a plant that grows in woodland shade, whereas the finest specimens of *M. sylvestris* will occur in full sun, at least in cooler gardens. Elsewhere light afternoon shade might help it with its struggles against extreme heat, which it does not enjoy.

Malva sylvestris grows quickly into a four-foot-tall, bushy erect plant, with two- to four-inch-wide, shallowly lobed leaves on long petioles. The flowers are borne in the axils of the upper leaves, generally in thick clusters, though in some select forms, clusters elongate into panicles or even spikes. Flowers are generally one to two inches across and, typically mallowlike, consist of five petals embraced by the prominent green calyx characteristic of the whole family. (These are best known as the papery surround to the boll of a cotton flower.) Flower color is usually a pale lavender but with dramatic veinings of a deeper tint, generally a dark purple intensifying almost to black in the center of the flower. This characteristic has given the plant a spurious botanical name, *M. zebrinus* (ze-BRI-nus), from the Portuguese "zebra," meaning striped. Several handsome selections have been made, including a subspecies native to North Africa, *Malva sylvestris* subsp. *mauritanica* (mo-ri-TA-ni-ka), called 'Bibor Fehlo', with two-inch, wavy petaled flowers of dark violet veined in deep purple. The late Sir David Scott, a great English gardener, discovered a chance seedling of *Malva sylvestris* in his garden at Boughton House, Kettering, when he was ninety-eight years old and named it 'Brave Heart'. It produces abundant, lavender-pink flowers on spikes rather than in clusters, each veined in deep purple with a dark purple center.

Whether technically annuals, biennials, or perennials, malvas will require pretty much the same treatment, flowering in their first season from an early spring sowing indoors about six to eight weeks before the last anticipated frost date. Seed should be chilled in the refrigerator at about 38 to 40°F before sowing, and as with most mallows, it should be planted in peat pots to minimize root constriction or disturbance. Seed should be barely covered and germination may be slow, taking as much as twenty days. Young seedlings should be grown on in bright, fresh conditions, and infestations of aphids or white flies—the general banes of this family—should be promptly eliminated. Young plants may be set out about twelve inches apart after all danger of frost is past. Growth will be slow until the heat of summer arrives, and indeed, in most gardens, good or even better results can be had by sowing seed directly in the ground. They will generally catch up with—or even surpass—seedlings started indoors. Bloom will occur over a very long time, from late June until September, and flowers may appear even after light frosts have struck the plants.

MARTYNIA PROBOSCIDEA (PROBOSCIDEA LOUISIANICA)

FAMILY: *Martyniaceae* or martynia family.

CLASSIFICATION: Tender annual.

COMMON NAMES: Unicorn plant, devil's claw, ram's horn, martynia, proboscidea.

HARDINESS: Sensitive to light frost.

GROWING CONDITIONS: Rich, fertile, well-drained soil. Full sun. Relishes heat.

PROPAGATION: By seed, sown indoors 6 to 8 weeks before frost.

HEIGHT: To 2' tall and as wide.

ORNAMENTAL VALUE: Grown for flower and for seed pods.

LEVEL OF CULTURAL DIFFICULTY: Easy in warmer gardens, moderately difficult in cool ones.

SPECIAL PROPERTIES: Seed pods may be pickled or dried for use in wreaths.

PRONUNCIATION: mar-TIN-ee-a pro-bo-SI-dee-a (loo-si-AN-i-ca)

Martynia proboscidea and *Proboscidea louisianica* are such close cousins within the family Martyniaceae that the genus name of the first becomes the species name of the second, and, where either is grown in gardens at all, one may pass for the other. The technical differences that have traditionally placed them in separate genera are very slight, consisting of whether the calyx is split into five sepals or fused (in *Martynia,* it is split), whether the flower possess two or four fertile stamens (*Proboscidea* possesses four), and whether there is a shorter or longer pointed beak on the seed pod (the beaks of *Proboscidea* are as much as three inches long, twice that of *Martynia*). Though both have a minor importance as a food crop in the deep South and the Caribbean, where their immature seed pods are sometimes pickled, in most North American gardens they are chiefly grown as curiosities.

Curious they are certainly, producing lax, sprawling, vinelike plants that, in a hot summer, may reach three or four feet in height and extend over as much as six feet of ground. The thick, dull green, triangular leaves are heavily veined, and are powdered over with fine, reddish hairs that give them a dusty appearance. The hairs, which occur on stems and unopened buds as well, have a cunning purpose, for they contain a tiny drop of sticky fluid that ensnares and immobilizes aphids and other predatory insects before they can do harm. When bruised, the leaves give off a curious smell that some people find mildly pleasant and others malodorous, as of an over-ripened peach that has fermented.

The bell-shaped flowers are borne in loose clusters in the axils of the upper leaves and consist of a tubed throat and five flaring lobes, the upper three separate and the lower two fused into a lip, with the lobes overlapping. Flowers may be up to two inches long and are generally whitish-pink or pale tangerine, with freckles of yellow, red, or purple in the throats, and sometimes orange-ish stripes brushed across the lower lobes. The flow-

ers strongly resemble those of florists' gloxinias or those of the caltapa tree, and are especially pretty when studied close, though care must be taken, as each may contain a drowsing bumblebee.

The seed capsules that follow the flowers are perhaps the most prominent part of the plants. They are fat, rounded pods to as much as five inches long, curved at the tip into a long, narrow beak. When the pods are ripe, the beak splits in half and curls away from the seed receptacles, quite dramatically in the case of *Proboscidea louisianica,* accounting for the popular names of "devil's claw" and "ram's horn." Both plants are sometimes grown for their pods, which may be pickled, but which are more frequently dried for use in wreaths and flower arrangements. (Alice McGowan, co-owner of Blue Meadow Farm in Montague, Massachusetts, has also noted that the woody, clawed fruit, with rattling seed inside, is a virtually perfect cat toy.)

Culturally, any member of the family Martyniaceae may be grown exactly like garden peppers and eggplants. Seed should be sown about six to eight weeks before the last anticipated frost date. Germination is speeded if the outer, blackish hull of each seed is carefully peeled away with a sharp knife, and the naked kernel within sown at warm temperatures, around 70°F. Young plants should be pricked out into individual pots and grown on in warm, sunny conditions until they may be hardened off and transplanted into the garden after all danger of frost is past. At all times in their growth, plants will be extremely sensitive to frosts and even to cool temperatures, and so transplanting should occur only when the weather is warm and settled. Even so, young plants may sulk until the warmth of midsummer occurs, when they will explode into growth. All species under cultivation are native to the warmest parts of North and Central America, and so require as much heat as possible for full development. Full sun is an absolute requirement, and soils should be fertile and rich with organic material, well drained but always evenly moist. Though species of *Martynia* and *Proboscidea* grow splendidly in the deep South, where they are sown directly into the garden in spring and may naturalize from year to year, in most American gardens, their requirements are best met by growing them in large pots, either in containers of mixed plants or as single specimens, where their stout but straggling stems may be tied to bamboo supports. But wherever they are grown, they will be greedy feeders, and so supplementary fertilizing with water-soluble plant food at regular intervals will encourage the finest growth, flower, and fruit.

Botanically, both *Martynia* and *Proboscidea* have a gaggle of names that may, in references and in commerce, pass back and forth among the two genuses and their species, all of which appear to be more-or-less confused in trade. *Martynia* is the signature genus of the family Martyniaceae, and commemorates a London physician, John Martyn (1699–1768), who was also a professor of botany at Cambridge, though it appears that he enjoyed all of the emoluments of that position and undertook none of its duties. (His son, also John Martyn [1725–1835], succeeded him.) *Proboscidea* speaks for itself, derived from the ancient Greek word for an elephant's trunk, *proboskis,* and referring to the snout or beak at the tip of the seed pods. The species of *Martynia* under most frequent cultivation may be listed as *M. annua* (though all species are annual) or *M. proboscidea,* in which case it may also be listed as *Proboscidea louisianica* or *P. louisiana,* for the state of Louisiana, where it was first found, and where native peoples wove its durable fibers into baskets. The name *jussieui* often appears as well, either for *Martynia proboscidea* or *Proboscidea louisianica,* or for a third species sometimes under cultivation, *Martynia* (or *Proboscidea*) *fragrans,* similar to the others but grown for the sweet smell of its flowers. That name commemorates Barnard de Jussieu (1699–1777), the great French botanist who laid the first foundation for the natural classification of species.

This maze of botanical names may interest botanists, botanical historians, or even gardeners concerned with the correct names of the plants they grow. If it has not so far, the family Martyniaceae might also form an admirable subject for a doctoral dissertation, for it tangles its complexity with another closely related family, Pedaliaceae, under which both *Martynia* and *Proboscidea* are also sometimes listed.

Meanwhile, most committed gardeners will grow plants within the family under whatever name, at least once, and perhaps for years, even to the point of accumulating and growing many within the closely related genuses and studying their differences. Culinary historians might also look at all these plants, in an attempt to recover and codify their kitchen uses in recipes before that knowledge is lost. In the never-ending search for newly discovered edible plants, seed pods of one, or many, might eventually be offered as a side dish in fashionable New York restaurants. But seed is seldom offered of any species, and so when plants are grown, it should always be saved and passed around.

MATRICARIA SPECIES

FAMILY: *Asteraceae* or aster or daisy family.

CLASSIFICATION: Weak perennials grown as hardy or half-hardy annuals.

COMMON NAMES: Feverfew, matricaria (other popular names vary with species).

HARDINESS: Withstands frost.

GROWING CONDITIONS: Ordinary to poor, well-
drained garden soil. Moderate moisture. Full
sun.

PROPAGATION: From seed, sown in site in autumn
or in very early spring, or indoors 6 to 8 weeks
before last frost date.

HEIGHT: To 12".

ORNAMENTAL VALUE: Grown for flower.

LEVEL OF CULTURAL DIFFICULTY: Easy.

SPECIAL PROPERTIES: Dried flowers of some species
used in herbal teas.

PRONUNCIATION: ma-tri-KA-ree-a

The genus *Matricaria* has a comfortable name, derived from the Latin word either for mother (*mater*) or for womb (*matrix*) and attesting to the use of various plants within the genus for a host of therapeutic purposes from ancient times to the present. It once contained about forty species of annuals, biennials, and perennials—all of Old World origins—but many have been shuffled out, first into the closely related genus *Chrysanthemum,* and then into *Pyrethrum, Tripleurospermum,* and *Tanacetum.* Still, however, *Matricaria* has treasures, at least three of which are grown in gardens as annuals.

By far the most important is *Matricaria recutita* (re-CU-ti-ta)—sometimes still listed under its old name as *M. camomile*—the uses of which have been handed down from ancient times to the present. It is principally employed to brew a mildly sedative, soothing drink that is believed to calm agitated children, alleviate nervous stress, assist digestion, and prevent insomnia and nightmares. Tea brewed from either the fresh or dried flowers of *M. recutita* has a sweeter, less bitter and astringent taste than that brewed from true chamomile (*Chamaemelum nobile*) and so is the main ingredient in modern packages of chamomile tea.

From a very early spring sowing as soon as the ground can be worked, *Matricaria recutita* will quickly form branching, bushy plants from one to two feet tall, with feathery, much-divided, aromatic foliage. Flowers should occur about sixteen weeks from seeding—usually midsummer in most northern gardens—and continue until frosts, or even after. Earlier flowers may be had by starting seed indoors, six to eight weeks before the last expected frost date, after which they may be transplanted into the garden. Full sun is preferred, though light afternoon shade may still produce pretty, long-flowering plants, particularly in warmer gardens, where otherwise, bloom may be reduced by summer heat. *M. recutita* seems indifferent to soil quality, provided it is well drained, and may often be seen occurring naturally on sandy roadside shoulders or in gravel drives. Where either garden display or abundant harvest is the goal, however, a single application of granular vegetable garden food when the plants are about six inches tall will produce finer flowers.

Also often still listed in seed catalogues among matricarias is *M. inodora* (in-O-do-ra), though it is now correctly lodged in the obscure genus *Tripleurospermum* (tri-plu-ro-SPER-mum), the

MATRICARIA (TANACETUM) *SPECIES*—TANACETUM PARTHENIUM *'AUREUM'* difficult name of which describes its three-ribbed seed, from ancient Greek *tri,* meaning three, *pleuron,* rib, and *sperma,* seed. A native of central and southern Europe, it is an old cottage garden favorite, usually called "bridal robe" from its immaculately white, almost two-inch-wide flowers. The species name *inodora,* which has clung to it in its present genus name as *Tripleurospermum maritimum* (ma-RI-ti-mum) subspecies *inodora,* attests to its lack of fragrant leaves, fragrance being a pronounced characteristic of most plants once in the genus *Matricaria.* It is a beautiful, clean-growing hardy annual to sixteen inches tall, producing fully double, fluffy white daisies from midsummer to frost from an early spring sowing. It makes a superb, long-lasting cut flower, and as such, is grown in winter in Dutch greenhouses for export to flower markets throughout the world.

Finally, *Matricaria matricarioides* (ma-tri-ca-ri-OY-dees) is a valuable little plant, mostly for the delicious pineapple smell of its leaves and flowers. A native probably of Asia Minor, it is widely naturalized throughout the temperate world, as it freely accepts farm tracks, barren ditch edges, roadsides, gravely banks, and other waste places. In appearance, it is mousy, forming a small bushy plant with green, divided leaves and producing knobby, yellowish-green buttons of flower with few ragged white ray petals. Fresh or dried, those buttons may be steeped in boiling water to make pineapple tea, and fresh leaves may be added to salads for a hint of the same flavor.

Like most matricarias, present and past, *M. matricariodes* is of very simple culture. Though it may be started indoors six to eight weeks before the last anticipated frost date, little is gained from that, as seed may be sown outdoors as soon as the soil is free of frost. Germination occurs quickly, within a week or two, and flowers will be produced by midsummer, when they make a valuable addition to iced tea. Like other garden matricarias and the feverfews now in the genus *Tanacetum,* once *Matricaria matricariodes* is grown in gardens it will faithfully reappear from one year to the next, although not always where it was first planted. Its species name *matricariodes* means resembles matricaria, though why it should be said to resemble itself is a mystery known only to C. L. Porter, the botanist who named it.

MATTHIOLA SPECIES

FAMILY: *Cruciferae* or mustard family.

CLASSIFICATION: Half-hardy biennials grown as hardy or half-hardy annuals.

COMMON NAMES: Stock, matthiola.

HARDINESS: Slightly frost-resistant when well established.

GROWING CONDITIONS: Rich, moist, well-drained soil. Good air circulation. Prefers cool. Full sun.

PROPAGATION: From seed, sown in late February or early March indoors in peat pots.

HEIGHT: To 2'.

ORNAMENTAL VALUE: For flowers and for strong fragrance.

LEVEL OF CULTURAL DIFFICULTY: Difficult except in cool gardens.

SPECIAL PROPERTIES: Excellent cut flowers.

PRONUNCIATION: ma-tee-O-la

Stock has never been as popular in North American gardens as in England and Europe, where it has been treasured for more than four centuries and was felt to be quaint and old-fashioned even by the seventeenth century. Natives of central and southern Europe, it was among the first garden flowers to be improved, particularly in the selection of double forms, and in the development of strains that would bloom reliably in a short period of time, as with the famous ten-week stock that is still the genetic base of many modern forms. Where it may be grown well, stock is a staple both of the simple cottage garden and of more elaborate bedding schemes. But grown well means first a climate in which springs are long and cool and summer nighttime temperatures do not get much above 60°F. Most American gardens do not offer such conditions, and so stock is generally either a brief spring and early summer pleasure, or an outright failure.

Of the fifty or so annual, biennial, perennial, and shrubby species contained in the genus *Matthiola,* only two are commonly cultivated in gardens, generally as annuals. *Matthiola incana* (in-CA-na), the plant usually imagined when stock is mentioned, is technically a hardy biennial, or even a weak perennial, though over almost three centuries of development, strains have been bred that will flower with relative rapidity from seed. However, as with most biennials adapted to becoming annuals, early sowing under glass is necessary, as plants require a long, slow growing period at temperatures around 50°F before producing flowers. When they are crowded or starved, or hurried into precocious flower for sale in garden centers, they never make the fine, bushy and floriferous plants they may become, reaching a height of as much as two feet and producing many clusters of flowers at the tips of branches. In addition to cool temperatures, *Matthiola incana* also demands rich, moist but well-drained soil and supplementary fertilizer (to move it on rapidly to flowering without a check), and fresh and buoyant air as wilts, crown rots, and other fungus diseases can carry it off quickly in muggy, stagnant weather. Transplanting should also be done with great care, as plants produce a strong taproot, and though they may accept a move even if it is damaged, they will never develop into perfect specimens.

The species name *incana* means gray or dusty, and describes the two- to four-inch-long leaves of the plant, each an elongated oval and somewhat succulent and felty to the touch. Branches are thick and woody, but can be brittle where they join the central stem, requiring that weeding among them be gentle. Flower color can be any shade of white, blue, mauve, purplish red, dark or light pink, cream or pale yellow. Double flowers, of many petals packed tight into shaggy little roses that touch on the stem, seem generally preferred, though no seed mix will give 100 percent double-flowering plants. Canny growers who want only double-flowering plants have therefore noted that even as small seedlings, double-flowered forms will be a lighter green than singles, which they eliminate. Seed strains also exist that carry a marker in the form of a notch in the leaf that signals a double-flowering plant, indicating in an unusual way how much can be done in breeding plants. But single-flowered stocks have their own ragged grace, each flower composed of four somewhat floppy-looking petals borne at widely spaced intervals along the stems. They have recently enjoyed more favor than ever before, perhaps because of a general trend toward simpler flower forms, and some of the finest colors, of peach and apricot and coral, exist only in singles.

In a mixed lot, however, one could harvest whichever form or color was not desired in the garden, as stocks make splendid cut flowers if taken just as the lower blossoms are opening. Successive flowers will open over as long as ten days in a vase if the water is changed daily and stems are re-cut. So treated, they will continue to release their magical fragrance, but if not so treated, they will become a malodorous dark green slime under water, much like a plastic bag of greens left too long in the refrigerator.

Matthiola incana, which at its best can be a vivid and luscious garden plant laden with bloom, has a shy cousin that wins no beauty prizes but possesses its own winsome grace (at least sometimes) and perhaps one of the most subtle fragrances of all annual plants. It has a very garbled botanical name, appearing usually as *Matthiola bicornis* (bi-KOR-nis), which notes its double-horned seed, or *M. longipetala* (lon-ji-PET-a-la), which notes its wispy, thin petals. Properly, however, all these characteristics are recorded in its correct but unwieldy botanical name, *Matthiola longipetala* subsp. *bicornis.* Most gardeners will prefer to call it simply "night-scented stock," for its most salient characteristic is the scent offered only at twilight and throughout the darkest hours of the night. Almonds predominate in its fragrance, though there is a strong undersmell of ripe fruit. It is actually quite pretty at twilight, when its slender, wavy petals open, tinted deep or light mauve at their tips and fading down to pinkish white in the center. The flowers are delicately borne up and down the stems, which tangle together in clumps of plants, producing enough of a show to justify growing them, though in daytime they shrivel up into little brown wisps. For that reason plants are usually grown in modest concealment behind taller, more floriferous annuals or perennials, but always near where one sits or strolls in the evening. Seed is sown in place, since plants resent root disturbance, and they are never thinned overmuch, no more than two or so inches one from another, in order to produce a tangle of wiry, flower-laden stems by midsummer, or two months from germination.

The genus *Matthiola* is named for the Italian physician and scholar of classical botany Pierandrea Mattioli (1500–1577). The popular name is a survival of the now archaic word *stock,* meaning a trunk or stick, and refers to the woody base of the plant that early gardeners felt distinguished it from gillyflowers, with which it shares a rich and spicy fragrance.

MELAMPODIUM SPECIES (*LEUCANTHEMUM SPECIES*)

FAMILY: *Asteraceae* or aster or daisy family.

CLASSIFICATION: Short-lived tender perennial grown as half-hardy annual.

COMMON NAMES: Blackfoot daisy, medallion flower, melampodium.

HARDINESS: Damaged by light frosts.

GROWING CONDITIONS: Rich, well-drained soil. Abundant moisture. Summer warmth. Full sun.

PROPAGATION: From seed, sown indoors 6 to 8 weeks before last frost.

HEIGHT: From 8" to 2', depending on cultivar.

ORNAMENTAL VALUE: Grown for flower.

LEVEL OF CULTURAL DIFFICULTY: Easy.

SPECIAL PROPERTIES: Excellent container plants.

PRONUNCIATION: me-lam-PO-dee-um (loo-KAN-thuh-mum)

Why few garden references discuss *Melampodium,* and seed of the plant is not commonly offered, is a mystery. The plant is of very easy culture, sprouting in ten days from seed and producing its inch-wide, chrome-yellow daisies practically with the first true leaves. From then on, if its cravings for warmth, rich well-drained but moist soil, and full sun can be met, it will produce little stars of flower from late spring until frost, creating an effect much like Lilliputian sunflowers. Compact and bushy of growth without pinching, it typically achieves a height of about a foot, though cultivars exist that form tight, tidy buns of growth scarcely eight inches tall. Its leaves are pointed ovals about three inches long, of a fresh green, raspy to the touch, and nicely set off its abundant flower. Groups of five or seven plants make pleasant masses of color in the summer border, and there are probably few other plants grown as annuals that do better in pots, containers, and window boxes, where warmth at the roots satisfies *Melampodium paludosum*'s love of heat.

Melampodium paludosum (pa-loo-DO-sum) is actually a native American wild flower, with a range extending across the southwestern United States and Mexico. It borrows its one common name from another plant within its small genus of twelve or so species, *Melampodium leucanthemum,* which is also called the "blackfoot daisy" after the Native American nation associated with the Algonquin and sharing their language. (*Melampodium* in botanical Greek comes from *melas,* meaning black, and *podos,* foot, which is an exact translation of the common name.) *M. leucanthemum* is also a perennial that may be grown as an annual, from an early spring sowing indoors at temperatures around 70°F. It forms a bushy, much-branched plant to about a foot and a half tall, covered with inch-wide daisies with white ray petals surrounding a bright yellow disk. Its species name, *leucanthemum,* means white, and always seems to be reserved for plants that look like daisies in the popular imagination, with white ray petals and a yellow center. In its native range, across Arizona, New Mexico, Texas, and northern Mexico, it grows in areas where the surface soil consists essentially of de-composed rock, with little humus. More-than-usually sharp drainage will be required to grow it successfully, therefore, and though it appreciates supplementary phosphorus and potassium, excess nitrogen will encourage growth at the expense of flower.

In contrast to *Melampodium leucanthemum,* the species name of *M. paludosum* is a bit of a mystery. The Latin *paludosus* means marsh-loving and usually designates a plant native to boggy conditions. But though *M. paludosum* demands a moister, more humus-rich soil than its cousin, it would perish in permanently waterlogged soils where slugs would also quickly shred it to pieces. Any situation that would please a marigold suits it to perfection, where it will bloom as long and as faithfully, and create as bright and cheerful an impression.

Seed of *Melampodium leucanthemum* is best sown in site, in very early spring in the place it is to grow, for it resents transplanting and is seldom successful when started indoors. *M. paludosum,* however, is easier to raise from seed. For the longest period of bloom it should be started under glass or on a sunny windowsill in sterile potting mix when even temperatures around 70°F can be ensured. Seedlings appear in about ten days and should be pricked out or thinned when the first true leaves appear, for as with many hairy leaved plants, damping off from crowding or from poor air circulation is always a threat. Sturdy seedlings can then be planted out in the garden or established in containers after danger of frost is past.

Like almost all plants included in or even associated with the genus *Chrysanthemum,* the melampodiums have been shifted about and are now lodged, for the moment, in the genus *Leucanthemum,* which also at present contains the shasta daisies.

MELIANTHUS MAJOR

FAMILY: *Melanthaceae* or melianthus family.

CLASSIFICATION: Tender shrub grown as tender annual.

COMMON NAMES: Honey flower, honey shrub, melianthus.

HARDINESS: Hardy to Zones 9 and 10. Intolerant of temperatures much below 40°F.

GROWING CONDITIONS: Rich, well-drained loam. Abundant moisture. Full sun to part shade. Summer heat.

PROPAGATION: From seed sown in February. Basal cuttings may be rooted at any time.

HEIGHT: To 10′ where hardy. Up to 4′ when treated as an annual.

ORNAMENTAL VALUE: Grown for its foliage.

LEVEL OF CULTURAL DIFFICULTY: Easy.

SPECIAL PROPERTIES: Excellent container plant.

PRONUNCIATION: mel-ee-AN-thus MA-jor

Though superlatives are always suspect in garden writing, still it must be said that *Melianthus major* is among the most beautiful of all foliage plants, and seems to attract words like "aristocratic," "bold," "handsome," and "architectural." A lax, soft-wooded shrub native to moist sandy grasslands in South Africa, it is treated as a perennial in gardens where winter temperatures do not fall below 25°F—Zones 8 to 10. In the warmer parts of that range, it will not die to the ground, and will produce its curious foot-long panicles of hooded, mahogany red flowers in spring. They are laden with nectar, and they attract hummingbirds and hosts of bees, which gives the genus both its common and botanical names, from ancient Greek *meli,* meaning honey, and *anthos,* flower. But however delicious they are to hummingbirds and bees, the flowers are malodorous to a human nose, giving off the musty, stale smell of an unaired room. In any case it is not for the flowers that the plant is grown, but for its incomparable form and the beauty of its leaves.

Where it is native, and in climates that experience no frost, melianthus will grow into a lax, sprawling plant with many shoots ascending from the base and falling outward, making a bold rounded clump up to ten feet tall. Each stem possesses a plume of leaves borne alternately, becoming progressively larger as they ascend up the stem until they reach a length of about ten inches, the whole arrangement creating a palmlike effect. The leaves are very beautiful, composed of seven to eleven toothed leaflets arranged as feathers along a central creased rib. Though large and bold, the leaves possess a curious delicacy and refinement, suggesting something even more beautiful than the stylized acanthus leaves on the capitals of Corinthian columns. Each leaf is heavily coated with a silvery wax over a dark green ground, giving it the look in some lights of old celadon porcelain and in others, of newly forged steel. The wax catches and holds water—from rain, irrigation, or even dew—in silver beads until it evaporates. So beautiful are the leaves that they almost have to be touched or fondled, but that rubs off the wax and then some of their beauty is ruined.

Though once rarely seen except in gardens where it was hardy or in botanical glasshouse collections, *Melianthus major* is now one of many tender plants avidly sought by gardeners to create tropical effects during summer in colder gardens. Young, single-stemmed plants grown from seed are therefore appearing in specialty nurseries and good garden centers in spring and can also be bought by mail. Though pretty enough, a youthful melianthus is not a melianthus in full sail, with several well-clad stems perhaps three feet tall and rich, palmlike, overlapping leaves. So, where budgetary considerations are not paramount, well-grown two-year-old plants in pots can be almost irresistible.

And in pots they may remain, either as single specimens in the garden or as the central, grand component of a large pot or tub containing other choice annual and tender plants. For melianthus grows well in containers and seems to relish the extra heat at its roots. Alternatively, a well-grown plant may be taken from its pot and planted as an accent in the perennial garden or as a single star in a bay of spring-flowering shrubs that may be undistinguished in summer.

Melianthus major is of very easy culture, and any situation that would please a common marigold will be suitable for it. Full sun is preferred, though light shade is acceptable, particularly in very hot gardens. Soil—whether in a container or the living earth—should be light and well drained but moist and rich. Supplementary nourishment in the form of water-soluble fertilizer applied according to the manufacturer's directions will quickly produce the most spectacular leaves, particularly in summer heat, which melianthus adores. Plants are very frost-sensitive, however, and so should be set out when the weather is warm and settled, and—if they are to be preserved—should be taken in before heavy freezes occur.

Though most melianthus plants will be acquired from commercial nurseries specializing in rare tender perennials and shrubs, they are easy to grow from seed with a little patience. If seed can be found, it should be sown in late winter or very early spring, at nighttime temperatures around 55°F. Young seedlings should be pricked out and grown on in the usual way, either in a sunny greenhouse with minimum nighttime temperatures around 50°F, or on a sunny windowsill. Plants quickly become weak and attenuated, however, in dim light and excessive, dry heat. In enclosed environments, aphids will also always be a problem and should be eliminated with organic insecticide soap. But where a cool, frost-free basement is available, both young and old plants flourish under fluorescent lights.

Many melianthus will be abandoned at first frost, withering down to the base on a night where the temperatures drop to 38°F. But if they are to be saved, the root mass (called by gardeners a "stool") can be dug, repotted, and stored in cool, frost-free conditions until new basal growth occurs in early spring, when pots must be stood in bright light but with cool conditions and liquid fertilizer applied. If additional plants are required, cuttings should be taken in early to mid-spring, just as basal growth occurs, and rooted in perlite or half perlite and half peat in a moist environment. Where "Irish cuttings" can be taken, with a bit of root already formed at the woody base of the new shoots, success is ensured. Young plants should then be grown on in bright and cool conditions, though the pinching that is often routinely recommended to encourage bushy growth, as with chrysanthemums, is no use here, as all new growth ascends from the base of the plant, which will never branch.

MELIANTHUS MAJOR

MENTZELIA LINDLEYI
(BARTONIA AUREA)

FAMILY: *Loasaceae* or false stinging nettle family.

CLASSIFICATION: Hardy annual.

COMMON NAMES: Blazing star, mentzelia.

HARDINESS: Resistant to light frosts.

GROWING CONDITIONS: Moist, well-drained soil. Full sun.

PROPAGATION: From seed, sown in place in warmer gardens in autumn, and in very early spring in cooler ones.

HEIGHT: To 18″.

ORNAMENTAL VALUE: Grown for flower.

LEVEL OF CULTURAL DIFFICULTY: Moderately difficult.

SPECIAL PROPERTIES: None.

PRONUNCIATION: min-ZEE-lee-a LIND-lee-ee (bar-TON-ee-a O-re-a)

Even within the incredible treasury of annuals native to California, *Mentzelia lindleyi* is a special jewel. Its flowers, beautifully shaped and of a vibrant chrome yellow, are often compared to poppies though they are not at all poppylike. If the flowers of other plants must be sought to describe them, they more resemble certain hypericons. Each two-inch-wide flower consists of five broad petals that touch but do not overlap, and are not pleated and rounded—as are those of most garden poppies—but are shaped like a broad mason's trowel curling into a spur at the tip. There is a magical satiny sheen to each petal, and where they meet in the center, they form a zone of orange-red. There a sort of explosion occurs, with many hair-fine stamens bursting outward like fireworks and perhaps accounting for their popular name.

Despite its floral beauty, *Mentzelia lindleyi* could never be wildly popular with most American gardeners. Its plant habit is ungainly, consisting often of a single, gaunt stem about eighteen inches tall, and its leaves are hardly enough to recommend it, though they are attractive in their way. Each is practically stemless, about three inches long and deeply divided, clothed with short hairs and raspy to the touch though not stinging as are other members of the Loasaceae family. It will never show up in garden centers to tempt browsers in spring and early summer, for like so many hardy annuals, it resents root disturbance and must be sown in place where it is to bloom. Finally, though it will bloom in as few as eight weeks from germinated seed sown in winter in mild gardens, and in April in cold ones, it remains in flower little more than a month and so cannot compete with other plants that offer bloom from early summer to frost. The English garden writer Christopher Lloyd recommends cutting plants back hard promptly after the first flowers are over (as close as two inches from the ground) and feeding well with a water-soluble plant food for a second flush of bloom. Anyone who grows the plant for a season and comes to love it will certainly want to try his method.

Mentzelia should be sown where it is to grow and thinned after healthy young seedlings develop to stand about eight inches apart. Full sun is an absolute requirement, and though native to dry climates, the plant experiences abundant vernal moisture where it grows naturally, and so should never be allowed to dry out at the roots. At all times, however, perfect drainage is necessary, and supplementary feedings of water-soluble fertilizer produce the most floriferous plants. Where the exacting art of annual wildflower meadows is practiced, seed of mentzelia is an interesting component, particularly near where it occurs natively. Elsewhere, mentzelia is best grown in open patches of the perennial garden, behind and between other plants that will develop and bloom later in the season. Alternatively, it is a superb specimen for early summer flower in the rock garden.

Mentzelia lindleyi commemorates two botanists who would probably never have seen the plant in flower. The genus name *Mentzelia* recognizes Christian Mentzel (1622–1701), a seventeenth-century German medical doctor and amateur. The species name *lindleyi* commemorates the great English botanist John Lindley (1799–1865), first professor of botany at the University of London.

MERREMIA AUREA

FAMILY: *Convolvulaceae* or morning glory family.

CLASSIFICATION: Tender perennial vine grown as half-hardy annual.

COMMON NAMES: Golden morning glory, merremia.

HARDINESS: Hardy in Zones 9 and 10. Frost-sensitive elsewhere.

GROWING CONDITIONS: Moderately rich, well-drained soil. Full sun.

PROPAGATION: By seed, sown indoors in peat pots in late March to early April. Seed must be nicked and soaked overnight. Seedlings resent root disturbance.

HEIGHT: To 8′ in one season.

ORNAMENTAL VALUE: Grown for flower.

LEVEL OF CULTURAL DIFFICULTY: Easy.

SPECIAL PROPERTIES: None.

PRONUNCIATION: muh-REE-mi-a AU-ree-a

*M*orning glories convey a freshness, simplicity, and beauty unequaled by any other flowers except daisies. Until about fifteen years ago, however, the only morning glories much cultivated were in the genus *Ipomoea,* with 'Heavenly Blue' as the standard. In Japan, however, the cultivation of the vines has amounted to a national passion for a hundred years, and many cultivars, species, and separate genuses—largely unknown to most American gardeners—are grown, including the genus *Merremia.*

Though *Merremia* includes seventy to eighty species of twining, herbaceous, or woody vines, only a few are worthy of cultivation. Of them the most familiar may be *M. tuberosa* (too-ber-O-sa [previously *Ipomoea tuberosa*]), called the "Hawaiian wood rose" because its curious, knobby seed receptacle surrounded by a ring of thick, woody sepals looks indeed like a rose carved of wood. Its large tuberous roots may be hardy at least to Zone 7 under ideal conditions, though bloom, if it occurs at all, will be so late that the decorative seed pods will not form before frost kills the vines.

For most American gardeners, a better choice within the genus would be *Merremia aurea,* the golden morning glory, for its profusion of two-inch-wide chartreuse yellow flowers borne in clusters in the upper leaf axils of the vine. *M. aurea* is actually a tender perennial hardy in Zones 9 and 10, though elsewhere it may be grown as a half-hardy annual, reaching its full height of eight feet or so and producing flower from mid- to late summer from an indoor sowing in early spring. Like many other morning glories, it has a very thick seed coat that might take at least a month to germinate unless it is nicked with a sharp knife, filed thin on one side, or rubbed between two pieces of sandpaper, and then soaked for a day or two. When the seed swells, it may be sown at temperatures around 55° to 60°F in peat pots to minimize root disturbance at transplant time. Germination should occur within two weeks, and young plants should be grown on in bright, fresh conditions until all danger of frost is past, after which they may be hardened off and transplanted. The best vines will develop in full sun, in moderately rich, well-drained soil, producing triangular or lobed, dark green leaves so much like those of the familiar 'Heavenly Blue' morning glory that the yellow-green flowers are a startling surprise.

More vigorous of growth than *Merremia aurea* is *M. siberica* (si-BER-i-ca), which is hardier, too, as its name suggests, though it is in fact a native of China. Its cultural requirements are the same as for *M. aurea,* though it produces strong twining vines to as much as twenty feet in a season, furnished with heart-shaped leaves two to three inches wide and about four inches long. Its flowers, borne in clusters from the axils of the upper leaves, are a pale, silvery pink, each about three-fourths of an inch wide and of typical morning glory shape. Vines come into flower about three months from seed and bloom through midsummer and into autumn, most profusely in August. Strikingly, both the stems and leaves of the vine will turn red as fall approaches.

MIMOSA PUDICA

FAMILY: *Leguminosae* or pea family.

CLASSIFICATION: Tender shrub grown as tender annual.

COMMON NAMES: Sensitive plant, humble plant, mimosa.

HARDINESS: Hardy to Zone 10. Extremely sensitive to temperatures below 40°F.

GROWING CONDITIONS: Lean, sandy, well-drained soil. Full sun.

PROPAGATION: From seed, soaked overnight and sown at 70°F.

HEIGHT: To 18″.

ORNAMENTAL VALUE: Grown for foliage.

LEVEL OF CULTURAL DIFFICULTY: Moderately easy.

SPECIAL PROPERTIES: Foliage collapses under gentle brushing.

PRONUNCIATION: mee-MO-sa PU-di-ca

Mimosa pudica is often grown and sold not as a plant of remarkable beauty, but simply as one that does a trick. It responds to touch, wind, the flame of a match, or any other tactile intrusion by folding together the tiny leaflets of its feathery leaves and collapsing them downward as if the petiole of each leaf were on a minute hinge. This characteristic, which has been much studied but is not well understood, earns *Mimosa pudica* both its popular name, "sensitive plant," and also the frequency with which it is cultivated. It is an oddity fascinating to children of all ages, and a gentle stroking of the leaves seems not to hurt the plant, which re-opens them after several minutes if it is left in peace. Most probably, this is a reaction contrived to cope with hostile environments, for when the leaves are shuttered up they are less vulnerable to drying winds, and possibly even less attractive to grazing animals (or malicious children).

Though a well-grown plant of *Mimosa pudica* can have a shy, gentle sort of charm, there is nothing about it one could call beautiful. It is an angular, gawky little shrub to about eighteen inches tall, with hairy stems that occasionally venture a protective spine. The whole plant is what gardeners call "sparsely furnished," for its dusty, gray-green leaves—composed of four delicate feathers of equal length, each about an inch and a half long—never occur in great abundance, and each one is widely separate from the other. At the tips of the stems of mature plants, little fuzzy powder puffs of flower will form in clusters, each flower less than an inch across, and of an indeterminate lilac to purplish pink.

The genus *Mimosa* is large, comprising some 400 to 500 species of annual, perennial, shrubby, or treelike plants variously native to the tropics worldwide. The name is derived from the ancient Greek word *mimos,* meaning mime or clown, and refers to the capacity of some species, most notably *M. pudica,* to counterfeit what humans call "feelings." The species name *pudica* is Latin for bashful, or shy, and accurately describes the downcast look of the leaves after collapse, though it might as easily describe the whole plant in its modest charms of leaf and flower. Young plants are the most dramatic in showing their feelings.

Though technically a shrub, *Mimosa pudica* is hardy only to Zone 10, where it is a widely escaped roadside weed. Elsewhere it is best grown as an annual or as a warm windowsill shrublet, though its culture over winter is not easy, since it requires precise watering and resents dry house atmospheres. For growth as an annual, the seeds should be soaked for a day or two until they swell, and then sown in very sandy, well-drained sterile compost at temperatures around 70°F. At all ages the plant resents root disturbance, and so three seed should be sown to a peat pot with the determination of eliminating all but the strongest after two or three sets of leaves have formed. If they have been presoaked, seed should germinate within two to three weeks, though at no time must the compost be either over-watered or allowed to dry out. After germination, young plants should be placed in bright, sunny conditions in temperatures around 70°F, and again watered carefully only when the soil is moderately dry, to prevent rot. (Most plants are lost to over-

watering, particularly by zealous young gardeners.) Applications of very weak, water-soluble fertilizer at two-week intervals will promote larger leaves. Plants prefer full sun, though they will tolerate some afternoon shade. As *M. pudica* has few physical beauties, it is best grown as single specimens in pots, one to play with and the others to give away to amused friends and guests.

MIMULUS SPECIES

FAMILY: *Scrophulariaceae* or snapdragon family.

CLASSIFICATION: Hardy or half-hardy perennials grown as hardy or half-hardy annuals.

COMMON NAMES: Monkey flower, mimulus.

HARDINESS: Varies with species. Most are tolerant of light frosts.

GROWING CONDITIONS: Rich, poorly drained, boggy soil. Some species prefer constantly moist but well-drained garden loam. Full to half-day sun.

PROPAGATION: From seed, sown indoors 8 weeks before last frost date, or in site in early spring. Cuttings root easily.

HEIGHT: From 12 to 18".

ORNAMENTAL VALUE: Grown for flowers.

LEVEL OF CULTURAL DIFFICULTY: Easy.

SPECIAL PROPERTIES: Unusually tolerant of wet soil. Good in containers, hanging baskets, and window boxes. Transplants easily at almost any stage.

PRONUNCIATION: mim-YEW-lus

*B*oth the popular and botanical names of *Mimulus* attest to the drollery of its flowers, for *Mimulus* is the Latin diminutive of *mimus,* a clown or comical mimic, and by extension, a monkey. With a little imagination, one can see the face of a

MIMULUS AURANTIACUS

modern seed strains (grouped as *Mimulus* x *hybridus* [HI-bri-dus]), demand constantly wet soils and will even grow in an inch or so of standing water. No other commonly grown annual tolerates such conditions, and so, where they obtain, mimulus is a treasure. But it is a treasure in any case, and so its particular needs should be met even if the garden does not contain a bog, streamside, or pond edge. Any humus-rich soil kept well watered will suit it, and there is no better choice for dank, partially shaded city gardens when *Impatiens capensis* and fibrous begonias have begun to weary the gardener. Where the need for moisture at its roots may be met, mimulus is also splendid in pots, hanging baskets, and window boxes.

Seed of *Mimulus* x *hybridus* should be sown about eight weeks before the last anticipated frost date for plants that will come into flower in late spring or early summer. Germination is very rapid, requiring only a week or two at most, though the fine brown seed should be sprinkled carefully over the top of moistened potting compost and not covered, as they require light to germinate. Young plants develop rapidly and are content in less than full sunlight indoors. They particularly thrive under fluorescent lights in a cool basement, where nighttime temperatures can be maintained at around 50°F, and few plants grown as annuals are more responsive to weekly applications of water-soluble plant food.

When young plants reach a height of five or six inches, terminal shoots may be pinched out and inserted in damp sand or half-sand and half-peat, where they will form roots in a little more than a week. The first flowers may well appear before plants can be hardened off and transplanted into the garden after danger of frost is past, a handy thing if one has sown seed of mixed colors and wants a particular color scheme. However, there

tiny grinning ape in each blossom, composed of five lobes flared out from a central tube or mouth, the upper two standing separately like ears and the lower three arranged so the one in the center sticks out like a snout above two cheeks. Colors range from white, cream, yellow, orange through red and mahogany, and the resemblance to a tiny, comic face is intensified in most forms by frecklings, splotchings, or streakings of a deeper tint—subtle or dramatic—over a lighter one. Monkey flowers thus take a recognizable place in the family Scrophulariaceae, which contains many other mimics such as snapdragons, toadflax, and turtleheads.

In addition to the charm of its flowers, mimulus possesses an attribute rare among plants grown as annuals. Individual species and the is no ugly *M. x hybridus*. The leaves are always a fresh pale or darker green, shiny, toothed, and pointed ovals about three inches long, clasping a watery, succulent stem, and plants may reach a height of a foot and a half, though generally they will topple over gracefully and root where they fall.

In addition to abundant moisture at its roots, *Mimulus x hybridus* prefers dappled shade, especially in warmer gardens. Where nights are cool, however, it will also thrive in full sun. With the arrival of full summer heat, plants are apt to cease flowering and begin the abundant setting of seed. New bloom may be encouraged by cutting them back to central rosettes of leaves, and fertilizing with a water-soluble plant food. If a few individuals are left to go to seed, however, abundant progeny will appear the following year, usually

quite thickly, though young plants can be taken up in plugs of three or more seedlings, spaced about six to eight inches one from another, and fertilized for quick-blooming adult plants. At all times *M. x hybridus* is easy to relocate, providing the work is done on a cloudy day and the transplants are well watered after they are moved. Cuttings may be rooted at almost any time before plants go to seed, and those rooted at the end of summer make excellent winter-flowering house plants. Alternatively, clumps of young seedlings, which generally appear around established plants in late summer, may be lifted and potted for indoor growth in winter. Those that remain may well overwinter to provide flower the following spring.

In addition to *Mimulus x hybridus,* seed is occasionally offered of *M. luteus* (LOO-tee-us), a na-

MIMULUS *X* HYBRIDUS

MIMULUS GUTTATUS 'CHEVRON'

tive of Chile though widely naturalized in temperate zones as a garden escapee, or of *M. guttatus* (gew-TA-tus), a native of the western coast of North America from Alaska to southern California. The two species are very similar in growth and flower, both bearing clear yellow blossoms sometimes freckled or streaked with red. They are hopelessly mixed up in trade and in gardens, and they may in fact simply be geographic variants of one single species. Alternatively, plants in gardens may be crosses of the two, for they hybridize freely. Once grown in a garden, both species or crosses between them will return faithfully from year to year, either regrowing from the roots or as volunteer seedlings.

Shrubby species of *Mimulus* are occasionally sometimes offered, most frequently *M. aurantiacus* (au-ran-tee-A-cus), previously listed as *Diplacus glutinosus* (DI-pla-cus glu-ti-NO-sus). Called the "sticky monkey flower" from its lance-shaped, dark green leaves, glossy but clammy to the touch, it forms a woody plant to as much as four feet tall, with open, funnel-shaped, inch-wide flowers that may range from tan to orange, yellow, dark red, or mahogany. Unlike perennial species of *Mimulus* grown as annuals, it does not relish soggy soils but prefers a humus-rich, well-

drained compost that may be kept evenly moist, such as would suit fuchsias. It flowers best in full sun, and it seems to be in flower from the time it is purchased as a rooted cutting until frost. Desirable color forms are propagated by cuttings, which should be taken from vigorous side shoots in late spring or early summer, inserted in damp sand and peat, and kept shaded until rooting occurs.

MIRABILIS SPECIES

FAMILY: *Nyctaginaceae* or four o'clock family.

CLASSIFICATION: Tender perennial grown as half-hardy annual.

COMMON NAMES: Four o'clock, marvel-of-Peru, mirabilis.

HARDINESS: Root-hardy to Zone 8. Seed-hardy to Zone 7. Leaves are frost-sensitive.

GROWING CONDITIONS: Moist, heavy to well-drained garden soil. Full sun in cool gardens, morning or afternoon shade in warmer ones.

PROPAGATION: From seed, sown indoors 6 to 8 weeks before last frost. Soak seed for 2 days before sowing.

HEIGHT: To 3'.

ORNAMENTAL VALUE: Grown for flower.

LEVEL OF CULTURAL DIFFICULTY: Easy.

SPECIAL PROPERTIES: Tubers may be stored over winter as for dahlias.

PRONUNCIATION: mi-RA-bi-liss

*E*ven given the sweet, primrose scent of their flowers, many gardeners are not very excited about four o'clocks—mostly because they do not offer the masses of vivid color expected from plants grown as annuals. Instead they open their flowers only in the late afternoon and close them the next morning with the heat of the sun. But as a subtle pleasure they can be wonderful.

Modern forms explode into a fascinating range of colors—white, cream, primrose and chrome yellow, orange, scarlet, magenta, deep and pale pink, salmon, purple, and lavender—all complexly marked with streaks, freckles, or shadowings of other colors. Sometimes flowers even occur that are half one color and half another, as if painted with precision on either side of a ruled line down the middle. When a plant is well furnished with its evening-borne flowers, it is easy to perceive different markings and colors, and to compare them with the flowers on other plants nearby. It is a little harder to remember what last evening's blooms looked like compared with this evening's, and so claims of fantastic variability of color on the same plant may be a little exaggerated. Nevertheless, even when individual flowers possess no distinctive markings but are all the same color, there is a great beauty in their two-inch-long tubes flaring out into five-lobed corollas, each about an inch wide. The five fused petals are also creased down the middle and creased again where they join one another, creating a star pattern. Even uniformly colored blooms, such as occur when the plant self-seeds in warmer gardens and has become naturalized, have a curious luminescence, the result of one color laid as a wash over a deeper ground—cerise over yellow, for example, or orange over cream. Five jewel-like orange anthers are always present, and at the base of each flower is a drop of nectar, enough to send a late-foraging hummingbird contentedly to bed or to provide enticement to ghostly night-flying moths.

Mirabilis jalapa (ha-LA-pa) is of very easy culture. It accepts almost any soil, though it is worthwhile to enrich planting places with compost or decayed leaf mold in order to achieve the handsome, multi-stemmed growth to four feet and the rich, dark green, five-inch-long oval leaves the plant can produce. That form is a value in itself, functioning as a sturdy shrub in the summer landscape, attractive even in daytime when all its flowers are newly closed or soon to open. In cooler gardens, full sun will produce the most abundant flower, but where summers are warmer, morning or afternoon shade is required. Plants are surprisingly drought-tolerant, though in dry weather the large leaves may lose both their thick leathery quality and their dark green color, becoming thin, pale, and anemic looking. They will recover quickly after a good, soaking rain, but four o'clocks are always best where soils stay evenly moist, even rather dank. Familiar to most southerners as the plants that grow behind the chicken house, they also seem to relish the sour soils of city backyards and are resistant to all forms of urban pollution, requiring only an occasional hosing to wash their leaves of dust, grime, and soot.

Mirabilis jalapa is technically a tender perennial hardy to Zone 8, though gardeners in colder zones might be surprised by its reappearance in late spring from underground storage roots much like those of dahlias, particularly where it has been grown against the greater winter

MIRABILIS JALAPA 'ALBA'

warmth of a house foundation. Normally, plants are raised each year from seed sown indoors about six to eight weeks before the last anticipated frost date. The large seeds possesses a thick, dark brown coat, and sprouting will be speeded if they are soaked for two days in water. So treated, germination should occur within two weeks, and young plants will develop quickly in a warm greenhouse, on a sunny windowsill, or under fluorescent lights in a heated basement. Plants grown indoors will be very frost-sensitive and so should be hardened off carefully before being planted about ten to fifteen inches from one another. Growth will be rapid when temperatures climb above 70°F, and gaps will quickly fill up.

One can never hope to reproduce any particularly lovely form of *Mirabilis jalapa* from seed, since any color may occur in the second generation, though most likely the plant will revert to the typical cherry red or orange yellow seen in most naturalized plants in Zones 7 and warmer. However, the thick, blackish-maroon tubers may be dug after frost, preserved in barely damp peat moss or perlite over the winter, and replanted the following spring about two weeks before the last anticipated frost. In addition to preserving fine color forms, this method has another advantage: Tuber-grown plants will be larger and more vigorous, and will flower much sooner than plants grown from seed, though abundant flower, which is produced at the tips of mature stems, can never be expected until the weather becomes settled and warm. Once flowers begin to be produced from terminal growths, a steady succession will continue until frost.

Mirabilis jalapa is the best-known member of its genus, the name of which is Latin for miracle. The species name *jalapa* is taken from the city of Jalapa, the capital of the eastern Mexican state of Veracruz, from which the plant is believed to originate. Plants were introduced to Europe by the Spanish early in the sixteenth century, and they created an immediate sensation. Despite their Central American origins, they were promptly named "marvel-of-Peru," reflecting perhaps the general sense of marvels the Inca Empire was reluctantly revealing to the Old World through brutal Spanish coercion. One can easily imagine seventeenth-century gardeners, bending over their plants as the sun declined in the afternoon sky, breathlessly awaiting the revelation of yet new colors or "breaks," as the streakings, splotchings, or mottlings on flowers were then called. Flowers of different colors or with different markings opening on a single plant was a phenomenon unknown in the plant kingdom at that time.

The genus comprises some sixty or more other species, of which two at least—*Mirabilis longiflora* (lon-ji-FLO-ra) and *M. multiflora* (multi-FLO-ra)—are also grown as perennials where they are hardy, and elsewhere as annuals, though both form thick tubers that may be lifted and stored as with *M. jalapa. M. longiflora* is native throughout west Texas, Arizona, and northern Mexico, where it forms a two- to three-foot-tall bushy plant furnished with heart-shaped leaves generally smaller than those of *M. jalapa* and somewhat more widely spaced along the stems. Flowers are narrow tubes nearly five inches long (as the species name *longiflora* indicates), flaring out at their ends into five fused petals about an inch across. The tube of the flower is white, though it shades to lavender pink at its open mouth. The effect is more delicate, more starlike than with the more familiar four o'clock, though flowers also open in late afternoon and close the following morning.

M. multiflora, by contrast, breaks its family pattern by opening in late morning and remaining open for the day. A native also of the southwestern United States and northern Mexico, it grows into a two- to three-foot bush with recognizable mirabilis leaves, though they are generally only three inches long at most. The tubular flowers, between one and two inches long, and about an inch and a half wide at the mouth, are variously described as crimson, purple, magenta, or rose pink, but in fact they are of an ineffable color somewhere among all those shades.

Species of *Mirabilis* are among those plants that were once treasured in gardens but that have fallen into neglect because they cut no figure at all in early spring, when most American gardeners browse the local garden center. If six-packs of promising young plants should be available, no precocious little blooms will be apparent, and an honest nurseryman will tell you that you cannot expect flower much before August. Further, young plants must be carefully handled since they are quite prepared to sulk if roughly treated and messed up at their roots, as too many gardeners still believe all "annuals" require. Compared to marigolds, then, or annual salvias, they would seem to have little going for them, at least in the garden center. But in gardens, when well grown, they are a great delight.

MOLUCELLA LAEVIS

FAMILY: *Lamiaceae* (*Labiatae*) or mint family.

CLASSIFICATION: Half-hardy annual.

COMMON NAMES: Bells of Ireland, shell flower, lady in the bath, balm of Molucca, molucella.

HARDINESS: Tolerant of light frosts when sown in site.

GROWING CONDITIONS: Fertile, well-drained garden loam. Full sun.

PROPAGATION: From seed, preferably sown in site in early spring. Sow indoors 6 to 8 weeks before last frost, in peat pots. Resents root disturbance.

HEIGHT: To 3′.

ORNAMENTAL VALUE: Grown for ornamental bracts.

LEVEL OF CULTURAL DIFFICULTY: Moderately difficult.

SPECIAL PROPERTIES: Valued as cut flower and for dried arrangements.

PRONUNCIATION: mo-loo-CHE-la (mo-lo-SELL-a) LAY-vis

*A*mong plants grown as annuals, there are very few that produce flowers in true shades of green. Notable among them are the tiny pendant trumpets of *Nicotiana langsdorffii* and the magnificent all-green *Zinnia elegans* called 'Envy'. Mostly, however, what one perceives as a green flower is actually some other part of the floral anatomy, the calyx or a set of modified leaves or bracts that surround the true flower. Of all the plants that have modified their floral furniture into green "flowers" in this way, none is more beautiful or more finely crafted than *Molucella laevis,* popularly called "bells of Ireland." It is called that not because it originated in that country—it comes in fact from Asia Minor—but because of the fresh, Irish green of its calyxes.

It has true flowers, of course, that begin as tiny pale-pink pearls nestled in the enlarged calyxes, and expand into funny, two-part blossoms consisting of a pink arching hood and a twice-divided lip of a pink so pale as to be almost white. But what is showy about the plant is the cup-shaped, fused calyx surrounding the flowers. The calyx is disproportionately large for the flower it shields, giving rise to the popular name "lady in the bath." The calyxes, each as much as an inch wide, elliptical and outfacing, are borne in whorls all up and down the stems, beginning practically at ground level, the largest at the bottom, graduating upward to perfectly formed but somewhat squashed ones at the top. The luminosity of bright, clear green comes from an overlay of fine, whitish-green veins on a yellow-green ground. Two or sometimes three fan-shaped leaves, each about one and three-quarter inches wide and lobed at the ends, accompany each whorl of bracts. Florists clip them away to reveal the shape of the inflorescences, though this is not to be done in the garden, where in any case they are part of the plant's charm.

Molucella laevis has been a popular garden plant since at least 1570, but it is seldom seen in the full magnificence it can attain. It should be a symmetrically branched, almost shrublike plant, three feet tall with relatively few leaves and many stems clothed in whorls of bells. Getting it to look that way requires that it be sown just where it is to grow as soon as the ground can be worked, usually April in most American gardens. As a hardy annual, it may also volunteer once it has been grown, and such self-seeded plants will always develop into the most magnificent specimens. One is frequently advised to start seed indoors six to eight weeks before the last frost date, and to transplant the young seedlings into the garden after danger of frost is past. However, *M. laevis* forms a long taproot, and like most such plants, resents any disturbance at the roots. If plants must be started indoors early, peat pots should be used, sowing three seed in each with the intention of later clipping out all but the strongest. Both light and cold are required for germination, which may take as long as three weeks, and so seed should be lightly pressed into the soil, not covered, and the peat pots placed in plastic bags and refrigerated for a week or so. Young plants should be grown on in a fresh buoyant atmosphere, ideally at temperatures around 60°F.

The ideal soil for *Molucella laevis* is good vegetable garden soil—humus rich, deeply tilled, and inclined to dry out on the surface a little between rains. The young plants should be thinned to stand nine to twelve inches apart and should be staked when young, as fully developed plants may fall over from their own weight, spoiling the desired effect. Supplementary feeding should occur just as for vegetables, with a side-dressing of granular food high in phosphorus and potassium. Though plants will accept part shade, the strongest, finest rods of bract and bloom are produced in full sun.

Most plants of bells of Ireland are actually grown in vegetable or cutting gardens, since the rods make superb and long-lasting cut flowers. Well-grown specimens, however, are very attractive in plantings of other flowers where their fresh color, interesting form, and substantial weight contribute beauty of their own and enhance the beauty of their neighbors. When stems are cut, florists know that they may be given almost any shape, by wilting them slightly, tying them to makeshift frames of canes or twiggy sticks, and then plunging them into water. They will stiffen into the forms they have been given, and the frames can then be removed. The plant is also treasured by dried flower arrangers, for if cut when fully developed and hung upside down in a dark, airy place, rods of bracts will keep for years, fading quickly from green to a beautiful ivory-gold.

The botanical name *Molucella* was applied from the mistaken notion that the plant originated in the Moluccas, the Spice Islands of the Malay Archipelago, because as a member of the mint family it gives off a haunting fragrance, something like lavender growing near a pine woods. From that it draws another popular name, "balm of Molucca." The species name *laevis,* meaning smooth, refers to the smooth, leaflike texture of the flower bracts.

The genus *Molucella* contains only four species, one other of which is sometimes grown in gardens, though it is very rare. *M. spinosa* (spi-NO-sa), a native of southern Europe and Eurasia, produces maroon-red to brownish-red stems developing into spikes of whitish flowers inside a two-part calyx. The calyx is furnished with eight long prickles or spines, giving the plant its species name. Seed of *M. spinosa* is worth seeking, for when well grown, it develops into a splendid plant five to seven feet tall, making it of excellent value at the back of a deep border. In its native range, the plant is biennial, though it is best grown as an annual in most American gardens. An early seeding indoors in March will be required for plants to develop flower by midsummer. Culture is the same as for *M. laevis*.

MOMORDICA SPECIES

FAMILY: *Cucurbitaceae* or cucumber family.

CLASSIFICATION: Tender perennial vine grown as tender annual vine.

COMMON NAMES: Balsam apple, balsam pear, bitter gourd, bitter cucumber, lizard fruit, momordica.

HARDINESS: Sensitive to frosts. Resents cool weather.

GROWING CONDITIONS: Rich, well-drained, humusy soil. Full sun. Relishes heat.

PROPAGATION: From seed, sown in peat pots 4 weeks before last frost.

HEIGHT: To 6' or more in a season, taller in very warm climates.

ORNAMENTAL VALUE: Grown for foliage and for ornamental fruit.

LEVEL OF CULTURAL DIFFICULTY: Moderately easy.

SPECIAL PROPERTIES: Fruits treasured in Asian cookery.

PRONUNCIATION: mo-MOR-di-ca

*T*he genus *Momordica* includes about forty tendril-bearing vines—variously native to the warmest parts of Africa and Asia. Exotic as they may seem, at least two of them have been grown for centuries in southern Asia, in tropical Africa, and in India, where their immature pods are treasured as an addition to rare dishes and curries most westerners have never tasted. Curious gardeners might cultivate either of them today, for they make handsome, cucumber-like vines, with rich, dark green, lobed leaves, and delicate, five-petaled gourdlike flowers of pale yellow or white, borne singly on threadlike stems in the axils of the leaves. The fruit of both, a sort of warted cucumber or snouted vegetable hedgehog, turns yellow or orange at maturity. When well grown, the vines—leaves, flowers, tendrils, and fruit—can look like a seventeenth-century botanical print of an exotic plant, no part of which would seem out of place in a Dutch still life.

Out of about forty species, only two momordicas are cultivated in gardens. The first, *M. balsamina* (bal-sa-MEE-na), is essentially a reduced version of the second, *M. charantia* (ka-RAN-tee-a). *Balsamina*'s slender stems climb to about six feet or more in the warmth of summer, bearing dark green, shiny but bristly, three- to five-lobed leaves, each about four inches wide and as long, very similar to those of its cousin, the garden cucumber. Like the cucumber, it bears both male and female flowers on the same plant, each of which is about an inch in diameter, bell-shaped or flared at the mouth, white or pale yellow, with a dark spot at its throat. Flowers of both sexes are borne on threadlike stems from the axils of the upper leaves. The fruit is a bumpy oval about two or three inches long that turns golden yellow when it is ripe and then splits into three segments, curling upward to reveal the seed. The species name *balsamina* would suggest a resinous scent similar to that of the balsam spruce *Abies balsamea,* but the leaves and fruit, even when crushed, only give off the smell of something green.

Momordica charantia is larger in all its parts and is perhaps the more desirable garden plant, reaching a height of twelve to twenty feet in a hot, steamy summer. Its three- to seven-lobed leaves are about four inches wide and long, and are attractively curled at their edges. The pale, primrose-yellow flowers are delicate and graceful, and the fruits, hanging from slender stems, can reach a length of as much as eight inches. They are torpedo-shaped, terminating in a pronounced slender snout, and the surface of their fruit is more warty than that of *M. balsamina.* The warts are arranged in five raised rows, with smaller bumps in between. The fruit turns yellow when it is ripe, and then splits into three segments and curls upward to expose the seed, surrounded by vivid orange pulp. As the opened fruit dries, it resembles nothing so much as fried pork rind. The prominent seed, which appear to be bitten off at their ends, perhaps explain the genus name *Momordica* from the Latin verb *mordere,* to bite, though more probably the bitterness of the flesh accounts for that name. The species name *charantia* is probably drawn from a vernacular Asian language.

Both *Momordica* grown in gardens are lovers of heat, and so little is gained by starting them too early indoors since, when transplanted into the garden, they will simply sulk until the settled warmth of summer arrives. Seed should be sown about a month before the last anticipated frost date and young plants grown on in the sunniest indoor conditions available until they may be transplanted into warm soil outdoors, generally when daytime temperatures remain at 70°F or more. Germination is erratic, but it may be hastened by soaking seed in tepid water for two days before sowing. Like all other garden cucurbits, momordica are entirely unwilling to be transplanted, even as small seedlings, and so peat pots should be used. As seed is apt to be scarce, however, economy suggests that only one seed be pressed sideways into moist potting compost, rather than the usual three. Except where plants are desired for culinary purposes, two or three vines will be enough for most gardeners. Again like cucumbers, momordica will happily scramble along the ground, though they are much more attractive if a scaffold of strings or an ornamental trellis of bamboo is provided for them to climb, thus displaying to advantage their handsome leaves, delicate flowers, and dangling fruits. Though vines will cling by tendrils to any support, an occasional tying in will prevent them from slipping down under their own weight.

Both species are prized in the cooking of India, Sri Lanka, Japan, China, and throughout Southeast Asia. In Asian markets, *Momordica balsamina* is generally offered under its Hindu name, *kantola,* and *M. charantia* as *karela,* though it is also known under the name *fu kwa* in Japanese, and in Mandarin Chinese as *Ku gua* (bitter gourd), *jin li zhi* (bright beautiful lichee), and *lao pu tao* (ugly grape).

MYOSOTIS SYLVATICA

FAMILY: *Boraginaceae* or borage family.

CLASSIFICATION: Hardy biennial grown as hardy annual or biennial.

COMMON NAMES: Forget-me-not, myosotis.

HARDINESS: Withstands frosts.

GROWING CONDITIONS: Humus-rich, moist, well-drained soil. Full sun in cool gardens. Part shade elsewhere.

PROPAGATION: By seed, sown in site in autumn or
in spring as soon as ground may be worked.
Sown indoors 6 to 8 weeks before last frost.

HEIGHT: To 12″.

ORNAMENTAL VALUE: Grown for flower.

LEVEL OF CULTURAL DIFFICULTY: Easy.

SPECIAL PROPERTIES: Useful as underbedding to
tulips or between emerging perennials.

PRONUNCIATION: my-o-SO-tis syl-VA-ti-ca

*P*eople seem always to have been busy constructing touching legends that explain why forget-me-nots bear the name they do. Most center on some tragedy in which a doomed lover extends a bouquet of the flowers to the loved one upon expiring, murmuring, "Forget me not!" Actually, however, the unforgettable china-blue of the tiny *Myosotis sylvatica,* each with its vibrant orange eye, seems quite enough to explain the popular name, even though ancient Greek botanists, who knew *Myosotis* as a vernal-flowering native plant, gave it quite a different and less poetic one, "mouse's ears," from *mus,* mouse, and *otos,* ear. That is a reasonably accurate description of the leaves, which are oblong to broadly oval, each about three-fourth to an inch long, furry or raspy to the touch, and folded down along their margins to form an inverted spoon or tiny upside-down boat. When grown in humus-rich, moist soil in part shade, the leaves are a healthy, vibrant green, borne thickly on bushy little plants hardly eight inches tall. But many gardeners have noted that *M. sylvatica* is one of the clearest indications of impoverished soil or inadequate drainage. Plants may survive in such conditions, but their leaves take on a chlorotic, yellowish appearance, or turn russet red, while growth and flower are poor. Time, then, to fork in extra humus and possibly sand.

There is much confusion, among both gardeners and seed companies, over whether *Myosotis sylvatica* is a hardy perennial, a hardy biennial, or a hardy annual. Actually, it may behave as any of the three, depending on climate and the conditions in which it is grown. Probably the best plants develop as biennials, germinating in midsummer and growing fat under cool late summer and early autumn conditions to flower abundantly the following spring. In any garden from Zones 4 to 8 where myosotis has once been grown, a few individuals will always be found that will behave this way, tucked under shrubbery and safe from weeding hands. In such gardens, however, seed may also germinate in very early spring, develop quickly, and flower around the time of the large tulips. Occasionally, also, a plant may persist for a year or two, becoming a short-lived perennial, though probably most plants considered perennial by gardeners are simply the seed-borne progeny of defunct plants grown in the same place. In any case, forget-me-nots are of such easy culture, and occur so faithfully as volunteer seedlings from year to year, that nothing much would be gained by preserving an elderly plant.

Though a limpid sky blue is the usual color

MYOSOTIS SYLVATICA

for the flowers, plants may occur that are white or pink, but always with an orange eye. Select seed strains also exist in deeper, richer blues that are not forget-me-not-blue at all, but closer to gentian. They can be magnificent in spring bedding though not necessarily to be preferred to the paler shade. If one wants a stand of pure white, all but white-flowered plants should be eliminated in one spot before they go to seed, thus building up, over several years, a population that will be mostly or entirely white. Some quite rich pink cultivars also exist, and solid stands of pink could be developed in the same way, though the pink of self-seeded plants tend to be weak.

Most gardeners will only plant forget-me-nots once, after which, if they are allowed to go to seed in late spring, yanked up, and shaken over the ground, young plants will always develop for the following spring. To start the sequence, however, seed may be sown in late autumn or in very early spring, where the plants are to grow, and the young plants thinned to stand about six inches one from another. Alternatively, seed may be sown indoors under glass about six to eight weeks before the last anticipated frost date, but the same seed could just as easily be sown outdoors as seedlings develop best in cold, raw weather. Once grown, seedlings of forget-me-nots may be transplanted from wherever they occur to where they are wanted, taking clumps of young seedlings up with a trowel full of earth and replanting them carefully with a minimum of root disturbance. For, though they accept transplanting, they do not really like it much.

For all its delicacy of appearance, *Myosotis sylvatica* is a tough, pest-free little garden plant that requires no coddling. It may be troubled by powdery mildew late in its blooming season, a fungus that turns the leaves a dusty gray. When this oc-

curs, however, most gardeners simply consider it a sign that it is time to pull up the plants and shake out the seed.

Though the species name *sylvatica* is Latin for "of woods," forget-me-nots will accept either full sun or partial shade, since even in gardens that experience blistering summer heat, their lovely, short life will be over before the onset of really hot weather. While they flourish, their delicate growth does little harm to other neighboring plants still developing, so that sprinklings of forget-me-nots among emerging perennials give an additional season of interest to the border. Finally, those gardeners lucky enough to have a cool greenhouse or minimally heated sun porch will find it worth the trouble to dig a few plants and pot them carefully in Pro-Mix to grow on through the winter.

NEMESIA SPECIES

FAMILY: *Scrophulariaceae* or snapdragon family.

CLASSIFICATION: Half-hardy annual.

COMMON NAME: Nemesia.

HARDINESS: Winter-blooming in Zones 9 and 10. Sensitive to frost elsewhere.

GROWING CONDITIONS: Moist, humus-rich, well-drained soil. Prefers cool weather.

PROPAGATION: From seed, sown in early March indoors.

HEIGHT: From 8 to 15″ tall.

ORNAMENTAL VALUE: Grown for flower.

LEVEL OF CULTURAL DIFFICULTY: Easy in cool gardens. Difficult elsewhere.

SPECIAL PROPERTIES: Excellent edging plant. Useful in containers and hanging baskets. Superb cool greenhouse plant for late winter-flowering.

PRONUNCIATION: ni-MEE-see-a

*A*mong annuals and tender perennials grown as annuals, *Nemesia strumosa* (stru-MO-sa) possesses a unique distinction. Its half-inch-wide flowers, often called jewel-like by horticultural writers, come in every color except green—white and cream to yellow, pink, crimson, true red, mahogany, and brown, with lavender, purple, and lilac shades, and (unusual in annuals with a wide color range) true blue. When one adds to this the fact that individual plants often bear flowers that are veined, shaded, or marked with a contrasting color in the center or even formed as perfect bicolors, one can understand why the most popular seed mix is called "Galaxy." Colors and combinations of colors are almost infinite.

Everything is attractive about nemesia's appearance. It forms a low, cushionlike but graceful little bush between eight and fifteen inches tall, nicely furnished with fresh green, lance-shaped leaves about two to three inches long, but becoming smaller where the stems begin to terminate in loose flower clusters. Individual flowers, which are generally about half an inch across, have all the personality typical of so many in the family Scrophulariaceae, such as foxgloves or snapdragons. Like them, the flowers of nemesia are composed of a corolla consisting of several fused lobes, in this case four smaller ones facing upward, and two broader ones turned down, with a pinched spur at the throat. The effect is often compared to a minute orchid, though the range and vibrancy of colors can be compared to nothing. When happy and in full bloom, individual plants smother themselves with flower.

But it takes a lot to make a nemesia happy, and most of it depends on geography. Almost no annual is more miserable in hot, dry conditions. It loves the cool but hates frost and is happiest in

NEMESIA FRUTICANS

sections of the country, such as the Pacific Northwest or the most climatically privileged parts of California that enjoy long, frost-free cool seasons in late winter, spring, and early summer. Predictably it is the darling of gardeners in the cooler parts of the British Isles, where it stays in flower from May almost to September.

Nemesias had an enormous vogue among Victorian gardeners, who thought nothing of re-making a bedding scheme four or five times in a season, beginning with bulbs, continuing with plants such as nemesias and stocks, proceeding from there to summer-flowering annuals and tender perennials, both for foliage and for colored leaf, and ending with chrysanthemums and other autumn-flowering perennials. Except for bulbs, all these plants were patiently grown in greenhouses, almost to the moment of perfection, and then dropped carefully into place. Nemesias were ideal for this treatment. Many distinct strains were developed that came true to color from seed, though they were thought to be lost when the popularity of nemesias declined with the disappearance of a trained garden staff and the subsequent demise of several-season bedding.

NEMESIA STRUMOSA *'NEBULA WHITE'*

Interestingly, however, some of the best of these cultivars survived, either in general mixes or in old cottage gardens. They have been reintroduced by seed companies, sometimes under their original name but more often with a catchy new name devised for marketing purposes. A new generation of plant scholars, however, is busy setting to rights this plagiarism of old plants under new names, and seed companies are discouraged from giving appealing but invalid names to plants merely in order to improve their sales.

A blend of well-grown nemesias in a wide array of colors has great charm, but the impact they may possess when grown as uniform flower colors is hard to describe. Particularly lovely are some of the bi-colors, such as 'Danish Flag' or 'KLM', with flowers divided neatly into two colors as with a ruler, the first red above and white below, and the second blue above and white below. For flowers of such startling beauty, one might even be willing to accept a bloom time of a month or less.

Although rigid as to climate preferences, the other needs of nemesias are not terribly difficult to satisfy. It is important to sow seed early in March so that young plants may develop freely before the onset of hot weather. Germination is somewhat erratic, however, taking anywhere from one to three weeks, so it is wise to sow the seed very thinly, making it possible to remove and prick out the first that appear while tardy ones are still too tiny to handle. Germination is improved if the seed is not too deeply covered. A fine sprinkling of sand will do, or the seed may be pressed lightly into moistened compost with the broad side of a board.

Plants develop best in temperatures as near to 50°F at night as can be managed, and on sunny days, good ventilation is required. When young plants reach a height of about six inches, the center should be pinched out to encourage bushiness. To promote optimum growth, water-soluble plant food should be applied once a week at half the strength recommended. Young plants should be set out as soon after the last anticipated frost date as possible. If plants are well hardened off, timing may be rushed a little, as the last frosts can usually be prevented from harming plants by a light covering of old sheets or burlap.

Nemesias are really full-sun plants, and the best specimens will develop under these conditions, though gardeners in warmer climates are often advised to plant them where they will be cooled by afternoon shade. They will develop into beautifully flowered plants in soil consisting of fibrous-rich, well-drained but moist loam. They are miserable, however, on heavy, poorly draining soil, which will cause them to "go off" in periods of prolonged, wet weather. In almost all gardens, nemesias are perhaps best when planted in gaps that will later be filled by other developing annuals or perennials, thereby avoiding the problem of what to plant when their brief season is done. But the gaps should be wide enough for several plants—five, seven, or more—because nemesias look best in drifts, and because they need the support of their companions or a scaffold of small twigs to stand upright.

The nemesia most commonly grown is offered as *Nemesia strumosa,* though in fact most plants are hybrids between that primarily orange-and-yellow-flowered species and *N. versicolor* (ver-SI-co-lor), which flowers in a cooler range of blue, white, and pale yellow. Both plants are natives of South Africa, and the genus name is derived from *nemesion,* a word used by Dioscorides to describe another snapdragon-like plant. The species name *strumosa* refers to small, cushionlike swellings along the squared, grooved stems. *Versicolor* means variously colored, which most nemesia are.

The genus *Nemesia* contains about fifty species, though only two others, both perennial sub-shrubs, are grown in gardens at present. The first is *Nemesia foetens* (FE-tens), a more delicate and wispy plant than *N. strumosa,* sometimes listed as *N. capensis* (ka-PEN-sis) from its place of origin, the Cape of Good Hope. A similar species that has only recently gained popularity is *Nemesia fruticans* (FRU-ti-cans), also from South Africa and also a bushy little plant, as the species name *fruticans* always indicates, though it must now correctly be listed as *N. caerulea* (suh-RU-lee-a).

All three species may be grown in cool greenhouses for bloom in late winter and very early spring, though for gardeners who have such a facility *Nemesia strumosa* is considered almost without competitors as a winter-flowering annual. For this purpose, seed should be sown in late August or early September, in five- or six-inch clay pots filled with a sandy, humus-rich compost that drains well. Several seed should be sprinkled across the compost of each pot, and all but the strongest eliminated. The pots should remain outdoors as long as possible, but be moved in just before the first autumn frost. The compost should be allowed to dry out slightly between waterings (though not to the point that plants wilt), for over-watering indoors will cause fatal rot at the crowns of plants. Plants should be pinched once or twice to form bushy specimens, and vigorous growth should be encouraged by light, weekly fertilizing with a water-soluble plant food. Flowers will arrive more slowly than with spring-grown outdoor plants, though the first should begin to appear in late December, and flowering should continue at least through February if spent bloom stems are removed and good culture maintained.

NEMOPHILA SPECIES

Insignis, the obsolete species name for *Nemophila menziesii* (men-ZEE-see-ee), might still serve as a description of it and also of *N. maculata* (ma-cu-LA-ta), for the Latin word indicates a quality of distinction, and *N. menziesii* and *N. maculata* both bear blooms so remarkable they seem invented by a fanciful Victorian painter. The five-petaled, cup-shaped flowers of *N. maculata* are popularly called "five spot" because each petal is marked by a rounded, violet-purple spot at its tip, as if made by a tiny thumb dipped in ink. Varieties—or possibly subspecies—exist with even more remarkable flowers, possessing deep black centers neatly banded with snow-white at their edges (*N. maculata* subsp. *discoidalis* [di-SKOY-da-lis]), white flowers banded in blue (*N. m.* 'Coelestis' [see-LES-tis]), or pure white flowers scattered over with tiny polka-dots of black (*N. m.* subsp. *atromarica* [a-tro-MA-ri-ka]).

By contrast, *N. menziesii* presents a simple, guileless appearance. Its inch-wide flowers, also cup- or bowl-shaped, are white in the center and shading outward to clear sky blue, giving each an animated look and supplying the popular name "baby blue eyes." (A pure white form, 'Alba', is, for once, almost as desirable as the blue.)

N. maculata and *N. menziesii* both belong to the incredibly rich trove of annuals native to California, which includes *Eschscholzia californica, Limnanthes douglasii, Phacellia campanularia,* and *Mentzelia lindleyi.* Though botanically unrelated, all these plants share a preference for fertile, light, well-drained soil, cool nights, warm bright days, and an intolerance of summer heat and transplanting. Where they occur natively, naturally dispersed seed germinate and grow slowly over a cool, frost-free winter to explode into bloom with the warmth of spring. Where nights remain fresh and cool, both species of *Nemophila* may stay in bloom for two months or more, though they will begin to fail when night temperatures reach about 70°F, and even a short period of drought will usually terminate their flowering. Though in gardens that approximate their native range seed may be sown in autumn or late winter, in most American gardens it is best sown in very early spring, two or so weeks before the last frosts may be anticipated. Seed should be scattered lightly over smooth-raked soil and barely pressed into the ground with a flat board or the palms of one's hands. Germination should occur in one to two weeks, and as soon as the young seedlings are growing on strongly, they should be thinned to stand about six to nine inches apart. Growth is rapid, and flowers should appear while the weather is still fresh and cool.

Alternatively, seed may be sown indoors about

six to eight weeks before the last anticipated frost date, using peat pots to minimize root disturbance at transplant time. Three or four seed should be sown to a pot, clipping out all but the strongest after two true sets of leaves have been formed. Young plants must be grown on in bright light in cool, well-ventilated conditions, with nighttime temperatures as close to 50°F as can be managed. When grown in such cool conditions, plants will require only a brief hardening-off period before being established in the garden. But whether direct-sown or started indoors, the soil in which plants are established should be light, fertile, well-drained loam that retains moisture at all times or that may be kept evenly moist by irrigation during times of drought. In cool coastal or high-altitude gardens, plants develop and flower best in dappled sun, with perhaps a little afternoon shade, as the genus name quite precisely indicates. (Ancient Greek *nemos* means a woodland glade or wooded pasture, and *phileo,* to love.) In warmer gardens, constant light shade may be required. When flowering begins to fail due to a temporary heat wave, as opposed to the permanent onset of summer heat, plants may be scissored back by about a third and fed with water-soluble plant food, to re-flower when cooler temperatures arrive. Plants will never recover, however, from even a brief period of drought at their roots.

Both *Nemophila maculata* and *N. menziesii* are small, bushy plants that may achieve as much as a foot of height when they find support but that tend to flop over in a pleasant way, flowering in sheets from upturned stems reaching about six inches. Leaves are downy, of a light, fresh green, slightly succulent, and composed of seven- to nine-lobed leaflets, sharper and more sawlike on *Nemophila menziesii,* broader and blunter on *N. maculata.* The flowers bloom briefly but are borne in great profusion in ideal growing conditions. Like most such delicate western North American wild flowers, nemophila are best when they may be established in generous drifts holding up one another without staking. Both species and their varieties are very beautiful in pots or hanging baskets if their need for cool temperatures and constant moisture at their roots may be met.

Like most annual plants that thrive best in even, cool temperatures, nemophila make excellent winter- and early-spring-flowering plants for the cool greenhouse. Seed should be sown in late September or early October directly into five- to six-inch clay pots. Compost should be rich with humus but made perfectly free-draining by a liberal amount of sharp sand. Several seed should be sown to a pot, very lightly covered with a sprinkling of sand, and all but the strongest one should be pinched or clipped out after several true leaves have developed. Plants should be grown on at nighttime temperatures around 45° to 50°F, perhaps ten or so degrees warmer in daytime sun, though they should be well ventilated on very warm days. Liquid plant food applied at weekly intervals at half the recommended strength will produce strong growth and abundant flower. Removing spent blossoms daily encourages a longer flowering period. Alternatively, plants may be

NEMOPHILA MENZIESII *'PENNY BLACK'*

sheared back when they show few blooms to re-flower into mid- and late spring.

N. menziesii, still occasionally listed as *N. insignis,* is named after Archibauld Menzies (1754–1842), the Scottish surgeon who accompanied Captain George Vancouver (1790–1795) on the voyage that created the first detailed survey of the Pacific Coast of North America.

NICANDRA PHYSALODES

FAMILY: *Solanaceae* or deadly nightshade family.

CLASSIFICATION: Half-hardy annual.

COMMON NAMES: Shoo-fly plant, apple of Peru, nicandra.

HARDINESS: Sensitive to light frosts when newly transplanted from indoor-grown plants.

GROWING CONDITIONS: Rich, well-drained loam. Abundant moisture. Full sun.

PROPAGATION: From seed, sown 6 to 8 weeks indoors before last expected frost. Sow outdoors in site after danger of frost.

HEIGHT: To 5'.

ORNAMENTAL VALUE: Grown for flower and for dense, shrubby growth.

LEVEL OF CULTURAL DIFFICULTY: Easy.

SPECIAL PROPERTIES: May be used as annual hedge. Believed to discourage flies and other disagreeable insects.

PRONUNCIATION: ni-KAN-dra fi-sa-LOW-dees

Gardeners who dislike annuals often accuse them of being graceless in form and garish in bloom, presenting little else in the garden but low mounds of perpetual color. Such gardeners, when they see nicandra, often ask "What perennial is that?" because its effect is as far from the modern petunia, marigold, or impatiens as a plant could get. Tall, for one thing, it makes a sturdy, much-branched bush up to five feet and almost as wide, generously clothed in oval, toothed, fresh green leaves about five inches long. Though it shares the need of many true annuals to bloom early and long, its flowers, borne singly in the axils of each leaf, appear small and subtle against the mass of the plant. Each is an upturned cup about an inch across and half as deep, formed of five fused lobes tinted at their edges an ethereal violet-blue, which gives way rather abruptly to greenish white in the center. Studied up close, the heart of each flower reveals a starlike arrangement of five black pistils surrounding a boss of pollen-thick yellow stamens. Each flower is clasped by a prominent, five-winged calyx, which enlarges after pollination to surround the seed—actually a berry made up of several seeds—into a papery, five-sided balloon, purple-green at first but maturing to a strawy beige. Certainly nicandra is not a plant appropriate to a bedding scheme that must be taken in at a glance, but its garden effect—in growth, leaf, bud, flower, and seed pod—has the charm of a beautifully detailed weed in an antique botanical print.

Nicandra was much cultivated in the nineteenth century, but it is only just beginning to make a reappearance in modern gardens. Nineteenth-century gardeners often grew it in the garden and in pots in greenhouses solely for its supposed power as a pestifuge (pest repellant), which earned it its most familiar name, "shoo-fly plant." It was assumed to lure aphids, white fly, and other plant pests to a poisoned death. Some gardeners still grow it for that reason, not so much on scientific evidence as on poetic faith, and where it is widely naturalized, around chicken yards and manure piles in the deep South, it is let be, on the sure conviction that common flies will be the scarcer there.

Nicandra is of very easy culture, requiring exactly the treatment accorded to tomatoes, a relative within the vast family Solanaceae. Seed germinates readily and may be sown indoors six to eight weeks before the last anticipated frost. Young plants should be grown on in bright, sunny conditions, hardened off, and planted in the garden after all danger of frost is past. Alternatively, seed may be sown outdoors in late April or early May, and young plants should be thinned or transplanted to stand about two feet apart for maximum development. Closer spacing—a foot or so apart—will result in shorter but still healthy plants, and pot-grown specimens may top out at about a foot in six-inch pots.

Nicandra develops best in fertile, well-drained loam in full sun—conditions found in the ideal vegetable garden. It requires abundant watering in dry periods. The finest shrubby growth and flower are promoted by a light dressing of balanced vegetable garden fertilizer—10-10-10—applied once in early summer, when direct-seeded or newly transplanted seedlings show strong growth. The pinching of terminal growth is unnecessary as the plants branch naturally, though plants grown singly will require staking. As with many annuals of bushy growth that are inclined to flop over under their own weight, a single stake inserted about eight inches and extending as much above ground will serve to keep them upright. Only a single tie is required, though it should be loose enough to accommodate the thickening of the main stem.

The single species within the genus *Nicandra* bears the name *physalodes,* which compares it to *Physalis* (FI-sa-lis), a genus of about eighty species also within the family Solanaceae, all of which bear fruits encased in five-winged inflated pods. The best known are the Tomatillo (*Physalis ixocarpa* [iks-o-KAR-pa]), an essential ingredient in salsa, and *P. alkekengi* (al-KEK-en-ji) (*P. franchetii*

NICANDRA PHYSALODES

[fran-CHET-ee-ee]), popularly called "Chinese lanterns." The fruit of nicandra is not palatable and when dried on the branch has none of the vividness of its cousin, the Chinese lantern. Still, branches of it are often included in dried arrangements, where its straw-colored, inflated pods create an effect best described as subtle.

The genus is named for Nicander of Colophon, a first-century B.C. Greek poet, though he could not have known the plant that commemorates him, for it is a native of Peru and was not introduced into European gardens until the eighteenth century.

NICOTIANA SPECIES

FAMILY: *Solanaceae* or deadly nightshade family.

CLASSIFICATION: Half-hardy perennials or annuals grown as half-hardy or tender annuals.

COMMON NAMES: Flowering tobacco, tobacco, nicotiana (other popular names vary with species).

HARDINESS: Withstand light frosts once established.

GROWING CONDITIONS: Moist, well-drained, humus-rich soil. Full sun to part shade.

PROPAGATION: From seed, sown indoors 6 to 8
weeks before last expected frost. Select forms
may be propagated by root cuttings.

HEIGHT: From 18" to 6', depending on species.

ORNAMENTAL VALUE: Grown for flower and for the
statuesque form of plants.

LEVEL OF CULTURAL DIFFICULTY: Easy.

SPECIAL PROPERTIES: Several species valued for narcotic properties. Excellent cool greenhouse
plant for late winter flowers.

PRONUNCIATION: ni-ko-shee-AN-a

For pleasure and pain, perhaps no single genus of plants has been more important to humanity than various species of *Nicotiana,* which—for smoking, chewing, or inhaling—are more widely used than any other narcotic or stimulant, excepting perhaps coffee. The genus name commemorates Jean Nicot (1530–1600), French ambassador to Portugal, who secured seed of some species from a Dutch merchant newly returned from the West Indies and sent it on to Queen Catherine de'Medici for cultivation in Paris. But knowledge of nicotiana's use as a narcotic and stimulant entered Europe practically with the first discovery of the Western Hemisphere. The inhaling of powdered tobacco was observed by a Franciscan friar who accompanied Columbus on his second voyage (1493–1496), and the chewing of dried tobacco leaves was noted by later Spanish explorers in 1502. Some form of tobacco was first brought to Europe in 1558 by Francisco Fernandez, a physician sent by King Philip II of Spain to investigate the medicinal properties of plants in the New World. And though Sir Walter Raleigh (c. 1552–1618) is credited with being the first smoker in England (taking a pipe of tobacco shortly before ascending the scaffold to be beheaded for treason under order

of Queen Elizabeth I), that title properly belongs to Ralph Lane, first governor of Virginia, who introduced Raleigh to the habit in 1586. Smoking tobacco and taking it in other forms spread quickly through Europe, though apparently from time immemorial its usage had also been bound up with the most sacred and solemn tribal ceremonies of peoples in the New World.

The future of species of *Nicotiana* as an agricultural crop is at present uncertain, for it has become abundantly clear that its habitual use is a direct cause of many dire ailments. Ironically, however, *Nicotiana rustica* (ROO-sti-ca)—the first species to enter Europe and probably the leaf Raleigh smoked shortly before his death—was originally assumed to possess almost magical powers as a curative and was called *herba panacea* ("Cure-All") and *herba sancta,* which the Elizabethan poet Spenser rendered as "divine tobacco." During its long history, various members of the genus *Nicotiana* have been used as poultices for sprains and severe bruises, to calm the inflammation of insect bites, to cure troubles of the skin, and as a soothing dressing for hemorrhoids. Finally, although the four chemical alkaloids present in most species of the genus have long been known to be poisonous to fish and to warm-blooded mammals, the chemical combination known as Nicotine has proven to be a safe, efficacious, and quickly bio-degradable organic pesticide.

As ornamental garden plants, many of the fifty to seventy species in the genus *Nicotiana* are valuable, including the two most used for their narcotic properties, *Nicotiana tabacum* (ta-BA-cum), the tobacco of commerce, and *N. rustica,* the Aztec, Mohawk, or Indian tobacco favored for ritual purposes by Native Americans. The former, which was treasured by Gertrude Jekyll, is a stately plant of majestic proportions, reaching a height of five feet or more. Its vast leaves—as much as two feet long and a foot wide—clasp the stem to form a rosette, from which the flower stalk rises, clad in progressively smaller leaves until they give way to a cluster of bloom. The tubular flowers are relatively small for so large a plant, each about three to three and a half inches long, and are borne individually down-hanging in a single terminal panicle. The color of the flowers may be white, whitish pink, rose, or purplish red, depending on variety. All parts of the plant are clothed with minute, sticky or clammy hairs, and oddly, for a plant known to be toxic, the leaves and stems are extremely attractive to aphids and white fly, which must be eliminated with chemical sprays.

In its association with humanity, *Nicotiana rustica* has an even longer history than *N. tabacum*. Perhaps native to Mexico and Texas, the plant was so widely disseminated in prehistoric times that its actual origins are uncertain, and its cultivation and use were widespread throughout North America before the arrival of Europeans. It looks like a smaller version of *N. tabacum*, reaching a height of about three feet, with alternate spoon- or paddle-shaped fleshy leaves from four to eight inches long, arranged in a basal rosette and extending up the flower stem. Flowers are quite small, scarcely a half to three-fourths of an inch long, consisting of down-hanging tubes of pink-tinted, pale green in a thick, blunt panicle like a club. All parts of the plant are covered with sticky hairs, clammy to the touch. Though *Nicotiana rustica* was quickly supplanted as a fumitory by *N. tabacum*, numerous heirloom varieties exist that have been in more-or-less continuous cultivation by Native Americans for many centuries. It is still cultivated, also, as a source for the insecticide Nicotine.

For many years, the most popular of all garden nicotianas was *Nicotiana alata* (a-LA-ta)—still sometimes listed as *N. affinis* (af-FIN-is),

native to Brazil, Uruguay, and Paraguay, and popularly known in old-fashioned gardens as "flowering tobacco" or "jasmine tobacco." It produces a basal rosette of oval, dark green leaves about sixteen or so inches long, which clasp the stem with two wings at the base, giving the plant its species name *alata,* meaning winged. As the weather warms in mid- to late June, a central stem is produced by each rosette that develops with surprising rapidity to a height of about four feet. Secondary stems are produced along its length, candelabra fashion. These eventually elongate to about two feet, forming flower buds at intervals of an inch, more or less, as they develop. From an indoor sowing in late March, the first flowers open in late June and early July and consist of three- to four-inch-long tubes that

NICOTIANA LANGSDORFFII

NICOTIANA LANGSDORFFII

flare at the end into a white star of five petals. In the variety 'Grandiflora', which has superseded the species, each flower may be as much as two inches across. The tube itself and the reverse of each flower are a clear lime green, with a darker green line down a crease in each petal. Faint shadowings of green can also be seen across the face of the flower that intensify in its center, where five nut-brown stamens and a green pistil nestle. During the day the flowers are limp and sad, but in the evening they become crisp, showing up with startling and wonderful clarity in dim nocturnal light. It is only then that they are fragrant, with a scent at once clean and strong, close to but not quite like the smell of jasmine, sweet but never cloying.

But it must be said that *Nicotiana alata* is a rather lax and undisciplined plant that throws its wiry stems about onto its neighbors. This easy attitude, along with its nocturnal tendencies, has caused it to be subjected to improvement since, until recently, gardeners tended to insist that annuals be trim, tidy, and self-supporting, and certainly as attractive in the daytime as at night. The modern bedding nicotianas—crosses between *N. alata* and several other species—achieve all these characteristics, though sadly at the loss of fra-

grance, most of them possessing at best the faintest whiff, or none at all. The original crosses bloomed in shades of pink, rose, and red, though subsequent breeding has achieved a very wide range of color, from green and white through cream, salmon, peach, crimson, and mulberry red to purple, often with a darker shade on the reverse of each bloom. Select forms produce plants anywhere from a foot to three feet tall, generally with abundant, up-turned flowers that remain open all day. As with the progeny of many distinguished parents, the modern improvements of *N. alata* are not necessarily better, but they are different. Their abundance of flower and compactness of growth suit them for situations where lots of bloom and lots of color are desired. A nice thing happens, also, the year after one has grown these highly bred versions of *Nicotiana alata*. Their offspring, either from self-seeded plants or from plants raised from saved seed, will begin to revert, producing plants of strange pale shades, faint or strong tinctures of mulberry or rose or green on a white ground. Often there will be a star of white marked on the joined five petals of a flower, or its face will show one odd and almost indefinable color and its back another.

For green, however, nothing is finer than *Nicotiana langsdorffii* (langs-DOR-fee-ee), native to Brazil and Chile, the species name of which commemorates the German botanist Georg Heinrich von Langsdorf (1774–1852). Though cultivated in gardens here and there for more than a century, within the last ten years it has begun to appear wherever interesting annuals are grown. It is certainly beautiful enough to justify this explosion into popularity, for its down-hanging bells are a wonderful, vibrant lime-green of perhaps the strongest shade to be found among true green flowers. Each flower, about an inch long, is a tube of polished green that swells into a little bulb before giving way to a tight cup of fused petals a third of an inch across. When the flower is turned upward, it reveals a face of a paler green, almost chartreuse, deepening down the tube where the color reflects on itself and gathering intensity from four cobalt-blue stamens. Hummingbirds adore the flowers, and a planting is never free for long from the whir of wings and the flash of a similar but iridescent green and perhaps the fine contrast of a ruby throat. For flower arrangers, *Nicotiana langsdorffii* is a joy: Its green bells are complementary to any other flower color, its graceful, wiry stems are easy to insert as a finishing grace to a composition, and it lasts a week or more in water. Its typically nicotiana-like leaves are about six to eight inches long, of a fresh, bright green. Recently, a variety has been introduced that carries splashes of cream across the leaves and that comes true from seed. When *Nicotiana langsdorffii* and *N. alata* are grown together in the same garden, interspecific hybrids often occur that may reach a stately height of five feet, possessing the rigid, upright character of *N. langsdorffii,* but bearing flowers closer to those of *N. alata.*

For both height and grace, however, *Nicotiana sylvestris* (sil-VES-tris), a native of Argentina, is perhaps without compare. It is called the "woodland nicotiana," from its species name *sylvestris,* meaning of woods, but it develops best in full sun or with no more than afternoon shade. From an indoor seeding in late March, plants develop by late June into large rosettes of grass-green leaves, each of which may be as much as two feet long and a foot across. One would suppose that something so vast would require a lot of space, but in fact the leaves, by facing upward where necessary, can tuck themselves against one another and into surprisingly small spaces of a foot or so without harming their neighbors. In midsummer, *N. sylvestris* produces a single thick stalk from the center of its first basal leaves that rapidly extends to five or six feet, clad at intervals by smaller leaves,

each of which clasps a side branch. Flowering stems terminate in a cob of many buds, which show white when half-formed, and from which flowers steadily emerge, beginning usually in mid-July and continuing until frost. Each flower is four or five inches long, down-hanging, consisting of a slender tube and a flared, half-inch-wide star of five joined petals at its end. From a single cob of buds there may be as many as fifty individual flowers over a period of a couple of months. Chalk white, they glow in the twilight and are sweetly scented. For decorating the summer border during the August slump, *Nicotiana sylvestris* is invaluable, for it develops best in the heat and humidity of late summer.

Though treated as annuals, most garden nicotianas are in fact tender perennials, the roots of

NICOTIANA SYLVESTRIS

which will persist in warm gardens to sprout new plants from year to year. Very desirable forms may also be propagated from root cuttings—thick, fleshy segments of root each about three inches long, stored in a cool place over winter and inserted upright in damp peat and sand in March.

Another nicotiana popular in gardens, however, is a woody shrub, *Nicotiana glauca* (GLAW-ka), the "tree tobacco" native to South America but naturalized throughout the warmer parts of Zone 9 in Texas and southern California, and elsewhere grown either as an annual or as a large tubbed plant carried over under glass from year to year. In its first year from seed, it forms a stout, upright plant to as much as five feet tall, with rounded or heart-shaped celadon green leaves, smooth to the touch, and terminates in a single stem of inch-and-a-half-long, tubular, yellowish-green flowers. Where it is hardy (or if carried over as a tubbed plant), the stem will branch in its second year, producing more cobs of flower, and will attain a greater height, to as much as twenty feet when grown in the ground in Zone 9. Plants may be pruned as a loose hedge or, when grown in pots, may be trained to standards—small single-trunked trees with a mop of growth at the top.

All nicotianas are easy to grow. Though they love full sun and will do their best in it, beautiful plants can be grown in half a day of shade, preferably falling in the afternoon. About soil they are not at all particular, provided it is moist but well drained, though they appreciate a starting diet rich in phosphorus and potassium, best applied when they are established in the garden and have produced their fourth or fifth set of leaves. Nicotianas grown for their large leaves and tall stature, such as *N. tabacum* and *N. sylvestris,* will be very greedy feeders and should have monthly applications of vegetable garden fertilizer from the time they are first established in the garden until bloom stems form.

NICOTIANA *SPECIES*

Seed of all nicotianas should be started by the end of March or earlier to produce blooming-size plants by the end of June. The seed is dust-fine and should be scattered very thinly over a sterile potting mix, pressed in lightly but not covered, as it needs light to germinate. Tiny plants will appear within ten days or so and should be pricked out as soon as they may be handled (generally after two or three sets of true leaves have appeared) and grown on in bright light at about 60°F until they may be hardened off and planted. Growth will be slow while the weather is cool and drizzly, though strong root systems will form under such conditions, and plants will develop extremely rapidly when warm and settled weather arrives.

Once any nicotiana has been grown, even in Zone 4, self-sown seedlings will appear in subsequent years, sometimes charmingly placed along paths or in stonework where the gardener's weeding hand has not been over-vigorous. Stands of volunteer seedlings should be thinned or transplanted, and though they will develop much more slowly than started plants, delaying their bloom until mid- or even late August, they are lusty and full of grace. And as all nicotianas are tolerant of light frost, they will provide an unlooked-for beauty to the late summer or early autumn garden. At the end of summer, the smaller seedlings can also be potted up and grown on, to be brought indoors where, with weekly doses of weak liquid fertilizer, they will flourish on a sunny windowsill or in a cool greenhouse, blooming into December. Plants may then be cut back hard and regrown for additional bloom in spring.

NIEREMBERGIA SPECIES

FAMILY: *Solanaceae* or deadly nightshade family.

CLASSIFICATION: Half-hardy perennials grown as half-hardy annuals.

COMMON NAMES: Cup flower, nierembergia.

HARDINESS: Occasionally hardy to Zone 7. Tolerant of light frosts when grown as an annual.

GROWING CONDITIONS: Humus-rich, well-drained, moist soils. Full sun. Afternoon shade in warmer gardens. Must not dry out.

PROPAGATION: From seed, sown indoors in late February. Young plants dislike root disturbance.

HEIGHT: Less than 1' in height, though spreading to 2'.

ORNAMENTAL VALUE: Grown for flower.

LEVEL OF CULTURAL DIFFICULTY: Easy.

SPECIAL PROPERTIES: Excellent edging plant. Useful in hanging baskets and window boxes.

PRONUNCIATION: near-em-BER-gee-a

The genus *Nierembergia* comprises somewhere between twenty-five and thirty species of mostly herbaceous plants native to the colder parts of South America, specifically the southern (and coldest) reaches of Chile and Argentina and into Uruguay. Of this number, only four perennial species are commonly grown in American gardens, mostly as annuals, but their charms are such that gardeners always hope they will prove hardy. Alas, few plants ever survive much beyond Zone 7, even with protection and perfect winter drainage, and if they do, they are so damaged and weakened by the cold that it would be better to start with fresh young plants in spring. Nierembergia, therefore, are usually treated as annuals in most North American gardens. Fortunately, all four species are willing to behave that way if seed is started quite early, in late February, and the young plants grown on vigorously in cool conditions under glass until they may be hardened off and planted.

Low plants of bushy to trailing growth, nierembergia seldom reach a foot in height, with narrow, irregularly spaced needle-like leaves from half an inch to an inch and a half long. The flowers—five-lobed fused cups—are borne upward and measure from half an inch to an inch across. Color is generally of a watery mauve, though richer, more purple forms exist, and some pure white cultivars are especially beautiful. Individual blossoms generally shade down to a rich, butter yellow at their throats, and a netting of deeper purple veins will extend across each silken petal, faint at the edges and deeper in the center, prominent in some species and selected cultivars, and barely a shadow in others. All four commonly grown species are superb in hanging baskets, window boxes, and large containers, where their flowers peek out daintily among other summer-bloomers and their airy growth smothers no other plants.

The best-known of the nierembergia is *N. repens* (RE-pens), from its trailing, carpetlike growth, though it was previously known as *N. rivularis* (ri-vu-LAR-is), a species name that means of rivers and streams, and signifies its preference for rich, constantly moist soil. A native of Argentina, it forms a dense mat of stems rooting at the joints and creating a carpet not much more than three or four inches tall but as much as ten inches in diameter in a single season. The tiny leaves are oblong, pointed at the ends, each about an inch long. Flowers are cup shaped, generally cream streaked with purple, though rose and blue-tinged forms exist. Barely an inch and a half wide, they seem surprisingly large for so small a plant. Where it is hardy, which is to say Zone 8, it is said to be invasive, and so is most often planted in cracks in pavement and other places where it may be confined. In colder gardens, it poses no such problem, though those who grow it might wish it did.

Nierembergia scoparia (sco-PA-ree-a) was previously listed as *N. frutescens* (fru-TES-ens), from Latin *frutex* signifying shrubby and attesting to its bushy growth. Its present species name, *scoparia,* means broomlike and offers simply another way of describing its form. It grows upright to as much as a foot tall, though it tends to sprawl. Its leaves are tiny needles, about an inch long, and its cupped flowers are each about an inch wide, borne singly at the ends of twigs. According to variety, their color may be light blue to mauve purple, though a magnificent pure white form, sometimes listed as 'Albiflora' (al-bi-FLO-ra) and sometimes as 'White Queen', is particularly to be treasured.

Nierembergia gracillis (gra-SI-lis) earns its species name, which means dainty, from its delicate, sprawling stems, never much more than six inches tall, clothed with half-inch-long, downy, needle-like leaves. Its flowers are also quite small,

less than half an inch across, generally white though delicately purple-veined in the center. Its fragile growth and flower suit it to the rock garden or to window boxes or containers that will show off its charm. Probably it is most beautiful when grown as single specimens in four- or five-inch clay pots, in which case it can be sheared back lightly for repeat bloom in late winter or early spring in a cool greenhouse.

By contrast, *Nierembergia caerulea* (see-RU-lee-a) is the tallest species in cultivation although still only nine inches to a foot in height. It forms an erect bush clad in fine, narrow leaves, each about three-eighths inch long. Inch-wide flowers are abundantly produced from June until frost, though a light shearing in midsummer will increase flower production and shapeliness of growth. The color of the flower in its wild form is a light mauve veined with darker purple, but very fine deep violet and pure white forms exist. A large drift planted to various intermingling shades is particularly beautiful, with plants spaced about six inches apart so that their airy growth supports one another and their flowers intermingle.

All nierembergia should be sown quite early— in February or in early March—for flowers from late June until frost. Though young plants are not positively averse to root disturbance, they do not like it much and so are best sown in peat pots or in plastic cell packs, rather than being pricked out from a pan sown to many seedlings. Plants may be expected to bloom about four months from seed if they may be grown on in bright sun and cool conditions, with nighttime temperatures of around 55°F being the ideal. Nierembergia are somewhat frost-tolerant, and so, if young seedlings are carefully hardened off to accustom them to outdoor temperatures, they may be planted in the garden two or three weeks before the last anticipated frost date.

NIEREMBERGIA SCOPARIA

They prefer full sun to part shade, a fertile soil that is evenly moist but well drained, and are particularly sensitive to drought, often withering beyond redemption when they dry out at the roots. They flower most abundantly in cool weather, tending to take a rest when nighttime temperatures climb much above 70°F. At this point, however, plants may be lightly sheared back for repeat flowering from late summer until frost.

As these four species of nierembergia under cultivation are actually half-hardy perennials that prefer cool conditions, they make superb flowering plants for the cool greenhouse. Cuttings, which root easily, should be taken in August and potted on so that each individual plant eventually occupies a pot five inches in diameter. Alternatively, seed may be sown in August, or whole plants may be cut back, lifted, and potted. Whatever method is used, however, plants should be encouraged to make as much growth as possible during autumn by weekly applications of liquid fertilizer at half the strength recommended on the package. Bright, sunny indoor conditions at nighttime temperatures around 55°F will produce strong plants that will flower abundantly from December until April. During the darker days of winter, however, plants should be watered very carefully, just when they begin to dry out, as over-watering, particularly in periods of dull weather, will cause the plants to develop fatal fungus diseases.

The genus name *Nierembergia* commemorates Juan Eusebio Nieremberg (1595–1658), a Spanish Jesuit who wrote a book celebrating the diversity of the natural world. The nierembergia cultivated in gardens, however, are not diverse enough to have claimed individual popular names in the gardener's imagination. So all four bear two common names, "cup flower" and "nierembergia" after Juan Eusebio himself.

NIGELLA DAMASCENA

FAMILY: *Ranunculaceae* or buttercup family.

CLASSIFICATION: Hardy annual.

COMMON NAMES: Love-in-a-mist, devil-in-the-bush, Catherine wheels, nigella.

HARDINESS: Withstands light frosts.

GROWING CONDITIONS: Moderately rich, well-drained loam. Full sun.

PROPAGATION: From seed, sown in place in autumn in warm gardens, in very early spring elsewhere. Sown indoors in peat pots 8 weeks before frost. Transplants resent root disturbance.

HEIGHT: To 2'.

ORNAMENTAL VALUE: Grown for flower and for interesting seed pods.

LEVEL OF CULTURAL DIFFICULTY: Easy in cool gardens, difficult elsewhere.

SPECIAL PROPERTIES: Excellent cut flower. Seed pods valued by flower arrangers. Seed occasionally used as substitute for pepper and as an aromatic spice.

PRONUNCIATION: nye-JEL-a da-ma-SEEN-a

Nigella damascena has been cultivated in English and European gardens since at least the sixteenth century, during which time it has accumulated a number of popular names. Most gardeners will know it as "love-in-a-mist," a name it takes from the fact that its limpid blue, white, or rose flowers nestle among threadlike leaves that extend upward into an embracing, prominent filamented calyx. But "devil-in-the-bush" is also current, acknowledging the plant's curious, inflated, egg-shaped seed pods much prized by flower arrangers. Long before it acquired these names, however, it was known as "Catherine wheels," from the supposed resemblance of its spoked blossoms to the fiery spinning circle on which Saint Catherine of Alexandria endured her martyrdom for refusing the advances of the Roman emperor Maximinus. It has also been known as *barbe-bleu* (bluebeard), after Charles Perrault's tale (published in 1697) of the monstrous *bête d'extermination* who murdered seven wives in quick succession, and a few small boys.

Despite the sometimes grisly names it has collected over the centuries, *Nigella damascena* is very beautiful, with an old-fashioned charm that always seems to earn it the vague but evocative description of a "cottage garden plant." At the start, it shows first a rosette of two-inch-long leaves, divided and re-divided into the finest filaments, which later gather into a green mist around a much-branched plant to about a foot tall, each stem thickening into a collar that surrounds the open flower and may be twice its width, an inch and a half. In the wild, flowers are single, made up of five notched petals surrounding a curious fused column of stamens that separates into five down-curved horns. They are almost always blue—actually white darkening to pale blue—though cultivated forms exist in pink, rose, red, deeper blue, and an elegant pure white. Perhaps the most popular cultivated form is 'Miss Jekyll's Blue', a double form with rich, gentian blue flowers selected by that lady herself, out of a swarm she grew from seed begged from a cottager in Kent. Many gardeners grow only this form, since, once grown in a garden, pure strains of nigella self-seed nicely from year to year, and the 'Miss Jekyll's Blue' form is of such a fine color that they are afraid of compromising it. But there is also a 'Miss Jekyll's White', which contributes luminescence wherever it is grown, particularly at night, and a 'Miss Jekyll's Rose' that carries a sweet, grandmotherly sort of charm. The modern series 'Persian Jewels' is a particu-larly rich mix of colors, and out of it a very fine form called 'Mulberry Rose' has been selected, with creamy white flowers aging to an almost indescribable shade of dusty pink.

Like so many other flowers cultivated over the centuries, however, *Nigella damascena* (of general Mediterranean origin, and not just "of Damascus") was grown not only for beauty but also for use. When pepper was scarce, the black seed that gives the genus its name (from the Latin *niger* for black) was used as a substitute and is still known in French as *poivrette*, little pepper. But another species within the genus of sixteen or so, *Nigella sativa* (sa-TEE-va), is of much more ancient cultivation, having been grown for more than two thousand years as an aromatic spice. (The species name, from the Latin *sativus*, means grown in gardens.) Its peppery flavor suggests at once nutmeg, lemon, carrot, coriander, and cumin, and so it is called in French *toute-épice*, all-spice, though it is not to be confused with true all-spice, which comes from the berry of the American tropical tree *Pimenta officinalis* (pi-MEN-ta off-i-si-NA-lis).

William Robinson, the great nineteenth-century English gardener, considered *Nigella his-*

NIGELLA DAMASCENA

NIGELLA DAMASCENA

panica (hi-SPAN-I-ca) to be the prettiest in the genus. In contrast to *N. damascena,* it is a sturdier plant, growing as tall as sixteen inches, with deeply divided dark green leaves. Its flowers, borne abundantly throughout July and early August from a spring seeding, are an unusually rich blue, made more so by a deepening in their centers almost to black, and by a column of dark red anthers. Like all nigella it makes an excellent cut flower, lasting up to fifteen days in water if picked just as the flowers are expanding.

Finally, another in the genus, *Nigella orientalis* (o-ree-en-TA-lis), is sometimes grown in gardens under the curious varietal name 'Transformer'. Its orientalism is no further away than Turkey and Asia Minor, since all species of *Nigella* are more-or-less Mediterranean. It is not a terribly prepossessing plant, forming a little bush about a foot tall with dark green, deeply divided foliage and yellowish-green flowers sometimes with red freckles, but both its claim to gardening space and its odd marketing name result from the fact that its ripe seed pods (large, as is always the case with nigella) can be carefully split into five lobes and turned backward, transforming them into a buff-colored "flower," in-

teresting in the garden and fascinating in dried arrangements.

Rather like that of African violets, the culture of all nigella is quite simple, once a few facts are understood. Though technically classed as annuals, they hover near to being biennials, in the sense that where they are native, they germinate in late summer or early autumn and quickly form deep taproots and rosettes of foliage that live over winter to flower magnificently in the cool wet weather of early spring. The best flowers and the longest period of bloom will therefore always be had where these conditions can be met, and so gardeners who live in Zones 7 and warmer should sow the seed in place in autumn but wait until the following spring to thin plants about seven inches apart, since some losses will occur, particularly on heavy clay soils. Elsewhere, seed should be sown in open, sunny places in the border in early spring as soon as the ground can be worked, and the seedlings thinned when they are about an inch in height. Little is probably gained by starting seed indoors, though it can be done, about eight weeks before the last anticipated frost date, using peat pots or flexible plastic cell packs, as nigella are very impatient of transplanting. Young seedlings should be grown vigorously, in cool, sunny conditions, and care should be taken to water them carefully, as too much water will cause damping off, and too little will quickly result in yellowed foliage and premature bud set.

The period of bloom for most nigella, particularly *N. damascena,* is very brief, extending for not more than a month in late June and early July from an outdoor sowing in April. Successive sowings may be made at the end of May, June, and—where nights are cool—even July, for flowers throughout the summer. Such a practice might be desirable if flowers are wanted for cutting or drying, for the decorative seed pods, fresh or dried, or for seed to be used in the kitchen. But for most gardeners, the chief value of nigella is as a delicate addition to the garden, sown in and among sturdier and later flowering perennials while their growth is developing in spring and early summer. The texture of leaf and stem is so fine that it crowds out nothing, and when plants are left in place after flowering, the curious seed pods are always interesting. Those that are allowed to ripen and shed their seed may even produce a second generation of plants and flower later in the summer and into early autumn.

NOLANA PARADOXA

FAMILY: *Nolanaceae* or nolana family.

CLASSIFICATION: Half-hardy perennial grown as half-hardy annual.

COMMON NAMES: Chilean bellflower, nolana.

HARDINESS: Root-hardy to Zone 8 with perfect drainage. Frost-sensitive elsewhere.

GROWING CONDITIONS: Thin, perfectly drained, sandy soils. Full sun. Abundant atmospheric moisture. Relishes cool weather.

PROPAGATION: From seed, sown indoors in peat pots in late winter. Plants resent root disturbance.

HEIGHT: To 6", but trailing to 1' or more.

ORNAMENTAL VALUE: Grown for flower.

LEVEL OF CULTURAL DIFFICULTY: Difficult.

SPECIAL PROPERTIES: Excellent in containers, large pots, or hanging baskets. Superb rock garden plant.

PRONUNCIATION: no-LA-na pa-ra-DOX-a

What the great English botanist John Lindley (1799–1865) meant precisely when he named the most popular species in the small genus *Nolana* "paradoxa" is uncertain. (In botany the Latin word generally means contrary to expectation.) Perhaps the paradox is that the flowers are often compared to diminutive morning glories, but they only open in dry, sunny weather. Each single bloom is composed of five fused petals, fluted and ruffled at their edges, and creased down the middle of each so they look like ten. The flowers resemble up-turned bells, giving both the family and the single genus of about sixteen species within it their name, from the Latin diminutive of *nola*, a bell. Pale violet and pure white cultivars exist, but the best form is a fresh, clear blue, with a deep band of pale yellow across the middle that gives way to a white throat.

Those who grow *N. paradoxa* will admire its trailing growth to six inches tall, its succulent, oval, dark green pointed leaves, to four inches long, and its spangling of charming, circular flowers, each about two inches across. But *N. paradoxa* is for several reasons not an easy plant to grow. A native of the coastal regions of Chile (hence its common name, Chilean bellflower), it thrives in thin, well-drained, sandy soils in full sun, but with abundant atmospheric moisture. It is very intolerant of heavy, clay soils or of excessive wetness at its roots. Actually a true perennial hardy to about 32°F, it can be superb in summer in seaside gardens that resemble its native habitat. Elsewhere, it is best grown as a hanging-basket, window-box, or container plant, in fertile but sandy, well-drained soil. Wherever it is grown, however, it will have to be protected from slugs and snails, which relish its succulent leaves and fleshy, maroon-striped stems.

Nolana paradoxa is often listed under the synonym *N. atriplicifolia* (a-tri-pli-si-FO-lee-a), an equally confusing species name, as it suggests a resemblance of the leaves of the plant to *Atriplex*

NOLANA PARADOXA

hortensis, the orach or mountain spinach. No resemblance whatsoever exists.

Other species within the genus are sometimes grown in gardens, the most common being *Nolana lanceolata* (lan-see-o-LA-ta), also called *N. acuminata* (a-ku-mi-NA-ta), a native of Peru. Both species names describe its lance- or spear-shaped leaves, tapering to a sharp point at the ends and measuring as much as five inches long. The entire plant is covered with fine white hairs, which nicely set off its two-inch-wide flowers of deep blue with white or primrose-yellow spots at their throats. Gardeners in search of interesting hanging basket or container plants might also grow *Nolana humifusa* (hu-mi-FU-sa), the species name of which ("fusing to the earth") attests to its ground-hugging capacities. It is similar to *Nolana paradoxa,* though it is smaller in all its parts, giving it the marketing name of "little bells." Its oval leaves are scarcely more than an inch long, and its purple-veined, blue flowers are less than an inch across.

Like other true perennials grown as annuals, nolana require an early start indoors, in late February or early March, as they may take as much as three months to flower from germination. The large seed is easy to handle and sprouts in about two weeks at temperatures around 70°F. Young seedlings quickly form a long, white, fleshy taproot, always a sign that transplanting will be difficult or impossible. Three seed should be sown to a peat pot and all but the strongest clipped away after two or three full sets of leaves are formed. Young plants must be grown on in full sun and watered only when they are moderately dry, as excess water in indoor conditions will quickly cause them to rot at the roots. They may be transplanted into the garden in sandy, well-aerated soil after all danger of frost is past. When conditions suit them, there is no prettier plant for the rock garden, or for establishing between stepping stones or in the cracks of pavement.

OCIMUM SPECIES

FAMILY: *Lamiaceae* (*Labiatae*) or mint family.

CLASSIFICATION: Short-lived tender perennial or tender shrub grown as tender annual.

COMMON NAMES: Sweet basil, basil.

HARDINESS: Sensitive to light frosts.

GROWING CONDITIONS: Rich, moist, well-drained soil. Full sun.

PROPAGATION: By seed, sown indoors 4 to 6 weeks before frost, or in place after soil warms in spring. Shrubby species propagated by cuttings.

HEIGHT: To 2½'.

ORNAMENTAL VALUE: Purple-leaved forms grown for ornament.

LEVEL OF CULTURAL DIFFICULTY: Easy.

SPECIAL PROPERTIES: Treasured as culinary herb.

PRONUNCIATION: o-SEE-mum

*A*fter parsley, basil is perhaps the most popular of all culinary herbs, though until recently, few gardeners have realized the extent of the horticultural possibilities within its genus, *Ocimum*. Common basil, *O. basilicum* (ba-SI-li-cum), derives its genus name from the ancient Greek word *okimon,* applied to some herb, most probably to it. The species name *basilicum* attests to the ancient reputation of the plant both for good and ill, since though it probably derives from the ancient Greek *basilokos* (Latin *basilicus*) meaning royal or princely, it carries also an allusion to the deadly dragon or giant lizard, the basilisk, which could kill men with a mere glance of its eye. *O. basilicum* is of very ancient cultivation and has been prized for many centuries as a culinary and medicinal herb, and also as one that possessed magical properties, aphrodisiac qualities, and, when rightly handled, baneful capacities. Over many centuries, distinct cultivars have been selected, which were often erroneously given species standing by botanists because they seemed so different from the typical plant native to the Old World Tropics. And in the last twenty-five years or so, there has been a positive explosion of varieties, some of which have been discovered in distant lands, and others of which have been hybridized for specific properties of flavor, pattern of growth, or coloration of leaf.

Even in its most common, typical form, sweet basil is a very attractive plant from its first emergence as a tiny seedling until it begins to initiate flower. Its oval, often quilted leaves are borne in pairs opposite each other on the stem, creating a rosette pattern apparent in quite small seedlings. Leaves are typically a fresh, grass green, about an inch or two long, slightly succulent and often with an iridescent sheen. Plants branch freely from the ground, and if spaced a foot or so apart, they will form shapely, self-supporting bushes one to two feet tall, slightly woody at their bases. Comeliness generally departs from basil plants as they initiate flower, however, for then the leaves become tatty and worn, all energy flowing upward from them to the raspy, columnar racemes at the tips of each branch in which the flowers are borne. The individual flowers are quite tiny, hardly more than a quarter of an inch long, consisting of whitish-pink tubes flaring into the lip and hood typical of all members of the mint family. The formation of flower not only disfigures the plant, but also robs its leaves of some of the pungency for which it is treasured. To a certain extent, the gardener can delay this decline by pinching out flower buds as they form, which also has the happy consequence of encouraging more leafy growth. At a certain point in the plant's life, however, usually in late summer or early autumn, no amount of pinching will cause the plant to recover from its frustration in failing to produce flower and seed, and it will shed its leaves and die.

Among the many forms of sweet basil available to gardeners, there are cultivars with larger or curled leaves, and with quite tiny leaves on small plants that may be so tidy of growth as to suggest topiary trimmed into perfect rounds. There are also several that are remarkable for their rich purple coloration. Plants with purple-tinged leaves and darker veins and stems occur in the wild, and are given the varietal name *purpurescens* (pur-pur-ES-sens) by botanists. Many of these have been selected for even darker coloration, the oldest and most frequently grown of which is 'Dark Opal', with rich, iridescent leaves of garnet red overcast with a leaden sheen. But other paler and darker purple forms have been developed, all very beautiful and all of which may serve the dual function of both culinary and ornamental plants. There is even at least one, called 'New Guinea', with purple veining on a green ground strong enough to qualify as variegated. And though the smell of the leaves of sweet basil is variously described as a blend of camphor, anise, clove, licorice, cinnamon, citrus, and mint, various cultivars have been developed in which one of these seems to predominate, so that connoisseurs of sweet basil may grow, for example, 'Anise', or 'Cinnamon', or the lemon-flavored 'Citriodora' (si-tri-o-DOR-a). Good seed catalogues that specialize in herbs will, among them, offer possibilities enough for a whole basil garden, varied not only in the scent of each form, but also in leaf coloration and plant growth.

As befits a plant of major culinary importance, sweet basil is very easy to grow, provided its needs for warmth, sun, and well-drained soil may be met. Seed germinates readily under indoor conditions comfortable to most people, at temperatures just above 70°F, though the young seedlings require full sun to develop, whether in a greenhouse or on a windowsill. Sweet basil is extremely sensitive to cold, however, and will blacken at even a whisper of frost, so seedlings, which germinate within a week, should not be sown until about four or five weeks before nighttime temperatures may be expected to remain reliably above 55°F and the soil is warm. Good results may also be had by sowing seed directly in the garden under the same weather conditions,

OCIMUM X 'AFRICAN BASIL'

later thinning the plants to stand about eight inches to a foot apart. Young seedlings are delicious added to salads, as are the tips of growth that should be pinched out to encourage branching. Sweet basil adapts easily to containers, even if one chooses not to follow the example of poor Isabella in Boccaccio's tale, who grew hers in a pot containing the severed head of her lover Ferdinand. Plants of sweet basil may be difficult to keep healthy indoors over winter for all but a short period of time, however, for the plant seems to decline rapidly in weak winter light, and no amount of severed heads seems to help.

Popular as sweet basil has been since classical times, it is not the only member of the genus *Ocimum* that has been grown, even anciently. Of equally antique culture is *O. sanctum* (SANK-tum), also known as *O. tenuiflorum* (ten-u-i-FLO-rum), the "holy basil" sacred to the gods Vishnu and Shiva in the Hindu religion. Occurring natively in India and Indonesia and usually called "tulsi," it has been planted around temples and grown by the pious for many centuries. Its dark to gray-green, downy, two-inch-long, oval leaves are also used fresh in salads, to ward off mosquitoes, and as a poultice that relieves the pain of insect bites. A tender perennial or bushy shrub, it may grow to three feet or more and persist from year to year in the warm gardens of Zones 9 and 10. Elsewhere it may be grown as an annual from seed or from cuttings, which root readily.

Ocimum kilimandsharicum (ki-li-mand-SHAR-i-cum), called "African basil," is also a tender, bushy perennial hardy to Zones 9 and 10, growing to about three feet tall and as wide. Though used in East African cookery, its strong camphor flavor is unpleasant to many people. In 1982, however, a spontaneous cross occurred between it and a purple-leaved sweet basil at Companion

Plants in Athens, Ohio, which was disseminated by the owner of the nursery, Peter Borchard, also under the popular name "African basil." It is a handsome plant, growing into a freely branched bush about two feet tall and as wide, with dark purple stems, purples leaves, and light pink flowers borne profusely in racemes of burgundy red. Unlike the flowers of some other basils, they are quite pretty, and as the plant is sterile, they need not be removed to keep it attractive. In flavor, the leaves are somewhat camphory, though not unpleasantly so, serving as an acceptable substitute in late summer and early autumn when sweet basil is past its prime. Since African basil does not set seed, it must be propagated by cuttings, which root with extreme ease. It also accepts indoor winter conditions far more readily than does sweet basil.

Though a native of Southeast Asia, another shrubby basil, *Ocimum gratissimum* (gra-TI-si-mum), is confusingly known as "East Indian basil," or sometimes "tea bush," from an infusion made of its richly clove-scented, felty, four-inch-long leaves. Another popular name, "tree basil," suits it, as it may grow to as tall as six feet in the privileged gardens of Zone 10, where it is hardy, and almost as tall when carried from summer to summer by overwintering it in a pot or tub indoors. Its species name, *gratissimum,* means excessively agreeable, and so it is, for it is used in cooking both in parts of China and in Ghana, but more important, as a medicinal herb throughout the world. Its leaves have variously been used to cure mange, scabies, and other parasitic skin diseases, inflammation of the eyes, diarrhea, whooping-cough and other bronchial difficulties, rheumatism, lower back pain, and even venereal diseases. Like many other species within its genus, *O. gratissimum* is said to be effective in warding off mosquitoes and in relieving the itch-ing symptoms of mosquito bites, and thus—though the plant is only modestly decorative—one or more plants are sometimes grown in pots, containers, or window boxes for the summer. As with other shrubby basils, propagation is by rooting tip cuttings.

Probably the most exciting of recently introduced basils, however, is a shrubby form marketed under the cultivar names 'Aussie Lassie' and 'Aussie Sweetie'. Its exact species status is presently unclear, as is its relationship to Australia, though the trail of circumstances that has caused it to explode on the American market may soon be known. It is a remarkable plant, for without trimming it forms a tight column of ascending woody branches to about three feet tall and less than half a foot wide in one season, furnished from top to bottom with arrow-shaped, half-inch-long, dark green leaves. It seems never to flower, in North American gardens at least, and its growth becomes richer and fuller as summer progresses into autumn, especially with frequent clipping for the kitchen. For though most shrubby basils are a less-than-perfect substitute for the best cultivars of sweet basil, 'Aussie Lassie' possesses a fine, light, pungent flavor equal to the very finest basils. It is closest, perhaps, to *O. basilicum* var. *minimum* (MIN-i-mum), the so-called Greek basil, the tiny leaves of which are preferred by many cooks for pesto and on slices of tomato. In addition to its culinary uses, the dramatic shape of 'Aussie Lassie' suits it for the center of a container of mixed herbs, as vertical accents in window boxes, and even for use as a small temporary hedge in the herb or flower garden. The plant would seem to have everything, except for the fact that it is difficult to carry successfully over the winter except in warm greenhouses. Even there, ventilation must be extremely good, and water carefully administered during the darkest months, to prevent leaves and stems from rotting off due to fungus diseases.

OMPHALODES LINIFOLIA

FAMILY: *Boraginaceae* or borage family.

CLASSIFICATION: Hardy annual.

COMMON NAMES: Venus's navelwort, annual omphalodes.

HARDINESS: Withstands light frost.

GROWING CONDITIONS: Moderately fertile, neutral to alkaline, well-drained soils. Full sun in cooler gardens, part shade in warmer ones.

PROPAGATION: By seed, sown in place in warmer gardens in autumn, and in cooler ones in very early spring.

HEIGHT: To 1'.

ORNAMENTAL VALUE: Grown for flower.

LEVEL OF CULTURAL DIFFICULTY: Moderately difficult.

SPECIAL PROPERTIES: None.

PRONUNCIATION: om-fa-LOW-des lin-i-FO-lee-a

*E*ven though a popular name such as Venus's navelwort would seem to make any plant irresistible, *Omphalodes linifolia* is seldom grown, and seed of it is difficult to acquire. It belongs to a genus of about twenty-eight species, most of which are true perennials, and two of which, *O. verna* (VER-na) and *O. cappadocica* (ka-pa-DO-si-ca), are grown in gardens from Zones 5 to 9 as sturdy, ground-hugging perennials that produce starry blue, forget-me-not-like flowers in spring. All three are collectively called "navelworts," a translation from the ancient Greek *omphalos,* a navel, and *-odes,* resembling, and referring to the small brown seed hollowed out on one side. Only *O. linifolia,* however, the narrow upper leaves of which resemble *Linum,* or flax, carries the special distinction of being Venus's own. A true annual native to Spain and Portugal, it is very charming, and very easy to grow, happily self-seeding in most gardens once it has been given a place for a season, rather in the manner of forget-me-nots (*Myosotis sylvatica*), a cousin within the borage family to which it is sometimes compared.

On light soils, and where winters are not too severe, Venus's navelwort develops best when it is sown in the autumn, usually in September or October. Quite early in the spring, its rosettes of silvery-gray, arrow-shaped leaves will be apparent, gradually elongating into hairy stems branched from the base, furnished with alternate, lance-shaped leaves, and terminating in one-sided racemes that bear from five to fifteen tiny, half-inch-wide starry white flowers. Each flower is composed of five rounded lobes fused at the center into a tube, and the plants, which prefer cool weather, will remain in bloom from early June until the end of July, when the weather becomes really warm. On heavy clay soil and in gardens that experience really cold winter weather (Zones 4 and colder) Venus's navelwort will not succeed if sown in autumn, and so it should be sown in very early spring, as soon as the ground may be worked, for slightly later flower by the end of June. Young seedlings are difficult to transplant, and little is gained by starting them early indoors.

Omphalodes linifolia prefers a neutral to slightly alkaline, well-drained soil of only moderate fertility. In cool gardens, it will flourish in full sun, though where the heat of summer arrives early, it will remain in bloom longer in part shade. Pinches of seed may be sown in and among other perennials where its early bloom will be appreciated and its delicate growth, to about a foot tall, will compete with no other plants. It is also both happy and attractive at the bases of taller shrubs, so long as it receives half a day of sun. Once grown in a garden and allowed to set seed, *O. linifolia* will generally appear from year to year, often just where it will look best, and never in an aggressive or smothering manner. Seedlings should be thinned to stand about six to eight inches apart to form mutually supporting patches of bloom. It is also a superb cut flower, lasting a week or more in water, and so a row or two might well be sown in the vegetable or cutting garden for that purpose. Rare as *O. linifolia* is in gardens, an even rarer form exists, *O. linifolia* var. *caerulescens* (se-ru-LES-cens), with pale blue flowers. The white and the blue are particularly lovely when grown together, as a certain percentage of *caerulescens* will always come true blue.

ONOPORDUM ACANTHIUM

FAMILY: *Asteraceae* or aster or daisy family.

CLASSIFICATION: Hardy biennial.

COMMON NAMES: Scots thistle, cotton thistle, down thistle, Robert Bruce, onopordum.

HARDINESS: Withstands heavy frosts. Winter-hardy to Zone 4.

GROWING CONDITIONS: Any well-drained garden soil. Full sun.

PROPAGATION: By seed, sown in place in autumn or very early spring.

HEIGHT: Usually from 5 to 8′.

ORNAMENTAL VALUE: Grown for silvery leaves.

LEVEL OF CULTURAL DIFFICULTY: Easy.

SPECIAL PROPERTIES: The national flower of Scotland.

PRONUNCIATION: on-o-POR-dum a-can-THEE-um

*I*f there were gardens on the moon, the ghostly *Onopordum acanthium* would surely grow there. And the moon, or any other place far away, is where some people might wish it to be. For it is frankly and fiercely a thistle, clad up and down—leaf tips, stem, and flower bud—with painfully sharp prickles. That is a lot of prickles, as it happens, for the plant can grow to ten feet when really happy, though five or six feet is more usual. Despite its fearsome armor, however, it is a very beautiful plant in all its parts. It was selected by James V of Scotland, father of Mary, Queen of Scots, as the national emblem of his country, and Queen Victoria, fond of all things Scots, had its flower stamped on the back of the fivepence piece. Sometimes in the British Isles it is still known as Robert Bruce, after the famous king who ruled Scotland from 1303 to 1309.

Though the Scots thistle is a true hardy biennial, many gardeners choose to grow it as an annual only for its first year's show, discarding it before it sends up a flower stalk in its second year. From a direct seeding outdoors as soon as the soil may be worked in spring, it produces a basal rosette or oval, acanthus-like leaves, each over a foot long at maturity and half as wide, with wavy margins edged with sharp spines. The whole plant seems covered over with silvery down or cobwebs, giving it two of its popular names, "cotton thistle" and "down thistle." Even from infancy, it is a striking plant, and it remains so throughout the autumn and winter when other plants have been cut down by cold.

In its second year, *Onopordum acanthium* sprouts a giant stalk, with foot-long deeply crinkled leaves clustering at the base and occurring scantily up the main stem. Each stem, great or small, is wrapped in four continuous wings, irregularly toothed, with each tooth ending in a spine. Branches are produced from a foot off the ground to near the top, candelabra fashion, and furnished with leaves that grow progressively

ONOPORDUM ACANTHIUM

out-of-the-way place—must be left to produce seed, which may germinate abundantly the following year, though always in the garden—not, as with the bull thistle, *Cirsium vulgare* (SEER-si-um vul-GAR-ay), stubbornly in the lawn—for seed must fall on open ground to germinate. Self-seeding is less of a nuisance in cooler gardens, though cultivation of the plant is forbidden in some states of the Southwest and the Pacific Northwest, where it may become a noxious field and roadside weed. Fortunately, where *Onopordum acanthium* is grown in gardens, the seedlings are easy to pull up. One might then leave one or two in place, if they are in the right place, or transplant them where they are wanted if they are not. Young seedlings may be easily moved in the first two months of their growth, though they make a single taproot, and when digging, one should try to get it all.

Onopordum acanthium always makes in the garden what landscape designers call a "statement," and that should not be blurred by packing the plant in too closely among others. Full profit should be taken from its bold appearance at all stages of its growth, and so plants should be spaced at least two feet apart. If it is in the flower border, a single specimen might be placed rather more forward than its great height would suggest, surrounding it with low and modest plants in order to create for it the greatest possible degree of presence. Onopordum is most wonderful when it looks as if it had chosen its own proper place to grow, at the edge of a gravel driveway or in a scattered, seemingly spontaneous drift along a board fence or the front of a barn.

The name of the genus *Onopordum* (sometimes erroneously spelled "Onopordon") is of ancient derivation, descending from the Greek *onos,* meaning a donkey or ass, and *porde,* fart, attesting to the supposed effects the plant has on donkeys when ingested. (One must assume,

smaller until they form a protective ruff around the flower bud. The spiny flower buds are perfectly round on their first appearance, until they fold outward to reveal a shaving brush of pale purple flowers, in its entirety about two inches across. Bloom is produced from early June until late August. As all parts of the plant are covered with cottony white down, the effect is of a vast plant cunningly carved of silver, white at midday and spectral at twilight. Many gardeners remove the plant, however, when its scaffold of branches begins to form, or later, when flower buds appear, so as to avoid unwanted seedlings. As plants come into full bloom, they grow shabby in any case, giving over leaves to produce more flower. A fresh, first-year plant should then be put in the vacated place.

Still, at least one individual—perhaps in an

from this derivation, that James V of Scotland was not much of a botanical scholar, and most probably had other aspects of the plant in mind.) Within the genus of forty species or more, only *Onopordum acanthium* is much grown. It takes its species name from the same word as the genus *Acanthus,* from the ancient Greek noun *acantha,* meaning thorn or prickle.

PAPAVER SPECIES

FAMILY: *Papaveraceae* or poppy family.

CLASSIFICATION: Hardy annuals, biennials, or weak perennials grown as hardy annuals.

COMMON NAME: Poppy (specific popular names vary with species).

HARDINESS: Withstand light frosts.

GROWING CONDITIONS: Moderately fertile to rich, well-drained soil. Full sun. Prefer cool weather.

PROPAGATION: From seed, sown in place in late autumn in warmer gardens and in very early spring in colder ones. Seedlings resent root disturbance.

HEIGHT: From 12" to 3'.

ORNAMENTAL VALUE: Grown for flower.

LEVEL OF CULTURAL DIFFICULTY: Easy.

SPECIAL PROPERTIES: *P. somniferum* is the source of opium, morphine, and heroin.

PRONUNCIATION: pa-PA-ver

Among the flowers that any gardener finds beautiful, some are purely personal favorites, others are reliable and sturdy, and others still are the equivalent of possessing the Holy Grail, if only their exacting cultural requirements can be met. But all gardeners would grant that among so many thousands of beautiful flowers that it is possible to grow, a small handful of aristocratic

genera exists, gathering together perfect beauty, relative ease of cultivation, and the deepest emotional resonances. Any gardener's list would probably include three flowers—the rose, the daisy, and the poppy. It is the poppy that is under consideration here.

Even though whole books have been written on it, *Papaver* is a relatively small genus, of some seventy species, distributed all over the globe, but primarily in the more temperate parts of the Old and New World. The name of the genus descends directly from classical Latin, and abundant evidence exists that members of it have been under cultivation for as long as there have been gardens. The most celebrated member of the family, *Papaver somniferum* (som-NI-fer-um), which provides both opium and morphine, has been associated with humanity for such a long time—for both good and ill— that its actual origins are uncertain. Within the genus are perennials, biennials, and true annuals, though—putting aside *P. orientale* (o-ree-en-TA-le), which can flourish for fifty years or more in the same spot when conditions suit it— many species cultivated in gardens waver rather uncertainly among those three categories, accepting a life that is brief or relatively long, depending on their environment and the conditions of their culture.

From a purely alphabetical point of view, the first of the poppies commonly grown as an annual is *P. commutatum* (co-mu-TA-tum), which draws its species name not from the fact that it may develop in thick communities of self-sown individuals, but from a curious Latin word of botanical convenience, *commutatus,* used to designate a species that possesses characteristics close to one already known. In fact, it does closely resemble the typical, pure red form of *Papaver rhoeas* (ro-EE-as), the Flanders field poppy, though each of its four two-inch-long petals is

PAPAVER NUDICAULE

marked with an ink-black stain at its base, sometimes rounded, like a thumbprint, and sometimes startlingly quite square. (The cultivar 'Ladybird' has been selected for the intense blackness of its markings.) Also, the rounded petals do not generally overlap, as is usually the case with *P. rhoeas,* but stand out singly, forming a cross. In other ways, the two species are similar, forming rosettes of oblong, downy, toothed leaves to six inches in length, and producing hairy bloom stems to as tall as eighteen inches, from which the brief-lived flowers are shaken out, and the curious pepper shakers of seed are formed. Whatever its species status, *Papaver commutatum* has been grown in gardens for almost a hundred years, having first been discovered in Russia in 1876 by William Thompson, one of the founders of the British seed company of Thompson & Morgan.

Though *Papaver commutatum* originates from very cold areas in northern Turkey, Iran, and Russia, it is not the hardiest of all poppies, a distinction that belongs to the Iceland or Arctic poppy, known still to gardeners as *P. nudicaule* (new-di-KA-lee), the species name of which means bare stemmed, though its correct botanical name is *P. croceum* (CRO-see-um), meaning golden. Hardy to Zone 2, where life-threatening winter temperatures as cold as −50°F obtain, it flourishes in places with short, cool summers where the sun hardly sets, and its four-petaled chalices of burning orange and yellow must, as Celia Thaxter remarked in *An Island Garden,* "warm the wind." Even if it lacked any other distinctions (which it possesses in plenty), *P. nudicaule* would be remarkable for being among the most cold-hardy plants commonly grown as annuals. And if one had to garden in Zone 2, a field of it in its brief moment of splendor would be some compensation. *Papaver croceum,* though fine enough in its original colors of citron yellow, orange, and tangerine red, has been developed into many other fine shades, including the pastels of 'Champagne Bubbles', some of which approach a biscuit tan.

It seems that all members of the genus *Papaver* have a birthright of great beauty, but within the clan, the Iceland poppy is precious for a quality of color and a poise of growth not quite matched by any of the others. From ferny, grayish-green rosettes of hairy leaves emerge thin rods of stem a foot and a half tall, as fine and strong as green wire. Each stem is eventually surmounted by a three-inch-wide bowl made up of four gossamer-thin overlapping petals surrounding a symmetrically arranged fringe of stamens, with the wheeled cap of the green ovary in the center. But the greatest distinction of these flowers is their curious quality of luminosity. Whether the flower is white, greenish white, ivory, coral, salmon pink, or scarlet, each flower possesses a vibrancy that occurs from the overlay of one color on another in the thinnest wash. In one cultivar at least, 'Oregon Rainbows', this overlay has been broken into distinct streaks and fadings, green into white, salmon into yellow, or coral into pale pink. Flowers of every random seedling of *P. nudicaule* will seem to glow from within, more so than any other poppy, though all of them are the children of light.

Despite its origins in the cold, subarctic climates of northern Europe and Asia, *P. nudicaule* is a little more difficult to grow than other poppies commonly cultivated as annuals. Technically it is a biennial, but if sown in late autumn or very early spring, it should flower in the first year. The fine seeds should be sown thinly in ground that has been well cultivated and raked smooth. Young plants should be thinned to stand about six to eight inches apart, and may be encouraged in their growth, once all danger of frost is past, with a light application of granular fertilizer high in phosphorus and potassium and low in nitrogen. Plants develop best in cool conditions, where temperatures hover around 50 to 60°F. Flowering should occur in mid-June and last for about a month. Gardeners who live in the deep South, in southern California, or the cooler parts of the Southwest can buy *P. nudicaule* already well developed in six-packs or peat pots to transplant into the garden for bloom in late winter and early spring. As with all members of the poppy family, *P. nudicaule* resents root disturbance and so should be shifted into the ground with great care.

Among the best loved of European wild flowers is *Papaver rhoeas,* called the "corn poppy" from the glorious way it colonizes European wheat fields—or used to, for now the widespread application of selective, pre-emergent weedkillers has made it very rare on cultivated land. The prototype of the Memorial Day poppy that was once given out in a crinkled paper form, it is an acknowledgment of contributions made on Memorial Day, May 30th. It is also called the "Flanders field poppy" because it grew and bloomed in untold numbers on battlefields the spring following the end of World War I. This rich flowering was caused by the fact that heavy artillery had deeply disturbed the earth, bringing to the surface seed that had lain buried and dormant for fifty years or more. It is a peculiarity of poppy seed that it retains viability for a very long time. *Papaver rhoeas* was also a favorite of the French painter Camille Corot, and dozens of his beautiful, brooding, gray-green canvases were made magical by its dots of scarlet.

No part of *P. rhoeas* is ugly, from its first ferny, glaucous leaves to its downy stems, clad in fine silver-green fur, to its shy goose-necked unopened buds that cast off their twin calyxes on a bright June morning to shake out the crumpled petals packed and folded within like the wings of a newly emerged butterfly. The individual life of each four-petaled, two- to three-inch-wide cup is short, but if spent flowers are carefully picked or snipped away, flowering may last from mid-June into early August.

For many gardeners, there can be no more beautiful *Papaver rhoeas* than the typical one with flowers of stained-glass red. A patch of plants in the flower border, surrounded by plenty of green and white, conveys the freshness of summer itself, especially when companioned with its traditional neighbor in grain fields, the blue cornflower, *Centaurea cyanus* (sin-TAW-ree-a si-AN-us). But *P. rhoeas* has been bred into many

PAPAVER SOMNIFERUM

PAPAVER SOMNIFERUM

wonderful strains, subtle of color and useful to those who do not enjoy clear red in the flower garden. The most famous is the Shirley poppy, bred by the Reverend W. Wilkes in his vicarage garden at Shirley, England. Around 1889, he noticed a single specimen of *P. rhoeas* that sported a fine band of white around each red petal, and a zone of pale pinkish white. By patiently selecting and re-selecting progeny of this plant, he succeeded in creating a strain with fantastic and wonderful shadings of carmine red, coral, peach, and ivory, many preserving the band of white that had been his original discovery. Eventually a double form occurred, with all the grace of the single four-petaled one, but with eight petals overlapping in an upturned cup. From this mutation, fully double forms were created. Though they may lack the essential elegance of the simple flower, they have a certain *fin-de-siècle* opulence about them, and a fair percentage will come true from seed.

A further wonderful advance on the appearance of *P. rhoeas* was made by the late English painter Sir Cedric Morris in his garden at Benton End in Suffolk. Working with the palest forms, he carefully selected only those plants that preserved a dusky, smoky color. His original aim was to produce a lavender form, but he eventually succeeded in producing a race that shows many strange and beautiful colors—from brooding purple and dove gray through palest mauve and lavender-white—in a mix called 'Sir Cedric Morris'. A similar strain is 'Mother of Pearl', which also includes bi-colors and picotees. Both strains come reasonably true from seed, though the occasional red or scarlet, though lovely in itself, should be immediately eliminated if the aim is to preserve the subtlest and most unusual colors. Those that show the desired shades can be left to self-seed, or seed may be gathered when ripe and sown in late autumn or very early spring.

Papaver rhoeas is one of the most beautiful cut flowers of summer, but individual blossoms should be conditioned carefully if they are to last well in water. Blooms should be cut in early morning, just as the twin calyxes have split apart to reveal the crinkled petals within. The stem ends should be dipped immediately into boiling water or held for a second or two over a flame. The stems should then be plunged as soon as possible into tepid water. Flowers will open almost immediately and will last for two or three days—longer, actually, than in the garden. They are so poised and graceful that it is almost impossible to arrange them clumsily.

The most opulent of all poppies generally grown as annuals must certainly be *Papaver somniferum,* the opium poppy anciently cultivated as a source of opium, and more recently, of morphine and heroin. But it is the irresistible beauty of its flowers that recommends it in gardens, not its narcotic properties. The Drug Enforcement Administration forbids the sale of seed of the plant in the United States (except in the sterilized form sold for culinary uses), and it is illegal to grow. It is doubtful, however, that the many beautiful forms of *P. somniferum* already established in gardens will be eliminated from them, and gardeners will continue to trade seed of desirable colors among themselves.

Papaver somniferum can be had in a wide range of soft colors—pale pink, rose, lavender, and grayish white—and in some stronger colors—vivid red and dark purple and wine. Flower shapes vary also, including elegant singles with the four petals characteristic of poppies in the wild, semi-doubles with eight petals, full doubles packed with many petals, and "pen wiper" sorts, in which all the petals have been modified into a soft, fluffy ball. Whatever their shape, the size of individual flowers is about four inches across, and almost all show a stain at the base of each petal, black in the more vivid colors but faded to a beautiful slate-gray in the paler ones and to a faint lavender in the whites.

For about half its life, *P. somniferum* is one of the most beautiful flowers of the summer garden. From a late autumn or early spring sowing directly where it is to grow, or from self-seeded plants, graceful rosettes of pale, bluish-green toothed leaves appear in April, each leaf down-curved into a reversed spoon. The rosettes will steadily enlarge and from the center of each will emerge a stout stem bearing the first bud. It will branch elegantly, producing a few more buds, many of which will open all together into a bush of glorious blossoms in late June. The life of each individual flower is short, scarcely more than two days, though the show will continue for two and sometimes three weeks as younger plants mature into bloom. After the petals have fallen, they leave behind neat little urns about an inch long and as much around, each surmounted by a pleated brown cap. (These seed pods are prized by arrangers of dried flowers.)

At this point, however, an ungraceful process of aging sets in. The handsome leaves begin to yellow, and the ripening seed pods stand up gaunt and naked. It is then that all but a few plants should be cleared away. But it is useful to know that in each of those urns are hundreds of seeds: They will scatter in midsummer winds, pepper-shaker fashion, to cover the ground the following spring with a thatch of progeny, most of which will have to be eliminated in the thinning process. Therefore, only a few pods need be left to ripen for next year's flowers, and those should be of the best and finest colors in whatever range and shape the gardener fancies. By such selection, over three or four years, wonderful color strains can be built up and kept pure, so long as one does not succumb to the temptation of sprinkling in seed of plants admired in someone else's garden.

Papaver somniferum, like all poppies, requires full sun and a good, open, well-drained soil not too rich in nitrogen. Thinning is essential, for plants will reach as much as two feet across when well grown, and need space to develop well. Nothing whatever is gained by spacing too close, which forces plants to become spindly and to flower poorly. A light dressing of granular fertilizer high in phosphorus and potassium and low in nitrogen, sprinkled lightly around each plant

PAPAVER SOMNIFERUM *'DANISH FLAG'*

PAPAVER SOMNIFERUM

HEIGHT: to 6 to 10′ when grown as an annual.

ORNAMENTAL VALUE: Grown for flower, and in some species, for ornamental leaf.

LEVEL OF CULTURAL DIFFICULTY: Easy to difficult, depending on species.

SPECIAL PROPERTIES: The fruit of some species is treasured as flavoring for ices and fruit drinks.

PRONUNCIATION: pass-i-FLO-ra

when the rosettes are about six inches across, will produce strong, free-flowering plants. Strains with heavy, fully double flowers may topple over from sheer weight after a summer shower, and it is worth the trouble to stake them individually just as the first buds are ready to open. If plants are likely to topple, they will do so at the point where the stem emerges from the ground, and so a single stake eight or so inches long fastened to the plant with a single tie will prevent such a mischance without disfiguring the display.

PASSIFLORA SPECIES

FAMILY: *Passifloraceae* or passion flower family.

CLASSIFICATION: Tender woody vines grown as tender annual vines.

COMMON NAMES: Passion flower, passion vine, granadilla, passiflora.

HARDINESS: Sensitive to frost.

GROWING CONDITIONS: Humus-rich, well-drained, moisture-retentive soil. Full sun.

PROPAGATION: From seed, cuttings taken in early summer, or by layering.

The genus *Passiflora* contains more than 400 species, originating mostly in the tropics and subtropics of the New World, with a few representatives in Asia, Australia, and New Zealand. The genus is so rich in beauty that many species are under cultivation, some for their magnificent flowers, some for curious and beautifully patterned leaves, and others for their richly perfumed fruit, which most Americans will know best as the dominant flavor in Hawaiian Punch. The hardiest passiflora is the North American May pop, *P. incarnata* (in-car-NA-ta), which may be found wild from Virginia south to Florida, and which is root-hardy as far north as Zone 6 with some winter protection. All other passiflora are tender vines to greater or lesser degree, depending on their origins. But most are of such quick and luxurious growth that they are becoming more and more commonly grown in summer gardens. No passiflora grown as an annual will ever produce sheets of bloom, but flowers will occur sparsely in the heat of summer and are so curiously crafted that even one is a thrill.

The most familiar passiflora is *P. caerulea* (see-RU-lee-a), which gave both the family and the genus its name, from Latin *passio,* meaning to suffer or endure, and *flos,* flower. It was first discovered by Spanish missionaries in Brazil, who saw in the curious structure of the flower a sort of notation of the crucifixion of Christ. The pious monks believed that the corona (a dense circle of filaments with fringy threads often fantastically curled or wavy, resting within the petals) represented the crown of thorns; the five stamens terminating the central column (the male organ that produces pollen) represented the five wounds inflicted on Christ by the Roman soldiers; and the three stigmas (the knobbed ends of which receive the pollen and transfer it to the ovary for fertilization), suggested the three nails that held him to the cross. A protective calyx surrounds the unopened bud and then splits to form five petal-like structures, and five true petals are arranged alternately with the lobes of the split calyx to form a ten-petaled flower. That the calyx and petals numbered only ten posed a problem for the missionaries, though its solution was to believe that they represented only the ten faithful apostles,

leaving out Peter because he denied Christ, and Judas, for his betrayal.

Passiflora caerulea is not actually blue, as its species name would suggest, but rather a greenish white brushed with mauve, with a dark purple band forming a circle at the base of the corona. For fifty years or so, it was the only passiflora offered to American gardeners, more as a pious curiosity than as the beautiful flower it is. It proved surprisingly hardy, however, well into areas where winter lows do not fall much below 0°F. Elsewhere, in the 1950s and 1960s, it was popular as a quick-growing vine cultivated as an annual and bought at nurseries or through mail order catalogues.

Though *Passiflora caerulea* is beautiful in flower, it is perhaps surpassed by many other species, not as hardy but as easy to grow for the summer gar-

PASSIFLORA COCCINEA

PASSIFLORA AMETHYSTINUM

den. All form vines that will reach from six to as much as ten feet in a season, clinging to any support by means of threadlike tendrils formed in the axils of the leaves. Though some passiflora are prized for their paddle-shaped leaves or leaves that form two curious, joined wings, most are grown for their flowers. Leaves are usually divided into three to five lobes, though sometimes as many as nine. Flowers are borne from the axils of the upper leaves, usually singly, and usually only when summer reaches its highest temperatures. The color may range from white through cream to pale pink, mauve and pale blue, purple, scarlet, and red, depending on species. As most passiflora cross freely among themselves, amateur breeders have added even richer coloring and flower form, to the extent that gardeners in the warmest climates of North America (where temperatures never drop lower than 30°F in winter) can make extensive collections.

Excepting the native American *Passiflora incarnata,* and possibly *P. caerulea,* all passiflora are quite tender and should not be set out in the garden, or established in pots or containers, until the weather is quite warm and settled, when nighttime temperatures reach at least 55°F. They prefer a very rich, fibrous, free-draining soil. Either

excessive moisture at the roots or prolonged periods of drought will cause them to become stunted or to die outright. They respond well to any fertilizer rich in phosphorus and potassium, but low in nitrogen, an excess of which encourages rampant, leafy growth at the expense of flower. Though vines will develop handsomely in part shade, full sun will produce the greatest number of flowers. Because vines will reach out tenaciously to cling to a support and scramble upward by means of their surprisingly strong tendrils, a tripod, trellis, or other structure must be provided early to prevent them from becoming entangled with their nearest neighbors.

Passiflora will generally be bought as well-started plants, perhaps already in flower. Gardeners may propagate their own, however, in three ways: by cuttings, by layering, or by seed. Cuttings are taken in summer of strong tip growth, ideally about four inches long, and severed just below a node from where a leaf has emerged. Lower leaves should be removed, and the cutting inserted in damp perlite, or a peat and perlite mix, covered with a tent made of a clear plastic bag supported away from the cutting by sticks and set in a warm place until roots form and growth resumes. At that point cuttings should be potted in fibrous, very well-draining compost, shaded for a day or two, and then gradually exposed to full sun. Layers may be taken at any time from a plant growing in someone else's garden. A side branch is bent to the ground and scraped or nicked just below a node, which is then buried and pegged down. When roots have formed, the branch may be severed entirely and potted up as for a cutting. Specialty sources occasionally offer seed of five or so species all popularly called "granadilla." They should be sown in early spring, indoors, in pots of well-draining compost, and covered with a pane of glass until germination occurs. Germination will be most rapid at temperatures around 70°F, and the young seedlings will develop quickly in full, bright sun until they may be established outdoors.

Though many of the rare passiflora are difficult to carry over the winter, those that are most often grown in gardens should be easy. Before frost, side growth on vines should be shortened to about eight inches, and the whole plant lifted and potted in very well-draining compost, ideally a soilless, peat-based compost such as Pro-Mix, made even lighter by the addition of one-third perlite by volume. A support will be required, and plants should be stood in bright light and kept at temperatures around 50°F. Very little water will be required until new growth begins in spring, at which point water should gradually be increased. When plants are growing well, they will benefit by weekly, half-strength application of water-soluble fertilizer. They may be returned to the garden as soon as nighttime temperatures become settled at about 55°F.

PELARGONIUM SPECIES

FAMILY: *Geraniaceae* or geranium family.

CLASSIFICATION: Tender shrubby perennials or sub-shrubs grown as tender annuals.

COMMON NAMES: Geranium, pelargonium.

HARDINESS: Sensitive to light frosts.

GROWING CONDITIONS: Moderately rich, well-drained, moisture-retentive soil. Full sun.

PROPAGATION: From seed, sown indoors in late winter or very early spring. Many choice varieties propagated by cuttings, which root readily.

HEIGHT: Variable with species and cultivar.

ORNAMENTAL VALUE: Grown for flower and sometimes for ornamental leaves.

LEVEL OF CULTURAL DIFFICULTY: Easy.

SPECIAL PROPERTIES: Many species and cultivars valued for fragrant leaves.

PRONUNCIATION: pe-lar-GO-nee-um

For the last hundred years or more, every discussion of pelargonium has had to begin with the fact that they travel under a borrowed name. So firmly fixed to them is the name "geranium" that all but the most pedantic gardeners use it. But geranium (from the classical Greek *geranion*, meaning crane's bill) properly belongs to a genus of about 300 largely hardy, herbaceous perennials, many of which are also extremely popular garden plants. And although pelargoniums (from classical Greek *pelargros,* signifying a stork's bill) are cousins within the family Geraniaceae and bear many resemblances to true geraniums, including the sharp-pointed, curved seed receptacles that give both their botanical names, they are still quite different plants. True geraniums—often called "border geraniums"—are mainstays of the perennial garden, blooming reliably in late spring or early summer throughout Zones 4 to 8. Pelargoniums, on the other hand, are killed by temperatures around 36°F but are favorites for summer bedding, containers, and as houseplants, where they will flower more-or-less continuously in bright, sunny conditions at temperatures above 50°F. This name confusion (even the painter's pigment is known as "Geranium Red") does no harm, provided everyone is aware of it.

Of the more than 230 species in the genus *Pelargonium* (about 10,000 varieties are registered by the American Pelargonium Society), those under general cultivation may be divided for convenience into five classes: Zonal, Martha Washington, Ivy Leaved, Scented, and (for want of a better word) Botanical.

Zonal geraniums are the ones most familiar

PELARGONIUM *X* PELTATUM

to gardeners and non-gardeners alike. They represent complex crosses, primarily between *Pelargonium inquinans* (in-KI-nans) and *P. zonale* (zo-NA-lee), though there is certainly the blood of other species in their lineage. *Pelargonium zonale,* cultivated in England as early as 1710, contributes the prominent, horseshoe-shaped marking, or zone, across the middle of the leaves of all cultivars except white-flowered ones. (A similar zone occurs across the leaves of some true geraniums, notably *Geranium phaeum* [FAY-um], and is a characteristic much sought after by breeders.) *P. inquinans,* with somewhat floppy, non-zoned green leaves and small red flowers, was probably the first geranium cultivated in North America, originally by the scientifically and artistically gifted Peale family. It is at least half the subject of the celebrated painting Rembrandt Peale made of his younger brother in 1801, titled "Reubens Peale with a Geranium." Both are lovingly painted, but the geranium pictured—gaunt of stem, loose of leaf, small of flower—although doubtless precious to the sitter and the painter at the time—could hardly claim room in any modern garden.

Peale would be stunned by the modern Zonal geraniums, which are short and compact of growth, crisp of leaf, and smothered with flowers in any shade from white to cream, through pale to deep orange, light to deep pink and carmine, magenta, and deep purple almost to black, with many bi-colors. Umbel-like clusters of bloom borne in each leaf axil may be composed of flowers with five to ten petals or more, resulting in fully double and rosebud forms, in which the central petals remain furled in a tight cone. A major breakthrough occurred in the 1960s, when F1 hybrids were bred that came true from seed, so now one can buy geraniums either as expensive, cutting-grown plants, just as always, or one can easily raise large numbers economically from seed sown early indoors, mid-February to mid-March, for young plants that will bloom the following summer. Lately, also, there has been tremendous interest in forms with vividly colored leaves, including white on mint green, bronze on yellow, or brown on gold. Cultivars such as 'Blazonry' represent this trend best, with complex leaves marked with pale and dark green, red, orange, and maroon on a clear, butter-yellow ground, making them as vivid as coleus.

It is a happy fact about the Zonal pelargoniums that they will continue to bloom as long as nighttime temperatures remain above 50°F, and so they have always been the quintessential kitchen windowsill plant. To carry them over winter as dormant plants, however, an old-fashioned method may be followed—digging whole plants in autumn just before frost, packing them upright in boxes with some earth about their roots, and storing them in a cool but frost-free place over winter to be planted out the following spring after all danger of frost is past. There is enough succulence in the stems to maintain life. The plants may look very wretched and depressing, but they will quickly regain an attractive appearance with the warmth of spring.

The Martha Washington geraniums are listed under the name *P.* x *domesticum* (do-MES-ticum), a designation that simply means domesticated, though it often suggests a houseplant with a complicated botanical lineage. In fact, any Martha Washington geranium also represents complex crosses—a series of crosses and back-crosses, principally of the species *cuculatum* (cu-cu-LA-tum), *angulosum* (an-gu-LO-sum), and *grandiflorum* (gran-di-FLO-rum). They are very showy plants, forming upright bushes to as much as three feet, with brown stems and cup-shaped, crinkled leaves as much as four inches long and across. Flowers are borne abundantly in very late spring to early summer and consist of clusters of single flowers composed of five petals, each from two to four inches across, in shades of white, cream, pink rose, red, or purple, usually with a dramatic stain of maroon on the upper petals. The splendor of their blooms has given them other popular names, including "Regal Geranium" and "Summer Azalea." Except in the warmer parts of Zones 9 and 10, where they may be treated as hardy, spring-flowering shrubs, their cultivation from year to year is difficult and is best left to specialists. Most gardeners will acquire them already in flower for spring and summer bloom, and then discard them at season's end.

The Ivy Leaved geraniums, selections and hybrids of *Pelargonium peltatum* (pel-TA-tum), have been popular for many years in Europe and are at present enjoying a huge vogue in North America. Also called "balcony geraniums," they are the plants one pictures tumbling out of window boxes and urns in Switzerland, along the Riviera, and in northern Italy, with shiny, ivy-leaved vines smothered with vivid, umbel-like clusters of flowers in shades of tangerine, pale and deep pink, scarlet and deep red, maroon, magenta, and white. Wherever they are grown, they seem to carry with them an atmosphere of clear, fresh mornings, blue skies, pristine beaches, and the sea. They are very sturdy, serviceable plants that will trail downward to as much as three feet in a season from a window box or hanging basket. Despite the resonances all pelargoniums carry of warm and sunny places, all are sensitive to intense sun and heat, none more so than the Ivy Leaved geraniums, which would prefer half a day of sun when grown in dry, warm gardens. Cool, fresh nights, such as one finds in Mediterranean climates or even in the desert, encourage maximum bloom.

Within the class of Scented (leaf) geraniums are more than fifty separate species and many hybrids. It is in fact true that no genus of plants contains so many species with distinctly scented leaves. Almost every pleasant herb or fruit scent known to humans is represented in one or another species or hybrid, ranging from clove and cinnamon, through anise, coconut, cucumber, pine, balsam, strawberry, apricot, orange, and spearmint with countless blends. Scented geraniums were the first brought under cultivation in Europe, beginning with *P. graveolens* (gra-ve-O-lens), the "rose geranium," which was grown in England as early as 1690. It was soon followed by *P. crispum* (CRISP-um), the crinkled-leaf "lemon geranium," by *P. tomentosum* (to-men-TO-sum), the "peppermint geranium," and by *P.* x *fragrans* (FRAY-grans), the

PELARGONIUM X DOMESTICUM

PELARGONIUM X HYBRIDUM 'FRANK KEDLEY'

"nutmeg geranium," all of which were in cultivation by the mid-eighteenth century. The eighteenth-century enthusiasm for scent in plants was perhaps a makeweight against the relative paucity of flower forms and colors, at least when judged by twentieth- or even nineteenth-century standards. Still, it is an enthusiasm that continues among modern gardeners, and many scented geraniums are very attractive in both leaf and in flower, making them admirable, quick-growing components of herb gardens. They have their table uses as well. A single leaf of flower- or fruit-scented geranium can be included in jams and jellies, and it may serve as both a garnish and flavoring to homemade ices, sherbet, cakes, and summer drinks. Many scented-leaf geraniums also bear pretty flowers, rather spidery and delicate, in shades of white, pinkish gray, mauve, or purple. They are much more modest than those of the showy Zonals or Martha Washingtons but are appropriate to the herbish growth of the plants. These, also, may be used as garnishes to sweets, savories, or salads, as no species of pelargonium is toxic, though very rarely, skin irritations have been reported. As all scented geraniums are easy to grow and to carry through the winter in a cool greenhouse or on a sunny windowsill, connois-

seurs of their scent might make large collections, adding ever more rarefied blends of fragrance as new plants became available.

The Botanical pelargoniums represent a fascinating group of plants that would, until quite recently, have been of interest only to collectors. Generally, they reflect some peculiarity, from forms possessed of so much fine, fringed foliage that one would take them for ferns, to others with swollen, elephantine, cactuslike limbs with hardly any leaves at all. They are all frankly oddities, more interesting than pretty, but they are very suitable to small dishes or other tabletop containers, and as such, have begun to appear more commonly in garden centers that cater to customers seeking rare and unusual plants as ornaments to the summer garden. They represent a very wide range of species, and generally, when one sees them for sale, it is love at first sight. Or not. Most certainly, however, they round out the appeal of pelargoniums, which begins with sturdy, reliable bedding plants chosen largely for color interest, through plants remarkable both for flower and for vivid coloration of leaf, to plants with leaves scented in strong or subtle ways, and ending with those that may have the most refined appeal, as does *Pelargonium sideroides* (si-de-ROY-des), with tiny fans of gray-green leaves topped by spidery flowers so dark a purple that they might as well be black.

PENSTEMON X GLOXINOIDES

FAMILY: *Scrophulariaceae* or snapdragon family.

CLASSIFICATION: Half-hardy perennials grown as half-hardy annuals.

COMMON NAMES: Beard tongue, border penstemon, gloxinia penstemon.

HARDINESS: Hardy to Zone 7, with perfect
    drainage.
GROWING CONDITIONS: Moderately fertile, neutral
    to slightly alkaline garden loam. Perfect
    drainage. Full sun.
PROPAGATION: From seed, sown in late February, or
    from tip cuttings taken in late spring and early
    summer.
HEIGHT: To 2'.
ORNAMENTAL VALUE: Grown for flower.
LEVEL OF CULTURAL DIFFICULTY: Difficult.
SPECIAL PROPERTIES: None.
PRONUNCIATION: PEN-ste-mon glox-i-NOY-des

The genus *Penstemon* contains perhaps as many as 300 species, all but one native to North America, generally occurring in the western half of the continent from Canada to Mexico. Within the group are some of the most beautiful of all American wild flowers, a very large number of which are grown in gardens. Of those that will submit to cultivation—many will not—*Penstemon* x *gloxinoides* is among the most splendid. The true botanical identity of the group is uncertain, and the name *gloxinoides,* though it aptly describes the flared, open, gloxinia-like bells of flower borne by the plant, has no botanical standing. It is thought that the group consists either of selections of *Penstemon hartwegii* (hart-WEG-ee-ee), a predominantly red-flowered species native to Mexico, or of crosses between it and *Penstemon cobaea* (co-BAY-ee-a), a larger-flowered species native from Missouri to Texas, with reddish-purple, lavender, or whitish-mauve blooms. Though plants have been grown under the name *gloxinoides* for a hundred years, modern botanists generally prefer to assign no species identity to the plant at all, rather than one that is inaccurate, so they list merely the genus and cultivar name, as, for example, *Penstemon* x 'Sour Grapes'.

Whatever their botanical identity, however, the border penstemon make magnificent garden plants, with many ascending stems thickly clasped by broad, bladelike, down-curved leaves of a dark rich shiny green that are extremely handsome in themselves. Flowers are borne in terminal panicles, often, though not always, one-sided, and may be as long as two feet with buds and open blooms occurring at pleasant intervals, creating a light, delicate effect. Buds color richly even when they are quite tiny, and open flowers are one- to two-inch-long tubes, flaring at the mouth into two lips, the lower one three-lobed and the upper two-lobed, though in some plants, the lobes are almost equal and

PENSTEMON 'WHITE BEDDER'

evenly spaced. Flowers may be any sumptuous shade of white, pink, scarlet, deep red, lavender, or purple, usually with a contrasting throat of white or pale yellow. Five anthers protrude prominently, four fertile and the fifth sterile and bearded, giving the genus its name, from the ancient Greek *pente,* five, and *stemon,* stamen. Any gardener who has seen a well-grown stand of border penstemon in full bloom would want them, for in addition to their beauty, they possess an upright grace that complements the rounded, bushy shapes of many other annuals and perennials.

The only thing certain about the lineage of the border penstemon is that they are true perennials, though in all but the most favored West Coast gardens they usually prove difficult or impossible to carry over from year to year. They can, however, be tricked into behaving as annuals, flowering in July from a very early sowing indoors in late February. Seed germinates more reliably if the seed packet is placed in a tightly lidded mason jar and chilled for three weeks in the refrigerator. It should then be scattered thinly over pots filled with a peat-based, soilless compost such as Pro-Mix and only barely pressed in as it needs light to germinate. Germination occurs best at around 60°F, though it is erratic, some seeds sprouting in a week and others taking as long as a month to appear. The compost should be kept only barely moist both while waiting for germination and after the infant seedlings appear, as they are subject to rot at all times. When seedlings are large enough to handle, they should be potted in very free-draining, soilless compost such as Pro-Mix, to which a liberal sprinkling of sharp sand has been added. They should then be grown on in good light and at temperatures around 60°F until they may be hardened off and planted outdoors.

When young seedlings are about five inches tall, pinching will encourage several rather than just one flowering stem.

Border penstemon grow best in full sun except in very hot gardens, where light shade will benefit them. Like virtually all members of their genus, they require a soil that is fertile, light, and very free draining, preferably on the alkaline side, or made so by a liberal sprinkling of lime. Heavy clay or extended periods of soil saturation will almost always induce root rot, which is fatal. Fertilizer of any kind should be avoided, as it is apt to produce leafy growth at the expense of flowers. As stems develop and form buds, each may need an individual stake, though it need not extend more than a foot upward. Flower panicles remain attractive for a very long time, as spent blossoms fall off and new buds open. When they are done, however, cutting the stems back to about half their leafy growth will sometimes encourage a second flush of bloom.

Mail order nurseries specializing in rare and unusual perennials offer many named forms of border penstemon that might be tried, if only as "annuals," to determine whether the plant may be made comfortable in one's garden. Successful plants should be propagated by tip cuttings three to four inches long, which root easily at any time from spring to fall when inserted into moist peat and sand, or peat and perlite, and kept shaded. Young rooted plants may then be carried over on a cool windowsill or in the cool greenhouse for planting out the following spring. They will also thrive unusually well under fluorescent light. But during the winter, the soil in which they are growing should be allowed to dry out slightly between waterings, and care should be taken not to over-water them at any time.

PENTAS LANCEOLATA

FAMILY: *Rubiaceae* or coffee family.

CLASSIFICATION: Tender shrubby perennial grown as tender shrubby annual.

COMMON NAMES: Star cluster, Egyptian star, pentas.

HARDINESS: Sensitive to light frosts.

GROWING CONDITIONS: Humus-rich, slightly dry, fertile soil. Full sun in cooler gardens, afternoon shade in warmer ones.

PROPAGATION: By seed, sown indoors in late winter. Most purchased plants are cutting-grown.

HEIGHT: To 6' where hardy. To 2' or less when grown as an annual.

ORNAMENTAL VALUE: Grown for flower.

LEVEL OF CULTURAL DIFFICULTY: Moderately difficult.

SPECIAL PROPERTIES: None.

PRONUNCIATION: PEN-tas lan-see-o-LA-ta

*M*ost gardeners will think of pentas as house-plants, grown for their clusters of starry flowers on sunny windowsills or in greenhouses, where they remain in bloom over a very long time, virtually as long as they are healthy. But the capacity of pentas to flower almost continuously also makes them excellent candidates for growing as annuals in northern gardens, and so they have joined a significant group of plants that have been liberated—if only for a brief summer—from the confines of indoor growing spaces. This is actually their second leap to freedom, for they were popular in Victorian and Edwardian gardens as components of elaborate bedding schemes that employed both many true annuals and also tender greenhouse plants.

As garden flowers, pentas possess many virtues. Technically sub-shrubs—a class of plants that wavers uncertainly between perennials and shrubs—they form tidy, upright bushes from one to four feet, depending on the cultivar. Their bright green, four- to six-inch-long leaves, borne thickly on the stems, are attractive in themselves and a handsome foil for the flowers. Bloom is produced at the tip of each branch, in thick clusters between three and five inches wide. Individual clusters are made up of many small flowers, each composed of a slender tube about three quarters of an inch long flaring open into a star of five narrow, pointed petals. (Hence, the common name "star cluster.") The range of colors is limited but includes red, deep and light pink, pinkish salmon, lavender, purple, and white. Selections have been made that emphasize lighter shading at the tips of petals and in the throat of each flower, such as the cultivar 'Tu-Tone', and though these are pretty up close, they may look bleached from a distance. The somewhat muddled colors of pentas have been purified in the New Look Series, plants of which are also compact at about a foot tall.

Pentas thrive in humus-rich, well-drained soil, slightly on the dry side, and in full sun. White fly is the only pest that attacks them, but as long as it

PENTAS LANCEOLATA *'PINK'*

PENTAS LANCEOLATA 'RED'

can be held in check, they make excellent garden plants. The ease with which they may be grown, and their continuous bloom throughout the summer until frost, have created a wave of popularity for them that will certainly result in future improvement. One will certainly be variegated foliage, for an old cultivar called 'Avalanche', with white-marked leaves and white flowers, would point the way.

The genus *Pentas* is relatively small, containing about thirty species native to tropical East Africa and Madagascar. It takes its name from ancient Greek *pentas,* a series of five, and refers to the five-petaled flowers typical of all members of the genus. *P. lanceolata* is the only species of any garden importance, though its leaves are not spear-shaped, as the specific name implies, but rather broad, pointed ovals. A very tender plant, it is hardy in gardens only in Zone 10, where winter temperatures remain above 30°F. In such privileged places, its tidy growth and almost perpetually produced bright flowers cause it to be extensively used (perhaps overused) in public parks, in street islands, and around commercial establishments. Outside Zone 10, however, pentas are novel enough to make them interesting additions to the summer garden, whether in con-

tainers, in hanging baskets, or in the open border. Pentas are also extremely popular with butterflies.

Although most gardeners will acquire pentas as single potted specimens already in bloom, plants can easily be grown from seed. It must be sown very early—in February—for plants large enough to be set out in early June. (Plants flower in about four months from seed.) The seed should not be covered with soil, as it requires light to germinate. Germination may be slow, taking as long as a month, during which time the seed flat should be kept at about 60°F, and moist but not soggy, for at all times pentas are extremely sensitive to poorly drained soil. When seedlings appear, they should be pricked out into individual pots or cell packs and grown on in bright light at temperatures between 55° and 65°F. Growth will be rapid and may be encouraged by weekly applications of half-strength water-soluble fertilizer. Older varieties should be pinched to encourage branching when about six inches tall.

In the garden, pentas flower most profusely in full sun, though they will accept light shade, particularly in the afternoon, and still produce some bloom. They are not particular as to soil, provided it is well drained and moderately moist, but they do appreciate regular supplementary feeding. Spent flower clusters should be removed by cutting branches back above two or so sets of leaves to encourage more branching and flower clusters. At the end of the season and before frost, individual plants may be lifted, cut back lightly, potted up, and brought indoors, where they will continue to grow and bloom on a sunny windowsill or in a greenhouse. Alternatively, cuttings may be taken, though rooting will be slow unless bottom heat can be supplied, and care must be taken to avoid wetting the foliage, which will be prone to rot until roots are formed. When grown in pots, pentas should be given as much light as possible, allowed to dry out slightly between waterings, and carefully watched for white fly, which multiplies very rapidly beneath their leaves. If white fly cannot be eliminated, infected plants should be destroyed and never returned to the garden where the white fly population will explode.

PERILLA FRUTESCENS

FAMILY: *Lamiaceae* (*Labiatae*) or mint family.

CLASSIFICATION: Hardy annual.

COMMON NAMES: Beefsteak plant, shiso, perilla.

HARDINESS: Withstands significant frost when young. Seed-hardy in all but the coldest gardens.

GROWING CONDITIONS: Almost any moisture-retentive, well-drained soil. Full sun to part shade.

PROPAGATION: From seed, sown in place in autumn or in very early spring. Rare cultivars propagated by cuttings.

HEIGHT: To 3'.

ORNAMENTAL VALUE: Grown for ornamental leaves.

LEVEL OF CULTURAL DIFFICULTY: Easy.

SPECIAL PROPERTIES: Aromatic foliage valued in Asian cooking.

PRONUNCIATION: pe-RILL-a fru-TES-ens

Perilla frutescens has actually been known to Western gardens since the mid-eighteenth century, and over 250 years of cultivation its fortunes have risen and fallen. Probably first grown in European botanical gardens merely as an oriental oddity, its bronze- or burgundy-leaved forms achieved some status in the Victorian period as a component of carpet bedding. As plants could easily be grown from seed or cuttings, and as they withstood the vagaries of summer weather well, they could be employed—along with other colored-leaf annuals and tender plants—in the complicated "florists'" designs popular on great Victorian estates and in public parks.

In late Edwardian gardens it fared better, for the richer-colored forms enhance every other color against which they are placed, from the brashest yellow to the palest mauve and silver, and so the followers of Gertrude Jekyll used it as a dot plant for occasional accent in the wildly opulent, tumbled perennial borders she made fashionable. For this reason also, it was much grown in America until the late 1950s, when what might be called the Hardy Perennial Movement caused all plants that had to be renewed from seed or cuttings each year to fall out of favor. Now, however, with the revival of interest in just such plants, and a renewed perception of the importance of foliage in flower borders, especially when it is purple, *Perilla frutescens* finds itself once again riding a crest of popularity.

Interestingly, however, these vagaries of fortune in Western gardens have co-existed with the very firm position *Perilla frutescens* has occupied for many centuries as one of the most important flavoring herbs in many Eastern cuisines. The plant occurs in the wild over a very wide geographic area, beginning in the Himalayas and extending through China to Japan, and southward to Indonesia, Myanmar, and Vietnam, though, as it is a valued culinary herb and naturalizes quickly wherever it is grown, its actual origins are in doubt. The genus name *Perilla* is also of uncertain origin, though it may be a corruption of the Hindi name for the plant, or possibly a diminutive of the Latin *pera,* meaning a small sack or wallet, and referring to the fact that the tiny, insignificant blossoms of the plant are borne in purselike calyxes packed together in two-inch-long, terminal racemes.

But whatever its origin or popular name, perilla has been put to almost every use one could think of. Its leaves are valued in many eastern countries as a salad, a cooked green, a fried vegetable, a garnish, a wrapping, or a coloring agent. It is apt to occur as a single leaf or two as an edible garnish on a plate of sushi, and its leaves and seed stems, when dipped in batter and fried quickly in hot oil, are popular components of tempura. It is also the coloring agent in pickled ginger, turning it pink.

Perilla frutescens belongs to a very small genus of only six species, of which it is the only one of any significance in cultivation. But over the centuries in which it has been valued, many varieties and cultivars have arisen. The natural form of the plant is shrubby, composed of many ascending branches, creating a bush that may reach a height of as much as four feet, but is usually closer to two and a half feet under cultivation. Its leaves are heart-shaped, about four to six inches long and four inches across, toothed along their edges and slightly raspy to the touch. They are borne alternately on the square stems typical of all members of the mint family. Generally, unless plants have naturalized from gardens, the color of the leaf is a medium green, but forms occur occa-

PERILLA FRUTESCENS

sionally in the wild in which the green is suffused with purple, or green on top and purple beneath, or purple throughout. The latter, known to botanists as *Perilla frutescens* var. *atropurpurea* (at-ro-pur-PUR-ee-a), provides the basis from which many cultivars, in various shades of burgundy, purple, and purplish brown, have been selected, some with deeply frilled or ruffled leaves. The ones most commonly grown in gardens are offered under the cultivar names 'Crispa', 'Laciniata' (la-sin-ee-A-ta), and 'Nankinensis' (nan-kin-EN-sis). These varietal names may in fact be synonymous, as all three are close enough in appearance to be essentially the same, though with a greater or lesser degree of ruffling, depending on seed source. (There is an extremely ruffled cultivar, 'Fancy Fringe', that is worth searching out wherever it may be found.) Most recently, a form of perilla with the catchy name 'Magilla Perilla' has appeared, with beet-red variegation on a purple ground, and with narrow, blade-shaped leaves that look like nothing so much as a coleus. Whether it has any aromatic or culinary value, or indeed, is within the variable species of *Perilla frutescens* at all, is yet to be determined.

Green forms of perilla are still preferred for culinary use, but generally it is the all-purple forms that gardeners cultivate for decorative purposes. And though the cultivars roughly grouped under 'Crispa', with ruffled leaves, are the ones most frequently encountered, the smooth-leaf forms of perilla have their advocates because they show off to best advantage the sheen across their leaves.

The smell of perilla, like that of cilantro, takes some getting used to. Lacking, as we do, a really descriptive language to describe smell, most people fall back on comparing it with a more familiar pungency, such as lemon and anise or cumin, basil, and cinnamon, variously mixed together.

All fall short of the mark. Most simply, perilla smells like perilla, and it is generally a smell one does or doesn't like. But a leaf nibbled as an experiment, whether in the garden or in a sushi restaurant, may lead to the craving for another leaf, and others still. For this reason, it is to be presumed, Vietnamese families that have immigrated to America almost always keep pots of perilla on balconies or back door porches and steps. Unusual among culinary herbs, however, perilla completely loses its pungency when dried and so is useful only when picked fresh from the plant.

Perilla frutescens is of very easy culture if its few needs may be met. It prefers a moderately rich, well-drained soil, abundant moisture during the growing season, and full sun, though it will accept very light shade. Because the plant makes very rapid growth, and because its leaves are effective practically from germination, it is seldom started early indoors. It may be, however, by sowing the seed about six to eight weeks before the last anticipated frost date, and pressing them only lightly into the potting compost, as they require light to germinate. The tiny seedlings should be pricked out into peat pots or plastic cell packs, for the older they get, the more unwillingly they will accept transplanting. Alternatively, seed may be sprinkled on prepared ground and raked smooth practically anytime in early spring. Plants should be thinned to stand about a foot from one another, though perilla is usually planted not so much in drifts as singly, here and there, individual plants providing the contrast for which they are valued without creating too funereal a tone.

Seed of perilla in any form is surprisingly hard to come by, appearing seldom in major seed catalogues. One's best sources for seed, therefore, are the small seed companies that specialize in Asian vegetables and herbs. The mystery of why seed is so infrequently offered is increased by the fact that perilla is a prolific self-seeder, and once grown in a garden, is apt to reappear from year to year, sometimes in a daunting abundance, though young seedlings are easy to eradicate simply by scratching or troweling them out. (Even when quite tiny, they make interesting additions to spring salads, so unwanted seedlings may be both eliminated and put to use in that way.) Perhaps the best source of perilla will be the garden of someone else who has grown it. For "starts," there will always be plenty to transplant, with a trowel of earth, in mid-spring. Or a fully mature, seed-heavy plant might be begged in autumn, taken home, and laid on the ground in a spot where perilla is wanted. Plants may also be easily reproduced from cuttings, taken from vigorous, nonflowering side shoots in summer. Perilla is a light-sensitive plant, flowering and setting seed only when the days shorten in late summer. That, as it happens, is a good thing, for, like coleus, plants quickly become shabby in the effort to flower and produce seed. One should not hasten to rip them out at that stage, however, unless volunteer plants are not wanted for the following year.

PERSICARIA SPECIES (*POLYGONUM* SPECIES)

FAMILY: *Polygonaceae* or knotweed family.

CLASSIFICATION: Hardy annuals.

COMMON NAMES: Prince's feather, annual knotweed, kiss-me-over-the-garden-gate, annual polygonum, annual persicaria.

HARDINESS: Withstand light frosts.

GROWING CONDITIONS: Humus-rich, well-drained, moisture-retentive soil for *P. orientale*. Lean, sandy, well-drained, dryish soil for *P. capitata*. Full sun for both.

PROPAGATION: By seed, sown in place in autumn in warmer gardens, in spring elsewhere, or indoors 6 weeks before last frost.

HEIGHT: *P. capitata* to 6″. *P. orientale* to 8′.

ORNAMENTAL VALUE: Grown for flower.

LEVEL OF CULTURAL DIFFICULTY: Easy.

SPECIAL PROPERTIES: None.

PRONUNCIATION: per-si-CAR-ee-a (po-LI-go-num)

Most gardeners will know polygonum either as climbing vines and perennials of garden value, or as noxious weeds colonizing roadsides to the exclusion of native flora. The genus once contained approximately 150 species, though many have now been shifted out into other genuses, chiefly *Reynoutria, Fallopia,* and *Persicaria.* It is in that latter genus that the only two plants grown as annuals are lodged, *Persicaria orientale* (o-ree-en-TA-le) and *P. capitata* (ca-pi-TA-ta). They are very different in appearance, for the former is a towering plant to as much as eight feet tall, and the latter forms a ground-hugging mat scarcely six or so inches high. Seed of either is very seldom offered, however, perhaps in part due to the noxious reputation of a former poly-

PERSICARIA CAPITATA

gonum, *P. cuspidatum* (cus-pi-DA-tum), now *Reynoutria japonica* (ree-new-TRI-a ja-PON-i-ca), the dreaded Mexican bamboo or Japanese knotweed that has proven almost impossible to eradicate along New England roadsides and in fields. This borrowed bad name is a pity, for both annuals are beautiful.

Persicaria orientale was actually a very popular garden plant a hundred years ago, when it was treasured for its ease of cultivation, its stately growth, and the vividness of its flower. It quickly forms a loosely branched plant that is typically four to five feet tall, but may grow much taller in moist, humus-rich soil. Its broadly lance-shaped, velvety leaves may be as long as ten inches, clasping the stem where it swells out into prominent joints. Leaves are a fresh grass green and are so thin of texture that light shines through them. Flowers are produced on slender, branched stems in terminal spikes, each about six inches long, that arch outward and downward, giving the plant, for all its size, a curious grace. (This height and arching habit account for the plant's more curious common name, "kiss-me-over-the-garden-gate," which it shares with another annual, *Amaranthus caudatus.*) Each flower is minute, though they are packed so tightly that the racemes look like lengths of plush or rope. As if to make up for their size, they are a vivid rich pink, made stronger by even deeper rose calyxes and unopened buds. It is a color that could be overpowering if it occurred in greater abundance or if it were not softened by the plant's large, thin leaves.

Persicaria orientale is widely native throughout Asia, which explains its species name. It is a very easy plant to grow, accepting almost any soil so long as it is not waterlogged, and indeed, it produces better foliage and finer-colored flowers on rather thin, poor soils. Classed as a hardy annual, it may be sown in all but the coldest gardens, either in autumn or in early spring as soon as the ground may be worked. It transplants easily, but growth is so rapid from seed sown where the plant is to grow that little is gained by an early seeding indoors. Plants should be spaced about a foot apart, so that their growth will interlace. In very rich soil, each plant must be prevented from toppling over by being tied to a single stake, though it need not extend more than two or so feet above ground. Plants of *P. orientale* are worth that trouble, however, for their height, endearingly awkward grace, and vivid flowers make them invaluable for planting at the back of deep flower borders. They are equally impressive, however, when grown alone, in a single colony against a barn or weathered fence or in a bay of shrubbery. Their only real liability is that they are very popular with Japanese beetles, which shred the handsome leaves while they are swarming and which must be picked off daily. In most gardens, *P. orientale* will self-seed freely once it has been grown but is never a nuisance as unwanted plants can be eliminated by a single tug.

Persicaria capitata owes all its charm to just the opposite characteristics of *P. orientale*. It is a low little plant, growing to a height of about six to eight inches, but creeping outward to form a dense, ground-hugging mat as much as a foot across in a single summer. It is hardy in Zones 8 and 9, where its vigorous, procumbent growth makes it useful as groundcover. Elsewhere, it is grown as an annual, as it develops and flowers rapidly from seed. Heart-shaped leaves, each about one to two inches long, clasp its jointed stems at close intervals and are attractively marked with a maroon chevron or inverted V in their center and often by a reddish midrib and red to orange coloration along the edges. Drought and poor soil accentuate this coloration. The flowers of the plant give it its species name, *capitata,* which means growing in a dense head, for

they are little rounded, marble-sized balls composed of many, tightly packed, tiny bells scarcely one-sixteenth inch across, standing well above the foliage on slender stems about two inches high. When immature, flower clusters are pinkish white though they deepen to a pretty, medium pink as the flowers open. Because of its small stature, *Persicaria capitata* is usually considered a rock garden plant, though it can look very fine in a hanging basket, window box, or container, where it will tumble gracefully over the edges. It roots with extreme ease, usually wherever the jointed stems touch the ground. Cuttings taken in August from tip growths will root quickly when inserted in moist sand, perlite, or a mixture of half perlite and half peat.

The genus name *Persicaria* is medieval English for a peach, the leaves of which the lance-shaped leaves of some species resemble. The previous genus name, *Polygonum,* is a Latinized form of the Greek word used by ancient botanists, *polygonon,* from *polys,* meaning much, and either *gonos,* meaning progeny or seed, or *gony,* knee joint, both of which apply to most previous members of the genus, as they are both jointed along their stems and very free in the production of seed.

PETUNIA SPECIES

FAMILY: *Solanaceae* or deadly nightshade family.

CLASSIFICATION: Tender perennial grown as tender or half-hardy annual.

COMMON NAME: Petunia.

HARDINESS: Sensitive to light frosts.

GROWING CONDITIONS: Widely variable, but best in moderately rich, well-drained, moisture-retentive soil. Full sun in cooler gardens to part shade in warmer ones.

PROPAGATION: By seed, sown indoors in late winter or early spring. Choice varieties and true species are propagated by cuttings.

HEIGHT: Variable, from 8" to 2', depending on cultivar and support.

ORNAMENTAL VALUE: Grown for flower.

LEVEL OF CULTURAL DIFFICULTY: Easy.

SPECIAL PROPERTIES: Excellent container, window box, and hanging basket plants.

PRONUNCIATION: pe-TOO-nee-a

Until about ten years ago, when they were supplanted by *Impatiens capensis,* petunias accounted for the largest number of sales in nurseries and garden centers. Their record-breaking popularity had been consistent since 1930, making petunias America's most popular annual for more than sixty years. Either because of this fact or as a result of complex genetic identity, no other plant grown as an annual exists in so bewildering a variety of forms and colors. In fact, with the recent breeding of excellent yellows, oranges, and blues, petunias alone may now be said to flower in every shade and color except (for the moment) green. Many bi-colors exist, either marked with stars of white against a darker ground, or picoteed with white at the edge of each petal, or heavily veined with a darker shade on a lighter one. "Haloed" forms have recently become very popular, in which a lighter color fades to a darker in the center of the flower, or a darker to a lighter. Flower size ranges from tiny, nickel-size blooms to grandifloras as much as five inches across, with open trumpets that may be smooth around the edges, deeply lobed, or crimped or frilled to resemble doubles, which also occur in plenty. So many colors exist that many sophisticated schemes may be executed with other annuals and perennials, or with petunias alone, the most delightful being combinations of closely related colors, such as deep and apple-blossom pink, dark and pale purple, or pink and deep red.

The forms in which petunias grow have also been modified, creating plants that produce tidy mounds, that sprawl among other plants or cover the ground, or that cascade in sheets from hanging baskets and window boxes. There is no breeding trend or garden fashion that petunias do not reflect, even including the recovery of native species and heirloom or "antique" forms. Among all the other flowers displayed in the new introductions section of most seed catalogues, petunias are sure to be present. That, added to their ease of culture and their reliable bloom from June to frost, attracts both the naïve and the sophisticated gardener alike. In fact, new introductions supplant older forms with such rapidity that gardeners are often disappointed when they are unable to find even last year's love in this year's crowded catalogue. It is wise, then, not to become too attached to any single cultivar, but to keep one's heart open and play the field, for something else is always sure to come along.

The genus *Petunia* contains about forty species, all native to South America, and takes its name from the Taipei Indian word for tobacco,

PETUNIA *X* HYBRIDA *'WHITE CASCADE'*

PETUNIA INTEGRIFOLIA

petunia. Until recently, all petunias sold in America were descended from two wild progenitors, *P. axilaris* (ax-i-LAR-is) and *P. violacea* (vi-o-LAY-see-a). Both species have always been overshadowed by their remarkable descendants, to the extent that if either species is mentioned at all in general garden references, it will be dismissed as unworthy of cultivation. That attitude appears to be changing, however, for *P. axilaris,* once generally discounted as a rangy plant with small, dingy white flowers, has begun to appear in sophisticated gardens, and its blossoms have been described by the English garden writer Graham Rice as "delicately patterned with speckled streaks the color of Dijon mustard." *P. violacea,* with violet, rose-red, or magenta flowers, is still waiting in the wings, but one suspects not for long. Its color range is what generally occurs

when hybrid petunias revert to earlier forms by self-seeding over several generations in gardens. Though previously scorned by garden writers as undesirable, forms of *P. violacea* have recently been offered, some with a pedigree of more than one hundred years.

The renewed interest in species, and in simpler, smaller-flowered forms of all annuals, has also brought into prominence another pure species, *Petunia integrifolia* (in-te-gre-FO-lee-a). It is a delicately branched, half-woody perennial with sparse, linear, two-inch leaves, but for all its lightness of construction, it may sprawl over as much as three feet by summer's end, or climb upward into any other plant or bush nearby. Its freely produced, inch-wide flowers are a rich, rose red shading down to a purple so deep in their throats that it appears black. Recently, also, a white form has become available, with delicate brown penciling within each flower. Both make wonderful components of large containers of mixed annuals and perennials, as they will scramble through other plants, unifying the whole with their delicate growth. *P. integrifolia* has also recently become important in breeding, to create a new race of petunia dubbed "Supertunias," which come in many fine colors. They are all cutting-grown and are excellent for containers or hanging baskets.

But perhaps the most interesting recent development in petunias—if indeed it is one—is the little plant that travels at present under the genus name *Calibrachoa* (cal-i-bra-KO-a) and under the popular name "million bells." In a short space of five years or so, it has come to be everywhere, tumbling from hanging baskets and window boxes, creating cascades of much-branched stems with tiny, inch-long, oval leaves and abundant, half-inch-wide flowers in many pretty colors, perhaps the nicest of which blends primrose yellow and coppery gold. It is an entirely amiable

CALIBRACHOA 'TERRA COTTA'

plant, rapid of growth and tireless in its flower production, seeming always to be fresh and perky, even in the hottest weather. Some plant experts simply assume that it is a diminutive petunia and list it as *Petunia milleflora* (mi-li-FLO-ra), though its chromosome count differs from that of most hybrids. Its wiry, vinelike habit and its tiny leaves and flowers are unlike the more succulent growth and rather blowzy flowers most people think of when they imagine a petunia. If, however, they are familiar with *Petunia integrifolia,* resemblances come clearer.

Petunias are among the easiest of all annuals to grow. They are not particular as to soil, and are reasonably tolerant of drought, though they will always do their best in a moderately rich, moist but well-drained loamy earth. They prefer full sun and bloom most abundantly there, though they will accept half a day of shade and still perform well. (They will in fact grow in fairly deep shade, though they will produce little or no flower.) Petunias transplant with ease, and indeed, even half-grown plants may be relocated with a generous ball of earth, provided the work is done on a cloudy day and they are well watered. They are therefore convenient for "dropping in," the practice of keeping plants in

reserve to fill gaps in the border left when early-flowering plants are done. Petunias will develop well without supplementary fertilizer, though they respond dramatically to monthly applications of a water-soluble fertilizer rich in phosphorus and potassium.

Petunias withstand heat very well, though in the height of summer they may produce fewer flowers and plants may begin to look tired. At that point, they may be sheared back by about a third, fed, and watered well to produce a reliable second flush. Bloom time is from late June even through the first light frosts, and though gardeners once believed that spent flowers should always be removed, it is not really necessary with newer hybrids. That is a good thing, as it happens, for all parts of the plant are covered with a sticky, clammy down that many people find extremely unpleasant to touch.

Given the ease with which petunias grow in the garden, it must still be said that they are among the most difficult plants for the home gardener to raise from seed. For one thing the seed is dust-fine, and one sneeze while holding it in the palm of the hand will disperse the whole crop. Experienced gardeners resort to mixing the seed with three or four teaspoons of fine dry sand sold as "canary gravel" in pet stores. The compost to be seeded should be very free draining, well moistened, and moderately dry before the seed is sprinkled across it. Its surface should also be pressed down lightly with a board, so that it has no crevices or pockets in which the tiny seed might become lost. After seeding, the soil is pressed down lightly again, but no soil is added over the seed, which will germinate best on top of the ground.

The seed pan should be covered with a pane of glass or plastic wrap, and then with a sheet of brown paper, and kept at temperatures around 70°F. When the young seedlings first germinate, it is helpful to sprinkle them very lightly with sifted compost or dry sand. They should be transplanted after the first set of true leaves develops and then grown on in cooler temperatures of 45°F or so, to produce sturdy, stocky young plants. Pinching out the top growth when plants reach about five inches tall encourages bushiness. At all times, seedlings are extremely prone to the fungus diseases called "damping off," and so they should always be watered from the bottom by standing the seed flat in a pan of water, and the environment in which the seedlings grow should be kept well ventilated. After germination and until they are ready for transplanting, young plants should be sprayed weekly with a fungicide specially formulated for use on seedlings.

All this is often more than most home gardeners can face, and so it is fortunate that forms and colors of petunias exist in greater variety as offerings at the garden center than any other plant grown as an annual. There is also the possibility of preserving and increasing one's stock through cuttings, which is sometimes the only way of being sure that a particularly loved form will be back in the garden the following year, as good varieties are supplanted by better ones—or at least newer ones—with incredible rapidity. Cuttings should be taken during the summer and inserted in an airy, free-draining compost, kept lightly shaded and moist until there is evidence of new growth, or until a cutting resists when tugged at gently. After roots are formed, the cuttings should be potted up in small, three-inch pots, and moved to six-inch pots after they have filled the first pot with roots. Once securely rooted, they should be grown on in sunny conditions and fertilized lightly. They should be brought into the house, greenhouse, or heated sun porch about two weeks before frost is anticipated, where they will often bloom sparingly through the winter. In spring they will serve as stock plants, from which additional cuttings may be taken for the summer garden.

Petunias are perhaps without parallel for use in pots, hanging baskets, containers, and window boxes. Some gardeners would say that is the best use for them, since in cool, wet weather they can be very depressing in open beds. The delicate flowers, spotted and shredded by rainfall, crumple up like used Kleenex, while the viscous leaves seem positively to attract mud to their surfaces. The worst are the *P. grandifloras,* and positively hopeless are the fully double forms with golf-ball-size flowers packed as full of petals as a carnation. They soak up moisture until they collapse. Better for open beds are the *multifloras,* but breeders have created cultivars that show progressively more resistance to weather, the Storm Series being one of the best to date.

What breeders have not given petunias, or rather, not given back to them, is fragrance. For many of the older forms were sweetly scented—always most apparent in the evening after a hot day. Among modern varieties, those with white or pale mauve flowers seem to have been left some scent, but the capacity is resident in the genes and is very apparent in heirloom varieties. Perhaps it will come back to modern hybrids soon.

PETUNIA *X* HYBRIDA

PHACELIA SPECIES

FAMILY: *Hydrophyllaceae* or waterleaf family.

CLASSIFICATION: Half-hardy or hardy annual.

COMMON NAMES: California bluebells, desert bluebells, gentianette, phacelia.

HARDINESS: Withstand very light frosts once established.

GROWING CONDITIONS: Moist, open, water-retentive, well-drained soil. Full sun.

PROPAGATION: By seed, sown in very early spring.

HEIGHT: To 12′.

ORNAMENTAL VALUE: Grown for flower.

LEVEL OF CULTURAL DIFFICULTY: Difficult outside native range.

SPECIAL PROPERTIES: None.

PRONUNCIATION: fa-CEE-lee-a

*A*ny gardener who sees a picture of *Phacelia campanularia* (cam-pan-yew-LA-ree-a) will want to grow it, for its inch-wide, cup-shaped flowers are of the purest gentian blue, made even more irresistible by five prominent sterile anther lobes that give each blossom a starry, almost animated look. The flowers nestle in loose, one-sided racemes that begin by being curled, then unwind gradually as each flower opens. (*Phacelia,* from ancient Greek *phakelos,* signifying a parcel or bundle, is a clumsy attempt to express this phenomenon.) Flowers stand well above the leaves, which are themselves very beautiful, consisting of delicately notched little fans that appear wrinkled because of their deep veining, and are dark green, though in some lights they have a purple sheen caused by a thick covering of velvetlike down. Like most members of the family Hydrophyllaceae, stems and leaves are succulent and if crushed emit a fresh, piney fragrance, though in some people, contact can cause skin rashes. The picture one generally sees of *Phacelia campanularia* shows it as a full, dense plant with many flowers, creating an effect that could only be described as "rich."

Alas, however, like so many splendid wild flowers native to California, *Phacelia campanularia* can be very difficult to grow well. Though always associated with California, it has a wider range, from the high deserts of Colorado to the Mojave, where it flowers in March or April, triggered by spring rains that fall briefly before aridity returns. One should not assume from its native habitat, however, that phacelia would flourish in a hot, dry garden, for during its brief life of a month or two, it enjoys moist but extremely well-drained soils, and also the cool that prevails in the desert at night in early spring. Gardeners who live in areas where spring nights are cool but days are mild and sunny may have a very easy time, but where heavy soils and wet and overcast days prevail, it will almost certainly be a disappointment. Nevertheless, its beauty is so great that one should always try.

Like many other annuals native to California and the Southwest, phacelia is also extremely impatient of transplanting. It produces a carrotlike, white taproot with minute root hairs, and any disturbance whatsoever will stunt the plant or cause it to die outright. Fortunately, there is no reason to start it early, or even to purchase it in plastic six-packs, for it grows extremely rapidly into a lax bush from eight to twelve inches tall, blooming six to eight weeks from germination, and so, from a sowing in mid-April, flowers may be had in mid-June and should continue for about a month thereafter. The plant is very light of growth, and so it may be seeded among clumps of emerging perennials. However, wherever phacelia grows very well, it is worth making successive sowings of seed at monthly intervals until August, in order to have the magic of its blue somewhere in the garden. There is also a pure white form, variety *alba,* but it can hardly compete with the blue.

Phacelia campanularia takes its species name from Latin *campana,* a bell, and is descriptive of its five-lobed petals fused into an up-facing cup, much like those of campanulas. It is by no means the only member of its genus of approximately 150 species that is worth growing, though it is considered the loveliest. *P. parryii* (PA-ree-ee), named for Charles Christopher Parry (1823–1890), an American botanical explorer, closely resembles it, though its flowers are nearer to lavender than to blue. Other species of phacelia are also sometimes offered, but they will be of more interest to wildflower enthusiasts than to other gardeners.

One other phacelia does deserve mention, however, not so much for its beauty, though it is pretty enough, but for its utility. *Phacelia tanacetifolia* (ta-na-see-TI-fo-lee-a), also a native of California, is a much taller plant, to three feet or slightly more, with tansylike, ferny foliage of dark green covered over with tiny, stiff bristles. It is popularly called "fiddleneck phacelia" from its curious clusters of flower composed of three racemes, each curled like the emerging fronds of fern. They are modestly showy, not for their petals, which are quite small, but for their fringy, lavender-colored anthers. The plant is very popular as a green manure to improve poor ground, where it is grown to maturity and then plowed into the soil just as the flowers appear. But it is also among the most valuable of bee plants, since it is rich in nectar, and the honey produced is of a very high quality. It is also very attractive to aphids, as indeed are all phacelias, and so organic gardeners sometimes plant it among vegetables in rows as a magnet for those insects and as an encouragement to populations of hover fly, which feed on them. It is much easier to grow than *Phacelia campanularia,* will accept even fairly heavy soils, and is often included in general seed mixes for annual wildflower meadows.

PHASEOLUS COCCINEUS

FAMILY: *Fabaceae* or bean family.

CLASSIFICATION: Tender perennial vine grown as tender annual vine.

COMMON NAMES: Scarlet runner bean, phaseolus coccineus.

HARDINESS: Sensitive to frost.

GROWING CONDITIONS: Humus-rich, deep, well-drained soil. Full sun.

PROPAGATION: By seed, sown in spring after weather settles.

HEIGHT: Vining to 10' in a single season.

ORNAMENTAL VALUE: Grown as flowering vine.

LEVEL OF CULTURAL DIFFICULTY: Easy.

SPECIAL PROPERTIES: Very young pods eaten as green beans.

PRONUNCIATION: fa-see-O-lus co-CHIN-ee-us

The current fashion for growing vegetables among flowers is not new. It represents a return to the practice common in old-fashioned gardens of growing everything all together. A few bright red zinnias or orange calendulas, some tall magenta cosmos, or a patch of marigolds were often considered as important a part of the vegetable garden as tomatoes or carrots. They dressed up the plot and made things cheerful as the gardener went about his work. There was always something to pick for visitors, or on Sunday.

Scarlet runner beans were always prominent in such plots, either as vegetables or as flowers. Most American gardeners have never quite made up their minds, though people certainly have eaten them for a long time. It appears that *Phase-*

olus coccineus was the bean that filled the granaries of the Aztecs. The first English colonists sent it home, where it rapidly became a popular table vegetable, and by the end of the seventeenth century it had been bred into a form with flowers half-white and half-red called 'Painted Lady'. From England it crossed to Holland, where an all-white flower called 'White Dutch Runner' or 'Dutch Case Knife Bean' was developed.

Scarlet runner beans are extremely free-flowering, bearing quantities of eight-inch-long stems furnished with inch-wide, translucent bean flowers of an unusually clear scarlet from late June until frost. On each flowering stem a few beans are borne, and if not taken when they are quite small (at which point they are delicious) they will develop into monster pods, sometimes a foot and a half long, covered with fine silver fur and swollen where the seeds are forming. The vines are handsome in themselves, able to scale a ten-foot pole or tripod by high summer and richly dressed with eight-inch-wide leaves divided into three lobes. Their fresh green color is the perfect foil for the scarlet blossoms that protrude showily among them. And though the fine scarlet of the typical form is among the best of garden colors, the white and warm pink blossoms of the cultivar 'Painted Lady' are also beautiful, and the two are stunning when grown together.

In old country gardens, the beauty of *Phaseolus coccineus* has always caused it to be liberated from the vegetable garden and brought closer to the house—planted on the supports of a sunny porch or trained over a split rail fence at the back of a perennial border. But it can also hold its own in sophisticated gardens, where it may be trained on tripods or a white-painted trellis. Wherever it is grown, it brings a strong note of rural charm, a sense of freshness and spontaneity.

To many English and European vegetable gardeners, *Phaseolus coccineus* is still the table bean of choice, eaten steamed when the pods are less than three inches long, shredded when they become a little longer but are still free of fibers, or shelled and boiled when they are mature. In North America, however, public favor passed over *Phaseolus coccineus* fifty years ago in preference to the climbing form of *Phaseolus vulgaris* (vul-GAR-is), called Kentucky Wonder—which is for many gardeners *the* pole bean. (Pole beans and runner beans both do the same thing, which is climb, though "pole" is American usage and "runner" is British.) But scarlet runner beans are still grown in many American gardens, whether as vegetable or ornamental or both.

Phaseolus coccineus is no more difficult to grow than any other bean. Like all of them, it resents transplanting, and as its growth is so rapid, little is gained by starting it early indoors. The fat beans should rather be pressed directly into well-cultivated, humus-rich soil in late May or early June to a depth of about three times their thickness, each two inches or so from the other. Such spacing is far too close for good growth, but not all the beans may germinate, and slugs or birds may take their toll. If, however, many do germinate and attain their first true set of leaves, all but the strongest ones should be removed so that the young plants stand about eight inches apart. When they have formed their second set of true leaves, they will be grateful for a side-dressing of granular vegetable-garden fertilizer applied in a circle around each plant and lightly scratched in. All beans are greedy feeders, so a second application might be made when the vines have twirled two or three times around their supports.

A sturdy support should be in place when the seeds are planted, as it is difficult to put it in once the vines begin to grow. Scarlet runner beans are traditionally trained on stout tripods of woodland saplings or bamboo poles about eight feet high, a design that gives support to the heavy vines. Though the supports may seem to loom at first, they will quickly be covered and it is important not to underestimate the heft of a well-grown vine. Drenched with summer dew or rain it can pull down a flimsy contrivance of thin twine or topple a slender cane. Young vines will need some training to catch hold of the poles, and as scarlet runners twine against the movement of the sun (unusual among vines), they should be guided from right to left. It is also a good idea to tie a length of garden twine to the top of each support when the vine is halfway up, twirling it down the length of the pole and tying it at the bottom. This supplies additional surface around which vines may twine, thus avoiding the depressing experience of having the mature vine slip to the ground just as it reaches the top.

With one exception—*Vicia fava* (VI-see-a FA-va), the broad bean—all beans are of New World origin. However, the genus name *Phaseolus* derives from the ancient Greek word for fava beans, Latinized into *phaseolus*. *Coccineus* means scarlet.

PHLOX DRUMMONDII

FAMILY: *Polemoniaceae* or phlox family.

CLASSIFICATION: Half-hardy anual.

COMMON NAMES: Annual phlox, Drummond phlox, Texas pride.

HARDINESS: Resists very light frosts once established.

GROWING CONDITIONS: Humus-rich, moist, well-drained soil. Full sun in cooler gardens, light afternoon shade in warmer ones.

PROPAGATION: By seed, sown indoors 6 to 8 weeks before frost.

HEIGHT: From 6" to 1½', depending on cultivar.

ORNAMENTAL VALUE: Grown for flower.

LEVEL OF CULTURAL DIFFICULTY: Easy.

SPECIAL PROPERTIES: Excellent container and window box plant. Useful late-winter flower in cool greenhouse.

PRONUNCIATION: flox drum-ON-dee-ee

Of the species in the genus *Phlox* that are commonly grown in gardens—sixty or so—only *Phlox drummondii* is an annual, and it enjoys practically every stellar virtue a flowering plant can possess. It is very easy to grow and essentially disease free, only very rarely afflicted by the powdery mildew that so disfigures the familiar perennial phlox, *Phlox paniculata* (pa-ni-cu-LA-ta). It forms compact, bushy plants to about a foot tall, with fresh, apple green leaves and stems, and it has an unusually long period of bloom for an annual, practically smothering itself with flowers from late June until even after the first light frosts. It is excellently suited to containers and window boxes, but it is equally attractive in the mixed flower border, planted in drifts among perennials and other annuals. Best of all, however, it displays a remarkable range of flower colors—perhaps broader than that of any other plant grown as an annual except petunias and sweet peas—and the colors themselves are often hauntingly unusual, even sometimes indescribable.

Victorian and Edwardian gardeners recognized all these virtues, and at one time as many as forty distinct varieties were offered. But the number of offerings steadily declined after World War I, with the increase in labor costs, and after World War II, when gardeners began to be more and more interested in perennials, it declined further still. By 1970 or so, most seed catalogues offered only one mix of colors—two at best—and

PHLOX DRUMMONDII

both were also almost certain to include a fair amount of strong red and magenta.

The renewed interest in plants grown as annuals has done much to retrieve the fortunes of *Phlox drummondii,* but probably even more has been done by the introduction of a strong-growing strain with delectable flowers in pastel shades of cream, pale pink and coral, salmon, rose, pale yellow, tan, light purple-mauve, and white, many marked at their throats with a contrasting eye. All these shades will likely be from a single pack of seed, and enough will be scented that a gentle fragrance will hang over them all. This cultivar has been engagingly named 'Phlox of Sheep', perhaps in acknowledgment of the gentleness of its colors, and it has come to be almost indispensable in the summer garden. It has been followed by other forms, in brighter, bolder colors, or with flowers uniformly shading from rose pink to white at the edges, and with double, or "rose bud" forms, which are both good in the garden and superb in pots. Heights also vary, from midget forms scarcely six inches tall, through plants growing to nine inches or a foot tall, up to cultivars that may reach a foot and a half. All *P. drummondii* last well in water, but the taller forms are particularly good as cut flowers.

Phlox drummondii is an American wild flower native to the moister, cooler parts of Texas and New Mexico. The genus name comes from ancient Greek *phlox,* meaning flame, and originally describing another now unknown plant with vividly colored flowers. The species name *drummondii* commemorates Thomas Drummond (c. 1790–1831), who botanized extensively throughout North America for the English nursery firm of Veitch, and who first discovered the plant growing in south-central Texas. The color range of the native plant extends from strong pink through red to magenta, though white forms occur. Flowers consist of five rounded petals fused together to form a wheel about an inch wide. They are borne at the ends of terminal growth, in umbel-like clusters, each flower close enough to its neighbor often to overlap. In the best cultivars, the clusters of flower are so profuse that the leaves beneath are barely visible, creating an effect of great luxuriance. In cooler gardens, flowering will continue from late June until frost, particularly if spent flower clusters are pinched off. It is tedious work but worth the effort, for the effect of increased flower production is dramatic. In warmer gardens, Drummond phlox will fail by midsummer, particularly if plants are allowed to dry out at the roots, for they flourish best in moist, well-drained loamy soils. When flower production begins to fail, it is often possible to achieve a second flush of growth and flower by shearing the plants back by about a third, thus removing all ripening seed heads. But in the very hottest gardens, Drummond phlox must be treated like pansies, and enjoyed as a spring and early summer flower.

Drummond phlox has become so popular that most gardeners will acquire their plants in six-packs. Plants bloom precociously so one can select six-packs with the prettiest shades. An unusually vigorous plant, perhaps with darker leaves, will almost certainly bear flowers of hard red or magenta that should be grown singly in a six-inch pot, where it will not overpower its delicate siblings. When grown from seed, Drummond phlox should be started six to eight weeks before the last anticipated frost date. Seedlings accept transplanting only when very young, and so they should be pricked off and grown on in cell packs. Plants develop best in cool, airy conditions with nighttime temperatures between 45° and 50°F. They may also be seeded directly where they are to grow as soon as the ground may be worked and later thinned to stand about six to eight inches apart. Weekly applications of water-soluble fertilizer at half the recommended strength will both encourage bloom and extend it.

Drummond phlox makes a superb late-winter- and spring-flowering plant for the cool greenhouse or heated sun porch where nighttime temperatures may be kept just above 45°F. For this purpose, seed is sown in late August, the young plants pricked out first into cell packs, then transplanted when they are about five inches high, three to a six-inch pot. Water early in the day gives plants a chance to dry by nightfall. Diluted water-soluble fertilizer applied weekly encourages precocious and abundant flowering.

PHYGELIUS X RECTUS

FAMILY: *Scrophulariaceae* or snapdragon family.

CLASSIFICATION: Half-hardy shrub.

COMMON NAMES: Cape fuchsia, cape figwort, phygelius.

HARDINESS: Possibly root-hardy to Zone 7, on well-drained soils and with protection. Leaves withstand light frosts in cooler gardens.

GROWING CONDITIONS: Humus-rich, moisture-retentive, well-drained soils. Full sun. Light shade in warmer gardens.

PROPAGATION: By seed, sown in late February or early March. Tip cuttings of nonflowering wood taken in early summer root readily. Older plants may be divided.

HEIGHT: To 4' where top hardy. To 2' when grown as an annual.

ORNAMENTAL VALUE: Grown for flower.

LEVEL OF CULTURAL DIFFICULTY: Easy.

SPECIAL PROPERTIES: None.

PRONUNCIATION: fy-GEE-lee-us REC-tus

The great nineteenth- and early-twentieth-century English garden writer William Robinson grew phygelius in his splendid garden at Gravetye Manor, but otherwise there is little record of its cultivation until the last ten years or so, when it began to appear in nurseries specializing in rare and unusual annuals and tender plants. It is hard to know why phygelius evaded popularity so long, for it is a superb garden plant, easy and adaptable in its cultural requirements and blooming from June until well after the first

PHYGELIUS AEQUALIS *'CREAM'*

PHYGELIUS AEQUALIS *'YELLOW TRUMPET'*

warm gardens. Native to South Africa, the genus is represented by only two species, *Phygelius aequalis* (e-KWA-lis) and *P. capensis* (ka-PEN-sis). In leaf, stem, and flower, they are so similar as to seem mere variants of one species. Both are often grown as pure species, but most phygelius now offered are crosses between the two and bear the botanical name *Phygelius* X *rectus,* suggesting an erect pattern of growth as typical of the parents as of their hybrid progeny.

Where temperatures do not fall much below 32°F, phygelius retains its growth through winter, particularly in the shelter of a warm wall, and forms a branched, woody-based shrub to as much as four feet tall. As far north as New York City, it will freeze to the ground, regrowing from the roots the following spring, behaving essentially as a perennial with many ascending stems that produce bloom late in the summer. North of Zone 7 plants may still persist, but growth will be weak, and flowers will be produced late in the season or not at all. In such gardens, phygelius is best treated as an annual, bought each year as rooted cuttings or well-established plants from nurseries and garden centers and set out after all danger of frost is past.

Whether species or hybrid, *Phygelius* is usually seen as a plant with three or more ascending stems, each terminating in a one-sided panicle of flower. Flowers occur along the stem in clusters of five or more, and each consists of a long, slender, down-hanging tube about two inches long, flared at the mouth into five rounded lobes, from which prominent stamens protrude. *Phygelius aequalis* produces shorter panicles, about eight inches in length, and its flowers are typically warm pink with crimson lobes and a yellow throat, though one cultivar, 'Yellow Trumpet', bears flowers of a clear banana-yellow. The panicles of *Phygelius capensis* are longer, to as much as a foot and a half, and the flowers, which are more

light frosts. It is even almost hardy, and gardeners who grow it in the open ground as an annual may find that it reappears the following spring as far north as Zone 7 if it is sited in well-drained soil and given a little protective mulch. It is superb in pots and containers, and may be successfully carried over indoors as an attractive, winter-flowering houseplant, from which cuttings may be taken for additional outdoor flowering plants the following summer.

As is so often the case when botanical names attempt to contain cultural advice, the genus name *Phygelius* misrepresents the culture of the plant. It derives from ancient Greek *phyge,* meaning flight, and *helios,* the sun, suggesting that it would prefer full shade. In fact, however, phygelius blooms most freely in full sun to very light shade, the latter being preferred in very loosely spaced along the stem, are a vivid scarlet, but also with yellow throats. It is a more sprawling plant than *Phygelius aequalis* and is also more commonly grown, spreading by stolons to the point that where it is hardy it can be something of a nuisance.

Except for one dwarf form, 'Pink Elf', which grows compactly to slightly more than a foot tall, crosses between *Phygelius aequalis* and *P. capensis* have been made to increase the color range of the flowers more than the growth pattern of the plant, though colors still exist in a narrow range of creamy white, yellow, salmon pink, brick red, and scarlet, usually with a contrasting yellow throat. Leaves are from three to five inches long, oval to lance-shaped, of an attractive laurel green, though in cream or yellow-flowered forms the leaves are paler. Generally, almost half the height of the plant will be flower panicle, and the flowers take on color even as small elongated buds, producing an effect that is attractive for a long time, as much as a month or more. In the darker colored forms, the flowering stems are reddish purple.

Seed of *Phygelius* in either species is sometimes offered and should be started quite early, in late February or early March, for plants that will flower by midsummer. Seed germinates best in warm conditions around 65° to 70°F, and young plants should be grown on in bright light and pinched once when they reach a height of about four inches to induce branching. They may be set out when the weather is warm and settled. The usual means of increase for *Phygelius,* however, and particularly of named varieties, is by cuttings, divisions, or rooted suckers. Tip cuttings are best taken in spring before flowering is initiated, much as one would with fuchsias. They require no special conditions beyond being inserted in half peat, half sharp sand or perlite, and kept moist and shaded until rooting

occurs. Often, young shoots or suckers will have formed roots near the base of the plants and may be taken as "Irish cuttings," with a bit of root attached, potted up, and grown on in shaded conditions until new growth is apparent. This method is easiest.

Though popularly called "cape fuchsia," *Phygelius* is unrelated to that genus, though it responds best to exactly the same conditions that fuchsias prefer. It is native to damp slopes and stream-sides in South Africa but is intolerant of heavy, poorly drained, or waterlogged soil. It prefers an evenly moist, humus-rich loam, though established plants will endure short periods of drought. It is very responsive to water-soluble fertilizers, particularly when grown in pots or containers. Except where it is hardy and

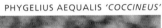

PHYGELIUS AEQUALIS *'COCCINEUS'*

becomes a small shrub, trimming or pruning is seldom necessary. Plants may be lifted two or three weeks before frost is anticipated, cut back to within six inches of soil level, potted up, and brought indoors for winter.

PLATYSTEMON CALIFORNICUS

FAMILY: *Papaveraceae* or poppy family.

CLASSIFICATION: Half-hardy to hardy annual.

COMMON NAMES: Cream cups, platystemon.

HARDINESS: Withstands light frosts once established.

GROWING CONDITIONS: Moderately fertile, light, perfectly drained soil.

PROPAGATION: From seed, sown in place in autumn in warmer gardens, in very early spring in cooler ones.

HEIGHT: To 1'.

ORNAMENTAL VALUE: Grown for flower.

LEVEL OF CULTURAL DIFFICULTY: Easy within natural range. Moderately difficult elsewhere.

SPECIAL PROPERTIES: None.

PRONUNCIATION: pla-ti-STEY-mon cal-i-FOR-ni-cus

*A*nnuals with relatively brief periods of flower have not been popular with most American gardeners, who have traditionally craved the "full summer of bloom" offered by petunias, impatiens, marigolds, zinnias, and the like. The present enthusiasm for annuals has somewhat altered that attitude, however, creating interest in plants that offer as little as three weeks to a month of flower, but which are so beautiful that they make their own argument for being grown. Usually they are small, not more than twelve or so inches high, and they mature quickly from seed to flower in late spring and early summer. Their delicate leaves and stems suit them for growing among other annuals or hardy perennials, for they do not crowd out their neighbors, and when they finish flowering they leave no unsightly gaps.

Among this group of plants, which might be called "annual ephemerals," no part of the world offers greater riches than the western and southwestern parts of the United States. *Platystemon californicus,* the California cream cup, is among the most beautiful and also among the easiest to grow. It is the single species in its genus, *Platystemon,* which takes its name from ancient Greek *platys,* meaning broad, and *stemon,* stamen, alluding to the thickened and flattened stamens in the center of the flower. Though its species name means of California, it has a much broader range, occurring from southern Oregon to western Colorado, Utah, Arizona, and south to Baja California. Where it grows naturally, it may colonize whole acres of thin, sandy soil, blooming from February through early June, depending on location.

Platystemon californicus is a true annual, producing a densely tufted little bush seldom more than a foot tall. Its narrow, gray-green, two-inch-long leaves cluster thickly at the base of the plant, above which the flowers stand up singly on stiff, wiry stems. Both leaves and stems are covered with short bristly hairs. The flowers are about an inch wide, consisting of six oval petals rounded at their ends and slightly concave, like tiny sea shells. They occur in two groups of three, one above and one below, alternating to very charming effect. In the center of the petals is a thick boss of stamens, some flattened to resemble additional petals and giving the flower an almost double appearance. The species is highly variable in the color of its flowers, one geographic population differing from another. Flowers may be an even, pale creamy yellow, often with a prominent, bright yellow spot at the base of each petal or the darker color may occur at the tips of petals and even sometimes be replaced by markings of pink or green. The hardiness of the plant probably also varies according to location, a fact that would be relevant to gardeners, since seed collected in colder areas might prove to be seed-hardy in colder gardens. Most seed presently available, however, is field-grown from seed collected in California, and so the plant is treated as a half-hardy annual.

Like almost all members of the poppy family, Papaveraceae, platystemon is difficult to transplant and so is usually sown in place where it will bloom. In milder gardens it may be sown in the fall, but elsewhere it is best sown in the spring, on cultivated patches raked smooth and leveled by being pressed slightly with a board. The seed is very fine and should not be sown too thickly, as plants must later be thinned to stand about four inches, one from another. As with other poppy-like plants, it is helpful to mix the seed with two or three teaspoons of fine dry sand, such as canary gravel, sprinkling the mixture across the soil with a salt shaker. Soils may be of ordinary fertility, but they should be very light and free draining, which may require mixing in liberal quantities of sand. Plants develop very quickly after germination, usually flowering about six weeks from their first appearance as tiny seedlings. They bloom best in cool, bright weather, and will begin to wither away when the settled heat of summer arrives. In areas that enjoy long springs and cool early summers, flowering may be prolonged by removing spent flowers before they set seed.

Platystemon californicus is only rarely offered by major seed firms, and so seed must be secured from small companies that specialize in western native wild flowers.

PLECTOSTACHYS SERPYLLIFOLIA

FAMILY: *Asteraceae* or aster or daisy family.

CLASSIFICATION: Tender perennials grown as half-hardy annuals.

COMMON NAMES: Dwarf helichrysum, dwarf licorice plant, plectostachys.

HARDINESS: Damaged by frost.

GROWING CONDITIONS: Any well-drained soil.

PROPAGATION: From cuttings, which root easily at any time.

HEIGHT: To 1 to 3' with support of other plants.

ORNAMENTAL VALUE: Grown for silvery leaves and scandent growth.

LEVEL OF CULTURAL DIFFICULTY: Easy.

SPECIAL PROPERTIES: None.

PRONUNCIATION: plec-to-STA-chis ser-pie-li-FO-lee-a (ser-pi-li-FO-lee-a)

The identity of plectostachys has been confused with that of *Helichrysum petiolare* (he-lee-KRI-sum pey-tee-o-LA-ray) for so long that garden references to it are very scarce. Superficially, it much resembles the popular *H. petiolare,* for both have silvery gray stems and leaves, both produce vigorous, procumbent growth, and both are valuable in containers and window boxes to soften the edges of the planting and also to provide a contrasting note of silver. Nevertheless, they are only distantly related within the vast daisy family, the Asteraceae.

Plectostachys is an extremely easy plant to grow. It seems indifferent to soil quality, accepting thin, dry, sandy soil and moist, humus-rich soil alike, though perfect drainage is always required. It prefers full sun but will put up with half a day of shade, so long as its foliage is able to dry off between waterings or rainfalls, for it is quick to rot if moisture is trapped in its dense mat of growth. On its own, a single plant will scarcely reach a foot in height, its stems overlaying themselves in a kind of hummock, with others crawling outward to start new colonies. If, however, it finds the support of other plants, some of its stems will weave gracefully in and out, climbing up to three feet. Both the creeping and the scrambling capacities of plectostachys make it very valuable for containers of mixed annuals and tender perennials because its scandent ways can knit a composition together while it also tumbles outward to soften edges. Plectostachys loves the heat of summer and grows the fastest when daytime temperatures climb toward 100°F. Like most downy, silver-leaved plants, it is resistant to drought, though if it is allowed to remain bone dry in a container for any significant length of time, its foliage will crisp and the plant will be disfigured. Its small clusters of pinkish-white daisy flowers are seldom produced in most American gardens, but they would most charitably be described as unshowy.

Seed is never available for plectostachys, and plants offered in nurseries and garden centers are all cutting-grown. Cuttings root easily at any time of the year, though care must be taken to keep the medium in which they are inserted evenly moist while never allowing moisture to remain on the foliage. Sensitive to frost, plectostachys is even discouraged by dank, cold weather. Young plants should therefore be held in a sunny windowsill or in the greenhouse until the weather is settled and warm. Easy to overwinter, plants readily accept the warm, dry conditions of most American homes and thus make excellent houseplants, provided they may be given some sun. Cuttings should be taken in August, potted up when they are well rooted, and pinched repeatedly to develop compact, bushy plants. Alternatively, plants established in the garden may be cut back severely, potted up, and brought indoors before first frosts have blackened their foliage.

Plectostachys serpyllifolia, a native of South Africa, is the only species in its genus under cultivation. Its botanical name seems applicable to no part of the plant—the genus designation *Plectostachys* derives from ancient Greek *plectos,* meaning braided or twisted, and *stachys,* an ear of wheat. The species name *serphyllifolia* compares the leaves of the plant to *Thymus serphyllum,* the mother-of-thyme often grown in cracks of paving or among rocks, but the two plants resemble each other only in their downy, silvery leaves. Those of *Thymus serphyllum* are minute, hardly an eighth of an inch in length, and are borne on wiry stems completely unlike the somewhat juicy, downy stems of plectostachys.

PLECTRANTHUS SPECIES

FAMILY: *Lamiaceae* (*Labiatae*) or mint family.

CLASSIFICATION: Tender perennials or sub-shrubs grown as tender annuals.

COMMON NAME: Plectranthus (other popular names vary with species).

HARDINESS: Sensitive to light frosts.

GROWING CONDITIONS: Humus-rich, fibrous, moisture-retentive, well-drained soil. Full sun in cooler gardens, part shade in warmer ones.

PROPAGATION: From seed, sown indoors 6 to 8 weeks before last frost. Nonflowering tip cuttings root readily at any time.

HEIGHT: To 4′ in upright-growing species; to 2′ in length in procumbent species.

ORNAMENTAL VALUE: Grown for foliage. Some
    species attractive in flower.
LEVEL OF CULTURAL DIFFICULTY: Easy.
SPECIAL PROPERTIES: Procumbent species excellent
    in hanging baskets and window boxes. All
    species adaptable as winter houseplants.
PRONUNCIATION: plek-TRAN-thus

As late as 1964, in his magnificent fourteen-volume *New Illustrated Encyclopedia of Gardening,* T. H. Everett summarized the genus *Plectranthus* by saying, "Those cultivated are grown chiefly in greenhouses and one or two as window-garden plants." He treats only three species, one of which, *Plectranthus oertendahlii* (or-ten-DAH-lee-ee), is probably the original Swedish ivy, an easily grown houseplant popular in the 1950s. But the genus contains more than 350 species distributed throughout the Old World tropics, Australia, and the Pacific Islands, a welter of which have proven to be not only good greenhouse and parlor plants but also excellent tender perennials for the summer garden. Plectranthus are generally grown for the beauty of their leaves, with many interestingly veined or variegated sorts, often with purple or mauve on the reverse of the leaf and the square stem typical of Lamiaceae (Labiatae), the mint family. Many emit a sweet, piney, or citrus odor when their leaves are crushed, and their flowers, generally borne in late summer, are also typically mintlike, consisting of small, two-lipped tubes borne on slender racemes of terminal growth. Though most are modest from a distance, they are attractive once one gets close to them. All willingly accept part shade.

At present, more than twenty species of plectranthus are in cultivation, with the promise that even more, with selected varieties and hybrids, will soon be offered. But though they are diverse in appearance, their cultural requirements are the same. They relish rich, fibrous soil that is moist but well drained, and they are extremely responsive to applications of diluted liquid fertilizer at two-week intervals throughout the growing season. In cool gardens, they will thrive in full sun, though they are also useful in part shade, which they prefer where summers are hot. If they are exposed to more sun than they like, the edges of the leaves will turn brown, and the plant may defoliate. Their growth is very rapid, attaining in the upright species a bushy height of three feet or so in a summer, and in the procumbent species, a length spreading or cascading to two feet or more.

The usual means of increase for all plectranthus is cuttings, taken of tip growth at almost any time, but preferably in early to midsummer when plants are growing most vigorously and have not yet initiated flower. Cuttings root with absurd ease in sand and peat, loose open soil, or even a glass of water on the windowsill. Seed is seldom offered, and when it is available, it is apt to come in mixes of several species, the varied results of which might be fun for only the botanically minded gardener, who will enjoy identifying them all. Seed should be sown six to eight weeks before the last anticipated frosts. It germinates most readily at fairly high temperatures, 65° to 70°F, and seedlings transplant easily and grow on vigorously in bright light at nighttime temperatures no lower than 55°F. Pinching encourages bushiness.

Some species, such as *Plectranthus oertendahlii,* may produce flower more or less continuously, though most species wait until late summer or early autumn to bloom. Plants may be dug and cut back severely before frost, potted up, and regrown as attractive houseplants. But as cuttings root so readily, it is often better to establish small, cutting-grown plants in August, taking

PLECTRANTHUS ARGENTATUS

more cuttings in spring for use in the summer garden. All plectranthus are sensitive to cold, suffering severely or dying outright when touched by frost, and so should not be established in the garden until temperatures are warm and settled.

Plectranthus amboinicus (am-BOY-ni-cus) is perhaps the species most frequently grown, not only for ornamental but also for culinary purposes. A native of the island of Amboinia in East Indonesia, it was brought from Spain to the New World, where it became an ingredient in Caribbean island cooking and in Mexico, as its popular names "Mexican basil" and "Cuban oregano" attest. It grows as a lax, spreading plant, thickly furnished with felty, rounded, succulent leaves attractively scalloped on their edges. Though the all-green form is pretty enough, it has largely been superseded by variegated forms, such as 'Goldheart', with a yellow blaze in the center of each leaf; 'Green Gold', with pale green leaves edged with cream and gold; and 'Spanish Thyme', with leaves irregularly splashed with gray and white. Though it is employed, along with other creeping plectranthus, as a groundcover in areas of southern California or Florida, elsewhere it is most attractive as a hanging basket or container plant, where its stems may reach two feet in length in a single summer.

Several species of plectranthus have been popular houseplants, all under the name "Swedish ivy," and are now also frequently used in hanging baskets or containers. *Plectranthus oertendahlii* was perhaps the first to be cultivated, with trailing growth to as much as three feet, purple stems and two-inch-long, almost perfectly round, dark green leaves, attractively netted with silver veins, purple and downy on their underside. It is also called "candle plant," from its abundantly produced racemes of foamy white flowers that stand well above the foliage. Another Swedish ivy is *Plectranthus australis* (aus-TRA-lis), a plant that begins by being upright and becomes procumbent as it develops, with shiny, dark green leaves, each up to two inches across and heavily scalloped along their margins. It is most frequently grown in the variegated form, with leaves attractively margined in white. A third Swedish ivy is *Plectranthus madagascariensis* (ma-da-gas-car-EE-en-sis), also usually grown in the smaller-leaved, variegated form 'Minimus Variegatus'. It is a delicate, trailing plant with small, inch-wide leaves, heavily veined and crinkled, margined in white and covered with tiny white bristles. Its leaves, when crushed or bruised, emit a clean, mint fragrance.

Other species of plectranthus, while not precisely creeping or ivylike, reach a height of about a foot and then spread outward by lateral growth, rapidly attaining a width of as much as three feet. *Plectranthus coleoides* (co-lee-OY-des), now correctly *P. forsteri* (FOR-ste-rie), also usually grown in its variegated form, 'Marginatus', bears two- to four-inch-long leaves attractively scalloped along their edges and lightly citrus scented when crushed. The plant is extremely fast growing, even for a plectranthus, and so is useful as filler among other plants, particularly in part shade. It may also be trained as a standard, grown on a single stem to three or four feet, and then pinched frequently to create a mop of down-hanging stems. *Plectranthus ciliatus* (cil-i-A-tus) is a shrubby, densely branched plant with oval, pointed, two- to three-inch-long leaves, toothed along their margins and deeply veined. The stems and the undersides of the leaves are a deep, mulberry red, and in late summer, attractive, two-lipped mauve flowers, each about half an inch long, are produced from purple panicles that stand well above the leaves. *Plectranthus fruticosus* (froo-ti-CO-sus) might be grown especially for its flowers, which are produced thickly in long, upright panicles in late summer, colored a pale mauve spotted over with purple, and measuring almost half an inch across. It attains a height of about four feet, with purple stems and large leaves up to seven inches long with rose-pink undersides.

Though most plectranthus bear green leaves, often with cream or pale yellow or with tints of purple or mauve on their stems and the undersides of their leaves, *Plectranthus argentatus* (ar-GEN-ta-tus) is silver all over. It forms a strong, upright, shrublike plant to as much as four feet tall in a single summer, with two- to four-inch-long, oval, pointed leaves, toothed along their margins and covered with fine down that makes them velvety to the touch. Six- to eight-inch-long, upright panicles bloom toward the end of summer, with pale, mauvish-pink flowers. In bloom, the plant takes on a somewhat ragged appearance, especially when seen from a distance, and so flower buds might be pinched out as soon as they form. Pinching also will make more compact plants. Still, *Plectranthus argentatus* is a valuable plant, alone among annuals and tender perennials with silver foliage in accepting part shade.

PLUMBAGO AURICULATA

FAMILY: *Plumbaginaceae* or plumbago family.

CLASSIFICATION: Tender scandent shrub grown as tender annual.

COMMON NAMES: Leadwort, plumbago.

HARDINESS: Sensitive to light frosts.

GROWING CONDITIONS: Fertile, well-drained, dryish soils. Full sun.

PROPAGATION: From cuttings taken from nonflowering shoots in spring or early summer.

HEIGHT: To 8' or more with support; to 3' when grown alone.

ORNAMENTAL VALUE: Valued for flower.

LEVEL OF CULTURAL DIFFICULTY: Moderately easy.

SPECIAL PROPERTIES: Drought tolerant once established.

PRONUNCIATION: plum-BA-go au-ri-kew-LA-ta

*I*t is difficult to believe that so cool and beautiful a plant as plumbago is native to hot, dry areas of South Africa, but such is the case. There, it colonizes large expanses of waste land, blooming profusely during the Southern Hemisphere summer—from November to May—and sporadically at other times of the year. Its old species name, *capensis,* meaning of the Cape of Good Hope, designates its origin, though that name has been superseded by the much less imaginative *auriculata,* ear-shaped, presumably descriptive of its oval leaves. However it is called, it is one of the loveliest flowers that may be grown in North American gardens, where it will be in bloom from the time young plants are first set out until frost, growing most luxuriously and flowering most abundantly in the hottest part of the summer.

Plumbago auriculata is the signature genus of its family, the Plumbaginaceae, and takes its curious

PLUMBAGO AURICULATA

by leaning on and weaving among other plants for support. As a plant for northern gardens, however, it may be expected to make about three feet of bushy growth in a summer, whether in the open ground or in a container. Its two- to three-inch-long leaves, borne alternately along the stems, are quite attractive, consisting of thin-textured ovals of a bright clear green. They make an excellent foil to the flowers, which are borne at the ends of stems in loose clusters of up to twenty blossoms. Each consists of a narrow tube an inch and a half long, flaring out into five oval petals to produce a flower about three-quarters inch across. The clusters of bloom are often compared to those of phlox, which the individual flowers also resemble, though their color is beyond compare, even to phlox, for it is typically a beautiful, limpid Wedgewood blue of a shade rare in any flower. For a plant dispersed naturally over so wide an area, it is surprising that there are few color variants. Cultivars do exist that are a slightly deeper blue, often with a streak of violet down the center of each petal that intensifies their color. There is also a white form, var. *alba,* that occurs in the wild and is crisp and pure, once a rival to the typical blue, though not to be mixed with it, because it creates from a distance a faded, washed-out effect.

Plumbago auriculata, for all the rarity of its beauty, is a very easy plant to grow. Seed is never offered, but young, cutting-grown plants are often available at nurseries and garden centers that specialize in unusual annuals and tender plants. They will generally be offered singly in five-inch pots as loosely branched plants about a foot tall, usually already sporting panicles of bloom. Plumbago is very frost sensitive, however, and also dislikes dank, cool weather. So young plants should be held on a sunny windowsill or in a greenhouse with a minimum nighttime temperature around 50°F until the

name from the Latin word for lead, *plumbum,* because of the supposed capacities of some species to cure lead poisoning. Its only popular name, "lead-wort," derives from the same belief. The twelve or so members of the genus are all tropical tender plants, and *Plumbago auriculata* is the only one much cultivated in gardens beyond Zones 9 and 10, where it is hardy. It is also deeply associated with Mediterranean gardens, where its tumble of growth and flower are as ubiquitous as pelargoniums, leading many tourists who see it there to cultivate a pot or two at home, just for the memory.

Plumbago auriculata grows naturally as a scandent shrub, throwing its woody stems up and out to form dense, rounded masses about eight feet tall, though when it finds support it can ascend to fifteen feet or more, not so much by climbing as weather is warm and settled. They may then be planted in the open border, where they look especially fine with almost any perennial or annual plant, or they may be grown in containers, either alone or as a component of a mixed composition.

Plumbago auriculata will accept a half day of shade, particularly in very warm gardens, but it flourishes best in as much sun and warmth as it can receive. It is therefore an excellent choice for south-facing window boxes, where its scandent growth will gracefully tumble downward. It is not overly particular about soil quality, though when grown in a container, it will perform best in a humus-rich, free-draining compost. As its provenance indicates, it is very tolerant of drought, though when it is grown in a pot or other container, one should always remember that the soil will both dry out and heat up much more quickly than in the open ground, which is always relatively cooler than the air and contains some residual moisture even in periods of drought. Plumbago should therefore never be allowed to dry out completely, though a slightly longer interval between waterings than one allows most plants, particularly in containers, will produce healthier leaf and flower. It is very intolerant of poorly drained or waterlogged soil, which at the least slows down flower production and at the worst produces root rot that quickly becomes fatal. Heavy soils should therefore be lightened by incorporating copious amounts of sand, and containers should be well crocked to facilitate rapid drainage. Maximum bloom may be encouraged by applications of water-soluble fertilizers fabricated for tomatoes and potatoes, according to the instructions on the box.

Plumbago is a tender woody shrub that is very easy to carry over the winter for an additional show of bloom the following year. In fact, when its needs for sun and warmth can be met, it will continue to flower attractively as an indoor houseplant throughout the winter. For this purpose, plants should be lifted in mid- to late August, cut back lightly, and potted in rich, free-draining compost. They should be shaded until growth resumes, which will indicate the formation of vigorous roots. They may then be placed in part or full sun, watered carefully, and fed with water-soluble fertilizer. Before frost, they should be moved indoors to a sunny windowsill, a heated sun porch, or a greenhouse with nighttime temperatures between 45 and 50°F. If kept slightly dry between waterings, they should flower modestly all winter. In late February or early March, they should be cut back hard to encourage fresh new growth that will flower the following summer. In this way, quite large plants, four or more feet tall, can be obtained for use in the summer border.

Cuttings taken in spring or early summer also root quite easily. They should be about three inches long, taken from vigorous side shoots that have not formed flower buds. The cuttings should be inserted in peat and perlite, or peat and sharp sand, and kept shaded and moist until roots form. They may then be potted up singly, and when they resume growth, they should be placed in the brightest possible conditions and pinched regularly to form stocky, compact plants for winter and for use later in the summer garden.

PORTULACA GRANDIFLORA

FAMILY: *Portulacaceae* or purslane family.

CLASSIFICATION: Half-hardy annual.

COMMON NAMES: Rock rose, rose moss, flowering purslane, wax plant, sun moss, sun rose, sun plant, eleven o'clock, portulaca.

HARDINESS: Withstands light frosts once established.

GROWING CONDITIONS: Dry, sandy, moderately fertile to poor soils. Full sun. Heat.

PROPAGATION: By seed, sown indoors in peat pots 6 to 8 weeks before last frost. By cuttings of choice varieties, which root readily.

HEIGHT: To 6".

ORNAMENTAL VALUE: Grown for flower.

LEVEL OF CULTURAL DIFFICULTY: Easy to moderately easy, depending on climate.

SPECIAL PROPERTIES: None.

PRONUNCIATION: por-too-LA-ca (por-choo-LA-ca) gran-di-FLO-ra

For an annual, *Portulaca grandiflora* has accumulated an unusually large number of common names, which attest to the popularity of the plant, and which, taken all together, also give a fairly accurate idea of its appearance and cultural preferences. A native of the more arid parts of Brazil, it is one of the few annuals that not only accepts dry, poor, sandy, or gravelly soil, but actually prefers it to the "moist, humus-rich loam" recommended for most annual plants. In its preferred growing conditions, the full sun it demands produces what the old gardeners called "baking conditions," a rigid preference that suits it not only for rocky or sandy banks, the edges of gravel driveways or paths, crevices in paving, and the hopelessly barren strips of earth along public sidewalks, but also for pots, containers, and window boxes, where soil may quickly dry out between waterings. Its flowers are indeed roselike, consisting of five overlapping petals and a prominent, central boss of stamens, though they have a beautiful silken sheen more reminiscent of poppies than of roses. However, put the characteristics of roses and poppies together in one blossom,

and the result will be a combination of perhaps the two most favorite flowers of gardeners the world over.

It is true that the flowers open when the sun hits them and close by noon (accounting for the curious popular name "eleven o'clock"), but that is merely a device of thrift, meant to waste no pollen on somnolent afternoon bees. That fault, if it is one, has been corrected by modern breeders, who have concentrated on producing cultivars that stay open later in the day and in cloudy weather.

The ease with which *Portulaca grandiflora* may be cultivated is best signaled by another common name, "flowering purslane," for it is first cousin to one of the peskiest weeds in North American gardens, *P. oleracea* (o-ler-A-cee-a) (common purslane), though as it happens, both are edible, and *P. grandiflora* is as excellent as common purslane when added to salads or soups.

Portulaca grandiflora is a small plant, hardly reaching six inches in height, but branching freely at ground level to produce a mat of growth as much as a foot across when it is growing happily. Its reddish-green stems and its inch-long, cylindrical, dark green leaves are succulent, adapted to storing water during periods of drought. Flowers are borne at the tips of the stems, in quick succession from early June until well into autumn where summers are bright and hot, but more sparingly in cool, damp gardens. They consist of five overlapping petals arranged in a shallow cup, at the center of which is a thick boss of orange-yellow stamens. Many modern strains are doubles, which does not mean packed with petals but signifies literally double the number of original petals to equal ten. The older varieties were as brashly colored as a Mexican paper toy, coming in scarlet, bright yellow, orange, magenta, purple, and white, and when portulaca self-seeds in a garden, which it is apt to do in conditions that suit it, these colors will occur. But modern breeders have developed a range of color lacking only true blue, and extending through white, cream, light and dark yellow, pale and rose pink, cerise, scarlet, orange, red, mauve, magenta, and purple. "Peppermint" forms exist, in which a darker color is streaked or speckled over a lighter, and one cultivar sports white flowers marked with stripes of red like a candy cane. Pastels, which may be any subtle shade of tangerine, apricot, peach, or melon, are particularly lovely, and those often have a blotch of orange at the base of each petal, adding to their beauty. There is also a magnificent, unusually large-flowered white cultivar appropriately called 'White Swan.'

Though seed of portulaca is occasionally offered in single colors, most seed packets will be "strains," in which one characteristic of another—doubling, say, or pastel shades, or the capacity to remain open throughout the day, or "pepperminting"—will characterize all, or a least most, of the plants that develop when the seed is sown. Usually, this poses no problem, for if the growth habit of plants is similar, they blend happily together, creating a pleasing crazy quilt of bright or subtle colors and shades. If, however, a particularly lovely form occurs that the gardener wishes to preserve from year to year, it is useful to know that the succulent stems root as easily as sedums when inserted into damp sand. Since portulaca will also readily accept indoor conditions on a sunny windowsill, cutting-grown plants may be carried over winter, to supply additional cuttings in spring for use in the summer garden.

Portulaca is quick of growth, flowering as soon as a month after germination if the weather is warm and settled, and so it is usually sown outdoors where it is to grow (especially if it is to grow in difficult places where the trowel cannot penetrate, such as cracks in pavement). Young plants should later be thinned to stand about six inches apart. Alternatively, seed may be started indoors about six to eight weeks before the last anticipated frost, though plants started early will never equal in beauty those sown in place. Portulaca accepts transplanting unwillingly, and so seed should be started in plastic six-packs or peat pots that will ensure a minimum of root disturbance. The seed of portulaca is very fine, and so dispersing it thriftily over the ground is most easily done by mixing it with three or so tablespoons of dry canary sand from the supermarket, perhaps using a salt shaker to spread it out evenly. Though portulaca is extremely drought tolerant at maturity, young plants benefit from irrigation in dry weather and from a light dressing of granular or water-soluble fertilizer such as is fabricated for tomatoes. Once flowering begins, however, plants are entirely self-sufficient.

The genus *Portulaca* derives its name from the ancient Greek name for garden purslane, and the species name *grandiflora* recognizes the fact that its flowers, at an inch across, are four or five times the size of those borne by purslane. The genus contains about 100 species, of which only one other, *P. umbraticola* (um-bra-TI-co-la), is grown as an annual in North American gardens, and that not until the last five years or so. It has been marketed both as a form of *P. oleracea*, called, then, "garden purslane," and also as *P. grandiflora*, though it is a distinct species, growing about six inches tall and with a spread of as much as two feet, with fat, succulent, medium green leaves about an inch long. The cultivar presently being marketed travels under the name 'Wild Fire', and bears single, inch-wide, cupped flowers of bright red, orange, hot pink, or white. Its species name is derived from Latin *umbra*, meaning shadow, and *cola*, resident of, and seems to suggest that the plant is more tolerant of shade than other portulaca. This is not in fact the case, however, for it shares the preference of other cultivated members of its genus for full sun and hot, baking conditions. *Portulaca umbraticola* develops rapidly and is apt to become a very popular plant for hanging baskets, window boxes, and other containers placed in hot, dry conditions.

REHMANNIA ELATA
(R. ANGULATA)

FAMILY: *Scrophulariaceae* or snapdragon family.

CLASSIFICATION: Half-hardy perennial grown as half-hardy annual.

COMMON NAMES: Beverly bells, Chinese foxglove, summer gloxinia, rehmannia.

HARDINESS: Hardy to Zone 7 with perfect drainage and protection. Grown as hardy annual elsewhere. Withstands light frosts.

GROWING CONDITIONS: Fertile, well-drained, moisture-retentive garden loam. Full sun in cooler gardens, part shade in warmer ones.

PROPAGATION: By division, basal cuttings, or stolons. Seed should be sown midsummer for bloom the following year.

HEIGHT: From 2 to 3'.

ORNAMENTAL VALUE: Grown for flower.

LEVEL OF CULTURAL DIFFICULTY: Moderately difficult.

SPECIAL PROPERTIES: None.

PRONUNCIATION: re-MAN-ee-a e-LA-ta (an-gu-LA-ta)

*B*otanically speaking, there is much confusion about the rehmannias, which commemorate Joseph Rehmann (1753–1831), a German physician who spent his professional life in St. Petersburg. Within the small genus of eight or nine species, two members are cultivated—*Rehmannia angulata,* the species name of which means angular and is of uncertain application, and *R. elata, elata* meaning tall. (It has been said to produce bloom stems five feet high, though no garden authority has actually seen it that tall.) Most botanists now believe that the two species are one, albeit highly variable in height, shape of flower, and flower color.

Whatever the name or the label, rehmannia are a recent and very valuable addition to the summer garden. The flowers—each a tube two to three inches long, flaring at the mouth into two lips, the upper two-lobed and the lower, three-lobed—resemble foxgloves, *Digitalis purpurea* (di-jee-TA-lis pur-PUR-ee-a), a close member in the family Scrophulariaceae. This accounts for one popular name, "Chinese foxglove," though rehmannia blooms are more widely spaced along the stems than those of foxgloves, and the stems are much more slender. Flower form varies from rather stodgy blooms with rounded lobes to quite elegant bells in which the lobes are narrow and face downward. Flower color is also highly variable, ranging from a reddish magenta with a yellow throat, marked with dark purple spots through medium to pale pink, the paler shades tending to possess throats of cream yellow with light purple spots. There is also a white form of unsurpassed elegance, 'Alba', with a cream-colored throat. From seed any of these variations may occur, though plants now offered in garden centers have been propagated vegetatively from suckers and will be of the best forms.

Several flower stems may arise from a single plant, usually to a height of two to three feet, sparsely clad with smaller leaves that reduce to little arrow-shaped, leaflike bracts where flowers are borne. The raspy leaves are oval, broad, and rather coarse, eight inches in length and four inches across, lobed on the edges, and often marked with prominent purplish-brown veins.

The rehmannia of gardens is a rather aggressive perennial plant native to stony and gravelly woodland in the temperate parts of China. Reliably

REHMANNIA ANGULATA

hardy in American gardens from Zones 8 to 10 (it may be brought through the winter in Zone 7 if it has perfect drainage and mulch), it is an easy, undemanding plant that will quickly form broad patches of ground-covering growth. Elsewhere, rehmannia is bought in spring as a well-established plant and used in the summer garden in containers, window boxes, or the open border, where it will bloom from mid-June to frost. Its identity as a true perennial causes it to blend perfectly with other hardier summer-flowering plants. It also makes a superb cut flower.

Most gardeners will acquire rehmannias in garden centers as single plants in quart pots. However, plants can be grown from seed, though seedlings will require a cool greenhouse with winter temperatures around 45°F. Seed, sown in midsummer to flower the following year, is easy to germinate, and seedlings transplant readily, though they must be potted up in free-draining soilless compost and watered carefully, as at all times of its life rehmannia resents waterlogged soil (which will occasion root rot). When pots are filled with roots, plants should be moved to larger ones, finishing with pots five or six inches across. As plants are highly variable in flower, any one that shows a particularly pretty color or flower form should be propagated vegetatively, which is easy to do in a cool greenhouse. Plants should be cut back hard, to within four inches of the basal leaf growth, which will quickly produce a number of suckers that can be taken in late summer as "Irish cuttings." Additional roots form quickly in half peat and half sharp sand or perlite, taking usually three weeks or so, after which the rooted cuttings can be potted up and grown on under cool greenhouse conditions. As rehmannias spread by underground stolons, small plants that appear at some distance from the mother may also be detached and potted up. Even a bundle of white roots scooped from the side of a plant will produce many plantlets over the winter if kept at about 45°F and watered carefully. Finally, just after frost has blackened their growth, whole plants may be lifted as "stools," with as much earth as clings about them, packed into boxes filled with barely damp peat moss, sand, or perlite, and stored in dark, frost-free but very cool conditions for replanting the following spring.

When in active growth, rehmannia are very responsive to water-soluble fertilizers applied according to the manufacturer's directions. They flourish outdoors in fertile, well-drained soil, with plenty of moisture at their roots, but always with perfect drainage. In northern gardens they may be grown in full sun, though where summers are hot, part shade suits them better.

RESEDA ODORATA

FAMILY: *Resedaceae* or mignonette family.

CLASSIFICATION: Half-hardy annual.

COMMON NAMES: Mignonette, sweet mignonette, reseda.

HARDINESS: Young plants resent frost.

GROWING CONDITIONS: Rich, well-drained, moisture-retentive garden loam. Full sun in cooler gardens, afternoon shade in warmer ones.

PROPAGATION: From seed, sown in place in early spring. Seed may be started indoors in peat pots 6 weeks before last frost. Seedlings resent root disturbance.

HEIGHT: From 1 to 2', depending on culture.

ORNAMENTAL VALUE: Little.

LEVEL OF CULTURAL DIFFICULTY: Moderately difficult.

SPECIAL PROPERTIES: Valued for intensely fragrant flowers.

PRONUNCIATION: res-EH-da o-do-RA-ta

"To be smelled but not seen" is the judgment of most garden authorities on *Reseda odorata,* a plant valued for its unmatchable fragrance for more than 200 years and treasured before that by the Romans, who gave the genus its botanical name, from the Latin verb *resedare,* meaning to heal or assuage pain. Seed of *Reseda odorata,* a native of North Africa, was sent to the Empress Josephine by Napoleon during his first Egyptian campaign. It became a favorite with her, and it is said that she gave it its common name, "mignonette," which translates into English as "little darling."

For modern gardeners, mignonette is a plant in which one virtue must stand for all. "It is not a pretty plant," British gardener Christopher Lloyd has bluntly said, and Larry Hodgson, French-speaking Canada's guide to gardening, has added, *"Qui achèterait une caissette de plantes si piteuses?"* ("Who would buy a flat of such pitiful plants?"). In its admittedly weedy sort of way, however, mignonette is not all that homely. A true annual, it forms a lax, branched plant up to two feet tall, furnished with thin-textured leaves up to three inches long, lance-shaped or three-lobed, though the actual form of an individual leaf is often lost in heavy rippling or puckering. Flowers are borne in racemes that begin as dense, broccoli-looking cobs, but elongate as individual flowers develop along the stem. In wild forms, the flowers are no more than a quarter of an inch across, with four to seven toothed petals of greenish yellow, rather ragged in effect, centered with anthers of stronger yellow. Since the late Victorian and Edwardian periods, when the plant reached its apex of popularity, every attempt has been made to develop forms of mignonette with prettier flowers, and forms have been selected with larger blooms. As often happens, however, when flowers of pronounced fragrance are improved in appearance, the fragrance gets lost along the way.

After the introduction of *Reseda odorata,* French *parfumiers* quickly realized the value of the plant, though its fragrance—powdery, piney, underlain with the smell of fresh raspberries and of carnations—proved difficult to fix and is still only used in the most costly of perfumes. But the plant, in all its homely splendor, became an almost obligatory fixture on Parisian balconies during the early part of the nineteenth century. It also became the darling of English florists, who raised it under glass in winter as a long-lasting cut flower and even perfected the art of training it into standards—tiny, intensely fragrant, mop-headed trees about a foot tall, perfect to line up and down the middle of tables set for formal dinners.

Mignonette is very easy to grow in the garden, provided one realizes that, like so many plants classed as hardy annuals, it is intolerant of transplanting. Seed may be started in peat pots or plastic cell packs about six weeks before the last anticipated frost date, though even when transplanted carefully into the garden after all danger of frost is past, the young plants will never equal those sown in place in very early spring as soon as the soil may be raked smooth. The seed is very fine and should be mixed with canary gravel for even distribution. It should be only lightly pressed into the soil with the broad side of a board, as it must be

RESEDA ODORATA

[387]

near the surface to germinate successfully. Rich, well-drained soil is required, and though in cool gardens plants develop well in full sun, where summers are very warm, half a day of shade will be preferred. When young seedlings have reached two or three inches in height, they should be thinned to within six or eight inches, taking care to pull unwanted plants through a V made by two fingers pressed against the soil so as not to disturb those that are to remain. Those seedlings left in place should be pinched once when they have reached six inches or so, to encourage branching and to promote a reasonable capacity to maintain themselves upright. Most will flop, however, and staking is of little use. It is better to allow the plant to right itself through strong lateral upright growths. Flowering stems should begin to appear within sixty days of germination, and flowers will open about ten days later, continuing until really hot summer weather causes plants to shrivel and die. In those lucky gardens where the heat of summer declines into a long, cool autumn, a successive sowing might be made in July for flowers from late summer to frost. If flowering stems are picked just before the first frost, they may last up to two months in water in a very cool room, giving off a gentler though still pleasant whiff of their summer fragrance.

Gardeners with cool greenhouses will certainly want to try mignonette as a late-winter- or early-spring-flowering plant. Plants develop very well at nighttime temperatures between 45° and 50°F, though they must be carefully watered to avoid fungus and root rot, which are fatal. Seed should be sown in August, three to a small pot, and all but the strongest seedlings eliminated after two or three true leaves have developed. Young plants must be grown on in good light and buoyant conditions, and pinched once to encourage bushiness. When the pots are full of roots, plants should be carefully repotted, first into three-inch pots, and then into five- or six-inch pots, where they may be expected to flower in late winter or early spring.

Gardeners who raise mignonette during the winter will certainly want to try making it into standards. For this purpose, cultural practices should be followed as for bushy plants, though all side growths of the chosen seedlings are eliminated and the single stem is trained to a stake. Growth of the central stem should not exceed much more than a foot, at which point it should be pinched at the top to encourage branching. Flower-bearing laterals should then occur at the top, and when they are well formed, leaves should be stripped from the central stem. The result will be a small, fragrant little tree, very charming, though its life will be brief, hardly a month, depending on growing conditions.

RHODANTHE SPECIES (*HELIPTERUM* SPECIES)

FAMILY: *Asteraceae* or aster or daisy family.

CLASSIFICATION: Tender annual.

COMMON NAMES: Everlasting, immortelle, strawflower, helipterum, rhodanthe.

HARDINESS: Extremely frost-sensitive.

GROWING CONDITIONS: Lean, sandy, well-drained, dryish soil. Full sun. Plants relish heat.

PROPAGATION: By seed, sown in place in April, or indoors in peat pots 6 to 8 weeks before frost. Seedlings resent root disturbance.

HEIGHT: From 10 to 20".

ORNAMENTAL VALUE: Grown for flower.

LEVEL OF CULTURAL DIFFICULTY: Easy under ideal conditions, difficult elsewhere.

SPECIAL PROPERTIES: Treasured for dried flowers.

PRONUNCIATION: ro-DAN-thee (he-LIP-te-rum)

Helipterum, grown and loved in gardens for more than a hundred years, have endured several name changes, first being shifted into the genus *Acroclinum* (ak-ro-CLI-num), with a few species temporarily in *Leucochrysum* (loo-co-CHRY-sum), and most recently into *Rhodanthe,* where, for the moment, those commonly grown in gardens are lodged. To gardeners, however—and more important, to seed companies—they have remained helipterum, from ancient Greek *helios,* meaning the sun, and *pteron,* a wing, and referring to the silky parachute by which the seed, dandelion fashion, travels on the wind. But helipterum, which must now be treated as a common name, is replaced by *Rhodanthe,* taken from a Latin adjective that simply means rosy red.

Only two rhodanthes have been generally available from seed companies, though where they may be made to thrive, even as annuals, they are such excellent and undemanding garden plants that more species will surely be introduced in the next few years. The rhodanthe most frequently grown is offered as *Rhodanthe rosea* (RO-see-a), though it is actually a subspecies, and so is correctly *R. chlorocephala* (klo-ro-CE-pha-la) subsp. *rosea,* a cumbersome phrase hardly ever listed. It bears the common name "rose everlasting," for like all cultivated members of the genus, its papery, daisylike flowers may be easily dried for use in winter bouquets. What seem to be its flowers, however, are not actually petals but rather a showy ring of papery bracts surrounding the true flowers—a tight button of disk florets. In the case of *Rhodanthe rosea,* the bracts may be colored white, pink, or a deep pink that sometimes approaches red. The disk flowers in the center are generally a strong yellow, though they are sometimes black and sometimes yellow with a black center. Flowers, one to three inches across, are borne singly on stiff, erect stems above grayish-green narrow, blade-shaped leaves that

thickly clasp the lower stems of the plant. The total height of plant and flowers is no more than two feet, and usually just fifteen inches. As with all rhodanthe, the bracts will close at night, in cloudy weather, or at the least touch of moisture, folding inward into a tight cone to protect the pollen of the disk flowers within. *Rhodanthe rosea* is best grown in masses, and selections that are several shades of pink are particularly attractive when their flowers blend together. Too much white or pinkish white spoils this effect, so specific blends are to be preferred above home-grown seed. There is, however, a splendid double white form with larger flowers that should be grown, particularly by dried flower enthusiasts.

A smaller, more delicate version of *Rhodanthe rosea* is *R. manglesii* (man-GLAY-see-ee), which produces inch-wide flowers borne in clusters on slender stems above densely bushy, upright plants to two feet tall, with oval to oblong leaves as much as four inches long. The true disk flowers are pale yellow, though the papery bracts surrounding them may be white, pink, red, or a deep almost purple-red. In the darker shades, the bracts begin to fade after a day or two, creating an attractive effect of many closely related shades in the same planting.

For drying, both species should be harvested just as the ray flowers unfold, for they will continue to open during the drying process. Single stems may be cut, or whole plants may be pulled and hung upside down to cure in a dark, airy place. The stems of both rhodanthe are stiffer when dried than are those of many other everlasting flowers, and so they do not require a strand of wire to keep them from nodding.

Species of *Rhodanthe* are easiest to grow in gardens that approximate their homeland, for both perennial and annual plants are mostly native to the arid parts of western and southwestern Australia. They thrive where summers are long, hot, and dry, and where soils are sandy and not over-rich. In such gardens they may be sown in place in April for flowers from late June until September. Elsewhere they may be started indoors, six to eight weeks before the last anticipated frost date. The seed should be sprinkled lightly over sterilized potting compost such as Pro-Mix combined equally with perlite or sharp sand, perfect drainage being a requirement of rhodanthes throughout their lives. Seed germinates best if it is not pressed into the soil, and it should be held at temperatures around 60°F. When very small, young plants will accept transplanting, though not readily, and so it is best to sow two or three seeds in peat pots or plastic cell packs, clipping out all but the strongest when one or two true sets of leaves have developed. They should be grown on in very bright, sunny conditions until all danger of frost has passed, when they may be hardened off and transplanted carefully.

RHODOCHITON
ATROSANGUINEUS

FAMILY: *Scrophulariaceae* or snapdragon family.

CLASSIFICATION: Tender perennial vine grown as tender annual vine.

COMMON NAMES: Purple bell vine, rhodochiton.

HARDINESS: Sensitive to light frosts.

GROWING CONDITIONS: Very rich, open, moisture-retentive, well-drained soil. Full sun. Relishes heat.

PROPAGATION: By seed, sown indoors in peat pots in mid-February. Young plants prefer no root disturbance.

HEIGHT: To 10′ when grown as an annual.

ORNAMENTAL VALUE: Grown for flower and for interesting character of vines.

LEVEL OF CULTURAL DIFFICULTY: Easy.

SPECIAL PROPERTIES: Excellent container plant.

PRONUNCIATION: ro-do-KI-ton a-tro-san-GWIN-ee-us

*A*mong the families most valued by gardeners, Scrophulariaceae is often noted for its wit and charm, for within it are located many plants that seem to have gone to extra trouble to make themselves especially engaging, such as snapdragons, *Antirrhinum* (an-ti-RI-num); toadflax, *Linaria* (lin-A-ree-a); wishbone flowers, *Torenia* (to-REE-nee-a); monkey flowers, *Mimulus* (mim-YEW-lus); and foxgloves, *Digitalis* (di-jee-TA-lis). Even in so droll a clan, *Rhodochiton atrosanguineus*—the only species in its genus—sets itself apart. For it forgoes the open-mouthed faces typical of its more famous relatives, which generally sport blossoms flaring into a mouth with a two-lobed upper lip and a three-lobed one below. The inflorescences of rhodochiton have something else in mind, for each hangs downward on a slender stem that may be as much as three or four inches long and is as fine as a coarse sewing thread. Dangling at the tip is a cup-shaped, four-pointed calyx about an inch across at maturity, billowing outward like a parachute and colored a vibrant fuchsia pink. Within is an inch-long, tubular flower of a purple so deep as to appear black. Each inflorescence, borne from the axils of heart-shaped, four-inch-long succulent, fresh green leaves, is beautiful in itself, but in mid-July they are borne in graduated sequence all along the upper stems from each leaf node. All are vividly colored, from the oldest and largest to tiny bells the size of a pea, and they look as if each could sound a progressively smaller silver note when struck. Calyxes remain in good condition and color long after the tubular inner flower has given way to a fat, spherical seed capsule, thus offering an ever-increasing show of bells until summer's end.

Rhodochiton atrosanguineus is a native of Mexico, and is actually a tender perennial vine hardy to Zones 8 to 10. At the northern limit of its range it dies to the ground each year, returning with greater vigor in the spring, though never so rampantly as to smother plants around it. Because it is perennial, gardeners who live in colder climates and wish to grow it as an annual should start it quite early—mid- to late February—for plants that will come into flower in early June. The flat, papery seed should be sown in a sterile potting mix to which a scattering of sharp sand has been added, for like most plants native to Mexico, rhodochiton requires perfect drainage at all stages of its life. Though it will accept transplanting when very young, plants should be grown on without a check to obtain the earliest flower, and so three seed should be sown to a peat pot, and all but the largest clipped away when young plants have achieved two or three sets of true leaves. Seed germinates rapidly at about 70°F, and young plants should be grown on at around that temperature in bright, sunny conditions, and fed weekly with half-strength liquid fertilizer. When roots show around the edges of the peat pots, plants should be shifted, peat pot and all, into five-inch clay pots, taking care to firm soilless potting mix (Pro-Mix lightened by about a third with sharp sand) gently but securely around the walls of the peat pot, working from the bottom up, so that all of its surface is in contact with the soil. Rhodochiton twines around any support it touches by means of its leaf petioles, and so supports of slender bamboo stakes should be provided to young vines.

As a Mexican native rhodochiton relishes heat, so young plants should be kept growing strongly indoors or in a greenhouse heated to a minimum nighttime temperature around 60°F until the weather is warm and settled. Plants develop best in full sun and in rich but well-drained soil, with protection from drying winds, conditions such as might be found on the sunny side of a garage or a board fence. A light grid of twine should be provided to support the vines, and where possible, lateral growths should be trained horizontally, so that the little bells of bud and flower will hang downward in a graded row. Alternatively, rhodochiton is light enough to train over an evergreen—yew or holly—or a spring-blooming deciduous shrub such as a forsythia or flowering quince, where its growth will do no harm and its charming flowers will provide interest in summer. It also makes a superb container plant, best grown as a single species in a very large pot, where a tripod of bamboo stakes perhaps six or

RHODOCHITON ATROSANGUINEUS

even eight feet tall has been inserted. Several young vines trained around the poles will make an obelisk of flower from early June until frost. Grown this way, vines may be cut back just before frost, stored in the kind of frost-free but very cool place suitable for storing cannas or dahlias, and brought back into growth in spring.

RICINUS COMMUNIS

FAMILY: *Euphorbiaceae* or spurge family.

CLASSIFICATION: Tender shrubs or trees grown as tender annuals.

COMMON NAMES: Castor bean, castor oil plant, palm of Christ, ricinus.

HARDINESS: Sensitive to light frosts.

GROWING CONDITIONS: Extremely rich, well-drained, moisture-retentive soil. Full sun. Relishes heat.

PROPAGATION: By seed, sown indoors in peat pots 6 weeks before last frost, or in place when weather becomes settled. Seedlings resent root disturbance.

HEIGHT: To 8′ or more in a season.

ORNAMENTAL VALUE: Grown for large ornamental leaves. Newer selections bear showy seed capsules.

LEVEL OF CULTURAL DIFFICULTY: Easy.

SPECIAL PROPERTIES: Grown as screen or annual hedge. Excellent for large containers.

PRONUNCIATION: ri-SIN-us com-MUN-is

*A*mong plants usually grown as annuals, *Ricinus communis* is without rival for its bold tropical appearance. From a fat bean inserted an inch into the ground as soon as all danger of frost has passed, a seedling will quickly sprout that can eventually achieve a height of eight feet in two months, creating a sturdy, branched plant with palmlike, outspreading leaves as large as two feet across. According to variety, leaves may be a fresh green or celadon gray-green, or they may be maroon, metallic bronze, or a deep burgundy red that is almost black. Leaves are borne alternately, held on long petioles well away from the plant and facing up to receive all the sun they can get. Each leaf may consist of five to eleven boldly cut, pointed lobes, arranged hand fashion and giving the plant the popular name it enjoyed in the late Middle Ages, and still does in Spanish-speaking countries—"*Palma Christi.*"

Why, precisely, the leaves of ricinus should suggest so gentle a name as "palm of Christ" is a mystery, however, for in tropical Africa, where it is native, its seriously toxic properties have been known since very ancient times. Everyone is wary of it throughout the tropical and subtropical parts of the world where it has become naturalized, because all parts of the plant contain the chemical *ricin,* a white, odorless protein. Most strongly concentrated in the fat, beanlike seed, it is a substance that can be fatal to humans and to all domestic livestock, including cattle, sheep, goats, chickens, and other poultry. The flowers of ricinus are insignificant, consisting of small, fringy, petalless blooms borne in a cob from the axils of upper leaves, but the seed capsules— many rounded and spined receptacles crowded densely along the stem—are often very attractive. Certain recent varieties, such as 'Carmencita', have been bred with highly colored cobs of seed in shades of rich orange and pink, but where any possibility exists that seed will be ingested, these should be removed and discarded at the first flower stage. Children should be firmly cautioned to avoid the plant, which can also cause severe skin rashes in people who are susceptible.

Ricinus communis is treasured as an ornamental

because it is the most tropical looking, and probably the fastest growing, of all plants grown as annuals. A single specimen can provide a striking accent in a planting of other annuals or perennials, and several plants, spaced from three to five feet apart, will quickly grow into an annual hedge that will conceal unsightly objects or will simply provide a bold pattern along a fence, at the side of a garage or barn, or at the edges of a property. Though one might not expect it of so vast a plant, ricinus also thrives in large tubs and other containers and may be very striking beside a pool or in the sunny corner of a terrace.

Ricinus is of very easy culture, accepting most soils and even tolerating considerable dryness at the roots, though it prefers a humus-rich, free-draining soil. Plants may struggle to survive in some shade, but they perform best in full sun. Heat is their friend, and they grow the fastest in summer temperatures that are uncomfortable to most people. Seed may be started indoors about six weeks before the last anticipated frost date, though young plants should be held in conditions with temperatures of at least 60°F until the weather is warm and settled, and transplanted at about the time one would plant out tomatoes and seed sweet corn. Alternatively, seed may be sown outdoors at around that time with very good results, as the growth of ricinus is very rapid, particularly when the weather becomes warm and settled. Germination, however, may be erratic, taking as little as a week or as long as fifteen days, though it may be speeded up considerably by soaking the seed overnight. As one might suppose with so massive a plant, ricinus is very responsive to supplementary fertilizer, in either granular or liquid form. Except with very small seedlings, transplanting is only grudgingly tolerated, and so it is best to start seed in peat pots, or to sow them outdoors where the plant is to grow. The root system of

RICINUS COMMUNIS

ricinus is surprisingly small for so large a plant, and mature plants in full sail are prone to blow over in summer storms. If they are likely to do so, they will topple just at ground level, and so a single but very stout stake firmly inserted in the soil and extending two feet or above will be sufficient.

Despite its seriously toxic properties, *Ricinus communis* has been grown as an economical medicinal herb by many cultures, beginning with the ancient Egyptians, who pressed its oil-rich beans for illumination in lamps, employed it as a treatment for inflamed eyes, and had a last recourse to it as a drastic purgative for victims of poisoning. In more recent times, oil from its seed has been used as a drying agent in paint and as an important ingredient in the fabrication of soap, linoleum, and ink. Its leaves, richly and freely produced, have been employed as a forage for silkworms, which are strangely immune to their toxic properties, and as an ingredient in organic insecticides. And, of course, oil from its seed, pressed out and freed of toxic properties, has been administered to generations of protesting children as a laxative.

Though there are many varieties of castor bean that are so distinct in appearance, one from another, as to suggest separate species, *Ricinus communis* is in fact the only species in its genus. It takes its name from the ancient Latin word for a tick, *ricinus,* because its flat, beanlike seed resemble that insect. *Communis* can mean common or frequently encountered, but it may also designate plants that grow in thick communities.

RUDBECKIA HIRTA

FAMILY: *Asteraceae* or aster or daisy family.

CLASSIFICATION: Weak hardy perennial or biennial grown as hardy annual.

COMMON NAMES: Black-eyed Susan, gloriosa daisy, annual rudbeckia.

HARDINESS: Withstands frosts.

GROWING CONDITIONS: Any soils, from moderately rich garden loam to poor, dryish roadside dirt. Full sun.

PROPAGATION: By seed, sown indoors 6 to 8 weeks before last frost date. Seedlings transplant easily.

HEIGHT: From 10″ to 3′, depending on culture.

ORNAMENTAL VALUE: Grown for flower.

LEVEL OF CULTURAL DIFFICULTY: Easy.

SPECIAL PROPERTIES: Excellent for naturalizing in rough grass.

PRONUNCIATION: rud-BEK-ee-a HIR-ta

*A*lmost everyone will recognize black-eyed Susan, the original form of *Rudbeckia hirta,* whose vivid, black-centered, chrome-yellow daisies, each about three inches across, decorate roadsides and fields throughout North America from mid-July until October. The range of the plant was once probably the Great Plains of the Midwest, but it has now naturalized throughout the continent after being widely dispersed in the nineteenth century by agriculturally produced hayseed. An upright plant as tall as two feet, the daisy has many-branched flower stems ascending from a basal rosette of mid-green, tongue-shaped leaves, each about five inches long and half as wide. Both leaves and stems are covered with short bristly hairs, which give the species its name, from Latin *hirta,* meaning hairy. Lovely though it is in its natural form, black-eyed Susan has been subjected to many improvements, creating a wide range of garden plants that are very easy to grow, very tolerant of less than the best cultural conditions, and very rewarding in their freely produced blooms from July to frost, especially if picked frequently or dead-headed. Choosing to dead-head may be a hard decision, however, for few plants produce food more palatable to small, seed-eating birds, which fatten on the ripe cones before beginning their arduous journeys of migration.

Dwarf forms of *Rudbeckia hirta,* about ten inches tall, are of dubious value, but the best known of the wild flower's descendants are anything but dwarf. Gloriosa daisies possess doubled chromosomes that produce plants of great sturdiness and vigor, with bloom stems that may reach three feet in height and blooms that may be as much as seven inches across. Both single, semidouble, and double forms occur, and in a wide variety of colors ranging from yellow and gold to orange, chestnut red, or mahogany. Often the darker color at the center shades out to yellow at the edges. Forty or so years ago, all these flower forms and colors were apt to appear from a single seed packet, and there was no great harm in that, for gloriosa daisies can hardly be described as subtle in their effect, and a crazy mix added to their mad appeal. Over the last few years, however, breeders have devoted great energy to standardizing the plant as much as possible by developing seed strains that would produce all single or all double flowers in consistent colors of clear yellow or orange, mahogany, or chestnut red. The central black cone of disk flowers has also been modified into a form with a startling lime-green center, called 'Green Eyes' in England and 'Irish Eyes' in America. For sophisticated planting schemes uniformity may be important, but for the ragged patch along the side of the barn or at the end of the perennial border where it blends into open field, the old mixes are to be preferred.

The twenty or so species within the genus *Rudbeckia* offer a good illustration of how uncertain the conventional classifications of perennial, biennial, and annual can be. For though the genus contains some sturdy, long-lived perennials, the very popular black-eyed Susans and gloriosa daisies may be weakly perennial, biennial, or annual, depending largely on cultural conditions. Gloriosa daisies, which are actually tetraploids, are likely to be more perennial than the black-eyed Susans, which are the diploid descendants of *Rudbeckia hirta*. But as the garden writer Allan Armitage has commented, ". . . regardless of the claims to the contrary, they should [all] be treated as annuals."

Rudbeckia hirta requires full sun but will accept almost any soil, even poor, dryish sandy loam, where plants remain free of powdery mildew, the one pest to which the plant is prone, and which it contracts most readily on rich soil after a period of drought followed by wet weather. Seed is easy to start indoors, about six to eight weeks before the last anticipated frost date. It should be pressed only gently into the soil and not covered, as it needs light to germinate. Young seedlings transplant easily, and should be grown on in bright, airy conditions at temperatures around 65° to 70°F until they may be hardened off and safely planted outdoors. Alternatively, seed may be sown in spring, as early as the ground may be worked, for plants that may be expected to bloom about fifteen weeks from germination.

Spacing may be as close as eight inches, but because these are essentially wild flowers, the distance from plant to plant need not be so very precise. Plants may be crowded even closer together, and one here, one there, also can be nice, for *Rudbeckia hirta* always seems to be a plant suited to very relaxed garden effects. Probably no annual looks better in beds that are less than perfectly tended. Even a patch of weeds can be made splendid by a few plants, the blooms of which always will carry a meadowy freedom, no matter how highly developed the seed strain may be. And if by chance, in such relatively neglected parts of the garden, plants return for a year or two, or self-seed spontaneously, then so much the better. Black-eyed Susans are especially lovely when seen along roadsides and in thin meadow grass in company with the yellow-centered, white-petaled European field daisy, *Leucanthemum maximum* (loo-CAN-thee-mum MAX-i-mum), now so widely naturalized across the North American continent that most people assume it to be a native plant. Both plants are popular components of wildflower mixes, and whether in the field or when picked together and

RUDBECKIA HIRTA

put naïvely in a vase or even a mason jar, they always carry a redolence of high summer.

The genus *Rudbeckia* commemorates a man who endured one of the most tragic experiences in botany. Olof Rudbeck (1630–1702), historian, antiquarian, professor at the University of Uppsala in Sweden, and perhaps the greatest botanist of his day, saw his life's work of 11,000 woodcut illustrations of plants destroyed by a great fire that swept Uppsala in 1702. His son, Olof Rudbeck the Younger (1660–1740), continued his father's work and befriended the young Linnaeus when he was a student at the university. The name of the genus was later assigned by Linnaeus in honor of both men.

RUELLIA SPECIES

FAMILY: *Acanthaceae* or acanthus family.

CLASSIFICATION: Tender shrubby perennials grown as tender annuals.

COMMON NAMES: Mexican petunia, Texas petunia, ruellia.

HARDINESS: Sensitive to light frosts. Dislikes cool weather.

GROWING CONDITIONS: Humus-rich, well-drained, moist soil. Relishes heat.

PROPAGATION: By seed, sown in late February, or by nursery-rooted cuttings.

HEIGHT: From 9″ to 3′, depending on species and cultivar.

ORNAMENTAL VALUE: Grown for flower.

LEVEL OF CULTURAL DIFFICULTY: Easy where climatic preferences may be met. Moderately difficult elsewhere.

SPECIAL PROPERTIES: None.

PRONUNCIATION: ru-EL-ee-a

*I*n their desperate search for common names, nurserymen and gardeners often resort clumsily to comparisons with other plants. So *Ruellia brittoniana* (bri-to-nee-A-na), a newly introduced and very handsome plant in its own right, must travel under the borrowed name of Mexican or Texas petunia. It is, in fact, a native of Mexico and has become widely naturalized in Texas, but there is really nothing petunia-like about it.

Ruellia brittoniana is a tender shrubby perennial that can, in its wild form, reach a bushy height of as much as four or five feet but is more often seen in gardens in its more compact form of two to three feet. (The cultivar 'Katie', or 'Katie's Dwarf', is smaller still at nine to twelve inches.) Plants branch from the ground into several ascending stems, woody at the base and furnished with closely spaced, blade-shaped leaves from four to six inches long. They are handsome in themselves, of a dark olive-green that is richly suffused with purple, and with mauvish-purple undersides. Flowers are borne from the upper leaf axils, in loose, purple-stemmed clusters, and though each individual flower remains open for only a day, it is quickly followed by others that are attractive even as furled buds. The flowers consist of a two-inch-long tube that flares outward into a mouth of five overlapping lobes, of a rich blue underlain with pink, making it close to true violet. Ruellia flowers most abundantly in really hot weather and so performs best in North American gardens that are near to its Mexican home, though its leaves and pattern of growth are so attractive that the few flowers it produces in northern gardens might simply be considered a bonus.

Another ruellia that has recently appeared in garden centers bears so little relationship to *Ruellia brittoniana* that one would hardly think them to be members of the same genus. *R. elegans* (EL-uh-gans) is, to begin with, scarlet-flowered, giving it its only popular name, "red ruellia." Its grass-green, oval leaves are about two inches long, and the plant bears many ascending stems to about a foot, each terminating in racemes of scarlet tubes. It is of very easy culture, preferring well-drained, humus-rich soil but relishing the warmth of summer.

Ruellia are likely to be acquired as rooted cuttings from nurseries that specialize in unusual annual and tender plants. They may, however, be started from seed, which should be sown quite early, in late February or early March, in temperatures around 75°F. Seedlings transplant easily and should be pricked out into plastic cell packs as soon as they have formed two sets of true leaves. They should then be grown on in bright, airy conditions and pinched once when they have reached a height of five inches or so to encourage bushiness. As ruellia are very sensitive to frost and even to cold, drizzly weather, young plants should be held in indoor conditions until the weather is quite warm and settled, when tomatoes, eggplants, and other tropical vegetables are set out. As with most plants native to Mexico, full sun is required for best development, though soils should be humus-rich, water-retentive, but well drained. Supplementary fertilizer, either liquid or granular, will encourage lush growth.

Ruellia are very attractive in the open border or in bays in the shrubbery, where their leafy stems and flowers suggest something other than annuals as that term is commonly understood. They are also excellent in pots, window boxes, or other containers, where their attractive flowers—even if sparsely produced—can be studied up close and where they thrive with warmth at their roots. Though native to Mexico, they pre-

RUELLIA BRITTONIANA

fer moist, well-drained fertile soil. Dryness will cause shriveling, poor flower production, and even death. At season's end, just before frost, plants may be lifted, cut back hard, and potted in free-draining compost, to be grown on over winter in a cool greenhouse with nighttime temperatures around 50°F. Cuttings taken in early summer also root readily, and young plants produced in this way may be pinched repeatedly throughout the summer to produce compact, well-branched plants that may flower shyly in winter in a cool greenhouse or on a sunny windowsill.

Ruellia belongs to a large genus, of as many as 200 species, variously native to the tropical, subtropical, and warmly temperate parts of the globe. The genus name commemorates Jean de la Ruelle (1474–1537), personal physician and herbalist to the gallant François I (1494–1547), King of France from 1515 until his death. The species now so suddenly popular in gardens, *R. brittoniana,* is named for Nathaniel Lord Britton (1859–1934), for many years director of the New York Botanical Garden in the Bronx, who botanized extensively in the southeastern part of the United States and northern Mexico.

SALPIGLOSSIS SINUATA

FAMILY: *Solanaceae* or deadly nightshade family.

CLASSIFICATION: Tender perennial grown as half-hardy annual.

COMMON NAMES: Painted tongue, salpiglossis.

HARDINESS: Sensitive to light frosts.

GROWING CONDITIONS: Humus-rich, well-drained, moisture-retentive soil. Full sun. Resents heat.

PROPAGATION: By seed, sown indoors in late February or early March.

HEIGHT: From 15" to 3', depending on cultivar.

ORNAMENTAL VALUE: Grown for flower.

LEVEL OF CULTURAL DIFFICULTY: Difficult.

SPECIAL PROPERTIES: None.

PRONUNCIATION: sal-pi-GLO-sis sin-u-A-ta

Despite their undeniable beauty and the praise heaped on them by a century of garden writers, salpiglossis have never been tremendously popular in America as summer-flowering annuals. Anyone who sees them for the first time might well wonder why, for though their foliage is unremarkable—four-inch-long, wavy or toothed lance-shaped leaves—no plant grown as an annual produces flowers quite like theirs. Borne in loose clusters on stems that may reach a height of three feet, each consists of a short tube flaring outward into five notched lobes, the whole measuring as much as two and a half inches in diameter. Their colors are remarkable, for they may be any shade from cream to pale and deep yellow, orange, chestnut or mahogany, rose, crimson red, violet, purple, and almost blue. The petals are heavily quilted and fantastically veined with a contrasting color—often a vibrant golden yellow, sometimes red or brown—which often assumes a distinct herringbone pattern.

But for various reasons, salpiglossis are not easy plants to grow. Closely related to petunias, they share that flower's tendency to become a bedraggled mess in wet weather. Even worse, water-soaked petals often develop a black, botrytus-like mold that can infect whole stems or the entire plant. They dislike damp cold and scorching heat alike, the first causing them to rot and the second causing them to cease blooming and even to shrivel away. Still, in gardens that suit them, where days are bright and sunny and nighttime temperatures do not climb above 70°F, they can be superb plants, for both borders and containers, blooming freely from early July until frost.

Seed of salpiglossis should be sown quite early, in late February or early March, for plants that may be set out after all danger of frost is past. It is difficult to evenly disperse the tiny seed—so minute it resembles a pinch of snuff—so it is best mixed with two or three tablespoons of fine sand, such as canary gravel, the whole sprinkled across the surface of sterilized potting compost. The seed should be only lightly pressed in, as the tiny seedlings are at first too fragile to break through a crust of earth. Still, they must be kept dark in order to germinate, and so seed pots should be covered with cardboard until the seedlings appear. When quite small, seedlings are extremely prone to damping off, a fatal malady that is best avoided by sowing the seed thinly and by keeping young seedlings in bright, open, airy conditions at temperatures around 55° to 60°F. When the seedlings are large enough to handle, they should be pricked off into individual pots or cell packs and grown on under similarly cool conditions until transplanted. Newer seed strains of salpiglossis tend to branch more freely than older varieties, but all seedlings should still be pinched once when they are about five inches tall to encourage several flower-bearing stems. Though seedlings transplant readily, gardeners sometimes grow them in peat pots to minimize transplant shock and thus secure early flowering before the heat of summer carries plants off. To make good garden plants, salpiglossis must be grown on without a check until they may be hardened off and established outdoors.

Salpiglossis requires well-drained humusy soil for best development, and plants respond to applications of water-soluble plant food every two weeks, preferably the sort fabricated for tomatoes. Newer varieties of salpiglossis are stockier and shorter than older forms, reaching a height of about fifteen inches and resisting the tendency to tumble over. Still, it is worth supporting each individual plant with a single stake or inserting brush among them to be certain that they remain upright. Plants should be spaced about a foot apart to allow room for full development. If flower production slows down in the heat of summer, a fresh flush of bloom in early autumn can sometimes be obtained by cutting the spent flower stems back. A thick mulch is often recommended to keep the soil cool and prolong flowering, though the slugs it encourages will have to be fought, as they are fond of salpiglossis flowers.

Though sometimes difficult in the garden, salpiglossis are among the easiest of all annuals to flower in late winter and spring in the cool greenhouse, heated sun porch, or even on a cool, sunny windowsill. (They also make superb cut flowers when whole stems are picked just as the lower buds have unfurled, smaller ones continuing to open for as long as ten days.) Plants that have remained vigorous into early autumn may be cut back, carefully dug, and potted singly into seven-inch pots, though better results are usually had by sowing fresh seed in late August or early September, growing the seedlings outdoors in pots and moving them in before they are touched by frost. They should be kept in vigorous growth by applications of liquid fertilizer, and main-

SALPIGLOSSIS SINUATA

tained at temperatures around 55° to 60°F. Bloom should begin in February and continue for three months or more, particularly if spent flowers are promptly removed.

Salpiglossis sinuata is the only member in its small genus of five or so species that is grown in gardens. Native to rocky slopes of the southern Andes, its unglamorous genus name is derived from classical Latin *salpinx,* signifying a trumpet, and *glossa,* tongue. The species name *sinuata* means rippled and refers to the wavy margins of the lower leaves. Though both names are moderately descriptive, neither captures the beauty of the flower any more than does its only common name, "painted tongue."

SALVIA SPECIES

FAMILY: *Lamiaceae* (*Labiatae*) or mint family.

CLASSIFICATION: Tender annuals, perennials, or shrubs grown as tender annuals.

COMMON NAME: Salvia (other common names vary with species).

HARDINESS: Varies with species.

GROWING CONDITIONS: Varies with species, though all prefer full sun.

PROPAGATION: From seed, sown 10 to 12 weeks before frost. Many desirable species propagated from cuttings or divisions.

HEIGHT: Variable, from 1 to 8′, depending on cultivar.

ORNAMENTAL VALUE: Grown for flower and sometimes for ornamental leaf.

LEVEL OF CULTURAL DIFFICULTY: Easy to difficult, depending on species.

SPECIAL PROPERTIES: *Salvia officinalis* is valued as a culinary herb.

PRONUNCIATION: SAL-vee-a

*A*mong its many other distinctions, *Salvia* is remarkable for possessing more garden-worthy species and hybrids than any other genus in the plant kingdom. Perhaps as many as 900 species are included within it, distributed throughout the tropical and temperate zones of the world, but mostly concentrated in the Western Hemisphere, chiefly in South America, Mexico, and in the southwestern United States. Within the genus are true annuals, perennials, sub-shrubs, and shrubs, many of which are highly decorative. Some European species have been cultivated from antiquity, particularly culinary sage, *Salvia officinalis* (off-i-si-NA-lis), grown for its pungent leaves, valuable as a seasoning but also believed to be health-giving, hence the name of the genus, from Latin *salvus,* meaning safe, well, sound, or healthy, but also carrying connotations of sanity and even wisdom. Other salvias, of New World origin, have been planted in gardens for a hundred years or more, and two at least, *Salvia splendens* (SPLEN-dens), the "scarlet bedder," and *Salvia farinacea* (fa-ri-NA-see-a), the "blue bedder," were important components of Victorian bedding schemes. But the genus *Salvia* was as modestly represented in gardens as many others until the late 1970s and early 1980s, when it achieved something like star status. During that time, and since, salvias have seemed to be everywhere, with new ones introduced each year, creating a sort of fever to the point that *The Sunset Western Gardening Book* (revised edition, 1995) estimated that "At least 60 species and an additional 40 to 50 selections are grown in the West."

Almost as many, it appears, are being grown elsewhere, for the tender salvia, when treated as annuals, are splendid additions to the late summer garden. The Mexican and South American species are particularly valuable, for they develop rapidly from rooted cuttings and are at their best in mid-August, when most American gardens need a boost. No general reference work can hope to keep up with their appearance in gardens, though two excellent books have been written on the genus: Betsy Clebsch's *A Book of Salvias: Sages for Every Garden* (1997) and John Sutton's *The Gardener's Guide to Growing Salvias* (1999), both of which are valuable references.

Diverse as they are, cultivated salvias share many physical characteristics and cultural needs that make it possible to describe them more-or-less accurately as a group. They are members of the large mint family, Lamiaceae (Labiatae), and usually they display the square stems and a pungency in their crushed leaves that are typical of the family. Almost to a species, they grow best in full sun, in well-drained loam of moderate fertility. Though they seem superficially to be drought-tolerant plants, almost all flourish in evenly moist conditions. Generally, they form a loose bush (made denser by pinching when they are young) and their branches, which are extremely brittle, often root where they touch ground, thus providing in their native habitats a ready means of increase when they are broken away from the mother plant. This characteristic makes it extremely easy to reproduce many of the shrubby sorts from cuttings, which root easily at almost any time they are in active growth, but it can be a problem in the garden, where the gardener's step or a strong wind can fracture an established plant. For this reason, even the shrubbier types benefit from tactful staking.

The leaves of salvias, whether large or tiny, are generally oval to heart- or lance-shaped, and are borne in opposite pairs along the stem. They are prominently or minutely toothed along the edges. Many bear leaves and even stems that are sticky or hairy, and some species are so thickly downed that they appear silver. The vein structure of the leaf is often very apparent, giving some species a quilted appearance. Flowers are borne in whorls that circle the generally slender racemes carried on terminal growths. Each individual flower is usually quite small and short-lived, but they emerge from prominent, cup-shaped, persistent calyxes that are often vividly colored, contributing greatly to the attractiveness of some species. Though some salvias flower generously from late June to frost, notably *Salvia farinacea, S. splendens, S. greggii* (GREG-ee-ee), and *S. coccinea* (co-CHIN-ee-a), the taller, more shrublike species wait until the shortened light and the heat of late summer to bloom, concentrating earlier on producing rapid growth, often to a height of five feet or more from a rooted cutting no more than ten inches tall at transplant time. This makes them invaluable in gardens where late summer is hot and steamy, and a long, frost-free autumn follows. In such conditions, bloom is generally opulent, with many racemes on a single large plant, each raceme producing flowers for a month or more.

The racemes are themselves often attractive, tinted vivid colors, retaining their decorative bracts long after individual flowers are spent.

Though the salvias most commonly grown as annuals are started from seed, many others are propagated from tip cuttings that root easily almost any time of the year, or from divisions of established clumps. Rare or newly introduced salvias are best bought as rooted cuttings from nurseries that specialize in unusual tender plants, though when seed is available, it should be started quite early, ten to twelve weeks before the last anticipated frost date, usually in late February or early March. The seed of most species requires light to germinate, and so it should be sprinkled thinly across damp, sterile compost, only lightly pressed in with a board, covered with plastic wrap, and kept in bright conditions at around 65° to 70°F until germination occurs. Young seedlings can be pricked out and grown on in bright, well-ventilated conditions, and develop best at nighttime temperatures around 50° to 55°F, with a ten-degree rise in the daytime. Most salvias are treated as tender annuals, which means that they will not tolerate frost and will be unhappy at temperatures that fall below 50°F. For that reason, they should not be transplanted into the garden until temperatures become warm and settled, at about the time eggplants and peppers may be transplanted. All salvias benefit from a single application of granular vegetable garden fertilizer that is weak in nitrogen but strong in phosphorus and potassium, such as is fabricated for tomatoes and potatoes. Perhaps because of the pungency of the leaves, whether weak or strong, or the hairy, sticky, or furry covering that often blankets all parts of plants, salvias seem impervious to most insects and diseases except white fly, heavy infestations of which will weaken or

SALVIA COCCINEA 'APPLE BLOSSOM'

gray-green, attractively quilted and felty leaves. In midsummer, pretty mauve flowers are borne on terminal growths. Though considered a hardy plant in its typical form, several choice varieties are tender, often failing to survive damp winters even in Zone 7. They are all useful for culinary purposes but are more often grown for their decorative foliage and treated as annuals planted at the front of the border, in the ornamental herb garden, or in containers of mixed plantings of true annuals and tender plants. The boldest of them is *Salvia officinalis* 'Berggarten', with very attractive, rounded leaves twice or more the size of the narrow, one-and-a-half-inch-long leaves of the typical species. A sterile cultivar, it never produces flowers, and its mild-flavored leaves, used fresh, have a lighter and more interesting flavor than the dry powdered sage traditionally added to the stuffing of the Thanksgiving turkey. Several cultivars also exist that replace the "sage green" leaf of the typical species with subtle or vivid colors. *Salvia officinalis* 'Icterina' (ik-ter-EE-na) bears narrow leaves splashed with gold and possesses the mildest pungency of any cultivar. *S. o.* 'Purpurea' (pur-PUR-ee-a) carries leaves of a rich, brownish maroon, favored by herbalists for a leaf tea used to soothe sore throats. *S. o.* 'Purpurescens Variegata' (pur-pur-ES-sens var-ee-GA-ta) possesses leaves that are carried on deep purple stems, and are felty white on their undersides, but irregularly marked with splotches of purple, rose, peach, and white on the surface. Finally, *S. o.* 'Tricolor' (TRI-co-lor) bears narrow leaves on pinkish stems that are a typical sage green but marked with white, pink, and purple on their margins, particularly on the newest leaves, which fade to irregularly white-margined green as they age.

Among other salvias, *Salvia argentea* (ar-GEN-

kill plants, and which must be fought when it first appears by whatever means one's conscience approves.

The salvia most familiar in gardens is *Salvia officinalis,* "culinary sage," which has been grown for many centuries, both as a flavoring to foods and as a medicinal herb that is believed to aid the digestion of fatty meats and to have a tonic effect on the blood. (The species name *officinalis* indicates always that a plant was important in the medieval pharmacopoeia, dispensed from the "officina" or pharmacy of a monastery.) Culinary sage is hardy from Zones 5 to 9, producing a low, mounded bush of many procumbent stems that root where they touch the ground, each richly furnished with pungent, tee-a) has an appearance all its own. Though technically a biennial or short-lived perennial native to the Mediterranean region, it may survive on light, well-drained soil for a year or two as far north as Zone 5, producing in its second year branched panicles of flowering stems in July, to a height of as much as three feet, and bearing small, white tubular flowers. Though flowering plants are more attractive, in their way, than most garden references allow, it is for its magnificent leaves that *Salvia argentea* is grown, often as an annual. Maturing to a length of as much as eight inches and five inches across, each leaf is broadly oval, beautifully lobed and rippled along its edges, and puckered across the surface with prominent veining. Leaves are borne alternately, creating a magnificent rosette no more than a foot tall but twice as broad, each leaf so thickly covered with velvety down that the plant is almost impossible to resist touching. The youngest leaves are a dramatic silvery white, giving the species both its botanical name, *argentea,* and its popular one, "silver sage," though older leaves age down to an attractive gray-green. Leaf color is always best on rather thin, sandy soil, and the survival of the plant to flower in its second year will also be improved by such conditions.

Salvia farinacea, a native of Texas, has been a staple of summer bedding for well over a hundred years. It also is a perennial hardy from Zones 7 to 10, though it flowers quickly from seed, and various cultivars are sold by thousands each spring in nurseries and garden centers. Plants typically reach a height of about two feet when mature and consist of many branches formed at the base to create a clumped effect. The leaves are narrowly lance-shaped and covered with silvery hairs that give them a soft, gray-green appearance. Generally, they are arched and pointing downward, an effect that is attractive in

itself but that can sometimes suggest a need for extra irrigation. Flowers are quite small, no more than a half-inch in length, though they are very numerous, borne in whorled racemes on stems a foot or more long. Typically they are a pale blue, though dark blue, white, and bi-colored cultivars are common. The darker blue forms bear flowers on purple-tinted stems, and the lighter forms may be quite ghostly looking, with flowers borne on stems of palest blue or chalk white. Of whatever color, however, flowers emerge from conspicuous calyxes that are densely covered with minute white hairs that give them a mealy or dusty effect. It is this characteristic that gives the plant both its species name, *farinacea,* meaning floury or mealy, and its common one, "mealy-cup sage."

Salvia splendens has also been grown in gardens for a hundred years or more, and is perhaps either the most popular or the most infamous species in the genus. Ruth Rogers Clausen and Nicolas H. Ekstrom, in their groundbreaking *Perennials for American Gardens* (1989), deviate from their usual neutrality to comment about the plant: "Not only ugly in its own right, it is often used in bedding schemes in insensitive and inap-

SALVIA FARINACEA

propriate combinations. . . ." Other great gardeners have disagreed with this judgment, for both Gertrude Jekyll and Russell Page employed it brilliantly (in both senses of the word), the latter as infilling of a uniform height within cool green boxwood parterres. The aesthetic of both designers, however, was naturally very far from that of the modern filling station, where *Salvia splendens* is typically planted with brash yellow dwarf marigolds and silver artemesias in a pattern of alternating dots. It deserves better treatment, for it is in fact an excellent plant, vigorous, disease-free, and reliably floriferous under almost any conditions so long as it enjoys full sun.

A native of Brazil, *Salvia splendens* is a much-branched plant that can, in its natural form, reach a shrubby height of as much as eight feet. The cultivars most usually grown are far shorter than that, producing in a single season stubby bushes to two feet or so, clad in heart-shaped, dark- to medium-green, heavily veined leaves that are carried sometimes in sad fashion, as if the plant were in an acute stage of dessication. Flowers consist of inch-long tubes, borne thickly on fat, coblike racemes, with vividly colored stems and calyxes. Flowering stems are decorative even

SALVIA COCCINEA *'LADY IN RED'*

when they first emerge, consisting of promising, tiny, curved growths already brightly colored, and they remain decorative when most of the flowers are past, only the colored calyxes remaining. They are borne at the tips of terminal growths, virtually from the time plants are purchased in six-packs in spring, though free branching is encouraged by pinching out that first precocious flower at transplant time. *Salvia splendens* is considered by many to be of such good value as a flowering plant that dozens of cultivars are offered. To the familiar screaming red, various other shades of orange, from deep reddish gold to pale tangerine, have been added, along with strong and pale pinks, salmon, white, lilac, and purple. Usually the decorative calyxes are the same color as the flowers, though some of the most interesting new cultivars produce flowers from calyxes of a deeper, lighter, or even contrasting tint.

Recent breeding efforts are also attempting to restore to plants something of their tall, angular grace, bred out of them at the turn of the century to make squat, uniform plants suitable for pattern bedding. The scarlet-flowered, French-bred cultivar unfortunately named 'Rambo' (one might have preferred "Rimbaud") is a step in this direction, with vigorous branched growth to two feet, and the plant marketed as 'Van Houttii', which is sometimes given independent species status, is perhaps closest to naturally occurring plants, with loose, bushy growth to as much as four feet in a season, and graceful racemes of brick- to orange-red flowers.

Though it also typically occurs in vivid scarlet and red, *Salvia coccinea,* a short-lived tender perennial native to the southwestern United States and Mexico, provides a delicate contrast to *Salvia splendens.* Popularly called "Texas sage," it forms a neat, densely branched plant to two feet tall and as wide, with oval to heart-shaped leaves of medium green that are prominently veined and slightly raspy on both sides. Flowering racemes occur in great profusion throughout the growing season, consisting of slender stems borne singly on terminal growths, with widely spaced whorls of inch-long flowers that possess a prominent, two-lobed lower lip. The most familiar cultivar of *Salvia coccinea* is 'Lady in Red', a name that explains itself. And though its species name is derived from the predominant color of the flowers (from Latin *coccineus,* meaning scarlet), more recently introduced cultivars may be bi-colors, with red calyxes and pink flowers, or consist of pale, pinkish-white tubes flaring into a beautiful, coral-colored lip and creating an apple or cherry blossom effect. A white form is offered that is particularly fresh and lovely, and may be one of the most reliable white annuals introduced in recent years. *Salvia coccinea* remains in flower from early June until frost cuts it down. It is a short-lived perennial hardy only from Zones 8 to 10, though once grown, self-seeded plants will appear in following years in all but the coldest gardens. Cuttings may be taken in midsummer for plants that will flower indoors or in a greenhouse throughout the winter if grown in very bright light at temperatures around 55° to 60°F.

A plant quite different in appearance but with a similar native range is *Salvia greggii*. It is popularly called "autumn sage" because in its desert habitats it flowers most freely after autumn and winter rains, though in gardens it will remain in bloom from first setting out in June until fairly heavy frosts cut it down in autumn. It forms a woody, branched sub-shrub to two feet tall, sparsely furnished with oblong to narrowly oval, inch-long rounded leaves. Flowers are borne in terminal racemes to six inches long and consist

SALVIA GREGGII

of an inch-long tube flaring out into a broad, pouting lower lip and a short, hooded upper one. Flowers are never numerously or thickly borne on racemes, but rather are sprinkled over the top of the plant like tiny, vivid butterflies. The typical color of the flowers is a warm, scarlet red, though lighter and darker shadings occur in nature.

Salvia greggii is quite similar in form and flower to *Salvia microphylla* (mi-cro-PHI-la), the "little-leaved autumn sage," which occupies an overlapping range from central Mexico north to southern Texas. It is a bushier, somewhat more robust plant, bearing flowers of brick to light red, magenta, mauve, or lilac-pink. Where both species occur together, natural hybrids often result, the first of which were identified by John Fairey, a dedicated explorer of southwestern American flora and a principal of Yucca Do Nursery in Hempstead, Texas. Listed as *Salvia* x *jamensis* (hi-MEN-sis), it probably includes many of the loveliest cultivars presently offered, with flowers ranging from cream through buff, peach and coral to light, clear scarlet, often shading from darker to lighter colors as they age, and sometimes borne on chocolate-colored stems. These crosses, first natural and now contrived,

SALVIA MICROPHYLLA *'RED VELVET'*

are offered as named cultivars in ever-increasing numbers, sometimes representing a significant increase in beauty over the two closely related species, which are in themselves often beautiful enough. And though *S. x jamensis* has also introduced great botanical confusion, it is not to be regretted, given the lovely plants that have resulted.

One or another species of *Salvia* may represent almost any flower color, but some of the most beautiful bear flowers that are blue. Perhaps the deepest, purest blue belongs to *Salvia patens* (PA-tens), a fact acknowledged by its popular name, "gentian sage." A tender perennial native to the mountains of Mexico and hardy only in Zones 9 and 10, it forms a spreading bush to three feet tall, with triangular, fresh green leaves from two to five inches long. The entire plant is covered with short, clammy hairs, more apparent to the touch than to the eye. The flowers, which are the largest of any cultivated salvia, consist of a curved tube about three inches long, flared at the mouth into two lobes, rather like a very skinny snapdragon. They are borne in pairs on racemes that may be a foot long, and though they are never very numerous, they are of an intense violet blue that makes them noticeable. A paler cultivar exists, called 'Cambridge Blue', and also a pure

white form, 'Alba', both of which would be lovely were they not overshadowed by the deeper, richer tint of the species.

Salvia patens is unusual among cultivated salvias in forming fleshy, tuberous roots that may be dug just after frost, dried off for a day or two, and stored with the earth clinging to them in a cool, frost-free place, exactly in the manner dahlias are stored. They may be potted up in March, held in temperatures around 50°F, and kept barely moist until growth appears. They should then be placed in bright light, though still at temperatures that hover around 50° to 55°F, watered more freely, and pinched once or twice to encourage branching. They may then be hardened off and transplanted into the garden when the weather has become warm and settled. Carrying tubers from year to year is worth the trouble, because the plants produced will be fuller and bear more numerous flowers than those started from seed or planted out as small rooted cuttings. *Salvia patens* always performs best in cool gardens that mimic its mountain homeland. More than almost any other species of *Salvia* in general cultivation, it demands light, open, moist soil and perfect drainage.

Among the taller blue salvias grown in gardens, perhaps the best is *Salvia guaranitica* (gwar-i-NI-ti-ca), a native of Brazil, Uruguay, and Argentina. It is reliably hardy in Zones 7 to 10 and cultivated elsewhere as an annual, since its growth is very rapid, reaching a height of as much as five feet in a single season. It forms a bushy, much branched plant, with oval, pointed, fresh green leaves to five inches long, with prominent veins that give them a wrinkled look. Flowers are borne on long terminal racemes from August until frost, tending to occur all on one side and consisting of two-inch-long tubes of dark blue, flaring into two lips, the top one hooded and the lower one tonguelike, creating a flower that looks somewhat like the open mouth of a snake. A very fine pale blue form was selected by Charles Cresson of Swarthmore, Pennsylvania, and nicely named by him 'Argentine Skies'. In some gardens, *S. guaranitica* may bloom so late in the summer that it is only briefly showy before frost cuts it down. The cultivar called 'Blue Enigma', syn. *S. ambigens* (AM-bi-gins), is very useful, as it bears earlier flowers, and it is also slightly hardier, possibly by one full zone. Among the *guaraniticas* should probably also be placed the hybrid known as 'Purple Majesty', which is of similar growth and bears flowers of a deep violet purple.

S. uliginosa (u-li-gi-NO-sa), also with blue flowers, is unusual among cultivated members of the genus in preferring poorly drained soil, giving it both its species name, from Latin *uliginosus,*

meaning of bogs and wet places, and its common one, "bog sage." Also a native of Brazil, Uruguay, and Argentina, it is hardy well into Zone 7, where it returns from fleshy, stoloniferous roots each year. Wherever it is hardy, it will spread rapidly, to the point of becoming something of a nuisance and requiring annual reduction and resetting just as the plants emerge in spring. It is useful for its tolerance of poorly drained, heavy soils, and it can be excellent along the edges of ponds, where it may be allowed to spread freely. *Salvia uliginosa* grows to about five feet tall in a season, creating slender, upright clumps with oblong, pointed, fresh green leaves to about three inches long, slightly clammy to the touch, and lightly aromatic when crushed. Flowers appear in late summer and autumn, borne on short, branched, cobby racemes about eight inches tall. They are

SALVIA PATENS

SALVIA GUARANITICA

quite small, hardly more than two-thirds inch long, of a fresh, light blue with a short upper lip and a two-lobed lower one, resembling, at a careless glance, the flowers of the creeping lobelia, *Lobelia erinus.* Where the plant is not hardy, it is very easy to store by potting up clumps of fleshy rhizomes and placing them for the winter in cool but frost-free conditions. Young shoots will begin to appear in March and can then be potted up, several to a container, to eventually make a clump. They should be grown on in bright conditions at temperatures around 50° to 55°F and transplanted into the garden after all danger of frost is past.

Among the taller blue salvias under cultivation, few grow faster or more vigorously than *Salvia* x 'Indigo Spires', a hybrid of *Salvia farinacea* and *S. longispicata* (lon-ji-spi-CA-ta)—or possibly *S. mexicana* (mex-i-CA-na), which may reach a height of four feet in two months from a rooted cutting six inches tall. Its unusually brittle, branching stems bear rather coarse, dark- to medium-green, arrow-shaped leaves to as long as five inches, toothed along their margins. In midsummer flowering stems begin to form on terminal growths extending steadily to reach a length of

as much as three feet. The individual flowers, of a deep, rich, somber blue, are borne from calyxes of the same color, and though they are quite small, less than three-quarters of an inch in length, stem, calyx, and flower, taken all together, make a very dramatic display. Cut flowering stems, though they last only for a day or two in water before shedding both calyxes and flowers, make interesting temporary additions to large bouquets.

Far less subtle in its effect, though very beautiful, is *Salvia leucantha* (loo-KAN-tha), a native of Mexico and tropical Central America that carries the popular name "Mexican bush sage." It forms a shrubby plant of many ascending stems, clad top to bottom in narrow, lance-shaped leaves about four inches long. Stems and leaves are densely covered with a thick white down, giving them a cottony appearance. The flowers, of a soft whitish pink, are tiny, hardly more than a half-inch long, borne densely on congested racemes from prominent calyxes, both covered in soft, pinkish-purple hairs that give them the appearance of antique faded plush velvet. *Salvia leucantha* is hardy only in Zones 9 and 10 (possibly Zone 8 in a sheltered site and with perfect drainage), where it flowers most abundantly from late summer well into winter, though it seems to bear some flowers almost all year. Elsewhere, it may be grown into opulent, five-foot-tall bushes in a single season from small rooted cuttings transplanted into the garden after all danger of frost is past and the weather is warm and settled. It is particularly fine in the hot, steamy gardens of the middle and upper South, where it will flower abundantly from early August until mid-October, or whenever it is cut down by frost. Stools may then be dug, potted, and stored in cool, frost-free conditions until March, when they may be divided, or basal cuttings taken, for fresh transplants into the garden.

In cool gardens, *S. leucantha* tends to flower too late in the season to make it useful in open borders, as it is very sensitive to frost. However, several plants may be established in a large pot, where they will produce felty, decorative growth throughout the summer, and showy racemes of flower in autumn. As the first frosts occur sporadically and often at widely spaced intervals, pots may be carried into shelter for protection and then brought out again in the warm, clear weather of Indian summer. The soft, dusty pink racemes that pot-grown plants form in abundance are very beautiful in autumn light, especially where the leaves of trees color richly in orange and red, and it is easy to store the plants in dormant condition to be divided and regrown the following year.

Among the taller shrubby salvia, perhaps the most dramatic is *Salvia involucrata* (in-vo-lu-CRA-ta), which takes its species name from the ring of bracts it bears on a flowering raceme, in common with many other salvias, called an "involucre" by botanists. It is native to southern Mexico, and therefore reliably hardy only in the warmest American gardens in Zones 9 and 10. Elsewhere, it grows rapidly from rooted cuttings into a substantial, open-branched bushy plant to as tall as five feet in a single season. Its rather rank foliage is handsome in its way, consisting of broadly arrow-shaped, velvety, light green leaves to five inches long, borne rather sparsely on thick, square, brittle stems. Chubby racemes begin to develop in August, eventually bearing numerous, two-inch-long flowers consisting of a swollen, seemingly inflated tube terminating in two lips, pinched tightly together as if to keep the air in. Flowers and calyxes are colored a shocking, intense pink, which might be intolerable in the early summer garden, but which is very lovely in late summer, just as the leaves turn and the late, tall asters, in blue, purple, and pinks just as intense, begin to appear.

Equally rank of growth though very different in effect is *Salvia confertiflora* (con-fer-ti-FLO-ra), a native of Brazil that is hardy only in Zones 9 and 10. Elsewhere, it grows rapidly from rooted cuttings into a loosely branched shrublike plant to as tall as six feet in a single season. Its coarse, dark green leaves are felty both above and below, attaining a length of about six inches and emitting a rank, unpleasant smell when crushed. From early August until frost, very slender, delicate flower spikes are produced from terminal growths, as much in contrast to the large foliage below as could be, and very nice for that. They are brick-red from the beginning, as are the tiny, half-inch-wide flowers, borne in a perfect circle of calyxes (involucrae) that are spaced one from the other at mathematically precise intervals up and down the flowering stems. The species name derives from Latin *confertiflorus,* signifying flowers that are crowded together, but it misrepresents this beautiful plant, the attenuated spires of which are unmatched for elegance among late-flowering perennials. In warmer gardens, racemes may remain in good flowering condition for two

SALVIA LEUCANTHA

SALVIA HORMINUM

months or more, from mid-August until mid-October. In cooler gardens the display will be shorter, hardly a month or less, though when frost threatens, racemes of whatever age should be cut, stripped of their coarse leaves, and placed alone in a vase, where they make a beautiful and surprisingly long-lasting arrangement.

Salvia elegans (EL-uh-gans), the "pineapple sage," was much loved by Victorian housewives as a sunny windowsill or conservatory plant, where one of its felty, four-inch-long, oval, pointed, bright green leaves might be pinched occasionally and crushed for its smell of fresh pineapple. It is so delightful that it has never gone out of favor, both as a houseplant and as an annual that may be transplanted into the summer herb garden after all danger of frost is past. A native of Guatemala and southern Mexico, it is quite tender, though small transplants will grow rapidly into bushy, four-foot-tall specimens by summer's end. In gardens where frosts arrive early, its slender racemes of delicate, inch-long scarlet flowers are seldom produced, though from Kentucky southward it can have a surprisingly long blooming period of two months or more, from late August until late October. But

even where it does not flower reliably in a single season, it is well worth growing, both for its bracing scent and as an addition to summer fruit salads and iced drinks. Nonflowering cuttings, taken at almost any time, root readily. If they are taken in June and grown vigorously through the summer, plants can be brought indoors before the first touch of frost and placed on a sunny windowsill or in a bright, cool greenhouse, where they will flower from Thanksgiving, or earlier, well into spring.

Of all the salvia commonly grown in gardens as annuals, it is perhaps surprising that only one actually fits that botanical definition, completing its entire life cycle from seed to seed in a single growing season. *Salvia viridis* (VI-ri-dis), however, is capable of doing that, and indeed, even where conditions are favorable for the winter survival of tender members of the genus, it will still wither away by summer's end, to appear, even in the colder gardens of Zone 4, as self-sown seedlings the following spring. In both its botanical and its common names, it suffers from some confusion, for it is often listed incorrectly as *Salvia horminum* (HOR-mi-num), the ancient Greek word for "culinary sage," and it is known in gardens as "clary." However, that medieval name properly belongs to a biennial relative, *Salvia sclarea* (SCLA-ree-a), the gelatinous seed of which was used to clear the sclarea, or white of the eye, of foreign particles. Hence its common name, "clear-eye," contracted to "clary." The seed of *Salvia viridis* is no good for that purpose, and indeed, as a wild-growing plant native to the Mediterranean region, it is good for little else as well, even for ornament, since it forms a rather nondescript bushy plant to eighteen inches tall, with tiny, pale pinkish-white flowers borne in greenish bracts. But in the natural variant, var. *comata* (co-MA-ta), the double, shell-shaped bracts from which flowers are produced enlarge to almost two inches and are richly colored rose, deep purple, blue, or greenish white, with prominent veins of a deeper shade. They persist long after the insignificant, half-inch-long flowers are gone, providing a dramatic display in most gardens from late June until the beginning of September. Florists treasure the plant, since bracts may be cut and stripped of their lower, oblong, hairy green leaves for use in fresh flower arrangements. They may also be hung upside down in dark, airy conditions, where they will preserve their color as they dry, making them valuable in winter arrangements of dried flowers and grasses, where they provide rich colors, especially blue and purple that are rare in other dried plants.

For the last ten years or so, salvia have enjoyed a remarkable vogue among American gardeners, and it is hardly over, as valuable new species are being introduced, familiar species are being selected into more subtle colors or growth patterns, and new hybrids are being created among closely or distantly related species. Novelty, of course, counts for a great deal in the summer garden, since it is always pleasant to grow something one has never grown before. Beyond this pleasure, however, the tender salvia offer something quite substantial, something that is apt to keep them in gardens long after their meteoric rise to popularity may have passed. They are easy and undemanding in their culture, quick of growth, and they relish the hot, humid conditions that cause most gardeners to give up on their garden in midsummer and go on vacation. A number of species are most spectacular from late August to October, and so are valuable in the many American gardens in Zones 5 through 8 that experience long, slow autumns. Once plants are triggered into bloom by the slanting light of the declining summer, they will continue to flower until frost

cuts them down. Only their other Central and South American counterparts, dahlias, for example, or cannas, can match them in that season for floral display. But unlike those others, salvia are somehow *comfortable* plants, "perennial"-looking—whatever that means—even when they are five-foot-tall haystacks of vivid flower, equal in height and girth to the best late-flowering native asters.

SANCHEZIA SPECIOSA

FAMILY: *Acanthaceae* or acanthus family.

CLASSIFICATION: Tropical shrub grown as a tender annual.

COMMON NAME: Sanchezia.

HARDINESS: Sensitive to light frosts. Resents cool weather.

GROWING CONDITIONS: Humus-rich, well-drained, moisture-retentive soil. Part shade.

PROPAGATION: By cuttings.

HEIGHT: To 4' when grown as an annual.

ORNAMENTAL VALUE: Valued for dramatic foliage.

LEVEL OF CULTURAL DIFFICULTY: Moderately easy.

SPECIAL PROPERTIES: None.

PRONUNCIATION: san-CHEEZ-ee-a spe-see-O-sa

The genus *Sanchezia* contains about twenty species of South American jungle and rainforest shrubs and perennials, of which only one, *Sanchezia speciosa*, is cultivated as an ornamental plant. "Ornamental" it certainly is, for sanchezia produces great, elliptical, pointed leaves that may, under perfect cultivation, reach a length of as much as a foot, and that are prominently marked with orange, cream, or yellow veins over a glossy, fresh green. The variety most often in cultivation, var. *glaucophylla* (glau-co-PHIL-a), bears leaves that are almost entirely yellow when they are new—and particularly if it is grown in strong light—though they fade down to green with a rich patterning of cream-yellow veins as they age. The plant is grown for its spectacular foliage, but flowers are borne in late summer, particularly in warmer gardens, in loose clusters at the tips of branches. Each chrome-yellow flower is about two inches long, emerging from a bright red bract, and consisting of a narrow tube flaring at the mouth into five, down-turned lobes.

Sanchezia, hardy only in the warmest American gardens of Zones 9 and 10, is grown elsewhere as a tender annual for summer decoration. It makes little or no growth until daytime temperatures rise into the sixties or higher, when it zooms upward, to a height of as much as four feet in a single season. Growth is encouraged by weekly feedings of water-soluble fertilizer, applied at half the strength recommended on the package. Like most plants of tropical origin, sanchezia prefer an evenly moist, well-drained soil rich in organic material. They must never be allowed to dry out, and they enjoy a daily wetting of their foliage, particularly early in the day, which increases the humidity around them and suggests the steamy jungles from which they come. Leaf color is best in bright light, but growth will be most luxuriant in part shade, especially in warmer gardens. In fact, leaf color gains in subtlety by some shading, which emphasizes the decorative, prominent veining for which the plant is grown, rather than a general suffusion of cream or yellow that can sometimes suggest a plant that is merely suffering from mineral deficiencies.

Sanchezia is one of many foliage plants that have been liberated from botanical collections for the contribution it can make to the summer garden. Usually it is grown from rooted cuttings purchased from nurseries specializing in unusual tender plants. Though it may be used in bedding schemes, where it looks particularly fine with ferns, it is most often grown in a container either singly or in mixed plantings. The subspecies *nana*—a compact, shrubby plant to no more than two feet tall in a single season—is useful in partly shaded window boxes or at the edges of large mixed containers.

Plants of sanchezia grown in containers may be carried through the winter as houseplants, though they seldom thrive, as they demand a higher humidity than is common in most American houses. In a dry atmosphere, leaves are apt to shrivel, particularly at the base of plants, and infestations of spider mite, mealy bug, and scale will be a constant problem. Plants are much more successfully overwintered in a warm greenhouse with a minimum nighttime temperature of 55°F, where they should be kept a little dryer than in summer, though never allowed to dry out entirely, and sprayed daily to maintain high humidity. With skill, plants can also be stored in a semi-dormant condition in dark, cool conditions at constant temperatures around 50°F. They will become quite shabby, and some top wood may die, though that is no loss, as sanchezia becomes leggy with age, and plants carried over in any condition will be more handsome for a very severe pruning in March. Soft wood tip cuttings can be taken from fresh growth, which root readily in a closed environment with gentle bottom heat. Most gardeners, however, will leave all this work to professionals, acquiring fresh plants in spring and discarding them at summer's end.

The genus *Sanchezia* commemorates José Sanchez, a nineteenth-century professor of botany at the University of Cádiz.

SANVITALIA PROCUMBENS

SANVITALIA PROCUMBENS

FAMILY: *Asteraceae* or aster or daisy family.

CLASSIFICATION: Half-hardy annual.

COMMON NAMES: Creeping zinnia, sanvitalia.

HARDINESS: Sensitive to light frosts.

GROWING CONDITIONS: Well-drained, lean, but moist soil. Full sun in cooler gardens, afternoon shade in warmer ones.

PROPAGATION: By seed, sown indoors 6 to 8 weeks before frost. Seedlings resent root disturbance.

HEIGHT: To less than 1', though creeping stems reach at least that length.

ORNAMENTAL VALUE: Grown for flower.

LEVEL OF CULTURAL DIFFICULTY: Easy.

SPECIAL PROPERTIES: Excellent in containers, window boxes, and hanging baskets.

PRONUNCIATION: san-vi-TA-lee-a pro-CUM-bens

When first seen tumbling from the edge of a container or window box or forming a small, mounded hummock along a path, *Sanvitalia procumbens* would instantly win a gardener's heart. In foliage and in flower, it so much resembles tiny yellow zinnias that gardeners who see it for the first time will assume that's what it is—shrunk to Lilliputian size. But, though the two genuses are relatives within the vast family Asteraceae, no zinnia is truly procumbent or so small. Above its raspy, tongue-shaped, two-inch-long leaves, sanvitalia produces hundreds of little yellow stars, each measuring scarcely three-quarters of an inch across and each composed of twelve ray petals, more or less, surrounding a disk of so dark a purple that it appears to be black. The effect of plants in full health is often described in seed catalogues as "cheerful," "perky," "adorable," and "cute."

Sanvitalia is all of these, and is, besides, easy to grow, making it an excellent candidate for very young gardeners who often have a special relish for flowers that are very large or very small. Seed germinates readily and may be sown indoors about six to eight weeks before the last anticipated frost date, or outdoors in autumn in very temperate gardens, or in colder ones about two weeks before the last frost. The seed needs light to germinate and so should be pressed only gently into the surface of the soil or potting compost. Unlike many members of the family Asteraceae grown in gardens, sanvitalia resents transplanting. When started indoors, seed should be sown three to a peat pot or the individual cells of plastic cell packs, and all but the strongest seedlings should be eliminated by a cruel clip of the scissors when the first true leaves appear. Seedlings grow on very readily on a sunny windowsill at temperatures comfortable to human beings, from where they may be hardened off and transplanted after all danger of frost is past. But they develop equally well when sown in place, beginning to flower about eight weeks from germination. Whether started indoors or seeded directly into the garden, however, young plants should be spaced about eight inches apart. When grown in the open border, they are always best in drifts of several plants to create a sheet of bloom. In window boxes, they may be tucked along the edges, where they will tumble down gracefully as much as sixteen inches.

As is usually the case with plants that produce blooms resembling sunflowers, however small, sanvitalias demand full sun, even in the hottest gardens, where, in fact, they perform their best. Native to the rocky slopes and dry riverbeds of the southeastern United States and northern Mexico, they relish what old gardeners called a "baking soil," making them admirably suited for hanging baskets and window boxes where soil temperatures are apt to be higher than in the open border. In such conditions, they will make graceful, down-hanging sheets of fresh green leaves starred with tiny flowers, either of clear yellow or of tangerine orange, depending on the cultivar. In the open border, they are useful as edging to beds of taller annuals or perennials, in the crevices of pavement, or to fill spaces in the rock garden after the foliage of ephemeral spring-blooming bulbs has disappeared.

Though plants develop best in rather lean, well-drained soils, deep irrigation in dry spells produces the lushest growth and flower. How-ever, plants should never go into a steamy night with foliage wet from overhead irrigation, as both mildew and stem rot may result. Sanvitalias are also surprisingly responsive to applications of water-soluble fertilizer low in nitrogen but high in phosphorus and potassium, a dosage that is particularly effective when plants are grown in containers.

Several cultivars of *Sanvitalia procumbens* are offered in seed catalogues and in nurseries and garden centers that specialize in annual and tender plants. The straight species cannot be surpassed in its appeal, with its tiny zinnia flowers of clearest yellow surrounding a dark purple disk. Double forms exist, however, both in bright yellow and in marmalade orange, though "double" usually signifies two rows of petals rather than a thick pom-pom. The disk in the center is still prominent, though it may be an olive green shading to brown as the flowers age. Fully double cultivars with many overlapping petals have begun to be offered by breeders, but sanvitalia's charm may be greatest in the unimproved species.

Sanvitalia procumbens belongs to a small genus of about seven species of annuals and perennials native to Central and South America. It is the only species in the genus commonly cultivated in gardens. The name commemorates Federico Sanvitali (1704–1761), a distinguished botanist belonging to an ancient Italian family who passed his productive years as a professor of botany in Brescia, Italy.

SCABIOSA ATROPURPUREA

FAMILY: *Dipsacaceae* or teasel family.
CLASSIFICATION: Tender, short-lived perennial grown as hardy annual.

SANVITALIA PROCUMBENS

COMMON NAMES: Pincushion flower, mourning
    widow, mourning bride, sweet scabious,
    scabiosa.
HARDINESS: Withstands light frosts once estab-
    lished.
GROWING CONDITIONS: Moist, well-drained alkaline
    soil. Full sun.
PROPAGATION: From seed, sown indoors in peat
    pots 6 to 8 weeks before last frost, or outdoors
    about 2 weeks before last frost. Seedlings re-
    sent transplanting.
HEIGHT: From 2 to 3'.
ORNAMENTAL VALUE: Grown for flower. *S. stellata*
    grown for ornamental seed heads.
LEVEL OF CULTURAL DIFFICULTY: Moderately easy.
SPECIAL PROPERTIES: Excellent cut flower. Interest-
    ing late-winter flower in cool greenhouse.
PRONUNCIATION: sca-bee-O-sa a-tro-pur-PUR-ee-a

Scabiosa atropurpurea is native to South Africa, but when the first seeds were sent from southern Europe to John Tradescant the Elder, gardener to King James I of England, the plant became an instant success. Its rounded, two-inch-wide umbels, standing well above a basal rosette of leaves and packed with tiny, tubular flowers, were an extraordinary purplish black, a color almost unknown in herbaceous plants at that time. So the plant received the species name *atropurpurea,* meaning dark purple, and its curious popular names, "mourning widow" and "mourning bride."

In addition to the velvet red and brooding purple flowers grown by Tradescant, modern forms of *Scabiosa atropurpurea* bloom in a much wider range, from white, cream, and light yellow to pale or rose pink, lavender blue, purple, light and dark crimson. Mixes sold in pastel shades are very pretty when grown in drifts, though they make a puzzle of the popular names cited above. Also,

they become unattractive when the darker shades are included, though those are still sumptuous when grown alone. Seed of sweet scabious is very easy to harvest, however, and by saving seed of the colors one likes best, sowing it the following year, and eliminating all other shades, one can create a range of colors that come reliably true from seed over three or four years.

Among species grown as annuals, *Scabiosa atropurpurea* is by far the most popular, though it is actually a biennial or weakly perennial plant hardy to Zones 8 to 10, where it flowers superbly when sown in the autumn and may persist for a year or two. Elsewhere, it may be sown indoors about six to eight weeks before the last anticipated frost or outdoors two weeks or so before frost. Since it performs best in cool summer weather, an indoor start is probably desirable, though, like all plants that produce a single taproot, it is difficult to transplant and should be seeded in peat pots or plastic cell packs, and relocated with minimal disturbance to its roots. For this reason, it is seldom found in nurseries.

Sweet scabious prefers full sun and evenly moist, well-drained soil that is slightly alkaline, so where soils are acid a dressing of powdered lime worked into the soil before seeding or transplanting will be beneficial. Young plants should be transplanted or thinned to stand about eight to ten inches apart and are best in drifts, where such spacing will help them keep their stems upright. Even so, twiggy brush should be inserted among the plants to prevent breaking of the thin, wiry flower stems, which may extend as much as two feet above the leaves. Dead-heading will prolong the period of bloom, but as sweet scabious is an excellent cut flower, lasting up to two weeks in water when picked just as the tiny florets have opened around the edges but not in the center, few may remain long enough to go to seed. Plants are responsive to fertilizers rich in phosphorus and potassium but low in nitrogen, too much of which will cause weak flower stems. Though the flowers are popular with butterflies and bees, seekers after intense fragrance should not be misled by the name sweet scabious, for modern varieties preserve only a faint honeylike smell, if any at all.

Scabiosa atropurpurea also makes a superb winter- and early-spring-blooming plant for gardeners with a cool greenhouse. Seed should be sown in early September and young seedlings moved on carefully as soon as their roots have filled smaller pots until they may be transplanted singly into six-inch pots. They should be moved into the greenhouse just before frost threatens and grown on in sunny, airy conditions at nighttime temperatures around 40°F. Flowering should begin in late winter and will continue into spring if flowers are removed before they go to seed.

In addition to *Scabiosa atropurpurea,* another annual species, *S. stellata* (ste-LA-ta), is also popular in gardens. In growth, it is very similar to sweet scabious, though its flowers, each about an inch and a half wide, rather ragged and of a watery lilac blue, are not the reason for growing the plant. Rather, it is cultivated for its curious seed heads, which are spherical and made up of many small, papery cups that begin by being a light olive green and age to parchment and then to a silvery straw color. When the seed heads are ripe, each shows a tiny black star in the center, the mature seed, which gives *Scabiosa stellata* one of its popular names, "star scabious." Its other popular name, "drumstick scabious," nicely describes the seed heads on their long stems—perfectly round and almost the size of a Ping-Pong ball—though a third popular name, "paper moon," is perhaps best of all. *Scabiosa stellata* is popular as a component of dried bouquets, for which purpose blossoms should be picked with stems as long as possible, just when they begin to turn from green to parchment, and hung upside down to dry in a dark, airy room. They are also attractive when left in the garden, though as they age they are easily shattered by late summer winds and rain.

The genus name *Scabiosa* had previously been assigned to a perennial relative, *Scabiosa caucasica* (cau-CA-si-ca), which was thought to cure scabies, a skin disease characterized by tormenting itching. Although the cure turned out to be without merit, the name stuck to the genus of about eighty species.

SCAEVOLA AEMULA

FAMILY: *Goodeniaceae* or scaevola family.

CLASSIFICATION: Tender perennial grown as tender annual.

COMMON NAMES: Fan flower, fairy fan flower, scaevola.

HARDINESS: Sensitive to light frosts.

GROWING CONDITIONS: Humus-rich, well-drained, moisture-retentive soil. Full sun.

PROPAGATION: From cuttings, preferably taken from nonflowering tips in late winter or early spring.

HEIGHT: From 6 to 9″, but sprawling to 2′ in a season.

ORNAMENTAL VALUE: Grown for flower.

LEVEL OF CULTURAL DIFFICULTY: Easy.

SPECIAL PROPERTIES: Excellent procumbent plant for hanging baskets, window boxes, and containers.

PRONUNCIATION: sca-VO-la ay-MEW-la

Until recently, none of the ninety-six species in the genus *Scaevola* was cultivated, either as houseplants or in gardens, but in only the last five years or so *Scaevola aemula* has shown up everywhere—in hanging baskets, in urns and containers, in window boxes, and even as tender "ground-cover" in the front of mixed borders. Its many excellent qualities explain its popularity, for it is quick of growth, relatively disease-free, reasonably tolerant of neglect, and it displays its tiny fans of flower from spring to fall. It has therefore quickly become the nurseryman's darling, and gardeners who have grown it once tend to grow it again, to the point that it has already become an essential plant in the summer landscape.

Native to Australia, *Scaevola aemula* would not create much excitement when seen growing wild. It forms a straggly sub-shrub with two-inch, lance-shaped toothed leaves and half-inch flowers of a dilute, bluish mauve scattered sparsely along its straggly stems. But someone had the good sense to select, or perhaps to hybridize, forms of more compact growth, with smaller leaves, and more abundant flowers of a deeper lilac-blue. Sadly, it is never a true blue, however, for there is always a hint of pink that keeps the flowers from being the color of *Lobelia erinus,* for example. But it is an acceptable blue, and this, along with its ease of cultivation, has made *Scaevola aemula* indispensable.

Two or three cultivars of scaevola are offered for sale, and more are sure to follow as other species are discovered and cultivars selected. Though accurate records have not been kept, it is assumed that the scaevolas presently on the market are hybrids of *S. aemula* and other species. 'Blue Wonder', which is apparently identical to 'Blue Fan', is a vigorous plant, with trailing stems to as much as two feet in length in a single season. Its flowers, borne in leafy racemes, occur as long as the plant is healthy but are most abundant from late spring to autumn. Each is about a half-inch wide, and of curious form, made up of five lobes of equal length arrayed on the lower side of the blossom like a fan or an outstretched hand. The lilac-blue of the flowers may be deepened by applications of iron chelates, a refined form of iron sulphate, which should be administered in strict accordance with the manufacturer's directions as a too generous dose will stunt or even kill the plant. The lilac tones of *S. aemula* are even more pronounced in the frequently offered cultivar 'Mauve Clusters'.

Scaevolas require full sun and humus-rich, well-drained, moist soil for best development. Though plants may be bushy in youth, they are naturally procumbent and will produce creeping or down-hanging stems to as much as two feet long in a single season, a growth habit that suits them admirably for window boxes or the edges of large containers of mixed plants. They relish heat and are reasonably tolerant of drying out at the roots, though when they become bone dry, they may shrivel past recovery. Supplementary fertilizer is seldom necessary to encourage bloom. Plants may be pinched or sheared to keep them in bounds and to encourage bushy growth, though they are naturally graceful and can be left

SCAEVOLA AEMULA

to sprawl as they will. In the warmest American gardens of Zones 9 and 10, scaevolas are perennial plants, forming dense mats of evergreen foliage and flowering virtually all the year round. Elsewhere, they may be cut back severely before frost and brought indoors to a sunny windowsill or cool greenhouse to regrow, though flowers will be scarce in the darker months of the year.

Except for those rare species grown from seed by specialists, scaevolas are propagated by soft tip cuttings, which may be taken at any time of the year, though late winter to early spring is best as cuttings root most easily if no flowers or flower buds have formed. Cuttings are inserted in half peat and half sharp sand or perlite, in a close, warm environment. Roots may form in as short a time as two weeks, after which the cuttings should be carefully potted in rich, fibrous, well-drained compost and pinched several times to encourage branching.

Scaevolas belong to a very small botanical family, the Goodeniaceae, with only thirteen genera, of which they are the only species cultivated for garden ornament. The genus name commemorates Samuel Goodenough (1743–1827), bishop of Carlisle, an avid botanist who was among the founders of the Linnean Society of London. The genus name derives from Latin *scaevus,* meaning left, and signifies the one-sided flowers typical of the genus. The species name *aemula* means imitating or rivaling, though imitating or rivaling what is not clear.

SCHIZANTHUS X WISETONENSIS

FAMILY: *Solanaceae* or deadly nightshade family.
CLASSIFICATION: Tender or half-hardy annual.

COMMON NAMES: Poor man's orchid, butterfly flower, schizanthus.
HARDINESS: Sensitive to light frosts.
GROWING CONDITIONS: Extemely rich, fibrous, well-drained but moisture-retentive soil. Full sun.
PROPAGATION: By seed, sown indoors 10 to 12 weeks before frost.
HEIGHT: From 9" to 2', depending on cultivar and culture.
ORNAMENTAL VALUE: Grown for flower.
LEVEL OF CULTURAL DIFFICULTY: Difficult.
SPECIAL PROPERTIES: None.
PRONUNCIATION: shi-ZAN-thus wi-seh-toe-NEN-sis

*E*xcept for regions that enjoy long, moist, cool summers—which is to say the upper West Coast of North America and parts of England and Scotland—schizanthus is rarely seen in the stunning perfection it can achieve, for it loathes summer heat and is subject to many diseases when under stress. Typically, plants are between one and two feet tall, though dwarf forms, at about nine inches in height, have been bred specifically for pot culture. The alternate leaves, occurring densely on the stems, are a soft, pale green, ferny and delicate, and are pretty in themselves. But they become almost invisible when smothered by the panicles of flower in any shade of pink, rose, red, white, cream, yellow, purple, or magenta, but always with prominent purple brushing and a deep purple throat.

The flowers are curiously structured, consisting of a shallow tube flaring into two lobes, accounting for the rather flat-footed genus name *Schizanthus,* made up of two ancient Greek words, *shizo,* to divide, and *anthos,* flower. Each flower is about an inch across, though giant strains exist with flowers that may be as much as three inches wide. The upper lobe is divided into two segments, and the lower one into three larger ones. A central, projecting tongue serves as a sort of landing strip for insects, the purple brushing guiding them in. The anthers, tucked beneath this tongue, have the curious ability to spring outward suddenly when the lower lip is lightly touched, showering a visiting insect with their pollen. The stigma emerges only after pollen is dispersed, thus ensuring the cross-pollination on which the plants depend. So finely particularized an evolution makes shizanthus a botanical curiosity, though hardly unique among plants that have contrived cunning ways to ensure their own fertility and increase.

It is very hard to believe that *Schizanthus* belongs to the vast family Solanaceae, which also of course includes tomatoes, peppers, potatoes, and eggplants, among which sturdy cousins it appears exotic indeed. All twelve species in the genus are native to Chile, and the first to be cultivated, in the late nineteenth century, was *S. pinnatus* (pi-NAY-tus). However, crosses were made at Wiseton, in England, between *S. pinnatus* and *S. retusus* (re-TOO-sus), producing the hybrids generally now grown, and carrying the sort of pseudo-Latin designation botanists hate, x *wisetonensis*. However that may be, the result of these crosses was hybrid vigor, producing compact plants with less brittleness, but also with an astonishing range of flower color. Crosses and back-crosses have since been made, to the point that probably no pure species of *Schizanthus* is now grown, except for scientific reasons in botanical gardens.

Even beyond its very pronounced climatic conditions, schizanthus is a difficult plant to grow from seed. It should be sown about ten to twelve weeks indoors before the last anticipated frost date, on perfectly sterile commercial seeding compost, as no plant is more susceptible to damping off, one of several fungal diseases that are fatal to young seedlings. Packaged compost is therefore best, though even it might be sterilized by baking in the oven at 350°F. (A potato should be buried in the center of the pan, and when it is soft, the compost will be sterile.) Seed germinates best around 60° to 70°F, though it should be barely pressed into the soil, and not covered, as it requires light to germinate. When young seedlings are large enough to handle, they should be pricked off into individual cell packs and grown on in somewhat cooler conditions, at temperatures from 55° to 60°F. The atmosphere around them must be kept airy and well ventilated, and they should be watered carefully, never being allowed to go into the night with wet foliage, which will encourage fungal diseases. Even with these precautions, it is wise to mist them occasionally with a fungicide specifically formulated to protect seedlings from fungus diseases. At all times in their life, but particularly when they are reaching flowering maturity, schizanthus are very brittle, and so plants must be handled with care to avoid the heartbreak of a splendid specimen snapping off just as it is about to flower.

Schizanthus develop best when fed regularly with water-soluble fertilizer, applied at half strength and twice as often as is recommended on the package. When young plants have reached a height of about four inches, they should be pinched to encourage branching, and pinched again at about eight inches. They may be transplanted into the garden or in outdoor containers after all danger of frost is past, in rich, moist, well-drained humusy earth—the best the gardener can manage. In open beds plants should be spaced about twelve inches apart, but in containers they may be spaced much closer, though they will then require regular supplementary fertilizer.

No plant is more splendid than schizanthus for growing in cool greenhouses for winter or late-spring display. Seed should be sown in late August or early September for plants that will flower from January to April. Young plants should be grown on in quite cool conditions, ranging from 45° to 55°F at night, and ten degrees warmer in the daytime. Plants should be pricked out and planted first in three-inch pots, and then moved on progressively until they occupy seven- or eight-inch pots, pinching out terminal growth at four inches and again at eight. For an extended flowering sequence, some plants may be delayed by a third pinching, though once the panicles of flower buds have formed, pinching should stop. Supplementary water-soluble fertilizer should be applied at regular intervals, and those high in potassium and phosphate, but low in nitrogen, will produce the richest panicles of flower. The result of this cosseting should be plants so full of bloom that they appear to be made up entirely of flower, no leaves apparent.

SCHIZOPETALON WALKERI

FAMILY: *Cruciferae* or mustard family.

CLASSIFICATION: Half-hardy annuals.

COMMON NAME: Schizopetalon.

HARDINESS: Sensitive to frosts.

GROWING CONDITIONS: Moderately rich, perfectly drained soil. Full sun.

PROPAGATION: By seed, sown indoors in peat pots 6 weeks before last frost, or outdoors just after frost.

HEIGHT: From 8″ to 1′.

ORNAMENTAL VALUE: Grown for flower.

LEVEL OF CULTURAL DIFFICULTY: Moderately difficult.

SPECIAL PROPERTIES: Frangrant, particularly at night.

PRONUNCIATION: ski-zo-PET-a-lon WAL-ker-i

For years seed of schizopetalon has been offered by mail order companies specializing in unusual annuals. Still, it is a plant almost never found in gardens, though its charm is undeniable, captivating any who see or smell it. Its delicate flowers, hardly more than an inch across, are beautifully crafted, consisting of four petals, each creased lightly down the middle, and cut into seven very narrow lobes, three on each side and one at the end, giving the blossom an ethereal, feathery effect. Their color is a creamy white with a slight green tinge, and flowers are borne in long racemes on the upper half of the plant. The magical fragrance of schizopetalon—like that of almonds but sweeter—is most apparent at night, so the plant, which merits close study in any case, should be planted in bedroom window boxes or in containers on terraces or wherever one lingers in the evening.

Schizopetalon is perhaps less often grown than it should be because it is among those annuals that do not accept transplanting and therefore seldom show up in garden centers or nurseries. It must be grown from seed sown at home, which should be started indoors in peat pots about six weeks from the last anticipated frost date. Three or so seed should be sown to a pot and covered with about a quarter of an inch of sifted compost. When the first true sets of leaves have formed, all but the strongest should be clipped away.

As schizopetalon blooms very quickly from seed, coming into flower about six weeks from germination, it may also be successfully sown outdoors in patches of the border after all danger of frost is past. Schizopetalon requires full sun and moderately rich, well-drained, light soil. The first central stem that forms will flop over to one side, an untidiness that should not be corrected with staking, since additional stems will sprout from the lower axils of the leaves. Eventually plants reach a height between eight inches and a foot, and if spaced between six and eight inches apart they will interweave to form a reasonably attractive mass. The period of bloom is relatively brief, six weeks or so, though if plants are cut back by about two-thirds before they have fully formed seed, and fed with water-soluble fertilizer, they will usually re-bloom.

In the early nineteenth century, schizopetalon was extremely popular as a winter-flowering plant for cool greenhouses, where both the delicacy of its flowers and their fragrance were greatly appreciated. As more Americans acquire greenhouses, schizopetalon may return to popularity for that purpose. Seed should be sown around the end of September for flowers in late winter and early spring. Young plants should be moved on when their pots are full of roots, taking great care not to damage the earth ball as it is gently transferred to a larger pot, ending with one about seven inches in diameter. Plants should be grown on at nighttime temperatures between 45° and 50°F, ten degrees higher in the daytime. Weak, water-soluble fertilizer should be applied every two weeks until bloom begins.

Schizopetalon walkeri is the only cultivated member of its genus of five species, all native to Chile. The genus name describes the fringed petals of the flower, from ancient Greek *schizo,* to divide, and *petalon,* a petal. The species name *walkeri* commemorates John Walker (1731–1804), about whom little else is known.

SELAGINELLA KRAUSSIANA

FAMILY: *Selaginellaceae* or selaginella family.

CLASSIFICATION: Tender perennial grown as tender annual.

COMMON NAMES: Club moss, trailing spikemoss, selaginella.

HARDINESS: Sensitive to frost.

GROWING CONDITIONS: Humus-rich, moist, well-drained soil. Full sun in cooler gardens, part shade in warmer ones.

PROPAGATION: By tip cuttings, taken at any time.

HEIGHT: To 6″.

ORNAMENTAL VALUE: Grown for mosslike appearance.

LEVEL OF CULTURAL DIFFICULTY: Easy.

SPECIAL PROPERTIES: Excellent for small pots and the sides of hanging baskets.

PRONUNCIATION: se-la-gi-NEL-la kraus-EE-a-na

*A*mong tender perennials, selaginella are, without contest, the most primitive plants cultivated by gardeners, more closely allied to ferns than to anything else generally grown as an annual. Their ancestors flourished when dinosaurs still roamed the forests and when the first true birds appeared among winged reptiles. Growing as huge treelike structures then, they fell and decayed in layers to form a significant component of the great coal deposits of the Mesozoic period. Now shrunk to modest mosslike plants, they show the tenacity of other survivors of that era, most notably cockroaches and palmlike cycads. In fact one species, *Selaginella lepidophylla* (le-pi-do-FI-la), a native of the deserts of Texas down into South America, is called the "resurrection plant" for its curious capacity in hard times to curl up into a tight, gray-brown ball to be blown by the wind until it settles into a moist hollow where it expands into a lacy, fresh green rosette and puts down roots. It is sometimes sold as a curiosity to delight children, for with a bit of moisture, it will attempt to resume its growing life many times, until it perishes from sheer exhaustion.

Selaginella were enormously popular with late-nineteenth-century gardeners, who grew many species in greenhouses or as parlor amusements in glass-enclosed Wardian cases along with ferns and other moisture-loving plants. There is an emphatic appeal to their growth, which extends outward in delicate fingers, completely covered with tiny one-eighth-inch-wide leaves that are more like scales and that lie flat over the tops of the stems, giving them the look of having been pressed in a Bible. Some are clumpy, some climb up moist supports to as much as six feet, and others form mosslike sheets upon the soil or hug the sides of pots or hanging baskets. The genus is surprisingly large, containing at least 700 species, one or more of which occurs on every continent except Antarctica, and in a range from steamy African and Asian jungles through all the temperate climes of the globe, even to the Arctic tundra.

The color of the scaly branched and fingered twigs ranges from a fresh, bright green through darker greens, almost to black. Some species—considered among the most choice by late-nineteenth-century gardeners—show a metallic sheen of gray, blue, or bronze, and were popularly called "peacock mosses." Toward the end of the Victorian era, perhaps as many as 200 species were in general cultivation, though most of them are now found only in the collections of major botanical gardens. Nevertheless, the 2000–2001 edition of *The Plant Finder,* a source book published by the Royal Horticultural Society for all plants available for purchase in the British Isles, lists twelve distinct species and four cultivars, of which a surprising five have received the

RHS Award of Garden Merit, proving again that selaginella are survivors, at least in horticultural circles.

One species, *Selaginella kraussiana,* has lately cut a modestly glamorous figure in nurseries specializing in annuals and tender plants, and for very good reason. Everyone loves a moss, and many gardeners crave them, but except on the upper West and East Coasts of North America, where soils are damp and nights are fresh and cool, the true mosses are difficult to grow. *Selaginella kraussiana* is far easier, flourishing in almost any garden in humus-rich, moist but well-drained soil, in full sun, dappled or full shade, preferring more sun in the north and more shadow farther south. It responds very well to weekly applications of water-soluble fertilizer, applied at half the strength recommended on the package. In steamy weather, it should be watered early in the day so it dries out before nightfall, thus avoiding its one great bane, which is fungal disease, but it must never be allowed to dry out completely at the roots, which will cause it to shrivel to death, nor must the soil be waterlogged, which will quickly cause it to rot.

Selaginella kraussiana is a true perennial, though it is hardy only where it experiences not a touch of frost—Zones 9 and 10. But it is quick of growth, and so it may be used in containers, hanging baskets, window boxes, or even in bedding schemes, where it offers a curious and wonderfully mossy effect where none is expected. The species form, which produces fluffy masses of medium green scaly stems, is not seen so often as the cultivar 'Aurea' (AU-ree-a), which is a bright, light green, closer to chartreuse in strong light. The cultivar 'Variegata' (var-ee-GA-ta), with foliage irregularly splashed with white, can sometimes be bought from nurseries that specialize in rare and unusual houseplants. And finally, the cultivar 'Brownii' (BROWN-ee-ee) does not creep, but rather forms small cushions making it attractive in dish gardens and miniature landscapes.

As primitive plants selaginella never flower, and so they do not form seed. The reproductive organs are tiny cones, technically called "strobili," which are borne in the axils of mature branches and which produce male spores at the top and female spores at the bottom. Like ferns, selaginella pass through two distinct phases of life. Quickening spores produce prothallia, small, scumlike growths across the surface of damp soil that may be male or female. Once contact is made between the two sexes of prothallia, however, a new baby selaginella is born. In favorable environments, such as occur on the punky, damp timbers of greenhouse benches, in the sour, damp soil beneath them, or even on the moist sides of clay pots, selaginella will often appear spontaneously. They are never a nuisance, and indeed, in nineteenth-century conservatories they were encouraged as a green fringe along the edges of benches and even as a decoration to the sides of pots of flowers.

Fortunately, one need not depend on the chance encounters of male and female strobili to secure new plants of selaginella. Plants are propagated from inch-long tip cuttings inserted into friable, well-drained but constantly moist compost, usually in the hanging basket or pot in which they will spend their whole life. They root with great ease, even if cuttings are simply scattered across suitably moist, well-drained soil, placed in the shade, and covered with a pane of glass. They thrive in all summer weathers, and before frost touches them they may be brought indoors or into a cool greenhouse for the winter, where they should be kept dryer than in summer, though not so dry as to cause them to shrivel.

The genus name *Selaginella* is a diminutive of a species in another related genus, *Lycopodium selago* (lye-co-PO-dee-um se-LA-go), the "princess" or "club moss" that, sadly, is harvested from eastern woodlands to make Christmas wreaths each year, a practice that is endangering the survival of native stands.

SENECIO SPECIES

FAMILY: *Asteraceae* or aster or daisy family.

CLASSIFICATION: Tender perennials grown as half-hardy or hardy annuals.

COMMON NAME: Senecio (other popular names vary with species).

HARDINESS: Varies according to species.

GROWING CONDITIONS: Ordinary, well-drained, dryish soil. Full sun. (Vining senecios require rich, moist, perfectly drained soil and will accept some shade.)

PROPAGATION: By seed, sown 10 to 12 weeks before last frost. Vining senecios propagated by tip cuttings taken at any time.

HEIGHT: To 1½', though vining types can extend up to 4' in a season.

ORNAMENTAL VALUE: Grown for foliage.

LEVEL OF CULTURAL DIFFICULTY: Easy.

SPECIAL PROPERTIES: None.

PRONUNCIATION: see-NEE-see-o

The large genus *Senecio*, which contains more than a thousand species, reflects possibly a greater diversity than any other genus in the plant kingdom, for it includes trees, shrubs, sub-shrubs, perennials, and annuals, many of very different appearance and some quite cactuslike, with swollen, succulent joints. All produce flowers, however, that are recognizable as daisies, though some lack ray petals and are merely buttons of disk florets. Their seeds all possess a silky white parachute, or pappus, which allows them to travel great distances and supplies the genus with its Latin name, reflecting a fancied resemblance of the silvery parachute to the hair of an old man, *senex* in Latin.

Within the genus are many species of ornamental value, as both greenhouse and hardy plants, though none is cultivated more than *Senecio cineraria* (sin-uh-RA-ree-a), the familiar "dusty miller" of summer gardens. It shares this popular name with a close relative, *S. viravira* (vi-ra-VI-ra), and with two other unrelated plants, *Artemisia stelleriana* (ar-ti-MEE-si-a ste-le-RI-a-na) and *Pyrethrum* (*Chrysanthemum*) *ptarmiciflorum* (pi-REE-thrum tar-mi-si-FLO-rum), but of them all, *Senecio cineraria* is the most beautiful as well as the most frequently cultivated. It flowers in late summer, producing half-inch yellow or cream-colored daisies in small terminal clusters, though it rarely blooms the first year from seed or cuttings. That is not a loss, as it happens, for the plant is grown entirely for its leaves, which are beautifully shaped and, because of the dense silvery hairs that cover them, a stark, grayish white. (The species name *cineraria* is Latin for ashy, which accurately describes their color.) The leaves are borne alternately along stems that are also felted and silver, and that vary in length according to their maturity from two to six inches long. They are always more or less lobed, though cultivars such as 'Cirrus' produce broad, oval leaves toothed along their edges, and those like 'Silver Dust' are so finely divided and re-divided that they resemble feathers.

Easily the most popular cultivar, however, is 'White Diamond', with very thick, almost succulent leaves that are divided and re-divided into rounded lobes. This is the plant that provides the "silver note" to brash annuals such as zinnias, marigolds, and scarlet salvia in public bedding schemes and in front of drive-in restaurants and filling stations. Discriminating gardeners sometimes turn away from it with a shudder, but, like many other badly or overused plants, it can be very beautiful when sensitively planted, perhaps with mauve, purple, or pale-pink flowers. It is also one of the hardiest of all annuals, surviving through the winter in protected places as far north as New York City. Native to the Mediterranean coast, it is actually a sub-shrub that may reach a height of four feet where it is hardy, though as a bedding annual it rarely exceeds a foot and a half, branching freely to form a bush almost as wide.

Recognizably related to *Senecio cineraria* is *S. viravira*, a native of Argentina whose curious species name is of native vernacular origin. Also hardy to Zones 8 to 10 (possibly 7 with protection), it can form—in late summer—a sprawling, much-branched bush to about four feet, producing small off-white or pale yellow buttons without ray petals. When used as a bedding plant, however, it reaches no more than fifteen inches and seldom blooms. Its leaves, typically about three inches long, are cut into numerous fine, pointed segments, creating a feathery, lacy appearance not unlike that of *Artemisia* x 'Powis Castle'. As with *S. cineraria,* both leaves and stems are covered thickly with a felty down that gives them a startlingly silver or white appearance. Though both will take some shade, the color develops most brilliantly in full sun and in ordinary, rather dry garden soil without supplementary fertilizer. Like most other silver-leaved plants, both are also surprisingly drought-tolerant once established.

Most gardeners will acquire both plants from nursery centers in spring, where *Senecio cineraria* is commonly offered in several forms. Cuttings taken in midsummer also root readily, providing a means of increase for rarer forms, such as the variegated form of *S. cineraria,* with cream- and yellow-margined leaves. *S. cineraria,* and more rarely *S. viravira,* are offered as seed, which should be sown early, ten to twelve weeks before the last anticipated frost date. Seed should be merely scattered over sterile compost as it needs bright light to germinate. Germination occurs quickest at temperatures around 70°F, and young seedlings transplant easily, as do plants of any age if the work is done carefully. Seedlings should be grown on in cooler temperatures of 55° to 60°F at night and slightly warmer in the daytime. The growing space should be well ventilated, and the young plants should be kept on the dry side, as too much moisture will induce root rot and other fungal diseases. When carefully hardened off, young plants may be transplanted two to three weeks before the last anticipated frost date, as they endure light frosts without damage.

Though neither of the silver-leaved species of *Senecio* is particularly prized for its flowers, several others in the genus are grown for their abundant and showy blooms. The best known of these is the florist's cineraria, now usually recognized as a hybrid between *S. cruentus* (cru-IN-tus) and *S. heritieri* (her-i-ti-ER-i) and listed as *S. x hybridus.* Both species are tender perennials originating in the Canary Islands. Plants range in height from eight inches to as much as two feet, the shorter forms growing as compact rosettes of broad, dark green leaves topped by a thick cob of daisies, and the taller ones producing more open growth and flower. It is the compact forms that are best known, offered in spring thickly budded and fully open flowers that look like a tight nosegay surrounded by carefully arranged leaves. Their colors can be stunning, ranging from white, cream, pink, purple, and red to particularly rich deep blues and purples, the latter two

shades being the most beautiful. If placed in a bright cool window or conservatory, protected from winter sun and kept evenly watered, they will remain in bloom for a month or more, after which time they should be discarded. Though both the hybrids and their parents are true perennials, they cannot be grown successfully outdoors in America except in the cooler but frost-free parts of the West Coast, where they will bloom for a long time in late winter and early spring, often self-seeding abundantly. Elsewhere, they are strictly for pot culture.

Easier to grow is another species cultivated for its flowers, *Senecio elegans* (EL-uh-gans), though it performs best in moist, cool gardens, particularly near the sea. A native of South Africa, it is also a tender perennial grown as an annual. Commonly called "purple groundsel," it forms erect, branching plants to two feet tall, clothed in three-inch, lance-shaped leaves of medium, bright green that are deeply cut or lobed into slender sections, rather as if an insect had chewed all but the veins away. Flowers, each of which is an inch wide, consist of typical, yellow-eyed daisies, which bloom from mid- to late summer, and are carried in loosely branched clusters. At one time, a range of colors was available, including white, rose pink, and deep purple, as well as double forms, though at present seed offered tends to be a strong purple close to magenta. Where it is happy, the plant is sturdy and carefree, so it is to be hoped that other shades will be recovered, particularly white. *Senecio elegans* should be seeded about six weeks before the last anticipated frost date and grown on under the same conditions required by *S. cineraria,* except that young plants should be pinched once when they are about five inches tall, to encourage branching.

Two species of *Senecio* have long been treasured as houseplants, and—like many other tender plants—have recently made the leap outdoors to be grown as "annuals." Both are twining vines that look far more like ivy (*Hedera helix*). The showiest of the two is the variegated form of *Senecio macroglossus* (ma-cro-GLO-sus), which, though native to South Africa, is sometimes called "Natal ivy," and sometimes more appropriately "Cape ivy." It is a succulent, twining, or sprawling vine with thick, leathery, broadly wedge-shaped leaves, each about three inches across, described by its species name as "large tongued," from the Latin *macro,* meaning large, and *glossa,* a tongue. Though the green form is pretty, the cultivar 'Variegata' (var-ee-GA-ta) is far more engaging, with irregular margins of cream or yellow, yellow veins, and a dusty overlay of cream over olive green. Since it is capable of scrambling or climbing up to twenty feet, it is usually grown as a cascade plant in window boxes or other containers, where it should be frequently pinched to hold it in bounds and create fresh lateral growths. It looks its best when grown in humus-rich soil, made very free-draining by the addition of grit, perlite, or sharp builder's sand, for it will quickly rot off in sodden, waterlogged soils. It performs beautifully as a houseplant in winter— sparingly producing two-inch-wide creamy yellow daisies—though it should be allowed to dry out slightly between waterings.

Similar in habit of growth is *Senecio mikanioides* (mi-kan-i-OY-des), also native to South Africa but cultivated for many years under the popular names "German ivy" and "parlor ivy." Its three-inch-wide, fleshy leaves are borne thickly and are broad wedges with five to seven pointed lobes, very like the leaves of English ivy though more succulent. They are of an attractive, dark, rich green, somewhat glossy, making the plant very effective when used to soften the edges of window boxes or containers. In Zones 9 and 10, it is sometimes used as a groundcover, where it will rapidly form thick, attractive mats of green, rooting as it goes, though in parts of coastal California it has become a pestiferous weed. Where it is hardy or when grown as a houseplant, in winter it will produce dense, three-inch-wide clusters of tiny yellow buttons made up entirely of disk florets. It grows in sun or semi-shade and will accept quite poor soil, though it looks lushest and most handsome when grown in fertile, well-drained sandy loam. Its leaves are more succulent than those of *Senecio macroglossus,* and plants should be even more carefully watered and protected from soggy soil. Seed of neither *Senecio* grown as "ivies" seems to be offered, but both root very easily when taken as tip cuttings about four inches long and inserted in moist sand and peat, or even in potting compost kept evenly moist.

SILENE SPECIES

FAMILY: *Caryophyllaceae* or carnation family.

CLASSIFICATION: Hardy biennals or annuals grown as hardy annuals.

COMMON NAMES: Catchfly, annual campion, annual silene.

HARDINESS: Resistant to light frosts once established.

GROWING CONDITIONS: Moderately fertile to poor, sandy, well-drained soil. Full sun.

PROPAGATION: From seed, sown in place in very early spring. Seedlings resent root disturbance.

HEIGHT: From 10 to 15″.

ORNAMENTAL VALUE: Grown for flower.

LEVEL OF CULTURAL DIFFICULTY: Moderately difficult.

SPECIAL PROPERTIES: None.

PRONUNCIATION: si-LEE-nee

*I*n the late nineteenth and early twentieth centuries, silenes were tremendously popular, and any good gardener would have been able to recognize half a dozen species at least, of which three or four would have been hardy annuals. Their long blooming season, the simple charm of their flowers, and their propensity to self-seed once established placed them among the essential cottager's flowers. That is to say, they might have graced simple dooryards and the borders of very sophisticated gardeners alike, for the cottage garden movement was a sublime democratization of gardening, based on the assumption that simple beauty in a flower is beauty always, whether in the eyes of the humble or the exalted (though the humble appear to have perceived that principle first).

The popularity of annual silenes fell off sharply just before World War II, perhaps because the cottagers were needed elsewhere and the gardening skills they possessed seemed irrelevant in a rapidly changing world. Many cultivars with specially attractive colors, or double flowers, or desirable growth patterns, seem to have been lost, though they may be persisting in very old gardens, waiting to be rediscovered. That may occur soon, as good American gardeners free themselves from the assumption that most annual plants can only be acquired from garden centers that perforce must specialize in species that transplant easily and show precocious bloom even as infants. Annual silenes will be among the first of neglected species to be rediscovered, for popular garden manuals are already describing them as "under-used" and "underrated."

The genus of about 500 species includes rank and pestiferous weeds, many desirable hardy perennials, several rock garden or alpine plants that are exceedingly difficult to grow, and at least three long-cultivated and beautiful annuals. *Silene armeria* (ar-MER-ee-a) is native to southern and central Europe, though it is widely naturalized both in England and in much of the eastern United States, where it is considered by many to be a native wild flower. The first of its popular names, "sweet William," is borrowed from another plant, the biennial *Dianthus barbatus*, though the second possesses a common name that is all its own: "none-so-sweet." It grows as an upright, wiry-stemmed plant to about fifteen inches tall, with celadon-green leaves that are rounded and cupped at the base and become lance-shaped farther up the stems, each measuring from one-half to one-and-a-half inches long. The flowers, borne in late summer, are produced in dense, rounded, somewhat flat-topped clusters to two inches wide and are typically of a deep, dusty rose with a yellow eye. Each tiny, five-petaled flower measures not much more than half an inch across. Petals are sometimes notched or even fringed, and each petal may be drawn into a thin neck at the base, a shape botanists call "clawed." The heads of flower bear a superficial resemblance to *Armeria maritima* (ar-MER-ee-a mah-RIT-i-ma), the sea-pink native to the British Isles, whose genus name is borrowed to designate this species. They also share its preference for seeding into old, crumbly, mortared walls. Of course, not every garden has an old wall, but it is probably true that all the annual silenes are prettiest when made to seem as if they had seeded naturally across the front of borders, along paths, among rocks in the rock garden, or in the crevices of pavement.

The second of the three annual species of cultivated silene, *Silene coeli-rosa* (chell-i-RO-sa), travels under several synonyms, and there seems to be no consensus among botanists as to which might be correct. A native of the Mediterranean coast, it is variously listed as *Viscaria elegans* (vis-CAR-ee-a EL-uh-gans), *Agrostemma coeli-rosa* (ag-ro-STEM-a), and *Lychnis coeli-rosa* (LICH-nis). (In older garden manuals, the plant is known by the popular name "viscaria.") There is, however, a consensus on the beauty of *Silene coeli-rosa,* whose species name means "rose of heaven." It is an erect, slender, hairless plant to about two feet tall, with gray-green, half-inch- to two-inch-long leaves that are lance-shaped and very narrow like blades of grass. Flowers are borne in loose, airy clusters, each measuring about an inch across and possessing four petals fused in the center to form a lovely cup. Often each petal is so deeply notched it seems like two, and there is always a prominent oval calyx beneath each flower. Typically, flowers

SILENE COELI-ROSA

open a delicate rose-pink shading down to white at the center. Freshly opened flowers bear the deepest tint, which soon fades to paler pink and then almost to white as each flower matures, so that a stand of plants will present a beautifully blended range of shades. At one time, seed strains were offered in cherry red, rose, purple, lavender, and white, the deeper shades displaying a contrasting eye of dark rose or purple. Some of the wide range of color inherent in the genetic make-up of the species has been recovered in the cultivar called 'Royal Celebration', which blooms in an engaging mixture of white, red, and rose, and in the fine cultivar 'Blue Angel', which is an unforgettable slatey, lavender blue.

The last of the annual silenes cultivated in gardens, *S. pendula* (pen-DU-la), received the greatest attention from late Victorian and Edwardian gardeners because its erect, bushy growth to about ten inches tall, covered in season with single or double, slightly nodding flowers, made it a perfect candidate for intricate bedding schemes. Its leaves are oval to lance-shaped, of velvety texture, and about two to two-and-a-half inches long. The flowers are each about half an inch wide, borne in loose clusters on terminal growths. Their form is highly variable, for some produce flowers in which the five petals are narrow ovals and widely separated, creating a very delicate, fringy effect, and in others, petals may be broad almost to overlapping, and charmingly saucer-shaped, with a single notch in each petal. Typically, the color of the flowers is rose-pink, though nineteenth-century seed catalogues listed forms that were white, lilac blue, crimson purple, crimson edged with white, and one cultivar with purple stems. Doubles were generally preferred for bedding, but the simple candor of the singles has its claims, especially as silenes belong to that group of annuals that seems half-wild, half-tamed, and whose wavering domesticity is a major part of their charm.

The annual silenes are of such quick growth that little is to be gained by sowing them indoors, especially as seed germinates and grows on best in quite cool, moist, outdoor conditions. As they are very impatient of transplanting, it is best to sow them where they are to bloom in the garden as soon as the soil may be worked, later thinning young plants to stand about five or six inches one from another. All species flower best in rather poor, well-drained sandy loam in full sun. They become rank and less floriferous in rich soils or when supplementary fertilizers are applied. Bloom should begin about eight to ten weeks from germination and will continue for six weeks or more, longest in gardens with cool nights and fresh, sunny days.

The etymology of the genus is obscure, though it is perhaps derived from ancient Greek *sialon,* meaning saliva, describing the mucous secretions on the stems of many species. This viscous, gluelike fluid traps small insects, providing the plants with a natural defense against sap-sucking pests, a bit of information useful to gardeners interested in intercropping natural pest-control plants among agricultural crops.

SILYBUM MARIANUM

FAMILY: *Asteraceae* or aster or daisy family.
CLASSIFICATION: Hardy biennial grown as hardy annual.
COMMON NAMES: Our Lady's thistle, milk thistle, holy thistle, silybum.
HARDINESS: Winter-hardy to Zone 4.

GROWING CONDITIONS: Average, well-drained soil. Full sun.
PROPAGATION: By seed, sown in place after last frost.
HEIGHT: From 8 to 10″ in first year. From 4 to 10′ in bloom.
ORNAMENTAL VALUE: Grown for first-year foliage.
LEVEL OF CULTURAL DIFFICULTY: Easy.
SPECIAL PROPERTIES: May contain substances important in treating liver diseases.
PRONUNCIATION: si-LI-bum ma-ree-A-num

*B*efore the birth of modern science in the seventeenth century, fanciful and wonderful explanations were constructed to account for the particular characteristics of plants. No clearer example exists than *Silybum marianum,* whose glossy leaves, veined and marbled in silvery white, were believed to have received their markings from the abundance of the Virgin Mary's milk, which splashed on them as she nursed the infant Jesus. Two of the plant's popular names, "holy thistle" and "Our Lady's thistle," were attached to it in the Middle Ages. The third, "milk thistle," attests to the use of the plant in medieval herbal medicine, to increase and regulate the milk of nursing mothers, following the Doctrine of Signatures, which argued that a Divine Providence had marked certain plants for the aid of a suffering humanity. Many plants bore the Virgin Mary's name *marianum* and were considered to be especially efficacious in the treatment of a wide range of diseases. *S. marianum* was commonly cultivated in medieval herb gardens throughout Europe and was variously used to treat coughs, depression, and a number of digestive and other internal problems. As has proven to be true surprisingly often with plants valued in

SILYBUM MARIANUM

ancient herbal medicine, *S. marianum* has recently received considerable attention for its possible value as a liver restorative. Its large, dark brown seeds contain a chemical isolated as silymarin, which appears to be efficacious in the treatment of damage to the liver from hepatitis, cirrhosis, alcohol and drug abuse, and cadmium poisoning.

Even without all this medical attention, ancient and modern, *Silybum marianum* would be a sufficiently noticeable plant, for its appearance is very dramatic. A native of the Mediterranean region but now widely naturalized in Europe and the West Coast of North America, it forms a broad rosette of alternate leaves that may be as wide as four feet across. Each basal leaf will typically be about two feet long, cut into lobes that undulate along the edges and are armed with many sharp spines. Their base color is a bright, shiny green, but they are heavily netted with silver veins, giving the plant a frosty look from a distance. When plants become mature, they send up several leafy stems that may be as tall as ten feet but are more typically nearer four feet, and that terminate in a recognizably thistly shaving brush surrounded by a sunburst of prominent bracts, each ending in a sharp thorn. The slightly nodding flowers vary in color from pale to deep rose-purple, though there is a white cultivar offered under the name 'Adriana'. Flowers are said to be sweetly scented by those who have gotten close to them. In most gardens, however, plants are pulled out just as they begin to flower, for then the decorative leaves become shabby, though removing flower stems as they form can keep foliage in good condition for perhaps a month longer than otherwise. Sometime in mid- to late summer, however, plants will have to be pulled, creating the problem of what may occupy their vacant spaces. For this reason, *Silybum marianum* is best established in the wild garden, or on rough banks and in waste places where its eventual shabbiness will not become a liability. Once grown, it will self-seed in all but the coldest gardens, sometimes quite aggressively. It has become a pernicious weed along roadsides and in open meadows in California, where it is routinely fought with herbicides, and where its cultivation in gardens is forbidden by law.

Because *Silybum marianum* grows very rapidly, and also because its flowering maturity should be delayed as long as possible, little is gained from seeding it early indoors. In any case, it germinates and grows best in cool weather, and so should be seeded outdoors where it is to grow just around the last anticipated frost date. Young plants possessing three or four true leaves transplant easily, though as they develop they may be more difficult to move. Individual plants should be spaced about two feet apart, eventually to create an interlocking and ground-covering mass of leaves. Plants develop best on average, well-drained soil in full sun, with no supplementary fertilizer, which causes the silver veining to be less pronounced. *Silybum marianum* looks best when mixed with other bold and architectural plants, particularly ornamental grasses.

The genus *Silybum* draws its curious name

from the ancient Greek word *silybon*, applied by Dioscorides to some thistly plant, perhaps to *S. marianum*. The genus contains only two species, of which it alone is cultivated. Its rich history includes its use as a culinary plant, for all parts of it except the thistles and seeds appear to be edible. Though virtually every authoritative reference on the plant includes this fact, recipes do not exist. Nevertheless, roots, peeled stems, and immature flower buds, when boiled, are said to taste like artichokes, and young leaves, before they develop spines, have been added to spring salads. Given the present enthusiasm for re-discovering lost vegetables, milk thistles may soon show up on the menus of fashionable restaurants, perhaps in an elegant gratin.

SOLANUM SPECIES

FAMILY: *Solanaceae* or deadly nightshade family.

CLASSIFICATION: Tender shrubs or climbers grown as tender annuals.

COMMON NAME: Solanum (other popular names vary with species).

HARDINESS: All species grown as annuals are sensitive to light frosts.

GROWING CONDITIONS: Light, fertile, moist but perfectly drained soil. Full sun in warmer gardens, afternoon shade in cooler ones. All species relish heat.

PROPAGATION: Usually by nursery-grown cuttings. Seed of ornamental varieties is scarce but should be sown, when available, indoors in late winter or very early spring.

HEIGHT: Varies with species.

ORNAMENTAL VALUE: Most species grown for flower, a few for decorative fruit.

LEVEL OF CULTURAL DIFFICULTY: Easy.

SPECIAL PROPERTIES: All parts of all ornamental species are toxic, particularly the fruit.

PRONUNCIATION: so-LA-num

*I*t seems very odd that a genus so vast as *Solanum*, with more than 1,500 species, contains no more than fifteen or so that are commonly cultivated. Four of these—tomatoes, peppers, eggplants, and potatoes—are of great economic importance, leaving little more than ten that are grown as ornamentals. Of that ten, five are similar enough in appearance (from the close resemblance of their flowers to those of the common potato) to bear the same popular name, "potato vine," and one that grows as a shrub, "potato bush." Another species, the popular "Jerusalem cherry," is sold by the hundreds of thousands as Christmas houseplants, along with its look-alike, the "false Jerusalem cherry." The remaining two, *S. quitoense* (kee-to-EN-see) and *S. pyracanthum* (pi-ra-CAN-thum), are cultivated usually as startling oddities. Though so large a genus may yet be rifled for additional ornamental species, especially given the current enthusiasm for tender plants grown as annuals, it may be said at the moment that solanum are not of great ornamental importance in American gardens.

That is not to say that the ones that are in cultivation are not very striking or very pretty, or both. Of them all, *Solanum jasminoides* (jas-min-OY-des), a potato vine native to Brazil, seems the most popular, especially in its elegant white form, 'Alba'. Like all other cultivated solanum, it is sensitive to frost and so is hardy only in Zones 9 and 10, where it will make a handsome, scrambling woody vine to thirty feet or more. Elsewhere, it is cultivated as an annual vine for its very rapid growth, capable of reaching six feet or more in a single season, especially in the heat of summer. Its

SOLANUM PYRACANTHUM

usually lance-shaped but sometimes lobed leaves are handsome in themselves, a dark laurel green often tinged with purple, and reaching a maximum length of three inches. Ten or more individual flowers are borne in loose, lax clusters from the axils of the leaves with each single flower, about an inch wide, consisting of five pointed petals joined at their base with, at their center, the bright orange-yellow, pointed, fused boss of stamens and pistil typical of most solanum. They are sweetly scented, a characteristic that gives the plant its species name *jasminoides,* like jasmine, and are freely produced from June until frost, occurring most abundantly in the heat of summer. The species bears flowers of a pale lilac, but it is seldom seen, having been supplanted by the white cultivar, 'Album', whose glistening, paper-white blossoms are substantial, but still thin enough that the light shows through them. A variegated form, 'Album Variegatum', has wide irregular margins of clear yellow and white along the edges of its leaves. (It might be considered a gilded lily.)

Solanum seaforthianum (see-for-thi-A-num) is similar to *S. jasminoides* in growth, but its leaves, while the same rich green, are larger, to as much as five inches long, and consist of rounded, oblong leaflets of irregular number from three to nine, very like those borne by true jasmines. Though native to Trinidad and parts of South America, *S. seaforthianum* has been cultivated in warm European gardens for more than a hundred years, where the English first experienced it and gave it its common name, "Italian jasmine." The scented flowers are borne from midsummer to frost in the axils of the leaves, on clusters of slender, branched stems made pendulous by the weight of the developing buds and open blooms. Each flower consists of five petals that are not fused but stand separate from one another, creating a starry effect. Typically, flowers are light lilac blue, though deeper purple and white cultivars exist. Where autumn is warm and long, clusters of pea-sized, decorative scarlet fruits will form, but—like other solanum grown for ornament—they would be toxic if ingested.

Solanum crispum (CRISP-um) is another beautiful climber within the genus, bearing oval, pointed, dark green leaves to four inches long, and, in late summer, elegant, clear lilac-blue flowers from much-branched clusters. Flowers consist of five petals fused together halfway down, but with each pointed tip separate, surrounding the typically orange-yellow boss of fused stamens and pistil. They begin to color when they are quite small buds, and open into bells that quickly flare out and backward as the flowers age. Where frost is delayed until October, abundant and decorative yellow berries may follow the flowers. The form of *Solanum crispum* most often sold is the cultivar 'Glasnevin' (glass-NE-vin), selected at the Dublin Botanical Garden for its deeper colored flowers.

It is hard to explain why *Solanum wendlandii* (wind-LAN-dee-ee), a native of Costa Rica, is not more widely grown, for it is the most magnificent of the climbing solanum. It bears several kinds of leaves. The lower ones are divided and consist of a large terminal leaflet and as many as twelve smaller leaflets arranged along the sides, though upper leaflets may consist of three lobes or be lance-shaped and pointed. All are a fresh, bright green, wavy along the margins, and varying in length from lower ones that may be as much as nine inches long to upper ones hardly longer than three. Flowers are borne from the axils of leaves in loose, bright green–stemmed panicles consisting of many buds that color when still unformed and open over a long period of time. Each flower is shaped into a shallow bowl about two inches wide, consisting of five fused petals with ruffled margins, brushed within which is a pale star. Flowers are unusually delicate in texture and are a magnificent, clear light violet, almost ethereal in its purity. Though sometimes also called "potato vine," the other common name of *Solanum wendlandii,* "paradise vine," is more suitable to its splendor.

Solanum rantonnetii (ran-to-NE-tee-ee), syn. *Lycrianthes rantonnetii* (li-CRAN-these), native to Argentina and Paraguay, produces rather ropey, weakly upright growths to six feet or so, giving it the popular name "blue potato bush." In Zones 9 and 10 where it is hardy, it looks best trained against some support, or shaped into a standard—a little, mop-headed tree four-and-a-half to five feet tall. In climates where it is not hardy it might also be trained that way, though it would have to be placed in a cool greenhouse in winter with temperatures of around 50° to 55°F. Otherwise, it will make two or three feet of growth in a single season. Its leaves, to four inches long, are lance-shaped with undulating margins of a glossy dark green. The lilac-blue flowers are borne from summer to autumn in clusters and consist of five petals completely fused into a little, inch-and-a-half-wide wheel, over which is superimposed a darker star that looks as if it is quilted onto them. The form most often offered in nurseries is the cultivar 'Royal Robe' with deep violet flowers that surpass the typical species in beauty. In warmer gardens, flowers will be followed by decorative—but toxic—red berries.

Quite unlike the climbing or scrambling solanum is *S. pseudocapsicum* (su-do-CAP-si-cum), the familiar Jerusalem cherry grown for winter holiday decoration. Widely native to eastern South America, it is a much-branched evergreen shrub that may grow to three feet or more, but that is typically seen as a year-old plant, established in a five-inch pot and heavily laden with fruit. Its leaves, to four inches long, are narrow and lance-shaped, dark green, smooth and glossy, and borne on purplish branches, which are gracefully carried outward from the main stem, creating a small, flat-topped bush. Tiny, inch-wide white, star-shaped flowers are borne in the axils of the leaves, each centered with the bright orange fused stamens and pistil typical of the genus. They are quickly followed by hard, perfectly round berries—carried in rows above the leaves—that look like marbles and are extremely persistent, lasting for six months or more in firm condition. Typically they color a bright orange, though yellow forms exist. Plants seem to bloom and set fruit virtually the year round, though most abundantly in summer.

SOLANUM PYRACANTHUM

A separate species, *Solanum capsicastrum* (cap-si-CAS-trum), is sometimes also grown. It differs from *S. pseudocapsicum* in possessing gray-green, downy leaves, and in bearing fruit that is not as persistent in staying on the plant. Its primary value may be in the cultivar 'Variegata', which bears leaves irregularly splashed with cream and white.

Two other solanum are grown for the oddness of their appearance, though one, *S. quitoense,* a native of Ecuador, and called *naranjilla* in Spanish, is valued for its large, bright orange, acid fruits, said to taste like a combination of pineapple, orange, and tomato. It bears dramatic, shallowly lobed leaves that are held outward from the plant, and that may reach a width of a foot or more. They are prominently veined with purple when they are young, and downed with maroon fuzz. Of rapid growth in the heat of summer, small plants may reach as much as four feet in height, bearing half-inch-wide pinkish-white, typically solanum-like flowers, followed by large, orange-red, tomato-like fruits that may reach a diameter of two inches. *Solanum quitoense* requires cool, humid conditions to develop and will need light shade in warmer gardens. Its large leaves give it away as a voracious feeder, benefiting by weekly doses of half-strength liquid fertilizer, without which it can otherwise be a poor thing indeed.

Solanum pyracanthum is usually grown merely as an oddity, though it has its own weird beauty. It is a branched shrub native to Madagascar, covered in all its vegetative parts with light orange spines. Its grayish-green leaves, which may reach a length of eight inches, are held laterally out from the stems, and are beautifully cut into many lobes of irregular length. But what makes the foliage unique among tender plants grown as annuals is a row of fierce, inch-long orange spines arranged down the center of each leaf that are as painfully sharp as they look. People have an al-most irresistible need to test them, just to see, in the manner that they seem compelled to touch any surface where there is a "Wet Paint" sign. In late summer, plants bear clusters of lavender flowers, pretty enough if one can get past the leaves to admire them.

As a group, the ornamental solanum thrive in approximately the same cultural conditions as their vegetable cousins: tomatoes, potatoes, peppers, and eggplants. Full sun is generally best, though in warmer gardens some light afternoon shade is beneficial, and *Solanum quitoense* may require it to survive at all. Soils should be light, fertile, and evenly moist, but perfect drainage is an absolute requirement. Plants should never be allowed to dry out completely, and they benefit by weekly feedings of water-soluble fertilizer applied at half the strength recommended on the package. Fertilizers rich in phosphorus and potassium will be ideal, as too much nitrogen encourages stem and leaf growth at the expense of flower. Plants need little pruning, though all but *S. quitoense* should have their terminal growths pinched once or twice when they are young, to encourage bushiness.

At season's end, solanum may be dug and potted just before they are touched by frost, the vining types cut back to a scaffold of branches and stood in a cool greenhouse with nighttime temperatures hovering around 50°F. Alternatively, plants may be forced into dormancy by storing them at 38° to 40°F in a dark, humid place, to be started back into growth in March. But however they are carried over winter, they should be kept moderately dry, though not so dry as to cause stems to shrivel. Water is gradually increased as growth begins in spring, and a regime of frequent feeding with diluted liquid fertilizer should then be begun.

The toxic properties of many solanum cannot

be over-emphasized, particularly since, unlike many other poisonous plants, their berrylike fruits may actually be tempting to children. Except for *Solanum pseudocapsicum* and *S. capiscastrum,* which are grown specifically for their ornamental berries, fruits can of course be removed as they form, though it is important to know that leaves and stems may also be toxic, particularly when wilted. The genus name *Solanum* is of classical Roman origin, applied to some specific plant, probably the black or deadly nightshade, known from antiquity for its dangerously poisonous properties, but also used by classical physicians in a numbing, painkilling salve that exercised a paralyzing effect on the nerve endings.

SPECULARIA SPECULUM (LEGOUSIA SPECULUM-VENERIS)

FAMILY: *Campanulaceae* or bellflower family.

CLASSIFICATION: Hardy annual.

COMMON NAMES: Venus's looking glass, specularia.

HARDINESS: Withstands light frosts once established.

GROWING CONDITIONS: Ordinarily fertile, well-drained garden soil. Full sun.

PROPAGATION: By seed, sown in place in late autumn in warmer gardens, in early spring in cooler ones.

HEIGHT: To 8″.

ORNAMENTAL VALUE: Grown for flower.

LEVEL OF CULTURAL DIFFICULTY: Moderately difficult.

SPECIAL PROPERTIES: None.

PRONUNCIATION: spe-cue-LA-ree-a SPE-cu-lum (li-GOU-see-a SPE-cu-lum-ve-NER-is)

Throughout the Mediterranean region, *Specularia speculum* is a common but very pretty roadside weed, to which the ancient Romans gave its original name, *speculum-veneris,* or "Venus's looking glass." Why, precisely, it carries that evocative common name, both in classical Latin and in modern English, is unclear, though obviously it invites speculation. Some have suggested that the hard, glossy spherical seed resembled a mirror to the Romans, though Jennifer Bennett and Turid Forsyth, in their excellent book, *The Harrowsmith Annual Garden* (Camden Press, 1990), suggest that the half-inch-wide flowers, of a true violet blue, resemble "tiny ponds in which one might imagine a goddess admiring her reflection." Whatever its explanation, the name has stuck—with never a rival—to a plant that is very charming, though sadly not often seen in modern gardens.

It is not that Venus's looking glass is difficult to grow, but rather, that it must be sown in place, as seedlings do not transplant easily. The round, shiny seeds may be sown in autumn in warm gardens, and in early spring in cold ones as soon as the frost is out of the ground. Ordinarily fertile, well-drained garden soil in full sun will suit them perfectly. Seed should be only lightly covered, or even simply pressed into the ground with a flat board, for it must lie close to the surface of the earth to germinate. Depending on weather conditions, seedlings should appear within one to three weeks. Once they are growing vigorously, they should be thinned to stand about three or four inches apart, though in warmer gardens, where germination may occur in autumn, thinning should wait until March, as some plants will be lost over the winter. In favorable conditions, flowering occurs as soon as eight weeks after germination. Flowers are borne successively for about six weeks before the plants expire. However, in cool gardens a second sowing may be made in late June for flowers well into autumn.

Specularia grows into a rather grassy looking plant about eight inches tall, with several ascending stems that bow outward from the center. These stems are sparsely furnished with alternate, oblong or lance-shaped, fresh green leaves, each about an inch long and saw-toothed along their margins. Flowers, borne singly or in clusters of two or three from the axils of upper leaves, are made up of five rounded petals arranged like a tiny bowl, each individual flower measuring about three-quarters of an inch across. Their color is generally described as violet purple, though in fact each petal shades from light purple to rich violet-blue and then to gray, creating a wistful effect. At one time, a cultivar called 'Grandiflora' was offered, with flowers more than an inch wide in shades of blue and also pure white, but it does not seem to be in commerce any longer. Both double and dwarf forms also existed, though the modern gardener will be lucky if he secures seed of the simple species. Still, the others may be lurking in old gardens waiting to be re-discovered, for once specularia has been grown in a favorable environment it self-seeds profusely, appearing on undisturbed ground spontaneously for many years.

Quite similar to *Specularia speculum* is *S. pentagonia* (pen-ta-GO-nee-a), which takes its species name from the fact that its flowers bear five-pointed petals, creating a pentangle or star. Gardeners who are familiar with the two plants often consider *S. pentagonia* superior, as it bears somewhat larger flowers, which shade beautifully from a rich, true violet at the edges through deep blue to white at the center. Its geographic range is the same as that of *Specularia speculum,* though the two plants do not appear to cross.

STACHYS SPECIES

FAMILY: *Lamiaceae* (*Labiatae*) or mint family.

CLASSIFICATION: Tender perennials grown as tender annuals.

COMMON NAMES: Stachys, scarlet stachys.

HARDINESS: Sensitive to light frosts.

GROWING CONDITIONS: Moderately rich, perfectly drained, dryish soil. Full sun.

PROPAGATION: From basal cuttings, taken at any time.

HEIGHT: To 2′.

ORNAMENTAL VALUE: Grown for decorative leaves and for flower.

LEVEL OF CULTURAL DIFFICULTY: Moderately easy.

SPECIAL PROPERTIES: None.

PRONUNCIATION: STA-chis

Some plants are grown in the summer garden because they look exotic, and others are grown precisely because they do not. Two tender members of the genus *Stachys* fit the latter category, for though they are hardy only to Zones 8 to 10 (and there only if winters are dry), they slip easily into most perennial borders without looking as if they are summer visitors from another climate. They are also excellent for use in containers, window boxes, and hanging baskets, remaining in bloom from June until frost, before which they may be brought indoors to flower on a sunny windowsill or in the greenhouse throughout the winter. Their culture is very undemanding and they are free of pests and diseases. At present, both plants are rare in America and must be gotten from mail order nurseries that specialize in unusual tender plants. But their considerable virtues guarantee that they will become more commonly available, and therefore more widely used.

Of the two, *Stachys albotomentosa* (al-bo-to-men-TO-sa) is the easier to acquire, though it is the newest to enter cultivation from wild material collected in Mexico, by Steve Brigham of Buena Creek Nursery in San Marcos, California. A true perennial, it forms a broad clump of several unbranched, lax, square stems that originate from the center of the plant but fall outward, rooting where they touch ground and producing new clumps of stems from the axils of their leaves. The leaves are up to three inches long, oval to arrow-shaped, toothed along their margins, and prominently veined. Stems and leaves are covered with downy white hairs that give the plant a silvery appearance and supply it with its species name, from Latin *albo,* signifying white, and *tomentosus,* meaning woolly. Both leaves and stems emit a strange, slightly unpleasant but not revolting odor when crushed. Flowers are produced in terminal spikes that stand upward from the lax stems that bear closely spaced, downy whorls dense with bud, from which individual blossoms are produced for up to two months, continuing to appear at the top after the bottom whorls display ripe black seed. Flowers are quite small, hardly longer than three-quarters of an inch, and consist of a tube that flares out into two lips, the lower larger, the upper shorter and hoodlike. Small though they are, they are very showy, for their color is a beautiful light warm coral pink that glows against the silver of leaves and stems.

Stachys coccinea (co-CHIN-ee-a) has been in gardens a much longer time, but though many named cultivars are grown in England, it is still rarely seen in America. Native from western Texas south to central Mexico, in its natural habitat it grows in fertile canyons and open scrub woodland, producing plants from twelve to eighteen inches tall, composed of several square, stiffly upright stems terminating in flowering spikes. The leaves, borne alternately on slender stems, are bright, medium green, heavily veined, toothed along their margins, and raspy to the touch. When crushed, they emit a faint but pleasant smell similar to that of ripe cantaloupes. Flowers are borne from whorls on the upper stems, widely spaced one from another, giving the plant a light, airy grace. Each flower is about three-quarters of an inch long and consists of a narrow tube that flares into two lips, the upper one short and hoodlike, the lower one broad and down-turned. The color of the native species is usually a vivid bright red, giving the species its name, from Latin *coccineus,* meaning scarlet, though natural variants occur in lighter red, tangerine, and orange-yellow. British gardeners have selected and named several cultivars with colors ranging from clear vermillion red through light orange to apricot, peach, and yellow. There is even a form with foliage splashed with white registered as 'Axminster Variegated'. Putting aside the variegated form, a mixed planting of all the flower colors available would be quite beautiful, as they are all shadings within the same scarlet range. Sadly, however, gardeners in America will be lucky at this point to locate one color form, and it will usually be the scarlet.

Both *Stachys albotomentosa* and *S. coccinea* are

STACHYS ALBOTOMENTOSA

easily propagated as "Irish cuttings," small non-flowering stems taken from the base of established clumps, usually with incipient roots already showing. Cuttings may also be taken from sections of stems containing two or three leaf nodes and sets of leaves, though in the case of *S. albotomentosa,* it is sometimes difficult (as with many downy-stemmed plants) to get such cuttings to root before they begin to rot. *S. coccinea* is also stoloniferous, and small, rooted bits at some distance from the mother plant can be easily detached and grown on. Seed of both species germinates readily at temperatures around 70°F, but it is seldom offered, as basal cuttings provide so easy a means of increase. Both species grow best in full sun, in moderately rich, well-drained soil, though *S. coccinea* will accept partial shade, particularly in warmer gardens. It also prefers damper though still perfectly drained soil, whereas *S. albotomentosa* must be kept fairly dry because its downy stems and leaves, meant to trap and conserve moisture in an arid climate, will quickly rot in heavy damp soils or when they remain wet for several days. It is therefore perhaps always best in a pot or container.

Both species are easy to overwinter indoors, either as established container-grown plants or as small basal cuttings potted up at the end of summer. Generally, such plants will make clumps that may be divided into separate rooted stems in late winter or early spring, for new plants to be grown outdoors the following summer.

The genus *Stachys* takes its name from ancient Greek *stachys,* meaning an ear of grain, but applied by both Dioscorides and Pliny to some member of the mint family with coblike inflorescences. The genus contains somewhere around 300 species, though relatively few are important in gardens. The best known, perhaps, are two hardy perennials, *Stachys byzantina* (bi-zan-TI-na),

the familiar, large-leaved, felty lamb's ears, and *S. grandiflora* (gran-di-FLO-ra), a beautiful, easily grown plant that produces racemes of lilac-pink to rich purple flower in late June or early July.

One other member of the genus, *Stachys sieboldii (S. affinis, S. tuberifera),* has been cultivated for centuries in China and Japan for its small, edible roots. It produces a lax, mintlike plant with small whorled racemes bearing pink flowers, pretty in their way but not really showy enough for inclusion in flower gardens.

STROBILANTHES SPECIES

FAMILY: *Acanthaceae* or acanthus family.

CLASSIFICATION: Tender perennials or tender sub-shrubs grown as tender annuals.

COMMON NAMES: Strobilanthes (*S. dyeriana* is popularly known as "Persian shield").

HARDINESS: Sensitive to light frosts.

GROWING CONDITIONS: Humus-rich, moist, well-drained soil. Full sun in warmer gardens, part shade in cooler ones.

PROPAGATION: From cuttings, which root readily.

HEIGHT: From 2 to 3′.

ORNAMENTAL VALUE: *S. atropurpurea* is grown for flower, *S. dyeriana* for ornamental leaves.

LEVEL OF CULTURAL DIFFICULTY: Easy.

SPECIAL PROPERTIES: None.

PRONUNCIATION: stro-bi-LAN-thes

Though the genus *Strobilanthes* contains more than 200 species, among them plants of great beauty, most are winter- or early-spring flowering, and so must be enjoyed in greenhouses. Two species, however, *Strobilanthes atropurpurea* (a-tro-pur-PUR-ee-a) and *S. dyeriana* (di-er-ee-A-na), are grown in the summer garden, the first for its flowers and the second for its foliage. Neither produces the conelike bloom structures that give the genus its name, from ancient Greek *strobilos,* signifying a cone, and *anthos,* flower. *Strobilanthes atropurpurea* bears small, tubular flowers in dense, long-flowering spikes with each flower about an inch and a half long, consisting of a curved throat that ends in five lobes at the mouth. *Strobilanthes dyeriana* is grown strictly as a foliage plant, its leaves being among the most dramatic in the summer garden, earning it the popular name "Persian shield." Both plants are very beautiful, in their separate ways, and are justifiably enjoying their recent popularity.

Strobilanthes atropurpurea, a native of northern India, is a bushy, perennial plant that is almost hardy, successfully overwintering in gardens as far north as Zone 6, provided the soil is light and free draining, and a mulch of evergreen boughs is placed over its crowns in late autumn. But in colder gardens it performs quite well as an annual, if it can be acquired as well-established plants from nurseries specializing in unusual tender species. Its leaves resemble nothing so much as the foliage of stinging nettles—coarse, opposite, oval and dark green, toothed along their margins, and as much as four inches long. The small, tubular flowers are a rich indigo purple when freshly opened, giving the plant its species name (from Latin *atro,* meaning dark, and *pur-pureus,* purple), though they shade down to a pale lavender pink at the throat and fade to a lighter purple with age. Seed does not seem to be offered in North America, the usual method of reproduction being by basal softwood cuttings taken in spring or early summer before flower buds form. Where plants are not hardy, one or two may be lifted in autumn, cut back, and stored in cold but

frost-free conditions until spring, when they may be brought into growth and cuttings taken for additional plants. These should be inserted in half peat, half perlite, kept warm and misted until roots form, and then potted up and grown on until all danger of frost is past, when they may be transplanted back into the garden.

Strobilanthes atropurpurea prefers full sun in cooler gardens and partial or afternoon shade in warmer ones. Soil should be humus-rich, free draining but evenly moist, and plants respond well to water-soluble fertilizer throughout the growing season. Pinching once or twice when plants are young will cause them to develop into much-branched, bushy specimens.

Strobilanthes dyeriana, a native of Burma, is a

STROBILANTHES DYERIANA

STROBILANTHES DYERIANA

much more tender plant, beginning to suffer at temperatures just below 50°F and surviving winters only in the warmest areas of North America. The plant is shrublike, with fleshy stems that bear oval, opposite, lance-shaped leaves typically about six inches long, toothed along their margins, and tapering sharply to a point at the ends. Their base color is a vivid green, though it is so thickly overlaid with magenta-purple and an iridescent silvery sheen that green is apparent only on the prominent veins. The undersides of the leaves are dark purple, adding significantly to their beauty. The vivid coloration fades down to silver as the plants age, but is still striking. Leaf color is best in light as bright as the plant can bear, which means full sun in northern gardens and light shade in warmer ones. Like all strobilanthes, Persian shield requires rich, friable, free-draining soil. It is a very greedy feeder and responds well to weekly feedings of half-strength water-soluble fertilizer. Growth is extremely rapid, especially in hot, humid weather, and plants may reach a height of as much as three feet from small, rooted cuttings transplanted when the weather is warm and settled. Pinching encourages free

branching as well as an abundance of brightly colored younger leaves. However, Dennis Schrader and Susan Roth, in their excellent book *Hot Plants for Cool Gardens* (2000), recommend planting three or so young plants in the same hole, thus creating a thick clumplike effect from the beginning. Though cuttings may be taken for young plants to carry through the winter in a warm greenhouse, most gardeners will find it more successful to start each season with rooted cuttings acquired from nurseries.

Strobilanthes dyeriana commemorates Sir William Turner Thiselton-Dyer (1843–1928), who was director of the Royal Botanic Garden at Kew from 1885 to 1905.

STYLOMECON HETEROPHYLLA

FAMILY: *Papaveraceae* or poppy family.

CLASSIFICATION: Hardy annual.

COMMON NAMES: California wind poppy, blood drop, flame poppy, stylomecon.

HARDINESS: Withstands light frosts once established.

GROWING CONDITIONS: Moderately fertile, light, gritty soil. Full sun.

PROPAGATION: From seed, sown in place as early in spring as soil may be worked.

HEIGHT: To 2′, half of which is bloom stem.

ORNAMENTAL VALUE: Grown for flower.

LEVEL OF CULTURAL DIFFICULTY: Moderately easy within natural range, difficult elsewhere.

SPECIAL PROPERTIES: None.

PRONUNCIATION: sti-LO-me-con he-te-ro-PHIL-a

Until 1930, when the botanist George Taylor transferred it into its own genus, the pretty California wind poppy *Stylomecon heterophylla* was classed in the genus *Meconopsis*. Such a family connection would make many gardeners come immediately to attention, for within that genus are some of the most sought-after perennials and biennials, most notably *Meconopsis betonicifolia* (meh-con-OP-sis be-to-ni-ci-FO-lee-a) and *M.* x *sheldonii* (shel-don-EE-i), the legendary Himalayan blue poppies. But stylomecon, now the solitary member of its own genus, is actually an annual, and—unlike many meconopsis, which are notoriously fussy about their environment—it is an easy plant to grow. Still, it is very seldom seen in gardens, and seed is rare. That is a great pity, for it partakes of its share of the beauty of all poppies, and once grown in all but the coldest gardens, it will faithfully reappear as self-sown plants from year to year.

Native to southern California, from the foothills of the Sierra Nevada mountains west to the Channel Islands, and south into Baja California, stylomecon grows as a delicate plant to two feet tall, with at least half of its height made up of slender flower stems, single or branching at the base. They rise gracefully from clumps of finely dissected, four- to six-inch-long leaves of celadon green, becoming lobed as they travel a bit of the way up the stems. Flowers are borne singly, in a nodding two-part calyx from which they shake out their petals, rather like a butterfly emerging from a cocoon. The flowers, which may face upward or turn modestly to one side, consist of four crinkly or satiny petals that slightly overlap, surrounding a prominent boss of golden anthers. Flowers are typically about two inches wide, though the slenderness of their stems makes them look larger. Their color is typically a rich brick red, and each petal is marked at the base with a prominent maroon red or dark purple spot, supplying another and

rather morbid common name, "blood drop." Many natural variants occur, however, from a brassy golden yellow through light and deep orange to coppery red. There is also a pure white form, 'Alba', which is registered as a cultivar under the descriptive name 'White Satin' and is extremely elegant. Rarely, plants occur that bear eight rather than the typical four petals, suggesting that double forms might be achieved through selective breeding. Unusual for a member of the poppy family, the flowers of stylomecon carry a sweet, mild fragrance, close to that of lily of the valley.

Stylomecon prefers a light, gritty, perfectly well-drained site in full sun, though it welcomes light afternoon shade in warmer gardens. Though called the "wind poppy" for the way its flowers dance on their slender stems at the slightest breeze, a sheltered location is preferred, since strong winds will quickly strip away the fragile petals and even damage the brittle, lower leaves. Like all members of the poppy family, stylomecon resents root disturbance, and though it may be sown indoors and transplanted carefully when very tiny, better plants usually occur from sowing the seed where it is to bloom, as early in spring as the ground may be worked. In its native habitat, it flowers in April and May, though as a cultivated plant in most American gardens, an early spring sowing will produce flowers in July and August. Near its native range, or in gardens that experience mild winters, it may be treated as a biennial, sown in autumn and overwintered for magnificent flower early in the following summer, though in gardens that are on heavy clay soils or that experience significant winter rains, spring sowing will produce better results. Plants should be thinned to stand about six inches, one from another, and a light dressing of granular, vegetable garden fertilizer applied a month or so after germination will produce stronger and more floriferous plants.

SUTERA CORDATA (BACOPA CORDATA)

FAMILY: *Scrophulariaceae* or snapdragon family.

CLASSIFICATION: Tender perennial grown as tender annual.

COMMON NAMES: Snowflake, bacopa, sutera.

HARDINESS: Sensitive to light frosts.

GROWING CONDITIONS: Humus-rich, water-retentive, well-drained soil. Full sun in cooler gardens, afternoon shade in warmer ones.

PROPAGATION: From tip cuttings, which root at any time.

HEIGHT: To 4", though stems extend laterally to 18" or more in a season.

ORNAMENTAL VALUE: Grown for flower and for draping habit of plant.

LEVEL OF CULTURAL DIFFICULTY: Easy.

SPECIAL PROPERTIES: Can be grown as winter house-plant.

PRONUNCIATION: soo-TER-a cor-DA-ta (ba-CO-pa)

Sutera cordata is an excellent example of many tender plants that were completely unknown in America ten years ago, but which, within that brief time, have become staples of the summer garden. In garden books published more than five years ago, references to the plant simply do not exist, though now it may be seen dangling as a basket plant even from the eaves of filling stations. Like several other genera and species that have attained a quite recent popularity, however, the botany of *Sutera cordata* is uncertain. The first to break on the market, the now ubiquitous 'Snowflake', was identified as *Bacopa cordata* although most botanists now consider it within the genus *Sutera*. But apparently *Sutera cordata* will always travel under the borrowed name *Bacopa*, and this confusion is apt to become more acute as other species within both *Bacopa* and *Sutera* reach the American market; for between them they contain as many as 186 species, many of which will prove garden-worthy.

By whatever name it is known, *Sutera cordata* is an enormously engaging little plant. Native to the South African cape, it is a tender, perennial sub-shrub with many procumbent stems that creep along the ground, seldom reaching a height of more than four inches unless they encounter some support to scramble up. The tiny rounded leaves, borne alternately on the stems, are about three-quarters of an inch long, scalloped or toothed along their margins, and of an unusually fresh bright green. The greatest charm of the plant, however, is its tiny, half-inch stars of flower, each composed of five snow-white lobes surrounding prominent golden anthers and borne in the axils of the leaves in great profusion. Where it is winter-hardy—Zones 9 and 10—it forms an excellent groundcover, blooming virtually all the year long. Elsewhere, it is valued as a container plant, where it may be expected to drape downward in a thick mat to as much as eighteen inches in a single season. It is also very attractive along paths or in the crevices of pavement, where it may be lightly sheared to keep it in bounds.

Seed of *Sutera cordata* seems never to be offered, most plants being professionally propagated by tip cuttings and grown in cell packs, small pots, or as fully developed specimens in hanging baskets. Full sun suits the plant best, though in gardens that experience blistering summer heat, light shade, particularly in the afternoon, will prolong growth and flower. A humus-rich, free-draining soil is required, though plants must never be allowed to dry out, which will cause them to yellow, shed their leaves, and possibly die. Though plants will grow well and bloom copiously with no supplementary fertilizer, biweekly applications of water-soluble plant food will make luxuriant and rapid growth. At the end of summer and before frost has touched the plants, one or two rooted bits may be dug from the edges of a container, potted up, and cut back to manageable size, for houseplants that will flower all winter long on a sunny windowsill with a minimum nighttime temperature around 50°F.

In addition to 'Snowflake', the flowers of which are a pristine white, other suteras have begun to appear in nurseries, bearing pale pink, brick red, mauve, or lilac blue flowers. All of them have botanists reeling with uncertainty as to where, from a scientific perspective, they belong.

A cultivar of *Sutera campanulata* (cam-pan-u-LA-ta), the "bellflower sutera," is also sometimes offered under the name 'Knysna Hills'. Native to the cape of South Africa, it forms a small shrubby plant to about twenty inches in height, with three-quarter-inch-long toothed, clammy leaves and terminal racemes of half-inch-wide, pale lavender-pink flowers borne from late spring until frost. Like other suteras, it readily accepts indoor growing conditions during the winter, though it may flower sparingly until the days lengthen in spring.

The suteras in commerce are all natives of South Africa, and the genus name commemorates the botanist Johan Rudolph Suter (1766–1827) about whom little else is known. The species name *cordata* means heart-shaped, though the leaves of all species grown at present are rounded and toothed or lobed.

TAGETES SPECIES

FAMILY: *Asteraceae* or aster or daisy family.

CLASSIFICATION: Annuals or short-lived perennials grown as tender annuals.

COMMON NAME: Marigold.

HARDINESS: Sensitive to frost when young, slightly resistant when mature.

GROWING CONDITIONS: Moderately fertile, well-drained, moisture-retentive soil. Full sun.

PROPAGATION: From seed, sown 6 to 8 weeks before last frost.

HEIGHT: From 6" to 3', depending on cultivar.

ORNAMENTAL VALUE: Grown for flower.

LEVEL OF CULTURAL DIFFICULTY: Easy.

SPECIAL PROPERTIES: Flowers are added to salads.

PRONUNCIATION: ta-JEE-tees (ta-GEE-tees)

Raising marigolds is child's play, often quite literally, since many children begin their love of gardening with a packet of this sturdy annual. It is a perfect way to begin, for the large seeds fit comfortably in a small hand, and germination is rapid. Infant marigolds are also unusually adaptable in their growth preferences and very precocious in flowering (producing their first bud sometimes as soon as five weeks after they make their appearance above ground), and are thus perfect plants for those who know little of time and are impatient of it. Also, their abundant, brashly colored flowers—in citron and chrome yellow, orange, and mahogany red—appeal to the love of bright color that all children have. Even their pungent, nose-wrinkling scent is interesting to a child, often the first experience of the fact that something can smell nice without necessarily smelling good.

It hardly matters to children, and, one suspects, to many adult gardeners, how a marigold is classed, though seed catalogues and garden references sometimes devote considerable space to explaining the various categories. There are four: African, French, Triploid, and Signet, of which the first two represent most marigolds grown in America. How, precisely, they acquired the nationalities attributed to them is a mystery, for of the fifty or so species included in the genus *Tagetes,* only one occurs natively in Africa and none in France. The genus name is also of uncertain application, originating from Tages, an Etruscan god who sprang from the first plowed field. But the several species most important in the development of modern forms of marigolds are all of Mexican heritage, though members of the genus occur from southern Arizona through Central America to Argentina. For most gardeners, who are apt in any case to pick their marigolds according to their brightly colored pictures in seed catalogues, it is sufficient to say that African marigolds are largely, though not exclusively, descendant from *Tagetes erecta* (ee-REC-ta) and contain the taller, bigger flowered sorts, and French marigolds have a preponderance of *T. patula* (PA-tu-la) in their make-up, and are shorter, with smaller flowers.

This distinction was very clear to nineteenth-century gardeners, but it is now blurred, for there are African marigolds that grow only six inches tall, with huge, carnation-like flowers on their terminal growths, and some French marigolds may produce airy, graceful plants to three feet or more, though still with single or semi-double flowers. The distinction between the two classes has also been further blurred by the increasing popularity of Triploid marigolds, which are crosses between cultivars of African and French marigolds. They display great hybrid vigor and, as they are mostly sterile, they produce a wealth of flower without tedious dead-heading. Extensive as the breeding work of marigolds has been, the time will shortly come when blood lines will be so tangled that it will be more convenient to list most marigold cultivars simply as *Tagetes* x *hybrida* (HI-bri-da), since, even at this point, most are probably that already.

An exception exists, however, in the fourth category, the Signet marigolds, all of which show descent from *Tagetes tenuifolia* (ten-u-i-FO-lee-a), and as yet have not been much crossed or back-crossed with other species or cultivars. They may be said to be connoisseurs' marigolds. They are elegant little plants, branching freely into graceful bushes, always carrying the fine, much-divided, threadlike foliage that gives the species its name, from the Latin adjective *tenuis,* meaning slender or thin, and *folius,* a leaf. Their flowers are far from the heavy, wadded, penwiper blooms of African marigolds, or even the stiff, almost plastic-petaled flowers of many of the French sorts. Signet marigolds look like real flowers, and many gardeners would agree that their common name, taken from Latin *signata,* a specific synonym meaning apparent or worth notice, is amply earned. Their flowers are always single, an inch wide or less, and consisting of five ray petals surrounding a tight bunch of disk florets above

TAGETES *'LEMON DROP'*

mounds of finely divided, grass-green leaves. To this group belong two very popular cultivars, 'Golden Gem' and 'Lemon Gem', the first orange and the second lemon. They are very beautiful when planted together, though 'Lemon Gem', with its paler flowers and greater subtlety, finds an easy place in many perennial gardens and containers planted with a mix of true annuals and tender plants.

Even cooks prefer marigolds in this group, for as Cathy Wilkinson Barash notes in her excellent book *Edible Flowers* (1993), "The flavor of the Signets is the best of any marigolds, almost like a spicy tarragon." But granting all their charms, the Signet group will never displace the brash, brilliant display made by African and French marigolds, which the late David Burpee thought should be the American national flower. (The rose won out.) Still their delicacy of growth and flower make them valuable additions to subtle combinations in mixed borders, in herb gardens, and in window boxes.

Quite similar in growth to the Signet group of marigolds is the species *filifolia* (fi-li-FO-lee-a), which draws its name from the fact that its leaves are reduced to the finest green filaments, creating a fluffy, much-branched little bush no more than a foot tall. It is very charming in itself, though one suspects that much of its appeal to snobbish gardeners is that it is a marigold that seldom produces flowers. When they do appear, often very late in the season, they are not worth much, consisting of tiny, ragged, few-petaled single white daisies. But the foliage is always beautiful and can provide a soothing counterpart to their more brashly colored cousins or to any plants grown in borders, window boxes, or containers of mixed annual and tender plants.

All marigold flowers are edible, though as Cathy Barash notes, some have a much milder flavor than others, and in any case, the petals of

TAGETES 'MR. MAJESTIC'

all of them are more palatable if one removes the bit of white where they join the stem, for it is very bitter. One marigold, however, *Tagetes lucida* (LU-ci-da), is cultivated specifically as a culinary herb, not for its flowers but for its leaves. Popularly called "Mexican tarragon," it forms an upright, unbranched plant to about two feet tall, with leaves that are not divided into leaflets as are those of most marigolds, but rather are narrow, dark green blades. They are smooth and shiny, which gives the plant its species name, from the Latin adjective *lucidus,* meaning bright, shining, or clear. The flavor of the leaves, when crushed, is very close to that of true tarragon, *Artemisia dracunculus* (ar-ti-MEE-si-a dra-CUN-cu-lus), for which they may be substituted. Though a true perennial hardy to Zones 9 and 10, *Tagetes lucida* is easily grown as an annual in the herb or vegetable garden.

Whatever class, height, flower shape, or color, the culture of all marigolds is the same. Though their quick germination and growth allow the gardener to sow them in place, a longer blooming season—in fact, among the longest of all plants grown as annuals—will result either from starting them indoors or from buying young plants from garden centers in plastic six-packs. Seed

TAGETES ERECTA *HYBRID*

should be sown about six to eight weeks before the last anticipated frost date, at temperatures around 70°F. They require dark to germinate, and so the seed should be lightly covered with sifted compost and placed away from the light until seedlings appear, at which time they should be shifted to full indoor light. They should be pricked out as soon as they may be easily handled, usually after the second set of true leaves has developed. As with tomatoes, cooler temperatures around 50° to 55°F produce the stockiest plants, though warmer temperatures are acceptable. Plants that are leggy may be stripped of their lower leaves and planted with only their top three or four sets of leaves above ground. They will quickly form additional roots along their buried stems, producing strong, upright plants.

Marigolds are classed as tender annuals, which means that they should not be transplanted into the garden until after all danger of frost is past and the weather is warm and settled, which is about the time that the petals of apple blossoms fall from the trees. Whatever their blood lines, they all originate from Mexican and Central American species, and, as is usual with ornamental plants from that region, they require full sun and the heat of summer to develop well. Soils should be of moderate fertility but always well drained. Marigolds prefer evenly moist soil, and benefit from deep soaking in times of drought. Soil rich in nitrogen produces rich leaf growth at the expense of flower, and so any supplementary fertilizer should be weak in nitrogen but strong in phosphorus and potassium. Fertilizer manufactured specifically for tomatoes will be ideal, and it is best applied in liquid form two or three times before the plants reach their full component of bloom. Some heavy-limbed plants, in both the African and French categories, are extremely brittle, and so should never be watered from above. A staking of twiggy brush inserted among the plants when they are about half grown will also provide extra support and prevent the tragedy of half a plant, heavy with dew or summer rain, splitting away from the mother stem.

Among plants classed as tender annuals, marigolds are unusual in being able to sustain light frosts with minimal protection. They are also never so splendid as in the declining light of late summer and early autumn, where their flowers both reflect and complement the turning leaves. So valuable are they at that season, which is perhaps their very best, that it is worth throwing covers over them when early frosts threaten, to preserve their beauty deep into Indian Summer. Then, even the most committed of marigold snobs will admire their rich colors and bend to sniff their pungent leaves.

TALINUM PANICULATUM (T. CRASSIFOLIUM)

FAMILY: *Portulacaceae* or purslane family.
CLASSIFICATION: Tender perennial grown as half-hardy annual.

COMMON NAMES: Jewels of Opar, flame flower, talinum.

HARDINESS: Young plants sensitive to light frost.

GROWING CONDITIONS: Moderately fertile to poor,
sandy, well-drained soil. Full sun.

PROPAGATION: From seed, sown indoors 8 to 10
weeks before last frost. Individual leaves may
be rooted.

HEIGHT: To 10″.

ORNAMENTAL VALUE: Grown for flower.

LEVEL OF CULTURAL DIFFICULTY: Easy.

SPECIAL PROPERTIES: Excellent winter windowsill
and cool greenhouse plant.

PRONUNCIATION: ta-LI-num pan-i-cu-LA-tum (crass-i-
FO-lee-um)

*T*alinum, a gentle plant native from the south-eastern United States into Mexico and Central America, is gradually making its shy way into American gardens. No gardener would want drifts of it, for it is far more beautiful when studied closely than when seen from a distance. It bears, also, a very charming common name, "jewels of Opar," though who, what, or where Opar might be remains a mystery. Its genus name is mysterious also, though some botanists have conjectured that it is derived from a vernacular Senegalese word for a quite different plant. There is nothing mysterious in the appearance of talinum, however, which has the open, guileless look of an antique botanical print.

Talinum paniculatum is a tuberous perennial hardy perhaps to Zone 8. It is worth growing as much for the character of its leaves as for its flowers. They are about four inches long and consist of broad, pointed ovals of a fresh, glossy, or waxy grass green. Like the leaves of most plants in the family Portulacaceae, they are fleshy and succulent, as are the smooth upper stems. Leaves are

borne close together, forming rosettes at the tops of the stems, from which the panicles of flowers are produced. These are much-branched, strong but almost threadlike in appearance, a striking contrast to the rather fat leaves beneath. Scattered through the panicle, each on its own wiry little stem, are first colored buds, then open cup-shaped flowers, and then hard, shiny little dull purple seed balls. Which are the jewels—buds, flowers, or seed balls—is uncertain, for all three are beautiful and very beautifully carried. The flowers are tiny, less than an inch across, and are usually red, strong or light pink, though reddish-yellow forms also exist. The flowers remain open only for a few hours, during which time the essential work of fertilization is completed, but buds are numerous, and other flowers follow in quick succession. Though the typical species is pretty enough, a gold-leaved cultivar also exists called 'Kingwood Gold', with butter-yellow leaves and bright pink flowers. At one time, a cultivar with white penciling along the edges of its leaves also existed, and though it does not seem to be offered now, it may still be waiting in some botanical collection for re-discovery.

Talinum requires full sun and well-drained, even sandy soil of only moderate fertility. It is easy to grow from seed, which should be sown about eight to ten weeks before the last anticipated frost date. Germination is rapid at temperatures around 70°F, and young plants should be pricked out and grown on as soon as they may be handled. Flower should occur about four months from seeding, though talinum is very frost sensitive, and so plants should not be established in the open garden until all danger of frost is past. They require no fertilizer, and once established are quite drought tolerant. It is a surprise in so tender a plant that once it has been grown in gardens even as cold as Zone 4, talinum will reappear the next spring as volunteer seedlings. Talinum is also easily grown as an attractive houseplant for a sunny windowsill or a bright spot in the home greenhouse or conservatory. Small plants may be carefully dug up in late summer and potted in free-draining, sandy compost to be brought indoors before frost. Alternatively, seed may be sown in midsummer and the young plants potted on until they may be moved into single, five-inch clay pots. Like many other plants grouped in the family Portulacaceae, the larger leaves at the base of the plant may be carefully detached from the stem and inserted only slightly in damp sand or perlite, where they will produce tiny, rooted plants.

TANACETUM SPECIES

FAMILY: *Asteraceae* or aster or daisy family.

CLASSIFICATION: Short-lived hardy perennials grown as hardy annuals.

COMMON NAME: Tanacetum (other common names vary with species).

HARDINESS: Withstands frost.

GROWING CONDITIONS: Lean, sandy, well-drained soil. Full sun.

PROPAGATION: From seed, sown 6 to 8 weeks before last frost. Cuttings root readily.

HEIGHT: From 4" to 4', depending on cultivar.

ORNAMENTAL VALUE: Grown for flower and for decorative foliage.

LEVEL OF CULTURAL DIFFICULTY: Easy.

SPECIAL PROPERTIES: Superb cut flower.

PRONUNCIATION: ta-na-SEE-tum

Though the old-fashioned, much-loved feverfews are easy to find in gardens, they are hard to find in modern garden references, for the plant now called *Tanacetum parthenium* (par-THI-nee-um) has been shifted about many times. It began its registered life as *Chrysanthemum parthenium,* but from that genus botanists have moved it, at one time or another, into both *Matricaria* (ma-tri-KA-ree-a) and *Pyrethrum* (pi-REE-thrum). Though *Tanacetum* is the genus in which it is correctly lodged—for the moment—it might still be located under the other three, particularly in older garden references. Its species name, however, *parthenium,* has stuck with it through many centuries, having been first assigned by ancient Greek botanists as *parthenion.*

That is the name they applied to a group of plants with aromatic foliage and small, white-petaled yellow-centered daisies that were used for various medicinal purposes, but especially as a purge of intestinal worms. The present genus name, *Tanacetum,* also descends through the medieval Latin *tanazita,* from the ancient Greek *athanasia,* signifying immortality, as the leaves of several related plants were incorporated into the winding sheets of corpses in the belief that they would delay infestations of maggots. (This practice continued in New England well into the early nineteenth century, but only in summer, as both leaves and maggots were apt to be present most abundantly then.) As the venerable common name of the plant attests, feverfew was also anciently used as a febrifuge.

But most gardeners will choose to grow *Tanacetum parthenium* as a decorative plant, for it is very pretty in its natural species form, and it has been bred into many attractive cultivars. Typically, it makes a woody-based, bushy plant, often with several stems ascending from a central crown. It may grow as tall as three feet, though much shorter dwarf forms exist in plenty. Flowers are borne in many-branched clusters at the tops of stems and consist usually of cheerful little daisies with a collar of pure white ray petals surrounding a thick boss of yellow disk florets. It may be argued that this simple form reflects the loveliest of all feverfews, though almost from the beginning of its cultivated life, forms were selected with double or fully double flowers. The former possess a ring of ray petals around a much thickened boss of disk florets, often dimpled in the middle and shaded green. Fully double forms produce tiny, half-inch, round buttons of undifferentiated petals, diminutive versions of pom-pom zinnias and dahlias. Flowers may be white and yellow and daisy-fresh, although attractive snow-white doubles are common, as well as all-yellow and golden forms, in both singles and doubles.

The foliage of feverfews is generally grass green, attractively lobed in the manner of florists' chrysanthemums, though forms exist with finer, more feather-cut leaves, and colored a lighter green. Very valuable is the cultivar 'Aureum' (O-ree-um) with butter-yellow leaves on a tight, cobby plant usually not more than eight inches tall. In colder gardens, its single flowers are scarce, consisting of small, yellow-centered white daisies, but there will generally be enough of them to ensure volunteer plants about the garden the following year. Several dwarf forms of feverfew will grow as wide as they are tall, spreading out, matlike, making them valuable for the front of the border, for containers of mixed plantings, and in the rock garden. The cultivar 'Santana' (san-TA-na) is one, at eight inches tall and as broad, with yellow-centered white daisies. They are colored golden in 'Santana Lemon'. 'Golden Moss' is tiny, at no more than four inches tall, with finely divided, mosslike yellow foliage that looks particularly good when it is established in the cracks of paving. At the other extreme, taller, more airy forms of feverfew exist, usually with single flowers, on plants that may be as tall as four feet. They have largely been bred in Holland for the cut flower trade, since sprays of feverfew always look

fresh and bright in an arrangement, and complement almost any other flower, much as baby's breath (*Gypsophila* species) does. As yet many of these forms have not made their way into general commerce, though it is to be hoped that they will get there eventually, for they would be superb mid-border subjects for the perennial garden.

Tanacetum parthenium is technically a perennial, originating in the Caucasus mountains, and though it is quite hardy, surviving winters well into Zone 4, it weakens after a season or two of growth. In colder gardens, it is therefore best grown as an annual, from seed sown in early spring, about six to eight weeks before the last anticipated frost date, for flowers about two months from germination. In warmer gardens—or indeed, in any garden, if one has seed enough to risk—it may be treated as a biennial, sown in August and overwintered outdoors for abundant flower in late June and early July. But either way, in all but the coldest climates, seedlings are apt to appear from year to year and may easily be transplanted where they are wanted.

Tanacetum parthenium demands full sun and grows best on well-drained, light soil of moderate fertility. It is very adaptable to soil conditions, but heavy, wet soils are almost always fatal and should be lightened with sharp sand, pigeon grit, or partially decayed litter. Young plants should be pinched once or twice early in their growth to encourage bushiness, but otherwise they are carefree, exempt from pests and diseases and requiring no supplementary fertilizing. Plants are generally grown from seed or bought as potted specimens from nurseries specializing in desirable perennials and annuals. Like most plants allied to chrysanthemums, however, feverfew is very easy to root at almost any time nonflowering growth occurs. Tip cuttings about two inches long should be taken, severed just beneath a node, and stripped of their lower leaves. They should then be inserted in a mixture of half peat, half sharp sand or perlite, and kept in a moist, shaded position. Rooting should occur within two weeks or so, at which point the cuttings should be potted up and gradually exposed to full sun. When growth is vigorous, they may be transplanted. Unusual or specially desirable cultivars, particularly doubles, may be acquired in this way, though as most feverfews self-seed abundantly, even in quite cold gardens, there will always be an ample number of young plants that transplant very easily at almost any time until they come into full flower. They may not be true to the named cultivar originally planted, but they will still be very lovely.

Quite unlike *Tanacetum parthenium* in appearance is the other member of the genus most commonly grown, *Tanacetum ptarmiciflorum* (tar-mi-ci-FLO-rum), which has also passed through several other genera, having been listed (and still) as *Chrysanthemum ptarmiciflorum* and *Pyrethrum ptarmiciflorum*. It is one of the "dusty millers," grown for its silvery, almost white foliage, and like all the rest, sometimes beautifully, but too often insensitively used among other plants grown as annuals. *Tanacetum ptarmiciflorum* differs from the most popular other dusty miller, *Senecio cineraria* (se-NEE-see-o cin-uh-RAR-i-a), in possessing very finely cut, feathery foliage that gives it its other popular names, "silver feather" and "silver lace." Each two- to four-inch-long leaf is cut into ten or so segments, which are then cut again into as many. The leaves are curiously carried on petioles that are almost upright on the branched stems, like hands about to be clasped in prayer. Each leaf is thickly coated with minute silvery hairs, as are the stems themselves, giving the entire plant a ghostly appearance.

Tanacetum ptarmiciflorum is native to a very lim-ited area in the Canary Islands and is thus hardy only to Zones 9 and 10, where it is a true perennial, growing into an erect, much-branched plant to two or more feet tall, and producing white-petaled daisies with a yellow center about an inch wide, recognizably feverfew-like. However, flowers rarely appear on plants grown in gardens farther north than Zone 8, though as the plant is cultivated for its foliage and not for its rather insignificant bloom, that is no loss.

Tanacetum ptarmiciflorum seems to thrive on neglect, flourishing and looking wonderful in the poorest soils and with almost no supplementary care. In that, it is not unlike other dusty millers, which are generally tough plants, conditioned to grow in difficult places, and wearing their protective coats of silver against the drought and harsh winds they experience in their native environments. But *Tanacetum ptarmiciflorum* has a distinctly different look from other dusty millers, beautiful as they are. It is far more delicate and refined, suitable for the most exquisitely drawn botanical study. One would therefore like to see the plant all by itself, grown singly in a six-inch clay pot or en masse in a large container.

The species name *ptarmiciflorum,* at which even the most botanically practiced must take a flying leap, probably derives from the ancient Greek *ptarmike,* used for some plant that caused sneezing. The dusty, powdered-over look of its leaves might reasonably suggest that response.

THUNBERGIA SPECIES

FAMILY: *Acanthaceae* or acanthus family.
CLASSIFICATION: Tender perennial vines grown as tender annual vines.

COMMON NAME: Thunbergia (other popular names vary with species).

HARDINESS: Sensitive to light frosts. Resent cool weather.

GROWING CONDITIONS: Deep, humus-rich, well-drained, moisture-retentive soil. Full sun in cooler gardens, light shade in warmer ones.

PROPAGATION: By seed, sown indoors in peat pots 8 to 10 weeks before frost. Seedlings resent root disturbance. Cuttings root easily.

HEIGHT: From 4 to 10′, depending on species.

ORNAMENTAL VALUE: Grown for flower and for attractive vines.

LEVEL OF CULTURAL DIFFICULTY: Moderately easy.

SPECIAL PROPERTIES: None.

PRONUNCIATION: thun-BER-gee-a

Thunbergia alata (a-LA-ta) has long been grown in gardens for its tidy, dark green triangular leaves, its amiable twining habit to six feet or so in a season, and its engaging, two-inch-wide flowers, consisting of five rounded, flared lobes surrounding a maroon-black mouth. (It is this center of deep black maroon that gives the species its most common popular name, "black-eyed Susan vine.") But the recent interest in sumptuous tropical perennials that may be grown as annuals well outside their range of hardiness has caused other thunbergia to receive attention. These perennial or woody vines originate in tropical Africa or Southeast Asia, and are reliably hardy only in Zones 9 and 10. But they are very fast growing, particularly in steamy summer weather, their foliage is always handsome, and even a few flowers, produced in late summer or early autumn, will be worth the trouble of planting them. Outside the areas where they are hardy, few are generally available as yet in America, and those that are must be acquired as rooted cuttings or established plants from nurseries specializing in unusual tender plants.

Thunbergia alata, however, is available everywhere, as is appropriate for so easily grown and so simply beautiful a plant. Though "black-eyed Susan" has stuck firmly to it as a popular name, it is sometimes also popularly called the "clock vine" from its habit of twining its stems with, rather than against, the clock. When grown as an annual, it seldom reaches a height above six feet or so, which makes it useful for twining up the wires from which hanging baskets are suspended, though it will also tumble gracefully over the edge of any container, catching hold of whatever it can. Its leaves are worth study, for they are broadly arrow-shaped, heavily veined, and glossy, each about three inches long. Sometimes they are curled into a shallow, pointed cup at the base of the stems and carry two wings, giving the species its name, from the Latin adjective *alata,* meaning winged or flying. The two-inch-wide flowers are borne in the axils of the leaves on quite long stems that curve gracefully outward. The flowers used to come only in a pretty golden orange, but now they may be any shade from that to deep and pale yellow, biscuit tan, and creamy white, and in fact several vines grown together with flowers of different shades can be very beautiful. This is apt to happen in any case when plants are grown from seed, for packets generally offer mixes of all available colors.

Seed of *Thunbergia alata* is very easy to germinate. It should be sown indoors at temperatures around 55°F, about eight weeks before the last anticipated frost date, or possibly even earlier, as plants require about three months to flower from germination. They resent transplanting, and so three or so seed should be sown to a single peat pot, and for once, all three may be allowed to develop together, intertwining to form one plant in appearance, but possibly with two or three different shades of flower. Young plants should be grown on in bright, cool conditions until they may be hardened off and transplanted into the garden when the weather is warm and settled. Native to tropical Africa, they will struggle and sulk until nights approach about 70°F and days become warmer. Then they will explode with growth and flower.

Thunbergia grandiflora (gran-di-FLO-ra), popularly called the "blue trumpet vine" or "sky flower," is native to the steamy jungles of Southeast Asia, and where temperatures do not dip much below 45°F in winter, it is capable of digesting whole houses, rapidly producing ropy stems to fifty feet or more. When grown in colder

THUNBERGIA GRANDIFLORA

gardens as an annual plant, however, eight to ten feet in a season from a rooted cutting is more usual. Its leaves alone make it worth cultivating, for they are luxuriant, dark green ovals, six to eight inches long, with wavy or slightly toothed margins and a down-pointed, sharp tip. Often, they are dusted over with purple. Flowers are produced in long chains from the axils of leaves and consist of three-inch-long tubes, flaring out into five clear lavender lobes, penciled white along their edges. The central, lower lobe stands as a platform, marked with whitish stripes that lead to the throat of the flower, providing both a landing strip and runway guidelines for pollinating insects. Where they are hardy, old vines will produce abundant flowers from early spring to late autumn, and even through the winter, though when grown as annuals in colder gardens, they may flower only at the very end of summer. When grown as an annual, *Thunbergia grandiflora* is therefore best where late summers are hot and steamy, and frost is delayed to give way to a long, slow autumn. Elsewhere, they are still a good bet, particularly when trained on tripods in large pots that may be whisked under cover when frosts threaten.

Equally splendid in flower, another thunbergia native to Kenya and Uganda, *Thunbergia battiscombei* (ba-tis-COM-bee-eye), has recently attained popularity. It hardly achieves vining status, but rather sprawls laxly along the ground or in a pot, with stems achieving about four feet of growth in a season. Its oval, pointed, dark green leaves, about five inches long and half as wide, are borne in widely spaced pairs along curious, jointed stems. Flowers appear from the upper leaf axils and consist of a curved tube flaring at the mouth into five squarish lobes. Their color— a magnificent rich deep blue set off by a clear yellow throat—ensures that the popular name of the plant, "blue glory," is not exaggerated praise.

Unaccountably rare in gardens is *Thunbergia gregorii* (gre-GOR-ee-ee), sometimes still listed under the previous name, *T. gibsonii* (gib-SO-nee-ee). Native to tropical Africa and hardy only to about 40°F, it is still capable of making annual growth to about six feet, with triangular, two- to three-inch-long leaves, toothed along their margins and of an attractive, fresh green. Both the stems and the prominent, bladderlike sepals that enclose unopened flowers are covered with short, bristly golden hairs. The two-inch-wide flowers are produced on long stems from the axils of the leaves and consist of four notched or scalloped lobes. Their color is a fine, clear tangerine shading to a deeper orange at the throat. Where vines are hardy, they seem never to be out of bloom, though when grown as an annual, flowers will be produced from midsummer to frost. Like *Thunbergia alata, T. gregorii* makes an excellent annual groundcover.

The culture of all thunbergia is essentially the same. In most gardens they develop best in full sun, though they appreciate light afternoon shade where summers are very warm. Soils should be deep, rich, and well drained, for heavy, waterlogged soil is almost always fatal. All species are very responsive to biweekly feeding with a general, all-purpose water-soluble fertilizer, and plants grown in containers, window boxes, or hanging baskets must be watched carefully to see that they never dry out. *Thunbergia battiscombei* may require a light scaffold of twigs or stakes to support its lax stems, which will otherwise lie unattractively on the ground or loll over the edge of a pot.

Thunbergia are evergreen perennials, so well-trained specimens in pots can be brought indoors or into a cool greenhouse, where they may overwinter at nighttime temperatures around 55° to 60°F. Plants should be kept somewhat dryer in the darkest months and not fertilized. *Thunbergia battiscombei* may yellow and wither away, but plants will resprout from potato-like tubers in early spring. All thunbergia root easily—within three weeks or so—as cuttings taken from non-flowering shoots and inserted into half peat and half sharp sand or perlite. Only *Thunbergia alata* and possibly *T. gregorii,* when it can be procured, are usually grown from seed. The other species are acquired as nursery-grown plants from rooted cuttings.

The genus *Thunbergia* commemorates Karl Peter Thunberg (1743–1828), a favorite student of Linnaeus, who followed his teacher as professor of botany at Uppsala, Sweden.

TIBOUCHINA SPECIES

FAMILY: *Melastomataceae* or melastoma family.

CLASSIFICATION: Tender shrubs or small trees grown as tender annuals.

COMMON NAMES: Princess flower, glory bush, spider flower, tibouchina.

HARDINESS: Sensitive to light frosts. Resents cool weather.

GROWING CONDITIONS: Humus-rich, moist, free-draining soil. Full sun.

PROPAGATION: By cuttings, which root readily.

HEIGHT: From 3 to 8′ in a season, depending on cultivar.

ORNAMENTAL VALUE: Grown for flower and for shrubby habit of growth.

LEVEL OF CULTURAL DIFFICULTY: Easy.

SPECIAL PROPERTIES: None.

PRONUNCIATION: ti-boo-CHEE-na (ti-boo-KINE-a)

The only genus in the family Melastomataceae grown in gardens north of Zone 10, *Tibouchina* is surprisingly large, containing approximately 350

TIBOUCHINA GRANDIFOLIA

species, mostly native to tropical South America, with the largest concentration of species found in Guiana and Brazil. (Tibouchina, taken whole into botanical Latin, is the Guianan vernacular name for the plants.) Only three or four of these species are in cultivation outside tropical gardens, however, though those have been popular since the Victorian period as greenhouse and conservatory plants and as large tubbed specimens in the summer garden. In the last fifteen years, they have also begun to appear in nurseries specializing in unusual annuals and tender plants, offered for containers and as tall specimens for the back of perennial borders. They are excellent for both uses, quick of growth and disease-free, with an open, shrubby look unusual in tender plants grown as annuals, and with sumptuous flowers, borne profusely from midsummer to autumn.

The nomenclature of the tibouchinas most frequently grown in gardens is very confused, for plants are sold under both *Tibouchina urvilleana* (er-vil-EE-a-na) and *T. organensis* (or-gan-EN-sis). Descriptions are offered that suggest one species is larger in leaf and flower than the other, though which is the large one and which is the small remains uncertain. There are, to be sure,

two sizes on the market, one with six-inch-long leaves, and one with leaves half that size, the first bearing flowers four inches across, and the second, flowers only two inches across. But putting size aside, both plants are so similar that they are perhaps variants of one species, in which case the smaller should be listed either as var. *nana* (meaning dwarf) or with a cultivar name, simply as 'Nana'.

Both plants are magnificent. They form loosely branched, rather open and gangly shrubs to as much as eight feet from a foot-tall, rooted cutting in a single northern summer, though in their native Brazil they can make stout trees to as tall as twenty feet. Their leaves, whether three or six inches long, are pointed ovals borne opposite on the stems, pleated down the center by three or more prominent veins, and covered across their surface with fine, velvety hairs that form tiny, reddish bristles along the edges. Upper stems are also covered with short hairs, though lower ones are woody and cinnamon colored, becoming square with age and trunklike on older plants. With maturity, under drought stress, or from cold, the leaves may turn a vivid pumpkin orange, suggesting an autumnal glory unusual in tender plants. The flowers, borne in loose panicles on terminal growth, consist of five slightly overlapping squarish lobes, seemingly folded in the center across a straight line of orange-red stamens. The flowers look as if they had somehow ingested all but the legs of a spider, which accounts for their least glamorous popular name, "spider flower." Whether four inches across or merely two, the color of the flowers is a rich, deep, velvety purple, almost unmatched in its intensity among annuals and tender plants grown as annuals. Toward the end of summer, these flowers create an even more magnificent effect among orange-tinted leaves.

Though the tibouchinas most often available are sometimes listed under the name "grandifolia," *T. grandifolia* (gran-di-FO-lee-a) is a quite distinct species, rarely cultivated in northern gardens but magnificent in its own right and probably soon to be much more popular. It bears huge leaves, to ten inches long and half as wide, pleated and downed as are those of its cousins. Its flowers are actually smaller than those of many other cultivated tibouchinas, scarcely achieving more than an inch in width. But relatively small though they are, they are also a deep, strong purple, though they are borne in huge terminal panicles, perhaps as much as sixteen inches long, with up to thirty flowers in a panicle, opening individually over a long period of time from midsummer to frost. *T. grandifolia* is very beautiful as a large, tubbed specimen with several ascending, flower-producing stems, but it is also wonderful at the back of a perennial border, in a bay of shrubbery, or placed singly among ornamental grasses.

Though most tibouchinas are grown for the color purple, one at least, *T. nandina* (nan-DI-na), produces pretty pink blossoms and is therefore predictably called the "pink princess flower." It is smaller in all its parts than any other cultivated tibouchina, growing into a lightly branched shrub to three feet or so in a single season, with velvety, silver green leaves, each about two inches long. It is virtually ever-blooming where it is hardy and, when in good health, produces silvery pink, half-inch-wide flowers. Unlike other tibouchinas, the pink princess flower

is compact enough to make an attractive house-plant for a sunny window, where it will flower all winter long.

Tibouchinas are of very easy culture, requiring only moist, fertile, well-drained soil and full sun. They are excellent subjects for pots or containers, as they seem to appreciate sharp drainage and a certain amount of heat at their roots. When in active growth, they respond dramatically to applications of general, water-soluble fertilizers at biweekly intervals. Generally, they grow into open, rangy shrubs, though they may be made more compact by frequent pinching when they are young or at any time before they initiate flowers in midsummer. Just before frost, if they are growing in open borders, they may be dug, root-and-top-pruned, potted up in free-draining soil, and brought indoors or into a cool greenhouse to overwinter. When grown in pots or containers, they should be pruned back only lightly, just enough to fit the spaces available to them. They are not particular about winter conditions, accepting a range from 55° to 75°F, and entering a semi-dormant condition that will allow them to survive quite happily even in the odd basement or laundry-room window. In the darkest months of the year, they should be watered only when the surface of the soil is dry, and they should not be fertilized. But when they resume growth in spring, they should be fertilized regularly, and the tips of new growth should be pinched once or twice to encourage branching. Softwood cuttings from overwintered plants root readily when inserted into half peat, half sand or perlite, and kept moist and shaded. Semi-ripe cuttings can also be rooted in early summer, taken from nonflowering lateral branches. Tibouchinas are rarely grown from seed, but rather are acquired as rooted cuttings or established plants.

TITHONIA ROTUNDIFOLIA

FAMILY: *Asteraceae* or aster or daisy family

CLASSIFICATION: Tender perennial shrub grown as tender annual.

COMMON NAMES: Mexican sunflower, torch flower, tithonia.

HARDINESS: Damaged by light frosts. Resents cool weather.

GROWING CONDITIONS: Moderately fertile, well-drained soil. Full sun.

PROPAGATION: From seed, sown indoors 6 weeks before last frost, or in place when weather becomes settled and warm.

HEIGHT: From 5 to 7'.

ORNAMENTAL VALUE: Grown for flower and for stately growth of plants.

LEVEL OF CULTURAL DIFFICULTY: Easy.

SPECIAL PROPERTIES: May be used as quick-growing annual hedge. Excellent as cut flowers.

PRONUNCIATION: ti-THON-i-a ro-tun-di-FO-li-a

The genus *Tithonia* commemorates Tithonus, a mortal youth so adored by Eos, goddess of the dawn, that she petitioned the gods to grant him immortal life. She neglected, however, to ask for perpetual youth, and so she rose from her couch each morning, renewed in beauty, only to see Tithonus shriveling into old age. Finally she was obliged to wrap the old man in swaddling clothes like a babe, though his voice *would* go on in unceasing complaint of his fate. Eventually, Zeus changed him into a grasshopper, the garrulous creature of an hour, in warning to all mortals to make use of their short day and not seek to extend it.

Nothing in the vigorous, fiery splendor of *Tithonia rotundifolia* suggests a parallel to this story.

The species name *rotundifolia* is not descriptively accurate either, for all up and down its hairy stems, the plant bears coarse, raspy, three- to twelve-inch-long leaves that may be triangular or three-lobed, wavy along their margins, but never round. Putting aside its name, however, *Tithonia rotundifolia* is a magnificent plant, unrivaled for height and splendor in the summer garden except by its cousins, the annual sunflowers. It grows tall, anywhere from five to seven feet, and at the ends of its abundant branches, it produces single flowers, each three or four inches wide, consisting of twelve or so slightly down-curved, velvet-textured, pleated ray petals surrounding a tight center of disk florets. The color of the species is a bright, fiery orange-red, though close examination reveals that the red is brushed over yellow, creating a curiously vibrant effect. In form, the blooms of tithonia are not unlike a single dahlia, though the stems, where they meet the flower, are hollow and flare out trumpetlike as if blowing a blast of scarlet sound. There are chrome-yellow forms as well, and mixes of yellow, orange, and red, but the untainted scarlet of the species is almost as rare as clear blue and is much to be preferred.

Tithonia rotundifolia is emphatically a flower for high summer, not only because of its color, but also because it relishes the hot weather of August. Native to Mexico and Central America, it will not really hit its stride until the weather in more temperate gardens begins to remind it of home. The worst of the dog days of August will cause it to grow with renewed strength and to produce abundant, single flowers on long stems, each of which will then be busy with honey-bees, bumblebees, wasps, hummingbirds, and butterflies.

Tithonia rotundifolia may be started in peat pots on a warm windowsill about six weeks before the last anticipated frost date. The large seeds germinate quickly, within one or two weeks, but the young plants must be grown on without a check, for if they dry out, or become attenuated from poor light, they will never make good garden specimens. In fact, except in the coldest gardens, or if one is aiming at plants large enough to be slipped in among perennials without becoming over-shaded by them, little is gained from starting tithonia early. Though they may be transplanted into the garden at about the time it is safe to transplant tomatoes, young plants will look sulky and turn yellow under the cool, damp conditions of spring in many northern gardens. Stronger, more steadily growing plants will be achieved by sowing seed where it is to grow, just about the time one would sow sweet corn. Germination will be rapid in warm soil, and young plants will quickly outstrip weaker specimens started indoors.

The species waits until late summer to flower, but modern varieties are precocious bloomers, beginning in midsummer on compact, branching plants about five feet tall. 'Torch' is still the cultivar to order, if one can find it. 'Goldfinger',

TITHONIA ROTUNDIFOLIA

which is frequently offered, has been bred into a short, three-foot-tall plant, as if in competition with a zinnia, and quite without the splendid height that makes tithonia so valuable. 'Acadian Blend' comes in all shades from yellow to orange and red, and can be beautiful when large drifts of mixed colors can be planted together. But where only two or three plants are wanted, differently colored flowers will create a haphazard, patchy look.

Tithonia rotundifolia is not particular about soils, though young plants do appreciate a scattering of all-purpose vegetable garden fertilizer when they are about four inches tall. Plants are astonishingly drought tolerant, but deep, thorough waterings are beneficial in dry spells while they are still achieving their great height and setting flower buds. Any check while plants are developing, whether from transplanting too early or from drought, may cause them to become stunted and prematurely deciduous along their shanks. In periods of extreme drought, they will be among the last flowers to cease blooming, though they can look fairly miserable with gaunt stems clad in wilted or withered leaves. Their greatest problem in gardens is that their massive, branched growth blows over easily in summer winds, particularly when plants are drenched with rain. Plants will support one another, and can be planted a foot or so apart to interlace into a tangled mass. Individual plants might still be given a single stake, inserted about two feet into the ground and extending as much above. For if they are likely to topple, they will topple just at ground level.

Tithonia rotundifolia is without compare at the back of a deep border, where its blood-red flowers will enliven the uniform yellow of the great, summer-blooming perennial daisies—the inulas, rudbeckias, coreopsis, and helianthemums, with which it shares a distant kinship. It has enough mass and density to form a quick-growing sum-mer hedge and would be splendid planted to screen a deck near the bright light of the sea. The plant is never so wonderful, however, as when it is planted alone in clumps of three or five, each plant spaced about a foot apart, against a weathered barn or towering over rough-mown grass in a pasture. Tithonia makes a superb cut flower, if single flowers are taken with long stems and the ends plunged briefly into boiling water just after they are picked. Without this scalding, the hollow stems will quickly collapse when placed in water, leaving the heavy flowers to dangle in a dejected manner to one side.

TOLPIS BARBATA

FAMILY: *Asteraceae* or aster or daisy family.

CLASSIFICATION: Half-hardy annual.

COMMON NAMES: Yellow hawkweed, bearded hawkweed, annual hawkbit, tolpis.

HARDINESS: Sensitive to light frosts.

GROWING CONDITIONS: Moderately fertile, well-drained soil. Full sun.

PROPAGATION: From seed, sown in place after last frost.

HEIGHT: To 8″.

ORNAMENTAL VALUE: Grown for flower.

LEVEL OF CULTURAL DIFFICULTY: Moderately easy.

SPECIAL PROPERTIES: None.

PRONUNCIATION: TOL-pis bar-BA-ta

Though *Tolpis barbata* is seldom seen in gardens, it always gets a recommendation in catalogues featuring unusual annuals because its simple, quiet charm sets it apart from so many other little yellow daisies. A true annual native to southern Europe, it is easy to grow, producing basal tufts of lobed or coarsely toothed, hairy leaves each about four inches long, from the center of which rise several scantly leaved flower stems topped with clusters of small, half-inch-wide, saucer-shaped daisies. Composed of a row of overlapping petals surrounding a brown disk, they look as if they have been clipped into a perfect circle with pinking shears. From first formation, buds carry a ring of threadlike bracts—eventually as long as an inch—that form an airy collar around the opened flowers and give the species its name, from Latin *barbatus,* meaning bearded or sporting long, thin hairs. Where *Tolpis barbata* is native, plants are of quick vernal growth, flowering from April to July. When sown in gardens, however, it will generally begin flowering in late June and continue into August or until frost if spent flowers are promptly removed. Stems bleed a milky white sap when cut, and so are not suitable as cut flowers.

It is almost impossible to transplant tolpis with success, and as it grows quickly from seed, little is gained by starting it early indoors. Seed should be scattered on prepared ground after all danger of frost is past, and lightly raked in. Full sun is required, and soils should be well drained, light, sandy, and of only moderate fertility. Young plants should be thinned to stand about six inches apart. Plants develop best and bloom most abundantly where summers are hot and relatively dry, though a deep soaking should be given in periods of extreme drought. Not showy enough for growing in window boxes, pots, or containers, tolpis is best thought of as a very pretty weed and so should be planted where it might look as if it came of itself—in rock gardens, as irregular patches in the wild garden, or along the edges of gravel paths or drives.

The genus *Tolpis,* containing between fifteen and twenty species all native to the Mediterranean region, bears a name assigned by the English botanist Michael Adanson (1727–1806), who left no explanation of its derivation or its applicability. *T. barbatus* is the only member within the genus that is cultivated in gardens.

TORENIA FOURNIERI

FAMILY: *Scrophulariaceae* or snapdragon family.

CLASSIFICATION: Tender annual.

COMMON NAMES: Wishbone flower, torenia.

HARDINESS: Sensitive to light frosts. Prefers heat and humidity.

GROWING CONDITIONS: Humus-rich, well-drained soil. Abundant moisture. Full sun.

PROPAGATION: From seed, sown indoors in peat pots 10 weeks before last frost. Plants resent root disturbance except when tiny.

HEIGHT: To 12".

ORNAMENTAL VALUE: Grown for flower.

LEVEL OF CULTURAL DIFFICULTY: Easy.

SPECIAL PROPERTIES: None.

PRONUNCIATION: to-REE-ni-a four-nee-AER-ee

$\mathcal{P}$rominent in the throat of each blossom of torenia is a curious structure—two stamens joined together into a wishbone that springs apart, as if pulled by tiny contending hands, when fertilization occurs. This distinction delights gardeners and children, but the plant has additional and abundant distinctions. Probably the greatest of these is its preference for growing in light, dappled shade. Torenias thus provide one answer at least for nursery owners, when patrons are bored with *Impatiens walleriana* and are averse to coleus because they want flowers, not leaves.

But torenia's preference for cool, shady spots would not get it very far were it not also a very well behaved and attractive plant with numerous pretty flowers. Typically, it grows into a much-branched

TORENIA FOURNIERI

bush to about twelve inches tall, with square stems and opposite leaves that are broadly lance-shaped, prominently toothed, slightly glossy, medium green, and often marked with prominent, purple-tinged veins. The flowers are borne from cobby clusters of bud on terminal growths, which from first formation show their prominent, lanternlike, four-winged calyxes, also often tinted purple on their edges. The flowers are slender tubes that flare out into two lips, the upper lip creased in the center, and the lower lip divided into three lobes. In the typical species, the color of the upper lip is an ineffable pale lilac, though all three lower lobes, and sometimes also the margin of the upper lobes, are a deep, velvety violet. The central, largest lower lobe carries a prominent blotch of golden yellow, presumably indicating a landing spot for pollinating insects, and there is an even deeper stain of gold in the heart of the flower, a false promise of rich pollen that tempts insects in, springing the wishbone of stamens when the flower has reached fertile maturity.

It would be hard to imagine an improvement on the naturally occurring form of torenia, which reveals such great beauty on close observation. Nevertheless, breeders have created numerous cultivars, with a range of colors from white and cream through pale and deep pink to rose red, with lilac forms predominating. At the same time, the plant has been made more compact, sometimes reducing the natural, rangy grace of older forms to mere dumpiness. The two strains that show the widest range of color are both "series," which means that any shade might occur, and what is more significant, sometimes any height from six inches to a foot. They are called the Clown series and the Panda series, and it is true that their flowers, on which the blotches of deep violet have been reduced to two patches on each of the lower side lobes, have the perky charm of clowns and panda bears. But, except where an odd individual comes closest to the typical species, they lack its ethereal beauty.

Torenias are adaptable and forgiving flowers in the garden, but they are not easy to get started. The seed is very fine, and it must be sown ten weeks or so before the last anticipated frost date for plants that will flower three months later. The seed should be only lightly covered and kept moist at temperatures around 60°F until germination occurs. When young seedlings have made two or three sets of true leaves, they should be pricked out singly into peat pots or plastic cell packs, for they accept root disturbance only when quite tiny. Plants should be protected from bright, scalding sunlight and grown on in airy conditions until they may be transplanted. Because *Torenia fournieri* is native to the steamy jungles of Vietnam, it possesses no frost tolerance whatsoever, so plants should be carefully hardened off and transplanted with a minimum of root disturbance when the weather is warm and settled. Ideally, they should be in full vegetative growth, but should show no flower, since once plants begin to bloom they adapt hesitantly to changes in their environment. Those that show precocious bloom in nurseries should therefore be passed over in favor of younger, leafy specimens that have not produced flower. Even those, however, might be given one terminal pinch, to encourage the production of several flowering stems.

Torenias grow best in evenly moist, humus-rich soil in dappled shade. They are excellent hot weather plants, blooming best in summers that are warm and steamy, which makes them ideal for gardens in the middle and lower South and sections of the Midwest. They must be kept well watered at all times, for they depend on even moisture for best development, and are very responsive to water-soluble fertilizers, particularly those rich in potassium. If flower production flags in mid- to late summer, a shearing back by about a third and a generous feeding will usually induce the formation of more flowers for late summer and early autumn.

The genus *Torenia* contains between forty and fifty species of tropical African and southeast Asian origin, though most American gardeners are familiar only with *T. fournieri* and its cultivars. Older garden references, however, include tantalizing references to a yellow-flowered, black-throated species named *Torenia baillonii* (by-ON-ee-ee), which has resurfaced recently and is apt to become prominent in gardens again. Technically a tender perennial also native to Vietnam, it grows as a sprawling, foot-high, somewhat succulent plant that roots freely at the leaf nodes wherever it touches moist ground. Its clean, oval, dark green leaves are toothed along their margins and prominently veined. It flowers profusely from early summer to frost, but if it is brought indoors it will continue flowering all winter long in a bright but not sunny windowsill. Its flowers resemble those of *Torenia fournieri* but are a striking, bright, chrome yellow with a dark maroon-purple throat.

Recently, also, there has appeared a splendid, trailing, almost ivylike form of torenia marketed under the trade name 'Summer Wave'. It quickly produces long stems of succulent, dark green, toothed, two-inch leaves, layered thickly one upon another and studded with recognizable torenia flowers with the usual flared upper and lower lobes, both of a light lilac marked with deeper violet. The flowers are not, however, borne from terminal panicles, but from the axils of the leaves, and as they appear to be sterile, they occur in succession as long as the plant remains in active growth. The exact botanical identity of the plant appears to be in question, and so it is sometimes listed in catalogues without species designation, simply as *Torenia* 'Summer Wave' or as *Torenia* x *hybrida*. Whatever its proper identity, however, it is a splendid addition to summer gardens, seeming always in flower as long as it is given moisture and a rich diet, though its trailing growth suits it far better for hanging baskets and window boxes than for use in the open border.

The genus *Torenia* honors Olof Torén (1718–1753), official chaplain to the Swedish East India Company and a friend and correspondent of Linnaeus, who botanized extensively in China. The species name *fournieri* commemorates Eugene Pierre Nicolas Fournier (1834–1884), a distinguished French botanist of his day. The species name *baillonii* commemorates his contemporary, Henri Baillon (1827–1895).

TRACHELIUM CAERULEUM

FAMILY: *Campanulaceae* or bellflower family.

CLASSIFICATION: Tender perennial or tender biennial grown as tender annual.

COMMON NAMES: Blue throatwort, trachelium.

HARDINESS: Damaged by light frosts. Resents cool weather.

GROWING CONDITIONS: Humus-rich, moisture-
    retentive, well-drained alkaline soil. Full sun.
PROPAGATION: From seed, sown 10 to 12 weeks be-
    fore last frost.
HEIGHT: From 1 to 3′.
ORNAMENTAL VALUE: Grown for flower.
LEVEL OF CULTURAL DIFFICULTY: Moderately diffi-
    cult.
SPECIAL PROPERTIES: Superb cut flower. Excellent in
    pots and containers.
PRONUNCIATION: tra-KEL-ee-um sa-ROO-lee-um

*A*ttractive perennials, annuals, and tender plants often make their way into gardens through the cut-flower trade. Such is the case with trachelium, which has always been attractive to florists, but not much cultivated since Victorian gardeners grew them as decorative pot plants in conservatories and greenhouses to supply cut flowers on large estates and for summer bedding. Trachelium disappeared from modern gardens because they are not plants that are easy to get started. Like most perennials and biennials grown as annuals, they must be seeded quite early, ten to twelve weeks before the last anticipated frost

TRACHELIUM CAERULEUM

date, in order to bloom the first season. The patient process required to bring plants to flower development is often beyond the skill of many home gardeners, especially if they lack working greenhouses and must depend on the "sunny windowsill." But the recent enthusiasm for unusual annuals has encouraged more specialty nurseries to grow exceptional plants for discriminating customers, and a whole range has become available that were once considered impossible to find.

Trachelium makes a valuable addition to any summer flower garden. An undemanding, carefree plant that produces strong, branching stems to as tall as three feet, it never requires staking. The three-inch, pointed, and sharply toothed oval leaves are a pleasant medium to dark green. Plants seeded in late February or early March will produce large, dome-shaped clusters of flowers, sometimes as much as eight inches across, from midsummer until frost. Each cluster contains many tightly packed individual flowers that are quite tiny, scarcely a third of an inch across, composed of five minute lobes and carrying a delicate, sweet fragrance. Prominent anthers extend well beyond the lobes, giving whole clusters an airy, cloudlike appearance. As the species name indicates, the typical color is a strong violet blue, although selections have been made that are a deeper, clearer blue, dark purple, or white. As Victorian gardeners knew, trachelium are very handsome when grown singly in clay pots, for each plant is of attractive, bushy growth, well furnished with disease-free leaves, and striking in flower. They would have envied us 'Passion in Violet', a dwarf form with compact growth to about a foot and abundant purple flower heads, because its short stature is especially suited to pot culture.

Trachelium will accept partial shade, but they develop much more strongly in full sun. Soil must be moist, rich, well drained, and alkaline, which may require the addition of lime at planting time. Plants should not be pinched since they are naturally bushy, and larger flower heads will develop on unpinched stems. Trachelium are native to the mildest areas of the Mediterranean coast, where they behave as short-lived perennials or as biennials. In gardens, they are classed as tender annuals, which means that they possess no frost tolerance at all, and so should not be established in the garden until the weather is warm and settled at about the time one would transplant peppers and eggplants.

TRACHYMENE COERULEA (DIDISCUS COERULEUS)

FAMILY: *Umbelliferae* or Queen Anne's lace family.

CLASSIFICATION: Tender annual.

COMMON NAMES: Blue lace flower, blue Queen Anne's lace, trachymene.

HARDINESS: Damaged by light frost.

GROWING CONDITIONS: Moderately fertile, well-drained garden soil. Prefers cool weather.

PROPAGATION: From seed, sown indoors in peat pots 6 to 8 weeks before last frost. Seedlings resent root disturbance.

HEIGHT: To 2′.

ORNAMENTAL VALUE: Grown for flower.

LEVEL OF CULTURAL DIFFICULTY: Moderately easy.

SPECIAL PROPERTIES: Excellent cut flower. Superb for late-winter flower in cool greenhouses.

PRONUNCIATION: tra-KI-me-nee sa-ROO-lee-uh (die-DIS-cus)

For all its life in gardens, the blue lace flower seems to have suffered under a name confusion, for though most garden references list it as *Tra-*chymeme coerulea, most catalogues usually offer it as *Didiscus coeruleus*. No matter, for gardeners who read its routine description as a "blue Queen Anne's lace" will have to have it. And though both its current genus names are dull, describing merely particular characteristics of its seed, the species name, taken from the classical Latin adjective *caeruleus,* means heavenly blue.

A native of western Australia, it produces a thin but strong-branched plant to two feet tall, sparsely furnished with handsome thrice-divided leaves, each of which is divided again at its end into notched lobes. Of a dull, silvery-veined olive green, the leaves alone would serve admirably for a photographic study of leaves close up, though few gardeners would grow the plant just for that. Flowers are produced in early to midsummer, and though each blossom is minute, hardly a fourth of an inch across, all of them open at more or less the same time, gathered together in flat or slightly dome-shaped umbels borne up-facing on long wiry stems, each umbel about three inches across. But heavenly blue they are not. Cloroxed lavender is a nearer description, and that color is always recessive in gardens, hardly noticed unless flowers are large or thick of petal, or unless close scrutiny is invited, as in an herb garden.

Still, blue lace flowers have their decided claims. They are probably better as cut flowers than in the garden. Like many blooms in the family Umbelliferae, they last unusually well in water, and sophisticated florists include them in mixed arrangements where they add a misty delicacy to more defined flower shapes. Bushels of them are grown each winter under glass in Holland for the international cut-flower market, and, indeed, American gardeners lucky enough to have a cool greenhouse or heated sun porch can produce beautiful pots of them for Christmas decoration from seed sown thinly in mid-

August. In an arrangement or grown for winter decoration in six-inch clay pots, blue lace flowers can be studied closely, and then their beauty is revealed.

Like most of the Umbelliferae, blue lace flowers transplant very unwillingly, since they are cousins to carrots and possess the long, fleshy taproot typical of the family. Seed should therefore be sown indoors in peat pots about six to eight weeks before the last anticipated frost date, grown in bright light, and transplanted with no root disturbance when the weather is settled and warm. Alternatively, seed may be sown in place after all danger of frost is past, usually late May in most American gardens. Seedlings should later be thinned to stand about six to eight inches apart. The plant is not particular about soil, though it requires good drainage and half to a full day of sun. It flowers best where summer nights are cool enough to sleep beneath a thin blanket and where days are bright and buoyant. One pinch when two or three true leaves have developed will make for bushy, well-flowered plants. Hot, muggy weather is generally their demise, though gardeners who can anticipate long autumns might find it worthwhile to make a second sowing of seed in August for flowers well into October.

The advice is often offered that as *Trachymene coerulea* is delicate of growth and flower, it looks better in the garden when grown in somewhat crowded stands, much like larkspurs. But if sturdy seedlings can be grown in peat pots, or bought from a local nursery center in flexible plastic six-packs, they can be slipped into spaces between developing perennials or late-flowering annuals to weave a magic haze among good things yet to come. Seed mixes of *Trachymene coerulea* are offered with pale blue, pink, and white flowers, and to make a tapestry over the garden, such mixes would be excellent. But in the cutting garden the typical lilac blue is probably to be preferred.

TRADESCANTIA SPECIES

FAMILY: *Commelinaceae* or commelina family.

CLASSIFICATION: Tender evergreen perennials grown as tender annuals.

COMMON NAMES: Spiderwort, tradescantia (other common names vary with species).

HARDINESS: Sensitive to light frost.

GROWING CONDITIONS: Almost any soil, though humus-rich, well-drained loam is preferred. Almost any light, though filtered, sun is preferred.

PROPAGATION: From tip cuttings, which root with ease at any time.

HEIGHT: To 6" or so, though trailing growths can achieve as much as 6' in a season.

ORNAMENTAL VALUE: Grown for vining habit and decorative leaves.

LEVEL OF CULTURAL DIFFICULTY: Easy.

SPECIAL PROPERTIES: Excellent for containers, window boxes, and hanging baskets. Good winter houseplants.

PRONUNCIATION: tra-des-CAN-tee-a

The genus *Tradescantia* commemorates two distinguished and intrepid seventeenth-century English gardeners, a father and son, who successively held the position of Royal Gardener to King Charles I. The elder, John Tradescant (died in 1638, though the date of his birth is unknown), made a botanical expedition to Russia in 1618, and another to North Africa two years later. Sometime shortly thereafter, he received material of *Tradescantia virginiana* (vir-gin-EE-ay-na). His son, John Tradescant II (1608–1662), occupied the position of Royal Gardener after his father's death, and made at least one voyage to the Virginia Colony in 1654. Both father and son were at the center of an expansion of botanical knowledge that, in the following century, led to the achievements of Carl Linnaeus (1707–1778), whose binomial system of nomenclature gave order to the entire plant world and who named the genus *Tradescantia* in honor of both father and son.

The genus *Tradescantia* is of entirely New World origin and includes about sixty-five species the majority of which occur in Mexico and Central and South America. The *T. virginiana* that the elder Tradescant grew is a hardy herbaceous plant but is rarely seen in gardens, having been supplanted by a complex swarm of much showier hybrids of it and other species, called by botanists *T. x andersoniana* (an-der-so-NI-a-na) or simply *T. Andersoniana* Group. The best-known tropical tradescantia are *T. fluminensis* and *T. zebrina,* both vining houseplants popularly known as "wandering Jew."

Tradescantia fluminensis (flu-min-EN-sis) derives its species name from the Latin *Flumen Januarrii,* the January River of Brazil, where it is native, and along the banks of which the City of Rio de Janeiro was established. A trailing, evergreen perennial of extremely rapid growth, achieving as much as six feet in a single season, it creeps along the earth in all directions, its succulent stems rooting at slightly swollen nodes wherever they touch moist ground. Its thin but watery leaves are about two and a half inches long and consist of pointed ovals clasping the stems. They occur alternately and lie flat on a plane, creating a beautiful shingled look that is reproduced by abundant side growths on the parent stem. In the typical species, the leaves are a bright, light lettuce-green, with a waxy sheen and with opalescent glands lying just beneath their surface that sparkle in bright light. Flowers—not an important component of the plant's ornamental value—are borne frequently from the axils of the leaves and consist of small, insignificant, three-petaled blossoms, each about half an inch across. Succulent cuttings of *Tradescantia fluminensis* or of any other tender tradescantia can live up to a week or more without water, and so bits can be pinched and brought home from winter vacations in warm places.

The *Tradescantia fluminensis* most often seen is the beautiful cultivar 'Albovittata' (al-bo-vi-TA-ta), which is similar to the typical species in growth, but which bears leaves brushed with irregular stripes of medium green on a white ground. (Hence its name, from Latin *alba,* meaning white, and *vittata,* a belt.) Some leaves will be almost all white, and occasionally a side shoot will occur that has no trace of green at all. The temptation to propagate these ghostly shoots—in the hope of producing a completely white plant—is great, but it always fails, because there is no chlorophyll whatsoever to complete the photosynthesis on which plant growth depends. And it is in fact the case that the cultivar 'Albovittata', though fast enough in its growth, is always slower than the all-green form. A rather lurid sport of *T. f.* 'Albovittata', with leaves striped in white, cream, green, and light and dark pink, is offered under the name 'Orchid Frost', and a quite pretty cultivar, 'Aurea' (O-ree-a), is also available, with chartreuse-yellow stripes on a pale green ground.

Tradescantia zebrina (zee-BRI-na), a native of southern Mexico, is so similar to *T. fluminensis* that most gardeners consider it simply a different variety and call it also by the name "wandering Jew." It is a somewhat larger plant, with trailing stems and oval, pointed, succulent leaves to four inches long, typically bluish green, marked by two brush strokes of silver on their surface and

TRADESCANTIA ZEBRINA

stained a rich purple beneath. Its flowers are modestly attractive, consisting of half-inch-wide, three-petaled, reddish-purple blossoms borne in the axils of the leaves from the boat-shaped bracts typical of the genus. A handsome, maroon-bronze cultivar exists called 'Purpusii' (pur-PU-see-ee) and—as with *Tradescantia fluminensis*—a variegated form, 'Quadricolor' (qua-dri-CO-lor), with leaves striped irregularly in green, silver, pink, and cream.

Tradescantia pallida, syn. *Setcresea pallida* (set-KRE-see-a PA-li-da), is quite different in appearance from either of the wandering Jews. A native of eastern Mexico, it grows into a lax tumble, its many stems remaining upright only at their tips, though when planted in the open, it can build up a haystack to two feet tall. Its three- to six-inch-long leaves clasp the thick stems closely and are narrowly lance-shaped, with their edges folded toward the center into a V. The flowers are borne all summer from the upper axils of the leaves, in two-part, boat-shaped bracts that are typical of the genus, but are here quite pronounced, giving the plant its popular name, "Moses-in-a-boat." The species carries the name *pallida,* which generally indicates a plant of pale leaves, though here the leaves are typically an olive green suffused

with purple. The pure species has been almost completely supplanted, however, by the cultivar 'Purpurea' (pur-PUR-ee-a), marketed as 'Purple Heart'. Both stems and leaves of 'Purple Heart' are an arresting dark wine red with shades of magenta, particularly where the undersides of leaves turn upward. Plants color most dramatically in full sun, in rather cramped positions, such as in a pot or window box, where they may be allowed to dry out between waterings, though in periods of great drought stress, they will turn an unattractive grayish purple and look shrunken and sad. In any situation, one might exercise some thought before planting *Tradescantia pallida* 'Purpurea' for, deficient in all grace, its dark, brownish-purple leaves and stems are its only value. And even those stems and leaves can sometimes look distinctly funereal.

By contrast, one other tender tradescantia sometimes offered is remarkable for its crafted appearance. *Tradescantia sillamontana* (si-a-mon-TA-na) comes from the Silla mountains of northeast Mexico, which give it its species name. Like many other tradescantia, it is half trailing, half upright, its stems reaching only a height of a foot or so before they tumble over to grow upright at the tips again—a device for self-propagation since stems that have reclined upon the soil root at each joint, making new plants. But the stems of *Tradescantia sillamontana* are not actually visible, since the opposite, oval, pointed leaves grow thickly in lateral pairs clasping the stem, each pair stacked above the one below, rather like shrimp *en brochette.* Each leaf is about three inches long, with a base color of bluish green, though both stems and leaves are covered thickly with long cobwebby silver hairs that give the plant a frosted appearance from a distance. As with many tradescantia, the flowers are a pleasant afterthought, consisting of three, hot-pink petals arranged in the triangle typical of the genus. Each flower is only about half an inch wide, but they are borne singly from the upper axils of the leaves all summer long, and though short-lived, they are doubly attractive against the silvery leaves.

The tender tradescantia, particularly the wandering Jews, are of such easy culture that they are predictable school room plants, handy for science experiments and otherwise very pleasant to look at, growing with little care on classroom windowsills. As a group, they prefer moist, humus-rich, fertile loam, though the wandering Jews will accept waterlogged soil and will even form roots and grow for a long time in a jar of water. Indeed, it is amazing what they will put up with, for plants of all species that have been allowed to dry out almost completely, causing their leaves to become paper thin and dusty looking, will plump out and begin to regain attractive vigor as soon as water is applied. With good cultural conditions, however, few plants are more lush and quick-growing. They are not particular as to light, though the trailing sorts prefer the bright, filtered sun that would occur under tall, leafy trees or beneath shrubs in high summer. With abundant water, however, they will accept full sun in the very warmest gardens in North America, where their prolific growth and their capacity to form new plants from each rooted joint can make them a pest. They are very responsive to liquid fertilizers, particularly in hanging baskets, applied at full strength to leaves and roots every two weeks. When well watered and regularly fed, sumptuous veils of growth will occur from surprisingly small pots or baskets. Without fertilizing, they will make more restrained but equally attractive cascades.

Cuttings of the tender tradescantia root with such ease that they are never grown from seed. *Tradescantia pallida* and *T. sillamontana* root at any time of year when taken as tip cuttings and in-serted into damp sand, or half sand, half peat and kept moist and shaded. The wandering Jews may also be inserted into damp soil, placed in a glass of water, or even scattered as tip cuttings over the earth.

There are rare jewels in the genus *Tradescantia* that will surely make their way eventually into North American gardens for summer decoration. Meanwhile, those available might be dismissed as common plants because of their ease of propagation, their undemanding cultural requirements, their abundant growth, and their consequent ubiquity. Nevertheless, few gardeners can resist a youthful, well-grown pot of any of the wandering Jews, lustily reaching out with graceful side branches from a central stem, its tip growths turned up optimistically.

TROPAEOLEUM SPECIES

FAMILY: *Tropaeolaceae* or nasturtium family.

CLASSIFICATION: Tender perennials grown as tender annuals.

COMMON NAMES: Nasturtium, tropaeoleum.

HARDINESS: Sensitive to light frost. Resents cool weather.

GROWING CONDITIONS: Moist, moderately fertile, well-drained soil. Full sun.

PROPAGATION: From seed, sown indoors in peat pots 4 weeks from last frost. Seedlings resent root disturbance. Cuttings root easily.

HEIGHT: Bushy sorts to 12". Scrambling sorts to 8' in a season.

ORNAMENTAL VALUE: Grown for flower.

LEVEL OF CULTURAL DIFFICULTY: Easy.

SPECIAL PROPERTIES: All parts of *T. majus* are edible as salad greens.

PRONUNCIATION: tro-pau-O-lee-um

TROPAEOLEUM MAJUS 'ALASKA'

*L*innaeus thought the rounded leaves of common nasturtiums looked like shields, and its spurred flowers like helmets, so he gave the genus the name *Tropaeoleum*. The word comes from the ancient Greek *tropaion,* for the trophy poles where victorious armies of ancient Greece and Rome hung the shields and helmets of their enemy's dead. Whether Linnaeus knew the bloody origins of the word or not, if modern gardeners did, it might make them more comfortable with the common name, nasturtium. That name, as it happens, is also classical Latin, from *nasus tortus,* literally "nose twister," and is the species name for watercress, *Rorippa nasturtium* (RO-ri-pa nas-TUR-tee-um), since the leaves, stems, flowers, unopened buds, and seeds of the garden nasturtium possess a refreshing, mustardy taste much like that of watercress and are often used as a substitute for it. The culinary attributes of *Tropaeoleum majus* have been known in Europe since the seventeenth century, but they have recently been given new attention by the current vogue for edible flowers. Nasturtium claim a great distinction, for in salads they are not merely decorative, but (unlike so many edible flowers) are actually delicious.

Although a perennial native to the mountains around Lima, Peru, *Tropaeoleum majus* (MA-jus) is widely naturalized throughout the globe where temperatures do not dip much below 40°F. It forms a scrambling, climbing plant to about eight feet in a season, with light green, fleshy stems and nearly rounded, lily-pad-like, grass-green leaves. The leaves—each about three inches across and beautifully marked with a net of white veins radiating out from the center—are carried on long stems that twine around any slender object they touch, lifting and holding up the plant as it grows. Flowers are borne singly from the axils of the upper leaves, on long but non-twining petioles, and each consists of five sepals joined at the base, three of which extend into a long spur at the back. The five rounded petals usually overlap slightly, but each one tapers down to a slender stem where it joins the sepals, a pattern botanists call "clawed." The flowers emit a fresh, clean fragrance, though it is stronger in some cultivars than in others. Unimproved plants produce flowers of a clear, vibrant orange-red, though modern forms have been bred in many beautiful colors from palest yellow and primrose through biscuit tan to apricot, tangerine, scarlet, clear deep red, and even brownish maroon. Lighter-flowered forms may display a neat, orange blotch on each petal, or petals may be veined and netted with scarlet red. Doubles also exist, which somewhat compromise the intrinsic elegance of the flowers. Finally, there is 'Alaska', a form with leaves beautifully splashed and mottled in white that now also flowers in several shades of yellow and orange-red.

The original nasturtium taken to Europe from Peru sometime before 1656 was a vine, though it was quickly bred into bushier forms suitable for bedding. The two forms have since developed side by side, and so it is important to choose a cultivar that is suitable to the situation in which it is to be grown. Most nasturtiums now in gardens are bush forms, though the climbing sorts are wonderful when they cascade from a balcony or

TROPAEOLEUM MAJUS

window box. This is the form that almost obscures the path under Monet's rose arbor at Giverny, and that tumbles in late winter from the balconies in the interior glassed-in courtyard of the Isabella Stewart Gardner Museum in Boston. Vining nasturtiums can also be very fine when trained up a fence, trellis, or tripod, though they need occasional tying in with organic fiber twine.

Tropaeoleum majus has a miniature look-alike, *T. minus* (MIN-us), which is a charming plant. Its leaves are approximately the same size as those of *T. majus,* but they are downy rather than smooth on their undersides, which gives them a grayish-green cast. The flowers possess a similar long spur at the back, though the five petals form a more pronounced funnel shape. They are a clear yellow, but the spur is orange-red, and that color is repeated in a blotch on the base of each petal.

Much worth cultivating is *Tropaeoleum peregrinum* (pe-re-GRI-num), for it has a look quite unlike that of *T. majus,* and a lovely charm all its own. It forms a tall vine to eight feet or more in a single season, with fleshy, waxy stems of pale green. Its two- to four-inch-wide leaves are borne on long petioles that twist firmly around any support. They are divided into five rounded, fingerlike lobes of bluish green, each promi-

nently marked with silver veins. Plants are beautiful in themselves, borne sparsely enough along the central stems to display their interestingly crafted leaves, as well as those that wander off on lateral growths. This habit gives the plant its species name, from classical Latin *peregrinus,* signifying an immigrant, a wanderer, or a pilgrim. The inch-wide, clear yellow flowers are borne on long, slender stems from the axils of the leaves and consist of two large, fringed, up-facing lobes and three very slender shorter lobes bundled together with the yellow stamens from which they are indistinguishable except on close examination. The flowers fancifully resemble tiny, bright yellow birds, giving the plant its popular name, "canary bird vine."

Both *Tropaeoleum majus* and *T. peregrinum* are actually tender perennials, though they possess no frost resistance whatsoever, and therefore, in all but the warmest gardens, are grown as annual plants. The cultural preferences of both are for moist, open soil, but it should not be too rich or augmented with fertilizers heavy in nitrogen, both of which will produce luxuriant foliage at the expense of flower. The large seed germinates very rapidly at temperatures around 60°F, but nasturtium will not accept disturbance at the roots and so are best seeded three to a peat pot. With *Tropaeoleum majus,* it does no harm to let all three seedlings develop together, provided they are spaced in the garden about one foot apart. However, all but the strongest seedling of *T. peregrinum* should be clipped away after two or three true leaves have developed, since the vine is most attractive when grown over a shrub as a single specimen. Neither plant benefits from pinching.

Generally, *Tropaeoleum majus* should not be hurried on indoors, as it grows best in cool, fresh conditions, and plants seeded directly in the garden about a week before the last anticipated frost date often surpass those that are cosseted indoors.

TROPAEOLEUM MAJUS

But if for some reason one must have plants to transplant as early as possible, seed should still be sown only about four weeks before the last frost date and grown on in bright, cool, sunny conditions until all danger of frost is past, when they may safely be transplanted. On the other hand, *T. peregrinum* might be started earlier, about six to eight weeks before the last anticipated frost date, so that young plants will be tall enough to establish beneath the sheltering branches of shrubs over which they will clamber.

Nasturtium make excellent cut flowers, lasting a week or longer in water, providing one of the prettiest bouquets of summer, asking simply to be gathered in the hand with a few leaves and placed in a vase. They might be kept on the kitchen counter until the evening salad is made, though their pungent flavor is always best within three or four hours of picking, which makes those bought in gourmet grocery markets hardly worth bothering with. *Tropaeoleum peregrinum,* the canary bird vine, is never mentioned as an edible plant, though it is a splendid cut flower. Whole side branches should be taken and placed in water a day or two before they are needed, so that leaves and flowers will turn upward.

In the nineteenth century, nasturtium were very popular as winter-flowering plants, both in the greenhouses of great estates and on the cottager's simple, white-washed windowsill. Gardeners who have a cool greenhouse, heated sun porch, or spare sunny window might still take pleasure even from a few brightly colored flowers in the dead of winter. For indoor winter growing, seed should be sown in early September for plants that will flower from December to spring. Alternatively, cuttings root with great ease, even in a glass of water, though stronger plants will result from inserting tip growths about four inches long into half peat, half perlite, and keeping the cuttings moist and shaded until rooting occurs,

TROPAEOLEUM PEREGRINUM

when they may be potted and grown on. Indoors in winter, nasturtium flower best in bright sun, and in cool conditions around 50°F at night and ten or so degrees warmer in the daytime.

Providing such conditions may be maintained, there is only one problem in growing them this way. For both indoors and out, there is no familiar garden pest that does not relish the succulent stems, leaves, and flowers of nasturtium: slugs, aphids of all sorts—particularly the nasty black ones called plant lice—white fly, and the slimy green cabbage worms that spoil the broccoli. For the cabbage worms, a good dose of *Bacillus thuringiensis,* an organic bacterium fatal to cabbage moths, will eliminate both nasty worms and their pretty little white moths. Slugs must be dealt with in saucers of beer or with strips of copper, or slug bait, judiciously applied. For other pests, only sprays will do. But putting aside serious ecological considerations, the problem is that nasturtium are notoriously intolerant of chemical sprays and may well shrivel up along with the bugs. Also, one does eat nasturtium, and so the chemicals with which they are sprayed must be considered an issue. Organically derived sprays based on nicotine or pyrethrum are kinder to both plant and salad-eater, and so should be used by preference.

But even then, it is good to wait a few days, not only for the spray to dissipate but also for the corpses of the insects it killed to fall away, and not be an unexpected garnish to one's salad.

TWEEDIA CAERULEA (OXYPETALUM CAERULEUM)

FAMILY: *Asclepiadaceae* or milkweed family.

CLASSIFICATION: Half-hardy perennial grown as half-hardy annual.

COMMON NAMES: Blue milkweed, southern star, oxypetalum, tweedia.

HARDINESS: Sensitive to light frost.

GROWING CONDITIONS: Moderately fertile, dryish garden soil. Full sun.

PROPAGATION: From seed, sown 10 to 12 weeks before last frost.

HEIGHT: From 1½ to 3′, depending on culture.

ORNAMENTAL VALUE: Grown for flower.

LEVEL OF CULTURAL DIFFICULTY: Moderately difficult.

SPECIAL PROPERTIES: Excellent cut flower. May be grown in cool greenhouse for winter flower.

PRONUNCIATION: TWEE-dee-a se-ROO-lee-a

TWEEDIA CAERULEA

Even the greatest admirers of *Tweedia caerulea* admit that the sole reason for cultivating the plant is its extraordinary flowers. As the adjective *caerulea* indicates, they are blue, but to call the inch-wide, strap-petaled, starry flowers merely blue is only to hint at their charm. When fully open they are a curious shade best described as turquoise. They assume that odd and beautiful color—rare among garden plants—only at one stage in their development. The buds are lavender pink, and as they mature, they change to turquoise tinted with green, then to clear turquoise, and finally to a light, lavender blue randomly freckled with purple spots. In fully opened flowers there is always a tiny cup of fused petals of deep marine surrounding a pointed pistil of white.

Because each flower is so great a treasure one can forgive the plant its lax, scandent stems that never quite succeed in becoming vines, and its narrow, dark green, lance-shaped leaves covered in short, white hairs that make them clammy to the touch. Plants grow to about three feet in a season, in the last foot of which they begin to produce loose clusters of flower from the upper axils of the leaves, appearing in midsummer and continuing until frost. After individual flowers complete their transition through several shades and colors (this takes a long time) the petals drop off to give way to a horn-shaped seed pod about two inches long at maturity that looks much like those of the familiar pasture milkweed, and like it, packed with many brown seeds, each possessing a silky white parachute. The blooms of *Tweedia caerulea* make excellent, long-lived cut flowers if one can bear to take whole stems from a plant that seldom produces many.

Tweedia caerulea is actually a tender perennial, native to southern Brazil and Uruguay, though it is usually grown as an annual. Like others of its class, it should be sown quite early, in late February or early March for the longest period of bloom. Seeds are sown sparingly over sterile potting mix and placed in temperatures around 60°F. Germination is rapid, and young plants should be pricked out as soon as they are large enough to handle, and then grown on in bright, airy conditions. When they are about five inches tall, they should be pinched to encourage branching, which will produce several stems to a crown rather than just one. After all danger of frost has passed, they may be transplanted into places that receive full sun. They grow best in a loose, open soil of moderate fertility, and bloom seems to be most abundant where the earth becomes slightly dry between rains. For this reason, though *Tweedia caerulea* lacks the overall distinction that should characterize most plants grown in pots, its aristocratic flowers, freely produced under pot culture, might justify growing it that way.

Pot culture offers an additional advantage, for just before frost, plants may be cut back by a third and carried indoors or into a cool greenhouse for late-winter flowering. They grow best at cool temperatures around 55° to 60°F at night, with an increase of ten or fifteen degrees in the day. The pots should be very free draining, and water should be applied only when the soil surface is dry to the touch. Toward the end of winter, plants that have been carried over indoors should be cut back again by about a third and fed with diluted liquid fertilizer. Treated this way, they will make small bushes, though still with rather lax branches, and they will produce abundant and earlier flowers.

Tweedia caerulea is the sole member of its genus, the previous name of which, *Oxypetalum*, described the pointed petals of the flower, from ancient Greek *oxys,* meaning sharp, and Latin *petalum,* a petal. The genus name *Tweedia* is believed to commemorate James Tweedie, head gardener at the beginning of the nineteenth cen-

TWEEDIA CAERULEA

tury at the Royal Botanic Gardens in Edinburgh, who later lived for many years in Argentina.

URSINIA SPECIES

FAMILY: *Asteraceae* or aster or daisy family.

CLASSIFICATION: Tender perennials grown as half-hardy annuals.

COMMON NAME: Ursinia.

HARDINESS: Sensitive to light frosts.

GROWING CONDITIONS: Moderately fertile to poor, well-drained garden soil. Full sun.

PROPAGATION: From seed, sown 6 to 8 weeks before last frost. Cuttings taken in midsummer root easily.

HEIGHT: From 1 to 2'.

ORNAMENTAL VALUE: Grown for flower.

LEVEL OF CULTURAL DIFFICULTY: Moderately easy.

SPECIAL PROPERTIES: None.

PRONUNCIATION: oor-SIN-ee-a

So many beautiful, low-growing daisies originate in the Cape Province of South Africa that one imagines it carpeted with them—arctotis, dimorphotheca, venidium, the bi-generic hybrid x venidioarctotis . . . and ursinia. All so closely resemble one another in flower that French gardeners are content with one popular name for them all, "Marguerites du cap." All are classic daisies, consisting of a single but fairly numerous circle of ray petals, twenty or so, surrounding a tight button of disk florets that is usually a darker and contrasting color. Often, also, there is a striking circle or "zone" of another color halfway down the ray petals, which adds great complexity and subtlety to their blooms. All are valuable gifts from a wealthy region, and it could be argued that ursinias, the least well-known of them all, are the most valuable, for they are of the easiest culture and—one may say—the sunniest disposition.

The genus consists of about forty species of tender perennial and annual plants, many of which have garden merit, and many of which are so close in their appearance as to be virtually interchangeable in the garden. Recognizing this fact, the distinguished English seed firm Chiltern's Seeds offers packets of mixed species, all of which, when they come to flowering size, will look like variations on one central theme.

As a genus, then, *Ursinia* may be said to have something of an identity crisis, and indeed, the four species most frequently cultivated have names that cannot do better than compare them to other plants. *Ursinia anethoides* (a-neth-OY-des), which has in the past been most commonly available, is said to resemble culinary dill, *Anethum graveolens* (A-NETH-um gra-vee-O-lens), for its much-divided, ferny, mid-green leaves—about two inches long—are very like dill in appearance. Flowers, however, when they come in midsummer, are most unlike the greenery-yallery flowers of dill, consisting of two-inch-wide, marigold-yellow daisies borne singly on stiff stems, each marked with a maroon-red,

red, or purple-black zone around the chestnut-red disk florets. In both leaf and flower, *Ursinia anethoides* sets the pattern for several other species, which, like it, are upright, bushy plants to about two feet tall, thickly clothed with attractive and fragrant ferny leaves and producing single daisies from midsummer to frost on wiry stems that stand well above the foliage.

Ursinia anthemoides (an-thuh-MOY-des), said by its botanical species name to resemble in leaf the genus *Anthemis,* the chamomiles, is significantly different from other ursinia only in producing flowers of lemon yellow that may be as wide as three inches, often with a very prominent and beautiful scarlet-red zone that occupies half the daisy and surrounds a deep, chestnut-red button of disk florets. *Ursinia pulchra* (PUL-chra) probably belongs in this species, though it is a somewhat smaller plant—perhaps a foot tall—and it is often listed separately.

Ursinia chrysanthemoides (chri-san-thuh-MOY-des) possesses leaves more lobed than fringy, similar to the florists' chrysanthemum, which are also a celadon green, nicely scented, and about two inches long. Though the two-inch-wide flowers are generally yellow with a darker chestnut red button of disk florets, white forms occasionally occur. Its variety, *greyeri* (GREY-er-i)—which is sometimes listed as a separate species, *U. greyeri*—is striking, with foliage that begins by being silver-downed and matures to flat green, producing two-inch-wide crimson flowers with a button of disk florets so dark a red as to appear black.

Ursinia calenduliflora (ca-len-dew-LI-flo-ra) derives its species name from *Calendula officinalis* (ka-lin-DEW-la off-i-si-NA-lis), the familiar pot marigold of gardens. Though it grows into a bushy plant about a foot and a half tall furnished with recognizably ursinia-like ferny leaves, its flowers do in fact resemble calendulas, consisting of two-inch-wide ray petals of light orange shad-

URSINIA ANTHEMOIDES

depends on the species, but all will behave as summer annuals if given an early start indoors.

Seed should be sown about six to eight weeks before the last anticipated frost date, for flowering plants about three months from germination. Like many Cape plants, seed germinates best— and plants grow best—in fairly cool temperatures, waiting to flower when the weather warms. Seed should therefore be sown at temperatures around 50° to 55°F, and seedlings should be transplanted and grown on in bright, airy conditions around that temperature range, or perhaps ten degrees higher. Young seedlings will possess no frost tolerance at all, however, and so should be established in the garden only after all danger of frost is past. They transplant readily, even when half-grown and carrying flower buds, if the work is done carefully in cloudy weather, and the plants are well watered in.

Ursinias demand full sun and perfectly drained soil, though they flower best on a rather lean diet and so should not be fertilized. Once established, they are drought tolerant, though they resent extreme summer heat, and certainly high humidity, both of which will cause them to cease flowering even if sheared back. They are superb in pots, particularly when three seedlings can be established in a six-inch pot where their delicate, ferny growth and their interesting daisies can be studied up close. They are also excellent winter-flowering plants for cool greenhouses or heated sun porches. For this purpose, cuttings should be taken in summer and grown on to be moved under glass before frost. They root almost as readily as marigolds, and indeed, side branches that have touched moist earth may already show incipient roots. Alternatively, seed can be sown from October to November for early spring bloom, and young seedlings pricked out directly into six-inch clay pots. They should be grown on in cool, buoyant conditions and watered only

ing down to a red-orange zone. Also sometimes offered is *Ursinia speciosa* (spe-see-O-sa), which derives its species name from the classical Latin adjective *speciosus,* meaning showy, which it is, but no more than others in the genus.

Whether there are great differences among these species, only the trained botanist—and not the gardener—could say. All are good bets if one can acquire seed, and they would probably hybridize freely among themselves, eventually resulting in a superb range of garden plants that might best be designated as *Ursinia* x *hybrida.* But little hybridizing work has been done with ursinias, and seed is scarcely ever offered. Both facts are a surprise, for among the African daisies, they are perhaps the easiest to grow. Whether they are true annuals or short-lived perennials when necessary until buds appear, when they may be watered more frequently, and even lightly fertilized with a water-soluble fertilizer high in phosphorus and potassium but low in nitrogen.

Like many daisies the flowers of ursinia will close up at night and on cloudy days, so though they are long-lasting cut flowers, they should not be counted on in arrangements for nighttime parties.

The genus *Ursinia* commemorates a distinguished German botanical author of the seventeenth century, Johannes Heinrich Ursinus (1608–1667).

VACCARIA HISPANICA

FAMILY: *Caryophyllaceae* or carnation family.

CLASSIFICATION: Hardy or half-hardy annual.

COMMON NAMES: Cow herb, cow cockle, dairy pink, vaccaria.

HARDINESS: Slightly frost hardy once established.

GROWING CONDITIONS: Moderately fertile, moist, well-drained soil. Full sun.

PROPAGATION: From seed, sown in place in very early spring.

HEIGHT: To 2′.

ORNAMENTAL VALUE: Grown for flower.

LEVEL OF CULTURAL DIFFICULTY: Easy.

SPECIAL PROPERTIES: Excellent cut flower. Used in herbal medicine to treat a number of ailments particular to women.

PRONUNCIATION: va-KA-ree-a his-PAN-i-ca

*E*ven a picture of *Vaccaria hispanica* would make gardeners want to grow it for its clouds of tiny pink to white flowers borne on hair-thin, wiry stems among buds that are already colored from first formation. But though it was once very popular in gardens, rivaling gypsophila, or baby's breath, which it much resembles, *Vaccaria hispanica,* like many annuals that are best sown in the open garden to grow in place, has slipped from popularity to the point that seed is seldom even offered. That is regrettable, for though it is difficult to transplant and so can never appear in spring in nurseries and garden centers, it is otherwise an extremely easy plant to grow, and very pretty in bloom.

A native of central Europe and temperate southeast Asia, vaccaria forms a slender, branched plant to about two feet tall, furnished with smooth, celadon-green, lance- or oval-shaped leaves, each about two and a half inches long, borne alternately and pointing upright to clasp the stems. Flowers are produced in airy, graceful clusters in loose terminal racemes. Each tiny flower, measuring hardly more than a fourth of an inch across, is composed of five notched, lightly veined petals flaring from a short tubed throat and overlapping slightly to form a circle. The typical color is a warm, cameo pink, though paler shades occur down to a pure white selection, *c. alba,* which, when grown alone, produces the effect of a froth of sudsy foam. As vaccaria is best grown in drifts of many interlacing plants, a blend of all the shades of pink with white is particularly attractive, looking even from a short distance very similar to stands of annual baby's breath. And like gypsophila, it is an excellent cut flower, adding grace and delicacy to any bouquet of summer flowers, and lasting a long time in water, if sprays are cut just as the first buds begin to open. Subsequent flowers will continue to open for as much as two weeks, if the water is kept fresh and the ends of stems are periodically recut.

It is difficult to raise seedlings of vaccaria indoors, and as it is best grown in drifts of many plants that develop quickly, seed should be sown where plants are wanted in early spring, about two weeks before the last anticipated frost date, or in autumn in milder gardens. Seed must experience a period of cold in order to germinate, and so in gardens that experience quick warming in spring, a chilling period of about ten days in the refrigerator will cause it to sprout within a week. Full sun is preferred, and soil should be well drained and fertile, though of only moderate fertility. When seedlings are about two inches tall, they should be thinned to stand about six to eight inches apart. Grown close together, they will mutually support one another, though, as the stems are very brittle, it is also wise to insert brushy twigs among young plants for additional support. Flowering should begin within eight to ten weeks from germination, commencing in most American gardens in mid-July and continuing for about six weeks. For cut flowers, a second sowing might be made toward the end of June for flowers in late summer and early autumn. Seed is abundantly produced in attractive, five-sided tear-drop-shaped pods that are easy to gather and store for plants the following year, and for seed to share with other gardeners, as vaccaria is now so rare in seed catalogues that it must continue in gardens as a pass-along. When dried, the seed capsules are also prized for use in dried flower arrangements.

Vaccaria hispanica is native to moist, fertile pasture land and was a familiar grain-field weed throughout Europe and eastern Asia before the advent of selective pre-emergent herbicides. It entered North America in colonial times as a component of animal fodder stored on board ships and has since naturalized across the temperate parts of the United States and Canada. Listed as an "invasive weed" by the United States

Department of Agriculture, it is so gentle a plant that it cannot cause much trouble and is always a pleasure when spotted along a roadside among other summer-flowering annuals and perennials. Botanically, it has gone through a surprising number of names, having been classed among the related genera of both *Saponaria* and *Lychnis,* and variously identified as *Saponaria vaccaria, Lychnis vaccaria, Vaccaria vulgaris, Vaccaria segitalis,* and finally as *Vaccaria hispanica.* The species name *hispanica* indicates the south-central European origins of the plant, though it is now widely dispersed throughout the globe. The genus name *Vaccaria* originates from the Latin word *vacca,* signifying a cow, and attesting to the palatability of the plant to ruminant animals. Two of its common names, "cow herb" and "dairy pink," also preserve the memory of its popularity in early agriculture as an easily grown forage crop. The popular name "cockle," meaning a shell, is shared with *Agrostemma lithago,* the more commonly grown corn cockle of fields and gardens, a recognizable cousin within the family Caryophyllaceae.

Vaccaria hispanica sometimes also carries the curious popular name "forbidden palace flower," for though it is native to the Mediterranean region, it was found growing in abundance in the Chinese imperial palace grounds after the death of the dowager empress Cixi and the removal of the royal family to Japan by the Japanese army before World War II. During the last years of the reign of Cixi, a soup made of the leaves of vaccaria was reported to have been fed to nursing mothers to increase their flow of milk, as the dowager empress preferred human milk in her tea to that of cows. *Vaccaria hispanica* is still used in Chinese medicine to treat a variety of complaints specific to women, including breast pain, benign breast tumors, the regulation of lactation in nursing mothers, difficulties attending menstruation, and delayed labor.

VERBENA SPECIES

FAMILY: *Verbenaceae* or verbena family.

CLASSIFICATION: Tender perennial grown as half-hardy annual.

COMMON NAMES: Verbena, vervain.

HARDINESS: Sometimes root-hardy to Zone 7. Plants withstand light frost once established.

GROWING CONDITIONS: Moderately fertile, well-drained soil. Full sun. Good air circulation.

PROPAGATION: From seed, sown indoors in late winter or very early spring. Cuttings root easily.

HEIGHT: Varies with species and cultivar.

ORNAMENTAL VALUE: Grown for flower.

LEVEL OF CULTURAL DIFFICULTY: Easy.

SPECIAL PROPERTIES: None.

PRONUNCIATION: ver-BEE-na

All of the familiar and showy verbenas grown in gardens are of New World origin, though both their genus and popular names are ancient, from classical Latin *verbena,* signifying all the herbs the ancient Romans considered holy and employed in religious ceremonies. The word, by extension, came to refer to branches held by priests in religious processions, usually of myrtle or bay, though other holy herbs, including *Verbena officinalis* (off-i-si-NA-lis), native to the Mediterranean region, were carried in baskets. Its specific function, when burned, was to purify holy sites and to induce visions. In the Middle Ages, it was later valued as a medicinal herb, from which it draws its species name, from *officina,* the office of a medieval monastery from which pharmaceuticals were distributed. Infusions of its leaves and flowers were prescribed for the treatment of a host of complaints, including depression, insomnia, and nervous headaches. The common name "vervain," hardly used anymore, is a descendant of the Latin through Middle to Modern English.

Verbena officinalis is not a particularly showy plant, consisting of several upright, wiry stems, sparsely furnished with arrow-shaped, deeply lobed leaves, and bearing minute, lavender-purple flowers from elongated, rat-tail-like racemes at the top. It is one of only two or three members of a large genus of 250 or so species that is native to the Old World.

The remaining species are often very decorative plants, native to both North and South America, and extensively hybridized and cross-hybridized to create the popular bedding plants gardeners know as verbenas and botanists know as *Verbena* x *hybrida* (hy-BRI-da). (They represent complex crosses, begun prior to 1830, between many species, chiefly *Verbena incisa, V. peruviana, V. platensis, V. phlogiflora, V. rigida,* and *V. teucrioides.*) Though they may vary in height, growth habit, and shape of leaf, gardeners will recognize in all of them a familiar plant, known to them (and, generally, to the clerk at the garden center) simply as "verbena."

Cultivars of *Verbena* x *hybrida* form clumping to spreading plants about a foot tall, with square, hairy stems on which raspy, dark green, oblong, toothed leaves are produced, usually between two and four inches long. Flowers occur from terminal growths practically from the time they are bought in six-packs at the nursery center until frost (or possibly disease) cuts them down. The "flower" is a flat-topped cluster, or umbel, composed of many tiny individual true flowers, each about a half-inch across, consisting of a short, nectar-filled tube that flares out into five lobes. Flowers open from the outside in, though buds color early, and the umbels are perhaps most attractive when a ring of open flowers surrounds a center of tightly closed buds. Many cultivars are sweetly scented, though it is not a fragrance that is carried on the wind, and one must bury one's nose in an umbel to pick up its faint but pleasant scent. The variety of flower colors offered by modern hybrids and cultivars is great, ranging from pure, pristine white, through pale and deep pink to carmine, cerise, and true red, and from there to rich purple, blue, lavender, and back to ice-blue white. Recently, cultivars have been bred even in colors of coral and pinkish orange, of which 'Peaches and Cream' is the most popular to date. There are also cultivars that are marked with a perky white eye in the center of each true flower, and others that show a deep, rich color in bud, but fade to paler shades as they mature, creating an attractive bi-colored effect.

Though the hybrid verbena are all derived from perennial species and are hardy in the very warm gardens of Zones 8 to 10, they are mostly grown as annuals, and most nurseries and garden centers will display an abundance of plants in a wide range of color. That is a very good thing, as it happens, for hybrid verbena seed is difficult to germinate successfully, even in the hands of experts. It should be sown about ten to twelve weeks before the last anticipated frost date, at temperatures around 60° to 70°F. Fluctuations between night- and daytime temperatures should be avoided, preferably by using electrically heated pads that deliver constant warmth. The seed requires darkness to germinate, and so seed pans should be covered with cardboard until young plants are apparent, at which point the seed pan should be brought into bright light, but still at warm conditions around 70°F, until young plants may be pricked out and grown on at cooler conditions around 60°F, then to be hardened off and transplanted into the garden after all danger of

VERBENA *X* HYBRIDA

frost is past. Watering must be very careful, preferably applied from the bottom by standing pots in water until they are moist, for various fungus diseases can be a problem in enclosed environments.

Most American gardeners will bypass this exacting process to purchase young plants in spring at nurseries and garden centers, where a wide variety of colors will be offered including some of the best cultivars, such as the pale pink 'Silver Anne', the deep, purplish-blue 'Homestead Purple', or the cherry-red 'Sissinghurst', all of which will in any case have been produced from cuttings, as they do not come true from seed. But all may show a first precocious bloom in the six-pack, which promises sheets and sheets of flower from midsummer to autumn, provided young plants are spaced about eight inches to a foot apart, in full sun, and in open, well-drained but not over-rich soil. A light feeding with a granular vegetable garden fertilizer low in nitrogen but high in potassium and phosphorus will encourage strong plants, and—one hopes—plenty of flower.

Verbena x *hybrida* would seem to be an almost perfect summer-flowering annual, as garden centers always promise, and so it will be, if one knows that it is subject to a number of diseases that must be fought. White fly seems to pick it out as a favorite and must be eradicated by whatever means one uses to combat that pest. More serious, powdery mildew can turn plants a sickly, powdery gray and eventually cause their demise. Organic sprays based on sulphur are available, as well as more potent sprays based on chemicals, some of which are "full spectrum," which means that they will kill almost anything except the plant itself. Summers do occur when both bugs and funguses stay miraculously away, but when they do come verbena will be under the first attack, which must be dealt with if they are to remain in the garden at all.

Though *Verbena* x *hybrida* represents most plants grown in gardens, two pure species are also sometimes offered, both sufficiently remarkable to hold their own against their more sophisticated and highly bred relations. *Verbena peruviana* (per-u-vee-A-na), a native of Peru as its species name indicates, rapidly forms a dense mat of stems, rooting where it goes. It is furnished with lance-shaped, lobed leaves to about two inches long, closely set along square stems. Umbels of flower about two inches wide are freely produced from the axils of the leaves, and they are typically

VERBENA 'POLARIS'

a vibrant geranium red that is among the purest of that tint gardeners may grow. There is, however, a very attractive pure white form, 'Alba', that could certainly claim equal space in a garden. The growth of both is far more delicate than that of most cultivars of *Verbena* x *hybrida,* and always looks best in a rock garden or grown in the cracks of pavement.

One would say the same about the equally delicate moss verbena, *Verbena tenuisecta* (ten-u-i-SEC-ta), from botanical Latin *tenuisectus,* meaning much-divided. Its ferny, inch-and-a-half-long leaves and delicate lilac-blue to purple flowers always look good when associated with stone. Lately, however, it has been offered as a hanging basket plant, where its mat-forming growth cascades gracefully, and its flowers, now selected in mauve, lilac, and deep purple-blue, are produced in great abundance, even in the hottest weather. As—like most verbena—it enjoys a little dryness at the roots and good air circulation, it is an almost perfect plant for hanging baskets, window boxes, and other containers, provided one does not allow it to wither to the point that leaves are crisp and turn to powder when rubbed between one's fingers. There is also a stunning white form of *Verbena tenuisecta,* 'Alba', which produces a froth of snow-white flowers above dark green, finely divided leaves.

Probably the most fashionable of verbena at the moment, however, is *Verbena bonariensis* (bon-air-ee-EN-sis). Unlike *V.* x *hybrida,* it cannot be expected to produce sheets of bloom, or sheets of anything. It is a stiff, upright, branching plant to four feet, embarrassingly ill clad in a few five-inch-long, narrow, toothed leaves. Indeed, given the sheer lack of foliar photosynthesizing surface, one wonders how it lives to grow so lustily. And seeing its tiny corymb of first flower in the nursery, borne at the top of a gawky stem, one might well ask what the bother is all about. The effect, at a quick glance, is hardly showy and furthermore seems distinctly inclined to magenta, a color many gardeners profess to hate. Nursery owners say it will not sell, and little wonder, for *Verbena bonariensis* is one of many plants grown as annuals whose first presentation is not its best.

With maturity, however, which arrives in midsummer, it gets better, with a skeletal grace unmatched in the summer garden. The adjective "airy" suits it perfectly, and by a happy pun, that is what it is botanically called, since the species name means "good air," from the city of Buenos Aires, where it was discovered in 1726. If the first angular, square-sided stem it produces is cut back to within three inches of the base, it will produce four to six new ones, to form a plant that branches and rebranches, each stem divid-

VERBENA *'AZTEC ROSE'*

VERBENA BONARIENSIS

ing many times and terminating in a flat, two-inch-wide corymb packed with tiny flowers hardly three times the size of a pinhead. To call those flowers magenta, however, is to be unobservant, for they are of the purest lavender, shaded at their bases into violet. Flowers last up to a week in water, where they may receive close study, and the plant will produce more branches and flowers wherever it is cut.

Verbena bonariensis is much easier to grow from seed than *Verbena* x *hybrida*. Seed should be sown about six to eight weeks before the last anticipated frost date, in warm conditions around 70°F, and shaded from light by sheets of newspaper or cardboard, as it needs dark to germinate. Young seedlings transplant easily (as, indeed, does the plant at almost any age) and should be pricked out as soon as they may be handled. They must be grown on in bright, buoyant conditions and pinched once to induce extra branching when they are about eight inches tall. Reducing each plant by half provides four-inch-long cuttings with a growing tip and two or so pairs of leaves, which will root within a week if inserted in half peat, half perlite, thereby supplying more plants. Cuttings of nonflowering side shoots may also be taken in late summer for stock plants overwintered under glass or on a sunny windowsill, where they will flower at the turn of the year and provide cuttings for additional plants the following spring. *Verbena bonariensis* is mildly frost tolerant, reaching its peak of beauty in late summer and early autumn, when it is visited constantly by bees and by migrating monarch butterflies. But young plants grown under glass will be frost sensitive and so should not be transplanted into the garden until the weather is warm and settled.

Verbena bonariensis has many uses in the garden. It can be stunning when planted in drifts of twenty or thirty plants, close enough that they all lace together into a shimmering curtain of violet. But its best use may be when placed here and there in sections of the perennial border, rather as if it had seeded in itself, which, in Zone 7 gardens and warmer, it will usually do. Its light, airy frame will never crowd out other plants, and though it can quickly achieve four feet in height, it is delicate enough to place rather far forward in the border, breaking the tedious rule of short, medium, and tall. As it grows very comfortably in pots, it is also an excellent "drop plant," grown on in an out-of-the-way place and used in midsummer to fill gaps left by earlier flowering annuals and perennials. Like all verbena grown in gardens, it is a true perennial and will persist from year to year in the warmer gardens of Zones 8 to 10.

VINCA MAJOR

FAMILY: *Apocynaceae* or periwinkle family.

CLASSIFICATION: Half-hardy perennial grown as hardy annual.

COMMON NAMES: Periwinkle, greater periwinkle, vinca major.

HARDINESS: Hardy to Zone 7 with protection. Withstands significant frost once established.

GROWING CONDITIONS: Accepts any soil but prefers moist, fertile, well-drained, humus-rich soil. Dislikes poor drainage.

PROPAGATION: From cuttings, taken at any time.

HEIGHT: To 6", but spreading to 6' or more in a season.

ORNAMENTAL VALUE: Grown for decorative foliage.

LEVEL OF CULTURAL DIFFICULTY: Easy.

SPECIAL PROPERTIES: Can be used as a sturdy winter houseplant.

PRONUNCIATION: VIN-ca MA-jor

*I*f one could, it would be interesting to locate the exact point at which *Vinca major* became an almost ubiquitous component of window boxes and mixed container plantings in America. Certainly it is part of a formula repeated over and over again, consisting of the spike plant (*Cordaline australis*) in the center, a ring of red geraniums or some color of petunia, and *Vinca major,* usually in the white-marbled form, trailing over the edges. One must suppose that gardeners (or nongardeners) who recompose this formula endlessly each spring find some sort of satisfying regularity in it, rather like attending church for purely social purposes. It is apparently simply something people do. And once poked into place, the plants are tough, furnishing "the planter" with a visible concession to decency and with little more fuss or bother.

It is of course easy to be scornful of a plant when one is actually scornful of the way it is used, and therefore many gardeners dismiss *Vinca major* from having seen it on the edges of simply too many planted whiskey barrels. But it is actually an excellent plant when looked at in its own right, and sensitively used, it can be very pretty.

Like many plants employed as annuals, it is actually a half-hardy perennial, surviving winters as far north as Zone 7 and providing useful groundcover on rough banks and under trees where lawn grass cannot be maintained or will not thrive. It is a lax, evergreen sub-shrub with many slender stems that arch along the ground, rooting as they go and giving rise to new plants. When mature, its alternate, flat-lying leaves are about three inches long, though they have the nice characteristic of being graded at the tips of the stems into progressively smaller and smaller sizes to minute but fully formed ones just born.

Of western Mediterranean origin, the plant was well known to the Romans, who wound its flexible stems into banquet wreaths, supplying it its genus name, a contraction of *vincapervinca,* from *vincio,* to wind (in this case, "round and round"). They would have used the typical form, with lustrous, dark green leaves and two-inch-wide flowers composed of five squarish petals arranged like a wheel surrounding a short tubular throat of bright yellow. But the whiskey barrel plant is most often the variegated form, *Vinca major* 'Variegata', with leaves margined in pure white and marbled in greenish white over celadon green. As with the green form, its flowers are produced sparingly over a long period of time from late spring to autumn, though they are a pale lilac blue rather than the deep, violet blue of the typical form. There is also a yellow-leaved form, 'Maculata', which can be useful when one wants to heat up, rather than cool down, a mixed composition of annual and tender plants. All forms bear the species name *major* to distinguish them from a similar but smaller cousin, *Vinca minor,* which, along with *Pachysandra procumbens,* is one of the most stalwart groundcover plants in gardens from Zones 3 to 9. The common name of both plants, "periwinkle," derives from the much-prized edible sea-snail, *Littorina littorea,* but the comparison has more to do with the wound shape of its shell than with its tint. Most people, however, will recognize the word *periwinkle* when applied to a color similar to the flowers of vinca, called "periwinkle blue."

Vinca major seems able to put up with almost any growing condition except permanently water-logged soil, though it prefers (and looks best when grown in) rich, well-drained but water-retentive humus or, when grown in containers, in commercial potting compost such as Pro-Mix. It will accept full shade to full sun, though in warmer gardens it will scorch without at least light afternoon shade. It responds dramatically to weekly, half-strength applications of a general water-soluble plant food such as Rapid Gro or Peters 20-20-20, as will all its companions when it is grown as the "trailer" in window boxes or containers of mixed compositions. It can, however, be quite striking when grown alone, carpeting the surface and tumbling from the sides of a large terra cotta pot placed in a shady corner of the terrace or patio. In any situation, however, its growth is apt to be stringy and benefits from an occasional clipping at the end to encourage branching and a thicker cascade of stems. That said, it should be noted that one of the most remarkable uses of *Vinca minor* 'Variegata' occurs each summer at the Red Lion Inn, in Stockbridge, Massachusetts, where window boxes on the top two stories of the antique red-painted inn are planted only in it. As a result of careful feeding and watering, by summer's end they form a two-story veil of vines, perhaps more remarkable for horticultural skill than for beauty.

All forms of *Vinca major* root so easily from cuttings that they are never grown from seed. Tip cuttings about six inches may be taken at almost any time and rooted in damp soil or even in a glass of water. The tender top growth is apt to wilt and so should be trimmed down to a pair of mature leaves, which will later encourage branching.

Plants should be set out in the garden after all danger of frost is past, though at season's end they will have hardened to the point that they can withstand several degrees of frost. *Vinca minor* also makes a sturdy and easily grown houseplant, useful for cascading down from plant shelves or for the edges of the benches of a cool greenhouse. For this purpose, cuttings should be taken in midsummer, pinched, and fed regularly to produce full, many-branched plants, and moved indoors just before frost. From indoor plants, cuttings may then be taken in February for use the following summer outdoors.

VIOLA SPECIES

FAMILY: *Violaceae* or violet family.

CLASSIFICATION: Short-lived perennials grown as hardy biennials or hardy annuals.

COMMON NAMES: Pansy, viola, heartsease.

HARDINESS: Resistant to frost when well hardened off. Older plants may persist over winter as far north as Zone 5, with protection.

GROWING CONDITIONS: Humus-rich, moist, well-drained soil. Full sun in cooler gardens, part-shade in warmer ones.

PROPAGATION: By seed, sown in July for October planting, in January for spring bedding.

HEIGHT: From 6″ to 1′.

ORNAMENTAL VALUE: Grown for flower.

LEVEL OF CULTURAL DIFFICULTY: Easy from started plants. Difficult from seed.

SPECIAL PROPERTIES: Edible flowers used in salads and as garnishes for cakes and pastries.

PRONUNCIATION: vi-O-la

Older garden references assure us that there is a clear distinction between pansies and violas, the former being large and relatively sparsely flowered, and the latter being small and profusely flowered. Pansies seldom persist from year to year, or self-sow, whereas violas will often settle down to become more-or-less perennial, will self-seed abundantly, and are more heat resistant. Satisfying as these distinctions are, however—and still roughly true—the line between pansies and violas is becoming so blurred that it is almost time to give it up. There are now so many small-flowered pansies and large-flowered violas, and the blood lines of cultivars offered are so complex, that placing them in one group or the other must be based simply on rough appearance and not on botany. The violas in the nursery center never had a clear botanical name in any case, but were grouped under one or the other of two species, *Viola tricolor* (TRI-col-or), the familiar "Johnny-jump-up," or *V. cornuta* (kor-NU-ta), the horned violet. Pansies came to be known botanically as *Viola* x *wittrockiana* (wit-rock-ee-A-na) after V. B. Wittrock (1839–1914), a Swedish botanist who studied them extensively, though their older name, *Viola tricolor hortensis* (hor-TEN-sis), allows room to tuck pansies and violas under one label, which is now probably best.

Whatever the confusions of their botany, however, pansies and violas are among the best loved of all flowers grown as annuals. Cultivated by both the newest and the most sophisticated gardeners alike, used by millions in park bedding schemes and under tulips within traffic islands, it is their distinction that, unlike other frequently used plants, they have never fallen out of favor. There are clear reasons for their popularity. The first is that they bloom at a time when one most needs their cheer—early spring. (Indeed, the genus name is a classical Latin word for all the sweet-smelling, long-awaited flowers of spring, including stocks and wallflowers as well as violas.) The second is the charm of their flowers, made up of five petals, two above and three below, with the middle lower one somewhat enlarged into a lip. Often—not always—they are marked with a deeper zone of color in the center or with radiating lines that give them a perky, animated look, like a musing stare on a small face. This appearance supplies the English popular name, from the French *pensée,* meaning thought.

And finally, the flowers, produced from the axils of the leaves, offer a range of color, and a play of color, unmatched by any annual, or, for that matter, any other flowering plant. It goes literally from white to black, with every intermediate color, tint, or shade in between, including startling bi-colors, picotees, traditional "faces," and shadowings. Colors can be deeply saturated, as with the rich purples, burgundies, oranges, and blacks, or they may be beautifully pale and faded, as with the Art Series. This infinite range makes possible the most sophisticated color schemes and blends as well as highly concentrated and intense effects of a single color. Even mixes, scorned by sophisticated garden colorists, can be wonderfully charming when viewed up close in a window box or other container or at the edge of a path.

Though pansies are of very easy culture as well-developed, precociously budded young plants, they are not easy to start from seed. There is the question, first, of when they should be seeded at all. In warmer gardens, where winter temperatures seldom dip much below 20°F, a July or August sowing will produce plants that may be set out in October, a great convenience if they are wanted to provide extra bloom and volume to the stems of tulips, as they can be bedded out just after the tulip bulbs are planted. The problem with such a sowing, however, is that pansy and viola seed sprouts best at a reasonably constant temperature around 60°F, and germination begins sharply to decline at temperatures

VIOLA *X* WITTROCKIANA

even five degrees warmer. Placing the seed pan in a cool, shaded spot under shrubbery, and being sure that it is kept moist, is therefore one's best hope if plants are wanted for autumn bedding. Germination will always also be improved by sowing seed onto very sterile seeding compost, covering it lightly, enclosing the seed pan in a plastic bag, and refrigerating it for a week or more. Where winter temperatures are sufficiently mild, a late-summer sowing is worth the venture, as there will be some autumn flowers and a positive explosion in very early spring. Strains have recently been bred, also, such as the Universal Series, that are unusually cold resistant.

Elsewhere, however, pansies and violas are usually sown in January and February for early spring bloom. Fresh seed germinates best and should be chilled for a week or so in the refrigerator before sowing. The seeding pans and compost must be absolutely sterile, as seedlings are very prone to damping off. Young plants are pricked out as soon as they may be handled and should be grown on in very bright, fresh, cool conditions that may dip just to freezing but should never get much higher than 50°F. Under warm and/or dim conditions, plants quickly become drawn and weak. As soon as winter tem-

VIOLA X WITTROCKIANA *AND* VIOLA TRICOLOR

peratures begin to moderate toward spring, young plants will benefit from being moved into cold frames, where they may experience outdoor light and cool conditions but may be covered if nighttime temperatures drop below freezing. Plants that have been conditioned in this way can be transplanted into permanent positions about a week or so before the last anticipated frost date.

Most gardeners will feel that the exacting regimen of growing pansies and violas from seed is best left to professional nurserymen, and will be content to buy their plants at just the time it is safe to transplant them. A good garden center will have a very wide range of colors, types, and bloom sizes from which to choose, and except with mixes, selection can be quite accurate, as a first precocious bloom or two is apt to show in each six-pack. Young plants transplant readily, providing one of the first truly pleasant jobs of early spring. Pansies and violas benefit from cool weather and will resist a degree or two of frost, and even a light dusting of snow, so they should be put in place as soon as heavy frosts are over. For best development, they require a fertile, well-drained but evenly moist soil that is never allowed to dry out between rains. In northern gardens, full sun produces the best flower, though in warmer gardens part shade prolongs bloom, and in the gardens of Zone 8 and warmer, they are best thought of as winter-blooming plants. Gardens in Zones 4 and 5 may have pansies and violas in bloom all summer, and in a mild winter where snow cover is reliable, plants may persist for a second season of flower.

In whatever conditions, however, flower production is significantly prolonged by the removal of spent flowers before they set seed. If plants become rangy, they may be cut back severely, to within two inches of the ground, and fed with a water-soluble fertilizer low in nitrogen, in the hope of encouraging new growth and flower.

Since the beginning of extensive hybridization of the genus *Viola* in the 1820s, pansies and violas have been valued as plants for bloom in winter and very early spring under glass. Gardeners who have a cool greenhouse or sun porch where temperatures hover around 40°F at night and ten or so degrees warmer in daytime will find them very rewarding plants, though some cultivars may wait stubbornly for the lengthening rays of the early spring sun to flower. Others, however, may flower as soon as ten weeks from germination and continue nonstop well into summer. For winter flower, seed should be sown in July according to the methods employed in warmer gardens for autumn bedding plants. Alternatively, pleasing varieties can be propagated by cuttings. For this purpose, selected plants should be cut back hard, and encouraged to form vigorous young shoots by an application of general, water-soluble fertilizer such as Rapid Gro or Peters 20-20-20. Two- to three-inch-long cuttings, if inserted into half peat, half perlite, and kept moist and shaded, should form roots within four weeks, after which they can be transplanted, eventually to be established singly in five- or six-inch clay pots.

A regular feeding with a water-soluble fertilizer low in nitrogen will encourage vigorous growth and abundant flower.

Pansies and violas are very beautiful when they may be made to flower in the depths of winter, but they are equally cheering in early spring, before the garden has waked, or they may be transplanted outdoors. For flowering plants at this time, it is usually possible to go to a garden center one patronizes regularly, even if they are closed for the season, and ask if one may select a six-pack or two for indoor bloom. Usually, the nursery owner will be pleased to offer a tour of his "pansy house," where abundant bloom may do him credit when there is nothing else to show. For the lift of the heart one may have at the sight of sheets of color at that season, and the unmistakable though gentle fragrance of a mass of pansies in bloom, it is worth a visit.

WAHLENBERGIA SPECIES

FAMILY: *Campanulaceae* or bellflower family.

CLASSIFICATION: Half-hardy to tender perennials grown as half-hardy annuals.

COMMON NAMES: Rock bells, wahlenbergia.

HARDINESS: Sensitive to light frosts.

GROWING CONDITIONS: Moderately fertile, moist, sandy, humus-rich soil. Perfect drainage. Full sun.

PROPAGATION: By seed, sown indoors in late winter or very early spring.

HEIGHT: From 1 to 8".

ORNAMENTAL VALUE: Grown for flower and for diminutive form.

LEVEL OF CULTURAL DIFFICULTY: Difficult.

SPECIAL PROPERTIES: None.

PRONUNCIATION: wa-len-BER-ji-a

Usually no more than six inches tall when mature, wahlenbergias are hardly plants for the open border, where they might easily be lost and where their delicacy could hardly compete even with those plants usually reserved for the front of a flower bed. Like other tiny treasures, they should be grown in places that will show them to advantage, and so they might be best in fine clay pots. Flowers are quite small, never more than an inch across, and often half that size, but because they are borne in profusion for about a month in midsummer, they often seem strikingly large for so small a plant.

Vegetative growth consists of a rosette or tuft never much more than eight inches tall, that being giant for the genus, as most species top out at half that height or less, down even to an inch. Leaves are mid- to dark green, often leathery, sometimes hairy and sometimes toothed, but generally lance- to broadly spoon-shaped, and scarcely three-quarters of an inch long. Many wiry stems extend above the basal growth, each producing a single, five-petaled, starry flower that is some variation of Confederate blue, deepening almost to violet in some species, and fading out almost to white in others, with an occasional veer toward a pale, slate gray. Often, where the five petals join at their base into a narrow tube, there will be a perky zone or "eye," almost of white, and petals are often marked with thin veinings of a darker blue or of green.

General garden references and seed catalogues that give wahlenbergia even a glance usually describe them as "choice," "rare," "gemlike," and "precious." Gardeners with a finely developed sense of catalogue language will then quickly add "hard to acquire" and "difficult to grow." The first conclusion is certainly true, though the second is not. Of the twenty or more species in gardens, only two or three are quite taxing, but most are easy to flower from seed if, like any other plant, their growing requirements are met.

Of the 150 to 200 widely disseminated species in the genus, some are native to Europe but the majority are found in South Africa, Australia, and New Zealand. In flower, leaf, and growth, all bear close resemblances to campanulas, to whose large family they belong, differing only in the botanical particularity of the way they release their ripened seed. The genus is made up of both true annuals and short-lived perennials, though the latter group contains species that will overwinter successfully only in Zones 8 to 10, and then only with perfect drainage. Perennial wahlenbergia are in the main rhizomatous, possessing swollen, tuberous roots that might suggest that they could be carried over and repropagated in the manner of potatoes or dahlias. They seem to resent root disturbance, however, a characteristic unusual in rhizomatous plants, and so are best propagated annually by seed. Even where they are hardy, they are apt to die out over winter or to persist only a year or two at best. In terms of culture, then, no distinction is made between perennial and annual species.

Seed of wahlenbergia should be sown quite early indoors, generally in March for plants that will flower from mid-July until frost, or about 110 days from germination. It should be sown on sterile potting compost lightened by a third with sharp sand or pigeon grit, as at all times wahlenbergia need open, free-draining soil. Seed should be barely covered by a dusting of about an eighth of an inch of sand, as it needs dark to germinate, but should not be smothered. Germination occurs best at temperatures around 55° to 60°F, and seedlings should be pricked out as soon as they may be handled. After they have begun to grow vigorously, they should experience bright, cool, sunny conditions at temperatures around 60°F until they may be transferred into the garden after all danger of frost is past. They require an open,

sunny location, and they grow best in moist but well-drained, sandy humus of moderate fertility. Though seed should be treasured, all but a few bloom stems should be pinched away after blossoms have withered in order to prolong flowering.

The genus *Wahlenbergia* commemorates Georg Wahlenberg (1780–1851), a Swedish botanist who continued Linnaeus's work at the University of Uppsala.

WEDELIA TRILOBA

FAMILY: *Asteraceae* or aster or daisy family.

CLASSIFICATION: Tender perennial grown as tender annual.

COMMON NAME: Wedelia.

HARDINESS: Extremely frost sensitive. Dislikes cool weather.

GROWING CONDITIONS: Any moderately fertile, well-drained soil. Sun to part shade.

PROPAGATION: By seed, sown indoors 6 to 8 weeks before frost. Cuttings root easily at any time.

HEIGHT: To 8", but spreading to 4' in a single growing season.

ORNAMENTAL VALUE: Grown for flower and for procumbent growth habit.

LEVEL OF CULTURAL DIFFICULTY: Easy.

SPECIAL PROPERTIES: Excellent container, hanging basket, or window box plant. Attractive as winter houseplant or cool greenhouse plant.

PRONUNCIATION: we-DEE-lee-a tri-LO-ba

One would suppose that there are enough small yellow daisies that may be grown as annuals without adding another, but wedelia has uses that set it apart from a host of others, especially as it is a trailing daisy, a distinction among so many that are bushlike or tufted in their growth.

A procumbent plant, its close-spaced, some-what succulent, dark, and lustrous green leaves borne alternately on stems, make it equal in foliage to *Vinca major, Hedera helix,* or various species of *Tradescantia.* Each leaf may eventually attain a length of four inches and half that in width, and consists of three lobes, coarsely toothed at their ends. When wedelia creeps along the ground, it attains a height of no more than eight inches but is capable of a spread of six to eight feet, and even in northern gardens can be expected to reach three to four feet in a single season. Its rapid, matted growth suits it as an annual groundcover. In sun or part shade, or in any bare corner of the garden, it will quickly cast its growth over the soil, achieving full cover by midsummer if plants are spaced about a foot apart. Two-inch-wide orange-yellow daisies are borne from the upper axils of the leaves, standing singly on wiry stems well above the foliage and appearing from late spring until frost, or indeed, at any time that the plant is in growth. Flowers are produced most abundantly in full sun, though in part shade there will still be a sprinkling of them, attractively set off by richer and more luxuriant foliage.

The genus commemorates the German botanist Georg Wolfgang Wedel (1645–1721), and though it contains about seventy species, *Wedelia triloba* is the single species under cultivation. Widely dispersed from southern Florida through Central and tropical South America, until recently it was known only to gardeners in Zones 9 and 10.

Wedelia seems indifferent to soil quality, so long as it is well drained and reasonably friable, though plants are responsive to applications every two weeks of a general water-soluble fertilizer such as Miracle-Gro, Rapid Gro, or Peters 20-20-20. When grown in containers, more abundant flowers are produced if plants are allowed to dry out slightly between waterings, though never to the point that they wither.

Cuttings of wedelia root so easily that plants are seldom grown from seed, but it is easy to germinate at temperatures around 65°F. Seed should be sown indoors about six to eight weeks before the last anticipated frost date. Young plants are pricked out as soon as they may be handled and grown on in bright, sunny conditions at about the same temperature, until they may be hardened off and transplanted. But as wedelia is classed as a tender annual, it is best to delay transplanting well beyond the last frost date, until the weather has become warm and settled. Plants will nevertheless benefit by experiencing full outdoor light, though they will need to be brought indoors during periods when temperatures remain below 55°F or so.

By far the more common way to acquire wedelia, however, is as small rooted cuttings. It is the nature of the plant to root wherever it touches moist ground, much in the manner of tradescantia, and therefore cuttings root with great ease, either in half peat, half perlite, moist sand, or even moistened potting compost. Cuttings may be taken at any time of the year, even from young plants newly acquired from a nursery or garden center. Wedelia makes a very attractive houseplant for a sunny windowsill, greenhouse, or conservatory, and so cuttings may also be taken in midsummer and grown on in six-inch clay pots to bring indoors before they are touched by frost. Given bright light and moderate applications of water-soluble fertilizer, they should produce a few of their cheerful yellow daisies all winter long. From plants wintered indoors or under glass, cuttings can be taken in early spring for additional plants outdoors in summer.

Excellent as wedelia is as a quick, attractive, and unusual groundcover, it is perhaps even more valuable when grown in containers, window boxes, or hanging baskets, where its cascading growth and yellow daisies are displayed to great advantage. Still rare in commerce but soon to be more available is an unusually beautiful cultivar, 'Outenreath Gold', which bears leaves attractively splashed and flecked with gold.

XANTHISMA TEXANUM

FAMILY: *Asteraceae* or aster or daisy family.

CLASSIFICATION: Half-hardy biennial grown as half-hardy annual.

COMMON NAMES: Star of Texas, sleepy daisy, xanthisma.

HARDINESS: Withstands light frost once established.

GROWING CONDITIONS: Friable, well-drained soil of only moderate fertility. Full sun. Prefers cool weather.

PROPAGATION: From seed, sown 8 to 10 weeks before last frost.

HEIGHT: To 2'.

ORNAMENTAL VALUE: Grown for flower.

LEVEL OF CULTURAL DIFFICULTY: Moderately difficult outside native range.

SPECIAL PROPERTIES: Useful as cut flower, but only in bouquets viewed during daytime.

PRONUNCIATION: zan-THIS-ma tex-A-num

Though *Xanthisma texanum* is yet one more little yellow daisy, its two-inch-wide flowers, consisting of a single row of about twenty ray florets surrounding a tight disk, are of an extraordinarily clear daffodil yellow, a characteristic signaled by its genus name, from ancient Greek *xanthos*, meaning dyed or tinted yellow. Each ray petal is sharply pointed and stands apart from the others, giving the flower a bright, starlike appearance and supplying it with one of its popular names, "star of Texas." The other name, "sleepy daisy," recognizes the tendency of the flowers to fold up in late afternoon, opening again slowly under the full force of the next morning's sun. Xanthisma is native to dry, open, sandy places in the warmer parts of Texas, where its habit is to germinate in autumn and flower the following spring and summer. But like many other plants technically classed as biennials, it does not positively require this jump on the season and will flower abundantly from midsummer to autumn if started indoors in March or April, about eight to ten weeks before the last anticipated frost.

Xanthisma grows into a much-branched but delicate bush to about two feet tall, with thin, brittle stems clad in bladelike or oblong, dull olive green leaves no more than two or so inches long. Flowers are borne at ends of branches but well above the plant, in a very showy abundance until cut down by heavy frost. Xanthisma requires full sun, and though it is native to places that experience extreme summer heat, it prefers cool weather, since in the wild it will generally have completed flowering and set seed by early summer. Light, sandy, alkaline soils suit it best, and it will be a dismal failure in gardens made on heavy clay, unless a patch can be made more friable through the addition of sharp sand and a generous sprinkling of gypsum. Xanthisma grows natively on soils that are poor in nitrogen but rich in mineral content, and so it responds to a single feeding with a granular fertilizer high in phosphorus and potassium but low in nitrogen, such as is formulated for tomatoes and potatoes.

Plants should be spaced about a foot apart, which will give them room to develop but still interlace attractively by the time they come into flower. If they have not grown fat from fertile, humusy soil or from over-feeding, they should be self-supporting, though branches are very brittle, and in exposed, open, or windy situations they will require staking with twiggy brush, inserted among the plants before they have interlaced. In cool gardens, flower production may be continued well into autumn by the removal of spent blooms before seed is formed, though seed of xanthisma is sufficiently rare that a plant or two should be designated as seed bearers.

Xanthisma is an excellent cut flower, lasting for up to a week or more in water. In gardens that experience high heat and humidity at midsummer, xanthisma will cease to flower no matter how it is treated. But in such gardens, it is worth sowing seed as soon as it is ripe for plants that may overwinter and flower abundantly in late spring and early summer of the following year. Young seedlings should not be thinned, however, until after the last frosts of spring, as there will be some winter losses, the chances of which are increased rather than eliminated by protective mulches. Even in gardens close to its native range, extra seed of xanthisma should be saved in the event that autumn-germinated seedlings do not survive the winter.

XERANTHEMUM ANNUUM

FAMILY: *Asteraceae* or aster or daisy family.

CLASSIFICATION: Hardy annuals.

COMMON NAMES: Immortelle, strawflower, everlasting, xeranthemum.

HARDINESS: Withstands light frost.

GROWING CONDITIONS: Moderately fertile, dryish, fast-draining soil. Full sun. Prefers cool weather.

PROPAGATION: By seed, sown in place just before last frost, or indoors in peat pots about 8 weeks before last frost. Resents root disturbance.

HEIGHT: To 30".

ORNAMENTAL VALUE: Grown for flower.

LEVEL OF CULTURAL DIFFICULTY: Moderately difficult.

SPECIAL PROPERTIES: Excellent as fresh and as dried cut flowers.

PRONUNCIATION: ze-RAN-the-mum AN-u-um

Xeranthemum annuum is one of several flowers that carry the evocative popular name "immortelle," from their capacity, when dried, to remain attractive for many years. Other annuals grown under that name (*Ammobium alatum, Helipterum roseum,* and *Helychrysum bracteatum*) are generally yellow-centered, with ray petals of white, yellow, or orange, but xeranthemum flowers in a range of colors from strong pink and cherry red through magenta, crimson, and purple to mauve and violet blue. There are also fine clear whites, the single 'Snow Lady' being perhaps the best. Such a range of color is invaluable in dried flower arrangements, where some of these tints are rare. Whatever their color, xeranthemum also look particularly fine with the tawny browns and beiges of grasses and other dried seed heads and leaves.

Though xeranthemum possesses most of its distinction as a dried flower, it is also very pretty in the summer and autumn garden. It grows into an upright, wiry plant to about thirty inches tall, branched at the base and sparsely furnished with narrow, blade-shaped leaves between one and two inches long. The whole plant has an ashy appearance, created by a thick cover of short, silvery hairs on the leaves and stems. Flowers are borne on wire-thin stems, each consisting of a single "daisy" about an inch and a half wide. But whereas the most familiar daisies consist of a row of ray petals surrounding a central knot of disk florets, the true flower of xeranthemum is only a boss of disk florets, and the "petals" of the flower are, in fact, vividly colored papery bracts. Depending on the cultivar, the bracts may form a single row, or be elegantly doubled into two or three layers. The bracts of single-flowered sorts are usually narrow and pointed, though doubles generally possess bracts that are rounded, often curved prettily toward the center to form a shallow bowl.

Xeranthemum is a very easy plant to grow, possessing only one difficulty, that it transplants unwillingly and so must usually be sown where it is to flower. Fortunately, however, it may be sown very early in spring, just around the last anticipated frost date. It germinates rapidly in cool soil, appearing above ground in three to ten days, and begins flowering about eleven weeks later. In most American gardens, therefore, little would be gained by starting plants indoors, since seed sown in late March should produce plants that will begin to bloom by mid-June and continue in flower for six weeks or more. Xeranthemum flourishes best in cool conditions, however, and so gardeners who experience brief springs and rapidly escalating summer heat might sow it in early March, three or so seed to a peat pot, allowing all three to develop in bright conditions around 55°F, and planting them in the garden, pot and all, after all danger of frost is past. Care must be taken, however, to be sure that the crowns of the plants are exactly level with the soil, for xeranthemum is very prone to rotting off at ground level, and even plants sown in place should never have their crowns covered with scratched or cultivated soil or with mulch. For the same reason, a rather dryish, fast-draining soil of moderate fertility produces the healthiest plants, which should be thinned to stand about six to eight inches from one another. As with all other everlasting daisies, full sun is an absolute requirement. And though xeranthemum grows rigidly upright and properly spaced plants will

generally support one another, in exposed and windy conditions one or several plants may topple over. Support should be supplied by inserting twiggy brush among colonies of plants just when they begin to form flower stems.

Xeranthemum is an excellent cut flower, both fresh and dried. For both purposes, stems should be cut just as the flowers begin to expand, using a sharp knife or scissors, and never a casual twist and yank, which will fail to sever the stem and may bring up the whole plant—bloom, stem, root, and all. The wiry stems of individual blossoms make them easy to insert in fresh arrangements of flowers as a last touch after all the heavier blooms and thorny or twiggy stems are in place. If they are wanted for winter arrangements, they should be gathered before they are fully opened, tied into small bunches, and hung upside down in a cool, dark, airy place to dry.

ZALUZIANSKYA CAPENSIS

FAMILY: *Scrophulariaceae* or snapdragon family.

CLASSIFICATION: Tender perennial grown as tender annual.

COMMON NAMES: Night phlox, star balsam, zaluzianskya.

HARDINESS: Sensitive to light frost.

GROWING CONDITIONS: Humus-rich, moist but perfectly drained soil. Brief dry periods between watering. Full sun.

PROPAGATION: By seed, sown 10 to 12 weeks before last frost.

HEIGHT: To 10', but often falling over and becoming procumbent at half that height.

ORNAMENTAL VALUE: Grown for night flower.

LEVEL OF CULTURAL DIFFICULTY: Moderately difficult.

SPECIAL PROPERTIES: Intense, night-borne fragrance. Excellent in containers and window boxes.

PRONUNCIATION: za-loo-zee-AN-skee-ya ca-PEN-sis

*L*ooked at in the broad light of day, nothing would seem to recommend zaluzianskyas. A short-lived tender perennial usually grown as an annual, it forms a lax, trailing, and branching plant to about ten inches tall that even charity would describe as "straggly." Its dark green leaves are narrowly oval, to no more than two inches long, and are slightly clammy to the touch. Somewhere around midsummer, however, zaluzianskya redeems its weedy anonymity by producing small half-inch-wide flowers in short spikes at the ends of branches. They are cunningly crafted in themselves, consisting of a short tube that flares into five lobes, each of which is notched halfway down its length into a Y, creating an unusual, pinwheel effect. The lobes are a dull, purplish black on their reverse and a sparkling white above. But it is their fragrance that makes zaluzianskyas remarkable, for they have one of the richest and most complex of all summer scents, at once fruitlike, sweet, and spicy, closest perhaps to the richly perfumed Asiatic lilies. But the flowers of zaluzianskya are quite small and never very numerous, making a mystery of how they convey so much fragrance over so great a distance. One pot, when in bloom, wafts its scent all about the garden and into the house. Flowers open late in the evening, though it is only with complete darkness that they begin to emit their fragrance for the delectation of night-pollinating insects.

Though perhaps no flowering plant is in greater need of a common name to replace the impossible cluster of consonants and vowels, nei-ther "night phlox" nor "summer balsam" catches the most remarkable characteristic of zaluzianskya, its fragrance. The British seed firm Chiltern Seeds does offer the plant under the trade name 'Midnight Candy', which may be thought an advance. Or not.

The genus name commemorates an important early Polish botanist, Adam Zaluziansky von Zalusian (1558–1613), who spent most of his productive life at Prague. It contains upwards of forty species, all native to South Africa, of which only two or three are grown in gardens. *Zaluzianskya capensis* is the most frequently cultivated, though the very similar species *Z. vilosa* (vi-LO-sa), with night-borne, fragrant flowers of pale lavender above and violet-purple beneath, is sometimes also grown.

Zaluzianskya ovata (o-VA-ta) is also occasionally available, usually cutting-grown, from nurseries specializing in unusual indoor plants. Shrubbier than the other two, and more reliably perennial, it forms a bushy, upright plant to about twelve inches tall, with narrowly oval, toothed leaves to two inches long. Both stems and leaves are covered with short, sticky hairs, which emit an unpleasant odor when touched or bruised. Flowers are as much as an inch across, with petals flaring from tubes. Long and rounded into two distinct lobes at their ends, they are arranged in the typical, five-petaled, pinwheel form of other zaluzianskyas. The petals are a dull maroon beneath and white above, and they remain slightly cupped when open, allowing both colors to be seen and giving the flowers great charm. Flowers may remain open during the day in dull weather, and though not as strongly scented as either *Zaluzianskya capensis* or *Z. vilosa*, they carry a sweet, almondlike fragrance, though in smelling them one must take care not to brush against the leaves, which have the odor of an old, wet dog.

The zaluzianskyas under cultivation are easy to raise from seed, which should be sown indoors about ten to twelve weeks before the last anticipated frost date, at cool temperatures of 50° to 55°F. Germination is rapid, and seedlings transplant easily when an inch or so tall, though juvenile plants should experience a minimum of root disturbance when they are established in the open garden or in containers, as too much disturbance may set them back severely or cause them to fail to establish. All zaluzianskyas require full sun and humus-rich but perfectly drained soil, and they benefit from being allowed to dry out slightly between waterings, as root and stem rot quickly set in when soils are soggy or plants are over-watered. Young plants profit from weekly applications of a general all-purpose water-soluble plant food such as Miracle-Gro, Rapid Gro, or Peters 20-20-20, at half the strength recommended on the package, though when bud formation occurs, fertilizers should be withheld. From a sowing in March, plants should begin to flower in early July and continue until frost. If flower production declines toward the middle of August, plants may be sheared back by about a third, and fertilized to encourage the production of a second flush of bloom for autumn.

No zaluzianskya is really a plant for the open border, as their undistinguished growth makes a patch of them look like a lapse of the weeding hand. For the mysterious fragrance that will waft about, however, a few plants might be tucked into plantings around a terrace, near a porch where people sit in the evening, or in a flower bed beneath windows that will be left open. Because of their rather exacting water requirements, zaluzianskyas are also excellent container plants, particularly where summers are unusually wet. They are perhaps most wonderful when combined with other plants in window boxes, for though they will show little during the day, they are everything on a warm midsummer night.

ZINNIA SPECIES

FAMILY: *Asteraceae* or aster or daisy family.

CLASSIFICATION: Tender annual.

COMMON NAMES: Youth-and-old-age, zinnia.

HARDINESS: Sensitive to light frost.

GROWING CONDITIONS: Deep, humus-rich, moisture-retentive but perfectly drained soil. Full sun. Plants resent cool weather and relish heat.

PROPAGATION: By seed, sown indoors in peat pots 4 to 6 weeks before last frost, or outdoors in place when weather is warm and settled.

HEIGHT: From 6" to 4', depending on cultivar.

ORNAMENTAL VALUE: Grown for flower.

LEVEL OF CULTURAL DIFFICULTY: Moderately easy.

SPECIAL PROPERTIES: Excellent cut flowers.

PRONUNCIATION: ZIN-ee-a

*U*ntil impatiens crowded them all aside, zinnias, along with marigolds and petunias, were the three most popular annual plants grown in American gardens. Natives of Mexico, zinnias are assumed to be both old-fashioned and easy to grow, though in fact neither assumption is completely true. They were not introduced into gardens until around 1861, when the narrow-leaved form, variously known as *Zinnia mexicana* (mexi-CA-na), *Z. linearis* (lin-ee-AR-is), *Z. angustifolia* (an-gus-ti-FO-lee-a), but now (correctly, for the moment) *Z. haageana* (hay-gee-A-na), first appeared. The larger-flowered *Zinnia elegans* (EL-uh-gans), the zinnia in most people's minds, did not appear until around 1886, though the genus was named by Linnaeus in honor of a brilliant professor of botany at the University of Göttengen, Johann Gottfried Zinn (1727–1759). Sadly, he could only have known his namesake from dried herbarium specimens and never from the cheerful masses of brightly colored, papery summer flowers that are so beloved of child gardeners and their grown-up counterparts, public park superintendents.

In much of North America, where summers are glaringly bright and hot, zinnias earn their reputation for being sturdy, desirable annuals, especially now that varieties have been bred that are resistant to powdery mildew, their one great bane. In England, however, they have always been plants to take a chance on, for, as natives to Mexico, they loathe a chill, damp summer and may pack off at their peak in a spell of bad weather, if indeed they ever get going at all. In one of his few confessions of personal defeat, the great English gardener William Robinson (1838–1935) comments in his landmark *The English Flower Garden,* "Zinnias have been a total failure with me, not showing a trace of their fine beauty as one sees it in Austria and Italy. . . . They are plants that wet weather disfigures very soon." It may be pleasant for American gardeners in the upper South and Midwest to know that English gardeners, who may grow such splendid delphiniums, foxgloves, and meconopsis, might envy them their success with a simple zinnia.

No commonly grown annual plant is quicker than zinnias from seed, which is large and easy to handle, and which should be sown only barely covered in rich but perfectly drained compost. Germination at around 60°F occurs after as few as four days, and young plants will be ready to move into their permanent positions after four weeks or so of growth. Under favorable weather conditions, they may be expected to produce their first flower bud as soon as six weeks after

ZINNIA HAAGEANA (ANGUSTIFOLIA) 'ALBA'

germination, though better plants and flowers will be had in the long run if this first precocious bud is pinched out as soon as it is apparent. Full flower should occur within eight to ten weeks from germination and continue all summer long, especially if spent flowers are promptly removed, or if plants are picked for indoor arrangements, where they are long-lived in a vase.

But the culture of zinnias, even in areas where they grow very well, is not to be taken entirely for granted. Though seedlings develop rapidly on a sunny windowsill or in a home greenhouse, they demand strong sunlight and relatively cool conditions. If, when they are small, they experience less than ideal conditions, they will quickly become drawn and spindly, never developing into good plants when transferred to their permanent homes. Even plants that thrive indoors will become tough and woody if they become mature under such conditions, filling their pots with roots and initiating premature flower. And though such plants are the darlings of roadside stands, where their perky first flower causes them to sell well, the best plants will always occur if seedlings are transplanted while still in their first flush of juvenile vigor, after only three or four sets of true leaves have developed. It is fortunate, then, that they are so rapid from seed. Indeed, gardeners who experience long, hot summers and frost-free early autumns may have the best success by sowing them in place, later thinning them to stand the appropriate distance one from another, according to whether they are tall, medium, short, or "Lilliputian" varieties.

One of the persistent myths associated with the culture of plants grown as annuals is that they benefit by having their roots mussed up at transplant time. The truth, however, is that perhaps 70 percent of all plants usually treated as annuals will be either killed outright by this practice or severely retarded in their growth. Zinnias are a clear case in point, for they hate root disturbance. It seldom causes them to perish but always sets them back irremediably, giving plants the

stunted, isolated look so familiar in park bedding schemes. Seed should therefore be sown three to a peat pot, clipping out all but the strongest after two sets of true leaves form, or individually in plastic cell packs that enable each plant to be eased out gently with all its roots intact.

Plants bought in cell packs from nurseries and garden centers should be transplanted as soon as possible. Whether grown at home or bought from a nursery, zinnias should also be transplanted just exactly at the level they grew, for, unlike other annuals that may form roots along their buried stems, such as marigolds, zinnias may quickly rot away, particularly in rainy weather. They are also very sensitive to cold. A touch of frost will kill them outright, but even damp, sulky "sweater weather" will discourage their growth to the point that their full potential

ZINNIA ELEGANS *'BRONZE'*

will never develop. Young plants should therefore not be transplanted until the weather is warm and settled, usually the second week of June in most American gardens.

Though heat- and sun-loving zinnias would appear to be drought-tolerant plants, they really reach the perfection of which they are capable when grown in deep, humus-rich, evenly moist but well-drained soil. At all times in their life, stagnant air and heavy, overly wet soils are their enemies, opening the way to mildew and various other molds and funguses that may carry off plants at any age, from tiny seedlings to mature flowering specimens. Powdery mildew, a scourge that has caused many gardeners to give up on the culture of zinnias, develops especially rapidly after a dry spell followed by a period of hot, rainy weather. Most modern varieties of zinnia have been bred with some resistance to this problem, though frequent treatments with copper sulfate, an organic remedy, will hold it at bay, as will deep, thorough waterings in dry spells. And though a deep organic mulch will retain necessary water near their roots, gardeners who follow this practice among annual plantings should always leave a zone about five inches wide around the central stem of zinnia plants to avoid fungal diseases that might strike just at ground level. Zinnias are also gross feeders, benefiting by the same regime followed for tomatoes, eggplants, peppers, and squashes, all of which share their Mexican heritage. A liberal dusting of general granular vegetable garden food, 10-10-10 or the like, works wonders when applied a few days after young seedlings have been transplanted and have "caught" and again just as flowering begins.

Most zinnias in commerce are complex crosses and back-crosses between the small, narrow-leaved *Zinnia haageana* and the taller, broader-leaved *Z. elegans.* For convenience in cat-

ZINNIA PERUVIANA

alogues, however, the species status of both is generally maintained. Cultivars listed under *Zinnia haageana* may be expected to grow about two feet tall, though usually they will flop over after about a foot of growth and send up branching and flowering stems from the axils of their leaves. This is actually a desirable characteristic as the end result is an attractive, profusely flowering, bushy plant to about a foot tall, suitable for drifts in the front of the border or for window boxes and containers. The original species produced single daisies about an inch and a half across, in shades from rich yellow through orange-red.

ZINNIA ELEGANS *'RED SAILS'*

ZINNIA HAAGEANA 'CHIPPENDALE'

Popular cultivars, such as 'Chippendale' and 'Persian Carpet', produce double flowers of orange and red marked with chestnut and maroon. But perhaps the most useful of the cultivars of *Zinnia haageana* offered is the white, single form with a central disk of yellow, which goes under many names, but most frequently as 'White Star'. It possesses all the freshness that a daisy should have, and individual flowers remain in good condition on the plant for a very long time, making dead-heading seldom necessary.

Cultivars listed under *Zinnia elegans* may grow to almost any size between tiny, bun-shaped, bushy plants no taller than six inches to giant-flowered strains that may reach four feet or even more (with staking). Flower form ranges from singles through semi-doubles to doubles so thick with petals that they should almost be reserved for some sport where balls are required. There are "cactus-flowered" forms also, where the broad, squared-off petals typical of the group have been curled into quills. Flower size may be anything from an inch or so across to five inches or more, and it is not always the case that the smaller flowers occur on the smaller plants, and larger on the larger. For there are grotesque midgets no taller than a foot with three-inch-wide flowers, and gi-

ants to four feet with single pinwheels of hardly an inch across. Flower color spans the entire range of the color spectrum except for true blue. According to cultivar, bloom may be any shade of white, cream, chartreuse or true green, palest yellow, chrome yellow or orange, pale to rich pink, lavender or purple, through every shade of red, crimson, and scarlet to maroon, chestnut, and mahogany brown, the deeper, brownish shades often bi-colored, splotched, or streaked.

All zinnias make superb cut flowers, which seem almost impossible to arrange badly. Indeed, a bunch of them in bright mixed colors, assembled in the hand as they are cut and then crammed into a simple mason jar, produces a lighthearted bouquet that is redolent both of summer itself, and of the reasons most people grow annuals at all.

ZINNIA HAAGEANA

TECHNIQUES FOR GROWING ANNUALS

Procuring Seeds and Plants

Until about ten years ago, a book such as this would have been very frustrating to most gardeners, for many of the plants it describes would simply not have been available. Over a little more than a decade, however, the sudden explosion of garden enthusiasm in North America has enormously increased the range of annuals and tender plants supplied by good local garden centers. Major seed houses seem to compete each year in offering rare species of annuals and tender plants, as well as unusual forms of familiar ones, and a host of small specialty seed companies have sprung up with lists that should always be scanned for some unexpected treasure. The mail order business, which experienced its great surge of growth also during this period, has made possible the delivery of good plants in excellent condition to the gardener's door. The sum of these advances has resulted in the conviction, among gardeners, that there never has been so exciting a time as right now.

On page 511 of this book, an extensive list of sources is offered, both for seed and for started plants. All are reputable firms that take care to provide material that is viable and true to name. It may still be the case, however, that some of the best annuals and tender plants will come from other gardeners. Most annuals set far more seed than is ever required, and most tender plants grown as annuals root easily from cuttings. So when visiting a garden, it never hurts to ask, though one's request is always more cheerfully granted if one has a few special seeds of one's own to offer, in small brown paper coin envelopes, clearly labeled.

Starting Seed Indoors

Starting plants from seed used to be a routine springtime activity for most gardeners. But the multiplication of good garden centers that offer plants in strong growth, just when they are needed, has resulted in a decline in home-grown plants. Most gardeners are relieved at that, for starting one's own plants from seed is a great deal of work, can be fraught with anxiety, and often produces results far less good than those achieved by professionals with highly efficient facilities. Still, there will always be plants that can be procured in no other way, perhaps because they are rare, or because the seed was a special gift or a family heirloom, or one gathered it on vacation and wants to remember that happy time. There are gardeners, too, who will always want to grow their own plants from seed, out of curiosity, or to know a plant intimately in all its phases, or from the sheer desire to nurture young life in the early days of the year. By far the most important thing to remember in starting seed indoors is that one is asking plants to germinate, grow, and develop in conditions that are usually far from those in which they originated. No plant, after all, is native to a sunny windowsill.

ESSENTIAL REQUIREMENTS

Sterile Potting Mix
Most of the diseases that affect young seedlings are soil borne, and so great care must be taken to maintain sterile conditions from the first. Gardeners who make their own compost swear by it as a principal ingredient for seed-starting mixes. It must still be sterilized, however, by first baking it in the oven at 350°F until an apple-sized potato buried in the middle tests done. When cool, it is sifted and combined with equal measures of peat and sharp sand or perlite.

Commercial growers, and many home growers, avoid this bother by using a soilless potting medium such as Pro-Mix, which is kept dry until use, and then moistened thoroughly before seeding occurs. Such mixes usually contain enough nutrients for germination and first growth, but as seedlings develop, they will exhaust the supply and so must receive supplementary fertilizers in water-soluble form. (See "Fertilizers," p. 507.) Soilless potting mix may not be reused to germinate seed, though it is a valuable soil improvement worked into the garden. It should not be confused with commercial potting soils, which generally contain earth and must be sterilized as compost is before use in germinating seedlings.

Pots and Containers

Almost anything that will hold earth and can be punctured at the bottom for drainage may be used for starting seed. Old-fashioned greenhouse gardeners depended on clay pans and wooden flats, though being porous, they required laborious scrubbing with strong chemicals before being reused. Most modern growers now use plastic seed trays, which are inexpensive, easy to store, and easy to clean. They are relatively shallow, about two inches in depth, because a greater volume of soil will hold too much moisture, which can cause rot to young seedlings. When plastic seed trays are reused, they should be scrubbed thoroughly with dishwashing liquid and allowed to air dry before being filled with fresh potting medium.

THE SEEDING PROCESS

Before cutting open a single packet of seed, sterile seed trays should be filled with potting medium, moistened thoroughly, and firmed gently, not with one's hands but with the flat side of a small board, as one's fingers may pit the surface unevenly, causing small seed to wash into the indentations. By far the most common cause of failure at starting young seedlings is sowing too thickly. Large seed pose no problems, for they can be shaken into the palm of one's hand, picked out, and evenly spaced over the top of the soil. Smaller seed, such as will tumble freely from a seed packet, are usually tapped from the packet's open end, though that is a skill that new gardeners may want to practice with an envelope of household grain—rice or mustard seed—before trying it with an actual seed packet. However, many annuals have seed that is dust-fine and tends to cling to one's open palm or even lodge in the crevices of the seed envelope. Such seed is best handled by mixing it with a tablespoon of fine bird gravel, available in the pet sections of most supermarkets, and dusting the mixture evenly over the soil surface. With seed of whatever size, however, it is always better to sow thinly, sometimes in two flats, or three, rather than to risk overcrowding, which encourages disease and makes young seedlings difficult to separate at transplant time.

Large and medium-sized seed should be covered lightly by sifting potting mix over them, and very small seed need only be gently pressed into the soil surface with a board. Some growers routinely cover seed with a light layer of vermiculite, a sterile product that seems to aid germination and discourage damping off. (See "Damping Off," p. 504.)

PRICKING OUT

"Pricking out" is a very old term in gardening, describing the process by which young seedlings are lifted from the pot in which they germinated and transferred to individual pots or plastic six-packs. It is usually done with a sharpened stick, a lead pencil, or a chopstick. Most seedlings, even those that do not transplant easily in adolescence, can be pricked out when quite small, though only after at least one set of true leaves has formed. Some, however, including several popular annual vines such as morning glories, moon vines, and sweet peas, will never accept root disturbance, and so should be sown three seed to a peat pot, with the intention of clipping out all but the strongest when two sets of true leaves have appeared.

Before any seedlings are disturbed, the small pots or plastic six-packs into which they will be transplanted should be filled, again with sterile potting mix, and watered well, for success often depends on exposing tiny roots as little as possible to drying air. Each seedling should be grasped very gently by thumb and forefinger as it is pried from the seed flat, and then, using the same sharpened stick, pencil, or chopstick to make a hole, gently inserted at the level it originally grew, and lightly firmed into place. Newly transplanted seedlings take very little time, a day or so, to make contact with the new soil and resume growth. During this adjustment period, they should be kept in a cool, moist, shaded location to minimize transpiration and wilt, which can be fatal.

Growing On Indoors

LIGHT

Of the three conditions necessary to adequate plant growth—water, nutrients, and adequate light—it is the latter that is by far the hardest to provide indoors. For it must be remembered that the early spring sunshine that comes through the windows of most houses is much reduced in intensity from that enjoyed by plants outdoors. For this reason, even plants that normally would prefer shaded conditions outdoors will benefit as seedlings by very good light indoors. They should also be as close to the natural source of light as possible, for plants distanced even a foot or two from windows will show a marked decline in vigor.

By far the best conditions in which to grow on seedlings is a small home greenhouse, and those gardeners who opt to grow their own plants from seed should seriously consider acquiring one. In addition to providing even and abundant light, greenhouses can usually be climatically controlled to supply the cool conditions in which most seedlings develop best. Lacking a greenhouse, however, many gardeners have great success with light units, which usually come with detailed instructions and which can be set up easily in any unused space, provided it is heated, such as a basement, frost-free garage, guest bedroom, or large closet.

Without either greenhouse or light units, however, gardeners will be left with the proverbial sunny windowsill, of which most houses do not have many, for such windowsills must face south or southeast and be without obstructions, such as deep overhanging eaves, shadowing trees or shrubs, or curtains. Modern household temperatures are also often too warm for seedlings, most of which prefer a range between

50° and 60°F in daytime, and even slightly cooler at night. Cold drafts from a window opened a crack must also be avoided, since seedlings of tropical origin will be harmed or killed outright by chilled air flowing over them.

An alternative to germinating and growing on seed at home is to farm it out to a friendly local nurseryman or garden center owner. For the same price they charge to produce their own plants for sale, they will usually grow seedlings for a customer, particularly of plants they are not familiar with, simply to get the experience. Establishing such a relationship allows one to search catalogues for an ever-growing number of rare or unusual species that would not be popular in garden centers, because they make a poor showing as young plants, are too subtle for general appeal, or are simply not yet well enough known.

PESTS AND DISEASES

Insects

Anyone who grows plants indoors will already know that closed environments provide marvelous breeding grounds for a number of insect pests. Fortunately, two of the most pernicious and most common—scale and mealy bug—are not interested in young seedlings, since they feed on the rich sap of mature plants. But white fly, aphids, and red spider mites will often attack young plants and can increase in enormous numbers among ranks of seedlings. White flies live and breed on the undersides of leaves but make their presence known by flying up in clouds when plants are disturbed. Red spider mites live there too, but it takes a keen eye or a magnifying glass to detect the individual insects. Their presence will usually be noted, though, by a dusty webbing on the undersides of leaves and a yellowed, anemic look on the upper sides. Aphids take no care to hide, but cluster on stems, usually the tender tips, in small, translucent globules. The appearance of any of these pests on seedlings calls for immediate action, for there isn't, usually, much in a seedling to spare, and all three insects can breed with astonishing rapidity. Further, white flies can be carried into the garden on young transplants, where they will be very difficult to eradicate.

All three insects may be controlled by chemicals sold in garden centers for this purpose, though when they are toxic to humans and pets, flats of seedlings should be carried into a well-ventilated, frost-free garage for treatment, or even outdoors if the weather is above freezing. Spider mites flourish best in arid conditions, and so raising atmospheric humidity by frequent misting or by growing seedlings in pots standing on gravel above—not in—trays filled with water will usually prevent them from multiplying. When young stems are strong and firm, aphids can often be rubbed off with thumb and forefinger or dislodged by a firm jet of water from the kitchen faucet. Nontoxic insecticidal soaps work to control both aphids and spider mites, but are not effective in controlling white fly, which requires a stronger chemical treatment.

Damping Off

Damping off is caused by a combination of conditions, but the operative villain is a soil-borne fungus that multiplies rapidly in moist and stagnant air. Completely invisible, it is recognized only when previously healthy seedlings topple over, showing a pinched stem near the ground. Once a few seedlings have been affected, usually in the middle of the flat, the disease will make its rapid way through all the rest. By working quickly, the gardener may save a few seedlings by transplanting them immediately into sterile soil and spacing them widely. Usually, however, when damping off strikes, it is best to begin again with fresh seed and fresh soil.

To avoid the possibility of damping off, care must be taken to be sure that both potting medium and pots are sterile at sowing time. Seed should be sown thinly, so that there is air space between and among seedlings. After germination, soil should be kept evenly moist, never sodden, and water is best applied from below, by standing the flats in a large pan or kitty litter tray, so that droplets do not cling to the leaves. Good ventilation is crucial, and if it cannot be secured naturally, a small fan trained just above the seedlings may be used. Finally, seed that is very small, or known to be especially prone to damping off, is often covered at sowing with a light layer of vermiculite, a commercial product made by expanding particles of mica at high temperatures, which remains sterile no matter how damp it becomes.

Establishing Plants Outdoors

HARDENING OFF

Hardening off is the process by which young plants are gradually exposed to outdoor conditions after having been grown in highly protected environments. When plants are bought from the outdoor benches of old-fashioned garden centers, that process has already occurred. More and more, however, plants are bought directly from large greenhouses, where they have been grown under carefully controlled conditions. Such plants will need the same hardening off required by seedlings raised on a sunny windowsill, in a home greenhouse, or in a lighted basement.

Young plants must be protected initially not only from the intensity of the outdoor sun, but also from wind, and so a sheltered spot should be found, such as the back wall of a garage or a well-protected nook along the north side of the house foundations. Provided the weather is above freezing at all times, they may stand there a day or two and then be gradually moved into more light, until they experience the exposure in which they are expected to grow. During this period, which may take as long as two weeks, depending on the weather, water-soluble fertilizers should be withheld, since it is not fresh tender growth that is desired, but rather a toughening and toning of plant tissue. At all times plants should also be kept well watered, since, in the dry atmosphere that can occur in spring, small pots and flats may desiccate much more rapidly than indoors.

TRANSPLANTING

Once the hardening off process has been completed, young annual plants are ready for their permanent positions in the garden. Though the urge to transplant will probably come to most gardeners on fine, bright days with no clouds in the sky, overcast days with the promise of a shower in the afternoon are far better, as the plants will transpire less moisture while their roots are attempting to reconnect with the sustaining earth. If transplanting must occur on a clear, bright day, however, then the work should be done as late in the afternoon as possible, and if the sun is still strong, young plants may be shaded by cardboard boxes or old sheets, but never with plastic bags or upturned plastic pots, which will heat up in the sun.

Many nurseries and many home gardeners now use flexible plastic six-packs to prick out and grow on young seedlings until they are ready for transplanting. They are a great convenience, for each seedling may be slipped gently out of its cell with minimum disturbance to its roots. However, the old practice is still sometimes followed of growing plants in flats or trays in which all the young seedlings share the same earth mass. If their roots are hopelessly entangled they may have to be cut apart with a sharp knife, though it is always better, where possible, to pry them apart with an old kitchen fork, or gently twist and tug with one's hands, so they preserve as much root as possible. But from whatever sort of container one is transplanting, it is best with most plants to ignore the old advice of "messing up the roots," which will be fatal to many, and a discouraging setback to most. It is far better to buy or grow plants that still have plenty of root room in their container and establish them with as little disturbance as possible.

Care should always be taken to establish all annuals with their necks just at the level they grew in the pot. A few, such as marigolds and verbenas, are able to root from buried stem tissue, but with many others, burying them too deeply may cause rotten stems or crowns. The native soil should be settled around each plant so that it is in direct contact with the root ball, and then pressed firmly and gently, never to the extent of hardening the soil into a cake. Finally, in wet weather or dry, plants should be well watered in, as water will complete the process of connecting the root ball to the surrounding soil. In very dry periods, water may also have to be reapplied daily, until the young plant's roots have begun to forage widely and can find their own moisture.

DIRECT SEEDING

A number of true annual plants always perform best when sown directly into the garden. Often they flower so quickly from seed that the bother of starting them indoors is not justified. Others resent transplanting so much that it is better to establish them in their permanent homes from the beginning. In this class, particularly, belong many "grain field annuals," such as poppies, larkspurs, bachelor's buttons, and corn cockles. Still others—little mat-forming annuals, such as sweet alyssum, toadflax, and portulaca—are most valuable just in those places one cannot trowel too deeply, such as the cracks in brick or stone paving or over dormant spring-flowering bulbs.

With some experience, gardeners learn which annuals may be safely seeded outdoors, thereby saving valuable space on the windowsill, in the greenhouse, or under the light units. Trouble, however, is not necessarily saved, for the areas in which annuals are sown outdoors must be cleared of weeds, enriched where appropriate with peat or humus, lightened with sand, and raked quite smooth before sowing can occur, so that tiny seed will not fall between clods of earth and fail to germinate. Then seed must be sprinkled carefully, never too thick, and pressed in lightly with a squarish board. Were this all the work, it would not be much. But the seed bed must be kept evenly moist in dry periods, and when the tiny seedlings appear, they must be protected against slugs and snails, which may find them delectable. As they grow older, usually when the second or third sets of true leaves appear, they must be thinned, according to species, and usually following the instructions on the back of the seed packet. A light application of granular fertilizer should then occur, by which point they should be approximately at the same stage as transplanted annuals, and receive the same care.

SELF-SEEDING ANNUALS

Even in quite cold gardens, many annuals need only to be planted for one season, after which they will reappear faithfully from year to year. Called "volunteers" by gardeners, notable examples include nicotianas, California and opium poppies, nigella, certain impatiens, and the beautiful Mexican prickly poppy, species of *Argemone.* Nervous gardeners always fear them, dreading that they may be introducing yet another noxious weed to plague their existence. But self-seeded annuals, when they are too numerous or simply no longer wanted at all, are much easier to eliminate than other weedy plants. None of them travel by underground stolons, shooting up into the hearts of desirable plants. Few have deep, carrotlike taproots, and if they do, they do not regenerate from deep within the ground when the crown is pulled. None are able to sprout from the tiniest root hairs left behind, as will many noxious perennial weeds. So if one is to have weeds in the garden, it is well that they be of introduced annual species.

Many gardeners count absolutely on the annual reappearance of some of their favorite plants as self-seeded individuals, which can either be eliminated where they are not wanted or moved to where they will be wanted. But though it is a happy gardener who finds young plants coming up just where they are wanted, it is a happier one still who finds them in unexpected spots where they look splendid nevertheless. Plants often have an uncanny ability to select their own best places to grow, and many beautiful effects from annual plants come quite on their own, giving the garden a valuable quality of spontaneity.

SOIL

With any garden plant, there is no substitute for the richest and finest soil one can contrive. Still, many gardeners erroneously believe that annuals require no special soil preparation and, in fact, will bloom more freely in poor soils. It is true that a few are treasured because of their preference for dry, gravelly, impoverished soil, but most annuals and certainly most tender plants will reward careful soil preparation with a greater exuberance of bloom, richer flower color, finer leaves, and even an increased resistance to disease and the vagaries of the weather. More than any other plants except vegetables, they also respond dramatically to supplementary fertilizers. Unless grown for their leaves, most prefer fertilizers strong in phosphorus and potassium and relatively low in nitrogen. Still, there is no substitute for good, friable earth, deeply tilled and rich in moisture-retentive humus. When taken up in the hand and squeezed lightly, it should form a compact mass that shows one's finger marks, but does not sit heavily in the palm, oozing moisture like a mud pie. Lightly rolled between the fingers, it should fall apart into crumbly particles, but never trickle away like sand.

By trial and error, every gardener must learn the techniques by which the dirt he or she is given can reach the ideal. If it is heavy or sticky, it may often require barrow loads of sharp sand or gravel, patiently dug in. If it is light and thin, then loam, manure, peat moss, decomposed leaves, or rotted wood chips may need to be added. In any type of soil, there is never a substitute for good, well-made compost, of which there can never be too much. Finally, soils should always be tested to determine whether they are deficient in essential nutrients, and whether lime should be added to bring the pH level close to neutral, which most annuals prefer.

FERTILIZERS

Even the most fabulous soil may be deficient in some of the elements plants need for good growth. Soils rich in organic matter should already have abundant nitrogen, but they may still be deficient in phosphorus, which develops strong root growth and which aids in ripening and maturing tissue, and in potassium, which increases resistance to disease and helps plants withstand unfavorable weather conditions. These elements may be supplied in organic form, which offers plants a slow and steady diet and increases the fertility of the soil incrementally over many years, building up a thriving world of beneficial microorganisms and earthworms, to the benefit of the entire garden.

But annuals have somewhat different needs from most other garden plants, from trees and shrubs and bulbs. They are plants of quick growth, expected to produce from seed or from tiny transplants lusty stems, leaves, and abundant flower in one short season, often no longer than two months' duration. Their needs are thus immediate, and those needs are often best answered by synthetically produced granular fertilizers or by water-soluble ones that can be absorbed almost immediately through growing tissue. Many are also what experienced gardeners call "greedy feeders," meaning that they require more than the usual ration of some elements, particularly phosphorus and potassium, to perform their best. Within individual plant portraits in this book, such requirements are noted where they apply. But almost all annual and tender plants seem to benefit tremendously from at least one application of granular fertilizer—10-10-10 or the like—given each transplant when it has adjusted to its new home and has begun to make fresh growth, or when self-seeded or direct seeded plants have been thinned and have formed two or three sets of true leaves. The amount used depends, of course, on the size of the plant, but approximately a tablespoon, sprinkled in a circle around each plant, should be enough for a three-inch-tall transplant or seedling. Great care must be taken to keep the fertilizer away from the stem of the plant or its leaves, for they are easily burned by direct contact with fertilizer salts. A deep soaking should be given after applications of granular food. Within a week, benefits should become apparent in quickened growth and the darkening of leaves. Should plants still appear thriftless, another application may be made after two or three weeks. But once plants appear to be growing strongly, no further applications should be made, lest plants "run to leaf" and fail to flower.

Water-soluble fertilizers differ from granular ones in that they are formulated to be absorbed almost immediately through all the growing tissue of the plant—leaf, stem, root, and even flower. They are very useful when a quick boost is needed for seedlings grown in a sterile medium, or in pots and window boxes, where many plants are grown in a constricted space, and also when plants are cut back to regrow for an additional display of flower. There are many excellent brands on the market, with careful instructions, though many experienced gardeners believe that water-soluble fertilizers are more beneficial to young seedlings and to container-grown plants when applied at half the strength recommended on the package, but twice as often.

SPACING

Unfortunately, no hard-and-fast rule can be given for spacing, since some annuals look and actually grow better when they are crowded enough to cover the ground between them. Others profit by close proximity with their own kind because their lax stems and heavy blooms can lean on one another for support. Still others, notably vines and weaving plants, will never show their best unless they have something to scramble on. Very tall annuals, such as sunflowers, *Impatiens glandulifera,* and *Nicotiana sylvestris,* will always look both gawky and lonely when grown with too much space between them. They may also be more vulnerable to toppling winds than when they are grown in mutually supporting communities.

Fortunately, the backs of seed packets usually offer specific advice, and they are always to be carefully filed for that reason. But still, it would be a comfort to all gardeners if someone could come up with a sure formula for spacing, such as "Plant all annuals at a distance apart of one third to one half the height each may be expected to achieve at maturity." Actually, that formula works well for a surprising number of plants grown as annuals, many of which achieve a height of one to three feet and so should accordingly be spaced six to eighteen inches apart. Only very tall plants, vines, and some self-seeding meadow annuals such as poppies and larkspurs seem to be exceptions. But when in doubt, it is always better, in the interest of the beauty of the plant—not just its flower, but its leaf and stem and general carriage—to space more rather than less generously.

STAKING

It is a blessing of annuals that many require little in the way of staking. Either they are independent by nature or they have been bred to stand on their own, asking only that they be spaced far enough apart to develop an upright character. Among annuals that do require some support, the easiest to provide for are those that weave in and among other plants, such as *Ammi majus, Nigella damascena,* or *Petunia integrifolia.* They are usually thin and wiry of stem and light of leaf, and should be deliberately planted so they can insinuate themselves into other plants for support.

Many annuals that are planted in drifts may require more elaborate staking. They are often bushy or shrublike in growth, and include such familiar plants as nicotianas, bells of Ireland, cleome, and *Lavatera trimestris.* It is useful to know about such bush-forming annuals that if they are likely to flop, they will flop just at ground level, and so a single stake inserted eight or so inches into the ground with as much showing above can be tied to their central stem for as much support as they will need.

An alternative to single, ground-level stakes for bushy annuals is to grow them among thickets of twiggy brush, usually harvested at pruning time and left to dry, and then inserted around the young plants while there is still space between them. Anyone visiting the great display gardens of England in late May or early June will notice these thickets around young annuals and perennials. By mid-June they are invisible, having been completely covered over by the developing foliage and flowers. It is perhaps the most effective of staking methods when well done, and like many old garden practices, it brings a sort of pleasure of its own.

Prolonging the Show

PINCHING

The first technique for securing the longest possible bloom season from annual plants is one that requires more courage than time, effort, or skill. It is to pinch out the premature, cheerful little bloom that showed so tantalizingly in the nursery or on the windowsill. Many annuals will produce their first bloom when quite small, an ingratiating characteristic in the minds of nursery owners, who count on that display to sell the plants. But if the first bloom or two is removed, the plant will then devote its energies into vegetative growth, thereby eventually producing much more flower, and over a longer period of time. Impatient as the average gardener is sure to be, it is a general rule that the more time an annual plant has to produce stem and leaf, the finer its eventual show of bloom will be.

DEAD-HEADING

"Dead-heading" is the gardener's term for removing spent flowers before they have had a chance to form seed. For most annuals, the production of flowers is really incidental. It is the production of seed on which they are most bent, since their mode of increase is to make quick use of their short day, peppering the earth with their progeny for the following season. By frustrating this drive, the gardener forces them to try and try again, producing more flowers and still more until either sheer exhaustion or the coming of autumn frosts puts an end to their efforts. Many plants, such as *Impatiens walleriana* or *Lavatera trimestris,* produce such abundance of bloom that it is hardly worth picking off the spent ones. More will come in any case. But with other annual plants, it is always best to dead-head if one has the leisure. It is pleasant work, and the rewards may be considerable.

SHEARING BACK

Shearing back is really only a radical variant of dead-heading, in which not only spent flowers are removed, but also whole tops of plants, in the hope that new flower-bearing growth will appear from stems and leaf nodes. This technique works best with mat-forming annuals such as sweet alyssum, with annuals (often actually tender perennials) that grow from a woody crown, such as snapdragons or species of *Diascia,* or with many plants grown in containers, such as argyranthemums and felicias. But with any plant grown as an annual, such drastic treatment is worth a try if the plant begins to look shabby and unproductive by midsummer.

Shearing back is most effective when only the top third or so of the plant is removed, just above the point where its scaffold of woody growth modifies into flower-bearing stems. But it is worth remembering that this sacrifice asks a lot of the plant, and so care should be taken to be sure that it is well watered and that a splash of water-soluble fertilizer is administered to encourage its future efforts.

MAIL ORDER SOURCES

Avant Gardens
710 High Hill Road
North Dartmouth, MA 02747
www.avantgardensne.com

W. Atlee Burpee & Co.
300 Park Avenue
Warminster, PA 18974
www.burpee.com

Chiltern Seeds
Bortree Stile, Ulverton
Cumbria LA12 7PB
England
www.chilternseeds.co.uk

Glasshouse Works
Church Street
PO Box 97
Stewart, OH 45778-0097
www.glasshouseworks.com

Johnny's Selected Seeds
955 Benton Avenue
Winslow, ME 04901-2601
www.johnnyseeds.com

Logee's Greenhouses
141 North Street
Danielson, CT 06239-1939
www.logees.com

Mr. Fothergill's Seeds
Gazeley Road
Kentford, Newmarket
Suffolk CB8 7QB
England
www.mr-fothergills.co.uk

Geo. W. Park Seed Co., Inc.
1 Parkton Avenue
Greenwood, SC 29647
www.parkseed.com

Pinetree Garden Seeds
Box 300
New Gloucester, ME 04260
www.superseeds.com

Plant Delights Nursery, Inc.
9241 Sauls Road
Raleigh, NC 27603
www.plantdelights.com

Seeds of Change
PO Box 15700
Santa Fe, NM 87592
www.seedsofchange.com

Seeds of Distinction
PO Box 86
Station A Etobicoke
(Etobicoke), Toronto, Ontario
Canada M9C 4V2
www.seedsofdistinction.com

Select Seeds
180 Stickney Hill Road
Union, CT 06076-4617
www.selectseeds.com

Singing Springs Nursery
8802 Wilkerson Road
Cedar Grove, NC 27231
www.singingspringsnursery.com

Territorial Seed Company
PO Box 158
Cottage Grove, OR 97424-0061
www.territorialseed.com

Thompson & Morgan
PO Box 1308
Jackson, NJ 08527-0308
www.thompson-morgan.com

K. van Bourgondien & Sons, Inc.
245 Route 109, PO Box 1000
Babylon, NY 11702-9004
www.kvbwholesale.com

Vermont Bean Seed Company
334 W. Stroud Street
Randolph, WI 53956
www.vermontbean.com

White Flower Farm
PO Box 50, Route 63
Litchfield, CT 06759
www.whiteflowerfarm.com

INDEX OF COMMON NAMES

African basil: *Ocimum kilimandsharicum*

African daisy: *Arctotis, Dimorphotheca (Osteospermum), Gazania, Gerbera jamesonii, Mezembrianthemum, Venedium, Echinacea purpurea*

African mallow: *Anisodontea hypomandarum*

African valerian: *Fedia cornucopia*

alewort: *Borago officinalis*

alkanet: *Anchusa capensis*

allgood: *Chenopodium bonus-henricus*

all-spice: *Pimenta officinalis*

althaea: *Hibiscus syriacus*

ambrosia plant: *Artemisia annua*

amethyst flower: *Browallia speciosa*

angels' trumpets: *Brugmansia, Datura*

anise hyssop: *Agastache foeniculum*

annual baby's breath: *Gypsophila paniculata*

annual campion: *Silene*

annual candytuft: *Iberis sempervirens*

annual carnations: *Dianthus*

annual hawkbit: *Crepis rubra, Tolpis barbata*

annual hop: *Humulus japonicus*

annual knotweed: *Persicaria* species, *Polygonum* species

annual lupine: *Lupinus hartwegii, Lupinus polyphyllus, Lupinus texensis, Lupinus varius*

annual mallow: *Malope trifida*

annual periwinkle: *Catharanthus roseus, Vinca rosea*

annual phlox: *Phlox drummondii*

annual pinks: *Dianthus*

apple of Peru: *Nicandra physalodes*

Arabian violet: *Exacum affine*

artichoke: *Cynara cardunculus*

autumn sage: *Salvia greggii*

baby blue eyes: *Nemophila menziesii*

baby-blue-eyes: *Browallia speciosa*

baby's tears: *Hypoestes phyllostachya, Soleirolia soleirolii*

bachelor's buttons: *Centaurea cyanus*

balcony geraniums: *Pelargonium peltatum*

balloon vine: *Cardiospermum halicacabum*

balm of Molucca: *Molucella laevis*

balsam apple: *Momordica* species

balsam impatiens: *Impatiens balsamina*

balsam pear: *Momordica* species

Barberton daisy: *Gerbera jamesonii*

basil: *Ocimum* species

bastard saffron: *Carthamus tinctorius*

beard tongue: *Penstemon* x *gloxinoides*

bearded hawkweed: *Tolpis barbata*
beef plant: *Iresine herbstii*
beefsteak plant: *Acalypha wilkesiana, Iresine herbstii, Perilla frutescens*
beet: *Beta vulgaris*
beggar's tick: *Bidens ferulifolia*
bellflower sutera: *Sutera campanulata*
bells of Ireland: *Molucella laevis*
Belvedere cypress: *Kochia scoparia*
Beverly bells: *Rehmannia elata*
billy buttons: *Craspedia globosa*
bindweed: *Convolvulus arvensis*
birds' eyes: *Gilia tricolor*
bishop's flower: *Ammi majus*
bitter cucumber: *Momordica* species
bitter gourd: *Momordica* species
black-eyed Susan: *Rudbeckia hirta*
black-eyed Susan vine: *Thunbergia alata*
blackfoot daisy: *Melampodium leucanthemum, Melampodium paludosum*
blanket flower: *Gaillardia* species
blazing star: *Mentzelia lindleyi, Bartonia aurea*
blister cress: *Erysismum*
blood drop: *Stylomecon heterophylla*
blood flower: *Asclepias curassavica*
blood leaf: *Iresine lendenii*
blood poppy: *Adonis aestivalis*
blue bedder: *Salvia farinacea*
blue bonnets: *Centaurea cyanus*
blue calico flower: *Downingia*
blue daisy: *Felicia amelloides*
blue daze: *Evolvulus glomeratus*
blue fleece flower: *Ageratum houstonianum*
blue glory: *Thunbergia battiscombei*
blue lace flower: *Didiscus coeruleus, Trachymene coerulea*
blue lips: *Collinsia grandiflora*
blue marguerite: *Felicia amelloides e*
blue milkweed: *Oxypetalum caeruleum, Tweedia caerulea*
blue potato bush: *Lycrianthes rantonneti, Solanum rantonneti*
blue star: *Isotoma, Laurentia, Pratia, Solenopsis*
blue thimble flowers: *Gilia capitata*
blue throatwort: *Trachelium caeruleum*
blue trumpet vine: *Thunbergia grandiflora*
bluebottle: *Centaurea cyanus*
blue-eyed Mary: *Collinsia verna*
bog sage: *Salvia uliginosa*
bonavist: *Dolichos lablab, Dipogon lablab, Lablab purpureus*
bonytip: *Erigeron karvinskianus*
boot jacks: *Bidens ferulifolia*

borage: *Borago officinalis*
bridal robe: *Tripleurospermum*
broad bean: *Vicia fava*
bugloss: *Anchusa capensis*
bull thistle: *Circium vulgare*
burning bush: *Kochia scoparia*
burr marigold: *Bidens ferulifolia*
bush mallow: *Malope trifida*
bush morning glory: *Convolvulus tricolor*
bush periwinkle: *Catharanthus roseus, Vinca rosea*
bush violet: *Browallia speciosa*
busy Lizzy: *Impatiens walleriana*
butterfly weed: *Asclepias tuberosa*

California bluebells: *Phacelia* species
California cream cup: *Platystemon californicus*
California golden bells: *Emmenanthe penduliflora*
California poppy: *Eschscholzia californica*
California wind poppy: *Stylomecon heterophylla*
canary bird vine: *Tropaeoleum peregrinum*
candle plant: *Plectranthus oertendahlii*
cape figwort: *Phygelius*
cape forget-me-not: *Anchusa capensis*
cape fuchsia: *Phygelius*
cape ivy: *Senecio macroglossus*
cape mallow: *Anisodontea hypomandarum*
cape stock: *Heliophila longifolia*
cardoon: *Cynara cardunculus*
carnations: *Dianthus caryophyllus*
castor bean: *Ricinus communis*
castor oil plant: *Ricinus communis*
catchfly: *Silene*
Catherine wheels: *Nigella damascena*
chain of love: *Antigonon leptopus*
chenille plant: *Acalypha hispida, Amaranthus caudatus*
cherry pie: *Heliotropium arborescens*
chickabiddy: *Asarina, Maurandya*
Chilean bellflower: *Nolana Paradoxa*
Chilean glory flower: *Eccremocarpus scaber*
Chilean nettle: *Loasa triphylla* var. *volcanica*
China aster: *Callistephus chinensis*
china-blue forget-me-nots: *Myosotis sylvestris*
Chinese forget-me-not: *Cynoglossom amabile*
Chinese foxglove: *Rehmannia elata*
Chinese holy lotus: *Nelumbian nelumbo*
Chinese houses: *Collinsia*
Chinese lantern bush: *Abutilon x hybridum*
Chinese lanterns: *Physalis alkekengi, Physalis franchetii*

chocolate cosmos: *Cosmos atrosanguineus*
Christmas poinsettia: *Euphorbia pulcherrima*
clary sage: *Salvia sclarea*
climbing gloxinia: *Asarina, Maurandya*
clock vine: *Thunbergia alata*
clove pink: *Dianthus plumarius, Dianthus* x
    alwoodii
club moss: *Lycopodium selago, Selaginella*
    kraussiana
cockle: *Agrostemma lithago, Vaccaria hispanica*
cockscomb: *Celosia cristata*
colt's foot: *Dichondra*
columbine: *Aquilegea* hybrids
common basil: *Ocimum basilicum*
common purslane: *Portulaca oleracea*
coneflower: *Dracopsis amplexicaulis*
confederate vine: *Antigonon leptopus*
cool tankard: *Borago officinalis*
copper leaf: *Acalypha wilkesiana*
coral vine: *Antigonon leptopus*
corallita: *Antigonon leptopus*
corn cockle: *Agrostemma githago*
corn poppy: *Papaver rhoeas*
cornflower: *Centaurea cyanus*
cotton thistle: *Onopordum acanthium*
cow cockle: *Vaccaria hispanica*
cow herb: *Vaccaria hispanica*
cream cups: *Platystemon californicus*
creeping gloxinia: *Asarina, Maurandya*
creeping zinnia: *Sanvitalia procumbens*
crown daisy: *Chrysanthemum coronarium*
Cuban oregano: *Plectranthus amboinicus*
culinary sage: *Salvia horminum, Salvia*
    officinalis
cup flower: *Nierembergia* species
cup-and-saucer vine: *Cobaea scandens*
cure all: *Fumaria officinalis*
cushion baby's breath: *Gypsophila muralis*
cypress vine: *Ipomoea quamoclit*

Dahlberg daisy: *Dyssodia tenuiloba*
dairy pink: *Vaccaria hispanica*
dame's rocket: *Hesperis matrionalis*
desert bluebells: *Phacelia* species
desert marigold: *Baileya multiradiata*
devil-in-the-bush: *Nigella damascena*
devil's apple: *Datura*
devil's claw: *Proboscidea louisianica*
devil's fig: *Argemone*
diamond flower: *Ionopsidium acaule*
dill: *Anethum graveolens*
distaff thistle: *Carthamus tinctorius*

down thistle: *Onopordum acanthium*
drug fumitory: *Fumaria officinalis*
Drummond phlox: *Phlox drummondii*
drumstick scabious: *Scabiosa stellata*
drumsticks: *Craspedia globosa*
dusty miller: *Artemisia stelleriana, Centaurea,*
    Chrysanthemum ptarmiciflorum, Cineraria,
    Pyrethrum ptarmiciflorum, Tanacetum ptarmi-
    ciflorum, Senecio cineraria, Senecio viravira
dwarf licorice plant: *Plectostachys serpyllifolia*
dwarf morning glory: *Convolvulus tricolor*

earth smoke: *Fumaria officinalis*
East Indian basil: *Ocimum gratissimum*
Egyptian bean: *Dolichos lablab, Dipogon lablab,*
    Lablab purpureus
Egyptian star: *Pentas lanceolata*
eleven o'clock: *Portulaca grandiflora*
elfin shrub: *Cuphea hysopifolia*
English daisy: *Bellis perennis*
English lawn daisy: *Bellis perennis*
English marigold: *Calendula*
epazote: *Chenopodium ambrosioides*
everlasting: *Helichrysum, Xeranthemum annuum*

fairy fan flower: *Scaevola aemula*
false hop: *Justicia brandegeeana*
false Queen Anne's lace: *Ammi majus*
false saffron: *Carthamus tinctorius*
fan flower: *Scaevola aemula*
farewell to spring: *Clarkia amoena*
fennel: *Foeniculum vulgare*
feverfew: *Tanacetum parthenium*
fiddleneck phacelia: *Phacelia tanacetifolia*
firebush: *Kochia scoparia*
firecracker plant: *Cuphea ignea*
five spot: *Nemophila maculata*
flame flower: *Talinum crassifolium, Talinum*
    paniculatum
flame poppy: *Stylomecon heterophylla*
flamingo plant: *Hypoestes phyllostachya*
Flanders field poppy: *Papaver rhoeas*
flax: *Linum grandiflorum, Linum narbonense,*
    Linum perenne, Linum usitatissimum
flax-leaved pimpernel: *Anagalis monellii*
Flora's paintbrush: *Emilia coccinea*
Florence fennel: *Foeniculum vulgare* 'Azoricum'
florist's mum: *Dendranthemum grandiflora*
floss flower: *Ageratum houstonianum*
flower of an hour: *Hibiscus trionum*
flowering cabbage: *Brassica oleracea*

flowering maple: *Abutilon* x *hybridum*
flowering purslane: *Portulaca grandiflora*
flowering tobacco: *Nicotiana affinis, Nicotiana alata*
forbidden palace flower: *Vaccaria hispanica*
forget-me-not: *Myosotis sylvatica*
four o'clock: *Mirabilis jalapa*
foxgloves: *Digitalis purpurea*
freckleface: *Hypoestes phyllostachya*
fried egg flower: *Limnanthes douglasii*
fumitory: *Fumaria officinalis*

garden hyssop: *Hyssopus officinalis*
garden mum: *Dendranthemum grandiflora*
garden pea: *Pisum sativum*
garden sorrel: *Rumex acetosa*
garland flower: *Chrysanthemum coronarium, Clarkia*
gentian sage: *Salvia patens*
gentianette: *Phacelia* species
German ivy: *Senecio mikanioides*
German violet: *Exacum affine*
giant fennel: *Ferula communis*
globe amaranth: *Gomphrena* species
globe candytuft: *Iberis umbellata*
globe gilia: *Gilia capitata*
gloriosa daisy: *Rudbeckia hirta*
glory bush: *Tibouchina*
godetia: *Clarkia amoena*
gold cups: *Hunnemannia fumariifolia*
gold flash: *Lotus* species
golden fleece: *Dyssodia tenuiloba*
golden morning glory: *Merremia aurea*
golden wave: *Coreopsis drummondii, Coreopsis basalis*
goldfield: *Lasthenia chrysostoma, Lasthenia glabrata*
good King Henry: *Chenopodium bonus-henricus*
goosefoot: *Chenopodium*
gopher plant: *Euphorbia lathyris*
granadilla: *Papaver* species
granny's bonnet: *Aquilegea* hybrids
greater periwinkle: *Vinca major*
Greek basil: *Ocimum* var. *minimum*
green-flowered sweet pea: *Lathyrus chloranthus*
gully lupine: *Lupinus densiflorus*

hairy morning glory: *Ipomoea hirta*
hardheads: *Centaurea cyanus*
hardy gloxinia: *Incarvillea delavayi*

hardy poinsettia: *Euphorbia cyathophora*
hare's ears: *Bupleurum rotundifolium*
Hawaiian snowbush: *Breynia nivosa*
Hawaiian wood rose: *Merremia tuberosa*
hawk's beard: *Crepis rubra*
hawkweed: *Crepis rubra*
heartsease: *Cardiospermum halicacabum, Viola*
heartseed: *Cardiospermum halicacabum*
hedge dolls: *Fumaria officinalis*
Himalayan balsam: *Impatiens glandulifera*
Himalayan blue poppies: *Meconopsis betonicifolia, Meconopsis grandis, Meconopsis* x *sheldonii*
Himalayan jewelweed: *Impatiens glandulifera*
Himalayan persimmon: *Diosporus lotus*
hollyhock: *Alcea rosea*
holy basil: *Ocimum sanctum*
holy thistle: *Silybum marianum*
honey flower: *Melianthus major*
honey shrub: *Melianthus major*
honeysuckle fuchsia: *Fuchsia triphylla*
honeywort: *Cerinthe major*
horn of plenty: *Fedia cornucopia*
horned violet: *Viola cornuta*
hound's tongue: *Cynoglossum amabile*
humble plant: *Mimosa pudica*
hummingbird vine: *Asarina*
hyacinth bean: *Dolichos lablab, Dipogon lablab, Lablab purpureus*
hyacinth-flowered candytuft: *Iberis amara*

ice plant: *Carpanthea pomeridiana*
Iceland poppy: *Papaver nudicaule*
immortelle: *Ammobium alatum, Helipterum roseum, Helychrysum bracteatum, Xeranthemum annuum*
India sorrel: *Hibiscus sabdariffa*
Indian blanket: *Gaillardia* species
Indian spinach: *Basella alba*
Indian wort: *Asclepias curassavica*
innocence: *Collinsia verna*
Italian jasmine: *Solanum seaforthianum*
ivy: *Hedera helix*

Jamaica sorrel: *Hibiscus sabdariffa*
Japanese hop: *Humulus japonicus*
Japanese knotweed: *Persicaria cispidatum, Reynoutria japonica*
Japanese thistle: *Cirsium japonicum*
jasmine tobacco: *Nicotiana affinis, Nicotiana alata*
Jerusalem cherry: *Solanum pseudocapsicum*

jewels of Opar: *Talinum crassifolium, Talinum paniculatum*
Jimson weed: *Datura stramonium*
Johnny-jump-up: *Viola tricolor*
Joseph's coat: *Acalypha wilkesiana, Alternanthera, Amaranthus tricolor*
jujube: *Zizyphus lotus*

Kentucky Wonder: *Phaseolus vulgaris*
kingfisher daisy: *Felicia bergeriana*
king's crown: *Dicliptera suberecta*
kiss-me-over-the-garden-gate: *Amaranthus caudatus*
knapweed: *Centaurea cyanus*

ladies' eardrops: *Fuchsia*
lady in the bath: *Molucella laevis*
lady's slippers: *Calceolaria*
lamb's ears: *Stachys byzantina*
lambs quarters: *Chenopodium album*
larkspur: *Consolida ajacis*
lawn daisy: *Bellis perennis*
lawn leaf: *Dichondra*
leadwort: *Plumbago auriculata*
leaf-flower: *Breynia nivosa*
lemon geranium: *Pelargonium crispum*
licorice plant: *Helichrysum petiolare*
licorice: *Glycyrrhiza glabra*
life-in-death: *Gomphrena* species
lion's ears: *Leonotis leonurus*
lion's tail: *Leonotis leonurus*
lisianthus: *Eustoma grandiflorum*
little bells: *Nolana humifusa*
little-leaved autumn sage: *Salvia microphylla*
lizard fruit: *Momordica* species
lobster claw vine: *Lotus* species
lotus vine: *Lotus* species
love lies bleeding: *Amaranthus caudatus*
love-in-a-mist: *Nigella damascena*
love-in-a-puff: *Cardiospermum halicacabum*

mad apple: *Datura*
Madagascar periwinkle: *Catharanthus roseus, Vinca rosea*
Madeira marigold: *Calendula maderensis, Calendula incana* subsp. *Maderensis*
madwort: *Lobularia maritima*
mahon: *Malcomia maritima*

Malabar spinach: *Basella alba*
Marguerite daisy: *Argyranthemum frutescens, Chrysanthemum frutescens*
marigold: *Tagetes* x *hybrida*
marvel-of-Peru: *Mirabilis jalapa*
mask flower: *Alonsoa warsewiczii*
match-me-if-you-can: *Acalypha wilkesiana*
May pop: *Passiflora incarnata*
meadow foam: *Limnanthes douglasii*
mealy-cup sage: *Salvia farinacea*
measles plant: *Hypoestes phyllostachya*
medallion flower: *Melampodium* species, *Leucanthemum* species
Mexican bamboo: *Persicaria cispidatum, Reynoutria japonica*
Mexican basil: *Plectranthus amboinicus*
Mexican bush sage: *Salvia leucantha*
Mexican cigar plant: *Cuphea ignea*
Mexican daisy: *Erigeron karvinskianus*
Mexican fleabane: *Erigeron karvinskianus*
Mexican petunia: *Ruellia*
Mexican prickly poppy: *Argemone grandiflora*
Mexican sunflower: *Tithonia rotundifolia*
Mexican tarragon: *Tagetes lucida*
Mexican tulip poppy: *Hunnemannia fumariifolia*
mignonette: *Reseda odorata*
milfoil: *Myriophyllum aquaticum*
milk thistle: *Silybum marianum*
million bells: *Calibrichoa*
mock cucumber: *Echinocystic lobata*
Moldavian balm: *Dracocephalum moldavicum*
Moldavian dragonhead: *Dracocephalum moldavicum*
mole plant: *Euphorbia lathyris*
monkey flower: *Mimulus*
moon vine: *Ipomoea alba*
morning glory: *Ipomoea purpurea*
Moses-in-a-boat: *Setcresea pallida*
mosquito flower: *Lopezia racemosa,*
moss verbena: *Verbena tenuisecta*
mother-of-thyme: *Thymus serphyllum*
mountain spinach: *Atriplex hortensis*
mourning bride: *Scabiosa atropurpurea*
mourning widow: *Scabiosa atropurpurea*

nasturtium: *Tropaeoleum*
natal ivy: *Senecio macroglossus*
night phlox: *Zaluzianskya capensis*
night-scented stock: *Matthiola longipetala* subsp. *bicornis*
none-so-sweet: *Silene armeria*

nun's scourge: *Amaranthus caudatus*
nutmeg geranium: *Pelargonium x fragrans*

oil plant: *Madia* species
okra: *Abelmoschus esculentus*
old maid: *Catharanthus roseus, Vinca rosea*
oldfield toadflax: *Linaria canadensis*
opal cups: *Anoda cristata*
opium poppy: *Papaver somniferum*
orach: *Atriplex hortensis*
orange cosmos: *Cosmos sulphureus*
ornamental cabbage: *Brassica oleracea*
ornamental kale: *Brassica oleracea*
ortiga: *Loasa triphylla* var. *volcanica*
Our Lady's thistle: *Silybum marianum*

pagoda flower: *Collinsia*
painted daisy: *Chrysanthemum carinatum*
painted tongue: *Salpiglosis sinuata*
palm of Christ: *Ricinus communis*
Palm Springs daisy: *Cladanthus arabicus*
pansy: *Viola*
paper daisy: *Helichrysum*
paper moon: *Scabiosa stellata*
paradise vine: *Solanum wendlandii*
Paris daisy: *Argyranthemum frutescens, Chrysan-themum frutescens*
parlor ivy: *Senecio mikanioides*
parlor maple: *Abutilon x hybridum*
parrot leaf: *Alternanthera*
parrot's beak: *Lotus* species
parrot's feather: *Gunnera manicata*
peacock mosses: *Selaginella*
pearly everlasting: *Ammobium alatum*
peppermint geranium: *Pelargonium tomentosum*
periwinkle: *Pachysandra procumbens, Vinca major*
Persian shield: *Strobilanthes dyeriana*
Persian violet: *Exacum affine*
pied daisy: *Gazania*
pimpernel: *Anagalis*
pincushion flower: *Scabiosa atropurpurea*
pineapple sage: *Salvia elegans*
pink pinheads: *Gomphrena dispersa*
pink pokers: *Limonium suworowi*
pink princess flower: *Tibouchina nandina*
pitchforks: *Bidens ferulifolia*
plume thistle: *Cirsium japonicum*
poached egg flower: *Limnanthes douglasii*

pocket book plant: *Calceolaria*
poinsettia: *Euphorbia pulcherrima*
pole bean: *Phaseolus vulgaris*
polka-dot plant: *Hypoestes phyllostachya*
poor man's weatherglass: *Anagalis arvensis*
poppy mallow: *Callirhoe*
pot marigold: *Calendula officinalis*
potato vine: *Solanum wendlandii*
pouch flower: *Calceolaria*
prairie gentian: *Eustoma grandiflorum*
pride of Madeira: *Echium fastuosum*
prince's feather: *Amaranthus cruentus, Amaran-thus hypochondriacus, Amaranthus paniculata; Celosia plumose, Persicaria* species, *Poly-gonum* species
princess flower: *Tibouchina*
princess moss: *Lycopodium selago*
purple bell vine: *Rhodochiton atrosanguineus*
purple groundsel: *Senecio elegans*
purple passion: *Gynura aurantiaca, Gynura sarmentosa*
purple velvet plant: *Gynura aurantiaca*

Queen Anne's lace: *Daucus carota*
Queen Anne's thimbles: *Gilia capitata*
queen's jewels: *Antigonon leptopus*
queen's wreath: *Antigonon leptopus*

ragged robin: *Centaurea cyanus*
ragged sailors: *Centaurea cyanus*
ram's horn: *Proboscidea louisianica*
red horned poppy: *Glaucium corniculatum*
red ruellia: *Ruellia elegans*
resurrection plant: *Selaginella lepidophylla*
Robert Bruce: *Onopordum acanthium*
rock bells: *Wahlenbergia*
rock jasmine: *Androsace*
rock purslane: *Calandrinia*
rock rose: *Portulaca grandiflora*
rocket candytuft: *Iberis amara*
rosa de Montana: *Antigonon leptopus*
rose everlasting: *Rhodanthe chlorocephala* subsp. *rosea*
rose geranium: *Pelargonium graveolens*
rose mallow: *Lavatera trimestis*
rose moss: *Portulaca grandiflora*
rose of Sharon: *Hibiscus syriacus*
rose thistle: *Cirsium japonicum*
roselle: *Hibiscus sabdariffa*
Russian sage: *Perovskia atriplicifolia*

safflower: *Carthamus tinctorius*
sage: *Salvia officinalis*
salt bush: *Atriplex hortensis*
sand verbena: *Abronia*
satin flower: *Clarkia*
scarlet bedder: *Salvia splendens*
scarlet pimpernel: *Anagalis arvensis*
scarlet runner bean: *Phaseolus coccineus*
Scots thistle: *Onopordum acanthium*
sea dahlia: *Coreopsis maritima*
sea lavender: *Limonium sinuatum*
sea pink: *Limonium sinuatum*
sea poppy: *Glaucium* species
sea purslane: *Atriplex hortensis*
sensitive plant: *Mimosa pudica*
shasta daisies: *Chrysanthemum, Leucanthemum*
     x *superbum*
shell flower: *Molucella laevis*
shepherd's clock: *Anagalis arvensis*
shiso: *Perilla frutescens*
shoo-fly plant: *Nicandra physalodes*
shrimp plant: *Justicia brandegeeana*
shrub verbena: *Lantana*
Siberian wallflower: *Erysimum perofskianum*
silver feather: *Tanacetum ptarmiciflorum*
silver lace: *Artemisia, Centaurea, Chrysanthe-mum ptarmiciflorum, Cineraria, Senicio, Tanacetum ptarmiciflorum*
silver sage: *Salvia argentea*
sky flower: *Thunbergia grandiflora*
sky lupine: *Lupinus nanus*
skyrocket: *Ipomopsis aggregata*
sleepy daisy: *Xanthisma texanum*
slipperwort: *Calceolaria*
snapdragon: *Antirrhinum majus*
snow in summer: *Euphorbia marginata*
snow on the mountain: *Euphorbia marginata*
snowflake: *Bacopa cordata, Sutera cordata*
southern star: *Oxypetalum caeruleum, Tweedia caerulea*
sow thistle: *Sonchus*
Spanish needles: *Bidens ferulifolia*
Spanish oyster plant: *Scolymus hispanicus*
spider flower: *Cleome hassleriana, Cleome spinosa, Tibouchina organensis, Tibouchina urvilleana,*
spiderwort: *Tradescantia*
spike plant: *Cordaline australis*
spurge: *Euphorbia*
standing cypress: *Ipomopsis rubra*
star balsam: *Zaluzianskya capensis*
star cluster: *Pentas lanceolata*

star of Texas: *Xanthisma texanum*
star scabious: *Scabiosa stellata*
statice: *Limonium sinuatum*
sticktights: *Bidens ferulifolia*
sticky monkey flower: *Mimulus aurantiacus*
stinkweed: *Datura*
stock: *Matthiola incana*
strawflower: *Helichrysum, Xeranthemum annuum*
summer cypress: *Kochia scoparia*
summer gloxinia: *Incarvillea sinensis* subsp. *Variabilis, Rehmannia elata*
sun moss: *Portulaca grandiflora*
sun plant: *Portulaca grandiflora*
sun rose: *Portulaca grandiflora*
sunflower: *Helianthus annuus*
swallow wort: *Asclepias curassavica*
Swan River daisy: *Brachycome*
Swedish ivy: *Plectranthus australis, Plectranthus madagascariensis, Plectranthus oertendahlii*
sweet alyssum: *Lobularia maritima*
sweet Annie: *Artemisia annua*
sweet basil: *Ocimum* species
sweet mignonette: *Reseda odorata*
sweet pea: *Lathyrus odoratus*
sweet potato: *Ipomoea batatas*
sweet scabious: *Scabiosa atropurpurea*
sweet William: *Dianthus barbatus, Silene armeria*
sweet woodruff (annual): *Asperula orientalis, Asperula asurea var. Setosa*
sweet woodruff (perennial): *Asperula odorota*
sweet wormwood: *Artemisia annua*
sweetheart vine: *Antigonon leptopus*
Swiss chard: *Beta vulgaris*

tansy: *Tanacetum vulgare*
tar weed: *Madia* species
tarragon: *Artemisia dracunculus*
tassel flower: *Emilia coccinea*
tea bush: *Ocimum gratissimum*
Texas bluebell: *Eustoma grandiflorum*
Texas bluebonnet: *Lupinus subcarnosus*
Texas petunia: *Ruellia*
Texas pride: *Phlox drummondii*
Texas sage: *Salvia coccinea*
thorn apple: *Datura*
thorow-wax: *Bupleurum rotundifolium*
tickseed: *Coreopsis grandiflora*
tiddly winks: *Exacum affin*
tidy tips: *Layia elegans, Layia platyglossa*

toadflax: *Linaria*
toatoa: *Haloragis erecta*
tobacco: *Nicotiana tabacum*
tomatillo: *Physalis ixocarpa*
torch flower: *Tithonia rotundifolia*
tower of jewels: *Echium pinnata*
trailing spikemoss: *Selaginella kraussiana*
Transvaal daisy: *Gerbera jamesonii*
treasure flower: *Gazania*
tree basil: *Ocimum gratissimum*
tree lupine: *Lupinus arboreus*
tree mallow: *Lavatera arborea*
tree tobacco: *Nicotiana glauca*
true chamomile: *Chamaemelum nobile*
true forget-me-not: *Myosotis sylvestris*
twinspur: *Diascia*

unicorn plant: *Martynia proboscidea, Proboscidea louisianica*

veldt daisy: *Gerbera jamesonii*
Venus's navelwort: *Omphalodes linifolia, Omphelodes verna*
Venus's looking glass: *Legousia speculum-veneris, Specularia speculum*
vervain: *Verbena officinalis*
Veterans Day poppy: *Papaver rhoeas*
violet cress: *Ionopsidium acaule*
viper's bugloss: *Echium lycopsis*
Virginia stock: *Malcomia maritima*

wallflower: *Erysismum*
wandering Jew: *Tradescantia fluminensis, Tradescantia zebrina*
watercress: *Rorippa nasturtium*
wax plant: *Portulaca grandiflora*
weasel snout: *Antirrhinum orontium*
weeping lantana: *Lantana montividensis*
whispering bells: *Emmenanthe penduliflora*
white bladder vine: *Araujia sericofera*
white daisies: *Layia glandulosa*
wild cucumber: *Echinocystic lobata*
wild lantana: *Abronia*
wild spinach: *Chenopodium bonus-henricus*
wind poppy: *Stylomecon heterophylla*
wine cups: *Callirhoe*
winged everlasting: *Ammobium alatum*
wishbone flower: *Torenia fournieri*
woodland nicotiana: *Nicotiana sylvestris*
wool flower: *Celosia*

yellow bachelor's buttons: *Craspedia globosa*
yellow hawkweed: *Tolpis barbata*
yellow horned poppy: *Glaucium flavum*

zarandaja: *Dolichos lablab, Dipogon lablab, Lablab purpureus*

INDEX

Page numbers given in bold refer to pages on which there are photographs. In plant entries, topics of general information relating to the main entries appear first; subentries for species and cultivars always follow the general subentries.

Abelmoschus, 3–5, 6, 288 89
    esculentus, 3–5
    manihot, **3,** 3–4
    moschatus, **4**
Abies balsamea, 310–11
Abronia, 5–6
    espaliers, 5–6
    fragrans, 5
    latifolia, 5
    umbellata 'Grandiflora', 5
Abutilon
    x *hybridum,* 6–7
        'Savitzii', **7**
    megapotamicum, **6**
Acalypha, 7–9
    hispida, **8**
    wilkesiana, 8–9, **9,** 26
Acanthus, 243, 341
acaule, 232
Acnistus australis, 9–11, **10**
    flowering requirements, 10
Adanson, Michael, 459
Adonis, 11
    aestivalis, 11

    annua, 11
    autumnalis, 11
Aegopodium podagraria, 27
aemula, 418
aeruginea, 267
African basil, 336–37
African daisy, 43, 148, 150, 195, 475
African mallow, 34–35
African valerian, 179
Agastache, 12–13
    anisata, 13
    aurantiaca 'Apricot Sunrise', **13**
    cana 'Heather Queen', 13
    coccinea x *mexicana,* 13
    foeniculum, 12
    x 'Fragrant Delight', 13
    mexicana, 13
    rupestris, **12**
Ageratum houstonianum, 13–15
    'Cut Wonder', 14
Agrostemma
    coeli-rosa, 428
    githago, 15–16, **16,** 97
        'Milas', 16

Agrostemma (*cont'd*):
    lithago, 477
alata, 323, 451
albotomentosa, 437
Alcea rosea, **17,** 17–18, 146
alewort, 66
alkaloids, 135–36, 219, 274, 322
alkanet, 31, 32
allgood, 101
Allioni, 244
all-spice, 331
Alonsoa, 18–21
    acutifolia, 19
    linearis, **19**
    meridionalis, 19
    warsewiczii, 19, **20**
Alstroemeria psittacina, 129–31
Alternanthera, 21–23
    amoena, 22
    bettzickiana, 22
    dentata 'Rubiginosa', **22,** 22–23
    ficoidea, 22–23
    purpurea 'Tricolor', 22
    versicolor, 22
althaea, 216
Alyssum, 274
amaranth, 23–27, 203
Amaranthaceae, 241
Amaranthus, 23–27
    albus, 23
    caudatus, 24–25
        'Viridis', 25, **26**
    cruentus, 25
    hybridus, 23, **25**
        var. *erythrostachys*, 25
    hypochondriacus, 25
    paniculata, 25
    tricolor, **24,** 25–26
ambrosia plant, 47
Amellus, 181
American black walnut, and *Helianthus*
    phytotoxicity, 210
amethyst flower, 73
Ammi
    majus, **27,** 27–28
    visnaga, 27–28,
        'Green Mist', **28**
Ammobium alatum, 28–29, **29,** 54, 210, 491
Anagalis, 29–31
    arvensis, 30
    monellii, 30–31
        subsp. *linifolia*, **30**

Anchusa
    azurea, 31
    capensis, 31–32
        'Alba', 32
        'Blue Bird', 31–32
        'Dawn', 32
        'Pink Bird', 31–32
    italica, 31
Androsace, 32–33
    lactiflora, 32–33
    septintrionalis, 32, 33
anesthetic, 136
Anethum graveolens, 474
Angel Wing begonia, 61
Angelonia angustifolio, 33–34, **34**
angels' trumpets, 75, 135
angulata, 384
Anisodontea, 6, 34–36
    capensis, 35
    hypomandarum, 34–36
    julii, 35
    scabrosa, 35
annual Adonis, 11
annual baby's breath, 205, 206
annual campion, 426
annual candytuft, 223
annual carnations, 137
annual hawkbit, 126, 458
annual hop, 219
annual knotweed, 359
annual lupine, 279–83
annual mallow, 287
annual periwinkle, 93
annual phlox, 369
annual pinks, 137
annual silene, 426
annual
    definition, *xviii*
    half-hardy, *xxii*
    hardy, *xxi*
    requirements for growing, *xx*
    transplanting, *xviii*
    true, *xviii*
Anoda cristata, 36–37, **37**
Antigonon leptopus, 37–38
Antirrhinum, 38–41, 49, 390
    braun-blanquettii, 40
    glutinosum, 40
    majus, 38–40, **39**
        'Floral Carpet', 39
        'Magic Carpet', 39
    molle, 40

orontium, 40
Rocket Series, 40
aphid, 86, 290, 291, 323, 367
    in *Lupinus*, 282–83
    repellant, 320
aphrodisiac, 335
apple of Peru, 320
Aquilegea hybrids, 41–42
Arabian violet, 177, 178
Araujia sericofera, 42–43
arborescens, 214
Arcoclinum, 389
Arctic poppy, 342
Arctotis, 43–45
    acaulis, 44
    breviscarpa, 44
    x *hybridus*, 43
        'Zulu Prince', 44
    stoechadifolia, **44**
        'Grandis', 44
    x *Venedium*, 45
Argemone, 45–47
    grandiflora, **46,** 92
    hispida, 46
    mexicana, 46
        'Alba', 46
        'Sanguinea', 46
    polyanthus, 46
argentea, 403
Argyranthemum frutescens,
    103–104
Armeria maritima, 427
Armitage, Allan, 395
Artemisia, 47–48, 105
    absinthium, 47
    annua, 47–48
    arborescens, 47
    dranunculus, 47, 445
    gmelinii, 47
        'Viridis', 48
    lactiflora, 47
    x 'Powis Castle', 47, 424
    saccrorum, 48
    stelleriana, 424
artichoke, 105, 130–32
Asarina, 48–50
    barlaiana, 49
    erubescens, 50
    procumbens, 48–49, **49,** 50
Asclepias, 50–51
    curassavica, 50–51
    tuberosa, 51

Asperula, 51–52
    asurea var. *Setosa*, 51–52
    odorato, 52
    orientalis, 51–52
assa-foetida, 183
assurgentiflora, 258–59
Aster amellus, 181
aster wilt, 86
aster yellows, 86
aster, 85–86, 283
Asteraceae, 59, 93, 105, 195, 375, 413
Atriplex hortensis, **52,** 52–54, **53,** 127, 333–34
atropurpurea, 415, 439
auriculas, 139
auriculata, 379
autumn sage, 405

baby blue eyes, 318
baby-blue-eyes, 73
baby's tears, 222
bachelor's buttons, 51, 97
Bacillus thuringiensis, 185, 471
Bacopa cordata, 442–43
Bailey, Vernon, 55
Baileya multiradiata, 54–55
Baillon, Henri, 461
baking soil, 414
balcony geraniums, 351
Balfour, Sir Isaac Bayley, 230
balloon vine, 89
Ballota, 55–56
    pseudodictamnus, 55–56
balm of Molucca, 309
balsam apple, 311
balsam pear, 311
balsamina, 311–12
Barash, Cathy Wilkinson, 445
Barbarea
    verna, 56–57
    vulgaris, 56–57
        'Flore pleno', 57
        'Variegata', 57
barbata, 459
barbe-bleu, 331
Barberton daisy, 195
Bartonia aurea, 300–301
Basella alba, 57–58, **58**
    'Rubra', 58
basil, 334–38
basilicum, 335
basilisk, 335

Bassi, Ferdinando, 244
Bassia scoparia, 244
bastard saffron, 92
batatas, 234
beard tongue, 352
bearded hawkweed, 458
beef plant, 242
beefsteak plant, 242, 357
bees, 157, 158, 246, 263, 298, 382
    plants, 367
beet, 63–64
beggar's tick, 64
Begonia, 58–61
    Angel Wing, 61
    fuchsioides, 61
    x *richmondensis,* 61
    semperflorens, 59
    x *semperflorens cultorum,* 61
    sutherlandii, **59,** 60–61
    tuberous begonia, 60–61
    wax begonia, 58–61
Begoniaceae, 58–61
bell peppers, 87
bellflower sutera, 443
Bellis perennis, 61–63, **62**
    and *Helianthus* phytotoxicity, 210
bells of Ireland, 309
Belvedere cypress, 244, **245**
Bennett, Jennifer, 435
Bertheolot, Sabin, 278
Beta vulgaris, 63–64
    'Bull's Blood', 63
    'Dracaenifolia', 63
    'MacGregor's Favorite', 63
Beverly bells, 384
Bidens
    atrosanguineus, 124–25
    ferulifolia, **64,** 64–65
biennial, 146
    definition, *xix*
billy buttons, 125
bindweed, 120
binomial system of nomenclature, 465
bird's eyes, 87, 199
birds, 246
bishop's flower, 27
bitter cucumber, 311
bitter gourd, 311
black nightshade, 435
black-eyed Susan, 394–96, **395**
black-eyed Susan vine, 451
blackfoot daisy, 296, 297
blanket flower, 191, 192–93

blazing star, 300
blister cress, 168
blood drop, 440
blood flower, 50
blood leaf, 241–42
blood poppy, 11
blue bedder, 400
blue bonnets, 97
blue calico flower, 156
blue daisy, 180
blue daze, 176
blue fleece flower, 13
blue glory, 452
blue lace flower, 463
blue lips, 116
blue marguerite, 180
blue milkweed, 472
blue potato bush, 433
blue Queen Anne's lace, 463
blue star, 254–55
blue thimble flowers, 198
blue throatwort, 462
blue trumpet vine, 451
bluebeard, 331
bluebottle, 97
blue-eyed Mary, 116
bog sage, 407
bonavist, 152, 153
bonytip, 166
Book of Salvias: Sages for Every Garden, The, 400
boot jacks, 64
borage, 66–67
Boraginaceae, 66–67
Borago officinalis, 66–67
    'Alba', 67
Borchard, Peter, 336–37
border geraniums, 349
Boston's 'Green Necklace', 157
Bouvard, Dr. Charles, 68
Bouvardia, 67–68
    'Alba', 68
    'Albatross', 67
    'Dazzler', 67
    longifolia, 67
    'President Cleveland', 67
    'President Garfield', 67
    'Princess of Wales', 67
    ternifolia, 67, **68**
Bowden, Wray, 273
Brachycome, 68–70
    iberidifolia, **69,** 69–70
        'Purple Splendor', 69
    melanocarpa, 70

multifida, 70

nivalis var. *alpina* 'Pink Mist', 70

tadgellii 'Tinkerbell', 70

Bracteantha bracteata, 210

bracts, 131, 173, 243, 459, 491–92

Brandegee, Townsend Stith, 243

Brassica oleracea, 70–71, **71**

'Osaka Mix', 71

Brassicaceae, 213

breeding modification, 123

Breyne, Jacob, 72

Breyne, Johann Phillip Breyne, 72

Breynia

'Atropurpurea', 72

disticha, 72

nivosa, 72

'Rosea Picta', 72

bridal robe, 294

Brigham, Steve, 437

Britton, Nathaniel Lord, 397

broad bean, 369

broccoli, 71

Broussonet, Pierre, 266

Browall, John, 74

Browallia

americana, **73,** 74

elata, 74

speciosa, 72–75

'Amethyst', **74**

'Major', 73

viscosa, 74

Brugmans, Sebald Justin, 75

Brugmansia, 10, 75–78, 136

aurea, 78

x *candida,* **77**

'Grand Marnier', **75**

x *insignis,* 78

suaveolens, 78

versicolor, **76**

Brussels sprouts, 71

Bt, 185

bugloss, 31, 32

bull thistle, 340

Bupleurum rotundifolium, 78–79

burning bush, 244, **245**

Burpee, David, 445

burr marigold, 64

bush mallow, 287

bush morning glory, 119

bush periwinkle, 93

bush violet, 73

busy Lizzy, 225, 226

butterflies, 185, 246

cabbage worms, 471

Cacalia coccinea, 165

cactus, 91–92

caerulea, 472

caeruleus, 463

Calandrini, Jean-Louis, 80

Calandrinia, 79–80

cilliata, 79, 80

discolor, 80

grandiflora, 80

nitida, 80

speciosa, 80

umbellata, **80**

Calceolaria, 80–82

crenatiflora, 81

fruitocohybrida, 82

x *hybrida,* 81

integrifolia, 82

mexicana, **81,** 81–82

rugosa, 82

scabiosaefolia, 82

tripartita, 82

Calendula, 82–84

arvensis, 84

incana subsp. *Maderensis,* 84

maderensis, 84

officinalis, **83,** 474

Calibrichoa, 363–64

'Terra Cotta', **364**

California bluebells, 366

California cream cup, 374

California golden bells, 164

California poppy, 92, 170–72

California wind poppy, 440

Calliopsis, 122

Callirhoe, 84–85

digitata, 84–85

involucrata, 84

papaver, 85

Callistephus chinensis, 85–86, **86**

calyx, 347, 390, 401, 403, 404, 408, 409, 428, 460

Canada thistle, 105–106

canary bird vine, 470, **471**

candida, 78

candle plant, 378

candytuft, 223–25

Cannabis sativa, 110

cape forget-me-not, 31

cape ivy, 426

cape mallow, 34–35

cape marigold, 148

cape stock, 212

capensis, 379
capitata, 361
Capparidaceae, 110
Capsicum
    annuum, 87–89, **88**
    cerasiforme, 87
    conoides, 87
    fasciculatum, 87
    frutescens, 87
    grossum, 87
    longum, 87
Cardiospermum halicacabum, 89–91, **90**
cardoon, 105, 130–32, **131**
Carduus, 105–106
carnations, 137, 138
Carophyllaceae, 477
Carpanthea pomeridiana, **80,** 80–81
Carthamus tinctorius, 92–93
castor bean, 392–94, **393**
castor oil plant, 392–94, **393**
catchfly, 426
Catharanthus roseus, 93–94, **94**
Catherine wheels, 330–31
Catherine, Saint, 330–31
cauliflower, 71
Celosia, 95–97
    argentea, 95
    cristata, 95
    plumosa, 95–97
    spicata, **96**
        'Flamingo', 96
Centaurea, 105
    cyanus, 51, 97–98, 343
Centradenia, 98–99
    grandiflora, **99**
    inaequilateralis, 98–99
Central Park, 157
cerasiforme, 87
Cerinthe major, 99–101, **100**
    var. *purpurescens,* 100
chain of love, 37
Chamaemelum nobile
    chamomile, 293
charantia, 312
chard, 63–64
Cheiranthus, 169–70
    allionii, 169
    linifolius, 168
Chenopodium, 101–102
    album, 101
    amaranticolor, 101–102
    ambrosioides, 101

    bonus-henricus, 101
    quinoa, 101
cherry pie, 214, 215
chickabiddy, 48
Chilean bellflower, 333
Chilean glory flower, 160–61
Chilean nettle, 270
China aster, 85–86
china-blue forget-me-nots, 146
Chinese forget-me-not, 31, 132–33
Chinese foxglove, 384
Chinese holy lotus, 278
Chinese houses, 115, 116
Chinese lantern bush, 6
Chinese lanterns, 321
chocolate cosmos, 124
Christ, 346–47
Christmas poinsettia, 172
Chrysanthemum, 102–105, 297, 424
    carinatum, 103–104
    coronarium, 103
    frutescens, 103–104
    multicaule, 104
    paludosum, 104
    parthenium, 104–105, 448–49
    ptarmiciflorum, 105, 450
    segetum, 103
    tenuilobum, 159–60
Churchill, Sir Winston, 185
Cineraria, 105
Cirsium
    arvense, 105–106
    japonicum, 105–106, **106**
    vulgare, 340
Cladanthus arabicus, 107
Clark, Captain William, 108
Clarkia, 107–109, **108**
    amoena, 108
    elegans, 108
    pulchella, 108
    unguiculata, 108
clary sage, 410
Clausen, Ruth Rogers, 403–404
claw, 109
clawed flowers, 193, 213
clawed petals, 427, 468
clear-eye, 410
Clebsch, Betsy, 400
Cleome
    hassleriana, 109–11, **110**
    spinosa, 109
climbing gloxinia, 48

clock vine, 451
clove pink, 138
club moss, 421, 423
Cobaea scandens, 111–12, **112**
 'Alba', 112
Cobo, Fr. Bernado, 111
coccinea, 405, 437
coccineus, 369
cockle, 477
cockscombs, 95–97
Cole, Silas, 250
Coleostephus myconis, 104
Coleus x *hybridus,* 113–15, **114**
collarette, 134
Collins, Zacheus, 115
Collinsia, 115–16
 bicolor, 115–16
 grandiflora, 116
 heterophylla, 115–16
  var. *candidissima,* 116
 verna, 116
colt's foot, 142
columbine, 41
comfrey, 66–67
common basil, 335
common purslane, 382
communis, 183, 393
coneflower, 158
confederate vine, 37
Connecticut Yankees' delphinium, 117
conoides, 87
Consolida species, **117,** 117–18
 ajacis, 118
 ambigua, 118
 orientalis, 118
 regalis, 118
Convolvulus
 arvensis, 120
 tricolor, **119**
  'Royal Blue', 119
  'Royal Ensign', 119
cool tankard, 66
copper sulfate, 497
coral vine, 37
corallita, 37
Cordaline australis, 482
cordata, 443
cordon method, 253
Coreopsis, 120–22
 basalis, 122
 drummondii, 122
 grandiflora, 121

lanceolata, 121
maritima, 121–22
tinctoria, 120, **121**
corn cockle, 15, 51, 97, 477
corn poppy, 97, 343
cornflower, 97, 343
corolla, 112, 186, 315
corona, 347
Corot, Camille, 343
corymb, 481
Cosmos
 atrosanguineus, 124–25
 bipinnatus, 123–24
 sulphureus, 123, **124**
cotton thistle, 339
cow cockle, 476
cow herb, 476
Craspedia, 125–26
 alpina, 126
 glauca, 126
 globosa, 125–26
 richea, 126
 uniflora, 126
cream cups, 374
creeping gloxinia, 48
creeping zinnia, 413
Crepis, 126–27
 incana, 126
 rubra, 126–27
  var. *alba,* 126
Cresson, Charles, 407
crown daisy, 103
Cruciferae, 232, 275
Cryptotaenia japonica, 127–28
Cuban oregano, 378
cucumber, 162, 311
Cucurbitaceae, 162
culinary sage, 402, 410
cup flower, 327
cup-and-saucer vine, 111–12, **112**
Cupani, Franciscus, 249
Cuphea, 128–30
 hysopifolia, 130
 ignea, **129**
 micropetala, 129
cure all, 189, 190
Cure-All, 322
cushion baby's breath, 206
Cynara cardunculus, 130–32, **131**
Cynoglossum amabile, 31, **132,** 132–33
 'Blue Showers', 132
cypress vine, 234–35

Dahlberg daisy, 159
Dahlia, 133–35
   'Bishop of Llandaff', **134**
   coccinea, 133
   x *hortensis,* 133–35
   pinnata, 133
dairy pink, 476
daisy, 120–21, 148, 159, 167, 182, 195,
     197, 210–12, 260, 283, 296–97,
     375, 394, 423, 425, 473–74, 476,
     491
dame's rocket, 146
damping off, 86, 92, 178, 365, 398, 504
Datura, 10, 75, 135–37
   inoxia subsp. *inoxia,* 137
     subsp. *quinquecuspidata,* 137
   metel, 136–37
   meteloides, **136,** 136–37
Daucus carota, 27
de Charentonneau, Gaillard, 193
de Jussieu, Barnard, 292
de la Ruelle, Jean, 397
de l'Obel, Mathias, 274
dead-heading, 510
deadly nightshade, 72, 75, 87, 135, 320, 321,
     327, 361, 398, 418, 431, 435
Delphinium, 117
   elatum, 117
     'Connecticut Yankees', 117
de'Medici, Catherine, 322
Dendranthemum grandiflora, 102
desert bluebells, 366
devil-in-the-bush, 330
devil's apple, 135
devil's claw, 290
devil's fig, 45
diamond flower, 232
Dianthus, 137–39
   x *alwoodii,* 138
   barbatus, 138–39, 427
   caryophyllus, 138
   chinensis, **138,** 139
     'Black and White Minstrels', 139
   heddewigii, 139
   plumarius, 138
   'Telstar', 139
Diascia, 139–42,
   rigescens, **141**
Dichondra, 142–43
   argentea, 143
   carolinensis, 143
   micrantha, 143
   repens, 143

Dichranostigma, 143–44
   franchetianum, 143–44
   lactuoides, 143–44
   leptopodum, 143–44
Dicliptera suberecta, 144–45, **145**
Didiscus coeruleus, 463–64
digitalin, 148
Digitalis purpurea, 146–48, **147,** 390
   and phytotoxicity, 210
   'Excelsior', 147
   'Foxy', 146–47
dill, 474
Dimorphotheca, 148–50
   annua, 148
   aurantiaca, 148–49
   ecklonis, 148
   x *hybrida,* **149**
   pluvialis, 148
Dioscorides, 33
Diosporus lotus, 278
Dipladenia, 150–52, **151**
   x *amabilis*
   'Alice Dupont', 151
   bouliviense, **151**
   'Red Riding Hood', 151
   suaveolens, 151
diploid, 395
Dipogon lablab, 152–54
diseases, 503–504
distaff thistle, 92
Doctrine of Signatures, 429
dogweeds, 159–60
Dolichos lablab, 152–54, **153**
Dorotheanthus, 154–56
   bellidiformis, 154, **155, 156**
     'Lunette', 155
     'Yellow Ice', 155
   gramineus, 154–55
Douglas, David, 264
douglasii, 264
down thistle, 339
Downing, Andrew Jackson, 157
Downingia, 156–57
   elegans, 156–57
   pulchella, 156–57
Dracocephalum moldavicum, 157–58
   'Album', 158
Dracopsis amplexicaulis, 158–59
Drake, Sir Francis, 170
drug fumitory, 189
Drummond phlox, 369–71
Drummond, Thomas, 370
drummondii, 370

drumstick scabious, 416
drumsticks, 125–26
duplexes, gerbera flower form, 197
dusty miller, 105, 424, 450
dwarf licorice plant, 375
dwarf morning glory, 119
dye plants, 92, 120, 190, 216
Dyssodia tenuiloba, 159–60

earth smoke, 189
East Indian basil, 337
Eccremocarpus scaber, 160–62, **161**
    'Tresco Cream', 161
    'Tresco Crimson', 161
Echinacea purpurea, 150
Echinocystis lobata, 162
Echium, 163–64
    fastuosum, 163
    lycopsis, 163–64
    pininana, 163
    plantagineum, 163
    vulgare, 163–64
    wildprettii, 163
Eckford, Henry, 249, 253
Edible Flowers, 445
eggplant, 431
Egyptian bean, 152, 153
Egyptian star, 355
Ekstrom, Nicolas H., 403–404
elata, 384
elegans, 285
eleven o'clock, 381, 382
elfin shrub, 130
Emilia, 165–66
    coccinea, 165–66, **166**
    flammea, 165
    javanica, 165
    sonchifolia, 166
Emmenanthe penduliflora, 164–65
English daisy, *xxi,* 61–62
English Flower Garden, The, 283, 495
English lawn daisy, and *Helianthus*
    phytotoxicity, 210
English marigold, 82
epazote, 101
Erigeron karvinskianus, 166–68, **167**
    'Profusion', 168
Erysimum, 168–70
    allionii, 169
    alpinum, 169
    'Bowles Mauve', 169
    hieracifolium, 169

    linifolium, 168, 169
    murale, 169
    perofskianum, 169
Eschscholtz, Johan Frederich, 172
Eschscholzia californica, 92, 170–72, **171**, 318
espaliers, 6–7
Euphorbia
    cyathophora, 172–73
    lathyris, 173
    marginata, 172–73, **174**
    pulcherrima, 172
Euphorbiaceae, 172
Eustoma grandiflorum, 174–76, **175**
Everett, T. H., 377
everlasting, 210, 388, 491
everlasting flowers, 24
Evolvulus
    glomeratus, 176, **177**
    nuttalianus, 176–77
    pilosus, 176
Exacum
    affine, 177–79
    grandiflorum, 178

Fairey, John, 405
fairy fan flower, 416
Fallopia, 360
false hop, 242
false Jerusalem cherry, 431
false Queen Anne's lace, 27
false saffron, 92
fan flower, 416
farewell to spring, 107, 108
fasciculatum, 87
fava beans, 369
febrifuge, 448
Fedia cornucopia, 179–80
Felicia
    amelloides, 180–82, **181, 182**
    'Read's White', 181
    bergeriana, 182
fennel, 182
Fernandez, Francisco, 322
fertilizers, 507–508
Ferula
    assa-foetida, 183
    communis, 65, 182–83
fetid marigolds, 159–60
feverfew, 104–105, 292, 448–50
fiddleneck phacelia, 367
filifolia, 445
firebush, 244, **245**

firecracker plant, 128, **129**
five spot, 318
flame flower, 447
flame poppy, 440
flamingo plant, 222
Flanders field poppy, 51, 341–42
flax, 265, 268–70, **269**
flax-leaved pimpernel, 30
fleabane, 166–68
Flora's paintbrush, 165
Florence fennel, 184
florist's mum, 102
floss flower, 13
flower of an hour, 126
flowering cabbage, 70–71
flowering maple, 6
flowering purslane, 381, 382
flowering tobacco, 321, 323
fluviatilis, 256
Foeniculum vulgare, 182, 183–185, **185**
    'Azoricum', 184
    'Bronze', 184
    'Dulce', 184
    'Giant Bronze', 184
    'Purpureum', 184
    'Rubrum', 184
    'Smokey', 184
Foerster, Karl, 117
forbidden palace flower, 477–78
forget-me-not, *xix,* 31, 32, 312
Forsyth, Turid, 435
four o'clock, 306, 307
Fournier, Eugene Pierre Nicolas, 461
foxgloves, 146–47, 384, 390
    and *Helianthus* phytotoxicity, 210
Franchet, Adrien Rene, 144
freckleface, 222
fried egg flower, 262, **263**
fu kwa, 312
Fuchs, Leonhart, 189
Fuchsia, 186–89
    fulgens, 186
    x *hybrida,* 186
    'Isis', **187**
    magellanica, 186
    splendens, 129–31
    triphylla, 186, **189**
    'Gartenmeister Bonstedt', 186, **188**
Fumaria officinalis, 189–91
fumariifolia, 222
fumitory, 189
fungal disease, 17–18, 86, 497

fungus, in *Lavatera,* 258
fused petals, 112

Gaillardia, 191–93
    aristata, 191
    x *grandiflora,* 191
    pulchella, 191–92, **192**
Gallium, 52
garden hyssop, 130
garden mum, 102
garden pea, 250
garden sorrel, 218–19
Gardener's Guide to Growing Salvias, The, 400
garland flower, 103, 107
Gaura lindheimeri, 193–94, **194**
Gazania, 150, 195–96
    x *hybrida,* 195
    'Sundrop', **196**
gentian sage, 406
Gentianaceae, 178
gentianette, 366
gentians, 175
Geraniaceae, 349
Geranium phaeum, 350
Gerber, Traugott, 198
Gerbera, 150, 196–98
    x *hybrida,* 198
    jamesonii, 196–98
German ivy, 426
German statice, 264
German violet, 177, 178
giant fennel, 65, 182
Gil, Philip Salvador, 199
Gili, Filippo Luigi, 199
Gilia
    capitata, 198–99
    rubra, 239
    tricolor, 198–99
gillyflowers, 296
ginger, 358
glabrata, 248
glandulosa, 261
Glaucium
    aurantiacum, 200–201
    corniculatum, 201
    flavum, **200,** 200–201, **201**
globe amaranth, 201, **203**
globe gilia, 198
gloriosa daisy, 394
glory bush, 453
gloxinoides, 353

Glycyrrhiza glabra, 212
Godetia, 107, 108
   amoena, 108
   grandiflora, 108
gold cups, 220
gold flash, 277
golden fleece, 159, 160
Golden Gate Park, 157
golden morning glory, 301
golden wave, 122
goldfield, 248
Gomphrena species, 201–203
   dispersa, 203
   globosa, 202–203, 210
   haagiana, 202–203
      'Strawberry Fields', 202, **203**
good King Henry, 101
Goodeniaceae, 418
Goodenough, Samuel, 418
goosefoot, 101
gopher plant, 173
Gossypium, 288–89
   hirsutum, 37
granadilla, 345, 348–49
grandiflora, 383
granny's bonnet, 41
gratissimum, 337
greater periwinkle, 482
Greek basil, 337
green-flowered sweet pea, 254
grossum, 87
gully lupine, 281
Gunnera manicata, 207
Gynura
   aurantiaca, 204–205
   sarmentosa, 204
Gypsophila, 205–207
   elegans, 205–207
   grandiflora var. 'Covent Garden', 205–206
   muralis, 206
   paniculata, 206

Haage, J. N., 202
hairy morning glory, 237
hallucinogen, 135–36
haloed petunias, 362
Haloradigaceae, 207
Haloragaceae, 207
Haloragis erecta, 127, 207–208
   'Rubra', 207
hardening off, *xxi,* 504

hardheads, 97
hardy annuals, *xxi*
   self seeding, *xxi*
hardy gloxinia, 231
hardy poinsettia, 172
hare's ears, 78
Harrowsmith Annual Garden, The, 435
Hartweg, Karl Theodor, 280
Hawaiian snowbush, 72
Hawker, Lieutenant, 227
hawk's beard, 126
hawkweed, 126
hayfever, 245
heartsease, 89, 484
heartseed, 89
Heddewig, Carl, 139
Hedera helix, 426
hedge dolls, 189
heirloom vegetables, 53
Helianthus
   phytotoxicity, 210
   annuus, 208–210, **209**
      'Italian White', 209–10
      'Russian Giant', 208
      'Stalla', 209
   debilis, 209
      subsp. *cucumerifolius,* 209
      'Flore Pleno', 209
Helichrysum, 210–12
   bracteatum, 210–11, **211**
   cassianum, 212
   davenportii, 212
   elatum, 212
   Monstrosum, 210–11
   petiolare, 210, 211–12, **212,** 375
      'Limelight', 212
      'Variegatum', 212
Heliophila, 212–14
   leptophylla, 213
   linearifolia, 213
   longifolia, 212–14, **214**
Heliotropium, 214–15
   arborescens, 214, **215**
   corymbosum, 214
   peruvianum, 214
Helipterum, 388–89
   roseum, 491
Helychrisum, 54
   bracteatum, 491
henna, 31
herba sancta, 322
Hesperis matrionalis, 146

Hibiscus, 4, 215–19
    acetosella, 218, **219**
        'Coppertone', 218
        'Red Shield', 218
    rosa-sinensis, 216, **217**
    sabdariffa, 218
    syriacus, 216
    trionum, 216, **217**
Himalayan balsam, 228
Himalayan blue poppies, 54
Himalayan jewelweed, *xxi,* 228
Himalayan persimmon, 278
Hodgson, Larry, 387
hollyhock, 17–18, 146
holy basil, 336
holy thistle, 429
honey flower, 298, **299**
honey shrub, 298, **299**
honeysuckle fuchsia, 186
honeywort, 99
hop, 219
horn of plenty, 179, 180
horned poppy, 199
horned violet, 484
Hot Plants for Cool Gardens, 440
hound's tongue, 132
Houstoun, Dr. William, 14
hover fly, 367
Hudson, J. L., 285
humble plant, 302
hummingbird vine, 48
hummingbirds, 145, 235, 298, 325
Humulus
    japonicus, 219–20, **220**
    lupulus, 219
Hunneman, John, 222
Hunnemannia fumariifolia, 220–21, **221**
    'Sunlite', 222
hyacinth bean, 152, 153, 154
hyacinth-flowered candytuft, 224
hyacinth-flowered larkspur, 118
Hydrophyllaceae, 366
hyoscyamine, 135–36
Hypoestes phyllostachya, 222–23
hyssop, 130

Iberis, 223–25
    affinis, 225
    amara, 224
    pinnata, 225
    sempervirens, 224
    umbellata, 224

ice plant, 91, 154, 155
Iceland poppy, 342
immortelle, 210, **211**, 388, 491
Impatiens, 225–30
    auricoma, 230
    balfourii, **229,** 230
    balsamina, 227
    glandulifera, xxi, **226,** 228, 230
        'Candida', 228
    hawkeri, 227
    linearifolia, 227
    New Guinea hybrids, 225
    niamniamensis, 230
    noli-me-tangere, 228–30
    walleriana, 225, 226–27
Incarvillea, 230–31
    delavayi, 231
    sinensis, **231**
        subsp. *variabilis,* 230
India sorrel, 218
Indian blanket, 191, 192–93
Indian spinach, 57
Indian wort, 50
innocence, 116
insects, 503
    attractors, 265
    trapping, 429
insecticides, 393
Insignis, 318
intercropping, 429
intercrossing, 42
International Code of Botanical Nomenclature,
    244
involucre, 409
Iochroma ausstrale, 9–11, **10**
Ionopsidium acaule, 232–33
Ipomoea, 233–39, 301
    alba, 237, 238–39
    batatas, 238–39
        'Ace of Spades', **234**
        'Margarita', **235**
    hederifolia, 235
    hirta, 237
        'Mini-Sky Blue', 237
    x *impereialis,* **236**
        'Chocolate', 236
    lobata, 235, **238**
    x *multifida,* 235
    nil, **236,** 238–39
    purpurea, 236
        'Kniola's Purple-black', 236
    quamoclit, 234–35
    setosa, 238–39

x *sloteri*, 235
  tricolor, 235, 238–39
    'Heavenly Blue', 233, 235–36
Ipomopsis
  aggregata, 239–40
  rubra, 239, **240, 241**
'Irene Nuss' begonia, 61
Iresine
  herbstii, 242
    'Aureoreticulata', 242
    'Brilliantissima', 242
  lendenii, 241–42
Irish cuttings, 192, 299, 373, 386, 437–38
Island Garden, An, 342
Isotoma, 255
Italian jasmine, 432
ivy, 425–26

jalapa, 308
Jamaica sorrel, 218
Japanese beetles, 361
Japanese hop, 219–20
Japanese knotweed, 360
Japanese thistle, 105
jasmine tobacco, 323
jasmine, 432
jasminoides, 431–32
Jekyll, Gertrude, 322, 357, 404
Jerusalem cherry, 431, 433
jewels of Opar, 447
Jimson weed, 136
jin li zhi, 312
Johnny-jump-up, *xxi*, 484
Joseph's coat, 21, 26
Juglans nigra, and *Helianthus* phytotoxicity,
    210
jujube, 278
Justice, James, 243
Justicia, 145
  brandegeeana, 242, **243**
  guttata, 242

kantola, 312
karela, 312
Kentucky Wonder, 368
kingfisher daisy, 182
king's crown, 144
kiss-me-over-the-garden-gate, 359,
    360
knapweed, 97
Koch, Wilhelm Daniel Josef, 244

Kochia, 244–45
  scoparia, 244, **245**
  trychophylla, 244
Ku gua, 312

Labiatae, 377, 400–401
Lablab purpureus, 152–54
ladies' eardrops, 186
lady in the bath, 309
lady's slippers, 80
laevis, 310
lamb's ears, 438
lambs quarters, 101
Lamiaceae, 377, 400–401
Lane, Ralph, 322
Lantana
  camara, **246**
  montividensis, 246–47
lao pu tao, 312
larkspur, *xxi*, **117**, 118
Lasthenia, 248–49
  chrysostoma, 248
  glabrata, 248
Lathyrus
  chloranthus, 254
  odoratus, 249–54, **251**
    'Countess Spencer', 250
    'Cupani', 249
    'Cupid', 250
    'Gladys Unwin', 250
    'Grandiflora', 249–50
    'Painted Lady', 249
    'Prima Donna', 250
  tingitanus, 254
Laurentia, 254–55
  axillaris, **255**
  fluviatilis, 255–56
  petraea, 256
Lavater, J. R. and M. M., 257
Lavatera, 6
  arborea, 258
  assurgentiflora, 258–59
  thuringiaca, 259
    'Barnsley', 259
  trimestis, 257–59, **258**
    'Mont Blanc', 257
    'Mont Rose', 257
    'Pink Beauty', 257
    'Ruby Regis', 257
    'Silver Cups', 257
lawn daisy, 61
lawn leaf, 142

lawns, 142–43
laxative, 393
Lay, George Tradescant, 260
Layia
    elegans, 259–61
        var. *Alba,* 260–61
    glandulosa, 260–61
    platyglossa, 259
leadwort, 379–80
leaf-flower, 72
Legousia speculum-veneris, 435–36
legumes, 154, 249–54
Leguminosae, 279
lemon geranium, 351
Leonotis
    dubia, 261–62
    dysophylla, 261–62
    leonurus, 261–62
        var. *albiflora,* 262
        'Harrismith White', 262
Leucanthemum, 102, 297
    maximum, 395
    paludosum, 104
    x *superbum,* 104
Leucochrysum, 389
Lewis, Captain Meriwether, 108
licorice plant, **212**
life-in-death, 201, 202, **203**
light
    for growing on indoors, 502–503
Lilium speciosum, 135
Limnanthaceae, 264
Limnanthes douglasii, 262–64, **263**, 318
Limonium
    latifolium, 264
    sinuatum, 264–65, **265**
    suworowi, 265
Linaria, 390
    aeruginea, 267
        var. *nevadensis,* 267
    amethystea, 266–67
    bipartita, 267
    broussonetti, 266
    canadensis, 267
    maroccana, **266**
    reticulata, 267
        'Aureo-purpurea', 267
    triornithophora, 267
Linden, Jean Jules, 241
Lindheimer, Ferdinand Jacob, 194
Lindley, John, 301, 333
lindleyi, 301
Linnaeus, Carl, 396, 465, 468

Linum, 265
    grandiflorum, 268–70, **269**
        'Alba', 270
        'Bright Eyes', 270
        'Caeruleum', 270
        'Coccineum', 270
        'Rubrum', 270
    narbonense, 168
    perenne, 268
    usitatissimum, 268
lion's ears, 261, 262
lion's tail, 261, 262
Lisianthus, 174, 176
little-leaved autumn sage, 405
liver restorative, 429–30
Livingstone daisy, 154
lizard fruit, 311
Lloyd, Christopher, 86, 300, 387
Loasa triphylla var. *volcanica,* 270–71
Loasaceae, 271, 300
Lobelia
    cardinalis, 273
    erinus, 271–74, **272, 274**
        'Kathleen Mallard', 272
    x *speciosa,* 273
    valida, 273
Lobeliaceae, 157
lobster claw vine, 277
Lobularia maritima, 274–76, **276**
longiflora, 308
longum, 87
Lopez, Tomas, 277
Lopezia racemosa, 276–77
Lophospermum, 49–50
    erubescens, 50
lotus vine, 277
Lotus, 277–79
    berthelotii, 278
    maculatus, 278
love-in-a-mist, 330
love-in-a-puff, 89
lucida, 445
Lupinus, 279–83
    arboreus, 279
    cruckshanksii, 280–82
    densiflorus, 281
    hartwegii, 280
        'Bianconeve', 280
        'New Snow', 280
    hirsutus, 282
    luteus, 282
    mutabilis, 280–81
    nanus, 281–82

polyphyllus, 279–80
pubescens, 281
subcarnosus, 279, 281
texensis, 281
varius, 282
lupulin, 219
Lychnis
coeli-rosa, 428
vaccaria, 477
Lycopodium selago, 423
Lycrianthes rantonnetii, 433

Macheranthema tanacetifolia, 283–84
maculatus, 278
mad apple, 135
Madagascar periwinkle, 93–94
Madeira marigold, 84
Madia, 284–85
elegans, 284
sativa, 284
madness, *Lobularia* for, 274–75
madwort, 274
maggots, 448
mahon, 285
Malabar spinach, 57, 58
Malcomia maritima, 285–87, **286**
'Lutea', 286
mallow, 36, 216, 287
Malope trifida, 287–88
Malva, 288–90
sylvestris, **289,** 289–90
'Bibor Fehlo', 290
'Brave Heart', 290
subsp. *mauritanica,* 290
verticillata, 289
'Crispa', 289
zebrinus, 290
Malvaceae, 4, 6, 36, 258, 288–89
Mandevilla, 150–52, **151**
Marguerite daisy, 103–104
marianum, 429
marigold, 443–46
maritima, 286
Martyn, John, 292
Martynia
annua, 292
fragrans, 292
proboscidea, 290–92
Martyniaceae, 290–91, 292
marvel-of-Peru, 306, 308
mask flower, 18–19
match-me-if-you-can, 26

Matricaria, 448
camomile, 293
capensis, 104
inodorata, 293–94
matricariodes, 294
parthenoides, 104
recutita, 293
Matthiola, 294–96
bicornis, 296
incana, 213, 295–96
longipetala, 296
subsp. *bicornis,* 296
Mattioli, Pierandrea, 296
Maurandella, 49
Maurandya, 48–50
barclaiana, 49, 50
erubescens, 50
scandens, 50
Maximinus, 330–31
May pop, 345
McGowan, Alice, 291
meadow foam, 262, **263**
mealy bug, 412
mealy-cup sage, 403
measles plant, 222, 223
Meconopsis
betonicifolia, 54, 441
grandis, 54
x *sheldonii,* 441
medallion flower, 296
Melampodium
leucanthemum, 296–97
paludosum, 296–97
Melastomataceae, 98, 453–54
Melianthus major, 298–99, **299**
Memorial Day poppy, 343
Mendel, Frederick, 252
Mentzel, Christian, 301
Mentzelia lindleyi, 300–301, 318
Menzies, Archibauld, 320
Merremia
aurea, 301–302
siberica, 302
tuberosa, 301
Mesembryanthemum criniflorum, 154–56
Mexican bamboo, 360
Mexican basil, 378
Mexican bush sage, 408
Mexican cigar plant, 128, **129**
Mexican daisy, 166
Mexican fleabane, 166
Mexican petunia, 396
Mexican prickly poppy, 45, 92

Mexican sunflower, 456
Mexican tarragon, 445
Mexican tulip poppy, 220
Mezembrianthemum, 150
Michaelmas daisies, 167
mignonette, 386, **387**
milfoil, 207
milk thistle, 429
millions bells, 363
mimics, 304
Mimosa pudica, 302
Mimulus, 303–306, 390
   aurantiacus, **304,** 306
   guttatus, 306
      'Chevron', **306**
   x *hybridus,* 304, **305**
   luteus, 305
Mina lobata, 235, **238**
mint, 377
Mirabilis, 306–309
   jalapa, 307
      'Alba', **307**
   longiflora, 308
   multiflora, 308–309
misticanza, 179–80
mock cucumber, 162
mold, 398
Moldavian balm, 157
Moldavian dragonhead, 157
mole plant, 173
Molucella, 309–11
   laevis, 309–11
   spinosa, 310–11
Momordica, 311–12
   balsamina, 311, 312
   charantia, 311, 312
Monet, Claude, 287
monkey flower, 303, 390
Monstrosum, 210–11
moon vine, 237
morning glory, 176, 233–39, 301–302
morphine, 341, 344
Morris, Sir Cedric, 344
Moses-in-a-boat, 466
mosquito bites, 337
mosquito flower, 276, 277
moss verbena, 480
mother-of-thyme, 376
mountain spinach, 52, 333–34
mourning bride, 415
mourning widow, 415
mouse's ears, 313
muralis, 206

mustard, 232
mutabilis, 280–81
Myosotis
   sylvatica, 312–14, **313**
   sylvestris, 31, 146
Myriophyllum aquaticum, 207

narcotic properties, 135–36, 322
nasturtium, 467, 468
natal ivy, 426
National Parks system, 157
navelworts, 338
Nemesia, 314–17
   caerulea, 317
   capensis, 317
   'Danish Flag', 316
   foetens, 317
   fruticans, **315,** 317
   'KLM', 316
   strumosa, 315, 317
      'Nebula White', **316**
   versicolor, 317
Nemophila, 318–20
   maculata, 318–20
      subsp. *Atromarica,* 318
      'Coelestis', 318
      subsp. *Discoidalis,* 318
   menziesii, 318–20
      'Alba', 318
      'Penny Black', **319**
New Guinea hybrid impatiens, 225, 227
New Illustrated Encyclopedia of Gardening, 377
Nicander, 321
Nicandra physalodes, 320–21, **321**
Nicot, Jean, 322
Nicotiana, 321–27, **326**
   affinis, 323–24
   alata, 323–24
      'Grandiflora', 324
   glauca, 326
   langsdorffi, 309, **324,** 324–25
   rustica, 322–23
   sylvestris, **325,** 325–26
   tabacum, 322–23, 326
nicotine, 322, 323, 471–72
Nieremberg, Juan Eusebio, 330
Nierembergia species, 327–30
   caerulea, 328
   frutescens, 328
   gracillis, 328

repens, 328
rivularis, 328
scoparia, 328, **329**
　　'Albiflora', 328
　　'White Queen', 328
Nigella, xxi, 330–33
　　damascena, 330–33, **331, 332**
　　　　'Miss Jekyll's Blue', 331
　　　　'Miss Jekyll's Rose', 331
　　　　'Miss Jekyll's White', 331
　　　　'Mulberry Rose', 331
　　　　'Persian Jewels', 331
　　hispanica, 331–32
　　orientalis, 332
　　　　'Transformer', 332
　　sativa, 331
night phlox, 492, 493
night-scented stock, 296
nightshade, 135, 435
Nolana
　　atriplicifolia, 333–34
　　humifusa, 334
　　paradoxa, 333–34
none-so-sweet, 427
nutmeg geranium, 351–52
Nuttall, Thomas, 84, 176–77
Nyctaginaceae, 5, 306

Ocimum, 334–38
　　basilicum, 335
　　　　'Anise', 336
　　　　'Aussie Lassie', 337
　　　　'Aussie Sweetie', 337
　　　　'Cinnamon', 336
　　　　'Citriodora', 336
　　　　var. *minimum*, 337
　　gratissimum, 337
　　kilimandsharicum, 336–37
　　purpurescens, 335
　　　　'Dark Opal', 335
　　　　'New Guinea', 335
　　sanctum, 336
　　tenuiflorum, 336
odoratus, 253
officina, 402, 478
officinalis, 190, 402
oil plant, 284
old maid, 93
oldfield toadflax, 267
Olmstead, Frederick Law, 157
Omphalodes
　　cappadocica, 338

linifolia, 338–39
　　var. *caerulescens*, 339
verna, 338
Onopordum acanthium, 339–41, **340**
opal cups, 36
opium, 341, 344
orach, 52, 179–80, 333–34
orange cosmos, 123, **124**
Orchidaceae, 59
Orczy, Baroness, 30
ornamental cabbage, 70–71
ornamental kale, 70–71
ortiga, 270
Osteospermum, 148–50
　　ecklonis, 148
Our Lady's thistle, 429
Oxypetalum caeruleum, 472–73, **473**

Pachysandra procumbens, 483
Pacific Giant series (delphinium), 117
Page, Russell, 404
pagoda flower, 115, 116
painted daisy, 103–104
painted tongue, 398, **399**
pallida, 466
palm of Christ, 392
Palm Springs daisy, 107
Palma Christi, 392
pansy, 484–87
Papaver, 15, 45, 341–46
　　commutatum, 341
　　croceum, 342
　　　　'Champagne Bubbles', 342
　　nudicaule, **342**, 342–43
　　orientale, 341
　　rhoeas, 15, 45, 51, 97, 341–43
　　　　'Ladybird', 342
　　　　'Mother of Pearl', 344
　　　　'Oregon Rainbows', 342
　　　　'Sir Cedric Morris', 344
　　somniferum, 45, 341–46, **343, 344, 346**
　　　　'Danish Flag', **345**
Papaveraceae, 45, 143, 144, 170, 201, 221, 375
paper daisy, 210
paper moon, 416
pappus, 423–24
paradise vine, 433
Paris daisy, 103–104
parlor ivy, 426
parlor maple, 6
parrot leaf, 21
parrot's beak, 277

parrot's feather, 207
Parry, Charles Christopher, 367
parthenium, 448
Passiflora
    amethystinum, 348
    caerulea, 346–48
    coccinea, 347
    incarnata, 346, 348
passion flower, 346
peacock mosses, 422
Peale, Rembrandt, 350
pearly everlasting, 28
Pedaliaceae, 292
Pelargonium
    classes
        Botanical, 349
        Ivy Leaved, 349, 351
        Martha Washington, 349, 350–51, 352
        Scented, 349, 351–52
        Zonal, 349–50, 352
    angulosum, 351
    crispum, 351
    cuculatum, 351
    x *domesticum,* 350–51, 351
    x *fragrans,* 351–52
    grandiflorum, 351
    graveolens, 351
    x *hybridum* 'Frank Kedley', 352
    inquinans, 350
    x *peltatum,* 350
    sideriodes, 352
    tomentosum, 351
    zonale, 350
Penstemon
    cobaea, 353
    x *gloxinoides,* 352–54
    hartwegii, 353
    x 'Sour Grapes', 353
    'White Bedder', **353**
Pentas lanceolata, 355
    'Avalanche', 356
    New Look Series, 355
    'Pink', **355**
    'Red', **356**
    'Tu-Tone', 355
peppermint geranium, 351
pepperminting, 383
peppers, 87–89, 431
Perault, Charles, 331
peregrinus, 470
perennial,
    half-hardy, *xviii–xix*
    tender, *xviii–xix*

Perennials for American Gardens, 403
Perilla frutescens, 23, 127, 357–59, **358**
    'Magilla Perilla', 358
    var. *atropurpurea,* 358
        'Crispa', 358
        'Fancy Fringe', 358
        'Lanciniata', 358
        'Nankinensis', 358
periwinkle, 93, 482, 483
Perovski, V. A., 169
Perovskia atriplicifolia, 169
Persian shield, 438, 439
Persian violet, 177, 178
Persicaria species, 359–61
    capitata, 359, **360,** 361
    cuspidatum, 360
    orientale, 359, 360–61
pest repellant, 320
pesticide, 322, 323
pests and diseases, 503–504
Petunia species, 361–65
    axilaris, 363
    grandifloras, 365
    x *hybrida,* **365**
        'White Cascade', **362**
    integrifolia, **363,** 364
    milleflora, 364
    multifloras, 365
    violacea, 363
Phacelia, 366–67
    campanularia, 318, 366, 367
    var. *alba,* 366–67
    parryii, 367
    tanacetifolia, 367
Phaseolus
    coccineus, 367–69
        'Dutch Case Knife Bean', 368
        'Painted Lady', 368
        'White Dutch Runner', 368
    vulgaris, 368
Phlox
    drummondii, 369–71, **370**
        'Phlox of Sheep', 370
    paniculata, 369
phosphorus, for abundant flower, 88
Phygelius
    aequalis, 371–73
        'Coccineus', **373**
        'Cream', **371**
        'Yellow Trumpet', **372**
    capensis, 372–73
    'Pink Elf', 373
    x *rectus,* 371–74

phyllostachya, 223
phyllotaxy, 208
Physalis, 321
    alkekengi, 321
    franchetii, 321
    ixocarpa, 321
phytotoxicity, 210
pied daisy, 195
Pimenta officinalis, 331
pimpernel, 29
pinching, 509
pincushion flower, 415
pineapple sage, 410
pink pinheads, 203
pink pokers, 265
pink princess flower, 455–56
Pisum sativum, 250
pitchforks, 64
Plant Finder, The, 422
Platystemon californicus, 374–75
Plectostachys serpyllifolia, 375–76
Plectranthus, 112–15, 376–79
    amboinicus, 378
        'Goldheart', 378
        'Green Gold', 378
        'Spanish Thyme', 378
    argentatus, **378,** 379
    ciliatus, 379
    coleoides, 378
    forsteri, 378
        'Marginatus', 378
    fruticosus, 379
    madagascariensis, 378
    'Minimus Variegatus', 378
    oertendahlii, 377–78
Plumbaginaceae, 379–80
Plumbago auriculata, 379–81, **380**
    var. *alba,* 380
plume thistle, 105
poached egg flower, 262, **263**
pocket book plant, 80
poinsettia, 172
pole bean, 368
polka-dot plant, 222
pollen, 245
Polygonaceae, 38
polygonon, 361
Polygonum, 359–61
poor man's orchid
poor man's weatherglass, 30
poppy mallow, 84
poppy, *xx,* 54, 143–44, 190, 199–200, 221,
    341–46, 375, 441

Portulaca
    grandiflora, 381–84
        'White Swan', 383
        'Wild Fire', 383
    oleracea, 382
    umbraticola, 383–84
Portulacaceae, 447, 448
pot marigold, 82, 83, 474
potato bush, 431, 433
potato vine, 433
pots, 501
potting soil, 500
pouch flower, 80
powdery mildew, 133, 480, 497
prairie gentian, 174
Pratia, 255
'President Carnot' begonia, 61
pricking out, 501–502
pride of Madeira, 163
prince's feathers, 25, 95–97, 359
princess flower, 453
princess moss, 423
Proboscidea louisianica, 290–92
proboskis, 292
propagation, 141
Psylliostachys, 265
ptarmiciflorum, 450
pudica, 303
puntarelle, 179–80
purple bell vine, 390
purple foliage, 127, 130, 204, 335–37, 352,
    358
purple groundsel, 425
purple passion, 204
purple velvet plant, 204
purpurescens, 335
purpurea, 147
purslane, 382
Pyrethrum, 293, 448, 471–72
    parthenium, 104
    ptarmiciflorum, 424, 450

Queen Anne's thimbles, 198
queen's jewels, 37
queen's wreath, 37
quilled flowers, 123

racemosa, 277
rage, *Lobularia* for, 274–75
ragged robin, 97
ragged sailors, 97

Raleigh, Sir Walter, 322
ram's horn, 290
red horned poppy, 201
red ruellia, 397
refrigerating seed, 288
Regal Geranium, 351
Rehmann, Joseph, 384
Rehmannia
    angulata, 384–86, 385
    elata, 384–86
        'Alba', 384
Reinelt, Frank, 117
Reseda odorata, 386–88, **387**
resurrection plant, 421–22
Reynoutria, 360
    japonica, 360
Rhodanthe, 388–90
    chlorocephala subsp. *rosea,* 389
    manglesii, 389
    rosea, 389
Rhodochiton atrosanguineus, 390–92, **391**
rhyzomatous plants, 488
Rice, Graham, 81, 155, 363
ricin, 392–93
Ricinus communis, 392–94, **393**
    'Carmencita', 392
rivularis, 328
Robert Bruce, 339
Robinson, William, 120, 156, 249, 250,
        253, 280, 281, 283, 331–32, 371,
        495
rock bells, 487
rock jasmine, 32
rock rose, 381
rocket candytuft, 224
root mass, 299
Rorippa nasturtium, 468
rosa de Montana, 37
rose everlasting, 389
rose geranium, 351
rose mallow, 257
rose moss, 381
rose of Sharon, 216
rose thistle, 105
Roselle, 218
Roth, Albrecht Wilhelm, 244
Roth, Susan, 440
rotundifolia, 457
Rudbeck, Olof, 396
Rudbeckia, 158–59
    hirta, 394–96, **395**
        'Green Eyes', 395
        'Irish Eyes', 395

Ruellia, 396–97
    brittoniana, 396–97, **397**
        'Katie', 396
        'Katie's Dwarf ', 396
    elegans, 397
Rumex acetosa, 218–19
Russell, George, 280
Russian sage, 169
rust, 17–18, 40

safflower, 92
sage, 402, 410
Saint Barbara, 56
Salpiglosis sinuata, 398–99, **399**
salt bush, 52
Salvia, 10, 399–410
    ambigens, 407
    argentea, 401–403
    coccinea, 401, 404–405
        'Apple Blossom', **402**
        'Lady in Red', **404,** 405
    confertiflora, 409
    elegans, 410
    farinacea, 400, 401, **403,** 408
    greggii, 401, **405**
    guaranitica, 406–407, **408**
        'Argentine Skies', 407
        'Blue Enigma', 407
        'Purple Majesty', 407
    horminum, 210, **410**
    x 'Indigo Spires', 408
    involucrata, 409
    x *jamensis,* 405–406
    leucantha, 408–409, **409**
    longispicata, 408
    mexicana, 408
    microphylla, 405
        'Red Velvet', **406**
    officinalis, 400
        'Berggarten', 402
        'Icterina', 402
        'Purpurescens Variegata',
            402
        'Tricolor', 402
    patens, 406, **407**
        'Alba', 406
        'Cambridge Blue', 406
    sclarea, 410
    splendens, 400, 401, 404–405
        'Rambo', 404
        'Van Houttii', 404
    uliginosa, 407–408

viridis, 410
    var. *comata,* 410–11
Sanchez, José, 412
Sanchezia speciosa, 411–12
    var. *glaucophylla,* 412
    subsp. *nana,* 412
sand verbena, 5
Sanvitali, Federico, 414
Sanvitalia procumbens, **413,** 413–16, **414**
Saponaria vaccaria, 477
sap-sucking pests, 429
satin flower, 107
sativa, 285
sativus, 331
Scabiosa
    atropurpurea, 414–16
    caucasica, 416
    stellata, 415, 416
Scaevola aemula, 416–18, **417**
    'Blue Fan', 417
    'Blue Wonder', 417
    'Mauve Clusters', 417
scale, 412
scarification, 238, 282
scarlet bedder, 400
scarlet pimpernel, 30
scarlet runner bean, 367–69
scarlet trompetilla, 67
Schizanthus
    pinnatus, 419
    retusus, 419
    x *wisetonensis,* 418–20
Schizopetalon walkeri, 420–21
Schrader, Dennis, 440
Schwantes, Dr. Martin Henrich, 154
Scolymus hispanicus, 131
scoparia, 244
Scots thistle, 339
Scott, Sir David, 290
Scrophularia aquatica, 116
Scrophulariaceae, 116, 140, 304, 315, 384, 390
sea dahlia, 121–22
sea lavender, 264
sea pink, 264
sea poppy, 199
sea purslane, 52
seeding
    direct, 505
    process, 501
seeds, starting indoors, 500–502
Selaginella
    kraussiana, 421–23
        'Aurea', 422

'Brownii', 422–23
'Variegata', 422
lepidophylla, 421–22
self-seeding annuals, 506
Senecio, 105, 423–26
    cineraria, 424–25
        'Cirrus', 424
        'Silver Dust', 424
        'White Diamond', 424
    cruentus, 425
    elegans, 425
    heritieri, 425
    x *hybridus,* 425
    macroglossus, 426
        'Variegata', 426
    mikanioides, 426
    viravira, 424
sensitive plant, 302
sepals, 186
serpyllifolia, 376
Setcresea pallida, 466
shasta daisies, 102, 104
shearing back, 510
shell flower, 309
shelled flowers, 123
shepherd's clock, 30
Shirley poppy, 344
shiso, 357
shoo-fly plant, 320
shrimp plant, 242, 243
shrub verbena, 245
shrubs, tender, *xix–xx*
    overwintering, *xx*
    standards, *xx*
shungiku, 103
Siberian wallflower, 169
signata, 444
Silene, 426–29
    armeria, 427
    coeli-rosa, 427–28, **428**
        'Blue Angel', 428
        'Royal Celebration', 428
    pendula, 428
silkworms, 393
silver feather, 450
silver lace, 105, 450
Silybum marianum, 429–31, **430**
    'Adriana', 430
silymarin, 430
sinensis, 231
sinuata, 399
sinuatum, 264
sky flower, 451

sky lupine, 282
skyrocket, 240
sleepy daisy, 490
slipperwort, 80
slugs, 471
snapdragon, 38–41, 48, 140, 390
snow in summer, 172–73, **174**
snow on the mountain, 172–73, **174**
snowflake, 442
soil, 506–507
Solanaceae, 136, 321, 419
Solanum, 431–35
   capsicastrum, 434
     'Variegata', 434
   crispum, 432
     'Glasnevin', 432
   jasminoides, 431–32
     'Alba', 431
     'Album', 432
     'Album Variegatum', 432
   pseudocapsicum, 433
   pyracanthum, 431–32, **432**, 434
   quitoense, 431, 434
   rantonnetii, 433
     'Royal Robe', 433
   seaforthianum, 432
   wendlandii, 432–33
Solenopsis, 255, 256
   axillaris, 256
   petraea, 256
Solenostemon scutellarioides, 113–15, **114**
southern star, 472
sowing very small seed, 276
spacing, 508
Spanish needles, 64
Spanish oyster plant, 131
speciosa, 475
Specularia
   pentagonia, 436
   speculum, 435–36
     'Grandiflora', 436
Spenser, 322
spider flower, 109–111, **110**, 453
spider mite, 239, 412
spiderwort, 464
spike plant, 482
spinach, 53
spores, 423
spurge, 172, 174
spurs, 140, 265
Stachys, 436–38
   affinis, 438
   albotomentosa, 436–38, **437**

   byzantina, 438
   coccinea, 437–38
     'Axminster Variegated', 437
   grandiflora, 438
   sieboldii, 438
   tuberifera, 438
staking, 509
standards, *xx,* 7, 36, 47, 128, 388
standing cypress, 239
star balsam, 492, 493
star cluster, 355
star of Texas, 490
star of the Veldt, 148
star scabious, 416
statice, 264
Steichen, Edward, 117
sterilizing packaged compost, 419
sticktights, 64
stimulant, 322
stinkweed, 135
stock flowered larkspur, 118
stock, 213, 294–95
stolon, 407, 438
stool (root mass), 299, 386, 408
strains, 383
strawflower, 210–11, 388, 491
Strobilanthes, 438–40
   atropurpurea, 438–40
   dyeriana, 438–40, **439, 440**
strobiles, 219
strobili, 423
Stylomecon heterophylla, 440–42
   'Alba', 441
   'White Satin', 441
subcarnosus, 281
succulents, 91–92
Summer Azalea, 351
summer cypress, 244, **245**
summer gloxinia, 230, 384
sun moss, 381
sun plant, 381
sun rose, 381
sunflower, 208–210, **209**
Sunset Western Gardening Book, The, 400
Superfinias, *xix*
Supertunias, *xix,* 363
Suter, Johan Rudolph, 443
Sutera
   campanulata, 443
     'Knysna Hills', 443
   cordata, 442–43
     'Snowflake', 442–43
Sutton, John, 400

swallow wort, 50
swallowtail butterflies, 185
Swan River daisy, 68–69
Swedish ivy, 378
sweet alyssum, 274–76
sweet Annie, 47
sweet basil, 334–38
sweet mignonette, 386, **387**
sweet pea, 249–54
sweet potato, 234
sweet scabious, 415–16
sweet William, 138–39, 427
sweet woodruff
    annual, 51
    perennial, 52
sweet wormwood, 47
sweetheart vine, 37
Swiss chard, 63–64
sylvatica, 314
sylvestris, 289, 325
Symphytum, 66–67

Tages, 444
Tagetes, 443–46
    classes
        African, 444
        French, 444
        Signet, 444
        Triploid, 444
    erecta, 444
        hybrid, 446
    filifolia, 445
    'Golden Gem', 445
    x *hybrida,* 444
    'Lemon Drop', **444**
    'Lemon Gem', 445
    lucida, 445
    'Mr. Majestic', **445**
    patula, 444
    tenuifolia, 444
Tahoka daisy, 283
Talinum
    crassifolium, 446–48
    paniculatum, 446–48
        'Kingwood Gold', 447
tampala, 26
Tanacetum, 104–105, 293
    parthenium, 104, 448–50
        'Aureum', **293,** 449
        'Golden Moss', 449
        'Santana', 449
        'Santana Lemon', 449

ptarmiciflorum, 450
vulgare, 283
tansy, 283
taproot, 131, 279, 282, 310, 334, 366, 464
tar weed, 284
tarragon, 445
tassel flower, 165
Taylor, George, 440–41
Taylor, Norman, 149
tea bush, 337
tenuifolia, 444
tenuisecta, 480
tetraploid, 395
Texas bluebell, 174
Texas bluebonnet, 279, 281
Texas petunia, 396
Texas plume, 239
Texas pride, 369
Texas sage, 404
Thaxter, Celia, 342
Theodore of Gaza, 196
Theophrastus, 253
Thiselton-Dyer, Sir William Turner, 440
thistle, 92, 93, 429–31
Thompson, William, 342
thorn apple, 135
thorow-wax, 78
Thunberg, Karl Peter, 453
Thunbergia, 450–53
    alata, 451, 453
    battiscombei, 452
    gibsonii, 453
    grandiflora, **452**
    gregorii, 453
Thymophylla tenuiloba, 159–60
Thymus serphyllum, 376
Tibouchina, 453–56
    grandifolia, **454,** 455
    nandina, 455
    organensis, 454
    urvilleana, 454, **455**
tickseed, 120
tiddly winks, 177
tidy tips, 259–60
Tithonia rotundifolia, 456–58, **457**
    'Acadian Blend', 458
    'Goldfinger', 457–58
    'Torch', 457
toadflax, 265, 390
toatoa, 207
tobacco, 321–27, 362–63

Tolpis barbata, 458–59
tomatillo, 321
tomatoes, 431
torch flower, 456
Toren, Olof, 461
Torenia, 390, 459–61
    baillonii, 461
    fournieri, 459–61, **460**
        Clown series, 460
        Panda series, 460
    x *hybrida,* 461
    'Summer Wave', 461
toute-epice, 331
tower of jewels, 163
toxicity, *Solanum,* 434–35
Trachelium caeruleum, 461–63, **462**
    'Passion in Violet', 462
Trachymene coerulea, 463–64
Tradescant II, John, 464–65
Tradescant, John, the Elder, 415,
    464
Tradescantia, 464–67
    x *andersoniana,* 465
    'Aurea', 465
    fluminensis, 465–66
        'Albovittata', 465
        'Orchid Frost', 465
    pallida, 466, 467
        'Purple Heart', 466
        'Purpurea', 466
    sillamontana, 466–67
    virginiana, 464–65
    zebrina, 465–66, **466**
        'Purpusii', 466
        'Quadricolor', 466
trailing spikemoss, 421
transplanting, *xxi,* 505
Transvaal daisy, 195
treasure flower, 195
tree basil, 337
tree lupine, 279
tree mallow, 257, 258
tree tobacco, 326
triornithophora, 267
triphylla, 271
Tripleurospermum, 293–94
Tripteris, 150
Tropaeoleum, 467
    majus, 467, 468, **469, 470**
        'Alaska', **468**
    minus, 470
    peregrinum, 470, **471**

trychophylla , 244
tuberous begonia, 60–61
tubers, 60–61, 134–35, 137, 152, 308, 406,
    447, 488
  care of, 60
tulsi, 336
Tweedia caerulea, 472–73, **473**
Tweedie, James, 473
twinspur, 139, 140

Umbelliferae, 79, 463–64
unicorn plant, 290
Unwin, William, 250
Ursinia, 473–76
    anethoides, 474, **475**
    calenduliflora, 474
    chrysanthemoides, 474
      var. *greyeri,* 474
    x *hybrida,* 475
    pulchra, 474
    speciosa, 475
Ursinus, Johannes Heinrich, 476

Vaccaria, 476–78
    hispanica, 476–78
    segitalis, 477
    vulgaris, 477
van Kotzebue, Otto, 172
Vancouver, Captain George, 320
veldt daisy, 195
Venedium, 45, 150
Venus's looking glass, 435–36
Venus's navelwort, 31, 338
Verbena, 478–82
    'Aztec Rose', **481**
    bonariensis, 480–82, **481**
    x *hybrida,* 478, **479,** 480
        'Homestead Purple', *xix ,* 479
        'Peaches and Cream', 479
        'Silver Anne', 479
        'Sissinghurst', 479
        'Sissinghurst Pink', *xix*
    incisa, 478
    officinalis, 478
    peruviana, 478, 480
        'Alba', 480
    phlogiflora, 478
    platenssis, 478
    'Polaris', **480**
    rigida, 478

tenuisecta, 480
    'Alba', 480
teucrioides, 478
Verey, Rosemary, 259
versicolor, 317
verticillata, 289
vervain, 478
Veterans Day poppy, 16
Viburnum, 247
Vicia fava, 369
Vinca
    major, 482–84
        'Maculata', 483
        'Variegata', 483
    minor, 483, 484
        'Variegata', 483
    rosea, 93–94, **94**
vincapervinca, 483
Viola, 484–87
    Art Series, 485
    cornuta, 484
    tricolor, 484, **486**
        hortensis, 484
    Universal Series, 485
    x *wittrockiana,* 484, **485, 486**
violet cress, 232, 233
viper's bugloss, 163, 164
Virginia stock, 285, 286
Viscaria elegans, 428
Vitamin C, 180
volcanica, 271
von Langsdorf, Georg Heinrich, 324
vulgare, 184

Wahlenberg, Georg, 488
Wahlenbergia, 487–88
Walker, John, 421
Waller, Horace, 226
wallflower, 168, 169
wandering Jew, 465–67
Warsczewicz, Joseph, 21
watercress, 468
wax begonia, 58–61
wax plant, 381
Wedel, Georg Wolfgang, 489
Wedelia triloba, 488–90
    'Outenreath Gold', 490
weeping lantana, 246–47
whispering bells, 164
white bladder vine, 42
white daisies, 260–61

white fly, 247, 290, 323, 355–56, 357, 401–402, 480
    repellant, 320
wild cucumber, 162
wild lantana, 5
wild spinach, 101
Wilkes, Reverend W., 344
wind poppy, 440
window, 140
wine cups, 84–85
winged everlasting, 28
wishbone flower, 390, 459
Wittrock, V. B., 484
woodland nicotiana, **325**

Xanthisma texanum, 490–91
Xeranthemum annuum, 491–92
    'Snow Lady', 491

yellow bachelor's buttons, 125
yellow hawkweed, 458
yellow horned poppy, **200, 201**
youth-and-old-age, 494

Zalusiansky von Zalusian, Adam, 493
Zaluzianskya, 492–494
    capensis, 492–94
        'Midnight Candy', 493
    ovata, 493
    vilosa, 493
Zanoni, Alonzo, 21
zarandaja, 152, 153
Zinn, Johann Gottfried, 495
Zinnia, 413–14
    angustifolia, 494
    elegans, 309, 494–98,
        'Bronze', **496**
        'Envy', 309
        'Red Sails', **497**
    haageana, 494, **495,** 498, **498**
        'Alba', **495,** 497
        'Chippendale', 498, **498**
        'Persian Carpet', 498
        'White Star', 498
    linearis, 494
    mexicana, 494
    peruviana, **497**
Zizyphus lotus, 278

WAYNE WINTERROWD, a native of Louisiana, now lives and gardens in Vermont. A writer, teacher, and frequent contributor to *Horticulture* magazine for many years, he began building the gardens at North Hill in southern Vermont in 1977 with gardening expert and writer Joe Eck. The two are now partners in North Hill Associates, a garden design firm. He is the author of *Living Seasonally: The Kitchen Garden and the Table at North Hill* (with Joe Eck); *A Year at North Hill: Four Seasons in a Vermont Garden* (with Joe Eck); *Annuals for Connoisseurs;* and editor of *Roses: A Celebration.*

ABOUT THE TYPE

This book was set in Bembo, a typeface based on an old-style Roman face that was used for Cardinal Bembo's tract *De Aetna* in 1495. Bembo was cut by Francisco Griffo in the early sixteenth century. The Lanston Monotype Machine Company of Philadelphia brought the well-proportioned letterforms of Bembo to the United States in the 1930s.